Classical Sociological Theory

SECOND EDITION

Michael S. Kimmel
State University of New York at Stony Brook

with Matthew Mahler,
State University of New York at Stony Brook

New York Oxford
OXFORD UNIVERSITY PRESS
2007

Oxford University Press, Inc., publishes works that further Oxford University's
objective of excellence in research, scholarship, and education.

Oxford New York
Auckland Cape Town Dar es Salaam Hong Kong Karachi
Kuala Lumpur Madrid Melbourne Mexico City Nairobi
New Delhi Shanghai Taipei Toronto

With offices in
Argentina Austria Brazil Chile Czech Republic France Greece
Guatemala Hungary Italy Japan Poland Portugal Singapore
South Korea Switzerland Thailand Turkey Ukraine Vietnam

Published by Oxford University Press, Inc.
198 Madison Avenue, New York, New York 10016
http://www.oup.com

Library of Congress Cataloging-in-Publication Data

Classical sociological theory / [edited] by Michael S. Kimmel with Matthew Mahler.—2nd ed.
p. cm.
Rev. ed. of: Social and political theory. c1998.
ISBN-13: 978-0-19-518785-4 (pbk. : alk. paper)
ISBN-10: 0-19-518785-7 (pbk. : alk. paper)
1. Sociology. 2. Political science. I. Kimmel, Michael S. II. Mahler, Matthew.
III. Social and political theory.

HM585.C59 2007
301—dc22

2006040136

9 8 7 6 5 4 3 2 1

Printed in the United States of America
on acid-free paper

CONTENTS

PART TWO The Critique of Capitalist Production, Industrial Society, and the Democratic State

PART THREE The Critique of Consumption, Rationality, and Imperialism

Preface

This book has its origins in a classroom. I'd been teaching classical sociological theory for over twenty years—first as a teaching assistant at the University of California, Berkeley, then at Rutgers and SUNY Stony Brook, where I've been a professor. In 1991, I returned to Berkeley as a Visiting Professor for a couple of years, teaching in both the Sociology Department and the program in the Political Economy of Industrial Societies, an interdisciplinary program in international studies.

In one particular class session of Classical Theories of Political Economy, early in the semester, we were discussing Locke's *Second Treatise on Government*, as I had in every theory class I had ever taught. Here Locke makes his case to expand the franchise by arguing that each man has property in his own person, a radical idea for the time, since property ownership was the basis for civic participation. I knew enough to modify Locke's seeming radicalism with an acknowledgment that women were still to be excluded from the franchise. One student, an African American man, posed a different question. "Locke theorizes about men owning property, or at his most radical, in possessing property in their own person," he said. "But how about his position on men who were themselves property? What does Locke say about slavery? How can he justify that?"

This was one of those moments of decision for me as a professor. Do I take the easy route, mumble some equivocating answer, and move on to the next topic? Do I toss it back his way by suggesting that he do some research on the topic and thus avoid being exposed for not knowing the answer? "I don't know," I said. "I'll get back to you on it in the next class."

I spent the next day in the library, rifling through several biographies of Locke and reading through other works I had not read since college. It turned out that Locke had financial interests in the Royal African Company, a slave-trading company, and helped to draft the *Fundamental Constitution of the Carolinas*, which explicitly granted citizens the right to own "negro slaves." His tepid sets of equivocations about slavery in his work struck me as so much academic weaseling, hardly a well-thought-out and coherent response.

I dutifully reported these findings to the class. I had bumped up against one of my own blind spots—or, rather, been pushed against it. I was surprised and somewhat thrilled by being pressed to return to the library, by having to do some homework myself. (I often think that much of the resistance to multiculturalism that is evident among the fiercest defenders of the traditional canon is just academic laziness masquerading as deference to the canon. Professors often feel themselves too busy, too harried, and too preoccupied with their research to do something as mundane as go to the library and reread texts that they have been teaching for what seems like an eternity.)

Here was the virtue of the multicultural classroom in sociological miniature—students of equal ability bringing their different life experiences into the classroom and using these experiences as resources, as the basis for interrogation of the canon. I was also curious: what else had I missed? What other perspectives had been missing from the way I had been taught the canonical texts?

I was already primed for such an inquiry. I had just completed a documentary history of men who had supported feminism throughout American history, and I knew from that research that many of the biographies of the more prominent of these "pro-feminist" men had scarcely mentioned their support of women's equality. Thus was the historical record shaped by biographers who wanted it clear that men like Thomas Paine, Thomas Wentworth Higginson, or even Frederick Douglass were "really" involved in far more pressing matters than the trivial pursuit of women's rights.

Now, it seemed, I knew better. I knew that the historical record is sanitized through revision as each generation of historians creates the history they feel is important for readers to have. And I came to know how some of the more prominent voices of the nineteenth century had been eliminated from that traditional canon as it was, itself, created in the first few decades of this century. That canon is, itself, a historical creation, a series of decisions about which works get in and which works are left out.

So I set about setting the record straight—or, at least, straighter. This anthology is the first result of that effort. We have not tried to elevate some second-rate thinkers into that hallowed pantheon of classical theorists, but rather tried to restore for contemporary readers the lively number of voices—voices of women, of people of color—who were actively engaged with the questions that define the terrain of classical social and political theory. Many of these theorists' contributions were effaced in the construction of the canon, their work omitted, their voices silenced. But at the time, their work was part of a larger theoretical conversation than has been acknowledged.

This anthology, then, has been motivated more by a sense of historical restoration than ideological purity. It is part of a project that questions the sacredness of the sacred texts, not because they are not, in themselves, meritorious, but because in the process of handing them down to us, other voices have been forgotten. This anthology, then, presents a more historically accurate classical canon—a canon that is informed by both the historical record and the needs of contemporary students.

I am grateful to the institutions at which I have taught for the past two decades. I'm especially grateful to Diane Barthel-Bouchier, who adopted the book in her classes and provided valuable feedback that helped me negotiate the revisions.

My family and friends have, as always, been supportive. Amy Aronson was in the final throes of dissertation writing when I assembled the first edition of this volume; now we're a (usually) smoothly functioning two-career family that, together with our seven-year-old son, Zachary, daily shows the limitations of any social theory that suggests that the personal and political are separate domains. But while we may need new and better theories to accommodate our lives, I wouldn't change a thing about the life we've made together.

I also acknowledge the work by my collaborators, Charles Stephen (on the first edition) and Matthew Mahler (on the second edition). I engaged each as an "assistant;" but they both became valued partners in the intellectual venture.

This book was born in that classroom at Berkeley, but it has been developing in all the Classical Social and Political Theory courses I have ever taught. I was deeply honored when those students nominated me as "Best Professor" at Berkeley in 1992–1993 (and thrilled when the article about me in *The Daily Californian* was placed next to the article about Jason Kidd, who had been voted "Best Athlete"). But I have learned far more from them than they can ever know. This book is for them.

M. S. K.

Introduction

Classical social and political philosophy forms the theoretical backbone of most disciplines in the social sciences and humanities. An introductory course in social and political theory presents the traditional canon of the development of western social theory from the Enlightenment to the end of the nineteenth century. A second course usually picks up the story from the turn of the century to the present day. This traditional canon of social and political theory seems to have solidified at the turn of the twentieth century, when academic social science sought its historical origins in the first centuries of Enlightenment thought. As academic social and political sciences distinguished themselves from philosophy, they appropriated Continental political and social philosophy as the foundation texts of their disciplines.

The classical sociological canon, consisting invariably of Durkheim, Weber, and Marx and usually of Comte, Freud, Veblen, Mead, Tocqueville, and Simmel, built on the chief insights of Hobbes, Locke, Rousseau, and Smith. Occasionally, works by Jefferson, Michels, Mill, Mosca, and Pareto might also have been added; these works were far more routinely included in courses on classical political theory offered by political science departments.

The traditional classical canon in social and political theory, therefore, did not fall out of the western European sky as a complete package ready for course adoption. It was an attempt by turn-of-the-century social scientists to claim a legacy within the canonical theories of Enlightenment philosophy in western Europe. Classics became classics because they were *declared* "classics" by intellectual specialists who were seeking to legitimate their own status. The canon has a history.

And it has politics. The creation of the canon was a political project from the start, seeking to locate these new discourses within the framework occupied by older, more respected and established academic fields, such as philosophy. In the process, certain themes were accentuated, such as the relationship of the individual to society, the development of the marketplace, and the relationship of that marketplace to the state. And certain themes were downplayed, such as the competing claims for inclusion by women or by African Americans; certain discourses were moved to the margins, such as the debates about woman suffrage or slavery. As we came to know them, the "Founding Fathers" of sociology, political science, anthropology, psychology, and economics were almost all white European men.

Of all the courses in the social science curriculum, those on classical social and political theory have been perhaps the most resistant to transformation in light of the current movements toward multiculturalism and diversity. In part, this is a generational issue as much as a political issue. In sociology, the classical canon was predominantly the work of Talcott Parsons in the 1930s and 1940s, and a subsequent generation of his students built the great sociology departments during the boom period of academic growth of the social sciences in the 1950s and 1960s. It was thus not until recently that sociology had such a classical canon.*

Increasingly, however, a new generation of scholars and students is seeking to disestablish that traditional canon, reevaluate the criteria for inclusion and exclusion, and redefine what constitutes the "classical" in classical social and political theory. We are interested in developing curricula that reflect the diversity and multicultural backgrounds of our students, our colleagues, and ourselves and, in so doing, in developing courses that more accurately reflect the subject matters we teach.

This movement is not simply a matter of historical resuscitation, by which formerly obscure theorists are elevated to the ranks of the great simply because they fill specific niches that had previously gone unfilled. It is more a project of setting the historical record straight, striving for a more inclusive and historically accurate presentation of the evolution of sociology's core ideas. Several of the theorists who are included here were far more influential in their time than they were subsequently declared to be as the canon was created. When Mary Wollstonecraft, Frederick Douglass, and W. E. B. Du Bois wrote, for example, their works were widely read and discussed as major contributions to the development of social and political theory. It was only later that they were pushed to the margins of the canon, declared to be derivative or second rate. This book restores them not only to a position that they *should* hold, but also to a position that they *did* hold.

This raises another issue in the study of classical social and political theory. Currently, most departments require their majors to take a course in classical theory—a course that the students invariably dread; put off for as long as possible; and, finally, grudgingly take. The students are convinced that such courses will be among the most esoteric in their collegiate curriculum and will speak less to their intellectual needs than to some perverse, possibly sadistic, need of professors to make students take unpleasant, boring, and irrelevant courses.

Social and political theory was not always considered an esoteric subject. Like any other cultural form, it was removed from everyday discussion to the rarified atmosphere of the university lecture hall. As intellectual elites at the turn of the twentieth century strove to legitimate their privileged access to knowledge, they removed from the emerging canon writers whose works were popular and widely read and debated by a large number of non-intellectuals. In their stead, the canon became increasingly composed of university professors who wrote, to be sure, about foundation issues in the social sciences, but in a language that was increasingly dense and impenetrable to ordinary people.

Such a process occurred in other cultural arenas as well. In the middle of the nineteenth century, ordinary people loved Shakespeare and the opera. Presentations of Shakespeare's plays and classical opera were raucous affairs, with full-fledged audience participation as viewers would shout their approval of particular scenes or especially delightful arias. The viewers would often even shout requests for their favorite scenes from *other* plays and often

* R. W. Connell, "Why Is Classical Theory Classical?" *American Journal of Sociology* 102, no. 6 (May 1997).

be obliged by a dedicated cast. As the eminent cultural historian Lawrence Levine shows in his brilliant book *Highbrow/Lowbrow*, it wasn't until the turn of the century that cultural and intellectual elites insisted on the reverential respect and utterly silent viewing that we now accord opera and Shakespearean drama.

So, too, with classical social and political theory. In the middle of the nineteenth century, local town meetings were held to discuss the writings of Frederick Douglass, arguably the premier public intellectual of the century. When Douglass publicly advocated woman suffrage in 1848, for example, it was seen as so newsworthy that the day after, the newspapers in Syracuse, New York, wrote vicious editorials denouncing his momentous position, calling him an "Aunt Nancy Man," the mid-nineteenth-century version of a wimp. Mary Wollstonecraft's writings were widely published in eighteenth-century newspapers and magazines, and her radical notions about women's rights were debated in coffeehouses, not seminar classrooms.

The selections in this book, then, paint a different picture of the historical development of classical social and political theory—a picture at once more historically accurate and more inclusive of the voices of those who have historically been marginalized. In doing so, they also suggest new questions to be posed to the Founding Fathers of the field. If, as Locke and Jefferson assert, human beings have an inalienable right to property, including property in their own person, then what are we to make of those people who are, themselves, property? Including the works of Frederick Douglass, Margaret Fuller, and Mary Wollstonecraft forces us to reexamine that question from a new angle. If human beings' experiences in the process of economic production hold the keys to both our enslavement and our liberation, as Marx argued, then, asked Charlotte Perkins Gilman, what of the realm of *reproduction*, the home and family? What does that separation of spheres look like from *women's* point of view? W. E. B. Du Bois and Gilman ask if the traditional community, however fundamentally moral (as Durkheim suggested it was), also includes "natural" hierarchies of race and gender.

These are not idle questions, offered to placate the marginalized. They were, and remain, among the most vital theoretical and political questions of our era, evidence that classical social and political theory continues to speak to new generations of students and scholars about the issues that most affect our lives. This it has always done, despite efforts of effete scholasticists to remove theory from the realm of the practical, to which it has always been linked. And as long as we continue to read these works in context, questioning always which voices are privileged and which are marginalized, classical social and political theory will continue to inform the everyday life of an enlightened citizenry.

PART ONE

The Rise of Society, the Market, and the State

Thomas Hobbes

Thomas Hobbes (1588–1679), English philosopher and scientist, is almost universally regarded as the founder of modern social thought. Hobbes attempted to use the new science of his day to explain the nature of man and society, without recourse to the religious and moral assumptions of the Greco-Christian tradition.

Hobbes was born in 1588 in Malmesbury, England, the son of a poor clergyman who deserted his family when Thomas was sixteen years old. He was recognized early as a brilliant boy and mastered the curriculum of the Renaissance grammar school, with its emphasis on Latin, Greek, and poetry. A fine linguist and translator, he was fluent in Latin, Greek, French, and Italian, and all his life wrote Latin and English verse. With these skills, a bright, lower-class boy could expect opportunities in the church, law, or medicine, or perhaps a place in an aristocratic household. Many seventeenth-century writers lived as bachelor secretaries, conducting correspondence, drafting speeches, giving advice, and tutoring the children. It was into the household of Sir William Cavendish that Hobbes was recruited in 1608, and he remained in such employment for the rest of his life, sitting in anterooms while his master and other great men discussed affairs of state, managing the lord's financial affairs, providing advice, and touring Europe with noblemen's sons.

Hobbes's first trip to Europe (1610–1615), particularly his stay in Venice, stimulated his interest in science and philosophy by bringing him into contact with the leaders of Renaissance thought in Europe. These men were skeptics grappling with the rise of the modern state and with deep divisions in the church. Modern political reality, based on deceit and intimidation, was a far cry from the recently rediscovered writings of Cicero and Aristotle, and also seemed to render traditional ethics irrelevant. Shaken by the Wars of Religion that followed the Reformation, these men condemned honor, patriotism, and religious principle as dangerous illusions, declaring that the only certain principle of human conduct was *self-preservation*. In one sense Hobbes's lifework was to transform this culture from within: What the skeptics regarded as a fact of human nature, Hobbes makes the fundamental *right* on which a new kind of ethics can be constructed.

Another visit to Europe from 1634 to 1636 gave Hobbes the tools he needed to answer skepticism without a retreat to Greco-Christian ethics, which he believed to be discredited. Whereas sixteenth-century skepticism had questioned the possibility of ever having true knowledge of anything, the new philosophers of Paris, led by René Descartes, insisted that human beings could still know reality even if there is no resemblance at all between our sense experience and the external world. Descartes's own solution rested on a complex argument about God that few found convincing. But the search for a firm basis of knowledge, not fallible like our senses, led others, including Hobbes, to the new physics of Galileo and to geometry. Hobbes visited Galileo at Florence in 1636, and during the next three years worked on a philosophy that would incorporate but go beyond Descartes. Entitled *The Elements of Philosophy* and written in Latin, it comprised three parts: a section on physics, showing that the causes of all things lay in diversity of motion; a section on psychology, showing that bodily motions were involved in human thinking and volition; and a section that developed the political implications of these arguments. The book was never published as a whole but was the basis of most of Hobbes's later work.

Increasing strife in England forced Hobbes to flee England for Paris, where he joined other Royalist exiles and found himself cut off from his English income. In 1640, hoping to avert civil war, he published the third part of his Latin treatise as *The Elements of Law, Natural and Politic*. Basing human rights on the principles of natural science, Hobbes argued that in a "state of nature," man's restless appetites drive him to seek his own preservation, and that whatever is necessary for this (provided it does not endanger other people's preservation) is therefore legitimate. Yet this is the *only* right man possesses, which means that in times of strife, an entire population might agree to renounce its freedoms in order to achieve social peace or harmony. Indeed, Hobbes intended his theory of rights as a defense of absolute monarchy—a view that was to irk John Locke and arouse the fury of Jean-Jacques Rousseau. Hobbes's views antagonized almost everyone in the England of his day: The believers in divine right of kings condemned his atheism and his effort to base sovereignty on a social contract, and parliamentarians were outraged by his advocacy of absolute monarchy.

Believing himself a marked man, Hobbes stayed in exile until 1651. He made his living as a mathematics tutor to the Prince of Wales, the future Charles II, but worked chiefly on his philosophy. *De cive* (1642) expanded *The Elements of Law*, focusing on the relation between church and state, and argued that because church and state were one body, with the ruler at the head, he thus had the right to interpret Scripture, to decide religious disputes, and to determine the form of public worship. In 1651 there appeared an English edition of *De cive* and, in the same year, Hobbes's masterpiece, *Leviathan*. Illness and poverty, together with difficulties stemming from his move back to England, delayed the completion of *The Elements of Philosophy*; as a result, Section One did not appear until 1655, under the title *Matter* (*De Corpore*), and Section Two in 1658, as *Man* (*De Homine*), published as Hobbes turned seventy. Both works show a decline in his powers and have never excited the enthusiasm that still greets his earlier works.

It can hardly be said that in the years after age seventy Hobbes retired from public life. He acquired a new prominence when the Prince of Wales, his former pupil, was restored to the throne as Charles II. He resumed his controversy with the church and entered into new ones over mathematics, physics, and constitutional law. He published an account of the English Civil War, *Behemoth* (1679), and in his eighties produced complete translations of the *Odyssey* and the *Iliad*. Hobbes died in Derbyshire on December 4, 1679.

Hobbes's reputation as a thinker rests on his social philosophy, in particular *Leviathan*. In accordance with his view that everything is matter in motion, Hobbes argues that all human desires are connected with the need to keep the body in motion and so avoid death. The most important passions are hope, or "appetite," and fear; the former impels people toward society, the latter drives them from it. All seemingly unselfish motives are seen as indirect ways of furthering our own interests, and human life is a constant struggle to satisfy desire.

To help them in this process, human beings are endowed with reason, which shows them the most effective ways to gain satisfaction and avoid disappointment. These strategies Hobbes calls "power," and power cannot be acquired without conflict. First people must struggle for scarce resources, then they must prevent others from taking the power they have obtained, and finally, even when they are secure in their possessions, they seek the feeling of superiority that springs from having power over others. As a result, in the absence of external controls they are in a chronic "state of war" with one another, and face a life that is "solitary, poore, nasty, brutish, and short."

Human beings need society and covet its benefits, yet by their nature they seem unable to cooperate. No one can be trusted to refrain from harming others when it benefits him to do so. Hobbes's solution to this paradox is that people in the "state of nature," before they make any other agreements, must first contract with one another to establish a power that will force them to keep their promises. This social contract makes it rational for them to act on their selfish desire for peaceful relationships because they are guaranteed the benefits they wish for as long as they themselves refrain from harming others. The power or "sovereign" can call on the collective strength of all other members of society to oppose any lawbreaker. With the assurance of security, industry, cultivation, and trading become possible.

Hobbes's theory holds that all social relationships are artificial in that they are the product of calculation rather than impulse or affection. Society is sustained not by a moral consensus but through a kind of cost–benefit analysis. Even the family is not based on natural affection but holds together because of the dominion of the father, which is based on force. It is important to note that the sovereign not only monopolizes the force that ensures social peace, he also determines what is right and wrong: the rules of social interaction. There is no moral authority higher than self-interest, and what matters for society is not that its rules are "correct" but that they are clearly and authoritatively determined. Thus people relinquish the right of private judgment just as they give up the right to defend themselves. Anything less will bring about a return to "perpetuale warre of every man against his neighbour."

From his descriptive sociology, then, Hobbes derives a moral conclusion: Human beings must give their consent to absolute government. Anything less makes government unstable and social life impossible.

LEVIATHAN

1651

THE INTRODUCTION

NATURE (the Art whereby God hath made and governes the World) is by the *Art* of man, as in many other things, so in this also imitated, that it can make an Artificial Animal. For seeing life is but a motion of Limbs, the begining whereof is in some principall part within; why may we not say, that all *Automata* (Engines that move themselves by springs and wheeles as doth a watch) have an artificiall life? For what is the *Heart*, but a *Spring*; and the *Nerves*, but so many *Strings*; and the *Joynts*, but so many *Wheeles*, giving motion to the whole Body, such as was intended by the Artificer? *Art* goes yet further, imitating that Rationall and most excellent worke of Nature, *Man*. For by Art is created that great LEVIATHAN called a COMMON-WEALTH, or STATE, (in latine CIVITAS) which is but an Artificiall Man; though of greater stature and strength than the Naturall, for whose protection and defence it was intended; and in which, the *Soveraignty* is an Artificiall *Soul*, as giving life and motion to the whole body; The *Magistrates*, and other *Officers* of Judicature and Execution, artificiall *Joynts*; *Reward* and *Punishment* (by which fastned to the seate of the Soveraignty, every joynt and member is moved

From *Leviathan* by Thomas Hobbes, ed. C. B. Macpherson (Baltimore: Penguin Inc., Pelican Books, 1968 [1651]).

to performe his duty) are the *Nerves*, that do the same in the Body Naturall; The *Wealth* and *Riches* of all the particular members, are the *Strength*; *Salus Populi* (the *peoples safety*) its *Businesse*; *Counsellors*, by whom all things needfull for it to know, are suggested unto it, are the *Memory*; *Equity* and *Lawes*, an artificiall *Reason* and *Will*; *Concord*, *Health*; *Sedition*, *Sicknesse*; and *Civill war*, *Death*. Lastly, the *Pacts* and *Covenants*, by which the parts of this Body Politique were at first made, set together, and united, resemble that *Fiat*, or the *Let us make man*, pronounced by God in the Creation.

To describe the Nature of this Artificiall man, I will consider

First, the *Matter* thereof, and the *Artificer*; both which is *Man*.
Secondly, *How*, and by what *Covenants* it is made; what are the *Rights* and just *Power* or *Authority* of a *Soveraigne*; and what it is that *preserveth* and *dissolveth* it.
Thirdly, what is a *Christian Common-wealth*.
Lastly, what is the *Kingdome of Darkness*.

Concerning the first, there is a saying much usurped of late, That *Wisedome* is acquired, not by reading of *Books*, but of *Men*. Consequently whereunto, those persons, that for the most part can give no other proof of being wise, take great delight to shew what they think they have read in men, by uncharitable censures of one another behind their backs. But there is another saying not of late understood, by which they might learn truly to read one another, if they would take the pains; and that is, *Nosce teipsum*, *Read thy self*: which was not meant, as it is now used, to countenance, either the barbarous state of men in power, towards their inferiors; or to encourage men of low degree, to a sawcie behaviour towards their betters; But to teach us, that for the similitude of the thoughts, and Passions of one man, to the thoughts, and Passions of another, whosoever looketh into himself, and considereth what he doth, when he does *think*, *opine*, *reason*, *hope*, *feare*, &c, and upon what grounds; he shall thereby read and know, what are the thoughts, and Passions of all other men, upon the like occasions. I say the similitude of *Passions*, which are the same in all men, *desire*, *feare*, *hope*, &c; not the similitude of *the objects* of the Passions, which are the things *desired*, *feared*, *hoped*, &c: for these the constitution individuall, and particular education do so vary, and they are so easie to be kept from our knowledge, that the characters of mans heart, blotted and confounded as they are, with dissembling, lying, counterfeiting, and erroneous doctrines, are legible onely to him that searcheth hearts. And though by mens actions wee do discover their designe sometimes; yet to do it without comparing them with our own, and distinguishing all circumstances, by which the case may come to be altered, is to decypher without a key, and be for the most part deceived, by too much trust, or by too much diffidence; as he that reads, is himself a good or evil man.

But let one man read another by his actions never so perfectly, it serves him onely with his acquaintance, which are but few. He that is to govern a whole Nation, must read in himself, not this, or that particular man; but Man-kind: which though it be hard to do, harder than to learn any Language, or Science; yet, when I shall have set down my own reading orderly, and perspicuously, the pains left another, will be onely to consider, if he also find not the same in himself. For this kind of Doctrine, admitteth no other Demonstration.

. . .

XII Of Man

Lastly, amongst the points by the Church of *Rome* declared necessary for Salvation, there be so many, manifestly to the advantage of the Pope, and of his spirituall subjects, residing in the territories of other Christian Princes, that were it not for the mutuall emulation of those Princes, they might without warre, or trouble, exclude all forraign Authority, as easily as it has been excluded in *England*. For who is there that does not see, to whose benefit it conduceth, to have it believed, that a King hath not his Authority from Christ, unlesse a Bishop crown him?

That a King, if he be a Priest, cannot Marry? That whether a Prince be born in lawfull Marriage, or not, must be judged by Authority from *Rome*? That Subjects may be freed from their Alleageance, if by the Court of *Rome*, the King be judged an Heretique? That a King (as *Chilperique* of *France*) may be deposed by a Pope (as Pope *Zachary*,) for no cause; and his Kingdome given to one of his Subjects? That the Clergy, and Regulars, in what Country soever, shall be exempt from the Jurisdiction of their King, in cases criminall? Or who does not see, to whose profit redound the Fees of private Masses, and Vales of Purgatory; with other signes of private interest, enough to mortifie the most lively Faith, if (as I sayd) the civill Magistrate, and Custome did not more sustain it, than any opinion they have of the Sanctity, Wisdom, or Probity of their Teachers? So that I may attribute all the changes of Religion in the world, to one and the same cause; and that is, unpleasing Priests; and those not onely amongst Catholiques, but even in that Church that hath presumed most of Reformation.

XIII Of the Naturall Condition of Mankind, as concerning their Felicity, and Misery

NATURE hath made men so equall, in the faculties of body, and mind; as that though there bee found one man sometimes manifestly stronger in body, or of quicker mind then another; yet when all is reckoned together, the difference between man, and man, is not so considerable, as that one man can thereupon claim to himselfe any benefit, to which another may not pretend, as well as he. For as to the strength of body, the weakest has strength enough to kill the strongest, either by secret machination, or by confederacy with others, that are in the same danger with himselfe.

And as to the faculties of the mind, (setting aside the arts grounded upon words, and especially that skill of proceeding upon generall, and infallible rules, called Science; which very few have, and but in few things; as being not a native faculty, born with us; nor attained, (as Prudence,) while we look after somewhat els,) I find yet a greater equality amongst men, than that of strength. For Prudence, is but Experience; which equall time, equally bestowes on all men, in those things they equally apply themselves unto. That which may perhaps make such equality incredible, is but a vain conceipt of ones owne wisdome, which almost all men think they have in a greater degree, than the Vulgar; that is, than all men but themselves, and a few others, whom by Fame, or for concurring with themselves, they approve. For such is the nature of men, that howsoever they may acknowledge many others to be more witty, or more eloquent, or more learned; Yet they will hardly believe there be many so wise as themselves: For they see their own wit at hand, and other mens at a distance. But this proveth rather that men are in that point equall, than unequall. For there is not ordinarily a greater signe of the equall distribution of any thing, than that every man is contented with his share.

From this equality of ability, ariseth equality of hope in the attaining of our Ends. And therefore if any two men desire the same thing, which neverthelesse they cannot both enjoy, they become enemies; and in the way to their End, (which is principally their owne conservation, and sometimes their delectation only,) endeavour to destroy, or subdue one an other. And from hence it comes to passe, that where an Invader hath no more to feare, than an other mans single power; if one plant, sow, build, or possesse a convenient Seat, others may probably be expected to come prepared with forces united, to dispossesse, and deprive him, not only of the fruit of his labour, but also of his life, or liberty. And the Invader again is in the like danger of another.

And from this diffidence of one another, there is no way for any man to secure himselfe, so reasonable, as Anticipation; that is, by force, or wiles, to master the persons of all men he can, so long, till he see no other power great enough to endanger him: And this is no more than his own conservation requireth, and is generally allowed. Also because there be some, that taking pleasure in contemplating their own power in the acts of conquest, which they pursue farther than their security requires; if others, that otherwise would be glad to be at ease within modest bounds, should not by invasion increase their power, they would not be able, long time, by standing only on their defence, to subsist. And by consequence, such augmentation of dominion over men, being necessary to a mans conservation, it ought to be allowed him.

Againe, men have no pleasure, (but on the contrary a great deale of griefe) in keeping company, where there is no power able to over-awe them all. For every man looketh that his companion should value him, at the same rate he sets upon himselfe: And upon all signes of contempt, or undervaluing, naturally endeavours, as far as he dares (which amongst them that have no common power, to keep them in quiet, is far enough to make them destroy each other,) to extort a greater value from his contemners, by dommage; and from others, by the example.

So that in the nature of man, we find three principall causes of quarrell. First, Competition; Secondly, Diffidence; Thirdly, Glory.

The first, maketh men invade for Gain; the second, for Safety; and the third, for Reputation. The first use Violence, to make themselves Masters of other mens persons, wives, children, and cattell; the second, to defend them; the third, for trifles, as a word, a smile, a different opinion, and any other signe of undervalue, either direct in their Persons, or by reflexion in their Kindred, their Friends, their Nation, their Profession, or their Name.

Hereby it is manifest, that during the time men live without a common Power to keep them all in awe, they are in that condition which is called Warre; and such a warre, as is of every man, against every man. For WARRE, consisteth not in Battell onely, or the act of fighting; but in a tract of time, wherein the Will to contend by Battell is sufficiently known: and therefore the notion of *Time*, is to be considered in the nature of Warre; as it is in the nature of Weather. For as the nature of Foule weather, lyeth not in a showre or two of rain; but in an inclination thereto of many dayes together: So the nature of Warre, consisteth not in actuall fighting; but in the known disposition thereto, during all the time there is no assurance to the contrary. All other time is PEACE.

Whatsoever therefore is consequent to a time of Warre, where every man is Enemy to every man; the same is consequent to the time, wherein men live without other security, than what their own strength, and their own invention shall furnish them withall. In such condition, there is no place for Industry; because the fruit thereof is uncertain: and consequently no Culture of the Earth; no Navigation, nor use of the commodities that may be imported by Sea; no commodious Building; no Instruments of moving, and removing such things as require much force; no Knowledge of the face of the Earth; no account of Time; no Arts; no Letters; no Society; and which is worst of all, continuall feare, and danger of violent death; And the life of man, solitary, poore, nasty, brutish, and short.

It may seem strange to some man, that has not well weighed these things; that Nature should thus dissociate, and render men apt to invade, and destroy one another: and he may therefore, not trusting to this Inference, made from the Passions, desire perhaps to have the same confirmed by Experience. Let him therefore consider with himselfe, when taking a journey, he armes himselfe, and seeks to go well accompanied; when going to sleep, he locks his dores; when even in his house he locks his chests; and this when he knows there bee Lawes, and publike Officers, armed, to revenge all injuries shall bee done him; what opinion he has of his fellow subjects, when he rides armed; of his fellow Citizens, when he locks his dores; and of his children, and servants, when he locks his chests. Does he not there as much accuse mankind by his actions, as I do by my words? But neither of us accuse mans nature in it. The Desires, and other Passions of man, are in themselves no Sin. No more are the Actions, that proceed from those Passions, till they know a Law that forbids them: which till Lawes be made they cannot know: nor can any Law be made, till they have agreed upon the Person that shall make it.

It may peradventure be thought, there was never such a time, nor condition of warre as this; and I believe it was never generally so, over all the world: but there are many places, where they live so now. For the savage people in many places of *America*, except the government of small Families, the concord whereof dependeth on naturall lust, have no government at all; and live at this day in that brutish manner, as I said before. Howsoever, it may be perceived what manner of life there would be, where there were no common Power to feare; by the manner of life, which men that have formerly lived under a peacefull government, use to degenerate into, in a civill Warre.

But though there had never been any time, wherein particular men were in a condition of warre one against another; yet in all times, Kings, and Persons of Soveraigne authority, because of their Independency, are in continuall jealousies, and in the state and posture of Gladiators; having their weapons pointing, and their eyes fixed on one another; that is, their Forts, Garrisons, and Guns upon the Frontiers of their Kingdomes; and continuall Spyes upon their neighbours; which is a posture of War. But because they uphold thereby, the Industry of their Subjects; there does not follow from it, that misery, which accompanies the Liberty of particular men.

To this warre of every man against every man, this also is consequent; that nothing can be Unjust. The notions of Right and Wrong, Justice and Injustice have there no place. Where there is no common Power, there is no Law: where no Law, no Injustice. Force, and Fraud, are in warre the two Cardinall vertues. Justice, and Injustice are none of the Faculties neither of the Body, nor Mind. If they were, they might be in a man that were alone in the world, as well as his Senses, and Passions. They are Qualities, that relate to men in Society, not in Solitude. It is consequent also to the same condition, that there be no Propriety, no Dominion, no *Mine* and *Thine* distinct; but onely that to be every mans that he can get; and for so long, as he can keep it. And thus much for the ill condition, which man by meer Nature is actually placed in; though with a possibility to come out of it, consisting partly in the Passions, partly in his Reason.

The Passions that encline men to Peace, are Feare of Death; Desire of such things as are necessary to commodious living; and a Hope by their Industry to obtain them. And Reason suggesteth convenient Articles of Peace, upon which men may be drawn to agreement. These Articles, are they, which otherwise are called the Lawes of Nature: whereof I shall speak more particularly, in the two following Chapters.

XIV Of the first and second Naturall Lawes, and of Contracts

The RIGHT OF NATURE, which Writers commonly call *Jus Naturale*, is the Liberty each man hath, to use his own power, as he will himselfe, for the preservation of his own Nature; that is to say, of his own Life; and consequently, of doing any thing, which in his own Judgement, and Reason, hee shall conceive to be the aptest means thereunto.

By LIBERTY, is understood, according to the proper signification of the word, the absence of externall Impediments: which Impediments, may oft take away part of a mans power to do what hee would; but cannot hinder him from using the power left him, according as his judgement, and reason shall dictate to him.

A LAW OF NATURE, (*Lex Naturalis*,) is a Precept, or generall Rule, found out by Reason, by which a man is forbidden to do, that, which is destructive of his life, or taketh away the means of preserving the same; and to omit, that, by which he thinketh it may be best preserved. For though they that speak of this subject, use to confound *Jus*, and *Lex*, *Right* and *Law*; yet they ought to be distinguished; because RIGHT, consisteth in liberty to do, or to forbeare; Whereas LAW, determineth, and bindeth to one of them: so that Law, and Right, differ as much, as Obligation, and Liberty; which in one and the same matter are inconsistent.

And because the condition of Man, (as hath been declared in the precedent Chapter) is a condition of

Warre of every one against every one; in which case every one is governed by his own Reason; and there is nothing he can make use of, that may not be a help unto him, in preserving his life against his enemyes; It followeth, that in such a condition, every man has a Right to every thing; even to one anothers body. And therefore, as long as this naturall Right of every man to every thing endureth, there can be no security to any man, (how strong or wise soever he be,) of living out the time, which Nature ordinarily alloweth men to live. And consequently it is a precept, or generall rule of Reason, *That every man, ought to endeavour Peace, as farre as he has hope of obtaining it; and when he cannot obtain it, that he may seek, and use, all helps, and advantages of Warre.* The first branch of which Rule, containeth the first, and Fundamentall Law of Nature; which is, *to seek Peace, and follow it.* The Second, the summe of the Right of Nature; which is, *By all means we can, to defend our selves.*

From this Fundamentall Law of Nature, by which men are commanded to endeavour Peace, is derived this second Law; *That a man be willing, when others are so too, as farre-forth, as for Peace, and defence of himselfe he shall think it necessary, to lay down this right to all things; and be contented with so much liberty against other men, as he would allow other men against himselfe.* For as long as every man holdeth this Right, of doing any thing he liketh; so long are all men in the condition of Warre. But if other men will not lay down their Right, as well as he; then there is no Reason for any one, to devest himselfe of his: For that were to expose himselfe to Prey, (which no man is bound to) rather than to dispose himselfe to Peace. This is that Law of the Gospell; *Whatsoever you require that others should do to you, that do ye to them.* And that Law of all men, *Quod tibi fieri non vis, alteri ne feceris.*

To *lay downe* a mans *Right* to any thing, is to *devest* himselfe of the *Liberty*, of hindring another of the benefit of his own Right to the same. For he that renounceth, or passeth away his Right, giveth not to any other man a Right which he had not before; because there is nothing to which every man had not Right by Nature: but onely standeth out of his way, that he may enjoy his own originall Right, without hindrance from him; not without hindrance from another. So that the effect which redoundeth to one man, by another mans defect of Right, is but so much diminution of impediments to the use of his own Right originall.

Right is layd aside, either by simply Renouncing it; or by Transferring it to another. By *Simply* RENOUNCING; when he cares not to whom the benefit thereof redoundeth. By TRANSFERRING; when he intendeth the benefit thereof to some certain person, or persons. And when a man hath in either manner abandoned, or granted away his Right; then is he said to be OBLIGED, or BOUND, not to hinder those, to whom such Right is granted, or abandoned, from the benefit of it: and that he *Ought*, and it is his DUTY, not to make voyd that voluntary act of his own: and that such hindrance is INJUSTICE, and INJURY, as being *Sine Jure*; the Right being before renounced, or transferred. So that *Injury*, or *Injustice*, in the controversies of the world, is somewhat like to that, which in the disputations of Scholers is called *Absurdity*. For as it is there called an Absurdity, to contradict what one maintained in the Beginning: so in the world, it is called Injustice, and Injury, voluntarily to undo that, which from the beginning he had voluntarily done. The way by which a man either simply Renounceth, or Transferreth his Right, is a Declaration, or Signification, by some voluntary and sufficient signe, or signes, that he doth so Renounce, or Transferre; or hath so Renounced, or Transferred the same, to him that accepteth it. And these Signes are either Words onely, or Actions onely; or (as it happeneth most often) both Words and Actions. And the same are the BONDS, by which men are bound, and obliged: Bonds, that have their strength, not from their own Nature, (for nothing is more easily broken than a mans word,) but from Feare of some evill consequence upon the rupture.

Whensoever a man Transferreth his Right, or Renounceth it; it is either in consideration of some Right reciprocally transferred to himselfe; or for some other good he hopeth for thereby. For it is a voluntary act: and of the voluntary acts of every man, the object is some *Good to himselfe*. And therefore there be some Rights, which no man can be understood by any words, or other signes, to have abandoned, or transferred. As first a man cannot lay down the right of resisting them, that assault him by force, to take away his life; because he cannot be understood to ayme thereby, at any Good to himself. The same may be sayd of Wounds, and Chayns, and Imprisonment; both because there is no benefit consequent to such patience; as there is to the patience of suffering another to be wounded, or imprisoned: as also because a man cannot tell, when he seeth men proceed against him by violence, whether they intend his death or not. And lastly the motive, and end for which this renouncing, and transferring of Right is introduced, is nothing else but the security of a mans person, in his life, and in the means of so preserving life, as not to be weary of it. And therefore if a man by words, or other signes, seem to despoyle himselfe of the End, for which those signes were intended; he is not to be understood as if he meant it, or that it was his will; but that he was ignorant of how such words and actions were to be interpreted.

The mutuall transferring of Right, is that which men call CONTRACT.

OF COMMON-WEALTH

XVII Of the Causes, Generation, and Definition of a Common-Wealth

The finall Cause, End, or Designe of men, (who naturally love Liberty, and Dominion over others,) in the introduction of that restraint upon themselves, (in which wee see them live in Common-wealths,) is the foresight of their own preservation, and of a more contented life thereby; that is to say, of getting themselves out from that miserable condition of Warre, which is necessarily consequent (as hath been shewn) to the naturall Passions of men, when there is no visible Power to keep them in awe, and tye them by feare of punishment to the performance of their Covenants, and observation of those Lawes of Nature set down in the fourteenth and fifteenth Chapters.

For the Lawes of Nature (as *Justice*, *Equity*, *Modesty*, *Mercy*, and (in summe) *doing to others, as wee would be done to,*) of themselves, without the terrour of some Power, to cause them to be observed, are contrary to our naturall Passions, that carry us to Partiality, Pride, Revenge, and the like. And Covenants, without the Sword, are but Words, and of no strength to secure a man at all. Therefore notwithstanding the Lawes of Nature, (which every one hath then kept, when he has the will to keep them, when he can do it safely,) if there be no Power erected, or not great enough for our security; every man will and may lawfully rely on his own strength and art, for caution against all other men. And in all places, where men have lived by small Families, to robbe and spoyle one another, has been a Trade, and so farre from being reputed against the Law of Nature, that the greater spoyles they gained, the greater was their honour; and men observed no other Lawes therein, but the Lawes of Honour; that is, to abstain from cruelty, leaving to men their lives, and instruments of husbandry. And as small Familyes did then; so now do Cities and Kingdomes which are but greater Families (for their own security) enlarge their Dominions, upon all pretences of danger, and fear of Invasion, or assistance that may be given to Invaders, endeavour as much as they can, to subdue, or weaken their neighbours, by open force, and secret arts, for want of other Caution, justly; and are remembred for it in after ages with honour.

Nor is it the joyning together of a small number of men, that gives them this security; because in small numbers, small additions on the one side or the other, make the advantage of strength so great, as is sufficient to carry the Victory; and therefore gives encouragement to an Invasion. The Multitude sufficient to confide in for our Security, is not determined by any certain number, but by comparison with the Enemy we feare; and is then sufficient, when the odds of the Enemy is not of so visible and conspicuous moment, to determine the event of warre, as to move him to attempt.

And be there never so great a Multitude; yet if their actions be directed according to their particular judgements, and particular appetites, they can expect thereby no defence, nor protection, neither against a Common enemy, nor against the injuries of one another. For being distracted in opinions concerning the best use and application of their strength, they do not help, but hinder one another; and reduce their strength by mutuall opposition to nothing: whereby they are easily, not onely subdued by a very few that agree together; but also when there is no common enemy, they make warre upon each other, for their particular interests. For if we could suppose a great Multitude of men to consent in the observation of Justice, and other Lawes of Nature, without a common Power to keep them all in awe; we might as well suppose all Man-kind to do the same; and then there neither would be, nor need to be any Civil. Government, or Common-wealth at all; because there would be Peace without subjection.

Nor is it enough for the security, which men desire should last all the time of their life, that they be governed, and directed by one judgement, for a limited time; as in one Battell, or one Warre. For though they obtain a Victory by their unanimous endeavour against a forraign enemy; yet afterwards, when either they have no common enemy, or he that by one part is held for an enemy, is by another part held for a friend, they must needs by the difference of their interests dissolve, and fall again into a Warre amongst themselves.

It is true, that certain living creatures, as Bees, and Ants, live sociably one with another, (which are therefore by *Aristotle* numbred amongst Politicall creatures;) and yet have no other direction, than their particular judgements and appetites; nor speech, whereby one of them can signifie to another, what he thinks expedient for the common benefit: and therefore some man may perhaps desire to know, why Man-kind cannot do the same. To which I answer,

First, that men are continually in competition for Honour and Dignity, which these creatures are not; and consequently amongst men there ariseth on that ground, Envy and Hatred, and finally Warre; but amongst these not so.

Secondly, that amongst these creatures, the Common good differeth not from the Private; and being by nature enclined to their private, they procure thereby the common benefit. But man, whose Joy consisteth in comparing himselfe with other men, can relish nothing but what is eminent.

Thirdly, that these creatures, having not (as man) the use of reason, do not see, nor think they see any fault, in the administration of their common businesse: whereas amongst men, there are very many, that thinke themselves wiser, and abler to govern the Publique, better than the rest; and these strive to reforme and innovate, one this way, another that way; and thereby bring it into Distraction and Civill warre.

Fourthly, that these creatures, though they have some use of voice, in making knowne to one another their desires, and other affections; yet they want that art of words, by which some men can represent to others, that which is Good, in the likenesse of Evill; and Evill, in the likenesse of Good; and augment, or diminish the apparent greatnesse of Good and Evill; discontenting men, and troubling their Peace at their pleasure.

Fiftly, irrationall creatures cannot distinguish betweene *Injury*, and *Dammage*; and therefore as long as they be at ease, they are not offended with their fellowes: whereas Man is then most troublesome, when he is most at ease: for then it is that he loves to shew his Wisdome, and controule the Actions of them that governe the Common-wealth.

Lastly, the agreement of these creatures is Naturall; that of men, is by Covenant only, which is Artificiall: and therefore it is no wonder if there be somewhat else required (besides Covenant) to make their Agreement constant and lasting; which is a Common Power, to keep them in awe, and to direct their actions to the Common Benefit.

The only way to erect such a Common Power, as may be able to defend them from the invasion of Forraigners, and the injuries of one another, and thereby to secure them in such sort, as that by their owne industrie, and by the fruites of the Earth, they may nourish themselves and live contentedly; is, to conferre all their power and strength upon one Man, or upon one Assembly of men, that may reduce all their Wills, by plurality of voices, unto one Will: which is as much as to say, to appoint one man, or Assembly of men, to beare their Person; and every one to owne, and acknowledge himselfe to be Author of whatsoever he that so beareth their Person, shall Act, or cause to be Acted, in those things which concerne the Common Peace and Safetie; and therein to submit their Wills, every one to his Will, and their Judgements, to his Judgment. This is more than Consent, or Concord; it is a reall Unitie of them all, in one and the same Person, made by Covenant of every man with every man, in such manner, as if every man should say to every man, *I Authorise and give up my Right of Governing my selfe, to this Man, or to this Assembly of men, on this condition, that thou give up thy Right to him, and Authorise all his Actions in like manner.* This done, the Multitude so united in one Person, is called a COMMON-WEALTH, in latine CIVITAS. This is the Generation of that great LEVIATHAN, or rather (to speake more reverently) of that *Mortall God*, to which wee owe under the *Immortall God*, our peace and defence. For by this Authoritie, given him by every particular man in the Common-Wealth, he hath the use of so much Power and Strength conferred on him, that by terror thereof, he is inabled to forme the wills of them all, to Peace at home, and mutuall ayd against their enemies abroad. And in him consisteth the Essence of the Common-wealth; which (to define it,) is *One Person, of whose Acts a great Multitude, by mutuall Covenants one with another, have made themselves every one the Author, to the end he may use the strength and means of them all, as he shall think expedient, for their Peace and Common Defence.*

And he that carryeth this Person, is called SOVERAIGNE, and said to have *Soveraigne Power*; and every one besides, his SUBJECT.

The attaining to this Soveraigne Power, is by two wayes. One, by Naturall force; as when a man maketh his children, to submit themselves, and their children to his government, as being able to destroy them if they refuse; or by Warre subdueth his enemies to his will, giving them their lives on that condition. The other, is when men agree amongst themselves, to submit to some Man, or Assembly of men, voluntarily, on confidence to be protected by him against all others. This later, may be called a Politicall Common-wealth or Common-wealth by *Institution*; and the former, a Common-wealth by *Acquisition*. And first, I shall speak of a Common-wealth by Institution.

XVIII Of the Rights of Soveraignes by Institution

A *Common-wealth* is said to be *Instituted*, when a *Multitude* of men do Agree, and *Covenant, every one, with every one*, that to whatsoever *Man*, or *Assembly of Men*, shall be given by the major part, the *Right* to *Present* the Person of them all, (that is to say, to be their *Representative*;) every one, as well he that *Voted for it*, as he that *Voted against it*, shall *Authorise* all the Actions and Judgements, of that Man, or Assembly of men, in the same manner, as if they were his own, to the end, to live peaceably amongst themselves, and be protected against other men.

From this Institution of a Common-wealth are derived all the *Rights*, and *Facultyes* of him, or them, on whom the Soveraigne Power is conferred by the consent of the People assembled.

First, because they Covenant, it is to be understood, they are not obliged by former Covenant to any thing repugnant hereunto. And Consequently they that have already Instituted a Common-wealth, being thereby bound by Covenant, to own the Actions, and Judgements of one, cannot lawfully make a new Covenant, amongst themselves, to be obedient to any other, in any thing whatsoever, without his permission. And therefore, they that are subjects to a Monarch, cannot without his leave cast off

Monarchy, and return to the confusion of a disunited Multitude; nor transferre their Person from him that beareth it, to another Man, or other Assembly of men: for they are bound, every man to every man, to Own, and be reputed Author of all, that he that already is their Soveraigne, shall do, and judge fit to be done: so that any one man dissenting, all the rest should break their Covenant made to that man, which is injustice: and they have also every man given the Soveraignty to him that beareth their Person; and therefore if they depose him, they take from him that which is his own, and so again it is injustice. Besides, if he that attempteth to depose his Soveraign, be killed, or punished by him for such attempt, he is author of his own punishment, as being by the Institution, Author of all his Soveraign shall do: And because it is injustice for a man to do any thing, for which he may be punished by his own authority, he is also upon that title, unjust. And whereas some men have pretended for their disobedience to their Soveraign, a new Covenant, made, not with men, but with God; this also is unjust: for there is no Covenant with God, but by mediation of some body that representeth Gods Person; which none doth but Gods Lieutenant, who hath the Soveraignty under God. But this pretence of Covenant with God, is so evident a lye, even in the pretenders own consciences, that it is not onely an act of an unjust, but also of a vile, and unmanly disposition.

Secondly, Because the Right of bearing the Person of them all, is given to him they make Soveraigne, by Covenant onely of one to another, and not of him to any of them; there can happen no breach of Covenant on the part of the Soveraigne; and consequently none of his Subjects, by any pretence of forfeiture, can be freed from his Subjection. That he which is made Soveraigne maketh no Covenant with his Subjects beforehand, is manifest; because either he must make it with the whole multitude, as one party to the Covenant; or he must make a severall Covenant with every man. With the whole, as one party, it is impossible; because as yet they are not one Person: and if he make so many severall Covenants as there be men, those Covenants after he hath the Soveraignty are voyd, because what act soever can be pretended by any one of them for breach thereof, is the act both of himselfe, and of all the rest, because done in the Person, and by the Right of every one of them in particular. Besides, if any one, or more of them, pretend a breach of the Covenant made by the Soveraigne at his Institution; and others, or one other of his Subjects, or himselfe alone, pretend there was no such breach, there is in this case, no Judge to decide the controversie: it returns therefore to the Sword again; and every man recovereth the right of Protecting himselfe by his own strength, contrary to the designe they had in the Institution. It is therefore in vain to grant Soveraignty by way of precedent Covenant. The opinion that any Monarch receiveth his Power by Covenant, that is to say on Condition, proceedeth from want of understanding this easie truth, that Covenants being but words, and breath, have no force to oblige, contain, constrain, or protect any man, but what it has from the publique Sword; that is, from the untyed hands of that Man, or Assembly of men that hath the Soveraignty, and whose actions are avouched by them all, and performed by the strength of them all, in him united. But when an Assembly of men is made Soveraigne; then no man imagineth any such Covenant to have past in the Institution; for no man is so dull as to say, for example, the People of *Rome*, made a Covenant with the Romans, to hold the Soveraignty on such or such conditions; which not performed, the Romans might lawfully depose the Roman People. That men see not the reason to be alike in a Monarchy, and in a Popular Government, proceedeth from the ambition of some, that are kinder to the government of an Assembly, whereof they may hope to participate, than of Monarchy, which they despair to enjoy.

Thirdly, because the major part hath by consenting voices declared a Soveraigne; he that dissented must now consent with the rest; that is, be contented to avow all the actions he shall do, or else justly be destroyed by the rest. For if he voluntarily entered into the Congregation of them that were assembled, he sufficiently declared thereby his will (and therefore tacitely covenanted) to stand to what the major part should ordayne: and therefore if he refuse to stand thereto, or make Protestation against any of their Decrees, he does contrary to his Covenant, and therfore unjustly. And whether he be of the Congregation, or not; and whether his consent be asked, or not, he must either submit to their decrees, or be left in the condition of warre he was in before; wherein he might without injustice be destroyed by any man whatsoever.

Fourthly, because every Subject is by this Institution Author of all the Actions, and Judgments of the Soveraigne Instituted; it followes, that whatsoever he doth, it can be no injury to any of his Subjects; nor ought he to be by any of them accused of Injustice. For he that doth any thing by authority from another, doth therein no injury to him by whose authority he acteth: But by this Institution of a Common-wealth, every particular man is Author of all the Soveraigne doth; and consequently he that complaineth of injury from his Soveraigne, complaineth of that whereof he himselfe is Author; and therefore ought not to accuse any man but himselfe; no nor himselfe of injury; because to do injury to ones selfe, is impossible. It is true that they that have Soveraigne power, may commit Iniquity; but not Injustice, or Injury in the proper signification.

Fifthly, and consequently to that which was sayd last, no man that hath Soveraigne power can justly be put to death, or otherwise in any manner by his Subjects punished. For seeing every Subject is Author of the actions of his Soveraigne; he punisheth another, for the actions committed by himselfe.

And because the End of this Institution, is the Peace and Defence of them all; and whosoever has right to the End, has right to the Means; it belongeth of Right, to whatsoever Man, or Assembly that hath the Soveraignty, to be Judge both of the meanes of Peace and Defence; and also of the hindrances, and disturbances of the same; and to do whatsoever he shall think necessary to be done, both before hand, for the preserving of Peace and Security, by prevention of Discord at home and Hostility from abroad; and, when Peace and Security are lost, for the recovery of the same. And therefore,

Sixthly, it is annexed to the Soveraignty, to be Judge of what Opinions and Doctrines are averse, and what conducing to Peace; and consequently, on what occasions, how farre, and what, men are to be trusted withall, in speaking to Multitudes of people; and who shall examine the Doctrines of all bookes before they be published. For the Actions of men proceed from their Opinions; and in the well governing of Opinions, consisteth the well governing of mens Actions, in order to their Peace, and Concord. And though in matter of Doctrine, nothing ought to be regarded but the Truth; yet this is not repugnant to regulating of the same by Peace. For Doctrine repugnant to Peace, can no more be True, than Peace and Concord can be against the Law of Nature. It is true, that in a Common-wealth, where by the negligence, or unskilfullnesse of Governours, and Teachers, false Doctrines are by time generally received; the contrary Truths may be generally offensive: Yet the most sudden, and rough busling in of a new Truth, that can be, does never breake the Peace, but only somtimes awake the Warre. For those men that are so remissely governed, that they dare take up Armes, to defend, or introduce an Opinion, are still in Warre; and their condition not Peace, but only a Cessation of Armes for feare of one another; and they live as it were, in the precincts of battaile continually. It belongeth therefore to him that hath the Soveraign Power, to be Judge, or constitute all Judges of Opinions and Doctrines, as a thing necessary to Peace; thereby to prevent Discord and Civill Warre.

Seventhly, is annexed to the Soveraigntie, the whole power of prescribing the Rules, whereby every man may know, what Goods he may enjoy and what Actions he may doe, without being molested by any of his fellow Subjects: And this is it men call *Propriety*. For before constitution of Soveraign Power (as hath already been shewn) all men had right to all things; which necessarily causeth Warre: and therefore this Proprietie, being necessary to Peace, and depending on Soveraign Power, is the Act of that Power, in order to the publique peace.

These Rules of Propriety (or *Meum* and *Tuum*) and of *Good, Evill, Lawfull*, and *Unlawfull* in the actions of Subjects, are the Civill Lawes, that is to say, the Lawes of each Common-wealth in particular; though the name of Civill Law be now restrained to the antient Civill Lawes of the City of *Rome*; which being the head of a great part of the World, her Lawes at that time were in these parts the Civill Law.

Eighthly, is annexed to the Soveraigntie, the Right of Judicature; that is to say, of hearing and deciding all Controversies, which may arise concerning Law, either Civill, or Naturall, or concerning Fact. For without the decision of Controversies, there is no protection of one Subject, against the injuries of another; the Lawes concerning *Meum* and *Tuum* are in vaine; and to every man remaineth, from the naturall and necessary appetite of his own conservation, the right of protecting himselfe by his private strength, which is the condition of Warre; and contrary to the end for which every Common-wealth is instituted.

Ninthly, is annexed to the Soveraignty, the Right of making Warre, and Peace with other Nations, and Common-wealths; that is to say, of Judging when it is for the publique good, and how great forces are to be assembled, armed, and payd for that end; and to levy mony upon the Subjects, to defray the expenses thereof. For the Power by which the people are to be defended, consisteth in their Armies; and the strength of an Army, in the union of their strength under one Command; which Command the Soveraign Instituted, therefore hath; because the command of the *Militia*, without other Institution, maketh him that hath it Soveraign. And therefore whosoever is made Generall of an Army, he that hath the Soveraign Power is alwayes Generallissimo.

Tenthly, is annexed to the Soveraignty, the choosing of all Councellours, Ministers, Magistrates, and Officers, both in Peace, and War. For seeing the Soveraign is charged with the End, which is the common Peace and Defence; he is understood to have Power to use such Means, as he shall think most fit for his discharge.

Eleventhly, to the Soveraign is committed the Power of Rewarding with riches, or honour; and of Punishing with corporall, or pecuniary punishment, or with ignominy every Subject according to the Law he hath formerly made; or if there be no Law made, according as he shall judge most to conduce to the encouraging of men to serve the Common-wealth, or deterring of them from doing dis-service to the same.

Lastly, considering what values men are naturally apt to set upon themselves; what respect they look for from others; and how little they value other men; from whence continually arise amongst them, Emulation, Quarrells, Factions, and at last Warre, to the destroying of one another, and diminution of their strength against a Common Enemy; It is necessary that there be Lawes of Honour, and a publique rate of the worth of such men as have deserved, or are able to deserve well of the Common-wealth; and that there be force in the hands of some or other, to put those Lawes in execution. But it hath already been shewn, that not onely the whole *Militia*, or forces of the Common-wealth; but also the Judicature of all Controversies, is annexed to the Soveraignty. To the Soveraign therefore it belongeth also to give titles of Honour; and to appoint what Order of place, and dignity, each man shall hold; and what signes of respect, in publique or private meetings, they shall give to one another.

These are the Rights, which make the Essence of Soveraignty; and which are the markes, whereby a man may discern in what Man, or Assembly of men, the Soveraign Power is placed, and resideth. For these are incommunicable, and inseparable. The Power to coyn Mony; to dispose of the estate and persons of Infant heires; to have præmption in Markets; and all other Statute Prærogatives, may be transferred by the Soveraign; and yet the Power to protect his Subjects be retained. But if he transferre the *Militia*, he retains the Judicature in vain, for want of execution of the Lawes: Or if he grant away the Power of raising Mony; the *Militia* is in vain: or if he give away the government of Doctrines, men will be frighted into rebellion with the feare of Spirits. And so if we consider any one of the said Rights, we shall presently see, that the holding of all the rest, will produce no effect, in the conservation of Peace and Justice, the end for which all Common-wealths are Instituted. And this division is it, whereof it is said, *a Kingdome divided in it selfe cannot stand*: For unlesse this division precede, division into opposite Armies can never happen. If there had not first been an opinion received of the greatest part of *England*, that these Powers were divided between the King, and the Lords, and the House of Commons, the people had never been divided, and fallen into this Civill Warre; first between those that disagreed in Politiques; and after between the Dissenters about the liberty of Religion; which have so instructed men in this point of Soveraign Right, that there be few now (in *England*,) that do not see, that these Rights are inseparable, and will be so generally acknowledged, at the next return of Peace; and so continue, till their miseries are forgotten; and no longer, except the vulgar be better taught than they have hetherto been.

And because they are essentiall and inseparable Rights, it follows necessarily, that in whatsoever, words any of them seem to be granted away, yet if the Soveraign Power it selfe be not in direct termes renounced, and the name of Soveraign no more given by the Grantees to him that Grants them, the Grant is voyd: for when he has granted all he can, if we grant back the Soveraignty, all is restored, as inseparably annexed thereunto.

This great Authority being Indivisible, and inseparably annexed to the Soveraignty, there is little ground for the opinion of them, that say of Soveraign Kings, though they be *singulis majores*, of greater Power than every one of their Subjects, yet they be *Universis minores*, of lesse power than them all together. For if by *all together*, they mean not the collective body as one person, then *all together*, and *every one*, signifie the same; and the speech is absurd. But if by *all together*, they understand them as one Person (which person the Soveraign bears,) then the power of all together, is the same with the Soveraigns power; and so again the speech is absurd: which absurdity they see well enough, when the Soveraignty is in an Assembly of the people; but in a Monarch they see it not; and yet the power of Soveraignty is the same in whomsoever it be placed.

And as the Power, so also the Honour of the Soveraign, ought to be greater, than that of any, or all the Subjects. For in the Soveraignty is the fountain of Honour. The dignities of Lord, Earle, Duke, and Prince are his Creatures. As in the presence of the Master, the Servants are equall, and without any honour at all; So are the Subjects, in the presence of the Soveraign. And though they shine some more, some lesse, when they are out of his sight; yet in his presence, they shine no more than the Starres in presence of the Sun.

But a man may here object, that the Condition of Subjects is very miserable; as being obnoxious to the lusts, and other irregular passions of him, or them that have so unlimited a Power in their hands. And commonly they that live under a Monarch, think it the fault of Monarchy; and they that live under the government of Democracy, or other Soveraign Assembly, attribute all the inconvenience to that forme of Common-wealth; whereas the Power in all formes, if they be perfect enough to protect them, is the same; not considering that the estate of Man can never be without some incommodity or other; and that the greatest, that in any forme of Government can possibly happen to the people in generall, is scarce sensible, in respect of the miseries, and horrible calamities, that accompany a Civill Warre; or that dissolute condition of masterlesse men, without subjection to Lawes, and a coërcive Power to tye their hands from rapine, and revenge: nor considering that the greatest pressure of Soveraign Governours, proceedeth not from any delight, or profit they can expect in the dammage, or weakening of their Subjects, in whose vigor, consisteth their own strength and glory; but in the restiveness of themselves, that unwillingly contributing to their own defence, make it necessary for their Governours to draw from them what they can in time of Peace, that they may have means on any emergent occasion, or sudden need, to resist, or take advantage on their

Enemies. For all men are by nature provided of notable multiplying glasses, (that is their Passions and Self-love,) through which, every little payment appeareth a great grievance; but are destitute of those prospective glasses, (namely Morall and Civill Science,) to see a farre off the miseries that hang over them, and cannot without such payments be avoyded.

. . .

XXI Of the Liberty of Subjects

Liberty, or Freedome, signifieth (properly) the absence of Opposition; (by Opposition, I mean externall Impediments of motion;) and may be applyed no lesse to Irrationall, and Inanimate creatures, than to Rationall. For whatsoever is so tyed, or environed, as it cannot move, but within a certain space, which space is determined by the opposition of some externall body, we say it hath not Liberty to go further. And so of all living creatures, whilest they are imprisoned, or restrained, with walls, or chayns; and of the water whilest it is kept in by banks, or vessels, that otherwise would spread it selfe into a larger space, we use to say, they are not at Liberty, to move in such manner, as without those externall impediments they would. But when the impediment of motion, is in the constitution of the thing it selfe, we use not to say, it wants the Liberty; but the Power to move; as when a stone lyeth still, or a man is fastned to his bed by sicknesse.

And according to this proper, and generally received meaning of the word, A Free-Man, *is he, that in those things, which by his strength and wit he is able to do, is not hindred to doe what he has a will to*. But when the words *Free*, and *Liberty*, are applyed to any thing but *Bodies*, they are abused; for that which is not subject to Motion, is not subject to Impediment: And therefore, when 'tis said (for example). The way is free, no liberty of the way is signified, but of those that walk in it without stop. And when we say a Guift is free, there is not meant any liberty of the Guift, but of the Giver, that was not bound by any law, or Covenant to give it. So when we *speak freely*, it is not the liberty of voice, or pronunciation, but of the man, whom no law hath obliged to speak otherwise then he did. Lastly, from the use of the word *Freewill*, no liberty can be inferred to the will, desire, or inclination, but the liberty of the man; which consisteth in this, that he finds no stop, in doing what he has the will, desire, or inclination to doe.

Feare and Liberty are consistent; as when a man throweth his goods into the Sea for *feare* the ship should sink, he doth it neverthelesse very willingly, and may refuse to doe it if he will: It is therefore the action, of one that was *free*: so a man sometimes pays his debt, only for *feare* of Imprisonment, which because no body hindred him from detaining, was the action of a man at *liberty*. And generally all actions which men doe in Common-wealths, for *feare* of the law, or actions, which the doers had *liberty* to omit.

Liberty and *Necessity* are Consistent: As in the water, that hath not only *liberty*, but a *necessity* of descending by the Channel; so likewise in the Actions which men voluntarily doe: which (because they proceed from their will) proceed from *liberty*; and yet because every act of mans will, and every desire, and inclination proceedeth from some cause, and that from another cause, which causes in a continuall chaine (whose first link is in the hand of God the first of all causes) proceed from *necessity*. So that to him that could see the connexion of those causes, the *necessity* of all mens voluntary actions, would appeare manifest. And therefore God, that seeth, and disposeth all things, seeth also that the *liberty* of man in doing what he will, is accompanied with the *necessity* of doing that which God will, & no more, nor lesse. For though men may do many things, which God does not command, nor is therefore Author of them; yet they can have no passion, nor appetite to any thing, of which appetite Gods will is not the cause. And did not his will assure the *necessity* of mans will, and consequently of all that on mans will dependeth, the *liberty* of men would be a contradiction, and impediment to the omnipotence and *liberty* of God. And this shall suffice, (as to the matter in hand) of that naturall *liberty*, which only is properly called *liberty*.

But as men, for the atteyning of peace, and conservation of themselves thereby, have made an Artificiall Man, which we call a Common-wealth; so also have they made Artificiall Chains, called *Civill Lawes*, which they themselves, by mutuall covenants, have fastned at one end, to the lips of that Man, or Assembly, to whom they have given the Soveraigne Power; and at the other end to their own Ears. These Bonds in their own nature but weak, may neverthelesse be made to hold, by the danger, though not by the difficulty of breaking them.

In relation to these Bonds only it is, that I am to speak now, of the *Liberty* of *Subjects*. For seeing there is no Common-wealth in the world, wherein there be Rules enough set down, for the regulating of all the actions, and words of men, (as being a thing impossible:) it followeth necessarily, that in all kinds of actions, by the laws prætermitted, men have the Liberty, of doing what their own reasons shall suggest, for the most profitable to themselves. For if wee take Liberty in the proper sense, for corporall Liberty; that is to say, freedome from chains, and prison, it were very absurd for men to clamor as they doe, for the Liberty they so manifestly enjoy. Againe, if we take Liberty, for an exemption from Lawes, it is no lesse absurd, for men to demand as they doe, that Liberty, by which all other men may be masters of their lives. And yet as absurd as it is, this is it they demand; not knowing that the Lawes are of no power to protect them, without a Sword in the hands of a man, or men, to cause those laws to be put in execution. The Liberty of a Subject, lyeth therefore only in those things, which in regulating their actions, the Soveraign hath prætermitted: such as is the Liberty to buy, and sell, and otherwise contract with one another; to choose their own aboad, their own diet, their own trade of life, and institute their children as they themselves think fit; & the like.

Neverthelesse we are not to understand, that by such Liberty, the Soveraign Power of life, and death, is either abolished, or limited. For it has been already shewn, that nothing the Soveraign Representative can doe to a Subject, on what pretence soever, can properly be called Injustice, or Injury; because every Subject is Author of every act the Soveraign doth; so that he never wanteth Right to any thing, otherwise, than as he himself is the Subject of God, and bound thereby to observe the laws of Nature. . . .

. . .

To come now to the particulars of the true Liberty of a Subject; that is to say, what are the things, which though commanded by the Soveraign, he may neverthelesse, without Injustice, refuse to do; we are to consider, what Rights we passe away, when we make a Common-wealth; or (which is all one,) what Liberty we deny our selves, by owning all the Actions (without exception) of the Man, or Assembly we make our Soveraign. For in the act of our *Submission*, consisteth both our *Obligation*, and our *Liberty*; which must therefore be inferred by arguments taken from thence; there being no Obligation on any man, which ariseth not from some Act of his own; for all men equally, are by Nature Free. And because such arguments, must either be drawn from the expresse words, *I Authorise all his Actions*, or from the Intention of him that submitteth himselfe to his Power, (which Intention is to be understood by the End for which he so submitteth;) The Obligation, and Liberty of the Subject, is to be derived, either from those Words, (or others equivalent;) or else from the End of the Institution of Soveraignty; namely, the Peace of the Subjects within themselves, and their Defence against a common Enemy.

First therefore, seeing Soveraignty by Institution, is by Covenant of every one to every one; and Soveraignty by Acquisition, by Covenants of the Vanquished to the Victor, or Child to the Parent; It is manifest, that every Subject has Liberty in all those things, the right whereof cannot by Covenant be transferred. I have shewn before in the 14. Chapter, that Covenants, not to defend a mans own body, are voyd. Therefore,

If the Soveraign command a man (though justly condemned,) to kill, wound, or mayme himselfe;

or not to resist those that assault him; or to abstain from the use of food, ayre, medicine, or any other thing, without which he cannot live; yet hath that man the Liberty to disobey.

If a man be interrogated by the Soveraign, or his Authority, concerning a crime done by himselfe, he is not bound (without assurance of Pardon) to confesse it; because no man (as I have shewn in the same Chapter) can be obliged by Covenant to accuse himselfe.

Again, the Consent of a Subject to Soveraign Power, is contained in these words, *I Authorise, or take upon me, all his actions*; in which there is no restriction at all, of his own former naturall Liberty: For by allowing him to *kill me*, I am not bound to kill my selfe when he commands me. 'Tis one thing to say, *Kill me, or my fellow, if you please*; another thing to say, *I will kill my selfe, or my fellow*. It followeth therefore, that

No man is bound by the words themselves, either to kill himselfe, or any other man; And consequently, that the Obligation a man may sometimes have, upon the Command of the Soveraign to execute any dangerous, or dishonourable Office, dependeth not on the Words of our Submission; but on the Intention; which is to be understood by the End thereof. When therefore our refusall to obey, frustrates the End for which the Soveraignty was ordained; then there is no Liberty to refuse: otherwise there is.

Upon this ground, a man that is commanded as a Souldier to fight against the enemy, though his Soveraign have Right enough to punish his refusall with death, may neverthelesse in many cases refuse, without Injustice; as when he substituteth a sufficient Souldier in his place: for in this case he deserteth not the service of the Common-wealth. And there is allowance to be made for naturall timorousnesse, not onely to women, (of whom no such dangerous duty is expected,) but also to men of feminine courage. When Armies fight, there is on one side, or both, a running away; yet when they do it not out of trechery, but fear, they are not esteemed to do it unjustly, but dishonourably. For the same reason, to avoyd battell, is not Injustice, but Cowardise. But he that inrowleth himselfe a Souldier, or taketh imprest mony, taketh away the excuse of a timorous nature; and is obliged, not onely to go to the battell, but also not to run from it, without his Captaines leave. And when the Defence of the Common-wealth, requireth at once the help of all that are able to bear Arms, every one is obliged; because otherwise the Institution of the Common-wealth, which they have not the purpose, or courage to preserve, was in vain.

To resist the Sword of the Common-wealth, in defence of another man, guilty, or innocent, no man hath Liberty; because such Liberty, takes away from the Soveraign, the means of Protecting us; and is therefore destructive of the very essence of Government. But in case a great many men together, have already resisted the Soveraign Power unjustly, or committed some Capitall crime, for which every one of them expecteth death, whether have they not the Liberty then to joyn together, and assist, and defend one another? Certainly they have: For they but defend their lives, which the Guilty man may as well do, as the Innocent. There was indeed injustice in the first breach of their duty; Their bearing of Arms subsequent to it, though it be to maintain what they have done, is no new unjust act. And if it be onely to defend their persons, it is not unjust at all. But the offer of Pardon taketh from them, to whom it is offered, the plea of self-defence, and maketh their perseverance in assisting, or defending the rest, unlawfull.

As for other Lyberties, they depend on the silence of the Law. In cases where the Soveraign has prescribed no rule, there the Subject hath the liberty to do, or forbeare, according to his own discretion. And therefore such Liberty is in some places more, and in some lesse; and in some times more, in other times lesse, according as they that have the Soveraignty shall think most convenient. As for Example, there was a time, when in *England* a man might enter in to his own Land, (and dispossesse such as wrongfully possessed it) by force. But in after-times, that Liberty of Forcible entry, was taken away by a Statute made (by the King) in Parliament. And in some places of the world, men have the Liberty of many wives: in other places, such Liberty is not allowed.

If a Subject have a controversie with his Soveraigne, of Debt, or of right of possession of lands or goods, or concerning any service required at his hands, or concerning any penalty corporall, or pecuniary, grounded on a precedent Law; He hath the same Liberty to sue for his right, as if it were against a Subject; and before such Judges, as are appointed by the Soveraign. For seeing the Soveraign demandeth by force of a former Law, and not by vertue of his Power; he declareth thereby, that he requireth no more, than shall appear to be due by that Law. The sute therefore is not contrary to the will of the Soveraign; and consequently the Subject hath the Liberty to demand the hearing of his Cause; and sentence, according to that Law. But if he demand, or take any thing by pretence of his Power; there lyeth, in that case, no action of Law: for all that is done by him in Vertue of his Power, is done by the Authority of every subject, and consequently, he that brings an action against the Soveraign, brings it against himselfe.

If a Monarch, or Soveraign Assembly, grant a Liberty to all, or any of his Subjects; which Grant standing, he is disabled to provide for their safety, the Grant is voyd; unlesse he directly renounce, or transferre the Soveraignty to another. For in that he might openly, (if it had been his will,) and in plain termes, have renounced, or transferred it, and did not; it is to be understood it was not his will; but that the Grant proceeded from ignorance of the repugnancy between such a Liberty and the Soveraign Power; and therefore the Soveraignty is still retayned; and consequently all those Powers, which are necessary to the exercising thereof; such as are the Power of Warre, and Peace, of Judicature, of appointing Officers, and Councellours, of levying Mony, and the rest named in the 18th Chapter.

The Obligation of Subjects to the Soveraign, is understood to last as long, and no longer, than the power lasteth, by which he is able to protect them. For the right men have by Nature to protect themselves, when none else can protect them, can by no Covenant be relinquished. The Soveraignty is the Soule of the Common-wealth; which once departed from the Body, the members doe no more receive their motion from it. The end of Obedience is Protection; which, wheresoever a man seeth it, either in his own, or in anothers sword, Nature applyeth his obedience to it, and his endeavour to maintaine it. And though Soveraignty, in the intention of them that make it, be immortall; yet is it in its own nature, not only subject to violent death, by forreign war; but also through the ignorance, and passions of men, it hath in it, from the very institution, many seeds of a naturall mortality, by Intestine Discord.

John Locke

John Locke (1632–1704) is the most representative thinker in the Anglo-American tradition of social thought. His ideas were not original but rather the articulation of centuries of political experience, the common currency of an enterprising middle class. Anointed the "father of the English Enlightenment," Locke's empiricist philosophy codified this experience: It gave expression to the English Revolution of 1688, established the major paradigm of eighteenth-century thought, especially in France, and stimulated the American Revolution of 1776. In the New World, free from European traditions of feudalism and state power, Locke's ideas became reality, shaping actual institutions, above all the law, as well as the "common sense" of a confident and ultimately triumphant bourgeoisie. Locke's writings enabled Americans to escape from their older biblical, especially Calvinist, tradition but without seeming to abandon it, and to forge an uneasy peace as the nation grew to include more ethnic groups and greater divisions of social class.

Like Hobbes, John Locke was born in the west of England. His father, a small landowner and attorney, was a Calvinist who fought in the parliamentary armies against the king during the Civil War of 1642–1646. The war was part of a constitutional struggle that late in the century led to a parliamentary government with limitations on the monarchy, as well as part of the last chapter in the religious strife between the Anglican church and the Protestants, resulting in the acceptance of toleration of most nonconformist sects. Both issues, constitutionalism and toleration, became important for Locke and figured prominently in his writings.

In 1652 Locke entered Christ Church College at Oxford, where he felt frustrated by the standard university curriculum and read widely outside its scope. He remained there as a student and later a tutor until forced into exile in 1684. At Oxford he found medicine more to his liking than classical texts, and he mingled with the scientists and doctors, such as his close friend Robert Boyle, who later formed the Royal Society. He also met a number of the English radicals whose ideas his final political doctrines resemble. His political and religious nonconformity aroused the ire of the inbred clergymen of Christ Church. Never happy at Oxford, Locke was on several occasions tempted to enter public affairs.

In 1667 Locke joined the household of Anthony Cooper (later Lord Shaftesbury) as secretary and family doctor. Shaftesbury was a wealthy landowner and powerful ally of Charles II, but in 1672 he fell out with the king and took an active role in opposition to him. This brought Locke into the heart of the political conflicts of the Restoration period. When Shaftesbury fled to Holland, Locke felt that he too was in jeopardy and followed his master there in 1684. Shortly before Locke sailed, there occurred the last burning of books in the history of England, including some of Locke's own library in his chambers at Christ Church. It is nearly certain that Locke was there himself, watching the smoke drift up between the church spires, as he prepared to flee the country. Soon after, a royal decree expelled him from his position.

As a result of the Glorious Revolution, William of Orange became king in 1689 and Locke returned, no longer an obscure exile but a man of high influence. His *Two Treatises on Government*, though composed before the Revolution, became its most persuasive justification before world opinion and made Locke famous. In the fifteen years left to him, he published all of his major works, which were to profoundly influence the eighteenth century.

Locke's political writing takes aim at two arguments for absolute government. In the first *Treatise*, his target is the patriarchal theory of divine right monarchy stated by Sir Robert Filmer in 1680. Filmer had argued that kings should be thought of as the direct heirs of Adam, that their sovereignty was indivisible, and that God had set some men above others, fathers above sons, men above women, the older above the younger, and masters above their servants. Locke refutes Filmer, partly by citing Scripture, but with empirical arguments as well; for example, some forms of authority, such as that of a father over his children, are only temporary and were intended to be overcome.

In the second *Treatise*, excerpted here, Locke takes issue with Hobbes (although without mentioning him), who in *Leviathan* had founded the concept of absolutism on consent. Hobbes assumed that, without the restraints of government, men would be in a chronic state of war and insecurity, the "war of all against all." Human beings are by nature so competitive, their desires so restless and unfixed, that only the strongest rule will restrain them. Their choice is between despotism and anarchy.

The second *Treatise* offers a rival account of human nature, one far more consistent with the outlook of enterprising landowners and rising bourgeoisie, who were acquiring economic if not political power as the century drew to an end. In the state of nature, Locke contends, men are more reasonable and more inclined to society than the selfish, calculating creatures that Hobbes describes. Locke sees men's condition as prepolitical but not presocial, because they are guided by a rule more fundamental than the laws of the state: the law of nature. Emanating from God and discernible by human reason, the law of nature binds human beings to obey just government once it has been inaugurated by consent. Thereby they can preserve the freedom, independence, and equality with which they are endowed by nature.

Locke draws on the natural law tradition, which extends from the Stoics to the Renaissance, but gives it a sharp, individualistic twist. It concerns mostly individual rights rather than individual responsibilities to society, and above all, the protection of property, which is seen as the chief function of government. Previous theories of natural law did not hold that property rights were prior to the creation of government. Significantly, Locke means by *property* the protection of persons as well as goods, and limits an individual's right to property to "as much land as a man tills, plants, improves, cultivates, and can use the product of. . . ." These qualifications made it possible for his theory to be used by a broad range of groups, including advocates of wide distribution of land and socialists who criticized capitalist society by means of a labor theory of value.

In Locke's version of the social contract, men retain all the rights of the state of nature and surrender only the right to enforce them. Consent must be unanimous and among free individuals, not between the people and their rulers. The latter are merely given a "trust" to be used for the good of the community. And because the contract can be drawn up only once, Locke relies on the notion that later generations give their "tacit consent" by accepting the protection and advantages of government instead of leaving for other communities or the open spaces of the New World. The doctrine of tacit consent is one of the weak points in Locke's theory.

The later chapters of the second *Treatise* are concerned with the limits to government. Locke argues for the separation of the executive and legislative functions, supremacy of the legislature, equality of all groups under the law, and taxation only by consent of the people or their representatives. In the last chapter, he justifies the people's right to revolution and to institute a new government if their rulers fail to exercise their trust in the interests of the governed.

TWO TREATISES ON GOVERNMENT

1690

Second Treatise

II OF THE STATE OF NATURE

4. To understand Political Power right, and derive it from its Original, we must consider what State all Men are naturally in, and that is, a *State of perfect Freedom* to order their Actions, and dispose of their Possessions, and Persons as they think fit, within the bounds of the Law of Nature, without asking leave, or depending upon the Will of any other Man.

A *State* also *of Equality*, wherein all the Power and Jurisdiction is reciprocal, no one having more than another: there being nothing more evident, than that Creatures of the same species and rank promiscuously born to all the same advantages of Nature, and the use of the same faculties, should also be equal one amongst another without Subordination or Subjection, unless the Lord and Master of them all, should by any manifest Declaration of his Will set one above another, and confer on him by an evident and clear appointment an undoubted Right to Dominion and Sovereignty.

5. This *equality* of Men by Nature, the Judicious *Hooker* looks upon as so evident in it self, and beyond all question, that he makes it the Foundation of that Obligation to mutual Love amongst Men, on which he Builds the Duties they owe one another, and from whence he derives the great Maxims *of Justice* and *Charity*. . . .

6. But though this be a *State of Liberty*, yet it is *not a State of Licence*, though Man in that State have an uncontroleable Liberty, to dispose of his Person or Possessions, yet he has not Liberty to destroy himself, or so much as any Creature in his Possession, but where some nobler use, than its bare Preservation calls for it. The *State of Nature* has a Law of Nature to govern it, which obliges every one: And Reason, which is that Law, teaches all Mankind, who will but consult it, that being all equal and independent, no one ought to harm another in his Life, Health, Liberty, or Possessions. For Men being all the Workmanship of one Omnipotent, and infinitely wise Maker; All the Servants of one Sovereign Master, sent into the World by his order and about his business, they are his Property, whose Workmanship they are, made to last during his, not one anothers Pleasure. And being furnished with like Faculties, sharing all in one Community of Nature, there cannot be supposed any such *Subordination* among us, that may Authorize us to destroy one another, as if we were made for one anothers uses, as the inferior ranks of Creatures are for ours. Every one as he is *bound to preserve himself*, and not to quit his Station wilfully; so by the like reason when

Reprinted from *Locke: Two Treatises of Government*, ed. Peter Laslett, 3rd ed. (Cambridge England: Cambridge University Press, 1988 [1690]).

his own Preservation comes not in competition, ought he, as much as he can, *to preserve the rest of Mankind*, and may not unless it be to do Justice on an Offender, take away, or impair the life, or what tends to the Preservation of the Life, Liberty, Health, Limb or Goods of another.

. . .

13. To this strange Doctrine, *viz.* That *in the State of Nature, every one has the Executive Power* of the Law of Nature, I doubt not but it will be objected, That it is unreasonable for Men to be Judges in their own Cases, that Self-love will make Men partial to themselves and their Friends. And on the other side, that Ill Nature, Passion and Revenge will carry them too far in punishing others. And hence nothing but Confusion and Disorder will follow, and that therefore God hath certainly appointed Government to restrain the partiality and violence of Men. I easily grant, that *Civil Government* is the proper Remedy for the Inconveniences of the State of Nature, which must certainly be Great, where Men may be Judges in their own Case, since 'tis easily to be imagined, that he who was so unjust as to do his Brother an Injury, will scarce be so just as to condemn himself for it: But I shall desire those who make this Objection, to remember that *Absolute Monarchs* are but Men, and if Government is to be the Remedy of those Evils, which necessarily follow from Mens being Judges in their own Cases, and the State of Nature is therefore not to be endured, I desire to know what kind of Government that is, and how much better it is than the State of Nature, where one Man commanding a multitude, has the Liberty to be Judge in his own Case, and may do to all his Subjects whatever he pleases, without the least liberty to any one to question or controle those who Execute his Pleasure? And in whatsoever he doth, whether led by Reason, Mistake or Passion, must be submitted to? Much better it is in the State of Nature wherein Men are not bound to submit to the unjust will of another: And if he that judges, judges amiss in his own, or any other Case, he is answerable for it to the rest of Mankind.

. . .

V PROPERTY

27. Though the Earth, and all inferior Creatures be common to all Men, yet every Man has a *Property* in his own *Person*. This no Body has any Right to but himself. The *Labour* of his Body, and the *Work* of his Hands, we may say, are properly his. Whatsoever then he removes out of the State that Nature hath provided, and left it in, he hath mixed his *Labour* with, and joyned to it something that is his own, and thereby makes it his *Property*. It being by him removed from the common state Nature placed it in, hath by this *labour* something annexed to it, that excludes the common right of other Men. For this *Labour* being the unquestionable Property of the Labourer, no Man but he can have a right to what that is once joyned to, at least where there is enough, and as good left in common for others.

. . .

31. It will perhaps be objected to this, That if gathering the Acorns, or other Fruits of the Earth, *&c.* makes a right to them, then any one may *ingross* as much as he will. To which I Answer, Not so. The same Law of Nature, that does by this means give us Property, does also *bound* that *Property* too. *God has given us all things richly*, 1 Tim. vi. 17. is the Voice of Reason confirmed by Inspiration. But how far has he given it us? *To enjoy*. As much as any one can make use of to any advantage of life before it spoils; so much he may by his labour fix a Property in. Whatever is beyond this, is more than his share, and belongs to others. Nothing was made by God for man to spoil or destroy. And thus considering the

plenty of natural Provisions there was a long time in the World, and the few spenders, and to how small a part of that provision the industry of one Man could extend it self, and engross it to the prejudice of others; especially keeping within the *bounds*, set by reason of what might serve for his *use*; there could be then little room for Quarrels or Contentions about Property so establish'd.

32. But the *chief matter of Property* being now not the Fruits of the Earth, and the Beasts that subsist on it, but the *Earth it self*; as that which takes in and carries with it all the rest: I think it is plain, that *Property* in that too is acquired as the former. *As much Land* as a Man Tills, Plants, Improves, Cultivates, and can use the Product of, so much is his *Property*. He by his Labour does, as it were, inclose it from the Common. Nor will it invalidate his right to say, Every body else has an equal Title to it; and therefore he cannot appropriate, he cannot inclose, without the Consent of all his Fellow-Commoners, all Mankind. God, when he gave the World in common to all Mankind, commanded Man also to labour, and the penury of his Condition required it of him. God and his Reason commanded him to subdue the Earth, *i.e.* improve it for the benefit of Life, and therein lay out something upon it that was his own, his labour. He that in Obedience to this Command of God, subdued, tilled and sowed any part of it, thereby annexed to it something that was his *Property*, which another had no Title to, nor could without injury take from him.

33. Nor was this *appropriation* of any parcel of *Land*, by improving it, any prejudice to any other Man, since there was still enough, and as good left; and more than the yet unprovided could use. So that in effect, there was never the less left for others because of his inclosure for himself. For he that leaves as much as another can make use of, does as good as take nothing at all. No Body could think himself injur'd by the drinking of another Man, though he took a good Draught, who had a whole River of the same Water left him to quench his thirst. And the Case of Land and Water, where there is enough of both, is perfectly the same.

34. God gave the World to Men in Common; but since he gave it them for their benefit, and the greatest Conveniencies of Life they were capable to draw from it, it cannot be supposed he meant it should always remain common and uncultivated. He gave it to the use of the Industrious and Rational, (and *Labour* was to be *his Title* to it;) not to the Fancy or Covetousness of the Quarrelsom and Contentious. He that had as good left for his Improvement, as was already taken up, needed not complain, ought not to meddle with what was already improved by another's Labour: If he did, 'tis plain he desired the benefit of another's Pains, which he had no right to, and not the Ground which God had given him in common with others to labour on, and whereof there was as good left, as that already possessed, and more than he knew what to do with, or his Industry could reach to.

. . .

46. The greatest part of *things really useful* to the Life of Man, and such as the necessity of subsisting made the first Commoners of the World look after, as it doth the *Americans* now, *are* generally things *of short duration*; such as, if they are not consumed by use, will decay and perish of themselves: Gold, Silver, and Diamonds, are things, that Fancy or Agreement hath put the Value on, more than real Use, and the necessary Support of Life. Now of those good things which Nature hath provided in common, every one had a Right (as hath been said) to as much as he could use, and had a Property in all that he could affect with his Labour: all that his Industry could extend to, to alter from the State Nature had put it in, was his. He that *gathered* a Hundred Bushels of Acorns or Apples, had thereby a *Property* in them; they were his Goods as soon as gathered. He was only to look that he used them before they spoiled; else he took more than his share, and robb'd others. And indeed it was a foolish thing, as well as dishonest, to hoard up more than he could make use of. If he gave away a part to any body else,

so that it perished not uselesly in his Possession, these he also made use of. And if he also bartered away Plumbs that would have rotted in a Week, for Nuts that would last good for his eating a whole Year, he did no injury; he wasted not the common Stock; destroyed no part of the portion of Goods that belonged to others, so long as nothing perished uselesly in his hands. Again, if he would give us Nuts for a piece of Metal, pleased with its colour; or exchanged his Sheep for Shells, or Wool for a sparkling Pebble or a Diamond, and keep those by him all his Life, he invaded not the Right of others, he might heap up as much of these durable things as he pleased; the *exceeding of the bounds of his* just *Property* not lying in the largeness of his Possession, but the perishing of any thing uselesly in it.

47. And thus *came in the use of Money*, some lasting thing that Men might keep without spoiling, and that by mutual consent Men would take in exchange for the truly useful, but perishable Supports of Life.

48. And as different degrees of Industry were apt to give Men Possessions in different Proportions, so this *Invention of Money* gave them the opportunity to continue to enlarge them. For supposing an Island, separated from all possible Commerce with the rest of the World, wherein there were but a hundred Families, but there were Sheep, Horses and Cows, with other useful Animals, wholsome Fruits, and Land enough for Corn for a hundred thousand times as many, but nothing in the Island, either because of its Commonness, or Perishableness, fit to supply the place of *Money*: What reason could any one have there to enlarge his Possessions beyond the use of his Family, and a plentiful supply to its Consumption, either in what their own Industry produced, or they could barter for like perishable, useful Commodities, with others? Where there is not something both lasting and scarce, and so valuable to be hoarded up, there Men will not be apt to enlarge their *Possessions of Land*, were it never so rich, never so free for them to take. For I ask, What would a Man value Ten Thousand, or an Hundred Thousand Acres of excellent *Land*, ready cultivated, and well stocked too with Cattle, in the middle of the in-land Parts of *America*, where he had no hopes of Commerce with other Parts of the World, to draw *Money* to him by the Sale of the Product? It would not be worth the inclosing, and we should see him give up again to the wild Common of Nature, whatever was more than would supply the Conveniencies of Life to be had there for him and his Family.

. . .

VIII OF THE BEGINNING OF POLITICAL SOCIETIES

95. Men being, as has been said, by Nature, all free, equal and independent, no one can be put out of this Estate, and subjected to the Political Power of another, without his own *Consent*. The only way whereby any one devests himself of his Natural Liberty, any *puts on the bonds of Civil Society* is by agreeing with other Men to joyn and unite into a Community, for their comfortable, safe, and peaceable living one amongst another, in a secure Enjoyment of their Properties, and a greater Security against any that are not of it. This any number of Men may do, because it injures not the Freedom of the rest; they are left as they were in the Liberty of the State of Nature. When any number of Men have so *consented to make one Community* or Government, they are thereby presently incorporated, and make *one Body Politick*, wherein the *Majority* have a Right to act and conclude the rest.

96. For when any number of Men have, by the consent of every individual, made a *Community*, they have thereby made that *Community* one Body, with a Power to Act as one Body, which is only by the will and determination of the *majority*. For that which acts any Community, being only the consent of the individuals of it, and it being necessary to that which is one body to move one way; it is necessary the Body should move that way whither the greater force carries it, which is the *consent of the majority*:

or else it is impossible it should act or continue one Body, *one Community*, which the consent of every individual that united into it, agreed that it should; and so every one is bound by that consent to be concluded by the *majority*. And therefore we see that in Assemblies impowered to act by positive Laws where no number is set by that positive Law which impowers them, the *act of the Majority* passes for the act of the whole, and of course determines, as having by the Law of Nature and Reason, the power of the whole.

97. And thus every Man, by consenting with others to make one Body Politick under one Government, puts himself under an Obligation to every one of that Society, to submit to the determination of the *majority*, and to be concluded by it; or else this *original Compact*, whereby he with others incorporates into *one Society*, would signifie nothing, and be no Compact, if he be left free, and under no other ties, than he was in before in the State of Nature. For what appearance would there be of any Compact? What new Engagement if he were no farther tied by any Decrees of the Society, than he himself thought fit, and did actually consent to? This would be still as great a liberty, as he himself had before his Compact, or any one else in the State of Nature hath, who may submit himself and consent to any acts of it if he thinks fit.

98. For if *the consent of the majority* shall not in reason, be received, *as the act of the whole*, and conclude every individual; nothing but the consent of every individual can make any thing to be the act of the whole: But such a consent is next impossible ever to be had, if we consider the Infirmities of Health, and Avocations of Business, which in a number, though much less than that of a Commonwealth, will necessarily keep many away from the publick Assembly. To which if we add the variety of Opinions, and contrariety of Interests, which unavoidably happen in all Collections of Men, the coming into Society upon such terms, would be only like *Cato's* coming into the Theatre, only to go out again. Such a Constitution as this would make the mighty *Leviathan* of a shorter duration, than the feeblest Creatures; and not let it outlast the day it was born in: which cannot be suppos'd till we can think, that Rational Creatures should desire and constitute Societies only to be dissolved. For where the *majority* cannot conclude the rest, there they cannot act as one Body, and consequently will be immediately dissolved again.

99. Whosoever therefore out of a state of Nature unite into a *Community*, must be understood to give up all the power, necessary to the ends for which they unite into Society, to the *majority* of the Community, unless they expressly agreed in any number greater than the majority. And this is done by barely agreeing to *unite into one Political Society*, which is *all the Compact that* is, or needs be, between the Individuals, that enter into, or make up a *Common-wealth*. And thus that, which begins and actually *constitutes any Political Society*, is nothing but the consent of any number of Freemen capable of a majority to unite and incorporate into such a Society. And this is that, and that only, which did, or could give *beginning* to any *lawful Government* in the World.

. . .

122. But submitting to the Laws of any Country, living quietly, and enjoying Priviledges and Protection under them, *makes not a Man a Member of that Society*: This is only a local Protection and Homage due to, and from all those, who, not being in a state of War, come within the Territories belonging to any Government, to all parts whereof the force of its Law extends. But this no more *makes a Man a Member of that Society*, a perpetual Subject of that Commonwealth, than it would make a Man a Subject to another in whose Family he found it convenient to abide for some time; though, whilst he continued in it, he were obliged to comply with the Laws, and submit to the Government he found there. And thus we see, that *Foreigners*, by living all their Lives under another Government, and enjoying the Priviledges and Protection of it, though they

are bound, even in Conscience, to submit to its Administration, as far forth as any Denison; yet do not thereby come to be *Subjects or Members of that Commonwealth*. Nothing can make any Man so, but his actually entering into it by positive Engagement, and express Promise and Compact. This is that, which I think, concerning the beginning of Political Societies, and that *Consent which makes any one a Member* of any Commonwealth.

IX OF THE ENDS OF POLITICAL SOCIETY AND GOVERNMENT

123. If Man in the State of Nature be so free, as has been said; If he be absolute Lord of his own Person and Possessions, equal to the greatest, and subject to no Body, why will he part with his Freedom? Why will he give up this Empire, and subject himself to the Dominion and Controul of any other Power? To which 'tis obvious to Answer, that though in the state of Nature he hath such a right, yet the Enjoyment of it is very uncertain, and constantly exposed to the Invasion of others. For all being Kings as much as he, every Man his Equal, and the greater part no strict Observers of Equity and Justice, the enjoyment of the property he has in this state is very unsafe, very unsecure. This makes him willing to quit a Condition, which however free, is full of fears and continual dangers: And 'tis not without reason, that he seeks out, and is willing to joyn in Society with others who are already united, or have a mind to unite for the mutual *Preservation* of their Lives, Liberties and Estates, which I call by the general Name, *Property*.

124. The great and *chief end* therefore, of Mens uniting into Commonwealths, and putting themselves under Government, *is the Preservation of their Property*. To which in the state of Nature there are many things wanting.

First, There wants an *establish'd*, settled, known *Law*, received and allowed by common consent to be the Standard of Right and Wrong, and the common measure to decide all Controversies between them. For though the Law of Nature be plain and intelligible to all rational Creatures; yet Men being biassed by their Interest, as well as ignorant for want of study of it, are not apt to allow of it as a Law binding to them in the application of it to their particular Cases.

125. *Secondly*, In the State of Nature there wants a *known and indifferent Judge*, with Authority to determine all differences according to the established Law. For every one in that state being both Judge and Executioner of the Law of Nature, Men being partial to themselves, Passion and Revenge is very apt to carry them too far, and with too much heat, in their own Cases; as well as negligence, and unconcernedness, to make them too remiss, in other Mens.

126. *Thirdly*, In the State of Nature there often wants *Power* to back and support the Sentence when right, and to *give* it due *Execution*. They who by any Injustice offended, will seldom fail, where they are able, by force to make good their Injustice: such resistance many times makes the punishment dangerous, and frequently destructive, to those who attempt it.

127. Thus Mankind, notwithstanding all the Priviledges of the state of Nature, being but in an ill condition, while they remain in it, are quickly driven into Society. Hence it comes to pass, that we seldom find any number of Men live any time together in this State. The inconveniences, that they are therein exposed to, by the irregular and uncertain exercise of the Power every Man has of punishing the transgressions of others, make them take Sanctuary under the establish'd Laws of Government, and therein seek *the preservation of their Property*. 'Tis this makes them so willingly give up every one his single power of punishing to be exercised by such alone as shall be appointed to it amongst them; and by such Rules as the Community, or those authorized by them to that purpose, shall agree on. And in this we have the original *right and rise* of both *the Legislative and Executive Power*, as well as of the Governments and Societies themselves.

128. For in the State of Nature, to omit the liberty he has of innocent Delights, a Man has two Powers.

The first is to do whatsoever he thinks fit for the preservation of himself and others within the permission of the *Law of Nature*: by which Law common to them all, he and all the rest of *Mankind are one Community*, make up one Society distinct from all other Creatures. And were it not for the corruption, and vitiousness of degenerate Men, there would be no need of any other; no necessity that Men should separate from this great and natural Community, and by positive agreements combine into smaller and divided associations.

The other power a Man has in the State of Nature, is the *power to punish the Crimes* committed against that Law. Both these he gives up, when he joyns in a private, if I may so call it, or particular Political Society, and incorporates into any Commonwealth, separate from the rest of Mankind.

129. The first *Power, viz. of doing whatsoever he thought fit for the Preservation of himself*, and the rest of Mankind, *he gives up* to be regulated by Laws made by the Society, so far forth as the preservation of himself, and the rest of that Society shall require; which Laws of the Society in many things confine the liberty he had by the Law of Nature.

130. *Secondly*, the *Power of punishing* he wholly *gives up*, and engages his natural force, (which he might before imploy in the Execution of the Law of Nature, by his own single Authority, as he thought fit) to assist the Executive Power of the Society, as the Law thereof shall require. For being now in a new State, wherein he is to enjoy many Conveniences, from the labour, assistance, and society of others in the same Community, as well as protection from its whole strength; he is to part also with as much of his natural liberty in providing for himself, as the good, prosperity, and safety of the Society shall require: which is not only necessary, but just; since the other Members of the Society do the like.

131. But though Men when they enter into Society, give up the Equality, Liberty, and Executive Power they had in the State of Nature, into the hands of the Society, to be so far disposed of by the Legislative, as the good of the Society shall require; yet it being only with an intention in every one the better to preserve himself his Liberty and Property; (For no rational Creature can be supposed to change his condition with an intention to be worse) the power of the Society, or *Legislative* constituted by them, *can never be suppos'd to extend farther than the common good*: but is obliged to secure every ones Property by providing against those three defects abovementioned, that made the State of Nature so unsafe and uneasie. And so whoever has the Legislative or Supream Power of any Commonwealth, is bound to govern by establish'd *standing Laws*, promulgated and known to the People, and not by Extemporary Decrees; by *indifferent* and upright *Judges*, who are to decide Controversies by those Laws; And to imploy the force of the Community at home, *only in the Execution of such Laws*, or abroad to prevent or redress Foreign Injuries, and secure the Community from Inroads and Invasion. And all this to be directed to no other *end*, but the *Peace, Safety*, and *publick good* of the People.

. . .

JEAN-JACQUES ROUSSEAU

Jean-Jacques Rousseau (1712–1778) was one of the most versatile and influential of modern thinkers. A figure of the Enlightenment as well as a pioneer of Romanticism, he left his mark on social philosophy, educational thought, and literature and authored the first truly modern autobiography. Of the philosophical writers in the century after Hobbes, it was he who stated the problem of civilization with the most rigor and force; indeed, more than anyone he lived out this problem in his own restless and defiant life.

Born in Geneva in 1712, Rousseau was the son of a watchmaker but was orphaned at age ten and left his native city at sixteen. A vagabond and adventurer for the rest of his life, Rousseau was to be imitated by a host of cultured travelers, especially by the Romantic poets, and his habits of direct observation were to impress and unsettle the literati of the ancien régime. From ages sixteen to twenty-nine, Rousseau worked as a footman, seminarist, music teacher, and tutor; became a Catholic convert at Turin; and found nurture and encouragement at the country house of Madame de Varennes, a hospitable widow whom he remembers fondly in his autobiography, *Les Confessions* (published 1782–1789).

In 1741 Rousseau moved on to Paris, hoping to make his name with a system of musical notation he had invented. He soon encountered the brilliant "philosophes," among them d'Alembert, Condillac, Marivaux, and especially Diderot, who commissioned him to write the musical articles for the *Encyclopedie*. He became a secretary to the French ambassador to Venice, but after a quarrel with his superior he was dismissed, returned to Paris, and supported himself by copying music. It was the last time Rousseau ever accepted work under another person's command.

Rousseau was lively, personable, and a brilliant if paradoxical conversationalist; his eloquence won him many upper-class admirers. His first opera was staged, and he was commissioned to retouch an opera ballet by Rameau for production at the court. In the meantime, he fathered five children by Therese Levasseur, a servant girl who remained with him for the rest of his life, and abandoned the children to a foundling home.

In 1749, while trudging to the prison of Vincennes to visit his friend Diderot, Rousseau experienced the bolt of inspiration that gave him both the identity he had been seeking through all of his wanderings and the theme for all of his future writings. Leafing through the newspaper, he fell upon the subject of an essay contest announced by the Academy of Dijon: "Has the advancement of civilization tended to corrupt or improve morals?" In his essay Rousseau argued that mounting corruption went hand in hand with the progress of the arts and sciences in a society lacking in justice and liberty. While primitive man had been naturally good and free, the present social order made men increasingly immoral and unhappy. Human beings must strive to recover the "rights of nature" and basic equality they once enjoyed. The sciences, industry, and the arts —here Rousseau pointed to his own friends, the proponents of Enlightenment—link men by bonds of self-interest instead of benevolence and mutual respect. With his *Discourse on the Arts and Sciences* (1750), Rousseau won the prize.

Rousseau entered a new essay contest in 1754, and the result of his meditations was the *Discourse on the Origin of Inequality*, one of his greatest works. In the state of nature, he argues, man is innocent, distinguished from the other animals only by capacities for self-improvement and compassion or sympathy. In the early stages, as human beings collaborate they develop their feelings of sympathy, but other things also ensue. Cultivation of the earth gives rise to the idea of property, which, given the inequality of people's skills, leads to inequality in their fortunes. The wealthy enslave the poor, conflict erupts, and demand arises for a system of law to impose order. With the establishment of law, which institutionalizes and increases inequality, human beings "run headlong into chains." They see the advantages of government but lack the experience to foresee the dangers. Rousseau dedicated this work to the Republic of Geneva, his native city. But, like most of his books, it offended the political authorities who were not nearly as democratic as he wished to believe; after a brief stay in Geneva, he took refuge in a cottage within the Forest of Montmorency.

The twelve years between the winning of the Dijon prize and the publication of *The Social Contract or Principles of Political Right* (1762) were Rousseau's most creative. He worked on *Emile* (1762), his treatise on pedagogy, and on his novel, *La Nouvelle Heloise* (1761), while he was working on the *Social Contract*. In rural peace, he also wrote *Lettre à d'Alembert*, his attack on the theater; *Lettre à Voltaire*, a defense of religious faith against Voltaire's mocking humanism; a defense of Italian music against the more artificial French style; and his *Essay on the Origin of Languages*.

The Social Contract, Rousseau's best-known work, opens with the famous sentence, "Man is born free, and is everywhere in chains." Following Hobbes, he argues that the social contract completely terminates the state of nature, with its natural freedom and equality. But in its place, Rousseau insists, mankind gains something even more precious: political freedom and civil equality. Point by point, he shows how civilization takes with one hand what it gives with another: how, for example, possession, which is purely an act of force, becomes property, a right that is both guaranteed and limited by the community. Most of all, Rousseau develops his idea of the general will, a kind of moral ethos that lives inside each person as well as in society as a whole. General will explains how a person who is punished by the community for breaking the law is, as Rousseau sees it, being brought back to an awareness of his own true will. Law is a means for helping the individual in his battle against his own passions, as well as a device for protecting society against its enemies. By establishing the general will—not tradition, positive law, or even individual conscience—as the highest moral authority, Rousseau pushed the liberal idea of freedom down a more democratic path, one that was to lead even to socialism.

After 1762, Rousseau, now chronically ill, was rewarded for his labors with persecution by the governments of France and other nations, who drove him from one place of exile to another. Religious fanatics burned his books in Paris and Geneva and forced him to flee, so Rousseau took refuge for a year in England at the invitation of David Hume. Suffering pain, harassed by misfortunes, he became querulous, even paranoid, in his later years, yet still summoned the energies to write his *Confessions* (completed in 1770), a magnificent polemic entitled "Letters from the Mountain," and the poignant and wistful reminiscences known posthumously as *The Reveries of the Solitary Walker*.

THE SOCIAL CONTRACT

1762

Or Principles of Political Right

BOOK I

Taking men as they are and laws as they can be, I propose to inquire whether there can be any legitimate and reliable rule of administration in the civil order. In this inquiry I shall try always to combine what right permits with what interest prescribes, so that justice and utility will not be divided.

I shall go directly to my subject without first demonstrating its importance. I may be asked if I am a ruler or a lawmaker, since I am writing on politics. I answer that I am neither, and that that is why I am writing on politics. If I were a ruler or a lawmaker, I would not waste time saying what ought to be done; I would either do it or remain silent.

Having been born a citizen of a free state and a member of its sovereign, I feel that however slightly my vote may affect public affairs, the right to vote on them is enough to make it my duty to inquire into them. When I reflect on governments, I am always happy to discover that my studies have given me new reasons to love the government of my own country.

I The Subject of This First Book

Man is born free, and is everywhere in chains. This or that man may regard himself as the master of others, but he is more of a slave than they. How did this change come about? I do not know. What can make it legitimate? I believe I can answer that question.

If I were to consider only force and the effects it produces, I would say, "As long as a people is compelled to obey and does so, it does well; as soon as it is able to throw off its yoke and does so, it does even better, for it has recovered its freedom by the same right as that by which it was taken away, so either it is justified in recovering it or there was no justification for taking it away." But the social order is a sacred right that serves as the basis of all others. Yet this right does not come from nature; it is therefore founded on agreements. The problem is to determine what those agreements are. First, however, I must substantiate what I have just stated.

. . .

III The Right of the Strongest

The strongest man is never strong enough to maintain his mastery at all times unless he transforms his strength into right and obedience into a duty. Hence the right of the strongest, a right that is taken ironically in appearance and established as a principle in reality. But will anyone ever explain what the term means? I do not see what morality can be derived from physical force. Yielding to force is an act of necessity, not of will; at the very most, it is an act of prudence. In what sense could it be a duty?

Let us suppose for a moment that this alleged right exists. I say that nothing results from it but a mass of nonsense. For if might makes right, the effect changes with the cause: Any might greater than the first will take over its right. As soon as one can disobey with impunity, one can disobey legitimately, and since the strongest is always in the right, one has only to act in such a way as to be the strongest. But what kind of right is it that ceases to exist when strength perishes? If a man is forced to obey, he no longer has any obligation to do so. It is clear that the word "right" adds nothing to force; in that connection, it means nothing at all.

"Obey the powers that be." If that means "Yield to force," it is a good precept, but superfluous, and I can guarantee that it will never be violated. All power comes from God. I acknowledge that; but all disease comes from him also. Does this mean that it is forbidden to call a doctor? If a bandit waylays me in the forest, I am forced to give him my money, but if it were possible for me to keep it, would I have a moral obligation to give it to him anyway? After all, the pistol he points at me is also a form of force.

Let us agree, then, that might does not make right, and that we are obligated to obey only legitimate powers. Thus my original question returns.

. . .

VI The Social Pact

I suppose men to have reached the point where the obstacles to their survival in the state of nature have a resistance that cannot be overcome by the forces each individual has at his disposal for preserving himself in that state. The time has thus come when that original state can subsist no longer, and the human race will perish if it does not change its way of living.

Since men cannot engender new forces, but can only unite and direct existing ones, they now have only one means of preserving themselves: to form by aggregation a sum of forces capable of overcoming the resistance, then direct them toward a single goal and make them act together.

Such a sum of forces can be produced only by the collaboration of a group of men. But since each man's strength and freedom are his primary means of self-preservation, how can he pledge them without harming himself, without neglecting the care he owes to himself? The problem that arises here can be stated as follows: "To devise a form of association which will defend and protect the person and possessions of each associate with all the collective strength, and in which each is united with all, yet obeys only himself and remains as free as before." Such is the fundamental problem that the social contract solves.

The terms of this contract are so determined by the nature of the agreement that the slightest alteration would make them null and void, so that even though they may never have been formally enunciated, they are everywhere the same, everywhere tacitly accepted and acknowledged, as long as the social pact is not violated, in which case each man regains his original rights and returns to his natural freedom, losing the contractual freedom for which he renounced it.

These terms, properly understood, can all be reduced to one, namely, the complete surrender of each associate, with all his rights, to the whole community. For in the first place, since each man gives himself entirely, the condition is equal for all; and since the condition is equal for all, it is to no one's interest to make it burdensome for others.

Furthermore, since the surrender is made without reserve, the union is as perfect as it can be and no associate has anything more to demand, for if individuals retained any rights, each would soon be his own judge on some point or other, there being no common superior to decide between him and the public; then eventually everyone would set himself up as his own judge on all points, the state of nature would subsist, and the association would necessarily become either tyrannical or ineffectual.

Finally, in giving himself to all, each man gives himself to no one, and since he acquires the same right over all the other associates as they acquire over him, he gains the equivalent of everything he loses, plus greater power to preserve what he has.

If, then, we exclude from the social pact everything that is not essential to it, we find that it reduces itself to this formulation: "Each of us puts his person and all his power in common under the supreme control of the general will, and we collectively receive each member as an indivisible part of the whole."

In place of the individual persons of the contracting parties, the act of association immediately creates a collective, artificial body, composed of as many members as the assembly has voters, and the same act gives this body its unity, its collective self, its life, and its will. Such a public person, formed by the union of all other persons, was formerly called a *city*, and is now known as a *republic* or a *body politic*. Its members call it the *state* when it is passive, the *sovereign* when it is active and a *power* when they compare it with others of its kind. They themselves collectively take the name of the *people*, and are individually called *citizens* as sharing in the sovereign authority, and *subjects* as owing obedience to the laws of the state. But these terms are often used indiscriminately, one in place of another; it is enough to know how to distinguish them when they are used precisely.

VII The Sovereign

This formulation shows that the act of association involves a reciprocal commitment between the public and the individuals who compose it, and that each individual, contracting with himself, so to speak, is under a double obligation: toward other individuals, as a member of the sovereign, and toward the sovereign, as a member of the state. But the principle of common law which says that a man cannot be held to a commitment he has made to himself does not apply here, for there is a great difference between assuming an obligation toward himself and assuming one toward a whole of which he is a part.

It should also be pointed out that while public decisions can obligate all subjects toward the sovereign, because of the two capacities in which each subject is considered, they cannot obligate the sovereign toward itself. It is therefore contrary to the nature of the body politic for the sovereign to impose a law on itself that it cannot infringe. Since it can be considered only in a single capacity, it is in the position of an individual contracting with himself. Hence we see that there neither is nor can be any kind of fundamental law binding on the people as a body—not even the social contract. This does not mean that the body politic cannot assume obligations toward others, insofar as they do not violate that contract, for in relation to outsiders it is an indivisible being, an individual.

But since the body politic or the sovereign draws its being only from the sanctity of the contract, it can never obligate itself, even to an outsider, to do anything contrary to that original agreement, such as alienating some portion of itself, or placing itself under the authority of another sovereign. To violate the agreement by which it exists would be to annihilate itself, and that which is nothing can do nothing.

Once a multitude is thus united in a body, no one can offend one of its members without attacking the body, much less offend the body without affecting its members. Duty and interest therefore equally oblige the two contracting parties to help each other, and the same men must seek to combine, in their double capacity, all the advantages that pertain to it.

The sovereign, being formed only by the individuals who compose it, neither has nor can have any interest contrary to theirs; consequently there is no need for the sovereign power to give guarantees to the subjects, because it is impossible for the body to want to harm all its members, and as we shall see later, it cannot harm any one of them in particular. Merely by virtue of existing, the sovereign is always what it should be.

This, however, is not true of the subjects in relation to the sovereign, which, despite the common interest, could not count on them to fulfill their obligations unless it devised means of making sure of their fidelity.

Each individual can, as a man, have a private will different from or even contrary to the general will which he has as a citizen. His private interest may speak to him quite differently from the common interest; his absolute and naturally independent existence may make him regard what he owes to the common cause as a gratuitous contribution, loss of which would be less harmful to others than payment of it is burdensome to him, and considering that the artificial person that constitutes the state is an imaginary being because it is not a man, he may want to enjoy the rights of a citizen without fulfilling the duties of a subject, an injustice that would bring about the ruin of the body politic if it were to spread.

In order, therefore, that the social pact shall not be an empty formality, it tacitly includes one stipulation without which all the others would be ineffectual:

that anyone who refuses to obey the general will shall be compelled to do so by the whole body. This means nothing else than that he shall be forced to be free, for such is the condition which gives each citizen to his country and thus secures him against all personal dependence. This condition is essential to the functioning of the political machine, and it alone legitimizes civil obligations, which would otherwise be absurd, tyrannical, and subject to the most outrageous abuses.

VIII The Civil State

The passage from the state of nature to the civil state produces a remarkable change in man by substituting justice for instinct in his conduct and giving his acts the morality they previously lacked. Only then, when physical impulses have yielded to the voice of duty, and appetite to right, does man, who so far had considered only himself, find that he is forced to act according to different principles and to consult his reason before listening to his inclinations. In this state he is deprived of some advantages given to him by nature, but he gains others so great—his faculties are exercised and developed, his ideas are broadened, his feelings are ennobled, his whole soul is uplifted—that if the abuses of this new state did not often degrade him below his previous level, he would constantly have reason to bless the happy moment when he was drawn out of the state of nature forever and changed from a stupid, shortsighted animal into an intelligent being and a man.

Let us reduce the balance to terms that can be easily compared. What man loses by the social contract is his natural freedom and an unlimited right to anything he wants and can get. What he gains is civil freedom and ownership of everything he possesses. To avoid error in evaluating this exchange, we must make two clear distinctions: first, between natural freedom, which is limited only by the individual's power, and civil freedom, which is limited by the general will; and second, between possession, which results only from force or the right of first occupancy, and ownership, which can be based only on juridical title.

Another gain can be added to those that come with the civil state: moral freedom, which alone makes man truly his own master, for impulsion by appetite alone is slavery, and obedience to self-imposed law is freedom. But I have already said too much on this point, and the philosophical meaning of the word "freedom" is not part of my subject here.

. . .

BOOK II

III Whether the General Will Can Err

It follows from what has been said above that the general will is always well-meaning and always tends toward the public good; but it does not follow that all decisions made by the people are equally sound. We always will our own good, but we do not always see what it is. The people is never corrupted, but it is often misled, and only then does it seem to will what is bad.

There is often a great difference between the will of all and the general will. The latter looks only to the common interest, while the former looks to private interest and is only a sum of individual wills. But take away from those same wills the pluses and minuses that cancel each other out, and the general will remains as the sum of the differences.

If the people always decided on the basis of adequate information, and with no discussion among the citizens beforehand, the general will would always result from the larger number of small differences and the decision would always be right. But when there are factions, lesser associations detrimental to the greater one, the will of each of them becomes general in relation to its members and particular in relation to the state. It can then be said that there are no longer as many voters as there are men, but only as many as there are associations. The differences become less numerous and give a less general result. Finally, when one of these associations is so large that it prevails over all the others, the result is no longer a sum of small differences, but a single difference; there is then no longer a general will, and the opinion that prevails is only a particular one.

Therefore, if the general will is to be clearly expressed, it is important that there be no partial societies within the state, and that each citizen form his opinion independently. Such was the unique and sublime system established by the great Lycurgus. When partial societies do exist, they must be made numerous and prevented from being unequal, as was done by Solon, Numa, and Servius. These are the only effective precautions that can be taken to ensure that the general will is always enlightened and the people never mistaken.

IV Limits of the Sovereign Power

If the state or body politic is only an artificial person whose life is in the union of its members, and if its most important concern is its own preservation, it must have a universal coercive power in order to move and direct each part in the manner most advantageous to the whole. Just as nature gives each man absolute power over the parts of his body, the social pact gives the body politic absolute power over its members, and it is this same power which, under the direction of the general will, bears the name of sovereignty, as I have already said.

But besides this public person, we must also consider the private persons who compose it, and whose life and freedom are naturally independent of it. We must therefore distinguish between the respective rights of the citizens and the sovereign, as well as between the duties which the citizens must fulfill as subjects and the natural rights they should enjoy as men.

It is acknowledged that the social pact requires each individual to relinquish only that part of his power, possessions, and freedom which it is important for the community to control; but it must also be acknowledged that the sovereign is the sole judge of that importance.

If a citizen is able to render certain services to the state, it is his duty to render them as soon as the sovereign requests them. But the sovereign, for its part, cannot place the subjects under any constraint useless to the community; it cannot even will to do so, for under the law of reason, as under the law of nature, nothing can occur without a cause.

The commitments that bind us to the social body are obligatory only because they are mutual, and their nature is such that, in fulfilling them, one cannot work for others without also working for oneself. Why is the general will always well-meaning, and why does everyone constantly will the happiness of each individual, if not because everyone applies the word "each" to himself and thinks of himself when he votes for the good of all? This proves that equality of rights, and the notion of justice it produces, stem from the preference that each man gives to himself, and therefore from the nature of man. It proves that in order to be truly general, the general will must be general in its object as well as in its essence, that it must come from everyone if it is to apply to everyone, and that it loses its natural rectitude when it tends toward a specific individual object, for we are then judging something alien to us, with no true principle of equity to guide us.

. . .

BOOK IV

I The General Will Is Indestructible

As long as a number of men, having joined together, consider themselves a single body, they have only one will, which is directed toward the common security and well-being. The forces that move the state are then simple and vigorous; its principles are clear and illuminating; there are no tangled, conflicting interests; the common good is always so obvious that it can be seen by anyone with common sense. Peace, unity, and equality are enemies of political guile. Simple, straightforward men are difficult to deceive because of their very simplicity. They are not taken in by blandishments and devious arguments; they are too unsophisticated to be dupes. When, in the world's happiest nation, one sees groups of peasants conducting the affairs of the state under an oak tree and always acting wisely, how can one help despising the refinements of other nations, which make themselves illustrious and wretched by such artful and mysterious means?

A state so governed requires very few laws, and whenever there is a need to promulgate new ones, that need is apparent to all. The first man who proposes them is only saying what everyone else already feels, and neither intrigue nor eloquence plays any part in enacting into law what each has already resolved to do as soon as he is sure that others will do the same.

What misleads glib theorizers is that, seeing only states which were badly constituted from the start, they are struck by the impossibility of conducting the affairs of such states in the way I have described. They laugh when they imagine all the foolish acts into which a clever scoundrel or an ingratiating orator could lead the people of Paris or London. They do not know that Cromwell would have been put to forced labor by the people of Berne, and the Duc de Beaufort imprisoned by the Genevans.

But when the social bond begins to loosen and the state to weaken, when private interests make themselves felt and smaller associations begin to influence the whole society, then the common interest becomes distorted and encounters opposition, voting is no longer unanimous, the general will is no longer the will of all, conflicts and debates arise, and even the wisest opinions are disputed.

Finally, when the state is close to ruin and exists only in an empty, illusory form, when the social bond has been broken in all hearts, when the vilest self-interest brazenly adorns itself with the sacred name of the public good, then the general will becomes mute, each man is guided by secret motives, the opinions he expresses are no more those of a citizen than if the state had never existed, and unjust decrees that have no other object than private interest are falsely presented as laws.

Does it follow from all this that the general will is annihilated or corrupted? No: It is still changeless, incorruptible, and pure; but it is subordinated to other wills that prevail over it. In detaching his interest from the common interest, each man clearly sees that he cannot separate the two completely, but his share of the public evil seems negligible to him, compared with the exclusive good that he intends to obtain for himself. Except where this private good is concerned, he wills the general good, in his own interest, as strongly as anyone else. Even if he sells his vote for money, he does not extinguish the general will in himself; he evades it. The transgression he commits is to change the formulation of the question, so that his answer concerns something other than what he was asked to decide; that is, instead of saying by his vote, "It is advantageous to the state," he says, "It is advantageous to a certain man or a certain faction that such and such a measure be adopted." Therefore the purpose of rules for regulating public assemblies is less to uphold the general will in them than to make sure that it is always questioned and always replies.

There are many observations that I could make here about the simple right of voting in every act of sovereignty, a right which nothing can take away from the citizens, and about the right of expressing opinions, making proposals, analyzing, and discussing, which the government always makes great efforts to reserve only for its members: but that important subject would require a separate treatise, and I cannot say everything in this one.

II Voting

From what has been said in the preceding chapter it can be seen that the manner in which public affairs are conducted is a reliable indication of the current state of public morality and the health of the body politic. The more agreement there is in the assemblies, that is, the closer opinions come to being unanimous, the more the general will is dominant; but long debates, dissension, and tumult herald the ascendancy of private interests and the decline of the state.

This seems less obvious when two or more orders enter into the constitution of the state. In Rome, for example, the assemblies were often disturbed by quarrels between the patricians and the plebeians, even in the finest days of the Republic. But this exception is more apparent than real, for in such cases, because of an inherent defect in the body politic, there are, so to speak, two states in one, and what is not true of both together is true of each separately. Even in the stormiest times, the decrees of the Roman people, when the Senate did not interfere, were always promulgated peacefully and by a large majority of votes. Since the citizens had only one interest, the people had only one will.

Unanimity returns at the opposite extreme, when the citizens have fallen into servitude and no longer have either freedom or will. Fear and obsequiousness then change voting into acclamation; there is no longer deliberation, but only worship or damnation. Such was the vile way in which the Roman Senate expressed itself under the emperors. It was sometimes done with ridiculous precautions: Tacitus writes that, during the reign of Otho, when the senators heaped abuse on Vitellius they made a great uproar at the same time, so that if he should happen to gain control of the empire he would not be able to learn what each of them had said.

These various considerations give rise to the principles by which the counting of votes and the comparing of opinions should be conducted, depending on the ease with which the general will can be recognized, and the extent to which the state is declining.

There is only one law which by its nature requires unanimous assent: the social pact. For civil association is the most voluntary act in the world; since each man is born free and his own master, no one can bind him to anything, on any pretext whatever, without his consent. To decide that the son of a slave woman is born a slave is to decide that he is not born human.

If, then, there are those who oppose the social pact at the time when it is made, their opposition does not invalidate the contract: It only excludes them from it. They are foreigners among the citizens. When the state is instituted, residence indicates consent; to live in its territory is to acknowledge the authority of its sovereign.

Apart from this original contract, the decision of the majority is always binding on the minority. This is a consequence of the contract itself. But it may be asked how a man can be free, and at the same time be forced to conform to wills that are not his own. How can dissenters be both free and subject to laws to which they have not consented?

I answer that the question is wrongly formulated. The citizen consents to all the laws, even those that are passed against his opposition, and even those that punish him if he dares to violate one of them. The unequivocal will of all the members of the state is the general will; it is through it that they are citizens and free. When a law is proposed in their assembly, what is asked of them is not precisely whether they accept or reject the proposal, but whether it is in conformity with the general will that is theirs. In voting, each man gives his opinion on this question, and the declaration of the general will is drawn from the count of the votes. When, therefore, the opinion contrary to mine prevails, it proves only that I was mistaken, that what I thought was the general will was not. If my private opinion had prevailed, I would have done something other than what I had willed, and then I would not have been free.

This presupposes, it is true, that all the characteristics of the general will are still present in the majority; when they cease to be there, no matter what decision is made, there is no longer any freedom.

When I showed earlier how particular wills were substituted for the general will in public decisions, I spoke at some length about the practical means of preventing that abuse, and I shall return to them later. As for the proportion of votes needed to declare the general will, I have also given the principles by which it can be determined. A difference of one vote breaks a tie, and one dissenting vote breaks unanimity; but between a tie and unanimity there are many unequal divisions, any one of which may be made the required proportion, depending on the condition and needs of the body politic.

Two general maxims may be used to determine the proportion. The first is that the more serious and important the decision is, the closer the prevailing opinion should approach unanimity. The second is that the shorter the time in which the decision must be made, the more the required majority should be reduced; in matters that must be decided without delay, a difference of one vote should be enough. The first of these maxims seems better suited to enacting laws, the second to conducting public affairs. In any case, it is by a combination of both that the best proportion to require for a decisive majority can be determined.

. . .

THOMAS JEFFERSON

Thomas Jefferson (1743–1826), third president of the United States, is the best-known spokesperson for political and spiritual liberty in his country's history. Jefferson won greatest fame at the age of thirty-three as the author of the Declaration of Independence. He also penned the Virginia Statute for Religious Freedom; founded the University of Virginia; and spent forty years in public service as a legislator, governor, congressman, diplomat, secretary of state, vice president, and president. Expert at any profession to which he put his mind, Jefferson also achieved success as a lawyer, farmer, translator, philosopher, architect, scientist, musician, and inventor.

While universally acclaimed as a revolutionary patriot, Jefferson was denounced as a radical and an atheist by his conservative foes, especially after he turned against the administration during George Washington's second term. Elected president in 1800, he became the first leader of an opposition party to win control of the national government from the party in power, thus vindicating the right of political opposition. His election blocked in the United States the tide of political reaction that was sweeping the rest of the world and revived the morale of democrats everywhere. Jefferson also established the right of an incoming president to remove his predecessor's major appointees, except for federal judges, and generally sought to conduct the government in the public interest rather than that of any privileged group.

Jefferson's father was a successful Virginia planter and county leader, whose death when the boy was fourteen left him thirty slaves and about 2,500 acres of land. Later Jefferson was to double these holdings by his marriage in 1772 to Martha Skelton. Two years after the death of his father, Jefferson enrolled at the College of William and Mary, where he was stimulated by mathematics and science, and read law with George Wythe, the greatest law teacher of his generation in Virginia.

After graduation in 1762, Jefferson studied law, was admitted to the bar in 1767, and practiced until 1774, when the courts were closed due to the American Revolution. Although successful at the law, he was drawn to the bustle of politics and in 1769 won election to the Virginia colonial legislature. For the next ten years he was re-elected regularly, fortifying a reputation for patriotic views and refining his skill at expressing them in writing. Jefferson's lifelong emphasis on local government grew directly out of this experience. When the governor of Virginia dissolved the legislature in 1774 because of its subversive activities, Jefferson wrote his first notable work, the pamphlet *A Summary View of the Rights of British America* (1774).

As a member of the Continental Congress (1775–1776), Jefferson was chosen to draft the Declaration of Independence. Summarizing current revolutionary thought, it declared that all men are equal in rights and that government is the servant, not the master, of human beings. During the next three years, Jefferson resumed his seat in the Virginia legislature and embarked upon the most creative period of his statesmanship. He wrote legislation to set up a new system of state courts, free public schools, and libraries; endeavored to abolish slavery; and authored the statute for religious freedom, which later became the basis for the First Amendment to the Constitution.

At age thirty-six Jefferson was elected by the legislature to succeed Patrick Henry as governor of Virginia, and he served two years during the bloodiest days of the Revolutionary War. Retiring in 1781, he began to compile his *Notes on the State of Virginia* (1785), an account of the resources, industries, and government of the state, which also contained reflections on religion, slavery, and Native

Americans. Several years later, while serving in the Continental Congress, Jefferson proposed that slavery be forbidden in all U.S. territories.

From 1784 to 1789 Jefferson served in France, first to negotiate trade treaties and then to succeed Benjamin Franklin as minister. He relished French culture; felt confirmed in his belief that France was a natural friend of the United States; and sent home a myriad of books, seeds and plants, statues and architectural models, maps and blueprints, and scientific information. Toward the end of his mission, he reported on the unfolding revolution and adopted a liberal-moderate stance.

Back home, as secretary of state in the Washington administration, Jefferson began his four-year contest with Alexander Hamilton, the champion of a strong centralized government armed with broad powers "implied" by the Constitution. Against Hamilton's support of merchants, bankers, and an expanding national debt, Jefferson reasserted his vision of the United States as a nation of small farms, widely distributed property, township government, and an active and literate citizenry, though one restricted to white males. But Hamilton's policies triumphed, and Jefferson reluctantly accepted his role as symbol of the opposition party.

Jefferson resigned in 1793 and threw himself into his private activities. He began rebuilding Monticello, his family home; set up a grist mill; experimented with the rotation of crops; and dabbled in the sciences. In 1796 his friends pressured him to run for president as head of the Democratic-Republican party. Narrowly defeated by John Adams, he became vice president and house critic, as it were, of the Adams administration. His major achievement was to thwart the Alien and Sedition Acts, which would have barred political opposition by fines and imprisonment, and to write the Kentucky Resolutions (1798), which articulated doctrines of states' rights against the federal government.

In 1800 Jefferson won the presidency from John Adams, vowing to reverse the expansion of executive power and restore the "spirit of 1776." His two administrations were notable for the serenity of their cabinets, the clarity of their policy, and the national unity that followed the Federalists' years of bitter partisan cleavage. His single greatest triumph was the Louisiana Purchase, which Jefferson had long desired. Although troubled by his belief that the treaty might be unconstitutional, he took pride in the journey of Lewis and Clark to the Pacific and relished the prospect that newly opened lands would help develop a yeoman democracy.

Jefferson's later years were devoted to his reading of the classic historians, to an extensive correspondence, particularly with his old friend John Adams, and to his lifelong dream of public education. After the University of Virginia was incorporated in 1819, he became the first rector, drew up architectural plans, supervised much of the instruction, and recruited capable teachers from abroad. Jefferson died, as did John Adams, on July 4, 1826, the fiftieth anniversary of the Declaration of Independence.

THE DECLARATION OF INDEPENDENCE

JULY 4, 1776

In Congress, July 4, 1776,

THE UNANIMOUS DECLARATION OF THE THIRTEEN UNITED STATES OF AMERICA

When in the Course of human events, it becomes necessary for one people to dissolve the political bands which have connected them with another, and to assume among the Powers of the earth, the separate and equal station to which the Laws of Nature and of Nature's God entitle them, a decent respect to the opinions of mankind requires that they should declare the causes which impel them to the separation.

We hold these truths to be self-evident, that all men are created equal, that they are endowed by their Creator with certain unalienable Rights, that among these are Life, Liberty and the pursuit of Happiness. That to secure these rights, Governments are instituted among Men, deriving their just powers from the consent of the governed. That whenever any Form of Government becomes destructive of these ends, it is the Right of the People to alter or to abolish it, and to institute new Government, laying its foundation on such principles and organizing its powers in such form, as to them shall seem most likely to effect their Safety and Happiness. Prudence, indeed, will dictate that Governments long established should not be changed for light and transient causes; and accordingly all experience hath shown, that mankind are more disposed to suffer, while evils are sufferable, than to right themselves by abolishing the forms to which they are accustomed. But when a long train of abuses and usurpations, pursuing invariably the same Object evinces a design to reduce them under absolute Despotism, it is their right, it is their duty, to throw off such Government, and to provide new Guards for their future security.—Such has been the patient sufferance of these Colonies; and such is now the necessity which constrains them to alter their former Systems of Government. The history of the present King of Great Britain is a history of repeated injuries and usurpations, all having in direct object the establishment of an absolute Tyranny over these States. To prove this, let Facts be submitted to a candid world.

He has refused his Assent to Laws, the most wholesome and necessary for the public good.

He has forbidden his Governors to pass Laws of immediate and pressing importance, unless suspended in their operation till his Assent should be obtained; and when so suspended, he has utterly neglected to attend to them.

He has refused to pass other Laws for the accommodation of large districts of people, unless those people would relinquish the right of Representation in the Legislature, a right inestimable to them and formidable to tyrants only.

He has called together legislative bodies at places unusual, uncomfortable, and distant from the depository of their Public Records, for the sole purpose of fatiguing them into compliance with his measures.

From *Documents of American History*, ed. Henry Steele Commager, 9th ed. (New York: Appleton-Century-Crofts, 1973).

He has dissolved Representative Houses repeatedly, for opposing with manly firmness his invasions on the rights of the people.

He has refused for a long time, after such dissolutions, to cause others to be elected; whereby the Legislative Powers, incapable of Annihilation, have returned to the People at large for their exercise; the State remaining in the mean time exposed to all the dangers of invasion from without, and convulsions within.

He has endeavoured to prevent the population of these States; for that purpose obstructing the Laws of Naturalization of Foreigners; refusing to pass others to encourage their migration hither, and raising the conditions of new Appropriations of Lands.

He has obstructed the Administration of Justice, by refusing his Assent to Laws for establishing Judiciary Powers.

He has made Judges dependent on his Will alone, for the tenure of their offices, and the amount and payment of their salaries.

He has erected a multitude of New Offices, and sent hither swarms of Officers to harass our People, and eat out their substance.

He has kept among us, in times of peace, Standing Armies without the Consent of our legislature.

He has affected to render the Military independent of and superior to the Civil Power.

He has combined with others to subject us to a jurisdiction foreign to our constitution, and unacknowledged by our laws; giving his Assent to their acts of pretended legislation:

For quartering large bodies of armed troops among us:

For protecting them, by a mock Trial, from Punishment for any Murders which they should commit on the Inhabitants of these States:

For cutting off our Trade with all parts of the world:

For imposing taxes on us without our Consent:

For depriving us in many cases, of the benefits of Trial by Jury:

For transporting us beyond Seas to be tried for pretended offences:

For abolishing the free System of English Laws in a neighbouring Province, establishing therein an Arbitrary government, and enlarging its Boundaries so as to render it at once an example and fit instrument for introducing the same absolute rule into these Colonies:

For taking away our Charters, abolishing our most valuable Laws, and altering fundamentally the Forms of our Governments:

For suspending our own Legislature, and declaring themselves invested with Power to legislate for us in all cases whatsoever.

He has abdicated Government here, by declaring us out of his Protection and waging War against us.

He has plundered our seas, ravaged our Coasts, burnt our towns, and destroyed the lives of our people.

He is at this time transporting large armies of foreign mercenaries to compleat the works of death, desolation and tyranny, already begun with circumstances of Cruelty & perfidy scarcely paralleled in the most barbarous ages, and totally unworthy the Head of a civilized nation.

He has constrained our fellow Citizens taken Captive on the high Seas to bear Arms against their Country, to become the executioners of their friends and Brethren, or to fall themselves by their Hands.

He has excited domestic insurrections amongst us, and has endeavoured to bring on the inhabitants of our frontiers, the merciless Indian Savages, whose known rule of warfare, is an undistinguished destruction of all ages, sexes and conditions.

In every stage of these Oppressions We have Petitioned for Redress in the most humble terms: Our repeated Petitions have been answered only by repeated injury. A Prince, whose character is thus marked by every act which may define a Tyrant, is unfit to be the ruler of a free People.

Nor have We been wanting in attention to our Brittish brethren. We have warned them from time to time of attempts by their legislature to extend an unwarrantable jurisdiction over us. We have reminded them of the circumstances of our emigration and settlement here. We have appealed to their native justice and magnanimity, and we have conjured them by the ties of our common kindred to disavow these usurpations, which, would inevitably interrupt our connections and correspondence. They too have been deaf to the voice of justice and of consanguinity. We must, therefore, acquiesce in the necessity, which denounces our Separation, and hold them, as we hold the rest of mankind, Enemies in War, in Peace Friends.

We, therefore, the Representatives of the united States of America, in General Congress, Assembled, appealing to the Supreme Judge of the world for the rectitude of our intentions, do, in the Name, and by Authority of the good People of these Colonies, solemnly publish and declare, That these United Colonies are, and of Right ought to be Free and Independent States; that they are Absolved from all Allegiance to the British Crown, and that all political connection between them and the State of Great Britain, is and ought to be totally dissolved; and that as Free and Independent States, they have full Power to levy War, conclude Peace, contract Alliances, establish Commerce, and to do all other Acts and Things which Independent States may of right do. And for the support of this Declaration, with a firm reliance on the Protection of Divine Providence, we mutually pledge to each other our Lives, our Fortunes and our sacred Honor.

LETTER TO JOHN ADAMS

1813

Monticello, October 28, 1813

Dear Sir,

According to the reservation between us, of taking up one of the subjects of our correspondence at a time, I turn to your letters of August the 16th and September the 2d.

The passage you quote from Theognis, I think has an ethical rather than a political object. The whole piece is a moral *exhortation*, *παραινεσις*, and this passage particularly seems to be a reproof to man, who, while with his domestic animals he is curious to improve the race, by employing always the finest male, pays no attention to the improvement of his own race, but intermarries with the vicious, the ugly, or the old, for considerations of wealth or ambition. It is in conformity with the principle adopted afterwards by the Pythagoreans, and expressed by Ocellus in another form; *περι δετης 'εκ τῶν αλληλων ανθρωπων γενεσεως* etc., —*ουχ ηδονης ενεκα η μιξις* which, as literally as intelligibility will admit, may be thus translated: "concerning the interprocreation of men, how, and of whom it shall be, in a perfect manner, and according to the laws of modesty and sanctity, conjointly, this is what I think right. First to lay it down that we do not commix for the sake of pleasure, but of the procreation of children. For the powers, the organs and desires for coition have not been given by God to man for the sake of pleasure, but for the procreation of the race. For as it were incongruous, for a mortal born to partake of divine life, the

From *Social and Political Philosophy: Readings from Plato to Ghandi*, eds. John Somerville and Ronald Santoni (Garden City, N.Y.: Anchor Books, 1963).

immortality of the race being taken away, God fulfilled the purpose by making the generations uninterrupted and continuous. This, therefore, we are especially to lay down as a principle, that coition is not for the sake of pleasure." But nature, not trusting to this moral and abstract motive, seems to have provided more securely for the perpetuation of the species, by making it the effect of the *oestrum* implanted in the constitution of both sexes. And not only has the commerce of love been indulged on this unhallowed impulse, but made subservient also to wealth and ambition by marriage, without regard to the beauty, the healthiness, the understanding, or virtue of the subject from which we are to breed. The selecting the best male for a harem of well-chosen females also, which Theognis seems to recommend from the example of our sheep and asses, would doubtless improve the human, as it does the brute animal and produce a race of veritable *ραιστοι*. For experience proves, that the moral and physical qualities of man, whether good or evil, are transmissible in a certain degree from father to son. But I suspect that the equal rights of men will rise up against this privileged Solomon and his harem, and oblige us to continue acquiescence under the "*Αμαυρωσις γενεος αστων*" which Theognis complains of, and to content ourselves with the accidental aristoi produced by the fortuitous concourse of breeders. For I agree with you that there is a natural aristocracy among men. The grounds of this are virtue and talents. Formerly, bodily powers gave place among the aristoi. But since the invention of gunpowder has armed the weak as well as the strong with missile death, bodily strength, like beauty, good humor, politeness and other accomplishments, has become but an auxiliary ground of distinction. There is also an artificial aristocracy, founded on wealth and birth, without either virtue or talents; for with these it would belong to the first class. The natural aristocracy I consider as the most precious gift of nature, for the instruction, the trusts, and government of society. And indeed, it would have been inconsistent in creation to have formed man for the social state, and not to have provided virtue and wisdom enough to manage the concerns of the society. May we not even say, that that form of government is the best, which provides the most effectually for a pure selection of these natural aristoi into the offices of government? The artificial aristocracy is a mischievous ingredient in government, and provision should be made to prevent its ascendency. On the question, what is the best provision, you and I differ; but we differ as rational friends, using the free exercise of our own reason, and mutually indulging its errors. You think it best to put the pseudo-aristoi into a separate chamber of legislation, where they may be hindered from doing mischief by their co-ordinate branches, and where, also, they may be a protection to wealth against the agrarian and plundering enterprises of the majority of the people. I think that to give them power in order to prevent them from doing mischief, is arming them for it, and increasing instead of remedying the evil. For if the co-ordinate branches can arrest their action, so may they that of the co-ordinates. Mischief may be done negatively as well as positively. Of this, a cabal in the Senate of the United States has furnished many proofs. Nor do I believe them necessary to protect the wealthy; because enough of these will find their way into every branch of the legislation, to protect themselves. From fifteen to twenty legislatures of our own, in action for thirty years past, have proved that no fears of an equalization of property are to be apprehended from them. I think the best remedy is exactly that provided by all our constitutions, to leave to the citizens the free election and separation of the aristoi from the pseudoaristoi, of the wheat from the chaff. In general they will elect the really good and wise. In some instances, wealth may corrupt, and birth blind them; but not in sufficient degree to endanger the society.

It is probable that our difference of opinion may, in some measure, be produced by a difference of character in those among whom we live. From what I have seen of Massachusetts and Connecticut myself, and still more from what I have heard, and the character given of the former by yourself, who know them so much better, there seems to be in those two States a traditionary reverence for certain families, which has rendered the offices of the government nearly hereditary in those families.

Adam Smith

Adam Smith (1723–1790), Scottish political economist and philosopher, is best known as the author of *The Wealth of Nations* (1776), the most influential economics book ever written. Published when Smith was a customs officer in Edinburgh, *The Wealth of Nations* set forth the doctrines of liberal capitalism and the ideology of laissez-faire or minimal government. Competition in the marketplace of each against all, a struggle despised by Rousseau, was for Smith the source of comfort and civilization and of the prosperity he saw in his native Scotland. Smith's most original idea is that society, as much as the individual, is a system, or machine, whose workings are not the product of human intentions but of the unconscious "invisible hand."

Smith was a central figure of the Scottish Enlightenment, a close friend of the skeptic David Hume, and an influence on such early sociologists as David Millar and Adam Ferguson. As chair of moral philosophy at Glasgow University, where he was appointed professor in 1751, he kept up lines of communication that tied Scotland closely to the Continent as well as to neighboring England. Smith lived in a society steeped in Reformation theology but that was also in the early stages of a commercial revolution that would come to represent the idea of progress. He was inspired by his teacher, the brilliant moralist Francis Hutcheson, to place the moral teachings of Protestantism on a scientific footing. Out of this endeavor came *Theory of Moral Sentiments* (1759), which made Smith famous in his own day. The book explains how each society evolves a moral consensus about what is proper, just, and prudent, which enables it to function as an "immense machine whose regular and harmonious movements produce a thousand agreeable effects." In so doing, society establishes and reestablishes certain natural balances by means of various hidden feedback mechanisms. Smith's description of these balances and mechanisms makes him a pioneer of functionalism in the social sciences.

In *Theory of Moral Sentiments*, one of these natural balances is represented by the moral sentiments: feelings that arise when one person imagines himself in the situation of another. A human being is by nature able to see himself from the outside, to "take the role of the other" in his attempt to share the opinions and feelings of others and so feel "at one" with them. On this basis there arises a moral agreement that restrains our tendencies to injure others and sets limits within which we naturally pursue our own welfare. Thus, Smith asserts that wealth and morals go hand in hand:

> Regard to our own private happiness and interest, too, appear upon many occasions very laudable principles of action. The habits of economy, industry, discretion, attention and application of thought, are generally supposed to be cultivated from self-interested motives, and at the same time are apprehended to be very praiseworthy qualities which deserve the esteem and approbation of everybody.

In 1763 Smith resigned his post at Glasgow to become tutor to a young duke, whom he accompanied on a tour of France (1764–1766). Thereafter, he lived mainly in Scotland, devoting himself to his magnum opus and being appointed commissioner of customs in 1778. Before his death in 1790, Smith apparently devoted a sizable portion of his income to many secret acts of charity.

Critics since Smith's day have debated whether his emphasis in the *Moral Sentiments* on sympathy as a basic human motive contradicts the key role of self-interest in his masterpiece, *The Wealth of Nations*. Despite praising the "invisible hand" that promotes the harmony of interests, Smith is by no means uncritical of capitalism; he finds countless occasions for conflict in the marketplace and notes the destructive effects of selfishness. *The Wealth of Nations* also stands apart from its successors in treating capitalism not merely as an economy, but as the outcome of a long historical process and a civilization with its own culture and political order.

In the first five chapters, Smith introduces the leading theme of his book—the value of goods is determined by the cost of their production, particularly the amount of labor involved, and that to increase productivity labor must become specialized, or "divided." The division of labor is limited by the extent of the market, but as exchanges multiply and money becomes a medium of exchange, the "natural" price, based on the cost of production, comes to diverge from the "market" price, based on short-run forces of supply and demand. Smith argues that in every society there is an average or natural level of wages, profit, and rent that comprises the natural price, and that therefore is the lowest price at which anyone will sell his goods for any length of time. If the market price is below the natural price, the former will rise; but if the market price is higher, other potential producers, looking for a share in the inflated profits, will set themselves up in the production of the overpriced goods and enter the market by selling at less than the current market price. Thus, other producers are forced to lower their prices, and the process continues until the natural price becomes the norm. The general tendency of this system is to produce a steady flow of consumer goods at the lowest feasible prices.

In later chapters Smith continues his defense of this "invisible hand," arguing for a "natural course of things" and against tariffs, monopolies, restrictions on free entry into occupations or free trade in land, and state control of the level of employment. (In one chapter, he attacks the monopolistic practices of colonialism.) Yet he leaves a considerable role for government as the provider of public works and suggests that "it is not very unreasonable that the rich should contribute to the public expense, not only in proportion to their revenue, but something more than in that proportion."

THE WEALTH OF NATIONS

1776

I OF THE DIVISION OF LABOUR

The greatest improvement in the productive powers of labour, and the greater part of the skill, dexterity, and judgement with which it is anywhere directed, or applied, seem to have been the effects of the division of labour.

The effects of the division of labour, in the general business of society, will be more easily understood by considering in what manner it operates in some particular manufactures. It is commonly supposed to be carried furthest in some very trifling ones; not perhaps that it really is carried further in them than in others of more importance: but in those trifling manufactures which are destined to supply the small wants of but a small number of people, the whole number of workmen must necessarily be small; and those employed in every different branch

From Everyman's Library edition (New York: Knopf, 1991).

of the work can often be collected into the same workhouse, and placed at once under the view of the spectator. In those great manufactures, on the contrary, which are destined to supply the great wants of the great body of the people, every different branch of the work employs so great a number of workmen that it is impossible to collect them all into the same workhouse. We can seldom see more, at one time, than those employed in one single branch. Though in such manufactures, therefore, the work may really be divided into a much greater number of parts than in those of a more trifling nature, the division is not near so obvious, and has accordingly been much less observed.

To take an example, therefore, from a very trifling manufacture; but one in which the division of labour has been very often taken notice of, the trade of the pin-maker; a workman not educated to this business (which the division of labour has rendered a distinct trade), nor acquainted with the use of the machinery employed in it (to the invention of which the same division of labour has probably given occasion), could scarce, perhaps, with his utmost industry, make one pin in a day, and certainly could not make twenty. But in the way in which this business is now carried on, not only the whole work is a peculiar trade, but it is divided into a number of branches, of which the greater part are likewise peculiar trades. One man draws out the wire, another straights it, a third cuts it, a fourth points it, a fifth grinds it at the top for receiving the head; to make the head requires three distinct operations; to put it on is a peculiar business, to whiten the pins is another; it is even a trade by itself to put them into the paper; and the important business of making a pin is, in this manner, divided into about eighteen distinct operations, which, in some manufactories, are all performed by distinct hands, though in others the same man will sometimes perform two or three of them. I have seen a small manufactory of this kind where ten men only were employed, and where some of them consequently performed two or three distinct operations. But though they were very poor, and therefore but indifferently accommodated with the necessary machinery, they could, when they exerted themselves, make among them about twelve pounds of pins in a day. There are in a pound upwards of four thousand pins of a middling size. Those ten persons, therefore, could make among them upwards of forty-eight thousand pins in a day. Each person, therefore, making a tenth part of forty-eight thousand pins, might be considered as making four thousand eight hundred pins in a day. But if they had all wrought separately and independently, and without any of them having been educated to this peculiar business, they could certainly not each of them have made twenty, perhaps not one pin in a day; that is, certainly, not the two hundred and fortieth, perhaps not the four thousand eight hundredth part of what they are at present capable of performing, in consequence of a proper division and combination of their different operations.

In every other art and manufacture, the effects of the division of labour are similar to what they are in this very trifling one; though, in many of them, the labour can neither be so much subdivided, nor reduced to so great a simplicity of operation. The division of labour, however, so far as it can be introduced, occasions, in every art, a proportionable increase of the productive powers of labour. The separation of different trades and employments from one another seems to have taken place in consequence of this advantage. This separation, too, is generally carried furthest in those countries which enjoy the highest degree of industry and improvement; what is the work of one man in a rude state of society being generally that of several in an improved one. In every improved society, the farmer is generally nothing but a farmer; the manufacturer, nothing but a manufacturer. The labour, too, which is necessary to produce any one complete manufacture is almost always divided among a great number of hands. How many different trades are employed in each branch of the linen and woollen manufactures, from the growers of the flax and the wool, to the bleachers and smoothers of the linen, or to the dyers and dressers of the cloth! The nature of agriculture, indeed, does not admit of so many subdivisions of labour, nor of so complete a separation of one business from another, as manufactures. It is impossible to separate so entirely the business of the grazier from that of the corn-farmer as the trade of the carpenter is commonly separated from that of the smith. The spinner is almost always a distinct person from the weaver; but the ploughman, the harrower, the sower of the seed, and the reaper of the corn, are often the same. The occasions for those different sorts of labour returning with the different seasons of the year, it is impossible that one man should be constantly employed in any one of them. This impossibility of making so complete and entire a separation of all the different branches of labour employed in agriculture, is perhaps the reason why the improvement of the productive powers of labour in this art does not always keep pace with their improvement in manufactures. The most opulent nations, indeed, generally excel all their neighbours in agriculture as well as in manufactures; but they are commonly more distinguished by their superiority in the latter than in the former. Their lands are in general better cultivated, and having more labour and expense bestowed upon them, produce more in proportion to the extent and natural fertility of the ground. But this superiority of produce is seldom much more than in proportion to the superiority of labour and expense. In agriculture, the labour of the rich country is not always much more productive than that of the poor; or, at least, it is never so much more productive as it commonly is in manufactures. The corn of the rich country, therefore, will not always, in the same degree of goodness, come cheaper to market than that of the poor. The corn of Poland, in the same degree of goodness, is as cheap as that of France, notwithstanding the superior opulence and improvement of the latter country. The corn of France is, in the corn provinces, fully as good, and in most years nearly about the same price with the corn of England, though, in opulence and improvement, France is perhaps inferior to England. The corn-lands of England, however, are better cultivated than those of France, and the corn-lands of France are said to be much better cultivated than those of Poland. But though the poor country, notwithstanding the inferiority of its cultivation, can, in some measure, rival the rich in the cheapness and goodness of its corn, it can pretend to no such competition in its manufactures; at least if those manufactures suit the soil, climate, and situation of the rich country. The silks of France are better and cheaper than those of England, because the silk manufacture, at least under the present high duties upon the importation of raw silk, does not so well suit the climate of England as that of France. But the hardware and the coarse woollens of England are beyond all comparison superior to those of France, and much cheaper too in the same degree of goodness. In Poland there are said to be scarce any manufactures of any kind, a few of those coarser household manufactures excepted, without which no country can well subsist.

This great increase of the quantity of work which, in consequence of the division of labour, the same number of people are capable of performing, is owing to three different circumstances; first, to the increase of dexterity in every particular workman; secondly, to the saving of the time which is commonly lost in passing from one species of work to another; and lastly, to the invention of a great number of machines which facilitate and abridge labour, and enable one man to do the work of many.

First, the improvement of the dexterity of the workman necessarily increases the quantity of the work he can perform; and the division of labour, by reducing every man's business to some one simple operation, and by making this operation the sole employment of his life, necessarily increases very much the dexterity of the workman. A common smith, who, though accustomed to handle the hammer, has never been used to make nails, if upon some particular occasion he is obliged to attempt it, will scarce, I am assured, be able to make above two or three hundred nails in a day, and those too very bad ones. A smith who has been accustomed to make nails, but whose sole or principal business has not been that of a nailer, can seldom with his utmost diligence make more than eight hundred or a thousand nails in a day. I have seen several boys under twenty years of age who had never exercised any other trade but that of making nails, and who, when they exerted themselves, could make, each of them, upwards of two thousand three hundred nails in a day. The making of a nail, however, is by no means one of the simplest operations. The same person blows the bellows, stirs or mends the fire as there is occasion, heats the iron, and forges every part of the nail: in forging the head too he is obliged to change his tools. The different operations into which the making of a pin, or of a metal button, is subdivided, are all of them much more simple, and the dexterity of the person, of whose life it has been the sole business to perform them, is usually much greater. The rapidity with which some of the operations of those manufactures are performed, exceeds what the human hand could, by those who had never seen them, be supposed capable of acquiring.

Secondly, the advantage which is gained by saving the time commonly lost in passing from one sort of work to another is much greater than we should at first view be apt to imagine it. It is impossible to pass very quickly from one kind of work to another that is carried on in a different place and with quite different tools. A country weaver, who cultivates a small farm, must lose a good deal of time in passing from his loom to the field, and from the field to his loom. When the two trades can be carried on in the same workhouse, the loss of time is no doubt much less. It is even in this case, however, very considerable. A man commonly saunters a little in turning his hand from one sort of employment to another. When he first begins the new work he is seldom very keen and hearty; his mind, as they say, does not go to it, and for some time he rather trifles than applies to good purpose. The habit of sauntering and of indolent careless application, which is naturally, or rather necessarily acquired by every country workman who is obliged to change his work and his tools every half hour, and to apply his hand in twenty different ways almost every day of his life, renders him almost always slothful and lazy, and incapable of any vigorous application even on the most pressing occasions. Independent, therefore, of his deficiency in point of dexterity, this cause alone must always reduce considerably the quantity of work which he is capable of performing.

Thirdly, and lastly, everybody must be sensible how much labour is facilitated and abridged by the application of proper machinery. It is unnecessary to give any example. I shall only observe, therefore, that the invention of all those machines by which labour is so much facilitated and abridged seems to have been originally owing to the division of labour. Men are much more likely to discover easier and readier methods of attaining any object when the whole attention of their minds is directed towards that single object than when it is dissipated among a great variety of things. But in consequence of the division of labour, the whole of every man's attention comes naturally to be directed towards some one very simple object. It is naturally to be expected, therefore, that some one or other of those who are employed in each particular branch of labour should soon find out easier and readier methods of performing their own particular work, wherever the nature of it admits of such improvement. A great part of the machines made use of in those manufactures in which labour is most subdivided, were originally the inventions of common workmen, who, being each of them employed in some very simple operation, naturally turned their thoughts towards finding out easier and readier methods of performing it. Whoever has been much accustomed to visit such manufactures must frequently have been shown very pretty machines, which were the inventions of such workmen in order to facilitate and quicken their own particular part of the work. In the first fire-engines, a boy was constantly employed to open and shut alternately the communication between the boiler and the cylinder, according as the piston either ascended or descended. One of those boys, who loved to play with his companions, observed that, by tying a string from the handle of the valve which opened this communication to another part of the machine, the valve would open and shut without his assistance, and leave him at liberty to divert himself with his play-fellows. One of the greatest improvements that has been made upon this machine, since it was first invented, was in this manner the discovery of a boy who wanted to save his own labour.

All the improvements in machinery, however, have by no means been the inventions of those who had occasion to use the machines. Many improvements have been made by the ingenuity of the makers of the machines, when to make them became the business of a peculiar trade; and some by that of those who are called philosophers or men of speculation, whose trade it is not to do anything, but to observe everything; and who, upon that account, are often capable of combining together the powers of the most distant and dissimilar objects. In the progress of society, philosophy or speculation becomes, like every other employment, the principal or sole trade and occupation of a particular class of citizens. Like every other employment too, it is subdivided into a great number of different branches, each of which affords occupation to a peculiar tribe or class of philosophers; and this subdivision of employment in philosophy, as well as in every other business, improves dexterity, and saves time. Each individual becomes more expert in his own peculiar branch, more work is done upon the whole, and the quantity of science is considerably increased by it.

It is the great multiplication of the productions of all the different arts, in consequence of the division of labour, which occasions, in a well-governed society, that universal opulence which extends itself to the lowest ranks of the people. Every workman has a great quantity of his own work to dispose of beyond what he himself has occasion for; and every other workman being exactly in the same situation, he is enabled to exchange a great quantity of his own goods for a great quantity, or, what comes to the same thing, for the price of a great quantity of theirs. He supplies them abundantly with what they have occasion for, and they accommodate him as amply with what he has occasion for, and a general plenty diffuses itself through all the different ranks of the society.

Observe the accommodation of the most common artificer or day-labourer in a civilized and thriving country, and you will perceive that the number of people of whose industry a part, though but a small part, has been employed in procuring him this accommodation, exceeds all computation. The woollen coat, for example, which covers the day-labourer, as coarse and rough as it may appear, is the produce of the joint labour of a great multitude of workmen. The shepherd, the sorter of the wool, the wool-comber or carder, the dyer, the scribbler, the spinner, the weaver, the fuller, the dresser, with many others, must all join their different arts in order to complete even this homely production. How many merchants and carriers, besides, must have been employed in transporting the materials from some of those workmen to others who often live in a very distant part of the country! How many merchants and carriers, besides, how many shipbuilders, sailors, sail-makers, rope-makers, must have been employed in order to bring together the different drugs made use of by the dyer, which often come from the remotest corners of the world! What a variety of labour, too, is necessary in order to produce the tools of the meanest of those workmen! To say nothing of such complicated machines as the ship of the sailor, the mill of the fuller, or even the loom of the weaver, let us consider only what a variety of labour is requisite in order to form that very simple machine, the shears with which the shepherd clips the wool. The miner, the builder of the furnace for smelting the ore, the seller of the timber, the burner of the charcoal to be made use of in the smelting-house, the brick-maker, the brick-layer, the workmen who attend the furnace, the mill-wright, the forger, the smith, must all of them join their different arts in order to produce them. Were we to examine, in the same manner, all the different parts of his dress and household furniture, the coarse linen shirt which he wears next his skin, the shoes which cover his feet, the bed which he lies on, and all the different parts which compose it, the kitchen-grate at which he prepares his victuals, the coals which he makes use of for that purpose, dug from the bowels of the earth, and brought to him perhaps by a long sea and a long land carriage, all the other utensils of his kitchen, all the furniture of his table, the knives and forks, the earthen or pewter plates upon which he serves up and divides his victuals, the different hands employed in preparing his bread and his beer, the glass window which lets in the heat and the light, and keeps out the wind and the rain, with all the knowledge and art requisite for preparing that beautiful and happy invention, without which these northern parts of the world could scarce have afforded a very comfortable habitation, together with the tools of all the different workmen employed in producing those different conveniencies; if we examine, I say, all these things, and consider what a variety of labour is employed about each of them, we shall be sensible that, without the assistance and co-operation of many thousands, the very meanest person in a civilized country could not be provided, even according to what we very falsely imagine the easy and simple manner in which he is commonly accommodated. Compared, indeed, with the more extravagant luxury of the great, his accommodation must no doubt appear extremely simple and easy; and yet it may be true, perhaps, that the accommodation of a European prince does not always so much exceed that of an industrious and frugal peasant as the accommodation of the latter exceeds that of many an African king, the absolute master of the lives and liberties of ten thousand naked savages.

II OF THE PRINCIPLE WHICH GIVES OCCASION TO THE DIVISION OF LABOUR

This division of labour, from which so many advantages are derived, is not originally the effect of any human wisdom, which foresees and intends that general opulence to which it gives occasion. It is the necessary, though very slow and gradual consequence of a certain propensity in human nature which has in view no such extensive utility; the propensity to truck, barter, and exchange one thing for another.

Whether this propensity be one of those original principles in human nature of which no further account can be given; or whether, as seems more probable, it be the necessary consequences of the faculties of reason and speech, it belongs not to our present subject to inquire. It is common to all men, and to be found in no other race of animals, which seem to know neither this nor any other species of contracts. Two greyhounds, in running down the same hare, have sometimes the appearance of acting in some sort of concert. Each turns her towards his companion, or endeavours to intercept her when his companion turns her towards himself. This, however, is not the effect of any contract, but of the accidental concurrence of their passions in the same object at that particular time. Nobody ever saw a dog make a fair and deliberate exchange of one bone for another with another dog. Nobody ever saw one animal by its gestures and natural cries signify to another, this is mine, that yours; I am willing to give this for that. When an animal wants to obtain something either of a man or of another animal, it has no other means of persuasion but to gain the favour of those whose service it requires. A puppy fawns upon its dam, and a spaniel endeavours by a thousand attractions to engage the attention of its master who is at dinner, when it wants to be fed by him. Man sometimes uses the same arts with his brethren, and when he has no other means of engaging them to act according to his inclinations, endeavours by every servile and fawning attention to obtain their good will. He has not time, however, to do this upon every occasion. In civilized society he stands at all times in need of the co-operation and assistance of great multitudes, while his whole life is scarce sufficient to gain the friendship of a few persons. In almost every other race of animals each individual, when it is grown up to maturity, is entirely independent, and in its natural state has occasion for the assistance of no other living creature. But man has almost constant occasion for the help of his brethren, and it is in vain for him to expect it from their benevolence only. He will be more likely to prevail if he can interest their self-love in his favour, and show them that it is for their own advantage to do for him what he requires of them. Whoever offers to another a bargain of any kind, proposes to do this. Give me that which I want, and you shall have this which you want, is the meaning of every such offer; and it is in this manner that we obtain from one another the far greater part of those good offices which we stand in need of. It is not from the benevolence of the butcher, the brewer, or the baker that we expect our dinner, but from their regard to their own interest. We address ourselves, not to their humanity but to their self-love, and never talk to them of our own necessities but of their advantages. Nobody but a beggar chooses to depend chiefly upon the benevolence of his fellow-citizens. Even a beggar does not depend upon it entirely. The charity of well-disposed people, indeed, supplies him with the whole fund of his subsistence. But though this principle ultimately provides him with all the necessaries of life which he has occasion for, it neither does nor can provide him with them as he has occasion for them. The greater part of his occasional wants are supplied in the same manner as those of other people, by treaty, by barter, and by purchase. With the money which one man gives him he purchases food. The old clothes which another bestows upon him he exchanges for other old clothes which suit him better, or for lodging, or for food, or for money, with which he can buy either food, clothes, or lodging, as he has occasion.

As it is by treaty, by barter, and by purchase that we obtain from one another the greater part of those mutual good offices which we stand in need of, so it is this same trucking disposition which originally gives occasion to the division of labour. In a tribe of hunters or shepherds a particular person makes bows and arrows, for example, with more readiness and dexterity than any other. He frequently exchanges them for cattle or for venison with his companions; and he finds at last that he can in this manner get more cattle and venison than if he himself went to the field to catch them. From a regard to his own interest, therefore, the making of bows and arrows grows to be his chief business, and he becomes a sort of armourer. Another excels in making the frames and covers of their little huts or moveable houses. He is accustomed to be of use in this way to his neighbours, who reward him in the same manner with cattle and with venison, till at last he finds it his interest to dedicate himself entirely to this employment, and to become a sort of house-carpenter. In the same manner a third becomes a smith or a brazier, a fourth a tanner or dresser of hides or skins, the principal part of the clothing of savages. And thus the certainty of being able to exchange all that surplus part of the produce of his own labour, which is over and above his own consumption, for such parts of the produce of other men's labour as he may have occasion for, encourages every man to apply himself to a particular occupation, and to cultivate and bring to perfection whatever talent or genius he may possess for that particular species of business.

The difference of natural talents in different men is, in reality, much less than we are aware of; and the very different genius which appears to distinguish men of different professions, when grown up to maturity, is not upon many occasions so much the cause as the effect of the division of labour. The difference between the most dissimilar characters, between a philosopher and a common street porter, for example, seems to arise not so much from nature as from habit, custom, and education. When they came into the world, and for the first six or eight years of their existence, they were perhaps very much alike, and neither their parents nor play-fellows could perceive any remarkable difference. About that age, or soon after, they come to be employed in very different occupations. The difference of talents comes then to be taken notice of, and widens by degrees, till at last the vanity of the philosopher is willing to acknowledge scarce any resemblance. But without the disposition to truck, barter, and exchange, every man must have procured to himself every necessary and conveniency of life which he wanted. All must have had the same duties to perform, and the same work to do, and there could have been no such difference of employment as could alone give occasion to any great difference of talents.

As it is this disposition which forms that difference of talents, so remarkable among men of different professions, so it is this same disposition which renders that difference useful. Many tribes of animals acknowledged to be all of the same species derive from nature a much more remarkable distinction of genius, than what, antecedent to custom and education, appears to take place among men. By nature a philosopher is not in genius and disposition half so different from a street porter, as a mastiff is from a greyhound, or a greyhound from a spaniel, or this last from a shepherd's dog. Those different tribes of animals, however, though all of the same species, are of scarce any use to one another. The strength of the mastiff is not in the least supported either by the swiftness of the greyhound, or by the sagacity of the spaniel, or by the docility of the shepherd's dog. The effects of those different geniuses and talents, for want of the power or disposition to barter and exchange, cannot be brought into a common stock, and do not in the least contribute to the better accommodation and conveniency of the species. Each animal is still obliged to support and defend itself, separately and independently, and derives no sort of advantage from that variety of talents with which nature has distinguished its fellows. Among men, on the contrary, the most dissimilar geniuses are of use to one another; the different produces of their respective talents, by the general disposition to truck, barter, and exchange, being brought, as it were, into a common stock, where every man may purchase whatever part of the produce of the other men's talents he has occasion for.

. . .

V OF THE REAL AND NOMINAL PRICE OF COMMODITIES, OR THEIR PRICE IN LABOUR, AND THEIR PRICE IN MONEY

Every man is rich or poor according to the degree in which he can afford to enjoy the necessaries, conveniences, and amusements of human life. But after the division of labour has once thoroughly taken place, it is but a very small part of these with which a man's own labour can supply him. The far greater part of them he must derive from the labour of other people, and he must be rich or poor according to the quantity of that labour which he can command, or which he can afford to purchase. The value of any commodity, therefore, to the person who possesses it, and who means not to use or consume it himself, but to exchange it for other commodities, is equal to the quantity of labour which it enables him to purchase or command. Labour, therefore, is the real measure of the exchangeable value of all commodities.

The real price of everything, what everything really costs to the man who wants to acquire it, is the toil and trouble of acquiring it. What everything is really worth to the man who has acquired it, and who wants to dispose of it or exchange it for something else, is the toil and trouble which it can save to himself, and which it can impose upon other people. What is bought with money or with goods is purchased by labour as much as what we acquire by the toil of our own body. That money or those goods indeed save us this toil. They contain the value of a certain quantity of labour which we exchange for what is supposed at the time to contain the value of an equal quantity. Labour was the first price, the original purchase-money that was paid for all things. It was not by gold or by silver, but by labour, that all the wealth of the world was originally purchased; and its value, to those who possess it, and who want to exchange it for some new productions, is precisely equal to the quantity of labour which it can enable them to purchase or command.

Wealth, as Mr. Hobbes says, is power. But the person who either acquires, or succeeds to a great fortune, does not necessarily acquire or succeed to any political power, either civil or military. His fortune may, perhaps, afford him the means of acquiring both, but the mere possession of that fortune does not necessarily convey to him either. The power which that possession immediately and directly conveys to him, is the power of purchasing; a certain command over all the labour, or over all the produce of labour, which is then in the market. His fortune is greater or less, precisely in proportion to the extent of this power; or to the quantity either of other men's labour, or, what is the same thing, of the produce of other men's labour, which it enables him to purchase or command. The exchangeable value of everything must always be precisely equal to the extent of this power which it conveys to its owner.

But though labour be the real measure of the exchangeable value of all commodities, it is not that by which their value is commonly estimated. It is often difficult to ascertain the proportion between two different quantities of labour. The time spent in two different sorts of work will not always alone determine this proportion. The different degrees of hardship endured, and of ingenuity exercised, must likewise be taken into account. There may be more labour in an hour's hard work than in two hours' easy business; or in an hour's application to a trade which it cost ten years' labour to learn, than in a month's industry at an ordinary and obvious employment. But it is not easy to find any accurate measure either of hardship or ingenuity. In exchanging, indeed, the different productions of different sorts of labour for one another, some allowance is commonly made for both. It is adjusted, however, not by any accurate measure, but by the higgling and bargaining of the market, according to that sort of rough equality which, though not exact, is sufficient for carrying on the business of common life.

Every commodity, besides, is more frequently exchanged for, and thereby compared with, other commodities than with labour. It is more natural, therefore, to estimate its exchangeable value by the quantity of some other commodity than by that of the labour which it can purchase. The greater part of people, too, understand better what is meant by a quantity of a particular commodity than by a quantity of labour. The one is a plain and palpable object; the other an abstract notion, which, though it can be made sufficiently intelligible, is not altogether so natural and obvious.

But when barter ceases, and money has become the common instrument of commerce, every particular commodity is more frequently exchanged for money than for any other commodity. The butcher seldom carries his beef or his mutton to the baker, or the brewer, in order to exchange them for bread or for beer; but he carries them to the market, where he exchanges them for money, and afterwards exchanges that money for bread and for beer. The quantity of money which he gets for them regulates, too, the quantity of bread and beer which he can afterwards purchase. It is more natural and obvious to him, therefore, to estimate their value by the quantity of money, the commodity for which he immediately exchanges them, than by that of bread and beer, the commodities for which he can exchange them only by the intervention of another commodity; and rather to say that his butcher's meat is worth threepence or fourpence a pound, than that it is worth three or four pounds of bread, or three or four quarts of small beer. Hence it comes to pass that the exchangeable value of every commodity is more frequently estimated by the quantity of money, than by the quantity either of labour or of any other commodity which can be had in exchange for it.

Gold and silver, however, like every other commodity, vary in their value, are sometimes cheaper and sometimes dearer, sometimes of easier and sometimes of more difficult purchase. The quantity of labour which any particular quantity of them can purchase or command, or the quantity of other goods which it will exchange for, depends always upon the fertility or barrenness of the mines which happen to be known about the time when such exchanges are made. The discovery of the abundant mines of America reduced, in the sixteenth century, the value of gold and silver in Europe to about a third of what it had been before. As it cost less labour to bring those metals from the mine to the market, so when they were brought thither they could purchase or command less labour; and this revolution in their value, though perhaps the greatest, is by no means the only one of which history gives some account. But as a measure of quantity, such as the natural foot, fathom, or handful, which is continually varying in its own quantity, can never be an accurate measure of the quantity of other things; so a commodity which is itself continually varying in its own value, can never be an accurate measure of the value of other commodities. Equal quantities of labour, at all times and places, may be said to be of equal value to the labourer. In his ordinary state of health, strength, and spirits; in the ordinary degree of his skill and dexterity, he must always lay down the same portion of his ease, his liberty, and his happiness. The price which he pays must always be the same, whatever may be the quantity of goods which he receives in return for it. Of these, indeed, it may sometimes purchase a greater and sometimes a smaller quantity; but it is their value which varies, not that of the labour which purchases them. At all times and places that is dear which it is difficult to come at, or which it costs much labour to acquire; and that cheap which is to be had easily, or with very little labour. Labour alone, therefore, never varying in its own value, is alone the ultimate and real standard by which the value of all commodities can at all times and places be estimated and compared. It is their real price; money is their nominal price only.

. . .

VIII OF THE WAGES OF LABOUR

The produce of labour constitutes the natural recompense or wages of labour.

In that original state of things, which precedes both the appropriation of land and the accumulation of stock, the whole produce of labour belongs to the labourer. He has neither landlord nor master to share with him.

Had this state continued, the wages of labour would have augmented with all those improvements in its productive powers to which the division of labour gives occasion. All things would gradually have become cheaper. They would have been produced by a smaller quantity of labour; and as the commodities produced by equal quantities of labour would naturally in this state of things be exchanged for one another, they would have been purchased likewise with the produce of a smaller quantity.

But though all things would have become cheaper in reality, in appearance many things might have become dearer than before, or have been exchanged for a greater quantity of other goods. Let us suppose, for example, that in the greater part of employments the productive powers of labour had been improved to tenfold, or that a day's labour could produce ten times the quantity of work which it had done originally; but that in a particular employment they had been improved only to double, or that a day's labour could produce only twice the quantity of work which it had done before. In exchanging the produce of a day's labour in the greater part of employments for that of a day's labour in this particular one, ten times the original quantity of work in them would purchase only twice the original quantity in it. Any particular quantity in it, therefore, a pound weight, for example, would appear to be five times dearer than before. In reality, however, it would be twice as cheap. Though it required five times the quantity of other goods to purchase it, it would require only half the quantity of labour either to purchase or to produce it. The acquisition, therefore, would be twice as easy as before.

But this original state of things, in which the labourer enjoyed the whole produce of his own labour, could not last beyond the first introduction of the appropriation of land and the accumulation of stock. It was at an end, therefore, long before the most considerable improvements were made in the productive powers of labour, and it would be to no purpose to trace further what might have been its effect upon the recompense or wages of labour.

As soon as land becomes private property, the landlord demands a share of almost all the produce which the labourer can either raise, or collect from it. His rent makes the first deduction from the produce of the labour which is employed upon land.

It seldom happens that the person who tills the ground has wherewithal to maintain himself till he reaps the harvest. His maintenance is generally advanced to him from the stock of a master, the farmer who employs him, and who would have no interest to employ him, unless he was to share in the produce of his labour, or unless his stock was to be replaced to him with a profit. This profit makes a second deduction from the produce of the labour which is employed upon land.

The produce of almost all other labour is liable to the like deduction of profit. In all arts and manufactures the greater part of the workmen stand in need of a master to advance them the materials of their work, and their wages and maintenance till it be completed. He shares in the produce of their labour, or in the value which it adds to the materials upon which it is bestowed; and in this share consists his profit.

It sometimes happens, indeed, that a single independent workman has stock sufficient both to purchase the materials of his work, and to maintain himself till it be completed. He is both master and workman, and enjoys the whole produce of his own labour, or the whole value which it adds to the materials upon which it is bestowed. It includes what are usually two distinct revenues, belonging to two distinct persons, the profits of stock, and the wages of labour.

Such cases, however, are not very frequent, and in every part of Europe, twenty workmen serve under a master for one that is independent; and the wages of labour are everywhere understood to be, what they usually are, when the labourer is one person, and the owner of the stock which employs him another.

What are the common wages of labour, depends everywhere upon the contract usually made between those two parties, whose interests are by no means the same. The workmen desire to get as much, the masters to give as little as possible. The former are disposed to combine in order to raise, the latter in order to lower the wages of labour.

It is not, however, difficult to foresee which of the two parties must, upon all ordinary occasions, have the advantage in the dispute, and force the other into a compliance with their terms. The masters, being fewer in number, can combine much more easily; and the law, besides, authorises, or at least does not prohibit their combinations, while it prohibits those of the workmen. We have no acts of parliament against combining to lower the price of work; but many against combining to raise it. In all such disputes the masters can hold out much longer. A landlord, a farmer, a master manufacturer, or merchant, though they did not employ a single workman, could generally live a year or two upon the stocks which they have already acquired. Many workmen could not subsist a week, few could subsist a month, and scarce any a year without employment. In the long-run the workman may be as necessary to his master as his master is to him; but the necessity is not so immediate.

We rarely hear, it has been said, of the combinations of masters, though frequently of those of workmen. But whoever imagines, upon this account, that masters rarely combine, is as ignorant of the world as of the subject. Masters are always and everywhere in a sort of tacit, but constant and uniform combination, not to raise the wages of labour above their actual rate. To violate this combination is everywhere a most unpopular action, and a sort of reproach to a master among his neighbours and equals. We seldom, indeed, hear of this combination, because it is the usual, and one may say, the natural state of things, which nobody ever hears of. Masters, too, sometimes enter into particular combinations to sink the wages of labour even below this rate. These are always conducted with the utmost silence and secrecy, till the moment of execution, and when the workmen yield, as they sometimes do, without resistance, though severely felt by them, they are never heard of by other people. Such combinations, however, are frequently resisted by a contrary defensive combination of the workmen; who sometimes too, without any provocation of this kind, combine of their own accord to raise the price of their labour. Their usual pretences are, sometimes the high price of provisions; sometimes the great profit which their masters make by their work. But whether their combinations be offensive or defensive, they are always abundantly heard of. In order to bring the point to a speedy decision, they have always recourse to the loudest clamour, and sometimes to the most shocking violence and outrage. They are desperate, and act with the folly and extravagance of desperate men, who must either starve, or frighten their masters into an immediate compliance with their demands. The masters upon these occasions are just as clamorous upon the other side, and never cease to call aloud for the assistance of the civil magistrate, and the rigorous execution of those laws which have been enacted with so much severity against the combinations of servants, labourers, and journeymen. The workmen, accordingly, very seldom derive any advantage from the violence of those tumultuous combinations, which, partly from the interposition of the civil magistrate, partly from the superior steadiness of the masters, partly from the necessity which the greater part of the workmen are under of submitting for the sake of present subsistence, generally end in nothing, but the punishment or ruin of the ringleaders.

But though in disputes with their workmen, masters must generally have the advantage, there is, however, a certain rate below which it seems impossible to reduce, for any considerable time, the ordinary wages, even of the lowest species of labour.

A man must always live by his work, and his wages must at least be sufficient to maintain him. They must even upon most occasions be somewhat more; otherwise it would be impossible for him to bring up a family, and the race of such workmen could not last beyond the first generation. Mr. Cantillon seems, upon this account, to suppose that the lowest species of common labourers must everywhere earn at least double their own maintenance, in order that one with another they may be enabled to bring up two children; the labour of the wife, on account of her necessary attendance on the children, being supposed no more than sufficient to provide for herself. But one-half the children born, it is computed, die before the age of manhood. The poorest labourers, therefore, according to this account, must, one with another, attempt to rear at least four children, in order that two may have an equal chance of living to that age. But the necessary maintenance of four children, it is supposed, may be nearly equal to that of one man. The labour of an able-bodied slave, the same author adds, is computed to be worth double his maintenance; and that of the meanest labourer, he thinks, cannot be worth less than that of an able-bodied slave. Thus far at least seems certain, that, in order to bring up a family, the labour of the husband and wife together must, even in the lowest species of common labour, be able to earn something more than what is precisely necessary for their own maintenance; but in what proportion, whether in that above mentioned, or in any other, I shall not take upon me to determine.

. . .

The demand for those who live by wages . . . necessarily increases with the increase of the revenue and stock of every country, and cannot possibly increase without it. The increase of revenue and stock is the increase of national wealth. The demand for those who live by wages, therefore, naturally increases with the increase of national wealth, and cannot possibly increase without it.

It is not the actual greatness of national wealth, but its continual increase, which occasions a rise in the wages of labour. It is not, accordingly, in the richest countries, but in the most thriving, or in those which are growing rich the fastest, that the wages of labour are highest. England is certainly, in the present times, a much richer country than any part of North America. The wages of labour, however, are much higher in North America than in any part of England. In the province of New York, common labourers earn three shillings and sixpence currency, equal to two shillings sterling, a day; ship carpenters, ten shillings and sixpence currency, with a pint of rum worth sixpence sterling, equal in all to six shillings and sixpence sterling; house carpenters and bricklayers, eight shillings currency, equal to four shillings and sixpence sterling; journeymen tailors, five shillings currency, equal to about two shillings and tenpence sterling. These prices are all above the London price; and wages are said to be as high in the other colonies as in New York. The price of provisions is everywhere in North America much lower than in England. A dearth has never been known there. In the worst seasons they have always had a sufficiency for themselves, though less for exportation. If the money price of labour, therefore, be higher than it is anywhere in the mother country, its real price, the real command of the necessaries and conveniences of life which it conveys to the labourer must be higher in a still greater proportion.

But though North America is not yet so rich as England, it is much more thriving, and advancing with much greater rapidity to the further acquisition of riches. The most decisive mark of the prosperity of any country is the increase of the number of its inhabitants. In Great Britain, and most other European countries, they are not supposed to double in less than five hundred years. In the British colonies in North America, it has been found that they double in twenty or five-and-twenty years. Nor in the present times is this increase principally owing to the continual importation of new inhabitants, but to the great multiplication of the species. Those who live to old age, it is said, frequently see there from fifty to a hundred, and sometimes many more, descendants from their own body. Labour is there so well rewarded that a numerous family of children, instead of being a burden, is a source of opulence and prosperity to the parents. The labour of each child, before it can leave their house, is computed to be worth a hundred pounds clear gain to them. A young widow with four or five young children, who, among the middling or inferior ranks of people in Europe, would have so little chance for a second husband, is there frequently courted as a sort of fortune. The value of the children is the greatest of all encouragements to marriage. We cannot, therefore, wonder that the people in North America should generally marry very young. Notwithstanding the great increase occasioned by such early marriages, there is a continual complaint of the scarcity of hands in North America. The demand for labourers, the funds destined for maintaining them, increase, it seems, still faster than they can find labourers to employ.

. . .

The real recompense of labour, the real quantity of the necessaries and conveniences of life which it can procure to the labourer, has, during the course of the present century, increased perhaps in a still greater proportion than its money price. Not only grain has become somewhat cheaper, but many other things from which the industrious poor derive an agreeable and wholesome variety of food have become a great deal cheaper. Potatoes, for example, do not at present, through the greater part of the kingdom, cost half the price which they used to do thirty or forty years ago. The same thing may be said of turnips, carrots, cabbages; things which were formerly never raised but by the spade, but which are now commonly raised by the plough. All sorts of garden stuff, too, has become cheaper. The greater part of the apples and even of the onions consumed in Great Britain were in the last century imported from Flanders. The great improvements in the coarser manufactures of both linen and woollen cloth furnish the labourers with cheaper and better clothing; and those in the manufactures of the coarser metals, with cheaper and better instruments of trade, as well as with many agreeable and convenient pieces of houshold furniture. Soap, salt, candles, leather, and fermented liquors have, indeed, become a good deal dearer; chiefly from the taxes which have been laid upon them. The quantity of these, however, which the labouring poor are under any necessity of consuming, is so very small, that the increase in their price does not compensate the diminution in that of so many other things. The common complaint that luxury extends itself even to the lowest ranks of the people, and that the labouring poor will not now be contented with the same food, clothing, and lodging which satisfied them in former times, may convince us that it is not the money price of labour only, but its real recompense, which has augmented.

Is this improvement in the circumstances of the lower ranks of the people to be regarded as an advantage or as an inconveniency to the society? The answer seems at first sight abundantly plain. Servants, labourers, and workmen of different kinds, make up the far greater part of every great political society. But what improves the circumstances of the greater part can never be regarded as an inconveniency to the whole. No society can surely be flourishing and happy, of which the far greater part of the members are poor and miserable. It is but equity, besides, that they who feed, clothe, and lodge the whole body of the people, should have such a share of the produce of their own labour as to be themselves tolerably well fed, clothed and lodged.

Poverty, though it no doubt discourages, does not always prevent marriage. It seems even to be favourable to generation. A half-starved Highland woman frequently bears more than twenty children, while a pampered fine lady is often incapable of bearing any, and is generally exhausted by two or three. Barrenness, so frequent among women of fashion, is very rare among those of inferior station. Luxury in the fair sex, while it inflames perhaps the passion for enjoyment, seems always to weaken, and frequently to destroy altogether, the powers of generation.

But poverty, though it does not prevent the generation, is extremely unfavourable to the rearing of children. The tender plant is produced, but in so cold a soil and so severe a climate, soon withers and dies. It is not uncommon, I have been frequently told, in the Highlands of Scotland for a mother who has borne twenty children not to have two alive. Several officers of great experience have assured me, that so far from recruiting their regiment, they have never been able to supply it with drums and fifes from all the soldiers' children that were born in it. A greater number of fine children, however, is seldom seen anywhere than about a barrack of soldiers. Very few of them, it seems, arrive at the age of thirteen or fourteen. In some places one half the children born die before they are four years of age; in many places before they are seven; and in almost all places before they are nine or ten. This great mortality, however, will everywhere be found chiefly among the children of the common people, who cannot afford to tend them with the same care as those of better station. Though their marriages are generally more fruitful than those of people of fashion, a smaller proportion of their children arrive at maturity. In foundling hospitals, and among the children brought up by parish charities, the mortality is still greater than among those of the common people.

Every species of animals naturally multiplies in proportion to the means of their subsistence, and no species can ever multiply beyond it. But in civilized society it is only among the inferior ranks of people that the scantiness of subsistence can set limits to the further multiplication of the human species; and it can do so in no other way than by destroying a great part of the children which their fruitful marriages produce.

The liberal reward of labour, by enabling them to provide better for their children, and consequently to bring up a greater number, naturally tends to widen and extend those limits. It deserves to be remarked, too, that it necessarily does this as nearly as possible in the proportion which the demand for labour requires. If this demand is continually increasing, the reward of labour must necessarily encourage in such a manner the marriage and multiplication of labourers, as may enable them to supply that continually increasing demand by a continually increasing population. If the reward should at any time be less than what was requisite for this purpose, the deficiency of hands would soon raise it; and if it should at any time be more, their excessive multiplication would soon lower it to this necessary rate. The market would be so much under-stocked with labour in the one case, and so much over-stocked in the other, as would soon force back its price to that proper rate which the circumstances of the society required. It is in this manner that the demand for men, like that for any other commodity, necessarily regulates the production of men; quickens it when it goes on too slowly, and stops it when it advances too fast. It is this demand which regulates and determines the state of propagation in all the different countries of the world, in North America, in Europe, and in China; which renders it rapidly progressive in the first, slow and gradual in the second, and altogether stationary in the last.

The wear and tear of a slave, it has been said, is at the expense of his master; but that of a free servant is at his own expense. The wear and tear of the latter, however, is, in reality, as much at the expense of his master as that of the former. The wages paid to journeymen and servants of every kind must be such as may enable them, one with another, to continue the race of journeymen and servants, according as the increasing, diminishing, or stationary demand of the society may happen to require. But though the wear and tear of a free servant be equally at the expense of his master, it generally costs him much less than that of a slave. The fund destined for replacing or repairing, if I may say so, the wear and tear of the slave, is commonly managed by a negligent master or careless overseer. That destined for performing the same office with regard to the free man, is managed by the free man himself. The disorders which generally prevail in the economy of the rich, naturally introduce themselves into the management of the former: the strict frugality and parsimonious attention of the poor as naturally establish themselves in that of the latter. Under such different management, the same purpose must require very different degrees of expense to execute it. It appears, accordingly, from the experience of all ages and nations, I believe, that the work done by freemen comes cheaper in the end than that performed by slaves. It is found to do so even at Boston, New York, and Philadelphia, where the wages of common labour are so very high.

The liberal reward of labour, therefore, as it is the effect of increasing wealth, so it is the cause of increasing population. To complain of it is to lament over the necessary effect and cause of the greatest public prosperity.

It deserves to be remarked, perhaps, that it is in the progressive state, while the society is advancing to the further acquisition, rather than when it has acquired its full complement of riches, that the condition of the labouring poor, of the great body of the people, seems to be the happiest and the most comfortable. It is hard in the stationary, and miserable in the declining state. The progressive state is in reality the cheerful and the hearty state to all the different orders of the society. The stationary is dull; the declining, melancholy.

. . .

Edmund Burke

Edmund Burke stands as one of the great conservative thinkers in the history of social and political thought. To this day, many consider his *Reflections on the Revolution in France* to be the most influential piece of conservative writing to be published in the past two hundred-plus years. Written as a response to a French acquaintance who had solicited Burke's reactions to the events in France, this work set forth what would become many of the standard themes of contemporary conservative thought, including a fear of social institutions unmoored from their linkages to the past and a distrust of abstract thought as a normative foundation for action.

At the heart of Burke's thinking was a rejection of the idea set forth by Rousseau and others, who believed that in a state of nature in which there were no "irrational" social or cultural influences, one would find contentment and equality. For Burke, nature was, at best, something fundamentally ambiguous and, at worst, something decidedly negative. Rather than encumbrances to be thrown off, social and cultural customs, Burke believed, served an important social function in that they "veiled" the unpolished character of our nature. While we may not fully understand their origins or the principles by which these customs operate, this does not mean that they are any less useful or necessary. In fact, Burke suggested that we should grant such traditions a degree of deference, even if they might not conform to the standards of rational inquiry, because they have managed to stand the test of time, which Burke interpreted as a testament to their value. Burke even warned that there were potentially disastrous consequences to political and social aims that overstretched their proper reach and did not respect the limits of human thinking or consider the recalcitrance of human nature. As he put it, "Politics ought to be adjusted, not to human reasonings, but to human nature; of which reason is but a part, and by no means the greatest part."

Another distinguishing characteristic of Burke's writing was his emphasis on the complexities and or contradictory nature of social life. Although he was a champion of the cause of liberty, Burke was not a blind advocate of democracy. Rather than seeing liberty and democracy as synonymous, Burke saw the two as existing in tension with one another. Thus, he defended systems of governance that protected aristocratic liberties as superior and preferable to full-fledged democracies that granted the same liberties to the masses; he believed that constitutional liberties established over time took precedence over new ones created, *ex nihilo*, from intellectual reasoning and that would extend new rights, including the right to vote, to the masses. At the same time, however, Burke also defended the rights of the masses, as long as those rights were ones that has been established over time. Similarly reflecting the complexity of his thought was Burke's insistence that strong governmental institutions needed to be accompanied by a sufficiently strong civil society so as not to lead to "austere and insolent domination," just as he argued that a strong civil society without the accompaniment of the appropriate governmental protections would tend toward unenlightened rule by the masses.

Notwithstanding the conservative tendencies inherent in much of his writings, Burke's thinking should not be seen as being characterized by a discomfort with all forms of change or a propensity for antirational romanticism of the past. In many ways, he sought to strike a middle ground between conservative and progressive thinking, advocating "prudence" as a more effective intellectual and political mode of thinking than either romanticism or rationalism. For Burke, then, the present should be seen as being connected not only to the past, but to the future, since "[a] state without the means of some change is without the means of its conservation."

Burke was born in Dublin, Ireland, in 1729, which was at the time a part of the British Empire. He attended Trinity College in Dublin and then, following the wishes of his father who was an attorney, left Ireland in 1750 to take on legal studies in London. By the time he was twenty-six, however, he had given up the idea of becoming a lawyer and had turned his attention to more strictly intellectual pursuits, immersing himself in the writing of Voltaire, Rousseau, and the English Deists. Shortly thereafter, Burke gained intellectual recognition upon publication of *A Vindication of Natural Society* in 1756 and again in 1757 with the publication of *A Philosophical Enquiry into the Origin of our Ideas of the Sublime and Beautiful*. In 1756, Burke married Jane Nugent, the daughter of a prominent physician, Christopher Nugent, and together they had two sons. The year 1759 marked the beginning of Burke's political career, when he became the secretary for a well-known parliamentarian William Gerald Hamilton. Six years later, Burke became private secretary to the Marquis of Rockingham, an influential landowner and politician (for whom the group of politicians known as the Rockingham Whigs was named), who had just gained the post of First Lord of the Treasury. In the same year, Burke was elected to the British House of Commons, and through his oratorical prowess, he quickly became one of its more prominent figures. Burke's efforts played a significant role in the creation of a coherent set of Whig party doctrines.

However, Burke was far from a wholehearted supporter of the British government. Throughout much of his life, he was known as much for his criticisms of the British government as for his support of it. Burke was particularly strident in criticizing the British East India Company and what he thought was its unprincipled and unjust treatment of the people of India. He also attacked the administration over its policies toward the American colonies. In such speeches as "On Conciliation with the Colonies" and "On American Taxation," he defended the American Revolution as a moderate revolution led by respectable Whig gentlemen, such as George Washington, who were fighting to defend traditional rights that protected individuals from the unlawful seizure of property and abuse of power.

While he saw the American Revolution as defensible, he threw the full weight of his rhetorical skills against the French Revolution, which he thought was a radical revolution spurred on by public mobs and led by intellectuals who were all too eager to throw away everything that was good in French tradition. Published on November 1, 1790—less than eighteen months after the storming of the Bastille—at a time when the full range of consequences from the revolution was far from certain, *Reflections on the Revolution in France* predicted not liberty and equality for France, as many intellectuals of the time did, but terror and dictatorship, a position that was at odds with the dominant views of most British parliamentarians. Burke argued that the French revolutionaries were fighting for historical innovations that directly threatened the traditional rights upon which French society was based. In destroying such important cultural institutions as the aristocracy and the church, he believed, the French Revolution threatened to reveal the "dishonourable circumstances of our Nature" and unleash its terrors on society—a prediction that proved all too true in the years and events to come, such as the Reign of Terror and the Vendée.

Burke's emphasis on the sanctity of long-enduring tradition remains one of the major pillars of contemporary conservatism, with its emphasis on traditional values and religion. Its libertarian pillar—based on unbridled individual freedom, unconstrained by concerns for environmental or moral restrictions (indeed, believing that individual freedom is a moral position that trumps all social and collective moralities) would be entirely foreign to him.

REFLECTIONS ON THE REVOLUTION IN FRANCE

1790

History will record, that on the morning of the 6th of October 1789, the king and queen of France, after a day of confusion, alarm, dismay, and slaughter, lay down, under the pledged security of public faith, to indulge nature in a few hours of respite, and troubled melancholy repose. From this sleep the queen was first startled by the voice of the centinel at her door, who cried out to her, to save herself by flight—that this was the last proof of fidelity he could give—that they were upon him, and he was dead. Instantly he was cut down. A band of cruel ruffians and assassins, reeking with his blood, rushed into the chamber of the queen, and pierced with an hundred strokes of bayonets and poniards the bed, from whence this persecuted woman had but just time to fly almost naked, and through ways unknown to the murderers had escaped to seek refuge at the feet of a king and husband, not secure of his own life for a moment.

This king, to say no more of him, and this queen, and their infant children (who once would have been the pride and hope of a great and generous people) were then forced to abandon the sanctuary of the most splendid palace in the world, which they left swimming in blood, polluted by massacre, and strewed with scattered limbs and mutilated carcases. Thence they were conducted into the capital of their kingdom. Two had been selected from the unprovoked, unresisted, promiscuous slaughter, which was made of the gentlemen of birth and family who composed the king's body guard. These two gentlemen, with all the parade of an execution of justice, were cruelly and publickly dragged to the block, and beheaded in the great court of the palace. Their heads were stuck upon spears, and led the procession; whilst the royal captives who followed in the train were slowly moved along, amidst the horrid yells, and shrilling screams, and frantic dances, and infamous contumelies [verbal abuse], and all the unutterable abominations of the furies of hell, in the abused shape of the vilest of women. After they had been made to taste, drop by drop, more than the bitterness of death, in the slow torture of a journey of twelve miles, protracted to six hours, they were, under a guard, composed of those very soldiers who had thus conducted them through this famous triumph, lodged in one of the old palaces of Paris now converted into a Bastile for kings. . . .

Although this work of our new light and knowledge, did not go to the length, that in all probability it was intended it should be carried; yet I must think, that such treatment of any human creatures must be shocking to any but those who are made for accomplishing Revolutions. But I cannot stop here. Influenced by the inborn feelings of my nature, and not being illuminated by a single ray of this new-sprung modern light, I confess to you, Sir, that the exalted rank of the persons suffering, and particularly the sex, the beauty, and the amiable qualities of the descendant of so many kings and emperors, with the tender age of royal infants, insensible only through infancy and innocence of the cruel outrages to which their parents were exposed, instead of being a subject of exultation, adds not a little to my sensibility on that most melancholy occasion. . . .

I hear, and I rejoice to hear, that the great lady, the other object of the triumph, has borne that day (one is interested that beings made for suffering should

Reprinted from *Reflections on the Revolution in France*, ed. L. G. Mitchell (New York: Oxford University Press, 1999 [1790]).

suffer well) and that she bears all the succeeding days, that she bears the imprisonment of her husband, and her own captivity, and the exile of her friends, and the insulting adulation of addresses, and the whole weight of her accumulated wrongs, with a serene patience, in a manner suited to her rank and race, and becoming the offspring of a sovereign distinguished for her piety and her courage; that like her she has lofty sentiments; that she feels with the dignity of a Roman matron; that in the last extremity she will save herself from the last disgrace, and that if she must fall, she will fall by no ignoble hand.

It is now sixteen or seventeen years since I saw the queen of France, then the dauphiness, at Versailles; and surely never lighted on this orb, which she hardly seemed to touch, a more delightful vision. I saw her just above the horizon, decorating and cheering the elevated sphere she just began to move in,—glittering like the morning-star, full of life, and splendor, and joy. Oh! what a revolution! and what an heart must I have, to contemplate without emotion that elevation and that fall! Little did I dream when she added titles of veneration to those of enthusiastic, distant, respectful love, that she should ever be obliged to carry the sharp antidote against disgrace concealed in that bosom; little did I dream that I should have lived to see such disasters fallen upon her in a nation of gallant men, in a nation of men of honour and of cavaliers. I thought ten thousand swords must have leaped from their scabbards to avenge even a look that threatened her with insult.—But the age of chivalry is gone.—That of sophisters, oeconomists, and calculators, has succeeded; and the glory of Europe is extinguished for ever. Never, never more, shall we behold that generous loyalty to rank and sex, that proud submission, that dignified obedience, that subordination of the heart, which kept alive, even in servitude itself, the spirit of an exalted freedom. The unbought grace of life, the cheap defence of nations, the nurse of manly sentiment and heroic enterprize is gone! It is gone, that sensibility of principle, that chastity of honour, which felt a stain like a wound, which inspired courage whilst it mitigated ferocity, which ennobled whatever it touched, and under which vice itself lost half its evil, by losing all its grossness.

This mixed system of opinion and sentiment had its origin in the antient chivalry; and the principle, though varied in its appearance by the varying state of human affairs, subsisted and influenced through a long succession of generations, even to the time we live in. If it should ever be totally extinguished, the loss I fear will be great. It is this which has given its character to modern Europe. It is this which has distinguished it under all its forms of government, and distinguished it to its advantage, from the states of Asia, and possibly from those states which flourished in the most brilliant periods of the antique world. It was this which, without confounding ranks, had produced a noble equality, and handed it down through all the gradations of social life. It was this opinion which mitigated kings into companions, and raised private men to be fellows with kings. Without force, or opposition, it subdued the fierceness of pride and power; it obliged sovereigns to submit to the soft collar of social esteem, compelled stern authority to submit to elegance, and gave a domination, vanquisher of laws, to be subdued by manners.

But now all is to be changed. All the pleasing illusions, which made power gentle, and obedience liberal, which harmonized the different shades of life, and which, by a bland assimilation, incorporated into politics the sentiments which beautify and soften private society, are to be dissolved by this new conquering empire of light and reason. All the decent drapery of life is to be rudely torn off. All the superadded ideas, furnished from the wardrobe of a moral imagination, which the heart owns, and the understanding ratifies, as necessary to cover the defects of our naked shivering nature, and to raise it to dignity in our own estimation, are to be exploded as a ridiculous, absurd, and antiquated fashion.

On this scheme of things, a king is but a man; a queen is but a woman; a woman is but an animal; and an animal not of the highest order. All homage paid to the sex in general as such, and without distinct views, is to be regarded as romance and folly. Regicide, and parricide, and sacrilege, are but fictions of superstition, corrupting jurisprudence by destroying its simplicity. The murder of a king, or a queen, or a bishop, or a father, are only common homicide; and if the people are by any chance, or in any way gainers by it, a sort of homicide much the most pardonable, and into which we ought not to make too severe a scrutiny.

On the scheme of this barbarous philosophy, which is the offspring of cold hearts and muddy understandings, and which is as void of solid wisdom, as it is destitute of all taste and elegance, laws are to be supported only by their own terrors, and by the concern, which each individual may find in them, from his own private speculations, or can spare to them from his own private interests. In the groves of their academy, at the end of every vista, you see nothing but the gallows. Nothing is left which engages the affections on the part of the commonwealth. On the principles of this mechanic philosophy, our institutions can never be embodied, if I may use the expression, in persons; so as to create in us love, veneration, admiration, or attachment. But that sort of reason which banishes the affections is incapable of filling their place. These public affections, combined with manners, are required sometimes as supplements, sometimes as correctives, always as aids to law. The precept given by a wise man, as well as a great critic, for the construction of poems, is equally true as to states. *Non satis est pulchra esse poemata, dulcia sunto.* There ought to be a system of manners in every nation which a well-formed mind would be disposed to relish. To make us love our country, our country ought to be lovely.

But power, of some kind or other, will survive the shock in which manners and opinions perish; and it will find other and worse means for its support. The usurpation which, in order to subvert antient institutions, has destroyed antient principles, will hold power by arts similar to those by which it has acquired it. When the old feudal and chivalrous spirit of *Fealty*, which, by freeing kings from fear, freed both kings and subjects from the precautions of tyranny, shall be extinct in the minds of men, plots and assassinations will be anticipated by preventive murder and preventive confiscation, and that long roll of grim and bloody maxims, which form the political code of all power, not standing on its own honour, and the honour of those who are to obey it. Kings will be tyrants from policy when subjects are rebels from principle.

When antient opinions and rules of life are taken away, the loss cannot possibly be estimated. From that moment we have no compass to govern us; nor can we know distinctly to what port we steer. Europe undoubtedly, taken in a mass, was in a flourishing condition the day on which your Revolution was compleated. How much of that prosperous state was owing to the spirit of our old manners and opinions is not easy to say; but as such causes cannot be indifferent in their operation, we must presume, that, on the whole, their operation was beneficial.

We are but too apt to consider things in the state in which we find them, without sufficiently adverting [paying attention] to the causes by which they have been produced, and possibly may be upheld. Nothing is more certain, than that our manners, our civilization, and all the good things which are connected with manners, and with civilization, have, in this European world of ours, depended for ages upon two principles; and were indeed the result of both combined; I mean the spirit of a gentleman, and the spirit of religion. The nobility and the clergy, the one by profession, the other by patronage, kept learning in existence, even in the midst of arms and confusions, and whilst governments were rather in their causes than formed. Learning paid back what it received to nobility and to priesthood; and paid it with usury, by enlarging their ideas and by furnishing their minds. Happy if they had all continued to know their indissoluble union, and their proper place! Happy if learning, not debauched by ambition, had been satisfied to continue the instructor, and not aspired to be the master! Along with its natural protectors and guardians, learning will be cast into the mire, and trodden down under the hoofs of a swinish multitude.

If, as I suspect, modern letters owe more than they are always willing to own to antient manners, so do other interests which we value full as much as they are worth. Even commerce, and trade, and manufacture, the gods of our oeconomical politicians, are themselves perhaps but creatures; are themselves but effects, which, as first causes, we choose to worship. They certainly grew under the same shade in which learning flourished. They too may decay with their natural protecting principles. With you, for the present at least, they all threaten to disappear together. Where trade and manufactures are wanting to a people, and the spirit of nobility and religion remains, sentiment supplies, and not always ill supplies their place; but if commerce and the arts should be lost in an experiment to try how well a state may stand without these old fundamental principles, what sort of a thing must be a nation of gross, stupid, ferocious, and at the same time, poor and sordid barbarians, destitute of religion, honour, or manly pride, possessing nothing at present, and hoping for nothing hereafter?

You see, Sir, that in this enlightened age I am bold enough to confess, that we [Englishmen] are generally men of untaught feelings; that instead of casting away all our old prejudices, we cherish them to a very considerable degree, and, to take more shame to ourselves, we cherish them because they are prejudices; and the longer they have lasted, and the more generally they have prevailed, the more we cherish them. We are afraid to put men to live and trade each on his own private stock of reason; because we suspect that this stock in each man is small, and that the individuals would be better to avail themselves of the general bank and capital of nations, and of ages. Many of our men of speculation, instead of exploding general prejudices, employ their sagacity to discover the latent wisdom which prevails in them. If they find what they seek, and they seldom fail, they think it more wise to continue the prejudice, with the reason involved, than to cast away the coat of prejudice, and to leave nothing but the naked reason; because prejudice, with its reason, has a motive to give action to that reason, and an affection which will give it permanence. Prejudice is of ready application in the emergency; it previously engages the mind in a steady course of wisdom and virtue, and does not leave the man hesitating in the moment of decision, sceptical, puzzled, and unresolved. Prejudice renders a man's virtue his habit; and not a series of unconnected acts. Through just prejudice, his duty becomes a part of his nature.

Your literary men, and your politicians, and so do the whole clan of the enlightened among us, essentially differ in these points. They have no respect for the wisdom of others; but they pay it off by a very full measure of confidence in their own. With them it is a sufficient motive to destroy an old scheme of things, because it is an old one. As to the new, they are in no sort of fear with regard to the duration of a building run up in haste; because duration is no object to those who think little or nothing has been done before their time, and who place all their hopes in discovery. They conceive, very systematically, that all things which give perpetuity are mischievous, and therefore they are at inexpiable war with all establishments. They think that government may vary like modes of dress, and with as little ill effect. That there needs no principle of attachment, except a sense of present conveniency, to any constitution of the state. They always speak as if they were of opinion that there is a singular species of compact between them and their magistrates, which binds the magistrate, but which has nothing reciprocal in it, but that the majesty of the people has a right to dissolve it without any reason, but its will. Their attachment to their country itself, is only so far as it agrees with some of their fleeting projects; it begins and ends with that scheme of polity which falls in with their momentary opinion. . . .

We know, and what is better we feel inwardly, that religion is the basis of civil society, and the source of all good and of all comfort. In England we are so convinced of this, that there is no rust of superstition, with which the accumulated absurdity of the human mind might have crusted it over in the course of ages, that ninety-nine in an hundred of the people of England would not prefer to impiety. We shall never be such fools as to call in an enemy to the substance of any system to remove its corruptions, to supply its defects, or to perfect its construction. If our religious tenets should ever want a further elucidation, we shall not call on atheism to explain them. . . .

We know, and it is our pride to know, that man is by his constitution a religious animal; that atheism is against, not only our reason but our instincts; and that it cannot prevail long. But if, in the moment of riot, and in a drunken delirium from the hot spirit drawn out of the alembick of hell, which in France is now so furiously boiling, we should uncover our nakedness by throwing off that Christian religion which has hitherto been our boast and comfort, and one great source of civilization amongst us, and among many other nations, we are apprehensive (being well aware that the mind will not endure a void) that some uncouth, pernicious, and degrading superstition, might take place of it. . . .

On these ideas, instead of quarrelling with establishments, as some do, who have made a philosophy and a religion of their hostility to such institutions, we cleave closely to them. We are resolved to keep an established church, an established monarchy, an established aristocracy, and an established democracy, each in the degree it exists, and in no greater. . . .

[O]ne of the first and most leading principles on which the commonwealth and the laws are consecrated, is lest the temporary possessors and life-renters in it, unmindful of what they have received from their ancestors, or of what is due to their posterity, should act as if they were the entire masters; that they should not think it amongst their rights to cut off the entail, or commit waste on the inheritance, by destroying at their pleasure the whole original fabric of their society; hazarding to leave to those who come after them, a ruin instead of an habitation—and teaching these successors as little to respect their contrivances, as they had themselves respected the institutions of their forefathers. By this unprincipled facility of changing the state as often, and as much, and in as many ways as there are floating fancies or fashions, the whole chain and continuity of the commonwealth would be broken. NO one generation could link with the other. Men would become little better than the flies of a summer.

And first of all the science of jurisprudence, the pride of the human intellect, which, with all its defects, redundancies, and errors, is the collected reason of ages, combining the principles of original justice with the infinite variety of human concerns, as a heap of old exploded errors, would be no longer studied. Personal self-sufficiency and arrogance (the certain attendants upon all those who have never experienced a wisdom greater than their own) would usurp the tribunal. Of course, no certain laws, establishing invariable grounds of hope and fear, would keep the actions of men in a certain course, or direct them to a certain end. Nothing stable in the modes of holding property, or exercising function, could form a solid ground on which any parent could speculate in the education of his offspring, or in a choice for their future establishment in the world. No principles would be early worked into the habits. As soon as the most able instructor had completed his laborious course of institution, instead of sending forth his pupil, accomplished in a virtuous discipline, fitted to procure him attention and respect, in his place in society, he would find everything altered; and that he had turned out a poor creature to the contempt and derision of the world, ignorant of the true grounds of estimation. Who would insure a tender and delicate sense of honour to beat almost with the first pulses of the heart, when no man could know what would be the test of honour in a nation, continually varying the standard of its coin? No part of life would retain its acquisitions. Barbarism with regard to science and literature, unskilfulness with regard to arts and manufactures, would infallibly succeed to the want of a steady education and settled principle; and thus the commonwealth itself would, in a few generations, crumble away, be disconnected into the dust and powder of individuality, and at length dispersed to all the winds of heaven.

To avoid therefore the evils of inconstancy and versatility, ten thousand times worse than those of obstinacy and the blindest prejudice, we have consecrated the state, that no man should approach to look into its defects or corruptions but with due caution; that he should never dream of beginning its reformation by its subversion; that he should approach to the faults of the state as to the wounds of a father, with pious awe and trembling solicitude. By this wise prejudice we are taught to look with horror on those children of their country who are prompt rashly to hack that aged parent in pieces, and put him into the kettle of magicians, in hopes that by their poisonous weeds, and wild incantations, they may regenerate the paternal constitution, and renovate their father's life.

Society is indeed a contract. Subordinate contracts for objects of mere occasional interest may be dissolved at pleasure—but the state ought not to be considered as nothing better than a partnership agreement in a trade of pepper and coffee, callico or tobacco, or some other such low concern, to be taken up for a little temporary interest, and to be dissolved by the fancy of the parties. It is to be looked on with other reverence; because it is not a partnership in things subservient only to the gross animal existence of a temporary and perishable nature. It is a partnership in all science; a partnership in all art; a partnership in every virtue, and in all perfection. As the ends of such a partnership cannot be obtained in many generations, it becomes a partnership not only between those who are living, but between those who are living, those who are dead, and those who are to be born. Each contract of each particular state is but a clause in the great primaeval contract of eternal society, linking the lower with the higher natures, connecting the visible and invisible world, according to a fixed compact sanctioned by the inviolable oath which holds all physical and all moral natures, each in their appointed place. . . .

. . .

We do not draw the moral lessons we might from history. On the contrary, without care it may be used to vitiate our minds and to destroy our happiness. In history a great volume is unrolled for our instruction, drawing the materials of future wisdom from the past errors and infirmities of mankind. It may, in the perversion, serve for a magazine, furnishing offensive and defensive weapons for parties in church and state, and supplying the means of keeping alive, or reviving dissensions and animosities, and adding fuel to civil fury. History consists, for the greater part, of the miseries brought upon the world by pride, ambition, avarice, revenge, lust, sedition, hypocrisy, ungoverned zeal, and all the train of disorderly appetites, which shake the public with the same

——troublous storms that toss
The private state, and render life unsweet.

These vices are the *causes* of those storms. Religion, morals, laws, prerogatives, privileges, liberties, rights of men, are the *pretexts*. The pretexts are always found in some specious appearance of a real good. You would not secure men from tyranny and sedition, by rooting out of the mind the principles to which these fraudulent pretexts apply? If you did, you would root out everything that is valuable in the human breast. As these are the pretexts, so the ordinary actors and instruments in great public evils are kings, priests, magistrates, senates, parliaments, national assemblies, judges, and captains. You would not cure the evil by resolving, that there should be no more monarchs, nor ministers of state, nor of the gospel; no interpreters of law; no general officers; no public councils. You might change the names. The things in some shape must remain. A certain *quantum* of power must always exist in the community, in some hands, and under some appellation. Wise men will apply their remedies to vices, not to names; to the causes of evil which are permanent, not to the occasional organs by which they act, and the transitory modes in which they appear. Otherwise you will be wise historically, a fool in practice. Seldom have two ages the same fashion in their pretexts and the same modes of mischief. Wickedness is a little more inventive. Whilst you are discussing fashion, the fashion is gone by. The very same vice assumes a new body. The spirit transmigrates; and, far from losing its principle of life by the change of its appearance, it is renovated in its new organs with the fresh vigour of a juvenile activity. It walks abroad; it continues its ravages; whilst you are gibbeting the carcass, or demolishing the tomb. You are terrifying yourself with ghosts and apparitions, whilst your house is the haunt of robbers. It is thus with all those, who, attending only to the shell and husk of history, think they are waging war with intolerance, pride, and cruelty, whilst, under colour of abhorring the ill principles of antiquated parties, they are authorizing and feeding the same odious vices in different factions, and perhaps in worse. . . .

When men are encouraged to go into a certain mode of life by the existing laws, and protected in that mode as in a lawful occupation—when they have accommodated all their ideas, and all their habits to it—when the law had long made their adherence to its rules a ground of reputation, and their departure from them a ground of disgrace and even of penalty—I am sure it is unjust in legislature, by an arbitrary act, to offer a sudden violence to their minds and their feelings; forcibly to degrade them from their state and condition, and to stigmatize with shame and infamy that character and those customs which before had been made the measure of their happiness and honour. If to this be added an expulsion from their habitations, and a confiscation of all their goods, I am not sagacious enough to discover how this despotic sport, made of the feelings, consciences, prejudices, and properties of men, can be discriminated from the rankest tyranny.

If the injustice of the course pursued in France be clear, the policy of the measure, that is, the public benefit to be expected from it, ought to be at least as evident, and at least as important. To a man who acts under the influence of no passion, who has nothing in view in his projects but the public good, a great difference will immediately strike him, between what policy would dictate on the original introduction of such institutions, and on a question of their total abolition, where they have cast their roots wide and deep, and where by long habit things more valuable than themselves are so adapted to them, and in a manner interwoven with them, that the one cannot be destroyed without notably impairing the other. He might be embarrassed, if the case were really such as sophisters represent it in their paltry style of debating. But in this, as in most questions of state, there is a middle. There is something else than the mere alternative of absolute destruction, or unreformed existence. *Spartam nactus es; hanc exorna.* This is, in my opinion, a rule of profound sense, and ought never to depart from the mind of an honest reformer. I cannot conceive how any man can have brought himself to that pitch of presumption, to consider his country as nothing but carte blanche, upon which he may scribble whatever he pleases. A man full of warm speculative benevolence may wish his society otherwise constituted than he finds it; but a good patriot and a true politician, always considers how he shall make the most of the existing materials of his country. A disposition to preserve, and an ability to improve, taken together, would be my standard of a statesman. Everything else is vulgar in the conception, perilous in the execution.

There are moments in the fortune of states when particular men are called to make improvements by great mental exertion. In those moments, even when they seem to enjoy the confidence of their prince and country, and to be invested with full authority; they have not always apt instruments. A politician, to do great things, looks for a *power*, what our workmen call a *purchase* and if he finds that power, in politics as in mechanics he cannot be at a loss to apply it. In the monastic institutions, in my opinion, was found a great *power* for the mechanism of politic benevolence. There were revenues with a public direction; there were men wholly set apart and dedicated to public purposes, without any other than public ties and public principles; men without the possibility of converting the estate of the community into a private fortune; men denied to self-interests, whose avarice is for some community; men to whom personal poverty is honour, and implicit obedience stands in the place of freedom. In vain shall a man look to the possibility of making such things when he wants them. The winds blow as they list. These institutions are the products of enthusiasm; they are the instruments of wisdom. Wisdom cannot create materials; they are the gifts of nature or of chance; her pride is in the use. The perennial existence of bodies corporate and their fortunes, are things particularly suited to a man who has long views; who meditates designs that require time in fashioning; and which propose duration when they are accomplished. He is not deserving to rank high, or even to be mentioned in the order of great statesmen, who, having obtained the command and direction of such a power as existed in the wealth, the discipline, and the habits of such corporations, as those which you have rashly destroyed, cannot find any way of converting it to the great and lasting benefit of his country. On the view of this subject a thousand uses suggest themselves to a contriving mind. To destroy any power, growing wild from the rank productive force of the human mind, is almost tantamount, in the moral world, to the destruction of the apparently active properties of bodies in the material. It would be like the attempt to destroy (if it were in our competence to destroy) the expansive force of fixed air in nitre, or the power of steam, or of electricity, or of magnetism. These energies always existed in nature, and they were always discernible. They seemed, some of them unserviceable, some noxious, some no better than a sport to children; until contemplative ability combining with practic skill, tamed their wild nature, subdued them to use, and rendered them at once the most powerful and the most tractable agents, in subservience to the great views and designs of men. Did fifty thousand persons, whose mental and whose bodily labour you might direct, and so many hundred thousand a year of a revenue, which was neither lazy nor superstitious, appear too big for your abilities to wield? Had you no way of using the men but by converting monks into pensioners? Had you no way of turning the revenue to account, but through the improvident resource of a spendthrift sale? If you were thus destitute of mental funds, the proceeding is in its natural course. Your politicians do not understand their trade; and therefore they sell their tools.

But the institutions savour of superstition in their very principle; and they nourish it by a permanent and standing influence. This I do not mean to dispute; but this ought not to hinder you from deriving from superstition itself any resources which may thence be furnished for the public advantage. You derive benefits from many dispositions and many passions of the human mind, which are of as doubtful a colour in the moral eye, as superstition itself. It was your business to correct and mitigate everything which was noxious in this passion, as in all the passions. But is superstition the greatest of all possible vices? In its possible excess I think it becomes a very great evil. It is, however, a moral subject; and of course admits of all degrees and all modifications. Superstition is the religion of feeble minds; and they must be tolerated in an intermixture of it, in some trifling or some enthusiastic shape or other, else you will deprive weak minds of a resource found necessary to the strongest. The body of all true religion consists, to be sure, in obedience to the will of the sovereign of the world; in a confidence in his declarations; and an imitation of his perfections. The rest is our own. It may be prejudicial to the great end; it may be auxiliary. Wise men, who as such, are not *admirers* (not admirers at least of the *Munera Terrae*) are not violently attached to these things, nor do they violently hate them. Wisdom is not the most severe corrector of folly. They are the rival follies, which mutually wage so unrelenting a war; and which make so cruel a use of their advantages, as they can happen to engage the immoderate vulgar on the one side or the other in their quarrels. Prudence would be neuter; but if, in the contention between fond attachment and fierce antipathy concerning things in their nature not made to produce such heats, a prudent man were obliged to make a choice of what errors and excesses of enthusiasm he would condemn or bear, perhaps he would think the superstition which builds, to be more tolerable than that which demolishes—that which adorns a country, than that which deforms it—that which endows, than that which plunders—that which disposes to mistaken beneficence, than that which stimulates to real injustice—that which leads a man to refuse to himself lawful pleasures, than that which snatches from others the scanty subsistence of their self-denial. Such, I think, is very nearly the state of the question between the ancient founders of monkish superstition, and the superstition of the pretended philosophers of the hour. . . .

[I]n these gentlemen there is nothing of the tender parental solicitude which fears to cut up the infant for the sake of an experiment. In the vastness of their promises, and the confidence of their predictions, they far outdo all the boasting of empirics [charlatans]. The arrogance of their pretensions, in a manner provokes, and challenges us to an enquiry into their foundation. . . .

. . .

But is it in destroying and pulling down that skill is displayed? Your mob can do this as well at least as your assemblies. The shallowest understanding, the rudest hand, is more than equal to that task. Rage and frenzy will pull down more in half an hour, than prudence, deliberation, and foresight can build up in an hundred years. The errors and defects of old establishments are visible and palpable. It calls for little ability to point them out; and where absolute power is given, it requires but a word wholly to abolish the vice and the establishment together. The same lazy but restless disposition, which loves sloth and hates quiet, directs these politicians, when they come to work, for supplying the place of what they have destroyed. To make everything the reverse of what they have seen is quite as easy as to destroy. No difficulties occur in what has never been tried. Criticism is almost baffled in discovering the defects of what has not existed; and eager enthusiasm, and cheating hope, have all the wide field of imagination in which they may expatiate with little or no opposition.

At once to preserve and to reform is quite another thing. When the useful parts of an old establishment are kept, and what is superadded is to be fitted to what is retained, a vigorous mind, steady persevering attention, various powers of comparison and combination, and the resources of an understanding fruitful in expedients are to be exercised; they are to be exercised in a continued conflict with the combined force of opposite vices; with the obstinacy that rejects all improvement, and the levity that is fatigued and disgusted with everything of which it is in possession. But you may object—"A process of this kind is slow. It is not fit for an assembly, which glories in performing in a few months the work of ages. Such a mode of reforming, possibly might take up many years." Without question it might; and it ought. It is one of the excellencies of a method in which time is amongst the assistants, that its operation is slow, and in some cases almost imperceptible. If circumspection and caution are a part of wisdom, when we work only upon inanimate matter, surely they become a part of duty too, when the subject of our demolition and construction is not brick and timber, but sentient beings, by the sudden alteration of whose state, condition, and habits, multitudes may be rendered miserable. But it seems as if it were the prevalent opinion in Paris, that an unfeeling heart, and an undoubting confidence, are the sole qualifications for a perfect legislator. Far different are my ideas of that high office. The true lawgiver ought to have an heart full of sensibility. He ought to love and respect his kind, and to fear himself. It may be allowed to his temperament to catch his ultimate object with an intuitive glance; but his movements towards it ought to be deliberate. Political arrangement, as it is a work for social ends, is to be only wrought by social means. There mind must conspire with mind. Time is required to produce that union of minds which alone can produce all the good we aim at. Our patience will achieve more than our force. If I might venture to appeal to what is so much out of fashion in Paris, I mean to experience, I should tell you, that in my course I have known, and, according to my measure, have co-operated with great men; and I have never yet seen any plan which has not been mended by the observations of those who were much inferior in understanding to the person who took the lead in the business. By a slow but well sustained progress, the effect of each step is watched; the good or ill success of the first, gives light to us in the second; and so, from light to light, we are conducted with safety through the whole series. We see, that the parts of the system do not clash. The evils latent in the most promising contrivances are provided for as they arise. One advantage is as little as possible sacrificed to another. We compensate, we reconcile, we balance. We are enabled to unite into a consistent whole the various anomalies and contending principles that are found in the minds and affairs of men. From hence arises, not an excellence in simplicity, but one far superior, an excellence in composition. Where the great interests of mankind are concerned through a long succession of generations, that succession ought to be admitted into some share in the councils which are so deeply to affect them. If justice requires this, the work itself requires the aid of more minds than one age can furnish. It is from this view of things that the best legislators have been often satisfied with the establishment of some sure, solid, and ruling principle in government; a power like that which some of the philosophers have called a plastic nature; and having fixed the principle, they have left it afterwards to its own operation. . . .

Old establishments are tried by their effects. If the people are happy, united, wealthy, and powerful, we presume the rest. We conclude that to be good from whence good is derived. In old establishments various correctives have been found for their aberrations from theory. Indeed they are the results of various necessities and expediencies. They are not often constructed after any theory; theories are rather drawn from them. In them we often see the end best obtained, where the means seem not perfectly reconcilable to what we may fancy was that original scheme. The means taught by experience may be better suited to political ends than those contrived in the original project. They again re-act upon the primitive constitution, and sometimes improve the design itself from which they seem to have departed. I think all this might be curiously exemplified in the British constitution. At worst, the errors and deviations of every kind in reckoning are found and computed, and the ship proceeds in her course. This is the case of old establishments; but in a new and merely theoretic system, it is expected that every contrivance shall appear, on the face of it, to answer its end; especially where the projectors are no way embarrassed with an endeavor to accommodate the new building to an old one, either in the walls or on the foundations. . . .

The effects of the incapacity shewn by the popular leaders in all the great members of the commonwealth are to be covered with the "all-atoning name" of liberty. In some people I see great liberty indeed; in many, if not in the most, an oppressive degrading servitude. But what is liberty without wisdom, and without virtue? It is the greatest of all possible evils; for it is folly, vice, and madness, without tuition or restraint. Those who know what virtuous liberty is, cannot bear to see it disgraced by incapable heads, on account of their having high-sounding words in their mouths. Grand, swelling sentiments of liberty, I am sure I do not despise. They warm the heart; they enlarge and liberalise our minds; they animate our courage in a time of conflict. Old as I am, I read the fine raptures of Lucan and Corneille with pleasure. Neither do I wholly condemn the little arts and devices of popularity. They facilitate the carrying of many points of moment; they keep the people together; they refresh the mind in its exertions; and they diffuse occasional gaiety over the severe brow of moral freedom. Every politician ought to sacrifice to the graces; and to join compliance with reason. But in such an undertaking as that in France, all these subsidiary sentiments and artifices are of little avail. To make a government requires no great prudence. Settle the seat of power; teach obedience: and the work is done. To give freedom is still more easy. It is not necessary to guide; it only requires to let go the rein. But to form *a free government*; that is, to temper together these opposite elements of liberty and restraint in one consistent work, requires much thought, deep reflection, a sagacious, powerful, and combining mind. This I do not find in those who take the lead in the national assembly. Perhaps they are not so miserably deficient as they appear. I rather believe it. It would put them below the common level of human understanding. But when the leaders choose to make themselves bidders at an auction of popularity, their talents, in the construction of the state, will be of no service. They will become flatterers instead of legislators; the instruments, not the guides of the people. If any of them should happen to propose a scheme of liberty, soberly limited, and defined with proper qualifications, he will be immediately outbid by his competitors, who will produce something more splendidly popular. Suspicions will be raised of his fidelity to his cause. Moderation will be stigmatized as the virtue of cowards; and compromise as the prudence of traitors; until, in hopes of preserving the credit which may enable him to temper and moderate on some occasions, the popular leader is obliged to become active in propagating doctrines, and establishing powers, that will afterwards defeat any sober purpose at which he ultimately might have aimed.

But am I so unreasonable as to see nothing at all that deserves commendation in the indefatigable labours of this assembly? I do not deny that among an infinite number of acts of violence and folly, some good may have been done. They who destroy everything certainly will remove some grievance. They who make everything new, have a chance that they may establish something beneficial. To give them credit for what they have done in virtue of the authority they have usurped, or which can excuse them in the crimes by which that authority has been acquired, it must appear, that the same things could not have been accomplished without producing such a revolution. Most assuredly they might; because almost every one of the regulations made by them, which is not very equivocal, was either in the cession of the king, voluntarily made at the meeting of the states, or in the concurrent instructions to the orders. Some usages have been abolished on just grounds; but they were such that if they had stood as they were to all eternity, they would little detract from the happiness and prosperity of any state. The improvements of the national assembly are superficial, their errors fundamental.

THOMAS PAINE

In January 1776, Tom Paine (1737–1809), an emigré journalist from England, published a pamphlet in the American colonies entitled *Common Sense*, which sold over 100,000 copies in three months. Paine's tract was the first public call for independence from Britain and had a profound impact on both public opinion and the deliberations of the Continental Congress then meeting in Philadelphia. Although a deist, Paine throughout his life was religious, and his language vibrates with the power of the Puritan jeremiad. The themes and rhetoric of *Common Sense* were familiar to the Calvinist ministers of New England and excited them and their flock as other Enlightenment writings did not. Under its banner, they set aside their innumerable sectarian quarrels to cooperate in the cause against the British and their bishops.

Paine was not only a rebel but a republican who considered insurrection to be the first step toward establishing a new government based on the innate rights of man. When revolution broke out in France, he defended it by formulating his principles in sharper, more systematic form. *The Rights of Man* (1791) established Paine as an international spokesman for political equality, natural rights, and the origin of government in a social contract among equals. In its concern for farmers, artisans, and the "middling" classes, Paine's defense of revolutions forms a bridge from Locke to the republican clubs of America and the nascent working-class movement in England.

Paine was born in England, a Quaker and the son of a poor corsetmaker. After a wayward career as a corsetmaker, schoolmaster, itinerant preacher, and customs inspector, he met Benjamin Franklin in London and on Franklin's recommendation sailed for Philadelphia in 1774. In the new land he became a journalist and an ardent patriot, though at first he advocated reconciliation in the conflict with Britain.

Paine became a revolutionary after the battles of Lexington and Concord and put the case for independence in savagely brilliant language:

> Can we but leave posterity with a settled form of government, an independent constitution of its own, the purchase at any price will be cheap. But to expend millions for the sake of getting a few vile acts repealed, and routing the present ministry only, is unworthy the charge, and is using posterity with the utmost cruelty; because it is leaving them the great work to do.

The immense influence of *Common Sense* is due to its flashy style, which is studded with striking metaphors and colloquial directness. Paine was also one of the first to insist that America adopt a new system of republican government, rather than simply reject British rule, and that the American Revolution was of philosophical significance, not just a change of regime. Paine was also among the first American men to actively and visibly support women's equality. In "An Occasional Letter on the Female Sex," he made the almost unheard of argument that if women were equally individuals, they were thus entitled to equal rights.

During the bleak first year of the Revolution, Paine's writings revived the flagging morale of both the troops and the civilian population. His propaganda also publicized the American cause throughout Europe. In April 1777 he was elected secretary of the congressional Committee of Foreign Affairs, though later dismissed when he published privileged information regarding treaty negotiations with France. He returned to Europe in 1787, living in England and France.

In 1791 Paine published *The Rights of Man*, a defense of the French Revolution against Edmund Burke's conservative *Reflections on the Revolution in France*, and thus indirectly a defense of republican liberties in England as well. Burke had emphasized the nonrational elements of authority—the role of custom, tradition, experience, and such deep-seated emotions as loyalty, love, and awe. According to Burke, no nation is the product of a contract but rather is the outcome of history, of a chain of generations making its impact by precedent and example, obligated to the past and responsible for the future. In reply, Paine reasserted that the rights of man were protected in antiquity, cultivated in the American colonies and secured by their revolution, and rooted in our nature. Striking a modern note, he also declared that Burke and his allies—who pretended to speak for the nation and indeed for the ages—were not above pursuing their selfish interests, if necessary, with rational and even revolutionary methods. Tradition may be in the eye of the beholder. Paine contended that the British government, like all monarchy, is itself the outcome of conquest and that it favors men of property, tries to exploit the forces of commerce, and reorganizes society with little regard for the customs and traditions of the common people. Thus, Paine's thought anticipates some themes of modern sociology, although it is grounded primarily in eighteenth-century deism and influenced by Rousseau.

As a result of his quarrel with Burke, Paine left England, where he was later declared a traitor and outlawed; he went to France, becoming a French citizen and in 1792 a delegate to the National Convention. His association with such moderates as Condorcet landed him in prison for one year under the Reign of Terror, and there he composed *The Age of Reason*, a statement of his deist principles.

In 1802 Paine returned to America, where he wrote articles that jointly defended the administration of Jefferson and the principles he espoused in 1776. He also proposed that the United States serve as a mediator between France and the black republic of Haiti. For the most part, however, Paine was ostracized for his radicalism; he lived in poverty until his death.

THE RIGHTS OF MAN

1791

PART FIRST

Among the incivilities by which nations or individuals provoke and irritate each other, Mr. Burke's pamphlet on the French Revolution is an extraordinary instance. Neither the people of France, nor the National Assembly, were troubling themselves about the affairs of England, or the English Parliament; and that Mr. Burke should commence an unprovoked attack upon them, both in Parliament and in public, is a conduct that cannot be pardoned on the score of manners, nor justified on that of policy. There is scarcely an epithet of abuse to be found in the English language, with which Mr. Burke has not loaded the French nation and the National Assembly. Every thing which rancor, prejudice, ignorance, or knowledge could suggest, are poured forth in the copious fury of near four hundred pages. In the strain and on the plan Mr. Burke was writing, he might have written on to as many thousands.

From *The Rights of Man* by Thomas Paine (Garden City, N.Y.: Doubleday Anchor Books, 1973 [1791]).

When the tongue or the pen is let loose in a frenzy of passion, it is the man and not the subject that becomes exhausted.

Hitherto Mr. Burke has been mistaken and disappointed in the opinions he had formed of the affairs of France; but such is the ingenuity of his hope, or the malignancy of his despair, that it furnishes him with new pretenses to go on. There was a time when it was impossible to make Mr. Burke believe there would be any revolution in France. His opinion then was, that the French had neither spirit to undertake it, nor fortitude to support it; and now that there is one, he seeks an escape by condemning it.

Not sufficiently content with abusing the National Assembly, a great part of his work is taken up with abusing Dr. Price (one of the best-hearted men that lives), and the two societies in England known by the name of the Revolution Society, and the Society for Constitutional Information.

Dr. Price had preached a sermon on the 4th of November, 1789, being the anniversary of what is called in England the Revolution, which took place in 1688. Mr. Burke, speaking of this sermon, says, "The political divine proceeds dogmatically to assert that, by the principles of the Revolution, the people of England have acquired three fundamental rights:

"1. To choose our own governors.
"2. To cashier them for misconduct.
"3. To frame a government for ourselves."

Dr. Price does not say that the right to do these things exists in this or in that person, or in this or in that description of persons, but that it exists in the *whole*; that it is a right resident in the nation. Mr. Burke, on the contrary, denies that such a right exists in the nation, either in whole or in part, or that it exists any where; and, what is still more strange and marvelous, he says, "that the people of England utterly disclaim such a right, and that they will resist the practical assertion of it with their lives and fortunes."

That men should take up arms, and spend their lives and fortunes, *not* to maintain their rights, but to maintain they have *not* rights, is an entirely new species of discovery, and suited to the paradoxical genius of Mr. Burke.

The method which Mr. Burke takes to prove that the people of England had no such rights, and that such rights do not now exist in the nation, either in whole or in part, or any where at all, is of the same marvelous and monstrous kind with what he has already said; for his arguments are, that the persons, or the generation of persons, in whom they did exist, are dead, and with them the right is dead also.

To prove this, he quotes a declaration made by Parliament about a hundred years ago, to William and Mary, in these words: "The Lords Spiritual and Temporal, and Commons, do, in the name of the people aforesaid," (meaning the people of England then living) "most humbly and faithfully *submit* themselves, their *heirs* and *posterities*, for EVER." He also quotes a clause of another act of Parliament made in the same reign, the terms of which, he says, "bind us," (meaning the people of that day) "our *heirs* and our *posterity*, to *them*, their *heirs* and *posterity*, to the end of time."

Mr. Burke conceives his point sufficiently established by producing these clauses, which he enforces by saying that they exclude the right of the nation for *ever*. And not yet content with making such declarations, repeated over and over again, he further says, "that if the people of England possessed such a right before the Revolution," (which he acknowledges to have been the case, not only in England but throughout Europe, at an early period,) "yet that the *English nation* did, at the time of the Revolution, most solemnly renounce and abdicate it, for themselves, and for *all their posterity, for ever*."

As Mr. Burke occasionally applies the poison drawn from his horrid principles, not only to the English nation, but to the French Revolution and the National Assembly, and charges that august, illuminated and illuminating body of men with the epithet of *usurpers*, I shall, *sans cérémonie*, place another system of principles in opposition to his.

The English Parliament of 1688 did a certain thing, which, for themselves and their constituents, they had a right to do, and which it appeared right should be done: But, in addition to this right, which they possessed by delegation, *they set up another right by assumption*, that of binding and controlling posterity to the end of time.

The case, therefore, divides itself into two parts; the right which they possessed by delegation, and the right which they set up by assumption. The first is admitted; but with respect to the second, I reply:—

There never did, there never will, and there never can exist a parliament, or any description of men, or any generation of men, in any country, possessed of the right or the power of binding and controlling posterity to the "*end of time*," or of commanding forever how the world shall be governed, or who shall govern it; and therefore, all such clauses, acts or declarations, by which the makers of them attempt to do what they have neither the right nor the power to do, nor the power to execute, are in themselves null and void.

Every age and generation must be as free to act for itself, *in all cases*, as the ages and generation which preceded it. The vanity and presumption of governing beyond the grave, is the most ridiculous and insolent of all tyrannies.

Man has no property in man; neither has any generation a property in the generations which are to follow. The Parliament or the people of 1688, or of any other period, had no more right to dispose of the people of the present day, or to bind or to control them *in any shape whatever*, than the Parliament or the people of the present day have to dispose of, bind, or control those who are to live a hundred or a thousand years hence.

Every generation is, and must be, competent to all the purposes which its occasions require. It is the living, and not the dead, that are to be accommodated. When man ceases to be, his power and his wants cease with him; and having no longer any participation in the concerns of this world, he has no longer any authority in directing who shall be its governors, or how its government shall be organized, or how administered.

I am not contending for nor against any form of government, nor for nor against any party here or elsewhere. That which a whole nation chooses to do, it has a right to do. Mr. Burke says, No. Where then *does* the right exist? I am contending for the rights of the *living*, and against their being willed away, and controlled and contracted for, by the manuscript assumed authority of the dead; and Mr. Burke is contending for the authority of the dead over the rights and freedom of the living.

There was a time when kings disposed of their crowns by will upon their death-beds, and consigned the people, like beasts of the field, to whatever successor they appointed. This is now so exploded as scarcely to be remembered, and so monstrous as hardly to be believed. But the parliamentary clauses upon which Mr. Burke builds his political church, are of the same nature.

The laws of every country must be analogous to some common principle. In England, no parent or master, nor all the authority of Parliament, omnipotent as it has called itself, can bind or control the personal freedom even of an individual beyond the age of twenty-one years. On what ground of right, then, could the Parliament of 1688, or any other parliament, bind all posterity for ever?

Those who have quitted the world, and those who are not yet arrived in it, are as remote from each other, as the utmost stretch of moral imagination can conceive. What possible obligation, then, can exist between them; what rule or principle can be laid down, that two nonentities, the one out of existence, and the other not in, and who never can meet in this world, that the one should control the other to the end of time?

In England, it is said that money cannot be taken out of the pockets of the people without their consent. But who authorized, or who could authorize the Parliament of 1688 to control and take away the freedom of posterity, and limit and confine their right of acting in certain cases for ever, who were not in existence to give or to withhold their consent?

A greater absurdity cannot present itself to the understanding of man, than what Mr. Burke offers to his readers. He tells them, and he tells the world to come, that a certain body of men, who existed a hundred years ago, made a law; and that there does not now exist in the nation, nor ever will, nor ever can, a power to alter it. Under how many subtilties, or absurdities, has the divine right to govern been imposed on the credulity of mankind!

Mr. Burke has discovered a new one, and he has shortened his journey to Rome, by appealing to the power of this infallible Parliament of former days;

and he produces what it has done, as of divine authority; for that power must certainly be more than human, which no human power to the end of time can alter.

But Mr. Burke has done some service, not to his cause, but to his country, by bringing those clauses into public view. They serve to demonstrate how necessary it is at all times to watch against the attempted encroachment of power, and to prevent its running to excess.

It is somewhat extraordinary, that the offense for which James II was expelled, that of setting up power by *assumption*, should be reacted, under another shape and form, by the Parliament that expelled him. It shows that the rights of man were but imperfectly understood at the Revolution; for certain it is, that the right which that Parliament set up by *assumption* (for by the delegation it had it not, and could not have it, because none could give it) over the persons and freedom of posterity for ever, was the same tyrannical, unfounded kind which James attempted to set up over the Parliament and the nation, and for which he was expelled.

The only difference is (for in principle they differ not), that the one was an usurper over the living, and the other over the unborn; and as the one has no better authority to stand upon than the other, both of them must be equally null and void, and of no effect.

From what, or from whence, does Mr. Burke prove the right of any human power to bind posterity for ever? He has produced his clauses; but he must produce also his proofs that such a right existed, and show how it existed. If it ever existed, it must now exist; for whatever appertains to the nature of man, cannot be annihilated by man.

It is the nature of man to die, and he will continue to die as long as he continues to be born. But Mr. Burke has set up a sort of political Adam, in whom all posterity are bound for ever; he must therefore prove that his Adam possessed such a power, or such a right.

The weaker any cord is, the less it will bear to be stretched and the worse is the policy to stretch it, unless it is intended to break it. Had a person contemplated the overthrow of Mr. Burke's positions, he would have proceeded as Mr. Burke has done. He would have magnified the authorities, on purpose to have called the *right* of them into question; and the instant the question of right was started, the authorities must have been given up.

It requires but a very small glance of thought to perceive, that although laws made in one generation often continue in force through succeeding generations, yet they continue to derive their force from the consent of the living. A law not repealed continues in force, not because it *cannot* be repealed, but because it is *not* repealed; and the non-repealing passes for consent.

But Mr. Burke's clauses have not even this qualification in their favor. They become null, by attempting to become immortal. The nature of them precludes consent. They destroy the right which they *might* have, by grounding it on a right which they *cannot* have. Immortal power is not a human right, and therefore cannot be a right of Parliament.

The Parliament of 1688 might as well have passed an act to have authorized themselves to live for ever as to make their authority to live for ever. All therefore that can be said of them is, that they are a formality of words, of as much import as if those who used them had addressed a congratulation to themselves, and in the oriental style of antiquity, had said, O Parliament, live for ever!

The circumstances of the world are continually changing, and the opinions of men change also; and as government is for the living, and not for the dead, it is the living only that has any right in it. That which may be thought right and found convenient in one age, may be thought wrong and found inconvenient in another. In such cases, who is to decide, the living, or the dead?

As almost one hundred pages of Mr. Burke's book are employed upon these clauses, it will consequently follow, that if the clauses themselves, so far as they set up on *assumed*, *usurped* dominion over posterity for ever, are unauthoritative, and in their nature null and void; that all his voluminous inferences, and declamation drawn therefrom, or founded thereon, are null and void also: and on this ground I rest the matter.

. . .

I will quote Mr. Burke's catalogue of barriers that he has set up between man and his Maker. Putting himself in the character of a herald, he says—"We fear God—we look with *awe* to kings—with affection to parliaments—with duty to magistrates—with reverence to priests, and with respect to nobility." Mr. Burke has forgotten to put in "*chivalry*." He has also forgotten to put in Peter.

The duty of man is not a wilderness of turnpike gates, through which he is to pass by tickets from one to the other. It is plain and simple, and consists but of two points. His duty to God, which every man must feel; and with respect to his neighbor, to do as he would be done by. If those to whom power is delegated do well, they will be respected; if not, they will be despised; and with regard to those to whom no power is delegated, but who assume it, the rational world can know nothing of them.

Hitherto we have spoken only (and that but in part) of the natural rights of man. We have now to consider the civil rights of man, and to show how the one originates from the other. Man did not enter into society to become *worse* than he was before, nor to have fewer rights than he had before, but to have those rights better secured. His natural rights are the foundation of all his civil rights. But in order to pursue this distinction with more precision, it is necessary to make the different qualities of natural and civil rights.

A few words will explain this. Natural rights are those which appertain to man in right of his existence. Of this kind are all the intellectual rights, or rights of the mind, and also all those rights of acting as an individual for his own comfort and happiness, which are not injurious to the natural rights of others. Civil rights are those which appertain to man in right of his being a member of society.

Every civil right has for its foundation some natural right pre-existing in the individual, but to the enjoyment of which his individual power is not, in all cases, sufficiently competent. Of this kind are all those which relate to security and protection.

From this short review, it will be easy to distinguish between that class of natural rights which man retains after entering into society, and those which he throws into the common stock as a member of society.

The natural rights which he retains, are all those in which the *power* to execute is as perfect in the individual as the right itself. Among this class, as is before mentioned, are all the intellectual rights, or rights of the mind: consequently, religion is one of those rights.

The natural rights which are not retained, are all those in which, though the right is perfect in the individual, the power to execute them is defective. They answer not his purpose. A man, by natural right, has a right to judge in his own cause; and so far as the right of the mind is concerned, he never surrenders it: but what availeth it him to judge, if he has not power to redress? He therefore deposits his right in the common stock of society, and takes the arm of society, of which he is a part, in preference and in addition to his own. Society *grants* him nothing. Every man is proprietor in society, and draws on the capital as a matter of right.

From these premises, two or three certain conclusions will follow.

First, That every civil right grows out of a natural right; or, in other words, is a natural right exchanged.

Secondly, That civil power, properly considered as such, is made up of the aggregate of that class of the natural rights of man, which becomes defective in the individual in point of power, and answers not his purpose, but when collected to a focus, becomes competent to the purpose of every one.

Thirdly, That the power produced from the aggregate of natural rights, imperfect in power in the individual, cannot be applied to invade the natural rights which are retained in the individual, and in which the power to execute is as perfect as the right itself.

We have now, in a few words, traced man from a natural individual to a member of society, and shown, or endeavored to show, the quality of the natural rights retained, and those which are exchanged for civil rights. Let us now apply those principles to governments.

In casting our eyes over the world, it is extremely easy to distinguish the governments which have arisen out of society, or out the social compact, from those which have not: but to place this in a clearer light than what a single glance may afford, it will be proper to take a review of the several sources from which the governments have arisen, and on which they have been founded.

They may be all comprehended under three heads. First, superstition. Secondly, power. Thirdly, the common interests of society, and the common rights of man.

The first was a government of priestcraft, the second of conquerors, and the third of reason.

When a set of artful men pretended, through the medium of oracles, to hold intercourse with the Deity, as familiarly as they now march up the back-stairs in European courts, the world was completely under the government of superstition. The oracles were consulted, and whatever they were made to say, became the law; and this sort of government lasted as long as this sort of superstition lasted.

After these a race of conquerors arose, whose government, like that of William the Conqueror, was founded in power, and the sword assumed the name of a sceptre. Governments thus established, last as long as the power to support them lasts; but that they might avail themselves of every engine in their favor, they united fraud to force, and set up an idol which they called *Divine Right*, and which, in imitation of the Pope, who affects to be spiritual and temporal, and in contradiction to the Founder of the Christian religion, twisted itself afterwards into an idol of another shape, called *Church and State*. The key of St. Peter, and the key of the Treasury, became quartered on one another, and the wondering, cheated multitude worshipped the invention.

When I contemplate the natural dignity of man; when I feel (for Nature has not been kind enough to me to blunt my feelings) for the honor and happiness of its character, I become irritated at the attempt to govern mankind by force and fraud, as if they were all knaves and fools, and can scarcely avoid disgust at those who are thus imposed upon.

We have now to review the governments which arise out of society, in contradistinction to those which arose out of superstition and conquest.

It has been thought a considerable advance toward establishing the principles of freedom, to say, that government is a compact between those who govern and those who are governed: but this cannot be true, because it is putting the effect before the cause; for as a man must have existed before governments existed, there necessarily was a time when governments did not exist, and consequently there could originally exist no governments to form such a compact with.

The fact therefore must be, that the *individuals themselves*, each in his own personal and sovereign right, *entered into a compact with each other* to produce a government: and this is the only mode in which governments have a right to arise, and the only principle on which they have a right to exist.

To possess ourselves of a clear idea of what government is, or ought to be, we must trace it to its origin. In doing this, we shall easily discover that governments must have arisen, either *out* of the people, or *over* the people. Mr. Burke has made no distinction.

He investigates nothing to its source, and therefore he confounds every thing; but he has signified his intention of undertaking at some future opportunity, a comparison between the constitutions of England and France.

As he thus renders it a subject of controversy by throwing the gauntlet, I take him upon his own ground. It is in high challenges that high truths have the right of appearing; and I accept it with the more readiness, because it affords me, at the same time, an opportunity of pursuing the subject with respect to governments arising out of society.

But it will be first necessary to define what is meant by a *constitution*. It is not sufficient that we adopt the word; we must fix also a standard signification to it.

A constitution is not a thing in name only, but in fact. It has not an ideal, but a real existence; and wherever it cannot be produced in a visible form, there is none. A constitution is a thing *antecedent* to a government, and a government is only the creature of a constitution. The constitution of a country is not the act of its government, but of the people constituting a government.

It is the body of elements, to which you can refer, and quote article by article; and which contains the principles on which the government shall be established, the manner in which it shall be organized, the powers it shall have, the mode of elections, the duration of parliaments, or by what other name such bodies may be called; the powers which the executive part of the government shall have; and, in fine, every thing that relates to the complete organization of a civil government, and the principles on which it shall act, and by which it shall be bound.

A constitution, therefore, is to a government, what the laws made afterwards by that government are to a court of judicature. The court of judicature does not make the laws, neither can it alter them; it only acts in conformity to the laws made: and the government is in like manner governed by the constitution.

Can then Mr. Burke produce the English Constitution? If he cannot, we may fairly conclude, that though it has been so much talked about, no such thing as a constitution exists, or ever did exist, and consequently that the people have yet a constitution to form. Mr. Burke will not, I presume, deny the position I have already advanced; namely, that governments arise, either *out* of the people, or *over* the people. The English Government is one of those which arose out of a conquest, and not out of society, and consequently it arose over the people; and though it has been much modified from the opportunity of circumstances since the time of William the Conqueror, the country has never yet regenerated itself, and is therefore without a constitution.

. . .

The French Constitution says, that the right of war and peace is in the nation. Where else should it reside but in those who are to pay the expense?

In England, this right is said to reside in a *metaphor*, shown at the Tower for six-pence or a shilling a-piece: So are the lions; and it would be a step nearer to reason to say it resided in them, for any inanimate metaphor is no more than a hat or a cap. We can all see the absurdity of worshipping Aaron's molten calf, or Nebuchadnezzar's golden image; but why do men continue to practise on themselves the absurdities they despise in others?

It may with reason be said, that in the manner the English nation is represented, it signifies not where this right resides, whether in the Crown or in the Parliament. War is the common harvest of all those who participate in the division and expenditure of public money, in all countries.

It is the art of *conquering at home*: the object of it is an increase of revenue; and as revenue cannot be increased without taxes, a pretense must be made for expenditures. In reviewing the history of the English Government, its wars and its taxes, a bystander, not blinded by prejudice, nor warped by interest, would declare, that taxes were not raised to carry on wars, but that wars were raised to carry on taxes.

Mr. Burke, as a member of the House of Commons, is a part of the English Government; and though he professes himself an enemy to war, he abuses the French Constitution, which seeks to explode it. He holds up the English Government as a model in all its parts, to France; but he should first know the remarks which the French make upon it.

They contend, in favor of their own, that the portion of liberty enjoyed in England, is just enough to enslave a country by, more productively than by despotism; and that as the real object of all despotism is revenue, a government so formed obtains more than it could do either by direct despotism, or in a full state of freedom, and is therefore, on the ground of interest, opposed to both.

They account also for the readiness which always appears in such governments for engaging in wars, by remarking on the different motives which produce them. In despotic governments, wars are the effect of pride; but in those governments in which they become the means of taxation, they acquire thereby a more permanent promptitude.

The French Constitution, therefore, to provide against both these evils, has taken away the power of declaring war from kings and ministers, and placed the right where the expense must fall.

When the question on the right of war and peace was agitating in the National Assembly, the people of England appeared to be much interested in the event, and highly to applaud the decision. As a principle, it applies as much to one country as to another. William the Conqueror, *as a conqueror*, held this power of war and peace in himself, and his descendants have ever since claimed it under him as a right.

Although Mr. Burke has asserted the right of the Parliament at the Revolution to bind and control the nation and posterity for *ever*, he denies, at the same time, that the Parliament or the nation had any right to alter what he calls the succession of the Crown, in any thing but in part, or by a sort of modification.

By his taking this ground, he throws the case back to the *Norman Conquest*; and by thus running a line of succession springing from William the Conqueror to the present day, he makes it necessary to inquire who and what William the Conqueror was, and where he came from; and into the origin, history, and nature of what are called prerogatives.

Every thing must have had a beginning, and the fog of time and antiquity should be penetrated to discover it. Let then Mr. Burke bring forward his William of Normandy, for it is to this origin that his argument goes. It also unfortunately happens, in running this line of succession, that another line, parallel thereto, presents itself, which is, that if the succession runs in the line of the Conquest, the nation runs in the line of being conquered, and it ought to rescue itself from this reproach.

. . .

Now, as all arguments respecting succession must necessarily connect that succession with some beginning, Mr. Burke's arguments on this subject go to show that there is no English origin of kings, and that they are descendants of the Norman line in right of the Conquest.

It may, therefore, be of service to his doctrine to make this story known, and to inform him that in case of that natural distinction to which all mortality is subject, kings may again be had from Normandy, on more reasonable terms than William the Conqueror; and consequently, that the good people of England, at the Revolution of 1688, might have done much better, had such a generous Norman as *this* known *their* wants, and they *his*.

The chivalric character which Mr. Burke so much admires, is certainly much easier to make a bargain with than a hard-dealing Dutchman. But to return to the matters of the Constitution—

The French Constitution says, *there shall be no titles*; and of consequence, all that class of equivocal generation, which in some countries is called "*aristocracy*," and in others "*nobility*," is done away, and the *peer* is exalted into *man*.

Titles are but nicknames, and every nickname is a title. The thing is perfectly harmless in itself, but it marks a sort of foppery in the human character which degrades it. It renders man diminutive in things which are great, and the counterfeit of woman in things which are little. It talks about its fine blue *riband* like a girl, and shows its new *garter* like a child. A certain writer, of some antiquity, says, "When I was a child, I thought as a child: but when I became a man, I put away childish things."

It is, properly, from the elevated mind of France, that the folly of titles has been abolished. It has outgrown the baby-clothes of *count* and *duke*, and breeched itself in manhood. France has not levelled, it has exalted. It has put down the dwarf to set up the man. The insignificance of a senseless word like *duke*, *count*, or *earl*, has ceased to please. Even those who possessed them, have disowned the gibberish, and, as they outgrew the rickets, have despised the rattle.

The genuine mind of man, thirsting for its native home, society, contemns the gewgaws that separate him from it. Titles are like circles drawn by the magician's wand, to contract the sphere of man's felicity. He lives immured within the Bastille of a word, and surveys at a distance the envied life of man.

Is it then any wonder that titles should fall in France? Is it not a greater wonder they should be kept up anywhere? What are they? What is their worth, and "what is their amount?" When we think or speak of a *judge* or a *general*, we associate with it the ideas of office and character; we think of gravity in the one, and bravery in the other; but when we use a word merely as a title, no ideas associate with it.

Through all the vocabulary of Adam, there is no such an animal as a duke or a count; neither can we connect any idea to the words. Whether they mean strength or weakness, wisdom or folly, a child or a man, or a rider or a horse, is all equivocal. What respect then can be paid to that which describes nothing, and which means nothing? Imagination has given figure and character to centaurs, satyrs, and down to all the fairy tribe; but titles baffle even the powers of fancy, and are a chimerical nondescript.

But this is not all. If a whole country is disposed to hold them in contempt, all their value is gone, and none will own them. It is common opinion only that makes them any thing or nothing, or worse than nothing. There is no occasion to take titles away, for they take themselves away when society concurs to ridicule them. This species of imaginary consequence has visibly declined in every part of Europe, and it hastens to its exit as the world of reason continues to rise.

There was a time when the lowest class of what are called nobility, was more thought of than the highest is now, and when a man in armor riding through Christendom in search of adventure was more stared at than a modern duke. The world has seen this folly fall, and it has fallen by being laughed at, and the farce of titles will follow its fate.

The patriots of France have discovered in good time, that rank and dignity in society must take a new ground. The old one has fallen through. It must now take the substantial ground of character, instead of the chimerical ground of titles; and they have brought their titles to the altar, and made of them a burnt-offering to Reason.

If no mischief had annexed itself to the folly of titles, they would not have been worth a serious and formal destruction, such as the National Assembly have decreed them: and this makes it necessary to inquire further into the nature and character of aristocracy.

That, then, which is called aristocracy in some countries, and nobility in others, arose out of the governments founded upon conquest. It was originally a military order, for the purpose of supporting military government (for such were all governments founded in conquest); and to keep up a succession of this order for the purpose for which it was established, all the younger branches of those families were disinherited, and the law of *primogenitureship* set up.

The nature and character of aristocracy shows itself to us in this law. It is a law against every law of nature, and nature herself calls for its destruction. Establish family justice, and aristocracy falls. By the aristocratical law of primogenitureship, in a family of six children, five are exposed. Aristocracy has never more than *one* child. The rest are begotten to be devoured. They are thrown to the cannibal for prey, and the natural parent prepares the unnatural repast.

As every thing which is out of nature in man, affects, more or less, the interest of society, so does this. All the children which the aristocracy disowns (which are all, except the eldest) are, in general, cast like orphans on a parish, to be provided for by the public, but at a greater charge. Unnecessary offices and places in governments and courts are created at the expense of the public, to maintain them.

With what kind of parental reflections can the father or mother contemplate their younger offspring? By nature they are children, and by marriage they are heirs; but by aristocracy they are bastards and orphans. They are the flesh and blood of their parents in one line, and nothing akin to them in the other. To restore, therefore, parents to their children, and children to their parents—relations to each other, and man to society—and to exterminate the monster, aristocracy, root and branch—the French Constitution has destroyed the law of *Primogenitureship*. Here then lies the monster; and Mr. Burke, if he pleases, may write its epitaph.

. . .

CONCLUSION

From the Revolutions of America and France, and the symptoms that have appeared in other countries, it is evident that the opinion of the world is changed with respect to systems of government, and that revolutions are not within the compass of political calculations. The progress of time and circumstances, which men assign to the accomplishment of great changes, is too mechanical to measure the force of the mind, and the rapidity of reflection, by which revolutions are generated. All the old governments have received a shock from those that already appear, and which were once more improbable, and are a greater subject of wonder, than a general revolution in Europe would be now.

When we survey the wretched condition of man under the monarchical and hereditary systems of government, dragged from his home by one power, or driven by another, and impoverished by taxes more than by enemies, it becomes evident that those systems are bad, and that a general revolution in the principle and construction of governments is necessary.

What is government more than the management of the affairs of a nation? It is not, and from its nature cannot be, the property of any particular man or family, but of the whole community, at whose expense it is supported; and though by force or contrivance it has been usurped into an inheritance, the usurpation cannot alter the right of things. Sovereignty, as a matter of right, appertains to the nation only, and not to any individual; and a nation has at all times an inherent indefeasible right to abolish any form of government it finds inconvenient, and establish such as accords with its interest, disposition, and happiness. The romantic and barbarous distinction of [making] men into kings and subjects, though it may suit the condition of courtiers, cannot that of citizens; and is exploded by the principle upon which governments are now founded. Every citizen is a member of the sovereignty, and, as such, can acknowledge no personal subjection; and his obedience can be only to the laws.

When men think of what government is, they must necessarily suppose it to possess a knowledge of all the objects and matters upon which its authority is to be exercised. In this view of government the republican system, as established by America and France, operates to embrace the whole of a nation; and the knowledge necessary to the interest of all the parts, is to be found in the center which the parts by representation form. But the old governments are on a construction that excludes knowledge as well as happiness; government by monks, who know nothing of the world beyond the walls of a convent, is as consistent as government by kings.

What were formerly called revolutions, were little more than a change of persons, or an alteration of local circumstances. They rose and fell like things of course, and had nothing in their existence or their fate that could influence beyond the spot that produced them. But what we now see in the world, from the revolutions of America and France, is a renovation of the natural order of things, a system of principles as universal as truth and the existence of man, and combining moral with political happiness and national prosperity.

> "I. *Men are born and always continue free and equal in respect to their rights. Civil distinctions, therefore, can be founded only on public utility.*
> "II. *The end of all political associations is the preservation of the natural and imprescriptible rights of man; and these rights are liberty, property, security, and resistance of oppression.*
> "III. *The Nation is essentially the source of all Sovereignty, nor can any individual or any body of men, be entitled to any authority which is not expressly derived from it.*"

. . .

"AN OCCASIONAL LETTER ON THE FEMALE SEX"

1775

O Woman! lovely Woman!
Nature made thee to temper man,
We had been Brutes without you.
—OTWAY

If we take a survey of ages and of countries, we shall find the women, almost—without exception at all times and in all places, adored and oppressed. Man, who has never neglected an opportunity of exerting his power, in paying homage to their beauty, has always availed himself of their weakness. He has been at once then tyrant and then slave.

Nature herself, in forming beings so susceptible and tender, appears to have been more attentive to their charms than to their happiness. Continually surrounded with griefs and fears, the women more than share all our miseries, and are besides subjected to ills which are peculiarly their own. They cannot be the means of life without exposing themselves to the loss of it; every revolution which they undergo, alters their health, and threatens their existence. Cruel distempers attack their beauty—and the hour which confirms their release from those is perhaps the most melancholy of their lives. It robs them of the most essential characteristic of their sex. They can then only hope for protection from the humiliating claims of pity, or the feeble voice of gratitude.

Society, instead of alleviating their condition, is to them the source of new miseries. More than one half of the globe is covered with savages; and among all these people women are completely wretched. Man, in a state of barbarity, equally cruel and indolent, active by necessity, but naturally inclined to repose, is acquainted with little more than the physical effects of love; and, having none of those moral ideas which only can soften the empire of force, he is led to consider it as his supreme law, subjecting to his despotism those whom reason had made his equal, but whose imbecility betrayed them to his strength. "Nothing" (says Professor Miller, speaking of the women of barbarous nations) "can exceed the dependence and subjection in which they are kept, or the toil and drudgery which they are obliged to undergo. The husband, when he is not engaged in some warlike exercise, indulges himself in idleness, and devolves upon his wife the whole burden of his domestic affairs. He disdains to assist her in any of those servile employments. She sleeps in a different bed, and is seldom permitted to have any conversation or correspondence with him."

The women among the Indians of America are what the Helots were among the Spartans, a vanquished people, obliged to toil for their conquerors. Hence on the banks of the Oroonoko, we have seen mothers slaying their daughters out of compassion, and smothering them in the hour of their birth. They consider this barbarous pity as a virtue.

"The men (says Commodore Byron, in his account of the inhabitants of South America) exercise a most despotic authority over their wives, whom they consider in the same view they do any other part of their property, and dispose of them

From *The Complete Writings of Thomas Paine*, ed. Philip S. Foner. 2 vols. (New York: Citadel, 1945). Reprinted in *Against the Tide*, eds. Michael S. Kimmel and Thomas E. Mosmiller (Boston: Beacon Press, 1992).

accordingly. Even their common treatment of them is cruel; for though the toil and hazard of procuring food lies entirely on the women, they are not suffered to touch any part of it till the husband is satisfied; and then he assigns them their portion, which is generally very scanty, and such as he has not a stomach for himself."

Among, the nations of the East we find another kind of despotism and dominion prevail—the Seraglio, and the domestic servitude of woman, authorized by the manners and established by the laws. In Turkey, in Persia, in India, in Japan, and over the vast empire of China, one half of the human species is oppressed by the other.

The excess of oppression in those countries springs from the excess of love.

All Asia is covered with prisoners, where beauty in bondage awaits the caprices of a master. The multitude of women there assembled have no will, no inclinations but his. Their triumphs are only for a moment; and their rivalry, their hate, and their animosities continue till death. There the lovely sex are obliged to repay even their servitude with the most tender affections; or, what is still more mortifying, with the counterfeit of an affection, which they do not feel. There the most gloomy tyranny has subjected them to creatures, who, being of neither sex, are a dishonor to both. There, in short, their education tends only to debase them; their virtues are forced; their very pleasures are involuntary and joyless; and after an existence of a few years—till the bloom of youth is over—their period of neglect commences, which is long and dreadful. In the temperate latitude where the climates, giving less ardor to passion, leave more confidence in virtue, the women have not been deprived of their liberty, but a severe legislation has, at all times, kept them in a state of dependence. One while they are confined to their own apartments, and debarred at once from business and amusement; at other times, a tedious guardianship defrauded their hearts, and insulted their understandings. Affronted in one country by polygamy, which gives them their rivals for their inseparable companions; enslaved in another by indissoluble ties, which often join the gentle to the rude, and sensibility to brutality. Even in countries where they may be esteemed most happy, constrained in their desires in the disposal of their goods, robbed of freedom of will by the laws, the slaves of opinion, which rules them with absolute sway, and construes the slightest appearances into guilt; surrounded on all sides by judges, who are at once tyrants and their seducers, and who, after having prepared their faults, punish every lapse with dishonor—nay, usurp the right of degrading them on suspicion! Who does not feel for the tender sex? Yet such, I am sorry to say, is the lot of women over the whole earth. Man with regard to them in all climates, and in all ages, has been either an insensible husband or an oppressor; but they have sometimes experienced the cold and deliberate oppression of pride, and sometimes the violent and terrible tyranny of jealousy. When they are not beloved they are nothing; and, when they are, they are tormented. They have almost equal cause to be afraid of indifference and of love. Over three-quarters of the globe nature has placed them between contempt and misery.

"The melting desires, or the fiery passions," says Professor Ferguson, "which in one climate take place between the sexes, are, in another, changed into a sober consideration, or a patience of mutual disgust. This change is remarked in crossing the Mediterranean, in following the course of the Mississippi, in ascending the mountains of Caucasus, and in passing from the Alps and the Pyrenees to the shores of the Baltic.

"The burning ardors and torturing jealousies of the seraglio and harem, which have reigned so long in Asia and Africa, and which, in the southern parts of Europe, have scarcely given way to the differences of religion and civil establishments, are found, however, with an abatement of heat in the climate, to be more easily changed, in one latitude, into a temporary passion, which engrosses the mind without enfeebling it, and which excites to romantic achievements. By a farther progress to the north it is changed into a spirit of gallantry, which employs the wit and fancy more than the heart, which prefers intrigue to enjoyment, and substitutes affection and vanity where sentiment and desire have failed. As it departs from the sun, the same passion is further composed into a habit of domestic connection, or frozen into a state of insensibility, under which the sexes at freedom scarcely choose to unite their society."

Even among people where beauty received the highest homage we find men who would deprive the sex of every kind of reputation. "The most virtuous woman," says a celebrated Greek, "is she who is least talked of." That morose man, while he imposes duties upon women, would deprive them of the sweets of public esteem, and in exacting virtues from them, would make it a crime to aspire at honor.

If a woman were to defend the cause of her sex, she might address him in the following manner:

"How great is your injustice? If we have an equal right with you to virtue, why should we not have an equal right to praise? The public esteem ought to wait upon merit. Our duties are different from yours, but they are not therefore less difficult to fulfil, or of less consequence to society: They are the fountains of your felicity, and the sweetness of life. We are wives, and mothers. 'Tis we who form the union and the cordiality of families. 'Tis we who soften that savage rudeness which considers everything as due to force, and which would involve man with man in eternal war. We cultivate in you that humanity which makes you feel for the misfortunes of others, and our tears forewarn you of your own danger. Nay, you cannot be ignorant that we have need of courage not less than you. More feeble in ourselves, we have perhaps more trials to encounter. Nature assails us with sorrow, law and custom press us with constraint, and sensibility and virtue alarm us with their continual conflict. Sometimes also the name of citizen demands from us the tribute of fortitude. When you offer your blood to the State think that it is ours. In giving it our sons and our husbands we give more than ourselves. You can only die on the field of battle, but we have the misfortune to survive those whom we love most. Alas! while your ambitious vanity is unceasingly laboring to cover the earth with statues, with monuments, and with inscriptions to eternalize, if possible, your names, and give yourselves an existence, when this body is no more, why must we be condemned to live and to die unknown? Would that the grave and eternal forgetfulness should be our lot. Be not our tyrants in all. Permit our names to be sometimes pronounced beyond the narrow circle in which we live. Permit friendship, or at least love, to inscribe its emblem on the tomb where our ashes repose; and deny us not that public esteem which, after the esteem of one's self, is the sweetest reward of well doing."

All men, however, it must be owned, have not been equally unjust to their fair companions. In some countries public honors have been paid to women. Art has erected them monuments. Eloquence has celebrated their virtues, and history has collected whatever could adorn their character.

Mary Wollstonecraft

Mary Wollstonecraft (1759–1797), a passionate advocate of the equality of the sexes, has been called the first major feminist. Many of her ideas, such as equal education for the sexes and the opening of the professions to women, and her critique of marriage as a form of legal prostitution, were shocking to her contemporaries but have proved remarkably prophetic. In her major work, *A Vindication of the Rights of Woman* (1792), she assails a host of male authorities, asserting that "liberty is the mother of virtue" and that one can exercise one's duties only if one has basic human rights.

Wollstonecraft was the first daughter of an unsuccessful farmer and resented the concentration of the family's dwindling resources on its eldest son. At age sixteen she met Fanny Blood, a painter two years older who became a powerful influence and later died in childbirth in her arms. To support herself, her sisters, and Fanny, Wollstonecraft established a small school; in her first work, *Thoughts on the Education of Daughters* (1787), she followed John Locke in stressing the power of environment in education. She also counsels women to seek happiness through reason and self-discipline, the paramount theme in her later work.

Following her dismissal as governess in an aristocratic household, Wollstonecraft became involved in a radical periodical, reviewing fiction and books on education; through its publisher she met William Blake, Thomas Paine, and William Godwin. On July 14, 1789, the Bastille fell, and with it England plunged into controversy over the French Revolution, a tumult that produced England's best sociopolitical writing in 150 years. After the publication of Edmund Burke's vehement denunciation of the French Revolution in 1790, political alignments became sharper and modem categories of social thought began to emerge. Over fifty replies to Burke followed, including Paine's *The Rights of Man* and Codwin's *Political Justice*, but the first to answer was Wollstonecraft, with *A Vindication of the Rights of Man* (1790).

From Paine and the English Dissenters, Wollstonecraft borrowed arguments regarding natural rights, ridiculing Burke's support of monarchy and hereditary honors and unmasking his praise of tradition as an obfuscatory and sentimental defense of power. Her original contribution was to link his chivalrous rhetoric to men's habit of speaking down to women; Burke's appeal to natural feeling and common sense demanded emotional acceptance without reason, and, as Janet Todd has argued, "put the reader in the place of the woman as the object (as well as subject) of his sentimental rhetoric." Wollstonecraft presented herself as rational and impartial, as unaffected clarity against Burke's elegant wit, and as principle against his opportunism. She charged Burke with the hypocrisy of belittling women by idealizing them and using a mystifying rhetoric to demand respect for irrational power.

In *A Vindication of The Rights of Woman*, Wollstonecraft turns from political privilege to social oppression. She argues that the tyranny of kingship is linked with that of the aristocracy, military, and church, and especially with the patriarchal family. The heart of her argument is the importance of equal education. She sees social interaction among children as a gender-shaping force and proposes that boys and girls be educated together in a program of physical as well as mental activity. Her critique of society is deeper than that of any of her contemporaries except Rousseau. Society, she argues, cannot progress if half its members are kept backward, yet the problem is more intractable because of women's collusion in their own oppression. Women accept their outward powerlessness in society because they can use their sexual power to seduce men, an enterprise made easier if they also deceive themselves. The social construction of women as sentimental—possessing superior sensitivity and delicacy of feeling—helps them compensate for their practical weakness but renders them childish and amoral, better suited to the fantasy world of books than to the realities of marriage or relationships based on mutual respect. Men who value women not as rational beings but as objects of pleasure and amusement allow themselves to be manipulated, and therefore the prison of self-indulgence corrupts both sexes.

Thus, Wollstonecraft joins other republicans of her time in condemning idleness, luxury, and "living in the eyes of others," all aristocratic traits that effeminize men and render them unfit for self-rule. But she goes beyond her contemporaries to consider the effects on women as well, arguing that in both the family and public life women are made frivolous and irresponsible. Perceiving the social debasement that results from the emphasis on female sexuality, Wollstonecraft denies that sex is a prime mover in human life, that women "desire to be desired," or that motherhood is rooted in superior female tenderness and nurturance. She declares that women, with a bracing sense of self, may develop a sexuality that is open and nonseductive and a form of mothering that is adult and unresentful. In this spirit she also commends friendship as an alternative to sexual dependence—an emphasis that may strike us as puritanical, but that was perhaps sensible in her time, particularly in the absence of birth control. Despite shocking readers who found the book licentious, *The Rights of Woman* is filled with tributes to masculine rationality and advances a concept of human rights that is individualistic and ahistorical.

Following the uproar caused by this work, Wollstonecraft traveled to Paris, where she observed the French Revolution and wrote a justification on its behalf. She also met her first husband and conceived two children, but was so mistreated that she twice attempted suicide before leaving him and renewing her friendship with William Godwin. Godwin was at the height of his fame as a philosopher and reformer and proved a match for Wollstonecraft intellectually and politically. Their friendship was a collaboration of equals, and in 1797 they married, embodying her dictum that "marriage will never be held sacred till women, by being brought up with men, are prepared to be their companions rather than their mistresses."

While pregnant, Wollstonecraft wrote *Maria: or, The Wrongs of Women*, published posthumously in 1798, and in the summer of 1797, she gave birth to Mary Godwin, the author of *Frankenstein* and future wife of the poet Percy Bysshe Shelley. However, as a result of the placenta that remained in her for several days and then became gangrenous, Wollstonecraft herself did not survive the birth: a victim, it may be said, of the very constraints she spent her life denouncing.

A VINDICATION OF THE RIGHTS OF MAN

1790

[T]here are rights which men inherit at their birth, as rational creatures, who were raised above the brute creation by their improvable faculties; and that, in receiving these, not from their forefathers but, from God, prescription can never undermine natural rights.

A father may dissipate his property without his child having any right to complain;—but should he attempt to sell him for a slave, or fetter him with laws contrary to reason; nature, in enabling him to discern good from evil, teaches him to break the ignoble chain, and not to believe that bread becomes flesh, and wine blood, because his parents swallowed the Eucharist with this blind persuasion.

. . .

Fully sensible as you must be of the baneful consequences that inevitably follow this notorious infringement on the dearest rights of men, and that it is an infernal blot on the very face of our immaculate constitution, I cannot avoid expressing my surprise that when you recommended our form of government as a model, you did not caution the French against the arbitrary custom of pressing men for the sea service. You should have hinted to them, that property in England is much more secure than liberty, and not have concealed that the liberty of an honest mechanic—his all—is often sacrificed to secure the property of the rich. For it is a farce to pretend that a man fights *for his country, his hearth, or his altars*, when he has neither liberty nor property.—His property is in his nervous arms—and they are compelled to pull a strange rope at the surly command of a tyrannic boy, who probably obtained his rank on account of his family connections, or he prostituted vote of his father, whose interest in a borough, or voice as a senator, was acceptable to the minister.

Our penal laws punish with death the thief who steals a few pounds; but to take by violence, or trepan, a man, is no such heinous offence.—For who shall dare to complain of the venerable vestige of the law that rendered the life of a deer more sacred than that of a man? But it was the poor man with only his native dignity who was thus oppressed—and only metaphysical sophists and cold mathematicians can discern this insubstantial form; it is a work of abstraction—and a *gentleman* of lively imagination must borrow some drapery from fancy before he can love or pity a *man*. Misery, to reach your heart, I perceive, must have its cap and bells; your tears are reserved, very *naturally* considering your character, for the declamation of the theatre, or for the downfall of queens, whose rank alters the nature of folly, and throws a graceful veil over vices that degrade humanity; whilst the distress of many industrious mothers, whose *helpmates* have been torn from them, and the hungry cry of helpless babes, were vulgar sorrows that could not move your commiseration, though they might extort an alms. "The tears that are shed for fictitious sorrow are admirably adapted," says Rousseau, "to make us proud of all the virtues which we do not possess."

. . .

Man has been termed, with strict propriety, a microcosm, a little world in himself.—He is so;—yet must, however, be reckoned an ephemera, or, to adopt your figure of rhetoric, a summer's fly. The perpetuation of property in our families is one of the privileges you most warmly contend for; yet it would not be very difficult to prove that the mind must have a very limited range that thus confines its benevolence to such a narrow circle, which, with great propriety, may be included in the sordid calculations of blind self-love.

A brutal attachment to children has appeared most conspicuous in parents who have treated them like slaves, and demanded due homage for all the property they transferred to them, during their lives. It has led them to force their children to break the most sacred ties; to do violence to a natural impulse, and run into legal prostitution to increase wealth or shun poverty; and, still worse, the dread of parental malediction has made many weak characters violate truth in the face of Heaven; and, to avoid a father's angry curse, the most sacred promises have been broken. It appears to be a natural suggestion of reason, that a man should be freed from implicit obedience to parents and private punishments, when he is of an age to be subject to the jurisdiction of the laws of his country; and that the barbarous cruelty of allowing parents to imprison their children, to prevent their contaminating their noble blood by following the dictates of nature when they chose to marry, or for any misdemeanor that does not come under the cognizance of public justice, is one of the most arbitrary violations of liberty.

Who can recount all the unnatural crimes which the *laudable, interesting* desire of perpetuating a name has produced? The younger children have been sacrificed to the eldest son; sent into exile, or confined in convents, that they might not encroach on what was called, with shameful falsehood, the *family* estate. Will Mr Burke call this parental affection reasonable or virtuous?—No; it is the spurious offspring of over-weening, mistaken pride—and not that first source of civilization, natural parental affection, that makes no difference between child and child, but what reason justifies by pointing out superior merit.

Another pernicious consequence which unavoidably arises from this artificial affection is, the insuperable bar which it puts in the way of early marriages. It would be difficult to determine whether the minds or bodies of our youth are most injured by this impediment. Our young men become selfish coxcombs, and gallantry with modest women, and intrigues with those of another description, weaken both mind and body, before either has arrived at maturity. The character of a master of a family, a husband, and a father, forms the citizen imperceptibly, by producing a sober manliness of thought, and orderly behaviour; but, from the lax morals and depraved affections of the libertine, what results?—a finical man of taste, who is only anxious to secure his own private gratifications, and to maintain his rank in society.

The same system has an equally pernicious effect on female morals.—Girls are sacrificed to family convenience, or else marry to settle themselves in a superior rank, and coquet, without restraint, with the fine gentleman whom I have already described. And to such lengths has this vanity, this desire of shining, carried them, that it is not now necessary to guard girls against imprudent love matches; for if some widows did not now and then *fall* in love, Love and Hymen would seldom meet, unless at a village church.

I do not intend to be sarcastically paradoxical when I say, that women of fashion take husbands that they may have it in their power to coquet, the grand business of genteel life, with a number of admirers, and thus flutter the spring of life away, without laying up any store for the winter of age, or being of any use to society. Affection in the marriage state can only be founded on respect—and are these weak beings respectable? Children are neglected for lovers, and we express surprise that adulteries are so common! A woman never forgets to adorn herself to make an impression on the senses of the other sex, and to extort the homage which it is gallant to pay, and yet we wonder that they have such confined understandings.

Have ye not heard that we cannot serve two masters? an immoderate desire to please contracts the faculties, and immerges, to borrow the idea of a great philosopher, the soul in matter, till it becomes unable to mount on the wing of contemplation.

It would be an arduous task to trace all the vice and misery that arise in society from the middle class of people apeing the manners of the great. All are aiming to procure respect on account of their property; and most places are considered as sinecures that enable men to start into notice. The grand concern of three parts out of four is to contrive to live above their equals, and to appear to be richer than they are. How much domestic comfort and private satisfaction is sacrificed to this irrational ambition! It is a destructive mildew that blights the fairest virtues; benevolence, friendship, generosity, and all those endearing charities which bind human hearts together, and the pursuits which raise the mind to higher contemplations, all that were not cankered in the bud by the false notions that "grew with its growth and strengthened with its strength," are crushed by the iron hand of property!

Property, I do not scruple to aver it, should be fluctuating, which would be the case, if it were more equally divided amongst all the children of a family; else it is an everlasting rampart, in consequence of a barbarous feudal institution, that enables the elder son to overpower talents and depress virtue.

Besides, an unmanly servility, most inimical to true dignity of character is, by this means, fostered in society. Men of some abilities play on the follies of the rich, and mounting to fortune as they degrade themselves, they stand in the way of men of superior talents, who cannot advance in such crooked paths, or wade through the filth which *parasites* never boggle at. Pursuing their way straight forward, their spirit is either bent or broken by the rich man's contumelies, or the difficulties they have to encounter.

The only security of property that nature authorizes and reason sanctions is, the right a man has to enjoy the acquisitions which his talents and industry have acquired; and to bequeath them to whom he chooses. Happy would it be for the world if there were no other road to wealth or honour; if pride, in the shape of parental affection, did not absorb the man, and prevent friendship from having the same weight as relationship. Luxury and effeminacy would not then introduce so much idiotism into the noble families which form one of the pillars of our state: the ground would not lie fallow, nor would undirected activity of mind spread the contagion of restless idleness, and its concomitant, vice, through the whole mass of society.

. . .

In what respect are we superior to the brute creation, if intellect is not allowed to be the guide of passion? Brutes hope and fear, love and hate; but, without a capacity to improve, a power of turning these passions to good or evil, they neither acquire virtue nor wisdom.—Why? Because the Creator has not given them reason.

But the cultivation of reason is an arduous task, and men of lively fancy, finding it easier to follow the impulse of passion, endeavour to persuade themselves and others that it is most *natural*. And happy is it for those, who indolently let that heaven-lighted spark rest like the ancient lamps in sepulchres, that some virtuous habits, with which the reason of others shackled them, supplies its place.—Affection for parents, reverence for superiors or antiquity, notions of honour, or that worldly self-interest that shrewdly shews them that honesty is the best policy: all proceed from the reason for which they serve as substitutes;—but it is reason at second-hand.

Children are born ignorant, consequently innocent; the passions, are neither good nor evil dispositions, till they receive a direction, and either bound over the feeble barrier raised by a faint glimmering of unexercised reason, called conscience, or strengthen her wavering dictates till sound principles are deeply rooted, and able to cope with the headstrong passions that often assume her awful form. What moral purpose can be answered by extolling good dispositions, as they are called, when these good dispositions are described as instincts: for instinct moves in a direct line to its ultimate end, and asks not for guide or support. But if virtue is to be acquired by experience, or taught by example, reason, perfected by reflection, must be the director of the whole host of passions, which produce a fructifying heat, but no light, that you would exalt into her place.—She must hold the rudder, or, let the wind blow which way it list, the vessel will never advance smoothly to its destined port; for the time lost in tacking about would dreadfully impede its progress.

. . .

What salutary dews might not be shed to refresh this thirsty land, if men were more *enlightened!* Smiles and premiums might encourage cleanliness, industry, and emulation.—A garden more inviting than Eden would then meet the eye, and springs of joy murmur on every side. The clergyman would superintend his own flock, the shepherd would then love the sheep he daily tended; the school might rear its decent head, and the buzzing tribe, let loose to play, impart a portion of their vivacious spirits to the heart that longed to open their minds, and lead them to taste the pleasures of men. Domestic comfort, the civilizing relations of husband, brother, and father, would soften labour, and render life contented.

Returning once from a despotic country to a part of England well cultivated, but not very picturesque—with what delight did I not observe the poor man's garden!—The homely palings and twining woodbine, with all the rustic contrivances of simple, unlettered taste, was a sight which relieved the eye that had wandered indignant from the stately palace to the pestiferous hovel, and turned from the awful contrast into itself to mourn the fate of man, and curse the arts of civilization!

Why cannot large estates be divided into small farms? these dwellings would indeed grace our land. Why are huge forests still allowed to stretch out with idle pomp and all the indolence of Eastern grandeur? Why does the brown waste meet the traveller's view, when men want work? But commons cannot be enclosed without *acts of parliament* to increase the property of the rich! Why might not the industrious peasant be allowed to steal a farm from the heath? This sight I have seen;—the cow that supported the children grazed near the hut, and the cheerful poultry were fed by the chubby babes, who breathed a bracing air, far from the diseases and the vices of cities. Domination blasts all these prospects; virtue can only flourish amongst equals, and the man who submits to a fellow-creature, because it promotes his worldly interest, and he who relieves only because it is his duty to lay up a treasure in heaven, are much on a par, for both are radically degraded by the habits of their life.

In this great city, that proudly rears its head, and boasts of its population and commerce, how much misery lurks in pestilential corners, whilst idle mendicants assail, on every side, the man who hates to encourage impostors, or repress, with angry frown, the plaints of the poor! How many mechanics, by a flux of trade or fashion, lose their employment; whom misfortunes, not to be warded off, lead to the idleness that vitiates their character and renders them afterwards averse to honest labour! Where is the eye that marks these evils, more gigantic than any of the infringements of property, which you piously deprecate? Are these remediless evils? And is the humane heart satisfied with turning the poor over to *another* world, to receive the blessings this could afford? If society was regulated on a more enlarged plan; if man was contented to be the friend of man, and did not seek to bury the sympathies of humanity in the servile appellation of master; if, turning his eyes from ideal regions of taste and elegance, he laboured to give the earth he inhabited all the beauty it is capable of receiving, and was ever on the watch to shed abroad all the happiness which human nature can enjoy;—he who, respecting the rights of men, wishes to convince or persuade society that this is true happiness and dignity, is not the cruel *oppressor* of the poor, nor a short-sighted philosopher—HE fears God and loves his fellow-creatures.—Behold the whole duty of man!—the citizen who acts differently is a sophisticated being.

Surveying civilized life, and seeing, with undazzled eye, the polished vices of the rich, their insincerity, want of natural affections, with all the specious train that luxury introduces, I have turned impatiently to the poor, to look for man undebauched by riches or power—but, alas! what did I see? a being scarcely above the brutes, over which he tyrannized; a broken spirit, worn-out body, and all those gross vices which the example of the rich, rudely copied, could produce. Envy built a wall of separation, that made the poor hate, whilst they bent to their superiors; who, on their part, stepped aside to avoid the loathsome sight of human misery.

What were the outrages of a day to these continual miseries? Let those sorrows hide their diminished head before the tremendous mountain of woe that thus defaces our globe! Man preys on man; and you mourn for the idle tapestry that decorated a gothic pile, and the dronish bell that summoned the fat priest to prayer. You mourn for the empty pageant of a name, when slavery flaps her wing, and the sick heart retires to die in lonely wilds, far from the abodes of men. Did the pangs you felt for insulted nobility, the anguish that rent your heart when the gorgeous robes were torn off the idol human weakness had set up, deserve to be compared with the long-drawn sigh of melancholy reflection, when misery and vice are thus seen to haunt our steps, and swim on the top of every cheering prospect? Why is our fancy to be appalled by terrific perspectives of a hell beyond the grave?—Hell stalks abroad;—the lash resounds on the slave's naked sides; and the sick wretch, who can no longer earn the sour bread of unremitting labour, steals to a ditch to bid the world a long good night—or, neglected in some ostentatious hospital, breathes his last amidst the laugh of mercenary attendants.

. . .

A VINDICATION OF THE RIGHTS OF WOMAN

1792

INTRODUCTION

After considering the historic page, and viewing the living world with anxious solicitude, the most melancholy emotions of sorrowful indignation have depressed my spirits, and I have sighed when obliged to confess, that either nature has made a great difference between man and man, or that the civilization which has hitherto taken place in the world has been very partial. I have turned over various books written on the subject of education, and patiently observed the conduct of parents and the management of schools; but what has been the result?—a profound conviction that the neglected education of my fellow-creatures is the grand source of the misery I deplore; and that women, in particular, are rendered weak and wretched by a variety of concurring causes, originating from one hasty conclusion. The conduct and manners of women, in fact, evidently prove that their minds are not in a healthy state; for, like the flowers which are planted in too rich a soil, strength and usefulness are sacrificed to beauty; and the flaunting leaves, after having pleased a fastidious eye, fade, disregarded on the stalk, long before the season when they ought to have arrived at maturity.—One cause of this barren blooming I attribute to a false system of education, gathered from the books written on this subject by men who, considering females rather as women than human creatures, have been more anxious to make them alluring mistresses than affectionate wives and rational mothers; and the understanding of the sex has been so bubbled by this specious homage, that the civilized women of the present century, with a few exceptions, are only anxious to inspire love, when they ought to cherish a nobler ambition, and by their abilities and virtues exact respect.

In a treatise, therefore, on female rights and manners, the works which have been particularly written for their improvement must not be overlooked; especially when it is asserted, in direct terms, that the minds of women are enfeebled by false refinement; that the books of instruction, written by men of genius, have had the same tendency as more frivolous productions; and that, in the true style of Mahometanism, they are treated as a kind of subordinate beings, and not as a part of the human species, when improveable reason is allowed to be the dignified distinction which raises men above the brute creation, and puts a natural sceptre in a feeble hand.

Yet, because I am a woman, I would not lead my readers to suppose that I mean violently to agitate the contested question respecting the equality or inferiority of the sex; but as the subject lies in my way, and I cannot pass it over without subjecting the main tendency of my reasoning to misconstruction, I shall stop a moment to deliver, in a few words, my opinion.—In the government of the physical world it is observable that the female in point of strength is, in general, inferior to the male. This is the law of nature; and it does not appear to be suspended or abrogated in favour of woman. A degree of physical superiority cannot, therefore, be denied—and it is a noble prerogative! But not content with this natural pre-eminence, men endeavour to sink us still lower, merely to render us alluring objects for a moment; and women, intoxicated by the adoration which men, under the influence of their senses, pay them, do not seek to obtain a durable interest in their hearts, or to become the friends of the fellow creatures who find amusement in their society.

I am aware of an obvious inference:—from every quarter have I heard exclamations against masculine women; but where are they to be found? If by this appellation men mean to inveigh against their ardour in hunting, shooting, and gaining, I shall most cordially join in the cry; but if it be against the imitation of manly virtues, or, more properly speaking, the attainment of those talents and virtues, the exercise of which ennobles the human character, and which raise females in the scale of animal being, when they are comprehensively termed mankind;—all those who view them with a philosophic eye must, I should think, wish with me, that they may every day grow more and more masculine.

This discussion naturally divides the subject. I shall first consider women in the grand light of human creatures, who, in common with men, are placed on this earth to unfold their faculties; and afterwards I shall more particularly point out their peculiar designation.

I wish also to steer clear of an error which many respectable writers have fallen into; for the instruction which has hitherto been addressed to women, has rather been applicable to *ladies*, if the little indirect advice, that is scattered through Sandford and Merton, be excepted; but, addressing my sex in a firmer tone, I pay particular attention to those in the middle class, because they appear to be in the most natural state. Perhaps the seeds of false-refinement, immorality, and vanity, have ever been shed by the great. Weak, artificial beings, raised above the common wants and affections of their race, in a premature unnatural manner, undermine the very foundation of virtue, and spread corruption through the whole mass of society! As a class of mankind they have the strongest claim to pity; the education of the rich tends to render them vain and helpless, and the unfolding mind is not strengthened by the practice of those duties which dignify the human character.—They only live to amuse themselves, and by the same law which in nature invariably produces certain effects, they soon only afford barren amusement.

But as I purpose taking a separate view of the different ranks of society, and of the moral character of women, in each, this hint is, for the present, sufficient; and I have only alluded to the subject, because it appears to me to be the very essence of an introduction to give a cursory account of the contents of the work it introduces.

My own sex, I hope, will excuse me, if I treat them like rational creatures, instead of flattering their *fascinating* graces, and viewing them as if they were in a state of perpetual childhood, unable to stand alone. I earnestly wish to point out in what true dignity and human happiness consists—I wish to persuade women to endeavour to acquire strength, both of mind and body, and to convince them that the soft phrases, susceptibility of heart, delicacy of sentiment, and refinement of taste, are almost synonymous with epithets of weakness, and that those beings who are only the objects of pity and that kind of love, which has been termed its sister, will soon become objects of contempt.

Dismissing then those pretty feminine phrases, which the men condescendingly use to soften our slavish dependence, and despising that weak elegancy of mind, exquisite sensibility, and sweet docility of manners, supposed to be the sexual characteristics of the weaker vessel, I wish to shew that elegance is inferior to virtue, that the first object of laudable ambition is to obtain a character as a human being, regardless of the distinction of sex; and that secondary views should be brought to this simple touchstone.

This is a rough sketch of my plan; and should I express my conviction with the energetic emotions that I feel whenever I think of the subject, the dictates of experience and reflection will be felt by some of my readers. Animated by this important object, I shall disdain to cull my phrases or polish my style;—I aim at being useful, and sincerity will render me unaffected; for, wishing rather to persuade by the force of my arguments, than dazzle by the elegance of my language, I shall not waste my time in rounding periods, or in fabricating the turgid bombast of artificial feelings, which, coming from the head, never reach the heart.—I shall be employed about things, not words!—and, anxious to render my sex more respectable members of society, I shall try to avoid that flowery diction which has slided from essays into novels, and from novels into familiar letters and conversation.

These pretty superlatives, dropping glibly from the tongue, vitiate the taste, and create a kind of sickly delicacy that turns away from simple unadorned truth; and a deluge of false sentiments and over-stretched feelings, stifling the natural emotions of the heart, render the domestic pleasures insipid, that ought to sweeten the exercise of those severe duties, which educate a rational and immortal being for a nobler field of action.

The education of women has, of late, been more attended to than formerly; yet they are still reckoned a frivolous sex, and ridiculed or pitied by the writers who endeavour by satire or instruction to improve them. It is acknowledged that they spend many of the first years of their lives in acquiring a smattering of accomplishments; meanwhile strength of body and mind are sacrificed to libertine notions of beauty, to the desire of establishing themselves,—the only way women can rise in the world,—by marriage. And this desire making mere animals of them, when they marry they act as such children may be expected to act:—they dress; they paint, and nickname God's creatures.—Surely these weak beings are only fit for a seraglio!—Can they be expected to govern a family with judgement, or take care of the poor babes whom they bring into the world?

If then it can be fairly deduced from the present conduct of the sex, from the prevalent fondness for pleasure which takes place of ambition and those nobler passions that open and enlarge the soul; that the instruction which women have hitherto received has only tended, with the constitution of civil society, to render them insignificant objects of desire —mere propagators of fools!—if it can be proved that in aiming to accomplish them, without cultivating their understandings, they are taken out of their sphere of duties, and made ridiculous and useless when the short-lived bloom of beauty is over. I presume that *rational* men will excuse me for endeavouring to persuade them to become more masculine and respectable.

Indeed the word masculine is only a bugbear: there is little reason to fear that women will acquire too much courage or fortitude; for their apparent inferiority with respect to bodily strength, must render them, in some degree, dependent on men in the various relations of life; but why should it be increased by prejudices that give a sex to virtue, and confound simple truths with sensual reveries?

Women are, in fact, so much degraded by mistaken notions of female excellence, that I do not mean to add a paradox when I assert, that this artificial weakness produces a propensity to tyrannize, and gives birth to cunning, the natural opponent of strength, which leads them to play off those contemptible infantine airs that undermine esteem even whilst they excite desire. Let men become more chaste and modest, and if women do not grow wiser in the same ratio, it will be clear that they have weaker understandings. It seems scarcely necessary to say, that I now speak of the sex in general. Many individuals have more sense than their male relatives; and, as nothing preponderates where there is a constant struggle for an equilibrium, without it has naturally more gravity, some women govern their husbands without degrading themselves, because intellect will always govern.

II THE PREVAILING OPINION OF A SEXUAL CHARACTER DISCUSSED

To account for, and excuse the tyranny of man, many ingenious arguments have been brought forward to prove, that the two sexes, in the acquirement of virtue, ought to aim at attaining a very different character: or, to speak explicity, women are not allowed to have sufficient strength of mind to acquire what really deserves the name of virtue. Yet it should seem, allowing them to have souls, that there is but one way appointed by Providence to lead *mankind* to either virtue or happiness.

If then women are not a swarm of ephemeron triflers, why should they be kept in ignorance under the specious name of innocence? Men complain, and with reason, of the follies and caprices of our sex, when they do not keenly satirize our headstrong passions and groveling vices.—Behold, I should answer, the natural effect of ignorance! The mind will ever be unstable that has only prejudices to rest on, and the current will run with destructive fury when there are no barriers to break its force. Women are told from their infancy, and taught by the example of their mothers, that a little knowledge of human weakness, justly termed cunning, softness of temper, *outward* obedience, and a scrupulous attention to a puerile kind of propriety, will obtain for them the protection of man; and should they be beautiful, every thing else is needless, for, at least, twenty years of their lives.

. . .

. . . The most perfect education, in my opinion, is such an exercise of the understanding as is best calculated to strengthen the body and form the heart. Or, in other words, to enable the individual to attain such habits of virtue as will render it independent. In fact, it is a farce to call any being virtuous whose virtues do not result from the exercise of its own reason. This was Rousseau's opinion respecting men: I extend it to women, and confidently assert that they have been drawn out of their sphere by false refinement, and not by an endeavour to acquire masculine qualities. Still the regal homage which they receive is so intoxicating, that till the manners of the times are changed, and formed on more reasonable principles, it may be impossible to convince them that the illegitimate power, which they obtain, by degrading themselves, is a curse, and that they must return to nature and equality, if they wish to secure the placid satisfaction that unsophisticated affections impart. But for this epoch we must wait—wait, perhaps, till kings and nobles, enlightened by reason, and, preferring the real dignity of man to childish state, throw off their gaudy hereditary trappings; and if then women do not resign the arbitrary power of beauty—they will prove that they have *less* mind than man.

I may be accused of arrogance; still I must declare what I firmly believe, that all the writers who have written on the subject of female education and manners from Rousseau to Dr. Gregory, have contributed to render women more artificial, weak characters, than they would otherwise have been; and, consequently, more useless members of society. I might have expressed this conviction in a lower key; but I am afraid it would have been the whine of affectation, and not the faithful expression of my feelings, of the clear result, which experience and reflection have led me to draw. When I come to that division of the subject, I shall advert to the passages that I more particularly disapprove of, in the works of the authors I have just alluded to; but it is first necessary to observe, that my objection extends to the whole purport of those books, which tend, in my opinion, to degrade one half of the human species, and render women pleasing at the expense of every solid virtue.

Though, to reason on Rousseau's ground, if man did attain a degree of perfection of mind when his body arrived at maturity, it might be proper, in order to make a man and his wife *one*, that she should rely entirely on his understanding; and the graceful ivy, clasping the oak that supported it, would form a whole in which strength and beauty would be equally conspicuous. But, alas! husbands, as well as their helpmates, are often only overgrown children; nay, thanks to early debauchery, scarcely men in their outward form—and if the blind lead the blind, one need not come from heaven to tell us the consequence.

Many are the causes that, in the present corrupt state of society, contribute to enslave women by cramping their understandings and sharpening their senses. One, perhaps, that silently does more mischief than all the rest, is their disregard of order.

To do every thing in an orderly manner, is a most important precept, which women, who, generally speaking, receive only a disorderly kind of education, seldom attend to with that degree of exactness that men, who from their infancy are broken into method, observe. This negligent kind of guess-work, for what other epithet can be used to point out the random exertions of a sort of instinctive common sense, never brought to the test of reason? prevents their generalizing matters of fact—so they do to-day, what they did yesterday, merely because they did it yesterday.

This contempt of the understanding in early life has more baneful consequences than is commonly supposed; for the little knowledge which women of strong minds attain, is, from various circumstances, of a more desultory kind than the knowledge of men, and it is acquired more by sheer observations on real life, than from comparing what has been individually observed with the results of experience generalized by speculation. Led by their dependent situation and domestic employments more into society, what they learn is rather by snatches; and as learning is with them, in general, only a secondary thing, they do not pursue any one branch with that persevering ardour necessary to give vigour to the faculties, and clearness to the judgment. In the present state of society, a little learning is required to support the character of a gentleman; and boys are obliged to submit to a few years of discipline. But in the education of women, the cultivation of the understanding is always subordinate to the acquirement of some corporeal accomplishment; even while enervated by confinement and false notions of modesty, the body is prevented from attaining that grace and beauty which relaxed half-formed limbs never exhibit. Besides, in youth their faculties are not brought forward by emulation; and having no serious scientific study, if they have natural sagacity it is turned too soon on life and manners. They dwell on effects, and modifications, without tracing them back to causes; and complicated rules to adjust behaviour are a weak substitute for simple principles.

. . .

I shall be told that woman would then lose many of her peculiar graces, and the opinion of a well known poet might be quoted to refute my unqualified assertion. For Pope has said, in the name of the whole male sex,

> Yet ne'er so sure our passion to create,
> As when she touch'd the brink of all we hate.

In what light this sally places men and women, I shall leave to the judicious to determine; meanwhile I shall content myself with observing, that I cannot discover why, unless they are mortal, females should always be degraded by being made subservient to love or lust.

To speak disrespectfully of love is, I know, high treason against sentiment and fine feelings; but I wish to speak the simple language of truth, and rather to address the head than the heart. To endeavour to reason love out of the world, would be to out Quixote Cervantes, and equally offend against common sense; but an endeavour to restrain this tumultuous passion, and to prove that it should not be allowed to dethrone superior powers, or to usurp the sceptre which the understanding should ever coolly wield, appears less wild.

Youth is the season for love in both sexes; but in those days of thoughtless enjoyment provision should be made for the more important years of life, when reflection takes place of sensation. But Rousseau, and most of the male writers who have followed his steps, have warmly inculcated that the whole tendency of female education ought to be directed to one point:—to render them pleasing.

Let me reason with the supporters of this opinion who have any knowledge of human nature, do they imagine that marriage can eradicate the habitude of life? The woman who has only been taught to please will soon find that her charms are oblique sunbeams, and that they cannot have much effect on her husband's heart when they are seen every day, when the summer is passed and gone. Will she then have sufficient native energy to look into herself for comfort, and cultivate her dormant faculties? or, is it not more rational to expect that she will try to please other men; and, in the emotions raised by the expectation of new conquests, endeavour to forget the mortification her love or pride has received? When the husband ceases to be a lover—and the time will inevitably come, her desire of pleasing will then grow languid, or become a spring of bitterness; and love, perhaps, the most evanescent of all passions, gives place to jealously or vanity.

I now speak of women who are restrained by principle or prejudice; such women, though they would shrink from an intrigue with real abhorrence, yet, nevertheless, wish to be convinced by the homage of gallantry that they are cruelly neglected by their husbands; or, days and weeks are spent in dreaming of the happiness enjoyed by congenial souls, till their health is undermined and their spirits broken by discontent. How then can the great art of pleasing be such a necessary study? it is only useful to a mistress; the chaste wife, and serious mother, should only consider her power to please as the polish of her virtues, and the affection of her husband as one of the comforts that render her task less difficult and her life happier.—But, whether she be loved or neglected, her first wish should be to make herself respectable, and not to rely for all her happiness on a being subject to like infirmities with herself.

To recommend gentleness, indeed, on a broad basis is strictly philosophical. A frail being should labour to be gentle. But when forbearance confounds right and wrong, it ceases to be a virtue; and, however convenient it may be found in a companion—that companion will ever be considered as an inferior, and only inspire a vapid tenderness, which easily degenerates into contempt. Still, if advice could really make a being gentle, whose natural disposition admitted not of such a fine polish, something towards the advancement of order would be attained; but if, as might quickly be demonstrated, only affectation be produced by this indiscriminate counsel, which throws a stumbling-block in the way of gradual improvement, and true melioration of temper, the sex is not much benefited by sacrificing solid virtues to the attainment of superficial graces, though for a few years they may procure the individuals regal sway.

As a philosopher, I read with indignation the plausible epithets which men use to soften their insults; and, as a moralist, I ask what is meant by such heterogeneous associations, as fair defects, amiable weaknesses, &c.? If there be but one criterion of morals, but one archetype for man, women appear to be suspended by destiny, according to the vulgar tale of Mahomet's coffin; they have neither the unerring instinct of brutes, nor are allowed to fix the eye of reason on a perfect model. They were made to be loved, and must not aim at respect, lest they should be hunted out of society as masculine.

But to view the subject in another point of view. Do passive indolent women make the best wives? Confining our discussion to the present moment of existence, let us see how such weak creatures perform their part. Do the women who, by the attainment of a few superficial accomplishments, have strengthened the prevailing prejudice, merely contribute to the happiness of their husbands? Do they display their charms merely to amuse them? And have women, who have early imbibed notions of passive obedience, sufficient character to manage a family or educate children? So far from it, that, after surveying the history of women, I cannot help, agreeing with the severest satirist, considering the sex as the weakest as well as the most oppressed half of the species. What does history disclose but marks of inferiority, and how few women have emancipated themselves from the galling yoke of sovereign man?—So few, that the exceptions remind me of an ingenious conjecture respecting Newton: that he was probably a being of a superior order, accidentally caged in a human body. Following the same train of thinking, I have been led to imagine that the few extraordinary women who have rushed in eccentrical directions out of the orbit prescribed to their sex, were *male* spirits, confined by mistake in female frames. But if it be not philosophical to think of sex when the soul is mentioned, the inferiority must depend on the organs; or the heavenly fire, which is to ferment the clay, is not given in equal portions.

But avoiding, as I have hitherto done, any direct comparison of the two sexes collectively, or frankly acknowledging the inferiority of woman, according to the present appearance of things, I shall only insist that men have increased that inferiority till women are almost sunk below the standard of rational creatures. Let their faculties have room to unfold, and their virtues to gain strength, and then determine where the whole sex must stand in the intellectual scale. Yet let it be remembered, that for a small number of distinguished women I do not ask a place.

. . .

JOHN STUART MILL

John Stuart Mill (1806–1873), the British philosopher and economist, is known for his writings on logic, utilitarianism, and political theory, and was perhaps the most prominent social reformer in nineteenth-century England. More than other figures in the Anglo-American tradition, Mill made overtures to rival currents of thought. His mature philosophy is an uneasy synthesis of utilitarianism with romantic, socialist, and feminist ideas.

His father was James Mill, a close friend of the reformer Jeremy Bentham and the economist David Ricardo, and leader of the philosophical radicals of early nineteenth-century England. James Mill subjected his eldest son to a notoriously rigid education designed to carry Bentham's crusade for utilitarianism into the next generation. John Stuart Mill began Greek at age three; Latin, arithmetic, and geometry at eight; logic at twelve; and political economy at thirteen. From his earliest years he discussed the issues on walks with his father and with Bentham himself, and at seventeen was debating in the Utilitarian Society, as well as writing articles for the *Westminster Review*.

Mill read law with the jurist John Austin and considered entering Cambridge. But the "Oxbridge" universities were no more palatable to radicals than was the Church of England itself. In 1823 he entered as a clerk in the India House and for over twenty years had charge of the East India Company's relation with the Indian states. He remained there until the India House was closed in 1858.

At age twenty, however, as he describes in his *Autobiography*, Mill found himself asking, "Suppose that all your objects in life were realized; that all the changes in institutions and opinions which you are looking forward to, could be completely effected at this very instant: would this be a great joy to you?" To this question Mill was forced to answer " 'No!' At this my heart sank within me: the whole foundation on which my life was constructed fell down." Mill was saved from his depression by his discovery of beauty, art, and nature, symbolized for him by William Wordsworth's *Miscellaneous Poems* (1815), which he thought the "very culture of the feelings." Breaking from his father, he began to work out a "new utilitarianism" in which feeling was to be "at least as valuable as thought, and Poetry not only on a par with, but the necessary condition of, any true and comprehensive Philosophy." In the next several years, he associated with Saint-Simonian leaders, read Samuel Taylor Coleridge and the Romantics, and initiated a lifelong correspondence with Thomas Carlyle. He also read Tocqueville and the French historians, who persuaded him of the shortcomings in his father's "abstract and unhistorical" political science. By the time of his first major book, *System of Logic* (1843), Mill had accepted poetry and history into his thought. To reconcile them with his father's scientific rigor and thus produce a genuine theory of society was to be the aim of all his future work.

In 1830 Mill met Harriet Taylor, the wife of a London merchant, with whom he carried on a celebrated friendship and married in 1851 after the death of her husband. Taylor not only gave him the sympathy and support he craved but influenced his ideals of life for the individual and society and directly inspired several works, notably *The Subjection of Women* (1869). Her death seven years after they married was a heavy blow to him, and Mill was forced to complete in solitude works they had enthusiastically planned together.

During the 1830s Mill contributed essays to the literary reviews and edited the *London and Westminster Review*. His twin essays on Bentham and Coleridge are perhaps the finest he wrote and show his extraordinary openness to alien forms of thought that he believed might enrich English social philosophy. In these years he also wrote his great systematic works on logic and political economy. The final version of *Principles of Political Economy* (1848) distinguished between the laws of production of wealth—which, following Adam Smith and David Ricardo, Mill understood to be "laws of nature"—and forms of distribution, which he held to be "subject to human will." Mill did not come to a socialist conclusion, but he did level the most severe criticism to date of the consequences of private property and the free market, made from within the "dismal science" of modern economics.

During the seven years of his marriage, Mill became increasingly occupied with the work of the East India Company and published less than at any other period in his life. His retirement in 1858 was followed almost immediately by Harriet Taylor's death, and he withdrew to the south of France, where "as a recluse who reads newspapers" he composed *On Liberty* (1859), *Considerations on Representative Government* (1861), and *Utilitarianism* (1863), works that comprise his mature philosophy. At the same time, he did not abstain from politics. He enlisted his energies in support of the North in the American Civil War, and in 1865 was elected to Parliament, where he took an active part in debates on the Reform bills of 1866–1867, the reform of land tenure in Ireland, and the representation of women. His reforming energies made him unpopular with moderates, however, and he was defeated for reelection in 1868. He died at Avignon on May 8, 1873.

ON LIBERTY

1859

I INTRODUCTORY

. . .

The object of this Essay is to assert one very simple principle, as entitled to govern absolutely the dealings of society with the individual in the way of compulsion and control, whether the means used be physical force in the form of legal penalties, or the moral coercion of public opinion. That principle is, that the sole end for which mankind are warranted individually or collectively, in interfering with the liberty of action of any of their number, is self-protection. That the only purpose for which power can be rightfully exercised over any member of a civilised community, against his will, is to prevent harm to others. His own good, either physical or moral, is not a sufficient warrant. He cannot rightfully be compelled to do or forbear because it will be better for him to do so, because it will make him happier, because, in the opinions of others, to do so would be wise, or even right. These are good reasons for remonstrating with him, or reasoning with him, or persuading him, or entreating him, but not for compelling him, or visiting him with any evil in case he do otherwise. To justify that, the conduct from which it is desired to deter him must be calculated to produce evil to some one else. The only part of the conduct of any one, for which he is amenable to society, is that which concerns others. In the part which merely concerns himself, his independence is, of right, absolute. Over himself, over his own body and mind, the individual is sovereign.

. . .

It is proper to state that I forego any advantage which could be derived to my argument from the idea of abstract right, as a thing independent of utility. I regard utility as the ultimate appeal on all ethical questions; but it must be utility in the largest sense, grounded on the permanent interests of man as a progressive being. Those interests, I contend, authorise the subjection of individual spontaneity to external control, only in respect to those actions of each, which concern the interest of other people. If any one does an act hurtful to others, there is a *prima facie* case for punishing him, by law, or, where legal penalties are not safely applicable, by general disapprobation. There are also many positive acts for the benefit of others, which he may rightfully be compelled to perform such as to give evidence in a court of justice; to bear his fair share in the common defence, or in any other joint work necessary to the interest of the society of which be enjoys the protection; and to perform certain acts of individual beneficence, such as saving a fellow-creature's life, or interposing to protect the defenceless against ill-usage, things which whenever it is obviously a man's duty to do, he may rightfully be made responsible to society for not doing. A person may cause evil to others not only by his actions but by his inaction, and in either case he is justly accountable to them for the injury. The latter case, it is true, requires a much more cautious exercise of compulsion than the former. To make any one answerable for doing evil to others is the rule; to make him answerable for not preventing evil is, comparatively speaking, the exception. Yet there are many cases clear enough and grave enough to justify that exception. In all things which regard the external relations of the individual, he is de jure amenable to those whose interests are concerned, and, if need be, to society as their protector. There are often good reasons for not holding him to the responsibility; but these reasons must arise from the special expediencies of the case: either because it is a kind of case in which he is on the whole likely to act better, when left to his own discretion, than when controlled in any way in which society have it in their power to control him; or because the attempt to exercise control would produce other evils, greater than those which it would prevent. When such reasons as these preclude the enforcement of responsibility, the conscience of the agent himself should step into the vacant judgement seat, and protect those interests of others which have no external protection; judging himself all the more rigidly, because the case does not admit of his being made accountable to the judgment of his fellow-creatures.

But there is a sphere of action in which society, as distinguished from the individual, has, if any, only an indirect interest; comprehending all that portion of a person's life and conduct which affects only himself, or if it also affects others, only with their free, voluntary, and undeceived consent and participation. When I say only himself, I mean directly, and in the first instance; for whatever affects himself, may affect others through himself; and the objection which may be grounded on this contingency, will receive consideration in the sequel. This, then, is the appropriate region of human liberty. It comprises, *first*, the inward domain of consciousness; demanding liberty of conscience in the most comprehensive sense; liberty of thought and feeling; absolute freedom of opinion and sentiment on all subjects, practical or speculative, scientific, moral, or theological. The liberty of expressing and publishing opinions may seem to fall under a different principle, since it belongs to that part of the conduct of an individual which concerns other people; but, being almost of as much importance as the liberty of thought itself, and resting in great part on the same reasons, is practically inseparable from it. *Secondly*, the principle requires liberty of tastes and pursuits; of framing the plan of our life to suit our own character; of doing as we like, subject to such consequences as may follow: without impediment from our fellow-creatures, so long as what we do does not harm them, even though they should think our conduct foolish, perverse, or wrong. *Thirdly*, from this liberty of each individual, follows the liberty, within the same limits, of combination among individuals; freedom to unite, for any purpose not involving harm to others: the persons combining being supposed to be of full age, and not forced or deceived.

No society in which these liberties are not, on the whole, respected, is free, whatever may be its form of government; and none is completely free in which they do not exist absolute and unqualified. The only freedom which deserves the name, is that of pursuing our own good in our own way, so long as we do not attempt to deprive others of theirs, or impede their efforts to obtain it. . . .

. . .

II OF THE LIBERTY OF THOUGHT AND DISCUSSION

The time, it is to be hoped, is gone by, when any defence would be necessary of the "liberty of the press" as one of the securities against corrupt or tyrannical government. No argument, we may suppose, can now be needed, against permitting a legislature or an executive, not identified in interest with the people, to prescribe opinions to them, and determine what doctrines or what arguments they shall be allowed to hear. This aspect of the question, besides, has been so often and so triumphantly enforced by preceding writers, that it needs not be specially insisted on in this place. Though the law of England, on the subject of the press, is as servile to this day as it was in the time of the Tudors, there is little danger of its being actually put in force against political discussion, except during some temporary panic, when fear of insurrection drives ministers and judges from their propriety; and, speaking generally, it is not, in constitutional countries, to be apprehended, that the government, whether completely responsible to the people or not, will often attempt to control the expression of opinion, except when in doing so it makes itself the organ of the general intolerance of the public. Let us suppose, therefore, that the government is entirely at one with the people, and never thinks of exerting any power of coercion unless in agreement with what it conceives to be their voice. But I deny the right of the people to exercise such coercion, either by themselves or by their government. The power itself is illegitimate. The best government has no more title to it than the worst. It is as noxious, or more noxious, when exerted in accordance with public opinion, than when in opposition to it. If all mankind minus one were of one opinion, and only one person were of the contrary opinion, mankind would be no more justified in silencing that one person, than he, if he had the power, would be justified in silencing mankind. Were an opinion a personal possession of no value except to the owner; if to be obstructed in the enjoyment of it were simply a private injury, it would make some difference whether the injury was inflicted only on a few persons or on many. But the peculiar evil of silencing the expression of an opinion is, that it is robbing the human race; posterity as well as the existing generation; those who dissent from the opinion, still more than those who hold it. If the opinion is right, they are deprived of the opportunity of exchanging error for truth: if wrong, they lose, what is almost as great a benefit, the clearer perception and livelier impression of truth, produced by its collision with error.

It is necessary to consider separately these two hypotheses, each of which has a distinct branch of the argument corresponding to it. We can never be sure that the opinion we are endeavouring to stifle is a false opinion; and if we were sure, stifling it would be an evil still.

First: the opinion which it is attempted to suppress by authority may possibly be true. Those who desire to suppress it, of course deny its truth; but they are not infallible. They have no authority to decide the question for all mankind, and exclude every other person from the means of judging. To refuse a hearing to an opinion, because they are sure that it is false, is to assume that *their* certainty is the same thing as *absolute* certainty. All silencing of discussion is an assumption of infallibility. Its condemnation may be allowed to rest on this common argument, not the worse for being common.

Unfortunately for the good sense of mankind, the fact of their fallibility is far from carrying the weight in their practical judgment which is always allowed to it in theory; for while every one well knows himself to be fallible, few think it necessary to take any precautions against their own fallibility, or admit the supposition that any opinion, of which they feel very certain, may be one of the examples of the error to which they acknowledge themselves to be liable. Absolute princes, or others who are accustomed to unlimited deference, usually feel this complete confidence in their own opinions on nearly all subjects. People more happily situated, who sometimes hear their opinions disputed, and are not wholly unused to be set right when they are wrong, place the same unbounded reliance only on such of their opinions as are shared by all who surround them, or to whom they habitually defer; for in proportion to a man's want of confidence in his own solitary judgment, does he usually repose, with implicit trust, on the infallibility of "the world" in general. And the world, to each individual, means the part of it with which he comes in contact; his party, his sect, his church, his class of society; the man may be called, by comparison, almost liberal and large-minded to whom it means anything so comprehensive as his own country or his own age. Nor is his faith in this collective authority at all shaken by his being aware that other ages, countries, sects, churches, classes, and parties have thought, and even now think, the exact reverse. He devolves upon his own world the responsibility of being in the right against the dissentient worlds of other people; and it never troubles him that mere accident has decided which of these numerous worlds is the object of his reliance, and that the same causes which make him a Churchman in London, would have made him a Buddhist or a Confucian in Pekin. Yet it is as evident in itself, as any amount of argument can make it, that ages are no more infallible than individuals; every age having held many opinions which subsequent ages have deemed not only false but absurd; and it is as certain that many opinions now general will be rejected by future ages, as it is that many, once general, are rejected by the present.

. . .

Let us now pass to the second division of the argument, and dismissing the supposition that any of the received opinions may be false, let us assume them to be true, and examine into the worth of the manner in which they are likely to be held, when their truth is not freely and openly canvassed. However unwillingly a person who has a strong opinion may admit the possibility that his opinion may be false, he ought to be moved by the consideration that, however true it may be, if it is not fully, frequently, and fearlessly discussed, it will be held as a dead dogma, not a living truth.

There is a class of persons (happily not quite so numerous as formerly) who think it enough if a person assents undoubtingly to what they think true, though he has no knowledge whatever of the grounds of the opinion, and could not make a tenable defence of it against the most superficial objections. Such persons, if they can once get their creed taught from authority, naturally think that no good, and some harm, comes of its being allowed to be questioned. Where their influence prevails, they make it nearly impossible for the received opinion to be rejected wisely and considerately, though it may still be rejected rashly and ignorantly; for to shut out discussion entirely is seldom possible, and when it once gets in, beliefs not grounded on conviction are apt to give way before the slightest semblance of an argument. Waiving, however, this possibility—assuming that the true opinion abides in the mind, but abides as a prejudice, a belief independent of, and proof against, argument—this is not the way in which truth ought to be held by a rational being. This is not knowing the truth. Truth, thus held, is but one superstition the more, accidentally clinging to the words which enunciate a truth.

If the intellect and judgment of mankind ought to be cultivated, a thing which Protestants at least do not deny, on what can these faculties be more appropriately exercised by any one, than on the things which concern him so much that it is considered necessary for him to hold opinions on them? If the cultivation of the understanding consists in one thing more than in another, it is surely in learning the grounds of one's own opinions. Whatever people believe, on subjects on which it is of the first importance to believe rightly, they ought to be able to defend against at least the common objections. But, some one may say, "Let them be *taught* the grounds of their opinions. It does not follow that opinions must be merely parroted because they are never heard controverted. Persons who learn geometry do not simply commit the theorems to memory, but understand and learn likewise the demonstrations; and it would be absurd to say that they remain ignorant of the grounds of geometrical truths, because they never hear any one deny, and attempt to disprove them." Undoubtedly: and such teaching suffices on a subject like mathematics, where there is nothing at all to be said on the wrong side of the question. The peculiarity of the evidence of mathematical truths is that all the argument is on one side. There are no objections, and no answers to objections. But on every subject on which difference of opinion is possible, the truth depends on a balance to be struck between two sets of conflicting reasons. Even in natural philosophy, there is always some other explanation possible of the same facts; some geocentric theory instead of heliocentric, some phlogiston instead of oxygen; and it has to be shown why that other theory cannot be the true one: and until this is shown, and until we know how it is shown, we do not understand the grounds of our opinion. But when we turn to subjects infinitely more complicated, to morals, religion, politics, social relations, and the business of life, three-fourths of the arguments for every disputed opinion consist in dispelling the appearances which favour some opinion different from it. The greatest orator, save one, of antiquity, has left it on record that he always studied his adversary's case with as great, if not still greater, intensity than even his own. What Cicero practised as the means of forensic success requires to be imitated by all who study any subject in order to arrive at the truth. He who knows only his own side of the case, knows little of that. His reasons may be good, and no one may have been able to refute them. But if he is equally unable to refute the reasons on the opposite side; if he does not so much as know what they are, he has no ground for preferring either opinion. The rational position for him would be suspension of judgment, and unless he contents himself with that, he is either led by authority, or adopts, like the generality of the world, the side to which he feels most inclination. Nor is it enough that he should hear the arguments of adversaries from his own teachers, presented as they state them, and accompanied by what they offer as refutations. That is not the way to do justice to the arguments, or bring them into real contact with his own mind. He must be able to hear them from persons who actually believe them; who defend them in earnest, and do their very utmost for them. He must know them in their most plausible and persuasive form; he must feel the whole force of the difficulty which the true view of the subject has to encounter and dispose of; else he will never really possess himself of the portion of truth which meets and removes that difficulty. Ninety-nine in a hundred of what are called educated men are in this condition; even of those who can argue fluently for their opinions. Their conclusion may be true, but it might be false for anything they know: they have never thrown themselves into the mental position of those who think differently from them, and considered what such persons may have to say; and consequently they do not, in any proper sense of the word, know the doctrine which they themselves profess. . . .

. . .

III OF INDIVIDUALITY, AS ONE OF THE ELEMENTS OF WELL-BEING

Such being the reasons which make it imperative that human beings should be free to form opinions, and to express their opinions without reserve; and such the baneful consequences to the intellectual, and through that to the moral nature of man, unless this liberty is either conceded, or asserted in spite of prohibition; let us next examine whether the same reasons do not require that men should be free to act upon their opinions —to carry these out in their lives, without hindrance, either physical or moral, from their fellow-men, so long as it is at their own risk and peril. This last proviso is of course indispensable. No one pretends that actions should be as free as opinions. On the contrary, even opinions lose their immunity when the circumstances in which they are expressed are such as to constitute their expression a positive instigation to some mischievous act. An opinion that corn-dealers are starvers of the poor, or that private property is robbery, ought to be unmolested when simply circulated through the press, but may justly incur punishment when delivered orally to an excited mob assembled before the house of a corn-dealer, or when handed about among the same mob in the form of a placard. Acts, of whatever kind, which, without justifiable cause, do harm to others, may be, and in the more important cases absolutely require to be, controlled by the unfavourable sentiments, and, when needful, by the active interference of mankind. The liberty of the individual must be thus far limited; he must not make himself a nuisance to other people. But if he refrains from molesting others in what concerns them, and merely acts according to his own inclination and judgment in things which concern himself, the same reasons which show that opinion should be free, prove also that he should be allowed, without molestation, to carry his opinions into practice at his own cost. That mankind are not infallible; that their truths, for the most part, are only half-truths; that unity of opinion, unless resulting from the fullest and freest comparison of opposite opinions, is not desirable, and diversity not an evil, but a good, until mankind are much more capable than at present of recognising all sides of the truth, are principles applicable to men's modes of action, not less than to their opinions. As it is useful that while mankind are imperfect there should be different opinions, so it is that there should be different experiments of living; that free scope should be given to varieties of character, short of injury to others; and that the worth of different modes of life should be proved practically, when any one thinks fit to try them. It is desirable, in short, that in things which do not primarily concern others, individuality should assert itself. Where, not the person's own character, but the traditions or customs of other people are the rule of conduct, there is wanting one of the principal ingredients of human happiness, and quite the chief ingredient of individual and social progress.

. . .

IV OF THE LIMITS TO THE AUTHORITY OF SOCIETY OVER THE INDIVIDUAL

What, then, is the rightful limit to the sovereignty of the individual over himself? Where does the authority of society begin? How much of human life should be assigned to individuality, and how much to society?

Each will receive its proper share, if each has that which more particularly concerns it. To individuality should belong the part of life in which it is chiefly the individual that is interested; to society, the part which chiefly interests society.

Though society is not founded on a contract, and though no good purpose is answered by inventing a contract in order to deduce social obligations from it, every one who receives the protection of society owes a return for the benefit, and the fact of living in society renders it indispensable that each should be bound to observe a certain line of conduct towards the rest. This conduct consists, first, in not injuring the interests of one another; or rather certain interests, which, either by express legal provision, or by tacit understanding, ought to be considered as rights; and secondly, in each person's bearing his share (to be fixed on some equitable principle) of the labours and sacrifices incurred for defending the society or its members from injury and molestation. These conditions society is justified in enforcing, at all costs to those who endeavour to withhold fulfillment. Nor is this all that society may do. The acts of an individual may be hurtful to others, or wanting in due consideration for their welfare, without going to the length of violating any of their constituted rights. The offender may then be justly punished by opinion, though not by law. As soon as any part of a person's conduct affects prejudicially the interests of others, society has jurisdiction over it, and the question whether the general welfare will or will not be promoted by interfering with it, becomes open to discussion. But there is no room for entertaining any such question when a person's conduct affects the interests of no persons besides himself, or needs not affect them unless they like (all the persons concerned being of full age, and the ordinary amount of understanding). In all such cases, there should be perfect freedom, legal and social, to do the action and stand the consequences.

It would be a great misunderstanding of this doctrine to suppose that it is one of selfish indifference, which pretends that human beings have no business with each other's conduct in life, and that they should not concern themselves about the well-doing or well-being of one another, unless their own interest is involved. Instead of any diminution, there is need of a great increase of disinterested exertion to promote the good of others. But disinterested benevolence can find other instruments to persuade people to their good than whips and scourges, either of a the literal or the metaphorical sort. I am the last person to undervalue the self-regarding virtues; they are only second in importance, if even second, to the social. It is equally the business of education to cultivate both. But even education works by conviction and persuasion as well as by compulsion, and it is by the former only that, when the period of education is passed, the self-regarding virtues should be inculcated. Human beings owe to each other help to distinguish the better from the worse, and encouragement to choose the former and avoid the latter. They should be forever stimulating each other to increased exercise of their higher faculties, and increased direction of their feelings and aims towards wise instead of foolish, elevating instead of degrading, objects and contemplations. But neither one person, nor any number of persons, is warranted in saying to another human creature of ripe years, that he shall not do with his life for his own benefit what he chooses to do with it. He is the person most interested in his own well-being: the interest which any other person, except in cases of strong personal attachment, can have in it, is trifling, compared with that which he himself has; the interest which society has in him individually (except as to his conduct to others) is fractional, and altogether indirect; while with respect to his own feelings and circumstances, the most ordinary man or woman has means of knowledge immeasurably surpassing those that can be possessed by any one else. The interference of society to overrule his judgment and purposes in what only regards himself must be grounded on general presumptions: which may be altogether wrong, and even if right, are as likely as not to be misapplied to individual cases, by persons no better acquainted with the circumstances of such cases than those are who look at them merely from without. In this department, therefore, of human affairs, Individuality has its proper field of action. In the conduct of human beings towards one another it is necessary that general rules should for the most part be observed, in order that people may know what they have to expect: but in each person's own concerns his individual spontaneity is entitled to free exercise. Considerations to aid his judgment, exhortations to strengthen his will, may be offered to him, even obtruded on him, by others: but he himself is the final judge. All errors which he is likely to commit against advice and warning are far outweighed by the evil of allowing others to constrain him to what they deem his good.

I do not mean that the feelings with which a person is regarded by others ought not to be in any way affected by his self-regarding qualities or deficiencies. This is neither possible nor desirable. If he is eminent in any of the qualities which conduce to his own good, he is, so far, a proper object of admiration. He is so much the nearer to the ideal perfection of human nature. If he is grossly deficient in those qualities, a sentiment the opposite of admiration will follow. There is a degree of folly, and a degree of what may be called (though the phrase is not unobjectionable) lowness or depravation of taste, which, though it cannot justify doing harm to the person who manifests it renders him necessarily and properly a subject of distaste, or, in extreme cases, even of contempt: a person could not have the opposite qualities in due strength without entertaining these feelings. Though doing no wrong to any one, a person may so act as to compel us to judge him, and feel to him, as a fool, or as a being of an inferior order: and since this judgment and feeling are a fact which he would prefer to avoid, it is doing him a service to warn him of it beforehand, as of any other disagreeable consequence to which he exposes himself. It would be well, indeed, if this good office were much more freely rendered than the common notions of politeness at present permit, and if one person could honestly point out to another that he thinks him in fault, without being considered unmannerly or presuming. . . .

. . .

To determine the point at which evils, so formidable to human freedom and advancement, begin, or rather at which they begin to predominate over the benefits attending the collective application of the force of society, under its recognised chiefs, for the removal of the obstacles which stand in the way of its well-being; to secure as much of the advantages of centralised power and intelligence as can be had without turning into governmental channels too great a proportion of the general activity—is one of the most difficult and complicated questions in the art of government. It is, in a great measure, a question of detail, in which many and various considerations must be kept in view, and no absolute rule can be laid down. But I believe that the practical principle in which safety resides, the ideal to be kept in view, the standard by which to test all arrangements intended for overcoming the difficulty, may be conveyed in these words: the greatest dissemination of power consistent with efficiency; but the greatest possible centralisation of information, and diffusion of it from the centre. Thus, in municipal administration, there would be, as in the New England States, a very minute division among separate officers, chosen by the localities, of all business which is not better left to the persons directly interested; but besides this, there would be, in each department of local affairs, a central superintendence, forming a branch of the general government. The organ of this superintendence would concentrate, as in a focus, the variety of information and experience derived from the conduct of that branch of public business in all the localities, from everything analogous which is done in foreign countries, and from the general principles of political science. This central organ should have a right to know all that is done, and its special duty should be that of making the knowledge acquired in one place available for others. Emancipated from the petty prejudices and narrow views of a locality by its elevated position and comprehensive sphere of observation, its advice would naturally carry much authority; but its actual power, as a permanent institution, should, I conceive, be limited to compelling the local officers to obey the laws laid down for their guidance. In all things not provided for by general rules, those officers should be left to their own judgment, under responsibility to their constituents. For the violation of rules, they should be responsible to law, and the rules themselves should be laid down by the legislature; the central administrative authority only watching over their execution, and if they were not properly carried into effect, appealing, according to the nature of the case, to the tribunals to enforce the law, or to the constituencies to dismiss the functionaries who had not executed it according to its spirit. Such, in its general conception, is the central superintendence which the Poor Law Board is intended to exercise over the administrators of the Poor Rate throughout the country. Whatever powers the Board exercises beyond this limit, were right and necessary in that peculiar case, for the cure of rooted habits of maladministration in matters deeply affecting not the localities merely, but the whole community; since no locality has a moral right to make itself by mismanagement a nest of pauperism, necessarily overflowing into other localities, and impairing the moral and physical condition of the whole labouring community. The powers of administrative coercion and subordinate legislation possessed by the Poor Law Board (but which, owing to the state of opinion on the subject, are very scantily exercised by them), though perfectly justifiable in a case of first-rate national interest, would be wholly out of place in the superintendence of interests purely local. But a central organ of information and instruction for all the localities, would be equally valuable in all departments of administration. A government cannot have too much of the kind of activity which does not impede, but aids and stimulates, individual exertion and development. The mischief begins when, instead of calling forth the activity and powers of individuals and bodies, it substitutes its own activity for theirs; when, instead of informing, advising, and, upon occasion, denouncing, it makes them work in fetters, or bids them stand aside and does their work instead of them. The worth of a State, in the long run, is the worth of the individuals composing it; and a State which postpones the interests of *their* mental expansion and elevation, to a little more of administrative skill, or of that semblance of it which practice gives, in the details of business; a State which dwarfs its men, in order that they may be more docile instruments in its hands even for beneficial purposes—will find that with small men no great thing can really be accomplished; and that the perfection of machinery to which it has sacrificed everything, will in the end avail it nothing, for want of the vital power which, in order that the machine might work more smoothly, it has preferred to banish.

THE SUBJECTION OF WOMEN

1869

I

The object of this Essay is to explain as clearly as I am able the grounds of an opinion which I have held from the very earliest period when I had formed any opinions at all on social or political matters, and which, instead of being weakened or modified, has been constantly growing stronger by the progress of reflection and the experience of life. That the principle which regulates the existing social relations between the two sexes—the legal subordination of one sex to the other—is wrong in itself, and now one of the chief hindrances to human improvement; and that it ought to be replaced by a principle of perfect equality, admitting no power or privilege on the one side, nor disability on the other.

. . .

The generality of a practice is in some cases a strong presumption that it is, or at all events once was, conducive to laudable ends. This is the case, when the practice was first adopted, or afterwards kept up, as a means to such ends, and was grounded on experience of the mode in which they could be most effectually attained. If the authority of men over women, when first established, had been the result of a conscientious comparison between different modes of constituting the government of society; if, after trying various other modes of social organisation—the government of women over men, equality between the two, and such mixed and divided modes of government as might be invented—it had been decided, on the testimony of experience, that the mode in which women are wholly under the rule of men, having no share at all in public concerns, and each in private being under the legal obligation of obedience to the man with whom she has associated her destiny, was the arrangement most conducive to the happiness and well-being of both; its general adoption might then be fairly thought to be some evidence that, at the time when it was adopted, it was the best: though even then the considerations which recommended it may, like so many other primeval social facts of the greatest importance, have subsequently, in the course of ages, ceased to exist. But

From *Essays on Sex Equality* by John Stuart Mill and Harriet Taylor Mill, ed. Alice S. Rossi (Chicago: University of Chicago Press, 1970).

the state of the case is in every respect the reverse of this. In the first place, the opinion in favour of the present system, which entirely subordinates the weaker sex to the stronger, rests upon theory only; for there never has been trial made of any other: so that experience, in the sense in which it is vulgarly opposed to theory, cannot be pretended to have pronounced any verdict. And in the second place, the adoption of this system of inequality never was the result of deliberation, or forethought, or any social ideas, or any notion whatever of what conduced to the benefit of humanity or the good order of society. It arose simply from the fact that from the very earliest twilight of human society, every woman (owing to the value attached to her by men, combined with her inferiority in muscular strength) was found in a state of bondage to some man. Laws and systems of polity always begin by recognising the relations they find already existing between individuals. They convert what was a mere physical fact into a legal right, give it the sanction of society, and principally aim at the substitution of public and organised means of asserting and protecting these rights, instead of the irregular and lawless conflict of physical strength. Those who had already been compelled to obedience became in this manner legally bound to it. Slavery, from being a mere affair of force between the master and the slave, became regularised and a matter of compact among the masters, who, binding themselves to one another for common protection, guaranteed by their collective strength the private possessions of each, including his slaves. In early times, the great majority of the male sex were slaves, as well as the whole of the female. And many ages elapsed, some of them ages of high cultivation, before any thinker was bold enough to question the rightfulness, and the absolute social necessity, either of the one slavery or of the other. By degrees such thinkers did arise; and (the general progress of society assisting) the slavery of the male sex has, in all the countries of Christian Europe at least (though, in one of them, only within the last few years) been at length abolished, and that of the female sex has been gradually changed into a milder form of dependence. But this dependence, as it exists at present, is not an original institution, taking a fresh start from considerations of justice and social expediency—it is the primitive state of slavery lasting on, through successive mitigations and modifications occasioned by the same causes which have softened the general manners, and brought all human relations more under the control of justice and the influence of humanity. It has not lost the taint of its brutal origin. No presumption in its favour, therefore, can be drawn from the fact of its existence. The only such presumption which it could be supposed to have, must be grounded on its having lasted till now, when so many other things which came down from the same odious source have been done away with. And this, indeed, is what makes it strange to ordinary ears, to hear it asserted that the inequality of rights between men and women has no other source than the law of the strongest.

. . .

But, it will be said, the rule of men over women differs from all these others in not being a rule of force: it is accepted voluntarily; women make no complaint, and are consenting parties to it. In the first place, a great number of women do not accept it. Ever since there have been women able to make their sentiments known by their writings (the only mode of publicity which society permits to them), an increasing number of them have recorded protests against their present social condition: and recently many thousands of them, headed by the most eminent women known to the public, have petitioned Parliament for their admission to the Parliamentary Suffrage. The claim of women to be educated as solidly, and in the same branches of knowledge, as men, is urged with growing intensity, and with a great prospect of success; while the demand for their admission into professions and occupations hitherto closed against them, becomes every year more urgent. Though there are not in this country, as there are in the United States, periodical conventions and an organised party to agitate for the Rights of Women, there is a numerous and active society organised and managed by women, for the more limited object of obtaining the political franchise. Nor is it only in our own country and in America that women are beginning to protest, more or less collectively, against the disabilities under which they labour. France, and Italy, and Switzerland, and Russia now afford examples of the same thing. How many more women there are who silently cherish similar aspirations, no one can possibly know; but there are abundant tokens how many *would* cherish them, were they not so strenuously taught to repress them as contrary to the proprieties of their sex. It must be remembered, also, that no enslaved class ever asked for complete liberty at once. When Simon de Montfort called the deputies of the commons to sit for the first time in Parliament, did any of them dream of demanding that an assembly, elected by their constituents, should make and destroy ministries, and dictate to the king in affairs of State? No such thought entered into the imagination of the most ambitious of them. The nobility had already these pretensions; the commons pretended to nothing but to be exempt from arbitrary taxation, and from the gross individual oppression of the king's officers. It is a political law of nature that those who are under any power of ancient origin, never begin by complaining of the power itself, but only of its oppressive exercise. There is never any want of women who complain of ill-usage by their husbands. There would be infinitely more, if complaint were not the greatest of all provocatives to a repetition and increase of the ill-usage. It is this which frustrates all attempts to maintain the power but protect the woman against its abuses. In no other case (except that of a child) is the person who has been proved judicially to have suffered an injury, replaced under the physical power of the culprit who inflicted it. Accordingly wives, even in the most extreme and protracted cases of bodily ill-usage, hardly ever dare avail themselves of the laws made for their protection: and if, in a moment of irrepressible indignation, or by the interference of neighbours, they are induced to do so, their whole effort afterwards is to disclose as little as they can, and to beg off their tyrant from his merited chastisement.

All causes, social and natural, combine to make it unlikely that women should be collectively rebellious to the power of men. They are so far in a position different from all other subject classes, that their masters require something more from them than actual service. Men do not want solely the obedience of women, they want their sentiments. All men, except the most brutish, desire to have, in the woman most nearly connected with them, not a forced slave but a willing one, not a slave merely, but a favourite. They have therefore put everything in practice to enslave their minds. The masters of all other slaves rely, for maintaining obedience, on fear; either fear of themselves, or religious fears. The masters of women wanted more than simple obedience, and they turned the whole force of education to effect their purpose. All women are brought up from the very earliest years in the belief that their ideal of character is the very opposite to that of men; not self-will, and government by self-control, but submission, and yielding to the control of others. All the moralities tell them that it is the duty of women, and all the current sentimentalities that it is their nature, to live for others; to make complete abnegation of themselves, and to have no life but in their affections. And by their affections are meant the only ones they are allowed to have—those to the men with whom they are connected, or to the children who constitute an additional and indefeasible tie between them and a man. When we put together three things—first, the natural attraction between opposite sexes; secondly, the wife's entire dependence on the husband, every privilege or pleasure she has being either his gift, or depending entirely on his will; and lastly, that the principal object of human pursuit, consideration, and all objects of social ambition, can in general be sought or obtained by her only through him, it would be a miracle if the object of being attractive to men had not become the polar star of feminine education and formation of character. And, this great means of influence over the minds of women having been acquired, an instinct of selfishness made men avail themselves of it to the utmost as a means of holding women in subjection, by representing to them meekness, submissiveness, and resignation of all individual will into the hands of a man, as an essential part of sexual attractiveness. Can it be doubted that any of the other yokes which mankind have succeeded in breaking, would have subsisted till now if the same means had existed, and had been so sedulously used, to bow down their minds to it? If it had been made the object of the life of every young plebeian to find personal favour in the eyes of some patrician, of every young serf with some seigneur; if domestication with him, and a share of his personal affections, had been held out as the prize which they all should look out for, the most gifted and aspiring being able to reckon on the most desirable prizes; and if, when this prize had been obtained, they had been shut out by a wall of brass from all interests not centring in him, all feelings and desires but those which he shared or inculcated; would not serfs and seigneurs, plebeians and patricians, have been as broadly distinguished at this day as men and women are? and would not all but a thinker here and there, have believed the distinction to be a fundamental and unalterable fact in human nature?

. . .

II

It will be well to commence the detailed discussion of the subject by the particular branch of it to which the course of our observations has led us: the conditions which the laws of this and all other countries annex to the marriage contract. Marriage being the destination appointed by society for women, the prospect they are brought up to, and the object which it is intended should be sought by all of them, except those who are too little attractive to be chosen by any man as his companion; one might have supposed that everything would have been done to make this condition as eligible to them as possible, that they might have no cause to regret being denied the option of any other. Society, however, both in this, and, at first, in all other cases, has preferred to attain its object by foul rather than fair means: but this is the only case in which it has substantially persisted in them even to the present day. Originally women were taken by force, or regularly sold by their father to the husband. Until a late period in European history, the father had the power to dispose of his daughter in marriage at his own will and pleasure, without any regard to hers. The Church, indeed, was so far faithful to a better morality as to require a formal "yes" from the woman at the marriage ceremony; but there was nothing to show that the consent was other than compulsory; and it was practically impossible for the girl to refuse compliance if the father persevered, except perhaps when she might obtain the protection of religion by a determined resolution to take monastic vows. After marriage, the man had anciently (but this was anterior to Christianity) the power of life and death over his wife. She could invoke no law against him; he was her sole tribunal and law. For a long time he could repudiate her, but she had no corresponding power in regard to him. By the old laws of England, the husband was called the *lord* of the wife; he was literally regarded as her sovereign, inasmuch that the murder of a man by his wife was called treason (*petty* as distinguished from *high* treason), and was more cruelly avenged than was usually the case with high treason, for the penalty was burning to death. Because these various enormities have fallen into disuse (for most of them were never formally abolished, or not until they had long ceased to be practised) men suppose that all is now as it should be in regard to the marriage contract; and we are continually told that civilisation and Christianity have restored to the woman her just rights. Meanwhile the wife is the actual bond-servant of her husband: no less so, as far as legal obligation goes, than slaves commonly so called. She vows a lifelong obedience to him at the altar, and is held to it all through her life by law. Casuists may say that the obligation of obedience stops short of participation in crime, but it certainly extends to everything else. She can do no act whatever but by his permission, at least tacit. She can acquire no property but for him; the instant it becomes hers, even if by inheritance, it becomes *ipso facto* his. In this respect the wife's position under the common law of England is worse than that of slaves in the laws of many countries: by the Roman law, for example, a slave might have his peculium, which to a certain extent the law guaranteed to him for his exclusive use. . . .

. . .

Whether the institution to be defended is slavery, political absolutism, or the absolutism of the head of a family, we are always expected to judge of it from its best instances; and we are presented with pictures of loving exercise of authority on one side, loving submission to it on the other—superior wisdom ordering all things for the greatest good of the dependents, and surrounded by their smiles and benedictions. All this would be very much to the purpose if anyone pretended that there are no such things as good men. Who doubts that there may be great goodness, and great happiness, and great affection, under the absolute government of a good man? Meanwhile, laws and institutions require to be adapted, not to good men, but to bad. Marriage is not an institution designed for a select few. Men are not required, as a preliminary to the marriage ceremony, to prove by testimonials that they are fit to be trusted with the exercise of absolute power. The tie of affection and obligation to a wife and children is very strong with those whose general social feelings are strong, and with many who are little sensible to any other social ties; but there are all degrees of sensibility and insensibility to it, as there are all grades of goodness and wickedness in men, down to those whom no ties will bind, and on whom society has no action but through its *ultima ratio*, the penalties of the law. In every grade of this descending scale are men to whom are committed all the legal powers of a husband. . . .

. . .

The equality of married persons before the law, is not only the sole mode in which that particular relation can be made consistent with justice to both sides, and conducive to the happiness of both, but it is the only means of rendering the daily life of mankind, in any high sense, a school of moral cultivation. Though the truth may not be felt or generally acknowledged for generations to come, the only school of genuine moral sentiment is society between equals. The moral education of mankind has hitherto emanated chiefly from the law of force, and is adapted almost solely to the relations which force creates. In the less advanced states of society, people hardly recognise any relation with their equals. To be an equal is to be an enemy. Society, from its highest place to its lowest, is one long chain, or rather ladder, where every individual is either above or below his nearest neighbour, and wherever he does not command he must obey. Existing moralities, accordingly, are mainly fitted to a relation of command and obedience. Yet command and obedience are but unfortunate necessities of human life: society in equality is its normal state. Already in modern life, and more and more as it progressively improves, command and obedience become exceptional facts in life, equal association its general rule. The morality of the first ages rested on the obligation to submit to power; that of the ages next following, on the right of the weak to the forbearance and protection of the strong. How much longer is one form of society and life to content itself with the morality made for another? We have had the morality of submission, and the morality of chivalry and generosity; the time is now come for the morality of justice. Whenever, in former ages, any approach has been made to society in equality, Justice has asserted its claims as the foundation of virtue. It was thus in the free republics of antiquity. But even in the best of these, the equals were limited to the free male citizens; slaves, women, and the unenfranchised residents were under the law of force. The joint influence of Roman civilisation and of Christianity obliterated these distinctions, and in theory (if only partially in practice) declared the claims of the human being, as such, to be paramount to those of sex, class, or social position. The barriers which had begun to be levelled were raised again by the northern conquests; and the whole of modern history consists of the slow process by which they have since been wearing away. We are entering into an order of things in which justice will again be the primary virtue; grounded as before on equal, but now also on sympathetic association; having its root no longer in the instinct of equals for self-protection, but in a cultivated sympathy between them; and no one being now left out, but an equal measure being extended to all. It is no novelty that mankind do not distinctly foresee their own changes, and that their sentiments are adapted to past, not to coming ages. To see the futurity of the species has always been the privilege of the intellectual élite, or of those who have learnt from them; to have the feelings of that futurity has been the distinction, and usually the martyrdom, of a still rarer élite. Institutions, books, education, society, all go on training human beings for the old, long after the new has come; much more when it is only coming. But the true virtue of human beings is fitness to live together as equals; claiming nothing for themselves but what they as freely concede to everyone else; regarding command of any kind as an exceptional necessity, and in all cases a temporary one; and preferring, whenever possible, the society of those with whom leading and following can be alternate and reciprocal. To these virtues, nothing in life as at present constituted gives cultivation by exercise. The family is a school of despotism, in which the virtues of despotism, but also its vices, are largely nourished. Citizenship, in free countries, is partly a school of society in equality; but citizenship fills only a small place in modern life, and does not come near the daily habits or inmost sentiments. The family, justly constituted, would be the real school of the virtues of freedom. It is sure to be a sufficient one of everything else. It will always be a school of obedience for the children, of command for the parents. What is needed is, that it should be a school of sympathy in equality, of living together in love, without power on one side or obedience on the other. This it ought to be between the parents. It would then be an exercise of those virtues which each requires to fit them for all other association, and a model to the children of the feelings and conduct which their temporary training by means of obedience is designed to render habitual, and therefore natural, to them. The moral training of mankind will never be adapted to the conditions of the life for which all other human progress is a preparation, until they practise in the family the same moral rule which is adapted to the normal constitution of human society. Any sentiment of freedom which can exist in a man whose nearest and dearest intimacies are with those of whom he is absolute master, is not the genuine or Christian love of freedom, but, what the love of freedom generally was in the ancients and in the middle ages—an intense feeling of the dignity and importance of his own personality; making him disdain a yoke for himself, of which he has no abhorrence whatever in the abstract, but which he is abundantly ready to impose on others for his own interest or glorification.

. . .

III

On the other point which is involved in the just equality of women, their admissibility to all the functions and occupations hitherto retained as the monopoly of the stronger sex, I should anticipate no difficulty in convincing anyone who has gone with me on the subject of the equality of women in the family. I believe that their disabilities elsewhere are only clung to in order to maintain their subordination in domestic life; because the generality of the male sex cannot yet tolerate the idea of living with an equal. Were it not for that, I think that almost everyone, in the existing state of opinion in politics and political economy, would admit the injustice of excluding half the human race from the greater number of lucrative occupations, and from almost all high social functions; ordaining from their birth either that they are not, and cannot by any possibility become, fit for employments which are legally open to the stupidest and basest of the other sex, or else that however fit they may be, those employments shall be interdicted to them, in order to be preserved for the exclusive benefit of males. In the last two centuries, when (which was seldom the case) any reason beyond the mere existence of the fact was thought to be required to justify the disabilities of women, people seldom assigned as a reason their inferior mental capacity; which, in times when there was a real trial of personal faculties (from which all women were not excluded) in the struggles of public life, no one really believed in. The reason given in those days was not women's unfitness, but the interest of society, by which was meant the interest of men: just as the *raison d'état*, meaning the convenience of the government, and the support of existing authority, was deemed a sufficient explanation and excuse for the most flagitious crimes. In the present day, power holds a smoother language, and whomsoever it oppresses, always pretends to do so for their own good: accordingly, when anything is forbidden to women, it is thought necessary to say, and desirable to believe, that they are incapable of doing it, and that they depart from their real path of success and happiness when they aspire to it. But to make this reason plausible (I do not say valid), those by whom it is urged must be prepared to carry it to a much greater length than anyone ventures to do in the face of present experience. It is not sufficient to maintain that women on the average are less gifted then men on the average, with certain of the higher mental faculties, or that a smaller number of women than of men are fit for occupations and functions of the highest intellectual character. It is necessary to maintain that no women at all are fit for them, and that the most eminent women are inferior in mental faculties to the most mediocre of the men on whom those functions at present devolve. For if the performance of the function is decided either by competition, or by any mode of choice which secures regard to the public interest, there needs be no apprehension that any important employments will fall into the hands of women inferior to average men, or to the average of their male competitors. The only result would be that there would be fewer women than men in such employments; a result certain to happen in any case, if only from the preference always likely to be felt by the majority of women for the one vocation in which there is nobody to compete with them. Now, the most determined depreciator of women will not venture to deny, that when we add the experience of recent times to that of ages past, women, and not a few merely, but many women, have proved themselves capable of everything, perhaps without a single exception, which is done by men, and of doing it successfully and creditably. The utmost that can be said is, that there are many things which none of them have succeeded in doing as well as they have been done by some men—many in which they have not reached the very highest rank. But there are extremely few, dependent only on mental faculties, in which they have not attained the rank next to the highest. Is not this enough, and much more than enough, to make it a tyranny to them, and a detriment to society, that they should not be allowed to compete with men for the exercise of these functions? Is it not a mere truism to say, that such functions are often filled by men far less fit for them than numbers of women, and who would be beaten by women in any fair field of competition? What difference does it make that there may be men somewhere, fully employed about other things, who may be still better qualified for the things in question than these women? Does not this take place in all competitions? Is there so great a superfluity of men fit for high duties, that society can afford to reject the service of any competent person? Are we so certain of always finding a man made to our hands for any duty or function of social importance which falls vacant, that we lose nothing by putting a ban upon one half of mankind, and refusing beforehand to make their faculties available, however distinguished they may be? And even if we could do without them, would it be consistent with justice to refuse to them their fair share of honour and distinction, or to deny to them the equal moral right of all human beings to choose their occupation (short of injury to others) according to their own preferences, at their own risk? Nor is the injustice confined to them: it is shared by those who are in a position to benefit by their services. To ordain that any kind of persons shall not be physicians, or shall not be advocates, or shall not be Members of Parliament, is to injure not them only, but all who employ physicians or advocates, or elect Members of Parliament, and who are deprived of the stimulating effect of greater competition on the exertions of the competitors, as well as restricted to a narrower range of individual choice.

Harriet Martineau

Harriet Martineau (1802–1876) was one of many foreigners who traveled to the United States during the early nineteenth century eager to examine the new democracy at firsthand. *Society in America*, the result of her two-year visit, ranks next to Tocqueville's *Democracy in America* as the best of these European accounts.

By the time Martineau set sail from England at the age of thirty-two, she was already an international figure whose essays and books sold well on both sides of the Atlantic. She wrote her first article at the age of twenty, became famous at the age of thirty when she published a series on political economy, and by the time of her death at seventy-four had produced some fifty books and pamphlets. Despite deafness, heart disease, and other disabilities, she was a spirited and incisive actor on the political scene, a feminist intellectual in a Victorian male world.

Martineau was fortunate to be born into a Unitarian family who believed that women's intellectual capacities were equal to men's. Despite poor health and the financial setbacks suffered by her father, she received a remarkably intensive education and grew deeply interested in religious and philosophical questions. Although her mother was a powerful figure, Harriet's strongest attachment was to her younger brother by three years, James; she studied with him when she could and consulting him on virtually every matter. It was James who suggested she try to write, and when at the age of seventeen he met and fell in love with his future wife, Harriet was deeply grieved.

Characteristically, Martineau's first published works were about women. Martineau was an ardent defender of women's rights all her life, although her plan to found a journal dedicated to women did not succeed. Long before Marx and Engels, she depicted women in England and America as household slaves, noting that the often harsh impact of marriage led to rapid aging and a shallowness of mind. Martineau was always eager to reach a working-class audience and hit upon a scheme of monthly stories that, though fictional, explained the principles of political economy in a popular style. She wrote several stories for children and a volume on "household education" that urged a more rational form of child care, and she proposed the publication of a 200-volume library of good, inexpensive books for the working classes; 140 were actually published.

Society in America (1837) is Harriet Martineau's masterpiece, a rich and sympathetic work that explains the points of difference and similarity between the American nation and its caste-divided European forebears. The book's comparative focus, its stress on the shaping power of history, and the accuracy and detail of its observations show Martineau to be a pioneer of "sociology" before Auguste Comte even coined the word. For each of her major topics—government, economy, family life, religion—she traces the way in which the values of the American nation both shape and respond to its institutional structure.

SOCIETY IN AMERICA

1837

WOMAN

If a test of civilisation be sought, none can be so sure as the condition of that half of society over which the other half has power,—from the exercise of the right of the strongest. Tried by this test, the American civilisation appears to be of a lower order than might have been expected from some other symptoms of its social state. The Americans have, in the treatment of women, fallen below, not only their own democratic principles, but the practice of some parts of the Old World.

The unconsciousness of both parties as to the injuries suffered by women at the hands of those who hold the power is a sufficient proof of the low degree of civilisation in this important particular at which they rest. While woman's intellect is confined, her morals crushed, her health ruined, her weaknesses encouraged, and her strength punished, she is told that her lot is cast in the paradise of women: and there is no country in the world where there is so much boasting of the "chivalrous" treatment she enjoys. That is to say,—she has the best place in stage-coaches: when there are not chairs enough for everybody, the gentlemen stand: she hears oratorical flourishes on public occasions about wives and home, and apostrophes to women: her husband's hair stands on end at the idea of her working, and he toils to indulge her with money: she has liberty to get her brain turned by religious excitements, that her attention may be diverted from morals, politics, and philosophy; and, especially, her morals are guarded by the strictest observance of propriety in her presence. In short, indulgence is given her as a substitute for justice. Her case differs from that of the slave, as to the principle, just so far as this; that the indulgence is large and universal, instead of petty and capricious. In both cases, justice is denied on no better plea than the right of the strongest. In both cases, the acquiescence of the many, and the burning discontent of the few, of the oppressed testify, the one to the actual degradation of the class, and the other to its fitness for the enjoyment of human rights. . . .

The intellect of woman is confined by an unjustifiable restriction of both methods of education,—by express teaching, and by the discipline of circumstance. The former, though prior in the chronology of each individual, is a direct consequence of the latter, as regards the whole of the sex. As women have none of the objects in life for which an enlarged education is considered requisite, the education is not given. Female education in America is much what it is in England. There is a profession of some things being taught which are supposed necessary because everybody learns them. They serve to fill up time, to occupy attention harmlessly, to improve conversation, and to make women something like companions to their husbands, and able to teach their children somewhat. But what is given is, for the most part, passively received; and what is obtained is, chiefly, by means of the memory. There is rarely or never a careful ordering of influences for the promotion of clear intellectual activity. Such activity, when it exceeds that which is necessary to make the work of the teacher easy, is feared and repressed. This is natural enough, as long as women are excluded from the objects for which men are

From *Society in America* by Harriet Martineau (New York: Saunders and Otley, 1837).

trained. While there are natural rights which women may not use, just claims which are not to be listened to, large objects which may not be approached, even in imagination, intellectual activity is dangerous: or, as the phrase is, unfit. Accordingly, marriage is the only object left open to woman. Philosophy she may pursue only fancifully, and under pain of ridicule: science only as a pastime, and under a similar penalty. Art is declared to be left open: but the necessary learning, and, yet more, the indispensable experience of reality, are denied to her. Literature is also said to be permitted: but under what penalties and restrictions? . . .

. . . Nothing is thus left for women but marriage. —Yes; Religion, is the reply.—Religion is a temper, not a pursuit. It is the moral atmosphere in which human beings are to live and move. Men do not live to breathe: they breathe to live. A German lady of extraordinary powers and endowments, remarked to me with amazement on all the knowledge of the American women being based on theology. She observed that in her own country theology had its turn with other sciences as a pursuit: but nowhere, but with the American women, had she known it make the foundation of all other knowledge. Even while thus complaining, this lady stated the case too favourably. American women have not the requisites for the study of theology. The difference between theology and religion, the science and the temper, is yet scarcely known among them. It is religion which they pursue as an occupation; and hence its small results upon the conduct, as well as upon the intellect. We are driven back upon marriage as the only appointed object in life: and upon the conviction that the sum and substance of female education in America, as in England, is training women to consider marriage as the sole object in life, and to pretend that they do not think so.

The morals of women are crushed. If there be any human power and business and privilege which is absolutely universal, it is the discovery and adoption of the principle and laws of duty. As every individual, whether man or woman, has a reason and a conscience, this is a work which each is thereby authorised to do for him or herself. But it is not only virtually prohibited to beings who, like the American women, have scarcely any objects in life proposed to them; but the whole apparatus of opinion is brought to bear offensively upon individuals among women who exercise freedom of mind in deciding upon what duty is, and the methods by which it is to be pursued. There is nothing extraordinary to the disinterested observer in women being so grieved at the case of slaves,—slave wives and mothers, as well as spirit-broken men,—as to wish to do what they could for their relief: there is nothing but what is natural in their being ashamed of the cowardice of such white slaves of the north as are deterred by intimidation from using their rights of speech and of the press, in behalf of the suffering race, and in their resolving not to do likewise: there is nothing but what is justifiable in their using their moral freedom, each for herself, in neglect of the threats of punishment: yet there were no bounds to the efforts made to crush the actions of women who thus used their human powers in the abolition question, and the convictions of those who looked on, and who might possibly be warmed into free action by the beauty of what they saw. It will be remembered that they were women who asserted the right of meeting and of discussion, on the day when Garrison was mobbed in Boston. Bills were posted about the city on this occasion, denouncing these women as casting off the refinement and delicacy of their sex: the newspapers, which laud the exertions of ladies in all other charities for the prosecution of which they are wont to meet and speak, teemed with the most disgusting reproaches and insinuations: and the pamphlets which related to the question all presumed to censure the act of duty which the women had performed in deciding upon their duty for themselves.—One lady, of high talents and character, whose books were very popular before she did a deed greater than that of writing any book, in acting upon an unusual conviction of duty, and becoming an abolitionist, has been almost excommunicated since. A family of ladies, whose talents and conscientiousness had placed them high in the estimation of society as teachers, have lost all their pupils since they declared their anti-slavery opinions. The reproach in all the many similar cases that I know is, not that the ladies hold anti-slavery opinions, but that they act upon them. The incessant outcry about the retiring modesty of the sex proves the opinion of the censors to be, that fidelity to conscience is inconsistent with retiring modesty. If it be so, let the modesty succumb. It can be only a false modesty which can be thus endangered. No doubt, there were people in Rome who were scandalised at the unseemly boldness of christian women who stood in the amphitheatre to be torn in pieces for their religion. No doubt there were many gentlemen in the British army who thought it unsuitable to the retiring delicacy of the sex that the wives and daughters of the revolutionary heroes should be revolutionary heroines. But the event has a marvellous efficacy in modifying the ultimate sentence. The bold christian women, the brave American wives and daughters of half a century ago are honoured, while the intrepid moralists of the present day, worthy of their grandmothers, are made the confessors and martyrs of their age.

. . .

How fearfully the morals of woman are crushed, appears from the prevalent persuasion that there are virtues which are peculiarly masculine, and others which are peculiarly feminine. It is amazing that a society which makes a most emphatic profession of its Christianity, should almost universally entertain such a fallacy: and not see that, in the case they suppose, instead of the character of Christ being the meeting point of all virtues, there would have been a separate gospel for women, and a second company of agents for its diffusion. It is not only that masculine and feminine employments are supposed to be properly different. No one in the world, I believe, questions this. But it is actually supposed that what are called the hardy virtues are more appropriate to men, and the gentler to women. . . .

. . . [T]he consequences are what might be looked for. Men are ungentle, tyrannical. They abuse the right of the strongest, however they may veil the abuse with indulgence. They want the magnanimity to discern woman's human rights; and they crush her morals rather than allow them. Women are, as might be anticipated, weak, ignorant and subservient, in as far as they exchange self-reliance for reliance on anything out of themselves. Those who will not submit to such a suspension of their moral functions, (for the work of self-perfection remains to be done, sooner or later,) have to suffer for their allegiance to duty. They have all the need of bravery that the few heroic men who assert the highest rights of women have of gentleness, to guard them from the encroachment to which power, custom, and education, incessantly conduce.

Such brave women and such just men there are in the United States, scattered among the multitude, whose false apprehension of rights leads to an enormous failure of duties. There are enough of such to commend the true understanding and practice to the simplest minds and most faithful hearts of the community, under whose testimony the right principle will spread and flourish. If it were not for the external prosperity of the country, the injured half of its society would probably obtain justice sooner than in any country of Europe. But the prosperity of America is a circumstance unfavourable to its women. It will be long before they are put to the proof as to what they are capable of thinking and doing: a proof to which hundreds, perhaps thousands of Englishwomen have been put by adversity, and the result of which is a remarkable improvement in their social condition, even within the space of ten years. Persecution for opinion, punishment for all manifestations of intellectual and moral strength, are still as common as women who have opinions and who manifest strength: but some things are easy, and many are possible of achievement, to women of ordinary powers, which it would have required genius to accomplish but a few years ago.

MARRIAGE

If there is any country on earth where the course of true love may be expected to run smooth, it is America. It is a country where all can marry early, where there need be no anxiety about a worldly provision, and where the troubles arising from conventional considerations of rank and connexion ought to be entirely absent. It is difficult for a stranger to imagine beforehand why all should not love and marry naturally and freely, to the prevention of vice out of the marriage state, and of the common causes of unhappiness within it. The anticipations of the stranger are not, however, fulfilled: and they never can be while the one sex overbears the other. Marriage is in America more nearly universal, more safe, more tranquil, more fortunate than in England: but it is still subject to the troubles which arise from the inequality of the parties in mind and in occupation. It is more nearly universal, from the entire prosperity of the country: it is safer, from the greater freedom of divorce, and consequent discouragement of swindling, and other vicious marriages: it is more tranquil and fortunate from the marriage vows being made absolutely reciprocal; from the arrangements about property being generally far more favorable to the wife than in England; and from her not being made, as in England, to all intents and purposes the property of her husband. The outward requisites to happiness are nearly complete, and the institution is purified from the grossest of the scandals which degrade it in the Old World: but it is still the imperfect institution which it must remain while women continue to be ill-educated, passive, and subservient: or well-educated, vigorous, and free only upon sufferance.

The institution presents a different aspect in the various parts of the country. I have spoken of the early marriages of silly children in the south and west, where, owing to the disproportion of numbers, every woman is married before she well knows how serious a matter human life is. She has an advantage which very few women elsewhere are allowed: she has her own property to manage. It would be a rare sight elsewhere to see a woman of twenty-one in her second widowhood, managing her own farm or plantation; and managing it well, because it had been in her own hands during her marriage. In Louisiana, and also in Missouri, (and probably in other States,) a woman not only has half her husband's property by right at his death, but may always be considered as possessed of half his gains during his life; having at all times power to bequeath that amount. The husband interferes much less with his wife's property in the south, even through her voluntary relinquishment of it, than is at all usual where the cases of women having property during their marriage are rare. In the southern newspapers, advertisements may at any time be seen, running thus:—"Mrs. A, wife of Mr. A, will dispose of &c. &c." When Madame Lalaurie was mobbed in New Orleans, no one meddled with her husband or his possessions; as he was no more responsible for her management of her human property than anybody else. On the whole, the practice seems to be that the weakest and most ignorant women give up their property to their husbands; the husbands of such women being precisely the men most disposed to accept it: and that the strongest-minded and most conscientious women keep their property, and use their rights; the husbands of such women being precisely those who would refuse to deprive their wives of their social duties and privileges. . . .

I have mentioned that divorce is more easily obtained in the United States than in England. In no country, I believe, are the marriage laws so iniquitous as in England, and the conjugal relation, in consequence, so impaired. Whatever may be thought of the principles which are to enter into laws of divorce, whether it be held that pleas for divorce should be one, (as narrow interpreters of the New Testament would have it;) or two, (as the law of England has it;) or several, (as the Continental and United States' laws in many instances allow,) nobody, I believe, defends the arrangement by which, in England, divorce is obtainable only by the very rich. The barbarism of granting that as a privilege to the extremely wealthy, to which money bears no relation whatever, and in which all married persons whatever have an equal interest, needs no exposure beyond the mere statement of the fact. It will be seen at a glance how such an arrangement tends to vitiate marriage: how it offers impunity to adventurers, and encouragement to every kind of mercenary marriages: how absolute is its oppression of the injured party: and how, by vitiating marriage, it originates and aggravates licentiousness to an incalculable extent. To England alone belongs the disgrace of such a method of legislation. . . .

Of the American States, I believe New York approaches nearest to England in its laws of divorce.

It is less rigid, in as far as that more is comprehended under the term "cruelty." The husband is supposed to be liable to cruelty from the wife, as well as the wife from the husband. There is no practical distinction made between rich and poor by the process being rendered expensive: and the cause is more easily resumable after a reconciliation of the parties. In Massachusetts, the term "cruelty" is made so comprehensive, and the mode of sustaining the plea is so considerately devised, that divorces are obtainable with peculiar ease. The natural consequence follows: such a thing is never heard of. A long-established and very eminent lawyer of Boston told me that he had known of only one in all his experience. Thus it is wherever the law is relaxed, and, *cæteris paribus*, in proportion to its relaxation: for the obvious reason, that the protection offered by law to the injured party causes marriages to be entered into with fewer risks, and the conjugal relation carried on with more equality. Retribution is known to impend over violations of conjugal duty. When I was in North Carolina, the wife of a gamester there obtained a divorce without the slightest difficulty. When she had brought evidence of the danger to herself and her children,—danger pecuniary and moral,—from her husband's gambling habits, the bill passed both Houses without a dissenting voice.

It is clear that the sole business which legislation has with marriage is with the arrangement of property; to guard the reciprocal rights of the children of the marriage and the community. There is no further pretence for the interference of the law, in any way. An advance towards the recognition of the true principle of legislative interference in marriage has been made in England, in the new law in which the agreement of marriage is made a civil contract, leaving the religious obligation to the conscience and taste of the parties. It will be probably next perceived that if the civil obligation is fulfilled, if the children of the marriage are legally and satisfactorily provided for by the parties, without the assistance of the legislature, the legislature has, in principle, nothing more to do with the matter. . . .

It is assumed in America, particularly in New England, that the morals of society there are peculiarly pure. I am grieved to doubt the fact: but I do doubt it. Nothing like a comparison between one country and another in different circumstances can be instituted: nor would any one desire to enter upon such a comparison. The bottomless vice, the all-pervading corruption of European society cannot, by possibility, be yet paralleled in America: but neither is it true that any outward prosperity, any arrangement of circumstances, can keep a society pure while there is corruption in its social methods, and among its principles of individual action. Even in America, where every young man may, if he chooses, marry at twenty-one, and appropriate all the best comforts of domestic life,—even here there is vice. Men do not choose to marry early, because they have learned to think other things of more importance than the best comforts of domestic life. A gentleman of Massachusetts, who knows life and the value of most things in it, spoke to me with deep concern of the alteration in manners which is going on: of the increase of bachelors, and of mercenary marriages; and of the fearful consequences. It is too soon for America to be following the old world in its ways. In the old world, the necessity of thinking of a maintenance before thinking of a wife has led to requiring a certain style of living before taking a wife; and then, alas! to taking a wife for the sake of securing a certain style of living. That this species of corruption is already spreading in the new world is beyond a doubt;—in the cities, where the people who live for wealth and for opinion congregate.

I was struck with the great number of New England women whom I saw married to men old enough to be their fathers. One instance which perplexed me exceedingly, on my entrance into the country, was explained very little to my satisfaction. The girl had been engaged to a young man whom she was attached to: her mother broke off the engagement, and married her to a rich old man. This story was a real shock to me; so persuaded had I been that in America, at least, one might escape from the disgusting spectacle of mercenary marriages. But I saw only too many instances afterwards. The practice was ascribed to the often-mentioned fact of the young men migrating westwards in large numbers, leaving those who should be their wives to marry widowers of double their age. The Auld Robin

Gray story is a frequently enacted tragedy here, and one of the worst symptoms that struck me was, that there was usually a demand upon my sympathy in such cases. I have no sympathy for those who, under any pressure of circumstances, sacrifice their heart's-love for legal prostitution, and no environment of beauty or sentiment can deprive the fact of its coarseness: and least of all could I sympathise with women who set the example of marrying for an establishment in a new country, where, if anywhere, the conjugal relation should be found in its purity.

The unavoidable consequence of such a mode of marrying is, that the sanctity of marriage is impaired, and that vice succeeds. Any one must see at a glance that if men and women marry those whom they do not love, they must love those whom they do not marry. There are sad tales in country villages, here and there, which attest to this; and yet more in towns, in a rank of society where such things are seldom or never heard of in England. I rather think that married life is immeasurably purer in America than in England: but that there is not otherwise much superiority to boast of. I can only say, that I unavoidably knew of more cases of lapse in highly respectable families in one State than ever came to my knowledge at home; and that they were got over with a disgrace far more temporary and superficial than they could have been visited with in England. I am aware that in Europe the victims are chosen, with deliberate selfishness, from classes which cannot make known their perils and their injuries; while in America, happily, no such class exists. I am aware that this destroys all possibility of a comparison: but the fact remains, that the morals of American society are less pure than they assume to be. If the common boast be meant to apply to the rural population, at least let it not be made, either in pious gratitude, or patriotic conceit, by the aristocratic city classes, who, by introducing the practice of mercenary marriages, have rendered themselves responsible for whatever dreadful consequences may ensue.

The ultimate and very strong impression on the mind of a stranger, pondering the morals of society in America, is that human nature is much the same everywhere, whatever may be its environment of riches or poverty; and that it is justice to the human nature, and not improvement in fortunes, which must be looked to as the promise of a better time. Laws and customs may be creative of vice; and should be therefore perpetually under process of observation and correction: but laws and customs cannot be creative of virtue: they may encourage and help to preserve it; but they cannot originate it.

OCCUPATION

The greater number of American women have home and its affairs, wherewith to occupy themselves. Wifely and motherly occupation may be called the sole business of woman there. If she has not that, she has nothing. The only alternative, as I have said, is making an occupation of either religion or dissipation; neither of which is fit to be so used: the one being a state of mind; the other altogether a negation when not taken in alternation with business.

It must happen that where all women have only one serious object, many of them will be unfit for that object. In the United States, as elsewhere, there are women no more fit to be wives and mothers than to be statesmen and generals; no more fit for any responsibility whatever, than for the maximum of responsibility. There is no need to describe such: they may be seen everywhere. I allude to them only for the purpose of mentioning that many of this class shirk some of their labours and cares, by taking refuge in boarding-houses. It is a circumstance very unfavourable to the character of some American women, that boarding-house life has been rendered compulsory by the scarcity of labour,—the difficulty of obtaining domestic service. The more I saw of boarding-house life, the worse I thought of it; though I saw none but the best. Indeed, the degrees of merit in such establishments weigh little in the consideration of the evil of their existence at all. In the best it is something to be secure of respectable company, of a good table, a well-mannered and courteous hostess, and comfort in the private apartments: but the mischiefs of the system throw all these objects into the background.

To begin with young children. There can be no sufficient command of proper food for them; nor any security that they will eat it naturally at the table where fifty persons may be sitting, a dozen obsequious blacks waiting, and an array of tempting dishes within sight. The child is in imminent danger of being too shy and frightened to eat at all, or of becoming greedy to eat too much. Next, it is melancholy to see girls of twelve years old either slinking down beside their parents, and blushing painfully as often as any one of fifty strangers looks towards them; or boldly staring at all that is going on, and serving themselves, like little women of the world. After tea, it is a common practice to hand the young ladies to the piano, to play and sing to a party, composed chiefly of gentlemen, and brought together on no principle of selection except mere respectability. Next comes the mischief to the young married ladies, the most numerous class of women found in boarding-houses. The uncertainty about domestic service is so great, and the economy of boarding-house life so tempting to people who have not provided themselves with house and furniture, that it is not to be wondered at that many young married people use the accommodation provided. But no sensible husband, who could beforehand become acquainted with the liabilities incurred, would willingly expose his domestic peace to the fearful risk. I saw enough when I saw the elegantly dressed ladies repair to the windows of the common drawing-room, on their husbands' departure to the counting-house, after breakfast. There the ladies sit for hours, doing nothing but gossiping with one another, with any gentlemen of the house who may happen to have no business, and with visitors. It is true that the sober-minded among the ladies can and do withdraw to their own apartments for the morning: but they complain that they cannot settle to regular employments as they could in a house of their own. Either they are not going to stay long; or they have not room for their books, or they are broken in upon by their acquaintances in the house. The common testimony is, that little can be done in boarding-houses: and if the more sober-minded find it so, the fate of the thoughtless, who have no real business to do, may be easily anticipated. They find a dear friend or two among the boarders, to whom they confide their husbands' secrets. A woman who would do this once would do it twice, or as often as she changes her boarding-house, and finds a new dear friend in each. I have been assured that there is no end to the difficulties in which gentlemen have been involved, both as to their commercial and domestic affairs, by the indiscretion of their thoughtless young wives, amidst the idleness and levities of boarding-house life. . . .

The study of the economy of domestic service was a continual amusement to me. What I saw would fill a volume. Many families are, and have for years been, as well off for domestics as any family in England; and I must say that among the loudest complainers there were many who, from fault of either judgment or temper, deserved whatever difficulty they met with. This is remarkably the case with English ladies settled in America. They carry with them habits of command, and expectations of obedience; and when these are found utterly to fail, they grow afraid of their servants. Even when they have learned the theory that domestic service is a matter of contract, an exchange of service for recompense, the authority of the employer extending no further than to require the performance of the service promised,—when the ladies have learned to assent in words to this, they are still apt to be annoyed at things which in no way concern them. If one domestic chooses to wait at table with no cap over her scanty chevelure, and in spectacles,—if another goes to church on Sunday morning, dressed exactly like her mistress, the lady is in no way answerable for the bad taste of her domestics. But English residents often cannot learn to acquiesce in these things; nor in the servants doing their work in their own way; nor in their dividing their time as they please between their mistress's work and their own. The consequence is, that they soon find it impossible to get American help at all, and they are consigned to the tender mercies of the low Irish; and every one knows what kind of servants they commonly are. Some few of them are the best domestics in America: those who know how to value a respectable home, a steady sufficient income, the honour of being trusted, and the security of valuable friends for life: but too many of them are unsettled, reckless, slovenly; some dishonest, and some intemperate. . . .

Many ladies, in the country especially, take little girls to train; having them bound to a certain term of service. In such a case, the girl is taken at about eleven years old, and bound to remain till she is eighteen. Her mistress engages to clothe her; to give her Sunday-schooling, and a certain amount of weekday schooling in the year; and to present her at the end of the term (except in case of bad behaviour) with fifty dollars, or a cow, or some equivalent. Under a good mistress, this is an excellent bargain for the girl; but mistresses complain that as soon as the girls become really serviceable, by the time they are fourteen or fifteen, they begin to grow restless, having usually abundance of kind friends to tell them what good wages they might get if they were free.

In several abodes in which I resided for a longer or shorter time, the routine of the house was as easy and agreeable as any Englishman's; elsewhere, the accounts of domestic difficulties were both edifying and amusing. At first, I heard but little of such things; there being a prevalent idea in America that English ladies concern themselves very little about household affairs. This injurious misapprehension the ladies of England owe, with many others, to the fashionable novels which deluge the country from New York to beyond the Mississippi. Though the Americans repeat and believe that these books are false pictures of manners, they cannot be wholly upon their guard against impressions derived from them. Too many of them involuntarily image to themselves the ladies of England as like the duchesses and countesses of those low books: and can scarcely believe that the wives of merchants, manufacturers, and shopkeepers, and of the greater number of professional men, buy their own provision, keep household accounts, look to the making and mending, the baking, making of preserves, &c., and sometimes cook, with their own hands, any dish of which their husbands may be fond. When it was found, from my revelations, that English and American ladies have, after all, much the same sort of things to do, the real state of household economy was laid open to me.

All American ladies should know how to clear-starch and iron: how to keep plate and glass: how to cook dainties: and, if they understand the making of bread and soup likewise, so much the better. The gentlemen usually charge themselves with the business of marketing; which is very fair. A lady, highly accomplished and very literary, told me that she had lately been left entirely without help, in a country village where there was little hope of being speedily able to procure any. She and her daughter made the bread, for six weeks, and entirely kept the house, which might vie with any nobleman's for true luxury; perfect sufficiency and neatness. She mentioned one good result from the necessity: that she should never again put up with bad bread. She could now testify that bread might always be good, notwithstanding changes of weather, and all the excuses commonly given. I heard an anecdote from this lady which struck me. She was in the habit of employing, when she wanted extra help, a poor woman of colour, to do kitchen-work. The domestics had always appeared on perfectly good terms with this woman till, one day, when there was to be an evening party, the upper domestic declined waiting on the company; giving as a reason that she was offended at being required to sit down to table with the coloured woman. Her mistress gently rebuked her pride, saying "If you are above waiting on my company, my family are not. You will see my daughter carry the tea-tray, and my niece the cake." The girl repented, and besought to be allowed to wait; but her assistance was declined; at which she cried heartily. The next day, she was very humble, and her mistress reasoned with her, quite successfully. The lady made one concession in silence. She had the coloured woman come after dinner, instead of before.

. . .

. . . For my own part, I had rather suffer any inconvenience from having to work occasionally in chambers and kitchen, and from having little hospitable designs frustrated, than witness the subservience in which the menial class is held in Europe. In England, servants have been so long accustomed to this subservience; it is so completely the established custom for the mistress to regulate their manners, their clothes, their intercourse with their friends, and many other things which they ought to manage for themselves, that it has become difficult to treat them any better. Mistresses who abstain from such regulation find that they are spoiling their servants; and heads of families who would make friends of their domestics find them little fitted to reciprocate the duty. In America it is otherwise: and may it ever be so! All but those who care for their selfish gratification more than for the welfare of those about them will be glad to have intelligent and disinterested friends in the domestics whom they may be able to attach, though there may be difficulty at first in retaining them; and some eccentricities of manner and dress may remain to be borne with. . . .

As for the occupations with which American ladies fill up their leisure; what has been already said will show that there is no great weight or diversity of occupation. Many are largely engaged in charities, doing good or harm according to the enlightenment of mind which is carried to the work. In New England, a vast deal of time is spent in attending preachings, and other religious meetings: and in paying visits, for religious purposes, to the poor and sorrowful. The same results follow from this practice that may be witnessed wherever it is much pursued. In as far as sympathy is kept up, and acquaintanceship between different classes in society is occasioned, the practice is good. In as far as it unsettles the minds of the visitors, encourages a false craving for religious excitement, tempts to spiritual interference on the one hand, and cant on the other, and humours or oppresses those who need such offices least, while it alienates those who want them most, the practice is bad. I am disposed to think that much good is done, and much harm: and that, whenever women have a greater charge of indispensable business on their hands, so as to do good and reciprocate religious sympathy by laying hold of opportunities, instead of by making occupation, more than the present good will be done, without any of the harm.

All American ladies are more or less literary: and some are so to excellent purpose: to the saving of their minds from vacuity. Readers are plentiful: thinkers are rare. Minds are of a very passive character: and it follows that languages are much cultivated. If ever a woman was pointed out to me as distinguished for information, I might be sure beforehand that she was a linguist. I met with a great number of ladies who read Latin; some Greek; some Hebrew; some German. With the exception of the last, the learning did not seem to be of much use to them, except as a harmless exercise. I met with more intellectual activity, more general power, among many ladies who gave little time to books, than among those who are distinguished as being literary. I did not meet with a good artist among all the ladies in the States. I never had the pleasure of seeing a good drawing, except in one instance; or, except in two, of hearing good music. The entire failure of all attempts to draw is still a mystery to me. The attempts are incessant; but the results are below criticism. Natural philosophy is not pursued to any extent by women. There is some pretension to mental and moral philosophy; but the less that is said on that head the better.

This is a sad account of things. It may tempt some to ask "what then are the American women?" They are better educated by Providence than by men. The lot of humanity is theirs: they have labour, probation, joy, and sorrow. They are good wives; and, under the teaching of nature, good mothers. They have, within the range of their activity, good sense, good temper, and good manners. Their beauty is very remarkable; and, I think, their wit no less. Their charity is overflowing, if it were but more enlightened: and it may be supposed that they could not exist without religion. It appears to superabound; but it is not usually of a healthy character. It may seem harsh to say this: but is it not the fact that religion emanates from the nature, from the moral state of the individual? Is it not therefore true that unless the nature be completely exercised, the moral state harmonised, the religion cannot be healthy?

One consequence, mournful and injurious, of the "chivalrous" taste and temper of a country with regard to its women is that it is difficult, where it is not impossible, for women to earn their bread. Where it is a boast that women do not labour, the encouragement and rewards of labour are not provided. It is so in America. In some parts, there are now so many women dependent on their own exertions for a maintenance, that the evil will give way before the force of circumstances. In the meantime, the lot of poor women is sad. Before the opening of the factories, there were but three resources; teaching, needle-work, and keeping boarding-houses or hotels. Now, there are the mills; and women are employed in printing-offices; as compositors, as well as folders and stitchers.

I dare not trust myself to do more than touch on this topic. There would be little use in dwelling upon it; for the mischief lies in the system by which women are depressed, so as to have the greater number of objects of pursuit placed beyond their reach, more than in any minor arrangements which might be rectified by an exposure of particular evils. I would only ask of philanthropists of all countries to inquire of physicians what is the state of health of sempstresses; and to judge thence whether it is not inconsistent with common humanity that women should depend for bread upon such employment. Let them inquire what is the recompense of this kind of labour, and then wonder if they can that the pleasures of the licentious are chiefly supplied from that class. Let them reverence the strength of such as keep their virtue, when the toil which they know is slowly and surely destroying them will barely afford them bread, while the wages of sin are luxury and idleness. During the present interval between the feudal age and the coming time, when life and its occupations will be freely thrown open to women as to men, the condition of the female working classes is such that if its sufferings were but made known, emotions of horror and shame would tremble through the whole of society.

For women who shrink from the lot of the needle-woman,—almost equally dreadful, from the fashionable milliner down to the humble stocking-darner,—for those who shrink through pride, or fear of sickness, poverty, or temptation, there is little resource but pretension to teach. What office is there which involves more responsibility, which requires more qualifications, and which ought, therefore, to be more honourable, than that of teaching? What work is there for which a decided bent, not to say a genius, is more requisite? Yet are governesses furnished, in America as elsewhere, from among those who teach because they want bread; and who certainly would not teach for any other reason. Teaching and training children is, to a few, a very few, a delightful employment, notwithstanding all its toils and cares. Except to these few it is irksome; and, when accompanied with poverty and mortification, intolerable. Let philanthropists inquire into the proportion of governesses among the inmates of lunatic asylums. The answer to this question will be found to involve a world of rebuke and instruction. What can be the condition of the sex when such an occupation is overcrowded with candidates, qualified and unqualified? What is to be hoped from the generation of children confided to the cares of a class, conscientious perhaps beyond most, but reluctant, harassed, and depressed?

The most accomplished governesses in the United States may obtain 600 dollars a-year in the families of southern planters; provided they will promise to teach everything. In the north they are paid less; and in neither case, is there a possibility of making provision for sickness and old age. Ladies who fully deserve the confidence of society may realise an independence in a few years by school-keeping in the north: but, on the whole, the scanty reward of female labour in America remains the reproach to the country which its philanthropists have for some years proclaimed it to be. I hope they will persevere in their proclamation, though special methods of charity will not avail to cure the evil. It lies deep; it lies in the subordination of the sex: and upon this the exposures and remonstrances of philanthropists may ultimately succeed in fixing the attention of society; particularly of women. The progression or emancipation of any class usually, if not always, takes place through the efforts of individuals of that class: and so it must be here. All women should inform themselves of the condition of their sex, and of their own position. It must necessarily follow that the noblest of them will, sooner or later, put forth a moral power which shall prostrate cant, and burst asunder the bonds, (silken to some, but cold iron to others,) of feudal prejudices and usages. In the meantime, is it to be understood that the principles of the Declaration of Independence bear no relation to half of the human race? If so, what is the ground of the limitation? If not so, how is the restricted and dependent state of women to be reconciled with the proclamation that "all are endowed by their Creator with certain inalienable rights; that among these are life, liberty, and the pursuit of happiness?"

PART TWO

The Critique of Capitalist Production, Industrial Society, and the Democratic State

AUGUSTE COMTE

Auguste Comte was born on January 19, 1798, in Montpellier, in the south of France. Both his father, a tax official for the government, and his mother were royalist Roman Catholics who were ill at ease with the ascendancy of republicanism and skepticism following the French Revolution. By the age of fourteen, however, Comte had not only denounced his family's religion, declaring that he had "naturally ceased believing in God," but had also distanced himself from its royalist tendencies by siding with republicans. These familial tensions and frustrations continued to rear their heads in Comte's adult life as well, with Comte calling his family "covetous and hypocritical" and complaining that if it was not for the persistent health issues that plagued his father and sister, his family would have been able to better support his intellectual endeavors and lessen the precariousness of his day-to-day existence.

Intellectually precocious, Comte was known to be one of the brightest students in his classes while he was growing up. In the summer of 1814, he took the entrance examination for the prestigious *École Polytechnique* in Paris and was the fourth person to be admitted in that year's class. At the same time, however, Comte also earned the reputation of being one of the most rebellious students in his classes. In 1816, a group of six *Polytechnique* students, with Comte as their leader, complained to the administration about the school's antiquated examination methods. After the school threatened to punish all six of the students, the entire student body expressed its dissatisfaction by protesting the proposed action against Comte and the others. The administration then asked the governmental minister in charge of the school for his opinion on the matter. It was determined that the *Polytechnique* would be reorganized and that students who were in good standing with the school could reapply. Comte was deemed not to be one of them.

With few other options open to him, Comte began tutoring and giving private mathematics lessons as a means of supporting himself. Although he briefly entertained the dream of emigrating to the United States, this possibility quickly faded when Congress indefinitely postponed the opening of the American version of the French *Polytechnique*. It was at this time that Comte struck up a serendipitous relationship with Henrí Saint-Simon. One of the first to recognize the significance that economic structures played in shaping modern societies and to offer a utopian socialist philosophy, Saint-Simon was the director of the periodical *Industrie* and an influential figure in French intellectual circles. Comte became Saint-Simon's secretary, and the two collaborated fruitfully until 1824 when they had a falling out and broke off their friendship. By the end of this partnership with Saint-Simon, Comte had earned a reputation as an up-and-comer in academic and journalistic settings. As valuable as this reputation may have been for Comte, however, he was still unable to secure a permanent academic position, and he was again forced to offer private lessons in mathematics to support himself.

One advantage of this arrangement, however, was that it enabled Comte to devote himself more fully to his studies and the development of his own ideas. In April 1826, he began a series of lectures, delivered to private audiences of acquaintances and important scientific and intellectual figures, in which he presented the rudiments of his positive philosophy. But before he could complete his lectures, Comte suffered a nervous breakdown and fell into an extended period of depression. At one point, Comte even went so far as to attempt suicide by jumping into the Seine river. But by 1829, he was on the mend and was again delivering lectures. Over the course of the next thirteen years, with little or no institutional support and with his marriage to Caroline Massin, increasingly troubled, Comte, nonetheless, managed to complete his masterwork *The Course of Positive Philosophy* (1830–1842).

In this work, Comte analyzed the evolution of intellectual thought over the course of human history and argued that it developed according to the Law of Three Stages. In the theological stage, supernatural forces are assumed to control the world; in the metaphysical stage, abstract forces and "personified abstractions" are thought to be the prime movers of history; and, finally, in the positive stage, events are explained through observation, experimentation, and analytical comparison. Just as humankind followed a set path in its development, Comte believed the same was true of the sciences, each of which he saw as progressing at different rates, depending on their relative complexity, generality, and independence from other subjects. Thus, Comte averred that astronomy was the first science to evolve, followed by physics, chemistry, biology, and eventually sociology. As the final science, sociology, a term that Comte himself coined, would shed light on the earlier sciences, synthesize all previous knowledge, and be able to reveal the principles and laws that affected the functioning of societies.

Following the publication of the *Course of Positive Philosophy*, Comte received increased attention for his work, not only in France, but in England, where John Stuart Mill became a vocal advocate of Comte's work. At one point, Mill even went so far as to have several of his associates, who were also admirers of Comte, send Comte money to ease his material difficulties. Comte's personal life also underwent significant changes in the years following the publication of *Positive Philosophy*. Shortly after its publication, his wife left him after several difficult years of marriage. Then in 1844, Comte met and fell in love with Clotilde de Vaux, an upper-class woman who was more than fifteen years has junior. The otherwise reserved and generally distant Comte showed an emotional and impetuous side to himself that had never been seen before. Although de Vaux died of tuberculosis, not even a year after they had met, Comte's work, especially his thinking on the role that women should play in a positivist society, continued to reflect the profound influence she had on his life, since he now placed much more emphasis on the importance that emotion should play in modern society.

Between 1851 and 1854, Comte finished his other major work, *System of Positive Polity*, in which he further elaborated his understanding of what sociology was and the role that it should play in modern society. The work's central thesis was that a concern for moral progress should be a central focus of the human sciences. As scientists, and more specifically sociologists, arrived at an understanding of how societies functioned, their keen insights should be used to make moral pronouncements of what was good and evil and how best individuals could fulfill their collective obligations to society. Thus, ultimately, a religion of humanity, shed of all supernatural assumptions and with sociologists as quasi-priests, would occupy the position of the highest science, according to Comte. By the end of his life, in 1857, Comte the humanist had won out over Comte the scientist as he came to see himself as the high priest of this religion and even took to signing his letters "The Founder of Universal Religion, Great Priest of Humanity." By the close of the century, England and France had both given birth to Positivistic Societies while Comtean churches had appeared as far away as Brazil.

POSITIVE PHILOSOPHY

1830–1842

INTRODUCTION

CHAPTER I. ACCOUNT OF THE AIM OF THIS WORK.—VIEW OF THE NATURE AND IMPORTANCE OF THE POSITIVE PHILOSOPHY

A GENERAL statement of any system of philosophy may be either a sketch of a doctrine to be established, or a summary of a doctrine already established. If greater value belongs to the last, the first is still important, as characterizing from its origin the subject to be treated. In a case like the present, where the proposed study is vast and hitherto indeterminate, it is especially important that the field of research should be marked out with all possible accuracy. For this purpose, I will glance at the considerations which have originated this work, and which will be fully elaborated in the course of it.

In order to understand the true value and character of the Positive Philosophy, we must take a brief general view of the progressive course of the human mind, regarded as a whole; for no conception can be understood otherwise than through its history.

Law of human progress

From the study of the development of human intelligence, in all directions, and through all times, the discovery arises of a great fundamental law, to which it is necessarily subject, and which has a solid foundation of proof, both in the facts of our organization and in our historical experience. The law is this:—that each of our leading conceptions—each branch of our knowledge—passes successively through three different theoretical condititions: the Theological, or fictitious; the Metaphysical, or abstract; and the Scientific, or positive. In other words, the human mind, by its nature, employs in its progress three methods of philosophizing, the character of which is essentially different, and even radically opposed: viz., the theological method, the metaphysical, and the positive. Hence arise three philosophies, or general systems of conceptions on the aggregate of phenomena, each of which excludes the others. The first is the necessary point of departure of the human understanding; and the third is its fixed and definite state. The second is merely a state of transition.

First Stage

In the theological state, the human mind, seeking the essential nature of beings, the first and final causes (the origin and purpose) of all effects—in short, Absolute knowledge—supposes all phenomena to be produced by the immediate action of supernatural beings.

Second Stage

In the metaphysical state which is only a modification of the first, the mind supposes, instead of supernatural beings, abstract forces, veritable entities (that is, personified abstractions) inherent in all beings, and capable of producing all phenomena. What is called the explanation of phenomena is, in this stage, a mere reference of each to its proper entity.

From *Positive Philosophy of Auguste Comte*, freely translated and condensed by Harriet Martineau (New York: Calvin Blanchard, 1855).

Third Stage

In the final, the positive state, the mind has given over the vain search after Absolute notions, the origin and destination of the universe, and the causes of phenomena, and applies itself to the study of their laws—that is, their invariable relations of succession and resemblance. Reasoning and observation, duly combined, are the means of this knowledge. What is now understood when we speak of an explanation of facts is simply the establishment of a connection between single phenomena and some general facts, the number of which continually diminishes with the progress of science.

Ultimate point of each

The Theological system arrived at the highest perfection of which it is capable when it substituted the providential action of a single Being for the varied operations of the numerous divinities which had been before imagined. In the same way, in the last stage of the Metaphysical system, men substitute one great entity (Nature) as the cause of all phenomena, instead of the multitude of entities at first supposed. In the same way, again, the ultimate perfection of the Positive system would be (if such perfection could be hoped for) to represent all phenomena as particular aspects of a single general fact—such as Gravitation, for instance.

The importance of the working of this general law will be established hereafter. At present, it must suffice to point out some of the grounds of it.

Evidence of the law

There is no science which, having attained the positive stage, does not bear marks of having passed through the others. Some time since it was (whatever it might be) composed, as we can now perceive, of metaphysical abstractions; and, further back in the course of time, it took its form from theological conceptions.

Actual

We shall have only too much occasion to see, as we proceed, that our most advanced sciences still bear very evident marks of the two earlier periods through which they have passed.

The progress of the individual mind is not only an illustration, but an indirect evidence of that of the general mind. The point of departure of the individual and of the race being the same, the phases of the mind of a man correspond to the epochs of the mind of the race. Now, each of us is aware, if he looks back upon his own history, that he was a theologian in his childhood, a metaphysician in his youth, and a natural philosopher in his manhood. All men who are up to their age can verify this for themselves.

Besides the observation of facts, we have theoretical reasons in support of this law.

Theoretical

The most important of these reasons arises from the necessity that always exists for some theory to which to refer our facts, combined with the clear impossibility that, at the outset of human knowledge, men could have formed theories out of the observation of facts. All good intellects have repeated, since Bacon's time, that there can be no real knowledge but that which is based on observed facts. This is incontestable, in our present advanced stage; but, if we look back to the primitive stage of human knowledge, we shall see that it must have been otherwise then. If it is true that every theory must be based upon observed facts, it is equally true that facts can not be observed without the guidance of some theory. Without such guidance, our facts would be desultory and fruitless; we could not retain them: for the most part we could not even perceive them.

Thus, between the necessity of observing facts in order to form a theory, and having a theory in order to observe facts, the human mind would have been entangled in a vicious circle, but for the natural opening afforded by Theological conceptions. This is the fundamental reason for the theological character of the primitive philosophy. This necessity is confirmed by the perfect suitability of the theological philosophy to the earliest researches of the human mind. It is remarkable that the most inaccessible questions—those of the nature of beings, and the origin and purpose of phenomena—should be the first to occur in a primitive state, while those which are really within our reach are regarded as almost unworthy of serious study. The reason is evident enough:—that experience alone can teach us the measure of our powers; and if men had not begun by an exaggerated estimate of what they can do, they would never have done all that they are capable of. Our organization requires this. At such a period there could have been no reception of a positive philosophy, whose function is to discover the laws of phenomena, and whose leading characteristic it is to regard as interdicted to human reason those sublime mysteries which theology explains, even to their minutest details, with the most attractive facility. It is just so under a practical view of the nature of the researches with which men first occupied themselves. Such inquiries offered the powerful charm of unlimited empire over the external world—a world destined wholly for our use, and involved in every way with our existence. The theological philosophy, presenting this view, administered exactly the stimulus necessary to incite the human mind to the irksome labor without which it could make no progress. We can now scarcely conceive of such a state of things, our reason having become sufficiently mature to enter upon laborious scientific researches, without needing any such stimulus as wrought upon the imaginations of astrologers and alchemists. We have motive enough in the hope of discovering the laws of phenomena, with a view to the confirmation or rejection of a theory. But it could not be so in the earliest days; and it is to the chimeras of astrology and alchemy that we owe the long series of observations and experiments on which our positive science is based. Kepler felt this on behalf of astronomy, and Berthollet on behalf of chemistry. Thus was a spontaneous philosophy, the theological, the only possible beginning, method, and provisional system, out of which the Positive philosophy could grow. It is easy, after this, to perceive how Metaphysical methods and doctrines must have afforded the means of transition from the one to the other.

The human understanding, slow in its advance, could not step at once from the theological into the positive philosophy. The two are so radically opposed, that an intermediate system of conceptions has been necessary to render the transition possible. It is only in doing this, that metaphysical conceptions have any utility whatever. In contemplating phenomena, men substitute for supernatural direction a corresponding entity. This entity may have been supposed to be derived from the supernatural action: but it is more easily lost sight of, leaving attention free from the facts themselves, till, at length, metaphysical agents have ceased to be anything more than the abstract names of phenomena. It is not easy to say by what other process than this our minds could have passed from supernatural considerations to natural; from the theological system to the positive.

The law of human development being thus established, let us consider what is the proper nature of the Positive Philosophy.

Character of the Positive Philosophy

As we have seen, the first characteristic of the Positive Philosophy is that it regards all phenomena as subjected to invariable natural *Laws*. Our business is,—seeing how vain is any research into what are called *Causes*, whether first or final,—to pursue an accurate discovery of these Laws, with a view to reducing them to the smallest possible number. By speculating upon causes, we could solve no difficulty about origin and purpose. Our real business is to analyse accurately the circumstances of phenomena, and to connect them by the natural relations of succession and resemblance. The best illustration of this is in the case of the doctrine of Gravitation. We say that the general phenomena of the universe are *explained* by it, because it connects under one head the whole immense variety of astronomical facts; exhibiting the constant tendency of atoms toward each other in direct proportion to their masses, and in inverse proportion to the squares of their distance; while the general fact itself is a mere extension of one which is perfectly familiar to us, and which we therefore say that we know;—the weight of bodies on the surface of the earth. As to what weight and attraction are, we have nothing to do with that, for it is not a matter of knowledge at all. Theologians and metaphysicians may imagine and refine about such questions; but positive philosophy rejects them. When any attempt has been made to explain them, it has ended only in saying that attraction is universal weight, and that weight is terrestrial attraction: that is, that the two orders of phenomena are identical; which is the point from which the question set out. Again, M. Fourier, in his fine series of researches on Heat, has given us all the most important and precise laws of the phenomena of heat, and many large and new truths, without once inquiring into its nature, as his predecessors had done when they disputed about calorific matter and the action of a universal ether. In treating his subject in the Positive method, he finds inexhaustible material for all his activity of research, without betaking himself to insoluble questions.

History of the Positive Philosophy

Before ascertaining the stage which the Positive Philosophy has reached, we must bear in mind that the different kinds of our knowledge have passed through the three stages of progress at different rates, and have not therefore arrived at the same time. The rate of advance depends on the nature of the knowledge in question, so distinctly that, as we shall see hereafter, this consideration constitutes an accessary to the fundamental law of progress. Any kind of knowledge reaches the positive stage early in proportion to its generality, simplicity, and independence of other departments. Astronomical science, which is above all made up of facts that are general, simple, and independent of other sciences, arrived first; then terrestrial Physics; then Chemistry; and, at length, Physiology.

It is difficult to assign any precise date to this revolution in science. It may be said, like everything else, to have been always going on; and especially since the labors of Aristotle and the school of Alexandria; and then from the introduction of natural science into the West of Europe by the Arabs. But, if we must fix upon some marked period, to serve as a rallying point, it must be that,—about two centuries ago,—when the human mind was astir under the precepts of Bacon, the conceptions of Descartes, and the discoveries of Galileo. Then it was that the spirit of the Positive philosophy rose up in opposition to that of the superstitious and scholastic systems which had hitherto obscured the true character of all science. Since that date, the progress of the Positive philosophy, and the decline of the other two, have been so marked that no rational mind now doubts that the revolution is destined to go on to its completion,—every branch of knowledge being, sooner or later, brought within the operation of Positive philosophy. This is not yet the case. Some are still lying outside: and not till they are brought in will the Positive philosophy possess that character of universality which is necessary to its definitive constitution.

In mentioning just now the four principal categories of phenomena,—astronomical, physical, chemical, and physiological,—there was an omission which will have been noticed. Nothing was said of Social phenomena.

New department of Positive Philosophy

Though involved with the physiological, Social phenomena demand a distinct classification, both on account of their importance and of their difficulty. They are the most individual, the most complicated, the most dependent on all others; and therefore they must be the latest,—even if they had no special obstacle to encounter. This branch of science has not hitherto entered into the domain of Positive philosophy. Theological and metaphysical methods, exploded in other departments, are as yet exclusively applied, both in the way of inquiry and discussion, in all treatment of Social subjects, though the best minds are heartily weary of eternal disputes about divine right and the sovereignity of the people. This is the great, while it is evidently the only gap which has to be filled, to constitute, solid and entire, the Positive Philosophy. Now that the human mind has grasped celestial and terrestrial physics,—mechanical and chemical; organic physics, both vegetable and animal,—there remains one science, to fill up the series of sciences of observation,—Social physics. This is what men have now most need of: and this it is the principal aim of the present work to establish.

Social Physics

It would be absurd to pretend to offer this new science at once in a complete state. Others, less now, are in very unequal conditions of forwardness. But the same character of positivity which is impressed on all the others will be shown to belong to this. This once done, the philosophical system of the moderns will be in fact complete, as there will then be no phenomenon which does not naturally enter into some one of the five great categories. All our fundamental conceptions having become homogeneous, the Positive state will be fully established. It can never again change its character, though it will be for ever in course of development by additions of new knowledge. Having acquired the character of universality which has hitherto been the only advantage resting with the two preceding systems, it will supersede them by its natural superiority, and leave to them only an historical existence.

Secondary aim of this work

We have stated the special aim of this work. Its secondary and general aim is this:—to review what has been effected in the Sciences, in order to show that they are not radically separate, but all branches from the same trunk. If we had confined ourselves to the first and special object of the work, we should have produced merely a study of Social physics: whereas, in introducing the second and general, we offer a study of Positive philosophy, passing in review all the positive sciences already formed.

To review the philosophy of the Sciences

The purpose of this work is not to give an account of the Natural Sciences. Besides that it would be endless, and that it would require a scientific preparation such as no one man possesses, it would be apart from our object, which is to go through a course of not Positive Science, but Positive Philosophy. We have only to consider each fundamental science in its relation to the whole positive system, and to the spirit which characterizes it; that is, with regard to its methods and its chief results.

The two aims, though distinct, are inseparable; for, on the one hand, there can be no positive philosophy without a basis of social science, without which it could not be all-comprehensive; and, on the other hand, we could not pursue Social science without having been prepared by the study of phenomena less complicated than those of society, and furnished with a knowledge of laws and anterior facts which have a bearing upon social science. Though the fundamental sciences are not all equally interesting to ordinary minds, there is no one of them that can be neglected in an inquiry like the present; and, in the eye of philosophy, all are of equal value to human welfare. Even those which appear the least interesting have their own value, either on account of the perfection of their methods, or as being the necessary basis of all the others.

Speciality

Lest it should be supposed that our course will lead us into a wilderness of such special studies as are at present the bane of a true positive philosophy, we will briefly advert to the existing prevalence of such special pursuit. In the primitive state of human knowledge there is no regular division of intellectual labor. Every student cultivates all the sciences. As knowledge accrues, the sciences part off; and students devote themselves each to some one branch. It is owing to this division of employment, and concentration of whole minds upon a single department, that science has made so prodigious an advance in modern times; and the perfection of this division is one of the most important characteristics of the Positive philosophy. But, while admitting all the merits of this change, we can not be blind to the eminent disadvantages which arise from the limitation of minds to a particular study. It is inevitable that each should be possessed with exclusive notions, and be therefore incapable of the general superiority of ancient students, who actually owed that general superiority to the inferiority of their knowledge. We must consider whether the evil can be avoided without losing the good of the modern arrangement; for the evil is becoming urgent. We all acknowledge that the divisions established for the convenience of scientific pursuit are radically artificial; and yet there are very few who can embrace in idea the whole of any one science: each science moreover being itself only a part of a great whole. Almost every one is busy about his own particular section, without much thought about its relation to the general system of positive knowledge. We must not be blind to the evil, nor slow in seeking a remedy. We must not forget that this is the weak side of the positive philosophy, by which it may yet be attacked, with some hope of success, by the adherents of the theological and metaphysical systems. As to the remedy, it certainly does not lie in a return to the ancient confusion of pursuits, which would be mere retrogression, if it were possible, which it is not. It lies in perfecting the division of employments itself,—in carrying it one degree higher,—in constituting one more speciality from the study of scientific generalities.

Proposed new class of students

Let us have a new class of students, suitably prepared, whose business it shall be to take the respective sciences as they are, determine the spirit of each, ascertain their relations and mutual connection, and reduce their respective principles to the smallest number of general principles, in conformity with the fundamental rules of the Positive Method. At the same time, let other students be prepared for their special pursuit by an education which recognises the whole scope of positive science, so as to profit by the labors of the students of generalities, and so as to correct reciprocally, under that guidance, the results obtained by each. We see some approach already to this arrangement. Once established, there would be nothing to apprehend from any extent of division of employments. When we once have a class of learned men, at the disposal of all others, whose business it shall be to connect each new discovery with the general system, we may dismiss all fear of the great whole being lost sight of in the pursuit of the details of knowledge. The organization of scientific research will then be complete; and it will henceforth have occasion only to extend its development, and not to change its character. After all, the formation of such a new class as is proposed would be merely an extension of the principle which has created all the classes we have. While science was narrow, there was only one class: as it expanded, more were instituted. With a further advance a fresh need arises, and this new class will be the result.

Advantages of the Positive Philosophy

The general spirit of a course of Positive Philosophy having been thus set forth, we must now glance at the chief advantages which may be derived, on behalf of human progression, from the study of it. Of these advantages, four may be especially pointed out.

Illustrates the Intellectual function

I. The study of the Positive Philosophy affords the only rational means of exhibiting the logical laws of the human mind, which have hitherto been sought by unfit methods. To explain what is meant by this, we may refer to a saying of M. de Blainville, in his work on Comparative Anatomy, that every active, and especially every living being, may be regarded under two relations—the Statical and the Dynamical; that is, under conditions or in action. It is clear that all considerations range themselves under the one or the other of these heads. Let us apply this classification to the intellectual functions.

If we regard these functions under their Statical aspect—that is, if we consider the conditions under which they exist—we must determine the organic circumstances of the case, which inquiry involves it with anatomy and physiology. If we look at the Dynamic aspect, we have to study simply the exercise and results of the intellectual powers of the human race, which is neither more nor less than the general object of the Positive Philosophy. In short, looking at all scientific theories as so many great logical facts, it is only by the thorough observation of these facts that we can arrive at the knowledge of logical laws. These being the only means of knowledge of intellectual phenomena, the illusory psychology, which is the last phase of theology, is excluded. It pretends to accomplish the discovery of the laws of the human mind by contemplating it in itself; that is, by separating it from causes and effects. Such an attempt, made in defiance of the physiological study of our intellectual organs, and of the observation of rational methods of procedure, can not succeed at this time of day.

The Positive Philosophy, which has been rising since the time of Bacon, has now secured such a preponderance, that the metaphysicians themselves profess to ground their pretended science on an observation of facts. They talk of external and internal facts, and say that their business is with the latter. This is much like saying that vision is explained by luminous objects painting their images upon the retina. To this the physiologists reply that another eye would be needed to see the image. In the same manner, the mind may observe all phenomena but its own. It may be said that a man's intellect may observe his passions, the seat of the reason being somewhat apart from that of the emotions in the brain; but there can be nothing like scientific observation of the passions, except from without, as the stir of the emotions disturbs the observing faculties more or less. It is yet more out of the question to make an intellectual observation of intellectual processes. The observing and observed organ are here the same, and its action can not be pure and natural. In order to observe, your intellect must pause from activity; yet it is this very activity that you want to observe. If you can not effect the pause, you can not observe: if you do effect it, there is nothing to observe. The results of such a method are in proportion to its absurdity. After two thousand years of psychological pursuit, no one proposition is established to the satisfaction of its followers. They are divided, to this day, into a multitude of schools, still disputing about the very elements of their doctrine. This interior observation gives birth to almost as many theories as there are observers. We ask in vain for any one discovery, great or small, which has been made under this method. The psychologists have done some good in keeping up the activity of our understandings, when there was no better work for our faculties to do; and they may have added something to our stock of knowledge. If they have done so, it is by practising the Positive method—by observing the progress of the human mind in the light of science; that is, by ceasing, for the moment, to be psychologists.

The view just given in relation to logical Science becomes yet more striking when we consider the logical Art.

The Positive Method can be judged of only in action. It can not be looked at by itself, apart from the work on which it is employed. At all events, such a contemplation would be only a dead study, which could produce nothing in the mind which loses time upon it. We may talk for ever about the method, and state it in terms very wisely, without knowing half so much about it as the man who has once put it in practice upon a single particular of actual research, even without any philosophical intention. Thus it is that psychologists, by dint of reading the precepts of Bacon and the discourses of Descartes, have mistaken their own dreams for science.

Without saying whether it will ever be possible to establish, a priori, a true method of investigation, independent of a philosophical study of the sciences, it is clear that the thing has never been done yet, and that we are not capable of doing it now. We can not, as yet, explain the great logical procedures, apart from their applications. If we ever do, it will remain as necessary then as now to form good intellectual habits by studying the regular application of the scientific methods which we shall have attained.

This, then, is the first great result of the Positive Philosophy—the manifestation by experiment of the laws which rule the Intellect in the investigation of truth; and, as a consequence, the knowledge of the general rules suitable for that object.

Must regenerate Education

II. The second effect of the Positive Philosophy, an effect not less important and far more urgently wanted, will be to regenerate Education.

The best minds are agreed that our European education, still essentially theological, metaphysical, and literary, must be superseded by a Positive training, conformable to our time and needs. Even the governments of our day have shared, where they have not originated, the attempts to establish positive instruction; and this is a striking indication of the prevalent sense of what is wanted. While encouraging such endeavors to the utmost, we must not however, conceal from ourselves that everything yet done is inadequate to the object. The present exclusive speciality of our pursuits, and the consequent isolation of the sciences, spoil our teaching. If any student desires to form an idea of natural philosophy as a whole, he is compelled to go through each department as it is now taught, as if he were to be only an astronomer, or only a chemist; so that, be his intellect what it may, his training must remain very imperfect. And yet his object requires that he should obtain general positive conceptions of all the classes of natural phenomena. It is such an aggregate of conceptions, whether on a great or on a small scale, which must henceforth be the permanent basis of all human combinations. It will constitute the mind of future generations. In order to this regeneration of our intellectual system, it is necessary that the sciences, considered as branches from one trunk, should yield us, as a whole, their chief methods and their most important results. The specialities of science can be pursued by those whose vocation lies in that direction. They are indispensable; and they are not likely to be neglected; but they can never of themselves renovate our system of Education; and, to be of their full use, they must rest upon the basis of that general instruction which is a direct result of the Positive Philosophy.

Advances sciences by combining them

III. The same special study of scientific generalities must also aid the progress of the respective positive sciences: and this constitutes our third head of advantages.

The divisions which we establish between the sciences are, though not arbitrary, essentially artificial. The subject of our researches is one: we divide it for our convenience, in order to deal the more easily with its difficulties. But it sometimes happens—and especially with the most important doctrines of each science—that we need what we can not obtain under the present isolation of the sciences—a combination of several special points of view; and for want of this, very important problems wait for their solution much longer than they otherwise need do. To go back into the past for example: Descartes' grant conception with regard to analytical geometry is a discovery which has changed the whole aspect of mathematical science, and yielded the germ of all future progress; and it issued from the union of two sciences which had always before been separately regarded and pursued. The case of pending questions is yet more impressive; as, for instance, in Chemistry, the doctrine of Definite Proportions. Without entering upon the discussion of the fundamental principle of this theory, we may say with assurance that, in order to determine it—in order to determine whether it is a law of nature that atoms should necessarily combine in fixed numbers—it will be indispensable that the chemical point of view should be united with the physiological. The failure of the theory with regard to organic bodies indicates that the cause of this immense exception must be investigated; and such an inquiry belongs as much to physiology as to chemistry. Again, it is as yet undecided whether azote is a simple or a compound body. It was concluded by almost all chemists that azote is a simple body; the illustrious Berzilius hesitated, on purely chemical considerations; but he was also influenced by the physiological observation that animals which receive no azote in their food have as much of it in their tissues as carnivorous animals. From this we see how physiology must unite with chemistry to inform us whether azote is simple or compound, and to institute a new series of researches upon the relation between the composition of living bodies and their mode of alimentation.

Such is the advantage which, in the third place, we shall owe to Positive philosophy—the elucidation of the respective sciences by their combination. In the fourth place.

Must reorganize society

IV. The Positive Philosophy offers the only solid basis for that Social Reorganization which must succeed the critical condition in which the most civilized nations are now living.

It can not be necessary to prove to anybody who reads this work that Ideas govern the world, or throw it into chaos; in other words, that all social mechanism rests upon Opinions. The great political and moral crisis that societies are now undergoing is shown by a rigid analysis to arise out of intellectual anarchy. While stability in fundamental maxims is the first condition of genuine social order, we are suffering under an utter disagreement which may be called universal. Till a certain number of general ideas can be acknowledged as a rallying-point of social doctrine, the nations will remain in a revolutionary state, whatever palliatives may be devised; and their institutions can be only provisional. But whenever the necessary agreement on first principles can be obtained appropriate institutions will issue from them, without shock or resistance; for the causes of disorder will have been arrested by the mere fact of the agreement. It is in this direction that those must look who desire a natural and regular, a normal state of society.

Now, the existing disorder is abundantly accounted for by the existence, all at once, of three incompatible philosophies—the theological, the metaphysical, and the positive. Any one of these might alone secure some sort of social order; but while the three co-exist, it is impossible for us to understand one another upon any essential point whatever. If this is true, we have only to ascertain which of the philosophies must, in the nature of things, prevail; and, this ascertained, every man, whatever may have been his former views, can not but concur in its triumph. The problem once recognised, can not remain long unsolved; for all considerations whatever point to the Positive Philosophy as the one destined to prevail. It alone has been advancing during a course of centuries, throughout which the others have been declining. The fact is incontestable. Some may deplore it, but none can destroy it, nor therefore neglect it but under penalty of being betrayed by illusory speculations. This general revolution of the human mind is nearly accomplished. We have only to complete the Positive Philosophy by bringing Social phenomena within its comprehension, and afterward consolidating the whole into one body of homogeneous doctrine. The marked preference which almost all minds, from the highest to the commonest, accord to positive knowledge over vague and mystical conceptions, is a pledge of what the reception of this philosophy will be when it has acquired the only quality that it now wants—a character of due generality. When it has become complete, its supremacy will take place spontaneously, and will re-establish order throughout society. There is, at present, no conflict but between the theological and the metaphysical philosophies. They are contending for the task of reorganizing society; but it is a work too mighty for either of them. The positive philosophy has hitherto intervened only to examine both, and both are abundantly discredited by the process. It is time now to be doing something more effective, without wasting our forces in needless controversy. It is time to complete the vast intellectual operation begun by Bacon, Descartes, and Galileo, by constructing the system of general ideas which must henceforth prevail among the human race. This is the way to put an end to the revolutionary crisis which is tormenting the civilized nations of the world.

Leaving these four points of advantage, we must attend to one precautionary reflection.

No hope of reduction to a single law

Because it is proposed to consolidate the whole of our acquired knowledge into one body of homogeneous doctrine, it must not be supposed that we are going to study this vast variety as proceeding from a single principle, and as subjected to a single law. There is something so chimerical in attempts at universal explanation by a single law, that it may be as well to secure this Work at once from any imputation of the kind, though its development will show how undeserved such an imputation would be. Our intellectual resources are too narrow, and the universe is too complex, to leave any hope that it will ever be within our power to carry scientific perfection to its last degree of simplicity. Moreover, it appears as if the value of such an attainment, supposing it possible, were greatly overrated. The only way, for instance, in which we could achieve the business, would be by connecting all natural phenomena with the most general law we know—which is that of gravitation, by which astronomical phenomena are already connected with a portion of terrestrial physics. Laplace has indicated that chemical phenomena may be regarded as simple atomic effects of the Newtonian attraction, modified by the form and mutual position of the atoms. But supposing this view proveable (which it can not be while we are without data about the constitution of bodies), the difficulty of its application would doubtless be found so great that we must still maintain the existing division between astronomy and chemistry, with the difference that we now regard as natural that division which we should then call artificial. Laplace himself presented his idea only as a philosophic device, incapable of exercising any useful influence over the progress of chemical science. Moreover, supposing this insuperable difficulty overcome, we should be no nearer to scientific unity, since we then should still have to connect the whole of physiological phenomena with the same law, which certainly would not be the least difficult part of the enterprise. Yet, all things considered, the hypothesis we have glanced at would be the most favorable to the desired unity.

The consideration of all phenomena as referable to a single origin is by no means necessary to the systematic formation of science, any more than to the realization of the great and happy consequences that we anticipate from the positive philosophy. The only necessary unity is that of Method, which is already in great part established. As for the doctrine, it need not be *one*; it is enough that it be *homogeneous*. It is, then, under the double aspect of unity of method and homogeneousness of doctrine that we shall consider the different classes of positive theories in this work. While pursuing the philosophical aim of all science, the lessening of the number of general laws requisite for the explanation of natural phenomena, we shall regard as presumptuous every attempt, in all future time, to reduce them rigorously to one.

FREDERICK DOUGLASS

Frederick Douglass (1817–1895) was the most important African American intellectual of the nineteenth century. He lived twenty years as a slave and nearly nine as a fugitive slave, then achieved international fame as an abolitionist, editor, orator, and the author of three autobiographies. His *Narrative of the Life of Frederick Douglass, an American Slave, Written by Himself* (1845), the first of the three, is the most widely read of all American slave narratives. This text is an imaginative look into the world of oppression, resistance, and subterfuge within which the slaves lived, as well as historical analysis and abolitionist argument.

Douglass was born in Tuckahoe, Maryland, in 1817. His mother was a black slave of exceptional intelligence, his father a white man. At the age of eight he was sent to the plantation where his father was a manager, and one year later to the Auld household in Baltimore where he was taught to read. In 1833 Douglass was returned to the plantation, from which he attempted to escape, then delivered again to Auld, who apprenticed him as a ship caulker. As he describes in the *Narrative*, his two decades in slavery were marked by harsh divisions: between the life of a favored slave youth in the city and that of a fieldhand, between brutality and decent treatment, between the promise of literacy and the bitterness of its suppression.

In 1838 Douglass obtained the papers of a free seaman by masquerading as a sailor and escaped on the Chesapeake shore in Maryland. He was joined by his fiancée, a free black woman, and with the help of David Ruggles, a black leader involved in the Underground Railroad, the two fled to New York City. Soon the Douglasses moved to New Bedford, Massachusetts, with its large free black population. For three years Douglass worked as a day laborer and discovered the growing circle of Massachusetts abolitionists.

From his first public speeches before a gathering of the Anti-Slavery Society on Nantucket Island in 1841, Douglass revealed the gift for language and fascination with its power that would earn him the title "America's black Jeremiah." As many historians have noted, writing and oratory became for him the act of creating a public and historical self. In the *Narrative*, writing also became a means to witness the fact that, contrary to popular belief, blacks too had histories and that their struggles and aspirations mattered to society. On hundreds of platforms in the 1840s and 1850s, Douglass linked his own story to the spiritual autobiographies familiar to nineteenth-century Americans: tales of men self-made in station and self-liberated in spirit. Even more significant, he linked it to the collective experience of slaves for whom bondage, however crushing, was always responded to in human terms: as a trial of the soul as well as the body. His political sermons not only transfixed audiences with their tales of captivity and escape, but they fitted into the nation's oldest literary tradition, the jeremiad, with its reminders of America's divinely appointed mission and its warnings of betrayals of that mission, such as slavery.

In important respects, the *Narrative* is an artful summary of the many speeches Douglass delivered on the abolitionist lecture circuit during his first three years of freedom. It is propagandistic and manipulates the reader with purple prose. But on close reading, the book reveals much about the psychological world of slaves: its sheer terror but also its complexities. Portraits of slaveowners range from parody to denunciation and, in one case, even respect, and all serve Douglass's principal theme—that slaveholding, no less than the slave's own condition, is learned behavior and presumably can be unlearned. Publication of the *Narrative* in 1845 was an enormous success internationally as well as at home. But by revealing his master's identity, the book forced Douglass to seek refuge in England, where friendly liberals managed to purchase his freedom.

From 1847, after his return to the United States, until 1863, Douglass published his own abolitionist newspaper, the *North Star*, in Rochester, New York. The paper also supported women's rights, a cause that Douglass had championed since his participation in the first women's rights convention in 1848. This support can be seen in his essay "The Rights of Women." In these years Douglass broke with his mentor, William Lloyd Garrison, and in the pages of the *North Star* called for more pragmatic, less evangelical, and less doctrinaire tactics for the antislavery movement. He came to believe that the Constitution could be used to exert federal power against slavery, especially its expansion into the West; he ultimately backed the Republican party. He used his lecture fees to aid fugitive slaves, headed the Rochester station of the Underground Railroad, and framed a plan for the establishment of an industrial college for African Americans. Yet despite his hopes for the political system and his status as international celebrity of the abolitionist movement, Douglass refused to disavow violence as a means of destroying slavery. Characteristically, he raised money for John Brown and remained an ally, even while opposing his friend's violent raid on Harper's Ferry in 1859.

During the Civil War, Douglass pushed for emancipation and enfranchisement and was an early advocate of the use of black troops by the Union Army. He passionately supported Reconstruction and campaigned for postwar Republican candidates. In 1871 President Grant appointed him assistant secretary of the Santo Domingo commission, and other federal appointments followed, including that of minister to Haiti (1889–1891). Douglass died in Washington on Februrary 20, 1895.

NARRATIVE OF THE LIFE OF FREDERICK DOUGLASS, AN AMERICAN SLAVE, WRITTEN BY HIMSELF

1845

I

I was born in Tuckahoe, near Hillsborough, and about twelve miles from Easton, in Talbot county, Maryland. I have no accurate knowledge of my age, never having seen any authentic record containing it. By far the larger part of the slaves know as little of their age as horses know of theirs, and it is the wish of most masters within my knowledge to keep their slaves thus ignorant. I do not remember to have ever met a slave who could tell of his birthday. They seldom come nearer to it than planting-time, harvest-time, cherry-time, spring-time, or fall-time. A want of information concerning my own was a source of unhappiness to me even during childhood. The white children could tell their ages. I could not tell why

Reprinted from *Narrative of the Life of Frederick Douglass, an American Slave, Written by Himself* by Frederick Douglass, ed. David Blight (Boston: Bedford Books of St. Martin's Press, Inc., 1993).

I ought to be deprived of the same privilege. I was not allowed to make any inquiries of my master concerning it. He deemed all such inquiries on the part of a slave improper and impertinent, and evidence of a restless spirit. The nearest estimate I can give makes me now between twenty-seven and twenty-eight years of age. I come to this, from hearing my master say, some time during 1835, I was about seventeen years old.

My mother was named Harriet Bailey. She was the daughter of Isaac and Betsey Bailey, both colored, and quite dark. My mother was of a darker complexion than either my grandmother or grandfather.

My father was a white man. He was admitted to be such by all I ever heard speak of my parentage. The opinion was also whispered that my master was my father; but of the correctness of this opinion, I know nothing; the means of knowing was withheld from me. My mother and I were separated when I was but an infant—before I knew her as my mother. It is a common custom, in the part of Maryland from which I ran away, to part children from their mothers at a very early age. Frequently, before the child has reached its twelfth month, its mother is taken from it, and hired out on some farm a considerable distance off, and the child is placed under the care of an old woman, too old for field labor. For what this separation is done, I do not know, unless it be to hinder the development of the child's affection toward its mother, and to blunt and destroy the natural affection of the mother for the child. This is the inevitable result.

I never saw my mother, to know her as such, more than four or five times in my life; and each of these times was very short in duration, and at night. She was hired by a Mr. Stewart, who lived about twelve miles from my home. She made her journeys to see me in the night, travelling the whole distance on foot, after the performance of her day's work. She was a field hand, and a whipping is the penalty of not being in the field at sunrise, unless a slave has special permission from his or her master to the contrary—a permission which they seldom get, and one that gives to him that gives it the proud name of being a kind master. I do not recollect of ever seeing my mother by the light of day. She was with me in the night. She would lie down with me, and get me to sleep, but long before I waked she was gone. Very little communication ever took place between us. Death soon ended what little we could have while she lived, and with it her hardships and suffering. She died when I was about seven years old, on one of my master's farms, near Lee's Mill. I was not allowed to be present during her illness, at her death, or burial. She was gone long before I knew any thing about it. Never having enjoyed, to any considerable extent, her soothing presence, her tender and watchful care, I received the tidings of her death with much the same emotions I should have probably felt at the death of a stranger.

Called thus suddenly away, she left me without the slightest intimation of who my father was. The whisper that my master was my father, may or may not be true; and, true or false, it is of but little consequence to my purpose whilst the fact remains, in all its glaring odiousness, that slaveholders have ordained, and by law established, that the children of slave women shall in all cases follow the condition of their mothers; and this is done too obviously to administer to their own lusts, and make a gratification of their wicked desires profitable as well as pleasurable; for by this cunning arrangement, the slaveholder, in cases not a few, sustains to his slaves the double relation of master and father.

I know of such cases; and it is worthy of remark that such slaves invariably suffer greater hardships, and have more to contend with, than others. They are, in the first place, a constant offence to their mistress. She is ever disposed to find fault with them; they can seldom do any thing to please her; she is never better pleased than when she sees them under the lash, especially when she suspects her husband of showing to his mulatto children favors which he withholds from his black slaves. The master is frequently compelled to sell this class of his slaves, out of deference to the feelings of his white wife; and, cruel as the deed may strike any one to be, for a man to sell his own children to human flesh-mongers, it is often the dictate of humanity for him to do so; for, unless he does this, he must not only whip them himself, but must stand by and see one white son tie up his brother, of but few shades darker complexion than himself, and ply the gory lash to his naked back; and if he lisp one word of disapproval, it is set down to his parental partiality, and only makes a bad matter worse, both for himself and the slave whom he would protect and defend.

Every year brings with it multitudes of this class of slaves. It was doubtless in consequence of a knowledge of this fact, that one great statesman of the south predicted the downfall of slavery by the inevitable laws of population. Whether this prophecy is ever fulfilled or not, it is nevertheless plain that a very different-looking class of people are springing up at the south, and are now held in slavery, from those originally brought to this country from Africa; and if their increase will do no other good, it will do away the force of the argument, that God cursed Ham, and therefore American slavery is right. If the lineal descendants of Ham are alone to be scripturally enslaved, it is certain that slavery at the south must soon become unscriptural; for thousands are ushered into the world, annually, who, like myself, owe their existence to white fathers, and those fathers most frequently their own masters.

I have had two masters. My first master's name was Anthony. I do not remember his first name. He was generally called Captain Anthony—a title which, I presume, he acquired by sailing a craft on the Chesapeake Bay. He was not considered a rich slaveholder. He owned two or three farms, and about thirty slaves. His farms and slaves were under the care of an overseer. The overseer's name was Plummer. Mr. Plummer was a miserable drunkard, a profane swearer, and a savage monster. He always went armed with a cowskin and a heavy cudgel. I have known him to cut and slash the women's heads so horribly, that even master would be enraged at his cruelty, and would threaten to whip him if he did not mind himself. Master, however, was not a humane slaveholder. It required extraordinary barbarity on the part of an overseer to affect him. He was a cruel man, hardened by a long life of slaveholding. He would at times seem to take great pleasure in whipping a slave. I have often been awakened at the dawn of day by the most heart-rending shrieks of an own aunt of mine, whom he used to tie up to a joist, and whip upon her naked back till she was literally covered with blood. No words, no tears, no prayers, from his gory victim, seemed to move his iron heart from its bloody purpose. The louder she screamed, the harder he whipped; and where the blood ran fastest, there he whipped longest. He would whip her to make her scream, and whip her to make her hush; and not until overcome by fatigue, would he cease to swing the blood-clotted cowskin. I remember the first time I ever witnessed this horrible exhibition. I was quite a child, but I well remember it. I never shall forget it whilst I remember any thing. It was the first of a long series of such outrages, of which I was doomed to be a witness and a participant. It struck me with awful force. It was the blood-stained gate, the entrance to the hell of slavery, through which I was about to pass. It was a most terrible spectacle. I wish I could commit to paper the feelings with which I beheld it.

. . .

II

My master's family consisted of two sons, Andrew and Richard; one daughter, Lucretia, and her husband, Captain Thomas Auld. They lived in one house, upon the home plantation of Colonel Edward Lloyd. My master was Colonel Lloyd's clerk and superintendent. He was what might be called the overseer of the overseers. I spent two years of childhood on this plantation in my old master's family. It was here that I witnessed the bloody transaction recorded in the first chapter; and as I received my first impressions of slavery on this plantation, I will give some description of it, and of slavery as it there existed. The plantation is about twelve miles north of Easton, in Talbot county, and is situated on the border of Miles River. The principal products raised upon it were tobacco, corn, and wheat. These were raised in great abundance; so that, with the products of this and the other farms belonging to him, he was able to keep in almost constant employment a large sloop, in carrying them to market at Baltimore. This sloop was named Sally Lloyd, in honor of one of the colonel's daughters. My master's son-in-law,

Captain Auld, was master of the vessel; she was otherwise manned by the colonel's own slaves. Their names were Peter, Isaac, Rich, and Jake. These were esteemed very highly by the other slaves, and looked upon as the privileged ones of the plantation; for it was no small affair, in the eyes of the slaves, to be allowed to see Baltimore.

Colonel Lloyd kept from three to four hundred slaves on his home plantation, and owned a large number more on the neighboring farms belonging to him. The names of the farms nearest to the home plantation were Wye Town and New Design. "Wye Town" was under the overseership of a man named Noah Willis. New Design was under the overseership of a Mr. Townsend. The overseers of these, and all the rest of the farms, numbering over twenty, received advice and direction from the managers of the home plantation. This was the great business place. It was the seat of government for the whole twenty farms. All disputes among the overseers were settled here. If a slave was convicted of any high misdemeanor, became unmanageable, or evinced a determination to run away, he was brought immediately here, severely whipped, put on board the sloop, carried to Baltimore, and sold to Austin Woolfolk, or some other slave-trader, as a warning to the slaves remaining.

Here, too, the slaves of all the other farms received their monthly allowance of food, and their yearly clothing. The men and women slaves received, as their monthly allowance of food, eight pounds of pork, or its equivalent in fish, and one bushel of corn meal. Their yearly clothing consisted of two coarse linen shirts, one pair of linen trousers, like the shirts, one jacket, one pair of trousers for winter, made of coarse negro cloth, one pair of stockings, and one pair of shoes; the whole of which could not have cost more than seven dollars. The allowance of the slave children was given to their mothers, or the old women having the care of them. The children unable to work in the field had neither shoes, stockings, jackets, nor trousers, given to them; their clothing consisted of two coarse linen shirts per year. When these failed them, they went naked until the next allowance-day. Children from seven to ten years old, of both sexes, almost naked, might be seen at all seasons of the year.

There were no beds given the slaves, unless one coarse blanket be considered such, and none but the men and women had these. This, however, is not considered a very great privation. They find less difficulty from the want of beds, than from the want of time to sleep; for when their day's work in the field is done, the most of them having their washing, mending, and cooking to do, and having few or none of the ordinary facilities for doing either of these, very many of their sleeping hours are consumed in preparing for the field the coming day; and when this is done, old and young, male and female, married and single, drop down side by side, on one common bed,—the cold, damp floor,—each covering himself or herself with their miserable blankets; and here they sleep till they are summoned to the field by the driver's horn. At the sound of this, all must rise, and be off to the field. There must be no halting; every one must be at his or her post; and woe betides them who hear not this morning summons to the field; for if they are not awakened by the sense of hearing, they are by the sense of feeling: no age nor sex finds any favor. Mr. Severe, the overseer, used to stand by the door of the quarter, armed with a large hickory stick and heavy cowskin, ready to whip any one who was so unfortunate as not to hear, or, from any other cause, was prevented from being ready to start for the field at the sound of the horn.

Mr. Severe was rightly named: he was a cruel man. I have seen him whip a woman, causing the blood to run half an hour at the time; and this, too, in the midst of her crying children, pleading for their mother's release. He seemed to take pleasure in manifesting his fiendish barbarity. Added to his cruelty, he was a profane swearer. It was enough to chill the blood and stiffen the hair of an ordinary man to hear him talk. Scarce a sentence escaped him but that was commenced or concluded by some horrid oath. The field was the place to witness his cruelty and profanity. His presence made it both the field of blood and of blasphemy. From the rising till the going down of the sun, he was cursing, raving, cutting, and slashing among the slaves of the field, in the most frightful manner. His career was short. He died very soon after I went to Colonel Lloyd's; and he died as he lived, uttering, with his dying groans, bitter curses and horrid oaths. His death was regarded by the slaves as the result of a merciful providence.

Mr. Severe's place was filled by a Mr. Hopkins. He was a very different man. He was less cruel, less profane, and made less noise, than Mr. Severe. His course was characterized by no extraordinary demonstrations of cruelty. He whipped, but seemed to take no pleasure in it. He was called by the slaves a good overseer.

. . .

III

. . .

To describe the wealth of Colonel Lloyd would be almost equal to describing the riches of Job. He kept from ten to fifteen house-servants. He was said to own a thousand slaves, and I think this estimate quite within the truth. Colonel Lloyd owned so many that he did not know them when he saw them; nor did all the slaves of the out-farms know him. It is reported of him, that, while riding along the road one day, he met a colored man, and addressed him in the usual manner of speaking to colored people on the public highways of the south: "Well, boy, whom do you belong to?" "To Colonel Lloyd," replied the slave. "Well, does the colonel treat you well?" "No, sir," was the ready reply. "What, does he work you too hard?" "Yes, sir." "Well, don't he give you enough to eat?" "Yes, sir, he gives me enough, such as it is."

The colonel, after ascertaining where the slave belonged, rode on; the man also went on about his business, not dreaming that he had been conversing with his master. He thought, said, and heard nothing more of the matter, until two or three weeks afterwards. The poor man was then informed by his overseer that, for having found fault with his master, he was now to be sold to a Georgia trader. He was immediately chained and handcuffed; and thus, without a moment's warning, he was snatched away, and forever sundered, from his family and friends, by a hand more unrelenting than death. This is the penalty of telling the truth, of telling the simple truth, in answer to a series of plain questions.

It is partly in consequence of such facts, that slaves, when inquired of as to their condition and the character of their masters, almost universally say they are contented, and that their masters are kind. The slaveholders have been known to send in spies among their slaves, to ascertain their views and feelings in regard to their condition. The frequency of this has had the effect to establish among the slaves the maxim, that a still tongue makes a wise head. They suppress the truth rather than take the consequences of telling it, and in so doing prove themselves a part of the human family. If they have any thing to say of their masters, it is generally in their masters' favor, especially when speaking to an untried man. I have been frequently asked, when a slave, if I had a kind master, and do not remember ever to have given a negative answer; nor did I, in pursuing this course, consider myself as uttering what was absolutely false; for I always measured the kindness of my master by the standard of kindness set up among slaveholders around us. Moreover, slaves are like other people, and imbibe prejudices quite common to others. They think their own better than that of others. Many, under the influence of this prejudice, think their own masters are better than the masters of other slaves; and this, too, in some cases, when the very reverse is true. Indeed, it is not uncommon for slaves even to fall out and quarrel among themselves about the relative goodness of their masters, each contending for the superior goodness of his own over that of the others. At the very same time, they mutually execrate their masters when viewed separately. It was so on our plantation. . . .

IV

Mr. Hopkins remained but a short time in the office of overseer. Why his career was so short, I do not know, but suppose he lacked the necessary severity to suit Colonel Lloyd. Mr. Hopkins was succeeded by Mr. Austin Gore, a man possessing, in an eminent degree, all those traits of character indispensable to what is called a first-rate overseer. Mr. Gore had served Colonel Lloyd, in the capacity of overseer, upon one of the out-farms, and had shown himself worthy of the high station of overseer upon the home or Great House Farm.

Mr. Gore was proud, ambitious, and persevering. He was artful, cruel, and obdurate. He was just the man for such a place, and it was just the place for such a man. It afforded scope for the full exercise of all his powers, and he seemed to be perfectly at home in it. He was one of those who could torture the slightest look, word, or gesture, on the part of the slave, into impudence, and would treat it accordingly. There must be no answering back to him; no explanation was allowed a slave, showing himself to have been wrongfully accused. Mr. Gore acted fully up to the maxim laid down by slaveholders,—"It is better that a dozen slaves suffer under the lash, than that the overseer should be convicted, in the presence of the slaves, of having been at fault." No matter how innocent a slave might be—it availed him nothing, when accused by Mr. Gore of any misdemeanor. To be accused was to be convicted, and to be convicted was to be punished; the one always following the other with immutable certainty. To escape punishment was to escape accusation; and few slaves had the fortune to do either, under the overseership of Mr. Gore. He was just proud enough to demand the most debasing homage of the slave, and quite servile enough to crouch, himself, at the feet of the master. . . .

. . .

I was probably between seven and eight years old when I left Colonel Lloyd's plantation. I left it with joy. I shall never forget the ecstasy with which I received the intelligence that my old master (Anthony) had determined to let me go to Baltimore, to live with Mr. Hugh Auld, brother to my old master's son-in-law, Captain Thomas Auld. I received this information about three days before my departure. They were three of the happiest days I ever enjoyed. I spent the most part of all these three days in the creek, washing off the plantation scurf, and preparing myself for my departure.

. . .

I look upon my departure from Colonel Lloyd's plantation as one of the most interesting events of my life. It is possible, and even quite probable, that but for the mere circumstance of being removed from that plantation to Baltimore, I should have to-day, instead of being here seated by my own table, in the enjoyment of freedom and the happiness of home, writing this Narrative, been confined in the galling chains of slavery. Going to live at Baltimore laid the foundation, and opened the gateway, to all my subsequent prosperity. I have ever regarded it as the first plain manifestation of that kind providence which has ever since attended me, and marked my life with so many favors. I regarded the selection of myself as being somewhat remarkable. There were a number of slave children that might have been sent from the plantation to Baltimore. There were those younger, those older, and those of the same age. I was chosen from among them all, and was the first, last, and only choice.

. . .

VI

My new mistress proved to be all she appeared when I first met her at the door,—a woman of the kindest heart and finest feelings. She had never had a slave under her control previously to myself, and prior to her marriage she had been dependent upon her own industry for a living. She was by trade a weaver; and by constant application to her business, she had been in a good degree preserved from the blighting and dehumanizing effects of slavery. I was utterly astonished at her goodness. I scarcely knew how to behave towards her. She was entirely unlike any other white woman I had ever seen. I could not approach her as I was accustomed to approach other white ladies. My early instruction was all out of place. The crouching servility, usually so acceptable a quality in a slave, did not answer when manifested toward her. Her favor was not gained by it; she seemed to be disturbed by it. She did not deem it impudent or unmannerly for a slave to look her in the face. The meanest slave was put fully at ease in her presence, and none left without feeling better for having seen her. Her face was made of heavenly smiles, and her voice of tranquil music.

But, alas! this kind heart had but a short time to remain such. The fatal poison of irresponsible power was already in her hands, and soon commenced its infernal work. That cheerful eye, under the influence of slavery, soon became red with rage; that voice, made all of sweet accord, changed to one of harsh and horrid discord; and that angelic face gave place to that of a demon.

Very soon after I went to live with Mr. and Mrs. Auld, she very kindly commenced to teach me the A, B, C. After I had learned this, she assisted me in learning to spell words of three or four letters. Just at this point of my progress, Mr. Auld found out what was going on, and at once forbade Mrs. Auld to instruct me further, telling her, among other things, that it was unlawful, as well as unsafe, to teach a slave to read. To use his own words, further, he said, "If you give a nigger an inch, he will take an ell. A nigger should know nothing but to obey his master—to do as he is told to do. Learning would *spoil* the best nigger in the world. Now," said he, "if you teach that nigger (speaking of myself) how to read, there would be no keeping him. It would forever unfit him to be a slave. He would at once become unmanageable, and of no value to his master. As to himself, it could do him no good, but a great deal of harm. It would make him discontented and unhappy. . . ." I now understood what had been to me a most perplexing difficulty—to wit, the white man's power to enslave the black man. It was a grand achievement and I prized it highly. From that moment, I understood the pathway from slavery to freedom. It was just what I wanted, and I got it at a time when I the least expected it. Whilst I was saddened by the thought of losing the aid of my kind mistress, I was gladdened by the invaluable instruction which, by the merest accident, I had gained from my master. Though conscious of the difficulty of learning without a teacher, I set out with high hope, and a fixed purpose, at whatever cost of trouble, to learn how to read. The very decided manner with which he spoke, and strove to impress his wife with the evil consequences of giving me instruction, served to convince me that he was deeply sensible of the truths he was uttering. It gave me the best assurance that I might rely with the utmost confidence on the results which, he said, would flow from teaching me to read. . . .

. . .

VII

. . .

The plan which I adopted, and the one by which I was most successful, was that of making friends of all the little white boys whom I met in the street.

As many of these as I could, I converted into teachers. With their kindly aid, obtained at different times and in different places, I finally succeeded in learning to read. When I was sent to errands, I always took my book with me, and by going one part of my errand quickly, I found time to get a lesson before my return. I used also to carry bread with me, enough of which was always in the house, and to which I was always welcome; for I was much better off in this regard than many of the poor white children in our neighborhood. This bread I used to bestow upon the hungry little urchins, who, in return, would give me that more valuable bread of knowledge. I am strongly tempted to give the names of two or three of those little boys, as a testimonial of the gratitude and affection I bear them; but prudence forbids; —not that it would injure me, but it might embarrass them; for it is almost an unpardonable offence to teach slaves to read in this Christian country. It is enough to say of the dear little fellows, that they lived on Philpot Street very near Durgin and Bailey's ship-yard. I used to talk this matter of slavery over with them. I would sometimes say to them, I wished I could be as free as they would be when they got to be men. "You will be free as soon as you are twenty-one, *but I am a slave for life*! Have not I as good a right to be free as you have?" These words used to trouble them; they would express for me the liveliest sympathy, and console me with the hope that something would occur by which I might be free.

. . .

VIII

In a very short time after I went to live at Baltimore, my old master's youngest son Richard died; and in about three years and six months after his death, my old master, Captain Anthony, died, leaving only his son, Andrew, and daughter, Lucretia, to share his estate. He died while on a visit to see his daughter at Hillsborough. Cut off thus unexpectedly, he left no will as to the disposal of his property. It was therefore necessary to have a valuation of the property, that it might be equally divided between Mrs. Lucretia and Master Andrew. I was immediately sent for, to be valued with the other property. Here again my feelings rose up in detestation of slavery. I had now a new conception of my degraded condition. Prior to this, I had become, if not insensible to my lot, at least partly so. I left Baltimore with a young heart overborne with sadness, and a soul full of apprehension. I took passage with Captain Rowe, in the schooner Wild Cat, and, after a sail of about twenty-four hours, I found myself near the place of my birth, I had now been absent from it almost, if not quite, five years. I, however, remembered the place very well. I was only about five years old when I left it, to go and live with my old master on Colonel Lloyd's plantation; so that I was now between ten and eleven years old.

We were all ranked together at the valuation. Men and women, old and young, married and single, were ranked with horses, sheep, and swine. There were horses and men, cattle and women, pigs and children, all holding the same rank in the scale of being, and were all subjected to the same narrow examination. Silvery-headed age and sprightly youth, maids and matrons, had to undergo the same indelicate inspection. At this moment, I saw more clearly than ever the brutalizing effects of slavery upon both slave and slaveholder.

After the valuation, then came the division. I have no language to express the high excitement and deep anxiety which were felt among us poor slaves during this time. Our fate for life was now to be decided. We had no more voice in that decision than the brutes among whom we were ranked. A single word from the white men was enough—against all our wishes, prayers, and entreaties—to sunder forever the dearest friends, dearest kindred, and strongest ties known to human beings. In addition to the pain of separation, there was the horrid dread of falling into the hands of Master Andrew. He was known to us all as being a most cruel wretch,—a common drunkard, who had, by his reckless mismanagement and profligate dissipation, already wasted a large portion of his father's property. We all felt that we might as well be sold at once to the Georgia traders, as to pass into his hands; for we knew that that would be our inevitable condition,—a condition held by us all in the utmost horror and dread.

I suffered more anxiety than most of my fellow-slaves. I had known what it was to be kindly treated; they had known nothing of the kind. They had seen little or nothing of the world. They were in very deed men and women of sorrow, and acquainted with grief. Their backs had been made familiar with the bloody lash, so that they had become callous; mine was yet tender; for while at Baltimore I got few whippings, and few slaves could boast of a kinder master and mistress than myself; and the thought of passing out of their hands into those of Master Andrew—a man who, but a few days before, to give me a sample of his bloody disposition, took my little brother by the throat, threw him on the ground, and with the heel of his boot stamped upon his head till the blood gushed from his nose and ears—was well calculated to make me anxious as to my fate. After he had committed this savage outrage upon my brother, he turned to me, and said that was the way he meant to serve me one of these days,—meaning, I suppose, when I came into his possession.

Thanks to a kind Providence, I fell to the portion of Mrs. Lucretia, and was sent immediately back to Baltimore, to live again in the family of Master Hugh. Their joy at my return equalled their sorrow at my departure. It was a glad day to me. I had escaped a worse than lion's jaws. I was absent from Baltimore, for the purpose of valuation and division, just about one month, and it seemed to have been six.

Very soon after my return to Baltimore, my mistress, Lucretia, died, leaving her husband and one child, Amanda; and in a very short time after her death, Master Andrew died. Now all the property of my old master, slaves included, was in the hands of strangers,—strangers who had had nothing to do with accumulating it. Not a slave was left free. All remained slaves, from the youngest to the oldest. If any one thing in my experience, more than another, served to deepen my conviction of the infernal character of slavery, and to fill me with unutterable loathing of slaveholders, it was their base ingratitude to my poor old grandmother. She had served my old master faithfully from youth to old age. She had been the source of all his wealth; she had peopled his plantation with slaves; she had become a great grandmother in his service. She had rocked him in infancy, attended him in childhood, served him through life, and at his death wiped from his icy brow the cold death-sweat, and closed his eyes forever. She was nevertheless left a slave—a slave for life—a slave in the hands of strangers; and in their hands she saw her children, her grandchildren, and her great-grandchildren, divided, like so many sheep, without being gratified with the small privilege of a single word, as to their or her own destiny. And, to cap the climax of their base ingratitude and fiendish barbarity, my grandmother, who was now very old, having outlived my old master and all his children, having seen the beginning and end of all of them, and her present owners finding she was of but little value, her frame already racked with the pains of old age, and complete helplessness fast stealing over her once active limbs, they took her to the woods, built her a little hut, put up a little mud-chimney, and then made her welcome to the privilege of supporting herself there in perfect loneliness; thus virtually turning her out to die! If my poor old grandmother now lives, she lives to suffer in utter loneliness; she lives to remember and mourn over the loss of children, the loss of grandchildren, and the loss of great-grandchildren. . . .

. . .

IX

I have now reached a period of my life when I can give dates. I left Baltimore, and went to live with Master Thomas Auld, at St. Michael's, in March, 1832. It was now more than seven years since I lived with him in the family of my old master, on Colonel Lloyd's plantation. We of course were now almost entire strangers to each other. He was to me a new master, and I to him a new slave. I was ignorant of his temper and disposition; he was equally so of mine. A very short time, however, brought us into full acquaintance with each other. I was made acquainted with his wife not less than with himself. They were well matched, being equally mean and cruel. I was now, for the first time during a space of more than seven years, made to feel the painful gnawings of hunger—a something which I had not experienced before since I left Colonel Lloyd's plantation. It went hard enough with me then, when I could look back to no period at which I had enjoyed a sufficiency. It was tenfold harder after living in Master Hugh's family, where I had always had enough to eat, and of that which was good. I have said Master Thomas was a mean man. He was so. Not to give a slave enough to eat, is regarded as the most aggravated development of meanness even among slaveholders. The rule is, no matter how coarse the food, only let there be enough of it. This is the theory; and in the part of Maryland from which I came, it is the general practice,—though there are many exceptions. . . .

Bad as all slaveholders are, we seldom meet one destitute of every element of character commanding respect. My master was one of this rare sort. I do not know of one single noble act ever performed by him. The leading trait in his character was meanness; and if there were any other element in his nature, it was made subject to this. He was mean; and, like most other mean men, he lacked the ability to conceal his meanness. Captain Auld was not born a slaveholder. He had been a poor man, master only of a Bay craft. He came into possession of all his slaves by marriage; and of all men, adopted slaveholders are the worst. He was cruel, but cowardly. He commanded without firmness. In the enforcement of his rules, he was at times rigid, and at times lax. At times, he spoke to his slaves with the firmness of Napoleon and the fury of a demon; at other times, he might well be mistaken for an inquirer who had lost his way.

He did nothing of himself. He might have passed for a lion, but for his ears. In all things noble which he attempted, his own meanness shone most conspicuous. His airs, words, and actions, were the airs, words, and actions of born slaveholders, and, being assumed, were awkward enough. He was not even a good imitator. He possessed all the disposition to deceive, but wanted the power. Having no resources within himself, he was compelled to be the copyist of many, and being such, he was forever the victim of inconsistency; and of consequence he was an object of contempt, and was held as such even by his slaves. The luxury of having slaves of his own to wait upon him was something new and unprepared for. He was a slaveholder without the ability to hold slaves. He found himself incapable of managing his slaves either by force, fear, or fraud, We seldom called him "master;" we generally called him "Captain Auld," and were hardly disposed to title him at all. I doubt not that our conduct had much to do with making him appear awkward, and of consequence fretful. Our want of reverence for him must have perplexed him greatly. He wished to have us call him master, but lacked the firmness necessary to command us to do so. His wife used to insist upon our calling him so, but to no purpose. In August, 1832, my master attended a Methodist camp-meeting held in the Bay-side, Talbot county, and there experienced religion. I indulged a faint hope that his conversion would lead him to emancipate his slaves, and that, if he did not do this, it would, at any rate, make him more kind and humane. I was disappointed in both these respects. It neither made him to be humane to his slaves, nor to emancipate them. If it had any effect on his character, it made him more cruel and hateful in all his ways; for I believe him to have been a much worse man after his conversion than before. Prior to his conversion, he relied upon his own depravity to shield and sustain him in his savage barbarity; but after his conversion, he found religious sanction and support for his slaveholding cruelty. He made the greatest pretensions to piety. His house was the house of prayer. He prayed morning, noon, and night. He very soon distinguished himself among his brethren, and was soon made a class-leader and exhorter. His activity in revivals was great, and he proved himself an instrument in the hands of the church in converting many souls. His house was the preacher's home. They used to take great pleasure in coming there to put up; for while he starved us, he stuffed them. We have had three or four preachers there at a time. . . .

. . .

X

I left Master Thomas's house, and went to live with Mr. Covey, on the 1st of January, 1833. I was now, for the first time in my life, a field hand. In my new employment, I found myself even more awkward than a country boy appeared to be in a large city. I had been at my new home but one week before Mr. Covey gave me a very severe whipping, cutting my back causing the blood to run, and raising ridges on my flesh as large as my little finger. The details of this affair are as follows: Mr. Covey sent me, very early in the morning of one of our coldest days in the month of January, to the woods, to get a load of wood. He gave me a team of unbroken oxen. He told me which was the in-hand ox, and which the off-hand one. He then tied the end of a large rope around the horns of the in-hand ox, and gave me the other end of it, and told me, if the oxen started to run, that I must hold on upon the rope. I had never driven oxen before, and of course I was very awkward. I, however, succeeded in getting to the edge of the woods with little difficulty; but I had got a very few rods into the woods, when the oxen took fright, and started full tilt, carrying the cart against trees, and over stumps, in the most frightful manner. I expected every moment that my brains would be dashed out against the trees. After running thus for a considerable distance, they finally upset the cart, dashing it with great force against a tree, and threw themselves into a dense thicket. How I escaped death, I do not know. There I was, entirely alone, in a thick wood, in a place new to me. My cart was upset and shattered, my oxen were entangled among the young trees, and there was none to help me. After a long spell of effort, I succeeded in getting my cart righted, my oxen disentangled, and again yoked to the cart. I now proceeded with my team to the place where I had, the day before, been chopping wood, and loaded my cart pretty heavily, thinking in this way to tame my oxen. I then proceeded on my way home. I had now consumed one half of the day. I got out of the woods safely, and now felt out of danger. I stopped my oxen to open the woods gate; and just as I did so, before I could get hold of my ox-rope, the oxen again started, rushed through the gate, catching it between the wheel and the body of the cart, tearing it to pieces, and coming within a few inches of crushing me against the gate-post. Thus twice, in one short day, I escaped death by the merest chance. On my return, I told Mr. Covey what had happened, and how it happened. He ordered me to return to the woods again immediately. I did so, and he followed on after me. Just as I got into the woods, he came up and told me to stop my cart, and that he would teach me how to trifle away my time, and break gates. He then went to a large gum-tree, and with his axe cut three large switches, and, after trimming them up neatly with his pocket-knife, he ordered me to take off my clothes. I made him no answer, but stood with my clothes on. He repeated his order. I still made him no answer, nor did I move to strip myself. Upon this he rushed at me with the fierceness of a tiger, tore off my clothes, and lashed me till he had worn out his switches, cutting me so savagely as to leave the marks visible for a long time after. This whipping was the first of a number just like it, and for similar offences.

I lived with Mr. Covey one year. During the first six months, of that year, scarce a week passed without his whipping me. I was seldom free from a sore back. My awkwardness was almost always his excuse for whipping me. We were worked fully up to the point of endurance. Long before day we were up, our horses fed, and by the first approach of day we were off to the field with our hoes and ploughing teams. Mr. Covey gave us enough to eat, but scarce time to eat it. We were often less than five minutes taking our meals. We were often in the field from the first approach of day till its last lingering ray had left us; and at saving-fodder time, midnight often caught us in the field binding blades. . . .

. . .

My term of actual service to Mr. Edward Covey ended on Christmas day, 1833. The days between Christmas and New Year's day are allowed as holidays; and, accordingly, we were not required to perform any labor, more than to feed and take care of the stock. This time we regarded as our own, by the grace of our masters; and we therefore used or abused it nearly as we pleased. Those of us who had families at a distance, were generally allowed to spend the whole six days in their society. This time, however, was spent in various ways. The staid, sober, thinking and industrious ones of our number would employ themselves in making combrooms, mats, horse-collars, and baskets; and another class of us would spend the time in hunting opossums, hares, and coons. But by far the larger part engaged in such sports and merriments as playing ball, wrestling, running foot-races, fiddling, dancing, and drinking whisky; and this latter mode of spending the time was by far the most agreeable to the feelings of our masters. A slave who would work during the holidays was considered by our masters as scarcely deserving them. He was regarded as one who rejected the favor of his master. It was deemed a disgrace not to get drunk at Christmas; and he was regarded as lazy indeed, who had not provided himself with the necessary means, during the year, to get whisky enough to last him through Christmas.

From what I know of the effect of these holidays upon the slave, I believe them to be among the most effective means in the hands of the slaveholder in keeping down the spirit of insurrection. Were the slaveholders at once to abandon this practice, I have not the slightest doubt it would lead to an immediate insurrection among the slaves. These holidays serve as conductors, or safety-valves, to carry off the rebellious spirit of enslaved humanity. But for these, the slave would be forced up to the wildest desperation; and woe betide the slaveholder, the day he ventures to remove or hinder the operation of those conductors! I warn him that, in such an event, a spirit will go forth in their midst, more to be dreaded than the most appalling earthquake.

The holidays are part and parcel of the gross fraud, wrong, and inhumanity of slavery. They are professedly a custom established by the benevolence of the slaveholders; but I undertake to say, it is the result of selfishness, and one of the grossest frauds committed upon the down-trodden slave. They do not give the slaves this time because they would not like to have their work during its continuance, but because they know it would be unsafe to deprive them of it. This will be seen by the fact, that the slaveholders like to have their slaves spend those days just in such a manner as to make them as glad of their ending as of their beginning. Their object seems to be, to disgust their slaves with freedom, by plunging them into the lowest depths of dissipation. For instance, the slaveholders not only like to see the slave drink of his own accord, but will adopt various plans to make him drunk. One plan is, to make bets on their slaves, as to who can drink the most whisky without getting drunk; and in this way they succeed in getting whole multitudes to drink to excess. Thus, when the slave asks for virtuous freedom, the cunning slaveholder, knowing his ignorance, cheats him with a dose of vicious dissipation, artfully labelled with the name of liberty. The most of us used to drink it down, and the result was just what might be supposed: many of us were led to think that there was little to choose between liberty and slavery. We felt, and very properly too, that we had almost as well be slaves to man as to rum. So, when the holidays ended, we staggered up from the filth of our wallowing, took a long breath, and marched to the field,—feeling, upon the whole, rather glad to go, from what our master had deceived us into a belief was freedom, back to the arms of slavery. . . .

. . .

On the first of January, 1834, I left Mr. Covey, and went to live with Mr. William Freeland, who lived about three miles from St. Michael's. I soon found Mr. Freeland a very different man from Mr. Covey. Though not rich, he was what would be called an educated southern gentleman. Mr. Covey, as I have shown, was a well-trained negro-breaker and slavedriver. The former (slaveholder though he was) seemed to possess some regard for honor, some reverence for justice, and some respect for humanity. The latter seemed totally insensible to all such sentiments. Mr. Freeland had many of the faults peculiar to slaveholders, such as being very passionate and fretful; but I must do him the justice to say, that he was exceedingly free from those degrading vices to which Mr. Covey was constantly addicted. The one was open and frank, and we always knew where to find him. The other was a most artful deceiver, and could be understood only by such as were skilful enough to detect his cunningly-devised frauds. Another advantage I gained in my new master was, he made no pretensions to, or profession of, religion; and this, in my opinion, was truly a great advantage. I assert most unhesitatingly, that the religion of the south is a mere covering for the most horrid crimes,—a justifier of the most appalling barbarity, —a sanctifier of the most hateful frauds,—and a dark shelter under which the darkest, foulest, grossest, and most infernal deeds of slaveholders find the strongest protection. . . .

. . .

The year passed off smoothly. It seemed only about half as long as the year which preceded it. I went through it without receiving a single blow. I will give Mr. Freeland the credit of being the best master I ever had, *till I became my own master*. For the ease with which I passed the year, I was, however, somewhat indebted to the society of my fellow-slaves. They were noble souls; they not only possessed loving hearts, but brave ones. We were linked and interlinked with each other. I loved them with a love stronger than any thing I have experienced since. It is sometimes said that we slaves do not love and confide in each other. In answer to this assertion, I can say, I never loved any or confided in any people more than my fellow-slaves, and especially those with whom I lived at Mr. Freeland's. I believe we would have died for each other. We never undertook to do any thing, of any importance, without a mutual consultation. We never moved separately. We were one; and as much so by our tempers and dispositions, as by the mutual hardships to which we were necessarily subjected by our condition as slaves.

At the close of the year 1834, Mr. Freeland again hired me of my master, for the year 1835. But, by this time, I began to want to live *upon free land* as well as *with Freeland*; and I was no longer content, therefore, to live with him or any other slaveholder. I began, with the commencement of the year, to prepare myself for a final struggle, which should decide my fate one way or the other. My tendency was upward. I was fast approaching manhood, and year after year had passed, and I was still a slave. These thoughts roused me—I must do something. I therefore resolved that 1835 should not pass without witnessing an attempt, on my part, to secure my liberty. But I was not willing to cherish this determination alone. My fellow-slaves were dear to me. I was anxious to have them participate with me in this, my life-giving determination. I therefore, though with great prudence, commenced early to ascertain their views and feelings in regard to their condition, and to imbue their minds with thoughts of freedom. I bent myself to devising ways and means for our escape, and meanwhile strove, on all fitting occasions, to impress them with the gross fraud and inhumanity of slavery. I went first to Henry, next to John, then to the others. I found, in them all, warm hearts and noble spirits. They were ready to hear, and ready to act when a feasible plan should be proposed. This was what I wanted. I talked to them of our want of manhood, if we submitted to our enslavement without at least one noble effort to be free. We met often, and consulted frequently, and told our hopes and fears, recounted the difficulties, real and imagined, which we should be called on to meet. At times we were almost disposed to give up, and try to content ourselves with our wretched lot; at others, we were firm and unbending in our determination to go. Whenever we suggested any plan, there was shrinking—the odds were fearful. Our path was beset with the greatest obstacles; and if we succeeded in gaining the end of it, our right to be free was yet questionable—we were yet liable to be returned to bondage. We could see no spot this side of the ocean, where we could be free. We knew nothing about Canada. Our knowledge of the north did not extend farther than New York; and to go there, and be forever harassed with the frightful liability of being returned to slavery—with the certainty of being treated tenfold worse than before—the thought was truly a horrible one, and one which it was not easy to overcome. The case sometimes stood thus: At every gate through which we were to pass, we saw a watchman—at every ferry a guard—on every bridge a sentinel—and in every wood a patrol. We were hemmed in upon every side. Here were the difficulties, real or imagined—the good to be sought, and the evil to be shunned. On the one hand, there stood slavery, a stern reality, glaring frightfully upon us,—its robes already crimsoned with the blood of millions, and even now feasting itself greedily upon our own flesh. On the other hand, away back in the dim distance, under the flickering light of the north star, behind some craggy hill or snow-covered mountain, stood a doubtful freedom—half frozen—beckoning us to come and share its hospitality. This in itself was sometimes enough to stagger us; but when we permitted ourselves to survey the road, we were frequently appalled. Upon either side we saw grim death, assuming the most horrid shapes. Now it was starvation, causing us to eat our own flesh;—now we were contending with the waves, and were drowned;—now we were overtaken, and torn to pieces by the fangs of the terrible bloodhound. We were stung by scorpions, chased by wild beasts, bitten by snakes, and finally, after having nearly reached the desired spot,—after swimming rivers, encountering wild beasts, sleeping in the woods, suffering hunger and nakedness,—we were overtaken by our pursuers, and, in our resistance, we were shot dead upon the spot! . . .

. . .

After a painful waiting, the Saturday morning, whose night was to witness our departure, came. I hailed it with joy, bring what of sadness it might.

Friday night was a sleepless one for me. I probably felt more anxious than the rest, because I was, by common consent, at the head of the whole affair. The responsibility of success or failure lay heavily upon me. The glory of the one, and the confusion of the other, were alike mine. The first two hours of that morning were such as I never experienced before, and hope never to again. Early in the morning, we went, as usual, to the field. We were spreading manure: and all at once, while thus engaged, I was overwhelmed with an indescribable feeling, in the fulness of which I turned to Sandy, who was near by, and said, "We are betrayed!" "Well," said he, "that thought has this moment struck me." We said no more. I was never more certain of any thing.

The horn was blown as usual, and we went up from the field to the house for breakfast. I went for the form, more than for want of any thing to eat that morning. Just as I got to the house, in looking out at the lane gate, I saw four white men, with two colored men. The white men were on horseback, and the colored ones were walking behind, as if tied. I watched them a few moments till they got up to our lane gate. Here they halted, and tied the colored men to the gate-post. I was not yet certain as to what the matter was. In a few moments, in rode Mr. Hamilton, with a speed betokening great excitement. He came to the door, and inquired if Master William was in. He was told he was at the barn. Mr. Hamilton, without dismounting, rode up to the barn with extraordinary speed. In a few moments, he and Mr. Freeland returned to the house. By this time, the three constables rode up, and in great haste dismounted, tied their horses, and met Master William and Mr. Hamilton returning from the barn; and after talking awhile, they all walked up to the kitchen door. There was no one in the kitchen but myself and John. Henry and Sandy were up at the barn. Mr. Freeland put his head in at the door, and called me by name, saying, there were some gentlemen at the door who wished to see me. I stepped to the door, and inquired what they wanted. They at once seized me, and, without giving me any satisfaction, tied me—lashing my hands closely together. I insisted upon knowing what the matter was. They at length said, that they had learned I had been in a "scrape," and that I was to be examined before my master; and if their information proved false, 1 should not be hurt. . . .

. . .

. . . We found the evidence against us to be the testimony of one person; our master would not tell who it was; but we came to a unanimous decision among ourselves as to who their informant was. We were sent off to the jail at Easton. When we got there, we were delivered up to the sheriff, Mr. Joseph Graham, and by him placed in jail. Henry, John, and myself, were placed in one room together—Charles, and Henry Bailey, in another. Their object in separating us was to hinder concert.

We had been in jail scarcely twenty minutes, when a swarm of slave traders, and agents for slave traders, flocked into jail to look at us, and to ascertain if we were for sale. Such a set of beings I never saw before! I felt myself surrounded by so many fiends from perdition. A band of pirates never looked more like their father, the devil. They laughed and grinned over us, saying, "Ah, my boys! we have got you, haven't we." And after taunting us in various ways, they one by one went into an examination of us, with intent to ascertain our value. They would impudently ask us if we would not like to have them for our masters. We would make them no answer, and leave them to find out as best they could. Then they would curse and swear at us, telling us that they could take the devil out of us in a very little while, if we were only in their hands.

While in jail, we found ourselves in much more comfortable quarters than we expected when we went there. We did not get much to eat, nor that which was very good; but we had a good clean room, from the windows of which we could see what was going on in the street, which was very much better than though we had been placed in one of the dark, damp cells. Upon the whole, we got along very well, so far as the jail and its keeper were concerned. Immediately after the holidays were over, contrary to all our expectations, Mr. Hamilton and Mr. Freeland came up to Easton, and took Charles, the two Henrys, and John, out of jail, and carried them home, leaving me alone. I regarded this separation as a final one. It caused me more pain than any thing else in the whole transaction. I was ready for any thing rather than separation. I supposed that they had consulted together, and had decided that, as I was the whole cause of the intention of the others to run away, it was hard to make the innocent suffer with the guilty; and that they had, therefore, concluded to take the others home, and sell me, as a warning to the others that remained. It is due to the noble Henry to say, he seemed almost as reluctant at leaving the prison as at leaving home to come to the prison. But we knew we should, in all probability, be separated, if we were sold; and since he was in their hands, he concluded to go peaceably home.

I was now left to my fate. I was all alone, and within the walls of a stone prison. But a few days before, and I was full of hope. I expected to have been safe in a land of freedom; but now I was covered with gloom, sunk down to the utmost despair. I thought the possibility of freedom was gone. I was kept in this way about one week, at the end of which, Captain Auld, my master, to my surprise and utter astonishment, came up, and took me out, with the intention of sending me, with a gentleman of his acquaintance, into Alabama. But, from some cause or other, he did not send me to Alabama, but concluded to send me back to Baltimore, to live again with his brother Hugh, and to learn a trade.

Thus, after an absence of three years and one month, I was once more permitted to return to my old home at Baltimore. My master sent me away, because there existed against me a very great prejudice in the community, and he feared I might be killed.

In a few weeks after I went to Baltimore, Master Hugh hired me to Mr. William Gardner, an extensive ship-builder, on Fell's Point. . . .

. . .

"THE RIGHTS OF WOMEN"

1848

One of the most interesting events of the past week, was the holding of what is technically styled a Woman's Rights Convention at Seneca Falls. The speaking, addresses, and resolutions of this extraordinary meeting was almost wholly conducted by women; and although they evidently felt themselves in a novel position, it is but simple justice to say that their whole proceedings were characterized by marked ability and dignity. No one present, we think, however much he might be disposed to differ from the views advanced by the leading speakers on that occasion, will fail to give them credit for brilliant talents and excellent dispositions. In this meeting, as in other deliberative assemblies, there were frequent differences of opinion and animated discussion; but in no case was there the slightest absence of good feeling and decorum. Several interesting documents setting forth the rights as well as the grievances of women were read. Among these was a Declaration of Sentiments, to be regarded as

Reprinted from *Against the Tide*, eds. Michael S. Kimmel and Thomas E. Mosmiller (Boston: Beacon Press, 1992). Originally published in *North Star* (28 July 1848).

the basis of a grand movement for attaining the civil, social, political, and religious rights of women. We should not do justice to our own convictions, or to the excellent persons connected with this infant movement, if we did not in this connection offer a few remarks on the general subject which the Convention met to consider and the objects they seek to attain. In doing so, we are not insensible that the bare mention of this truly important subject in any other than terms of contemptuous ridicule and scornful disfavor, is likely to excite against us the fury of bigotry and the folly of prejudice. A discussion of the rights of animals would be regarded with far more complacency by many of what are called the *wise* and the *good* of our land, than would a discussion of the rights of women. It is, in their estimation, to be guilty of evil thoughts, to think that woman is entitled to equal rights with man. Many who have at last made the discovery that the Negroes have some rights as well as other members of the human family, have yet to be convinced that women are entitled to any. Eight years ago a number of persons of this description actually abandoned the anti-slavery cause, lest by giving their influence in that direction they might possibly be giving countenance to the dangerous heresy that woman, in respect to rights, stands on an equal footing with man. In the judgment of such persons the American slave system, with all its concomitant horrors, is less to be deplored than this *wicked* idea. It is perhaps needless to say, that we cherish little sympathy for such sentiments or respect for such prejudices. Standing as we do upon the watch-tower of human freedom, we cannot be deterred from an expression of our approbation of any movement, however humble, to improve and elevate the character of any members of the human family. While it is impossible for us to go into this subject at length, and dispose of the various objections which are often urged against such a doctrine as that of female equality, we are free to say that in respect to political rights, we hold woman to be justly entitled to all we claim for man. We go farther, and express our conviction that all political rights which it is expedient for man to exercise, it is equally so for woman. All that distinguishes man as an intelligent and accountable being, is equally true of woman, and if that government only is just which governs by the free consent of the governed, there can be no reason in the world for denying to woman the exercise of the elective franchise, or a hand in making and administering the laws of the land. Our doctrine is that "right is of no sex." We therefore bid the women engaged in this movement our humble Godspeed.

MARGARET FULLER

Margaret Fuller (1810–1850), American writer, critic, and feminist, was born in Cambridgeport, Massachusetts. A child prodigy and an immensely erudite adult, she became a respected literary critic, a close friend of Ralph Waldo Emerson, and America's first female foreign correspondent. Today she is best known for her treatise, *Woman in the Nineteenth Century*, which inspired the 1848 Declaration of Sentiments in Seneca Falls, New York, that became the intellectual foundation of the American feminist movement.

Fuller was the eldest child of a Harvard-educated lawyer and congressman who was acquainted with Mary Wollstonecraft's educational views. While her mother was engaged in housework and raising the younger children, her father tutored her in a rigorous classical education. She began the study of Latin at age six; read Ovid at eight; and was introduced to the works of Shakespeare, Cervantes, and Moliere before she entered her teens. This regimen left Fuller with unshakable confidence, branded by many as arrogance, and with formidable intellectual standards that she applied to herself as well as to others. Much later she would blame her broken health on her father and say that a childhood lived through books was no substitute for actual experience and sympathetic relations with others.

Although early nineteenth-century colleges excluded women, Margaret Fuller pursued her studies, becoming widely admired and sometimes feared for her learning. A legend grew around her that homeliness and disappointment in love drove her to excel, and she was the object of many personal attacks. This gave her a different perspective on the American individualism her colleagues extolled, and for years she was to criticize Emerson, who could not admit the difficulty a woman faced in being self-reliant and earning a living. Called a "whetstone of genius" because of her stimulus to other thinkers and writers, Fuller's conversation was legendary. She is remembered more as a teacher and a personality than for any particular works.

As a young woman, Fuller assisted Bronson Alcott at his experimental Temple School in Boston, then conducted her own school in Providence, Rhode Island (1837–1839). In 1839 she published a translation of *Eckermann's Conversations with Goethe* and embarked on her most cherished project, a biography of Goethe that was never completed. Fuller was capable of intense attachments; and male intellectuals found her vehement and demanding in her personal relationships. She initiated a friendship with Emerson—a charged, ambiguous relationship that he seemed to find threatening—and participated in his circle of transcendentalists. From 1840 to 1842 she edited the transcendentalist periodical *Dial*. About this time, she developed her "Conversations," discussions of the culture and controversies of the day that women from leading Boston families paid to attend. Ideas that arose in these seminars foreshadowed the American feminist movement and stimulated Fuller to write *Woman in the Nineteenth Century* (1845).

Publication of *Woman* brought Fuller international celebrity and notoriety. Her dissident ideas were ridiculed by opponents but not seriously addressed, and she was often vilified in personal terms. (When the book was first published, Fuller was mocked as an old maid; after she took a lover, critics labeled her a fallen woman.) The book itself is a bracing call for complete freedom and equality, a call that "every path be open to woman as freely as to man." In the spirit of the transcendentalists, it posits universal principles of good and evil, stresses the need for educational reform and spiritual rebirth, and sounds an optimistic tone for the future. Fuller calls on women to become self-reliant and not expect help from men and introduces the concept of sisterhood—women must help one another, no matter whether they are scholars, servants, or prostitutes.

Fuller's original contribution in *Woman* is to document female capabilities from an immense catalog of mythology, folklore, the Bible, classical antiquity, fiction, and history. She explores the image of woman, in all its ambiguity, within literature and myth, and asserts that "no age was left entirely without a witness of the equality of the sexes in function, duty, and hope." She also suggests the androgynous character of sexuality and calls for an end to sexual stereotyping and the sexual double standard.

In 1844 Fuller joined the staff of Horace Greeley's New York *Tribune* as a book reviewer and became known for her trenchant criticism of European as well as American literature. Two years later she sailed for Europe as a correspondent and interviewed Thomas Carlyle, George Sand, and Guiseppe Mazzini. The latter piqued her interest in the Roman Republic, and in 1847 she returned to Rome as a partisan of the revolution against the Papal States. She later secretly married one of the revolutionaries, Giovanni Angelo, the Marquis of Ossoli, and joined him in the unsuccessful defense of Rome against the French in 1849. When the republic fell, Fuller and her husband fled with their eighteen-month-old son for America. They were lost at sea when their ship foundered in a storm off Fire Island, New York.

Margaret Fuller was swiftly recognized as a significant figure in American letters, despite the fact that her writings were diffuse and incomplete. Her brother Arthur collected them into two volumes: *At Home and Abroad* (1856) and *Life Without and Life Within* (1858).

WOMAN IN THE NINETEENTH CENTURY

1845

A better comment could not be made on what is required to perfect Man, and place him in that superior position for which he was designed, than by the interpretation of Bacon upon the legends of the Syren coast. "When the wise Ulysses passed," says he, "he caused his mariners to stop their ears with wax, knowing there was in them no power to resist the lure of that voluptuous song. But he, the much experienced man, who wished to be experienced in all, and use all to the service of wisdom, desired to hear the song that he might understand its meaning. Yet, distrusting his own power to be firm in his better purpose, he caused himself to be bound to the mast, that he might be kept secure against his own weakness. But Orpheus passed unfettered, so absorbed in singing hymns to the gods that he could not even hear those sounds of degrading enchantment."

Meanwhile, not a few believe, and men themselves have expressed the opinion, that the time is come when Eurydice is to call for an Orpheus, rather than Orpheus for Eurydice; that the idea of Man, however imperfectly brought out, has been far more so than that of Woman; that she, the other half of the same thought, the other chamber of the heart of life,

Reprinted from *Woman in the Nineteenth Century*, W. W. Norton edition, 1971. Originally published by John Jewett & Comany, Cleveland, 1855.

needs now take her turn in the full pulsation, and that improvement in the daughters will best aid in the reformation of the sons of this age.

It should be remarked that, as the principle of liberty is better understood, and more nobly interpreted, a broader protest is made in behalf of Woman. As men become aware that few men have had a fair chance, they are inclined to say that no women have had a fair chance. The French Revolution, that strangely disguised angel, bore witness in favor of Woman, but interpreted her claims no less ignorantly than those of Man. Its idea of happiness did not rise beyond outward enjoyment, unobstructed by the tyranny of others. The title it gave was "citoyen," "citoyenne;" and it is not unimportant to Woman that even this species of equality was awarded her. . . .

. . .

Here, as elsewhere, the gain of creation consists always in the growth of individual minds, which live and aspire, as flowers bloom and birds sing, in the midst of morasses; and in the continual development of that thought, the thought of human destiny, which is given to eternity adequately to express, and which ages of failure only seemingly impede. Only seemingly; and whatever seems to the contrary, this country is as surely destined to elucidate a great moral law, as Europe was to promote the mental culture of Man.

Though the national independence be blurred by the servility of individuals; though freedom and equality have been proclaimed only to leave room for a monstrous display of slave-dealing and slave-keeping; though the free American so often feels himself free, like the Roman, only to pamper his appetites and his indolence through the misery of his fellow-beings; still it is not in vain that the verbal statement has been made, "All men are born free and equal." There it stands, a golden certainty wherewith to encourage the good, to shame the bad. The New World may be called clearly to perceive that it incurs the utmost penalty if it reject or oppress the sorrowful brother. And, if men are deaf, the angels hear. But men cannot be deaf. It is inevitable that an external freedom, an independence of the encroachments of other men, such as has been achieved for the nation, should be so also for every member of it. That which has once been clearly conceived in the intelligence cannot fail, sooner or later, to be acted out. . . .

. . .

It may well be an Anti-Slavery party that pleads for Woman, if we consider merely that she does not hold property on equal terms with men; so that, if a husband dies without making a will, the wife, instead of taking at once his place as head of the family, inherits only a part of his fortune, often brought him by herself, as if she were a child, or ward only, not an equal partner.

We will not speak of the innumerable instances in which profligate and idle men live upon the earnings of industrious wives; or if the wives leave them, and take with them the children, to perform the double duty of mother and father, follow from place to place, and threaten to rob them of the children, if deprived of the rights of a husband, as they call them, planting themselves in their poor lodgings, frightening them into paying tribute by taking from them the children, running into debt at the expense of these otherwise so overtasked helots. Such instances count up by scores within my own memory. I have seen the husband who had stained himself by a long course of low vice, till his wife was wearied from her heroic forgiveness, by finding that his treachery made it useless, and that if she would provide bread for herself and her children, she must be separate from his ill fame—I have known this man come to install himself in the chamber of a woman who loathed him, and say she should never take food without his company. I have known these men steal their children, whom they knew they had no means to maintain, take them into dissolute company, expose them to bodily danger, to frighten the poor woman, to whom, it seems, the fact that she alone had borne the pangs of their birth, and nourished their infancy, does not give an equal right to them. I do believe that this mode of kidnapping—and it is frequent enough in all classes of society

—will be by the next age viewed as it is by Heaven now, and that the man who avails himself of the shelter of men's laws to steal from a mother her own children, or arrogate any superior right in them, save that of superior virtue, will bear the stigma he deserves, in common with him who steals grown men from their mother-land, their hopes, and their homes.

. . . Men must soon see that as, on their own ground, Woman is the weaker party, she ought to have legal protection, which would make such oppression impossible. . . .

. . .

"That can never be necessary," cry the other side. "All men are privately influenced by women; each has his wife, sister, or female friends, and is too much biased by these relations to fail of representing their interests; and, if this is not enough, let them propose and enforce their wishes with the pen. The beauty of home would be destroyed, the delicacy of the sex be violated, the dignity of halls of legislation degraded, by an attempt to introduce them there. Such duties are inconsistent with those of a mother;" and then we have ludicrous pictures of ladies in hysterics at the polls, and senate-chambers filled with cradles.

But if, in reply, we admit as truth that Woman seems destined by nature rather for the inner circle, we must add that the arrangements of civilized life have not been, as yet, such as to secure it to her. Her circle, if the duller, is not the quieter. If kept from "excitement," she is not from drudgery. Not only the Indian squaw carries the burdens of the camp, but the favorites of Louis XIV, accompany him in his journeys, and the washerwoman stands at her tub, and carries home her work at all seasons, and in all states of health. Those who think the physical circumstances of Woman would make a part in the affairs of national government unsuitable, are by no means those who think it impossible for negresses to endure field-work, even during pregnancy, or for sempstresses to go through their killing labors.

As to the use of the pen, there was quite as much opposition to Woman's possessing herself of that help to free agency as there is now to her seizing on the rostrum or the desk; and she is likely to draw, from a permission to plead her cause that way, opposite inferences to what might be wished by those who now grant it.

As to the possibility of her filling with grace and dignity any such position, we should think those who had seen the great actresses, and heard the Quaker preachers of modern times, would not doubt that Woman can express publicly the fulness of thought and creation, without losing any of the peculiar beauty of her sex. What can pollute and tarnish is to act thus from any motive except that something needs to be said or done. Woman could take part in the processions, the songs, the dances of old religion; no one fancied her delicacy was impaired by appearing in public for such a cause.

As to her home, she is not likely to leave it more than she now does for balls, theatres, meetings for promoting missions, revival meetings, and others to which she flies, in hope of an animation for her existence commensurate with what she sees enjoyed by men. Governors of ladies'-fairs are no less engrossed by such a charge, than the governor of a state by his; presidents of Washingtonian societies no less away from home than presidents of conventions. If men look straitly to it, they will find that, unless their lives are domestic, those of the women will not be. A house is no home unless it contain food and fire for the mind as well as for the body. The female Greek, of our day, is as much in the street as the male to cry, "What news?" We doubt not it was the same in Athens of old. The women, shut out from the market-place, made up for it at the religious festivals. For human beings are not so constituted that they can live without expansion. If they do not get it in one way, they must in another, or perish.

As to men's representing women fairly at present, while we hear from men who owe to their wives not only all that is comfortable or graceful, but all that is wise, in the arrangement of their lives, the frequent remark, "You cannot reason with a woman,"—when from those of delicacy, nobleness, and poetic culture, falls the contemptuous phrase "women and children," and that in no light sally of the hour, but in works intended to give a permanent statement of the best experiences,—when not one man, in the million, shall I say? no, not in the hundred million, can rise above the belief that Woman was made *for Man*,—when such traits as these are daily forced upon the attention, can we feel that Man will always do justice to the interests of Woman? Can we think that he takes a sufficiently discerning and religious view of her office and destiny *ever* to do her justice, except when prompted by sentiment,—accidentally or transiently, that is, for the sentiment will vary according to the relations in which he is placed? The lover, the poet, the artist, are likely to view her nobly. The father and the philosopher have some chance of liberality; the man of the world, the legislator for expediency, none.

Under these circumstances, without attaching importance, in themselves, to the changes demanded by the champions of Woman, we hail them as signs of the times. We would have every arbitrary barrier thrown down. We would have every path laid open to Woman as freely as to Man. Were this done, and a slight temporary fermentation allowed to subside, we should see crystallizations more pure and of more various beauty. We believe the divine energy would pervade nature to a degree unknown in the history of former ages, and that no discordant collision, but a ravishing harmony of the spheres, would ensue.

Yet, then and only then will mankind be ripe for this, when inward and outward freedom for Woman as much as for Man shall be acknowledged as a *right*, not yielded as a concession. As the friend of the negro assumes that one man cannot by right hold another in bondage, so should the friend of Woman assume that Man cannot by right lay even well-meant restrictions on Woman. If the negro be a soul, if the woman be a soul, apparelled in flesh, to one Master only are they accountable. There is but one law for souls, and, if there is to be an interpreter of it, he must come not as man, or son of man, but as son of God.

Were thought and feeling once so far elevated that Man should esteem himself the brother and friend, but nowise the lord and tutor, of Woman,—were he really bound with her in equal worship,—arrangements as to function and employment would be of no consequence. What Woman needs is not as a woman to act or rule, but as a nature to grow, as an intellect to discern, as a soul to live freely and unimpeded, to unfold such powers as were given her when we left our common home. If fewer talents were given her, yet if allowed the free and full employment of these, so that she may render back to the giver his own with usury, she will not complain; nay, I dare to say she will bless and rejoice in her earthly birth-place, her earthly lot. Let us consider what obstructions impede this good era, and what signs give reason to hope that it draws near.

. . .

. . . [C]ivilized Europe is still in a transition state about marriage; not only in practice but in thought. It is idle to speak with contempt of the nations where polygamy is an institution, or seraglios a custom, while practices far more debasing haunt, well-nigh fill, every city and every town, and so far as union of one with one is believed to be the only pure form of marriage, a great majority of societies and individuals are still doubtful whether the earthly bond must be a meeting of souls, or only supposes a contract of convenience and utility. Were Woman established in the rights of an immortal being, this could not be. She would not, in some countries, be given away by her father, with scarcely more respect for her feelings than is shown by the Indian chief, who sells his daughter for a horse, and beats her if she runs away from her new home. Nor, in societies where her choice is left free, would she be perverted, by the current of opinion that seizes her, into the belief that she must marry, if it be only to find a protector, and a home of her own. Neither would Man, if he thought the connection of permanent importance, form it so lightly. He would not deem it a trifle, that he was to enter into the closest relations with another soul, which, if not eternal in themselves, must eternally affect his growth. Neither, did he believe Woman capable of friendship, would he, by rash haste, lose the chance of finding a friend in the person who might, probably, live half a century by his side. Did love, to his mind, stretch forth into infinity, he would not miss his chance of its revelations, that he might the sooner rest from his weariness by a bright fireside, and secure a sweet and graceful attendant "devoted to him alone." Were he a step higher, he would not carelessly enter into a relation where he might not be able to do the duty of a friend, as well as a protector from external ill, to the other party, and have a being in his power pining for sympathy, intelligence and aid, that he could not give.

What deep communion, what real intercourse is implied in sharing the joys and cares of parentage, when any degree of equality is admitted between the parties! It is true that, in a majority of instances, the man looks upon his wife as an adopted child, and places her to the other children in the relation of nurse or governess, rather than that of parent. Her influence with them is sure; but she misses the education which should enlighten that influence, by being thus treated. It is the order of nature that children should complete the education, moral and mental, of parents, by making them think what is needed for the best culture of human beings, and conquer all faults and impulses that interfere with their giving this to these dear objects, who represent the world to them. Father and mother should assist one another to learn what is required for this sublime priesthood of Nature. But, for this, a religious recognition of equality is required.

Where this thought of equality begins to diffuse itself, it is shown in four ways.

First;—The household partnership. In our country, the woman looks for a "smart but kind" husband; the man for a "capable, sweet-tempered" wife. The man furnishes the house; the woman regulates it. Their relation is one of mutual esteem, mutual dependence. Their talk is of business; their affection shows itself by practical kindness. They know that life goes more smoothly and cheerfully to each for the other's aid; they are grateful and content. The wife praises her husband as a "good provider;" the husband, in return, compliments her as a "capital housekeeper." This relation is good so far as it goes.

Next comes a closer tie, which takes the form either of mutual idolatry or of intellectual companionship. The first, we suppose, is to no one a pleasing subject of contemplation. The parties weaken and narrow one another; they lock the gate against all the glories of the universe, that they may live in a cell together. To themselves they seem the only wise; to all others, steeped in infatuation; the gods smile as they look forward to the crisis of cure; to men, the woman seems an unlovely syren; to women, the man an effeminate boy.

The other form, of intellectual companionship, has become more and more frequent. Men engaged in public life, literary men, and artists, have often found in their wives companions and confidants in thought no less than in feeling. And, as the intellectual development of Woman has spread wider and risen higher, they have, not unfrequently, shared the same employment; as in the case of Roland and his wife, who were friends in the household and in the nation's councils, read, regulated home affairs, or prepared public documents together, indifferently. It is very pleasant, in letters begun by Roland and finished by his wife, to see the harmony of mind, and the difference of nature; one thought, but various ways of treating it.

This is one of the best instances of a marriage of friendship. It was only friendship, whose basis was esteem; probably neither party knew love, except by name. Roland was a good man, worthy to esteem, and be esteemed; his wife as deserving of admiration as able to do without it.

. . .

Mary Wolstonecraft [*sic*], like Madame Dudevant (commonly known as George Sand) in our day, was a woman whose existence better proved the need of some new interpretation of Woman's Rights than anything she wrote. Such beings as these, rich in genius, of most tender sympathies, capable of high virtue and a chastened harmony, ought not to find themselves, by birth, in a place so narrow, that, in breaking bonds, they become outlaws. Were there as much room in the world for such, as in Spenser's poem for Britomart, they would not run their heads so wildly against the walls, but prize their shelter rather. They find their way, at last, to light and air, but the world will not take off the brand it has set upon them. The champion of the Rights of Woman found, in Godwin, one who would plead that cause like a brother. . . .

This author, beginning like the many in assault upon bad institutions, and external ills, yet deepening the experience through comparative freedom, sees at last that the only efficient remedy must come from individual character. These bad institutions, indeed, it may always be replied, prevent individuals from forming good character, therefore we must remove them. Agreed; yet keep steadily the higher aim in view. Could you clear away all the bad forms of society, it is vain, unless the individual begin to be ready for better. There must be a parallel movement in these two branches of life. And all the rules left by Moses availed less to further the best life than the living example of one Messiah.

Still the mind of the age struggles confusedly with these problems, better discerning as yet the ill it can no longer bear, than the good by which it may supersede it. But women like Sand will speak now and cannot be silenced; their characters and their eloquence alike foretell an era when such as they shall easier learn to lead true lives. But though such forebode, not such shall be parents of it. Those who would reform the world must show that they do not speak in the heat of wild impulse; their lives must be unstained by passionate error; they must be severe lawgivers to themselves. They must be religious students of the divine purpose with regard to man, if they would not confound the fancies of a day with the requisitions of eternal good. Their liberty must be the liberty of law and knowledge. But as to the transgressions against custom which have caused such outcry against those of noble intention, it may be observed that the resolve of Eloisa to be only the mistress of Abelard, was that of one who saw in practice around her the contract of marriage made the seal of degradation. Shelley feared not to be fettered, unless so to be was to be false. Wherever abuses are seen, the timid will suffer; the bold will protest. But society has a right to outlaw them till she has revised her law; and this she must be taught to do, by one who speaks with authority, not in anger or haste.

. . .

In naming these instances, I do not mean to imply that community of employment is essential to the union of husband and wife, more than to the union of friends. Harmony exists in difference, no less than in likeness, if only the same key-note govern both parts. Woman the poem, Man the poet! Woman the heart, Man the head! Such divisions are only important when they are never to be transcended. If nature is never bound down, nor the voice of inspiration stifled, that is enough. We are pleased that women should write and speak, if they feel need of it, from having something to tell; but silence for ages would be no misfortune, if that silence be from divine command, and not from Man's tradition.

While Goetz Von Berlichingen rides to battle, his wife is busy in the kitchen; but difference of occupation does not prevent that community of inward life, that perfect esteem, with which he says,

> Whom God loves, to him gives he such a wife.

Manzoni thus dedicates his "Adelchi."

"To his beloved and venerated wife, Enrichetta Luigia Blondel, who, with conjugal affection and maternal wisdom, has preserved a virgin mind, the author dedicates this 'Adelchi,' grieving that he could not, by a more splendid and more durable monument, honor the dear name, and the memory of so many virtues."

The relation could not be fairer, nor more equal, if she, too, had written poems. Yet the position of the parties might have been the reverse as well; the Woman might have sung the deeds, given voice to the life of the Man, and beauty would have been the result; . . .

The fourth and highest grade of marriage union is the religious, which may be expressed as pilgrimage toward a common shrine. This includes the others: home sympathies and household wisdom, for these pilgrims must know how to assist each other along the dusty way; intellectual communion, for how sad it would be on such a journey to have a companion to whom you could not communicate your thoughts and aspirations as they sprang to life; who would have no feeling for the prospects that open, more and more glorious as we advance; who would never see the flowers that may be gathered by the most industrious traveller! It must include all these.

Such a fellow-pilgrim Count Zinzendorf seems to have found in his countess, of whom he thus writes:

"Twenty-five years' experience has shown me that just the help-meet whom I have is the only one that could suit my vocation. Who else could have so carried through my family affairs? Who lived so spotlessly before the world? Who so wisely aided me in my rejection of a dry morality? Who so clearly set aside the Pharisaism which, as years passed, threatened to creep in among us? Who so deeply discerned as to the spirits of delusion which sought to bewilder us? Who would have governed my whole economy so wisely, richly and hospitably, when circumstances commanded?". . . .

. . .

And now I have designated in outline, if not in fulness, the stream which is ever flowing from the heights of my thought.

In the earlier tract I was told I did not make my meaning sufficiently clear. In this I have consequently tried to illustrate it in various ways, and may have been guilty of much repetition. Yet, as I am anxious to leave no room for doubt, I shall venture to retrace, once more, the scope of my design in points, as was done in old-fashioned sermons.

Man is a being of two-fold relations, to nature beneath, and intelligences above him. The earth is his school, if not his birth-place; God his object; life and thought his means of interpreting nature, and aspiring to God.

Only a fraction of this purpose is accomplished in the life of any one man. Its entire accomplishment is to be hoped only from the sum of the lives of men, or Man considered as a whole.

As this whole has one soul and one body, any injury or obstruction to a part, or to the meanest member; affects the whole. Man can never be perfectly happy or virtuous, till all men are so.

To address Man wisely, you must not forget that his life is partly animal, subject to the same laws with Nature.

But you cannot address him wisely unless you consider him still more as soul, and appreciate the conditions and destiny of soul.

The growth of Man is two-fold, masculine and feminine.

So far as these two methods can be distinguished, they are so as

Energy and Harmony;
Power and Beauty;
Intellect and Love;

or by some such rude classification; for we have not language primitive and pure enough to express such ideas with precision.

These two sides are supposed to be expressed in Man and Woman, that is, as the more and the less, for the faculties have not been given pure to either, but only in preponderance. There are also exceptions in great number, such as men of far more beauty than power, and the reverse. But, as a general rule, it seems to have been the intention to give a preponderance on the one side, that is called masculine, and on the other, one that is called feminine.

There cannot be a doubt that, if these two developments were in perfect harmony, they would correspond to and fulfil one another, like hemispheres, or the tenor and base in music.

But there is no perfect harmony in human nature; and the two parts answer one another only now and then; or, if there be a persistent consonance, it can only be traced at long intervals, instead of discoursing an obvious melody.

What is the cause of this?

Man, in the order of time, was developed first; as energy comes before harmony; power before beauty.

Woman was therefore under his care as an elder. He might have been her guardian and teacher.

But, as human nature goes not straight forward, but by excessive action and then reaction in an undulated course, he misunderstood and abused his advantages, and became her temporal master instead of her spiritual sire.

On himself came the punishment. He educated Woman more as a servant than a daughter, and found himself a king without a queen.

The children of this unequal union showed unequal natures, and, more and more, men seemed sons of the handmaid, rather than princess.

At last, there were so many Ishmaelites that the rest grew frightened and indignant. They laid the blame on Hagar, and drove her forth into the wilderness.

But there were none the fewer Ishmaelites for that.

At last men became a little wiser, and saw that the infant Moses was, in every case, saved by the pure instincts of Woman's breast. For, as too much adversity is better for the moral nature than too much prosperity, Woman, in this respect, dwindled less than Man, though in other respects still a child in leading-strings.

So Man did her more and more justice, and grew more and more kind.

But yet—his habits and his will corrupted by the past—he did not clearly see that Woman was half himself; that her interests were identical with his; and that, by the law of their common being, he could never reach his true proportions while she remained in any wise shorn of hers.

And so it has gone on to our day; both ideas developing, but more slowly than they would under a clearer recognition of truth and justice, which would have permitted the sexes their due influence on one another, and mutual improvement from more dignified relations.

Wherever there was pure love, the natural influences were, for the time, restored.

Wherever the poet or artist gave free course to his genius, he saw the truth, and expressed it in worthy forms, for these men especially share and need the feminine principle. The divine birds need to be brooded into life and song by mothers.

Wherever religion (I mean the thirst for truth and good, not the love of sect and dogma) had its course, the original design was apprehended in its simplicity, and the dove presaged sweetly from Dodona's oak.

I have aimed to show that no age was left entirely without a witness of the equality of the sexes in function, duty and hope.

Also that, when there was unwillingness or ignorance, which prevented this being acted upon, women had not the less power for their want of light and noble freedom. But it was power which hurt alike them and those against whom they made use of the arms of the servile,—cunning, blandishment, and unreasonable emotion.

That now the time has come when a clearer vision and better action are possible—when Man and Woman may regard one another as brother and sister, the pillars of one porch, the priests of one worship.

I have believed and intimated that this hope would receive an ampler fruition, than ever before, in our own land.

And it will do so if this land carry out the principles from which sprang our national life.

I believe that, at present, women are the best helpers of one another.

Let them think; let them act; till they know what they need.

We only ask of men to remove arbitrary barriers. Some would like to do more. But I believe it needs that Woman show herself in her native dignity, to teach them how to aid her; their minds are so encumbered by tradition.

. . .

I think women need, especially at this juncture, a much greater range of occupation than they have, to rouse their latent powers. A party of travellers lately visited a lonely hut on a mountain. There they found an old woman, who told them she and her husband had lived there forty years. "Why," they said, "did you choose so barren a spot?" She "did not know; *it was the man's notion*."

And, during forty years, she had been content to act, without knowing why, upon "the man's notion." I would not have it so.

In families that I know, some little girls like to saw wood, others to use carpenters' tools. Where these tastes are indulged, cheerfulness and good-humor are promoted. Where they are forbidden, because "such things are not proper for girls," they grow sullen and mischievous.

Fourier had observed these wants of women, as no one can fail to do who watches the desires of little girls, or knows the ennui that haunts grown women, except where they make to themselves a serene little world by art of some kind. He, therefore, in proposing a great variety of employments, in manufactures or the care of plants and animals, allows for one third of women as likely to have a taste for masculine pursuits, one third of men for feminine.

Who does not observe the immediate glow and serenity that is diffused over the life of women, before restless or fretful, by engaging in gardening, building, or the lowest department of art? Here is something that is not routine, something that draws forth life towards the infinite.

I have no doubt, however, that a large proportion of women would give themselves to the same employments as now, because there are circumstances that must lead them. Mothers will delight to make the nest soft and warm. Nature would take care of that; no need to clip the wings of any bird that wants to soar and sing, or finds in itself the strength of pinion for a migratory flight unusual to its kind. The difference would be that *all* need not be constrained to employments for which *some* are unfit.

I have urged upon the sex self-subsistence in its two forms of self-reliance and self-impulse, because I believe them to be the needed means of the present juncture.

I have urged on Woman independence of Man, not that I do not think the sexes mutually needed by one another, but because in Woman this fact has led to an excessive devotion, which has cooled love, degraded marriage, and prevented either sex from being what it should be to itself or the other.

I wish Woman to live, *first* for God's sake. Then she will not make an imperfect man her god, and thus sink to idolatry. Then she will not take what is not fit for her from a sense of weakness and poverty. Then, if she finds what she needs in Man embodied, she will know how to love, and be worthy of being loved.

. . .

KARL MARX (AND FRIEDRICH ENGELS)

Karl Marx (1818–1883) was the most important of all socialist thinkers, a sociologist and economist who supported himself by journalism but lived the life of an independent intellectual and revolutionary. He was the author (with Friedrich Engels) of *The Communist Manifesto* (1848)—the most celebrated pamphlet in the history of socialism—as well as of socialism's most important book, the three-volume *Capital* (1867, 1885, 1894).

Marx was born in 1818 in the city of Trier, Germany, one of seven children of middle-class Jewish parents. After a year at the University of Bonn, where he studied the humanities, fought a duel, and spent a day in jail (the only imprisonment he suffered in his life), he left for the University of Berlin to study law and philosophy. There, in 1837, he was introduced to Georg Hegel's philosophy and to the Young Hegelians, whose leader, Bruno Bauer, was developing the idea that the Christian gospels were a record not of history but of fantasies arising from men's emotional needs. By 1841 the young Hegelians had become leftist republicans, the Prussian police were driving them from the universities, and Marx's hopes for a teaching position were dim. After completing his doctoral thesis, he turned to journalism and began writing for the *Rheinische Zeitung*, a liberal daily the authorities closed down in 1843. That summer, Marx married Jenny von Westphalen, an intelligent and cultivated woman whose own father was a socialist. Unemployable in Germany, Marx decided they must emigrate to Paris.

In Paris Marx met Friedrich Engels (1820–1895), his lifelong friend, collaborator, and benefactor. In the famous "Economic and Philosophical Manuscripts" of 1844, he began to unite Hegelian theory with the progressive politics of France and finally espoused communism. Marx's article "Toward the Critique of the Hegelian Philosophy of Right" asserts that religion is the "opium of the people" and calls for an "uprising of the proletariat" to realize the conceptions of philosophy, a point also made in "Theses on Feuerbach" (1845). Once more the government thwarted Marx; he was expelled from Paris in the autumn of 1844.

For the next three years Marx lived in Brussels, where he developed his views through confrontations with chief figures of the working-class movement, such as Mikhail Bakunin, Wilhelm Weitling, and Pierre Proudhon. He and Engels published *The Holy Family* (1845) and wrote *The German Ideology*, their first full exposition of the materialist philosophy of history (which found no publisher in their lifetimes). Marx also visited England, with Engels as a guide, and in London met the leaders of the League of the Just, a clandestine group of émigré German artisans. Given the task of composing the League of the Just program, Marx and Engels worked from December 1847 until the end of January 1848 and produced *The Communist Manifesto*. Asserting that all history had "hitherto been the history of class struggles," the Manifesto linked the victory of the proletariat to the development of capitalism itself, which dissolved traditional bonds and replaced them with the naked ties of self-interest. It ruthlessly criticized "social utopias" and all forms of socialism based on abstract ideals, rather than on the inevitable unfolding of the dialectical, historical process.

A month later revolution erupted in Paris, then spread to Prussia. Marx returned to Cologne, revived his newspaper, now entitled *Neue Rheinische Zeitung*, and supported an alliance between the German workers' movement and the progressive elements of the middle class. These years also inspired *The Eighteenth Brumaire of Louis Bonaparte* (1852), his subtle analysis of the relation between social classes and the state and the nature of bureaucracy. When the German revolution collapsed in 1849, he was once again expelled, this time sailing for England where he was to spend the rest of his life in exile.

Marx settled in London, where for the next decade he and his family suffered in grinding poverty. Often they subsisted on a diet of bread and potatoes; once they were evicted and their belongings seized. Several of the children died. For a short time Marx rejoined the Communist League and resumed his journalistic activities. But the study of economics convinced him that a new revolution hinged upon a new crisis—an economic crisis. He retreated from politics into the public reading room of the British Museum and devoted himself to exposing the "laws of motion of capitalist society as a whole." Except for occasional largesse from Engels, Marx's only source of income came from articles he wrote on contemporary politics for the *New York Daily Tribune*, a radical paper with the largest circulation in the United States.

In 1859 Marx published his first book on economic theory, *A Contribution to the Critique of Political Economy*, and in 1867 the first volume of *Capital*. (The second and third volumes, edited by Engels, were published posthumously in 1885 and 1894.) The pamphlets *Wage Labor and Capital* and *Value, Price and Profit* summarized his economic theories. In these works he found the key to understanding the capitalist system in the fact that the exchange of money and services between capital and labor is unequal. Workers must work longer than is necessary to pay for the costs of their upkeep, producing what Marx called "surplus value." And because of competition, capitalists must try to increase the rate of surplus value, replace human labor with machinery, and centralize the means of production until the system reached a crisis. Thus, capitalism was driven toward destruction, but its downfall was not automatic: It would require a revolutionary act in which the workers overturned the existing state and abolished private property and thus the class system. Marx expected that the revolution would occur in the industrialized nations of Western Europe, that it was imminent and would likely be violent, but that capitalism had the potential of delaying or even appeasing the workers' movement.

Marx resumed his political activity in 1864 as the founder of the International Workingman's Association, commonly known as the First International. For the eight years of its life, he was its dominant personality, drafting pronouncements on a number of European movements, including the Paris Commune of 1871. Immediately following the Commune's bloody suppression, Marx issued an eloquent pamphlet, *On the Civil War in France*, which defended the insurgents.

The final decade of Marx's life was financially secure, thanks to Engels, but plagued with health problems. Marx worked on new editions of *Capital* and followed closely the rise of the German Social Democratic Party. The death of his wife in 1881 was a devastating blow, and Marx himself died two years later, on March 14, 1883.

"THESES ON FEUERBACH"

1845

I

The chief defect of all hitherto existing materialism —that of Feuerbach included—is that the thing, reality, sensuousness, is conceived only in the form of the object or of *contemplation*, but not as *human sensuous activity, practice*, not subjectively. Hence, it happened that the *active* side, in contradistinction to materialism, was developed by idealism—but only abstractly, since, of course, idealism does not know real, sensuous activity as such. Feuerbach wants sensuous objects, really distinct from the thought objects, but he does not conceive human activity itself as *objective* activity. Hence, in *Das Wesen des Christentums*, he regards the theoretical attitude as the only genuinely human attitude, while practice is conceived and fixed only in its dirty-judaical manifestation. Hence he does not grasp the significance of "revolutionary," of practical-critical, activity.

II

The question whether objective truth can be attributed to human thinking is not a question of theory but is a *practical* question. Man must prove the truth, that is, the reality and power, the this-sidedness of his thinking in practice. The dispute over the reality or non-reality of thinking which is isolated from practice is a purely *scholastic* question.

III

The materialist doctrine that men are products of circumstances and upbringing, and that, therefore, changed men are products of other circumstances and changed upbringing, forgets that it is men who change circumstances and that it is essential to educate the educator himself. Hence, this doctrine necessarily arrives at dividing society into two parts, one of which is superior to society (in Robert Owen for example).

The coincidence of the changing of circumstances and of human activity can be conceived and rationally understood only as revolutionising practice.

IV

Feuerbach starts out from the fact of religious self-alienation, of the duplication of the world into a religious, imaginary world and a real one. His work consists in resolving the religious world into its secular basis. He overlooks the fact that after completing this work, the chief thing still remains to be done. For the fact that the secular basis detaches itself from itself and establishes itself in the clouds as an independent realm can only be explained by the cleavage and self-contradictions within this secular basis. The latter must itself, therefore, first be understood in its contradiction and then, by the removal of the contradiction, revolutionized in practice. Thus, for instance, after the earthly family is discovered to be the secret of the holy family, the former must then itself be criticised in theory and revolutionised in practice.

V

Feuerbach, not satisfied with *abstract thinking*, appeals to *sensuous contemplation*; but he does not conceive sensuousness as practical, humansensuous activity.

VI

Feuerbach resolves the religious essence into the human essence. But the human essence is no abstraction inherent in each single individual. In its reality it is the ensemble of the social relations.

Feuerbach, who does not enter upon a criticism of this real essence, is consequently compelled:

(1) To abstract from the historical process and to fix the religious sentiment as something by itself and to presuppose an abstract—*isolated*—human individual.

(2) The human essence, therefore, can with him be comprehended only as "genus," as an internal, dumb generality which merely *naturally* unites the many individuals.

VII

Feuerbach, consequently, does not see that the "religious sentiment" is itself a *social product*, and that the abstract individual whom he analyses belongs in reality to a particular form of society.

VIII

Social life is essentially *practical*. All mysteries which mislead theory into mysticism find their rational solution in human practice and in the comprehension of this practice.

IX

The highest point reached by *contemplative* materialism, that is, materialism which does not comprehend sensuousness as practical activity, is the contemplation of single individuals in "civil society."

X

The standpoint of the old materialism is civil society; the standpoint of the new is human society, or socialised humanity.

XI

The philosophers have only *interpreted* the world, in various ways; the point, however, is to *change* it.

A CONTRIBUTION TO THE CRITIQUE OF POLITICAL ECONOMY

1859

XX OUTLINE OF THE THEORY

In the social production which men carry on they enter into definite relations that are indispensable and independent of their will; these relations of production correspond to a definite stage of development of their material powers of production. The sum total of these relations of production constitutes the economic structure of society—the real foundation, on which rise legal and political superstructures and to which correspond definite forms of social consciousness. The mode of production in material life determines the general character of the social, political and spiritual processes of life. It is not the consciousness of men that determines their existence, but, on the contrary, their social existence determines their consciousness. At a certain stage of their development, the material forces of production in society come in conflict with the existing relations of production, or—what is but a legal expression for the same thing—with the property relations within which they had been at work before. From forms of development of the forces of production these relations turn into their fetters. Then comes the period of social revolution. With the change of the economic foundation the entire immense superstructure is more or less rapidly transformed. In considering such transformations the distinction should always be made between the material transformation of the economic conditions of production which can be determined with the precision of natural science, and the legal, political, religious, aesthetic or philosophic—in short ideological forms in which men become conscious of this conflict and fight it out. Just as our opinion of an individual is not based on what he thinks of himself, so can we not judge of such a period of transformation by its own consciousness; on the contrary, this consciousness must rather be explained from the contradictions of material life, from the existing conflict between the social forces of production and the relations of production. No social order ever disappears before all the productive forces, for which there is room in it, have been developed; and new higher relations of production never appear before the material conditions of their existence have matured in the womb of the old society. Therefore, mankind always takes up only such problems as it can solve; since, looking at the matter more closely, we will always find that the problem itself arises only when the material conditions necessary for its solution already exist or are at least in the process of formation. In broad outlines we can designate the Asiatic, the ancient, the feudal, and the modern bourgeois methods of production as so many epochs in the progress of the economic formation of society. The bourgeois relations of production are the last antagonistic form of the social process of production—antagonistic not in the sense of individual antagonism, but of one arising from conditions surrounding the life of individuals in society; at the same time the productive forces developing in the womb of bourgeois society create the material conditions for the solution of that antagonism. This social formation constitutes, therefore, the closing chapter of the prehistoric stage of human society. . . .

. . .

MANIFESTO OF THE COMMUNIST PARTY

1848

A spectre is haunting Europe—the spectre of Communism. All the Powers of old Europe have entered into a holy alliance to exorcise this spectre: Pope and Czar, Metternich and Guizot, French Radicals and police-spies.

Where is the party in opposition that has not been decried as Communistic by its opponents in power? Where the Opposition that has not hurled back the branding reproach of Communism, against the more advanced opposition parties, as well as against its reactionary adversaries?

Two things result from this fact.

I. Communism is already acknowledged by all European Powers to be itself a Power.

II. It is high time that Communists should openly, in the face of the whole world, publish their views, their aims their tendencies, and meet this nursery tale of the Spectre of Communism with a Manifesto of the party itself.

To this end, Communists of various nationalities have assembled in London, and sketched the following Manifesto, to be published in the English, French, German, Italian, Flemish and Danish languages.

I BOURGEOIS AND PROLETARIANS

The history of all hitherto existing society is the history of class struggles.

Freeman and slave, patrician and plebeian, lord and serf, guild-master and journeyman, in a word, oppressor and oppressed, stood in constant opposition to one another, carried on an uninterrupted, now hidden, now open fight, a fight that each time ended, either in a revolutionary re-constitution of society at large, or in the common ruin of the contending classes.

In the earlier epochs of history, we find almost everywhere a complicated arrangement of society into various orders, a manifold gradation of social rank. In ancient Rome we have patricians, knights, plebeians, slaves; in the Middle Ages, feudal lords, vassals, guild-masters, journeymen, apprentices, serfs; in almost all of these classes, again, subordinate gradations.

The modern bourgeois society that has sprouted from the ruins of feudal society has not done away with class antagonisms. It has but established new classes, new conditions of oppression, new forms of struggle in place of the old ones.

Our epoch, the epoch of the bourgeoisie, possesses, however, this distinctive feature: it has simplified the class antagonisms: Society as a whole is more and more splitting up into two great hostile camps, into two great classes directly facing each other: Bourgeoisie and Proletariat.

From the serfs of the Middle Ages sprang the chartered burghers of the earliest towns. From these burgesses the first elements of the bourgeoisie were developed.

The discovery of America, the rounding of the Cape, opened up fresh ground for the rising bourgeoisie. The East-Indian and Chinese markets, the colonisation of America, trade with the colonies, the increase in the means of exchange and in commodities generally, gave to commerce, to navigation, to industry, an impulse never before known, and thereby, to the revolutionary element in the tottering feudal society, a rapid development.

The feudal system of industry, under which industrial production was monopolised by closed guilds, now no longer sufficed for the growing wants of the new markets. The manufacturing system took its place. The guild-masters were pushed on one side by the manufacturing middle class; division of labour between the different corporate guilds vanished in the face of division of labour in each single workshop.

Meantime the markets kept ever growing, the demand ever rising. Even manufacture no longer sufficed. Thereupon, steam and machinery revolutionised industrial production. The place of manufacture was taken by the giant, Modern Industry, the place of the industrial middle class, by industrial millionaires, the leaders of whole industrial armies, the modern bourgeois.

Modern industry has established the worldmarket, for which the discovery of America paved the way. This market has given an immense development to commerce, to navigation, to communication by land. This development has, in its turn, reacted on the extension of industry; and in proportion as industry, commerce, navigation, railways extended, in the same proportion the bourgeoisie developed, increased its capital, and pushed into the background every class handed down from the Middle Ages.

We see, therefore, how the modern bourgeoisie is itself the product of a long course of development, of a series of revolutions in the modes of production and of exchange.

Each step in the development of the bourgeoisie was accompanied by a corresponding political advance of that class. An oppressed class under the sway of the feudal nobility, an armed and self-governing association in the mediaeval commune; here independent urban republic (as in Italy and Germany), there taxable "third estate" of the monarchy (as in France), afterwards, in the period of manufacture proper, serving either the semi-feudal or the absolute monarchy as a counterpoise against the nobility, and, in fact, cornerstone of the great monarchies in general, the bourgeoisie has at last, since the establishment of Modern Industry and of the world-market, conquered for itself, in the modern representative State, exclusive political sway. The executive of the modern State is but a committee for managing the common affairs of the whole bourgeoisie.

The bourgeoisie, historically, has played a most revolutionary part.

The bourgeoisie, wherever it has got the upper hand, has put an end to all feudal, patriarchal, idyllic relations. It has pitilessly tom asunder the motley feudal ties that bound man to his "natural superiors," and has left remaining no other nexus between man and man than naked self-interest, than callous "cash payment." It has drowned the most heavenly ecstasies of religious fervour, of chivalrous enthusiasm, of philistine sentimentalism, in the icy water of egotistical calculation. It has resolved personal worth into exchange value, and in place of the numberless indefeasible chartered freedoms, has set up that single, unconscionable freedom—Free Trade. In one word, for exploitation, veiled by religious and political illusions, it has substituted naked, shameless, direct, brutal exploitation.

The bourgeoisie has stripped of its halo every occupation hitherto honoured and looked up to with reverent awe. It has converted the physician, the lawyer, the priest, the poet, the man of science, into its paid wage-labourers.

The bourgeoisie has torn away from the family its sentimental veil, and has reduced the family relation to a mere money relation.

The bourgeoisie has disclosed how it came to pass that the brutal display of vigour in the Middle Ages, which Reactionists so much admire, found its fitting complement in the most slothful indolence. It has been the first to show what man's activity can bring about. It has accomplished wonders far surpassing Egyptian pyramids, Roman aqueducts, and Gothic cathedrals; it has conducted expeditions that put in the shade all former Exoduses of nations and crusades.

The bourgeoisie cannot exist without constantly revolutionising the instruments of production, and thereby the relations of production, and with them the whole relations of society. Conservation of the old modes of production in unaltered form, was, on the contrary, the first condition of existence for all earlier industrial classes. Constant revolutionising of production, uninterrupted disturbance of all social conditions, everlasting uncertainty and agitation distinguish the bourgeois epoch from all earlier ones. All fixed, fast-frozen relations, with their train of ancient and venerable prejudices and opinions, are swept away, all new-formed ones become antiquated before they can ossify. All that is solid melts into air, all that is holy is profaned, and man is at last compelled to face with sober senses, his real conditions of life, and his relations with his kind.

The need of a constantly expanding market for its products chases the bourgeoisie over the whole surface of the globe. It must nestle everywhere, settle everywhere, establish connexions everywhere.

The bourgeoisie has through its exploitation of the world-market given a cosmopolitan character to production and consumption in every country. To the great chagrin of Reactionists, it has drawn from under the feet of industry the national ground on which it stood. All old-established national industries have been destroyed or are daily being destroyed. They are dislodged by new industries, whose introduction becomes a life and death question for all civilised nations, by industries that no longer work up indigenous raw material, but raw material drawn from the remotest zones; industries whose products are consumed, not only at home, but in every quarter of the globe. In place of the old wants, satisfied by the productions of the country, we find new wants, requiring for their satisfaction the products of distant lands and climes. In place of the old local and national seclusion and self-sufficiency, we have intercourse in every direction, universal inter-dependence of nations. And as in material, so also in intellectual production. The intellectual creations of individual nations become common property. National one-sidedness and narrow-mindedness become more and more impossible, and from the numerous national and local literatures, there arises a world literature.

The bourgeoisie, by the rapid improvement of all instruments of production, by the immensely facilitated means of communication, draws all, even the most barbarian, nations into civilisation. The cheap prices of its commodities are the heavy artillery with which it batters down all Chinese walls, with which it forces the barbarians' intensely obstinate hatred of foreigners to capitulate. It compels all nations, on pain of extinction, to adopt the bourgeois mode of production; it compels them to introduce what it calls civilisation into their midst, i.e., to become bourgeois themselves. In one word, it creates a world after its own image.

The bourgeoisie has subjected the country to the rule of the towns. It has created enormous cities, has greatly increased the urban population as compared with the rural, and has thus rescued a considerable part of the population from the idiocy of rural life. Just as it has made the country dependent on the towns, so it has made barbarian and semi-barbarian countries dependent on the civilised ones, nations of peasants on nations of bourgeois, the East on the West.

The bourgeoisie keeps more and more doing away with the scattered state of the population, of the means of production, and of property. It has agglomerated population, centralised means of production, and has concentrated property in a few hands. The necessary consequence of this was political centralisation. Independent, or but loosely connected provinces, with separate interests, laws, governments and systems of taxation, became lumped together into one nation, with one government, one code of laws, one national class-interest, one frontier and one customs-tariff.

The bourgeoisie, during its rule of scarce one hundred years, has created more massive and more colossal productive forces than have all preceding generations together. Subjection of Nature's forces to man, machinery, application of chemistry to industry and agriculture, steam-navigation, railways, electric telegraphs, clearing of whole continents for cultivation, canalisation of rivers, whole populations conjured out of the ground—what earlier century had even a presentiment that such productive forces slumbered in the lap of social labour?

We see then: the means of production and of exchange, on whose foundation the bourgeoisie built itself up, were generated in feudal society. At a certain stage in the development of these means of production and of exchange, the conditions under which feudal society produced and exchanged, the feudal organisation of agriculture and manufacturing industry, in one word, the feudal relations of property became no longer compatible with the already developed productive forces; they became so many fetters. They had to be burst asunder; they were burst asunder.

Into their place stepped free competition, accompanied by a social and political constitution adapted to it, and by the economical and political sway of the bourgeois class.

A similar movement is going on before our own eyes. Modern bourgeois society with its relations of production, of exchange and of property, a society that has conjured up such gigantic means of production and of exchange, is like the sorcerer, who is no longer able to control the powers the nether world whom he has called up by his spells. For many a decade past the history of industry and commerce is but the history of the revolt of modern productive forces against modern conditions of production, against the property relations that are the conditions for the existence of the bourgeoisie and of its rule. It is enough to mention the commercial crises that by their periodical return put on its trial, each time more threateningly, the existence of the entire bourgeois society. In these crises a great part not only of the existing products, but also of the previously created productive forces, are periodically destroyed. In these crises there breaks out an epidemic that, in all earlier epochs, would have seemed an absurdity—the epidemic of over-production. Society suddenly finds itself put back into a state of momentary barbarism; it appears as if a famine, a universal war of devastation had cut off the supply of every means of subsistence; industry and commerce seem to be destroyed; and why? Because there is too much civilisation, too much means of subsistence, too much industry, too much commerce. The productive forces at the disposal of society no longer tend to further the development of the conditions of bourgeois property; on the contrary, they have become too powerful for these conditions, by which they are fettered, and so soon as they overcome these fetters, they bring disorder into the whole of bourgeois society, endanger the existence of bourgeois property. The conditions of bourgeois society are too narrow to comprise the wealth created by them. And how does the bourgeoisie get over these crises? On the one hand by enforced destruction of a mass of productive forces; on the other, by the conquest of new markets, and by the more thorough exploitation of the old ones. That is to say, by paving the way for more extensive and more destructive crises, and by diminishing the means whereby crises are prevented.

The weapons with which the bourgeoisie felled feudalism to the ground are now turned against the bourgeoisie itself.

But not only has the bourgeoisie forged the weapons that bring death to itself; it has also called into existence the men who are to wield those weapons—the modern working class—the proletarians.

In proportion as the bourgeoisie, i.e., capital, is developed, in the same proportion is the proletariat, the modern working class, developed—a class of labourers, who live only so long as they find work, and who find work only so long as their labour increases capital. These labourers, who must sell themselves piece-meal, are a commodity, like every other article of commerce, and are consequently exposed to all the vicissitudes of competition, to all the fluctuations of the market.

Owing to the extensive use of machinery and to division of labour, the work of the proletarians has lost all individual character, and consequently, all charm for the workman. He becomes an appendage of the machine, and it is only the most simple, most monotonous, and most easily acquired knack, that is required of him. Hence, the cost of production of a workman is restricted, almost entirely, to the means of subsistence that he requires for his maintenance, and for the propagation of his race. But the price of a commodity, and therefore also of labour, is equal to its cost of production. In proportion, therefore, as the repulsiveness of the work increases, the wage decreases. Nay more, in proportion as the use of machinery and division of labour increases, in the same proportion the burden of toil also increases, whether by prolongation of the working hours, by increase of the work exacted in a given time or by increased speed of the machinery, etc.

Modern industry has converted the little workshop of the patriarchal master into the great factory of the industrial capitalist. Masses of labourers, crowded into the factory, are organised like soldiers. As privates of the industrial army they are placed under the command of a perfect hierarchy of officers and sergeants. Not only are they slaves of the bourgeois class, and of the bourgeois State; they are daily and hourly enslaved by the machine, by the over-looker, and, above all, by the individual bourgeois manufacturer himself. The more openly this despotism proclaims gain to be its end and aim, the more petty, the more hateful and the more embittering it is.

The less the skill and exertion of strength implied in manual labour, in other words, the more modern industry becomes developed, the more is the labour of men superseded by that of women. Differences of age and sex have no longer any distinctive social validity for the working class. All are instruments of labour, more or less expensive to use, according to their age and sex.

No sooner is the exploitation of the labourer by the manufacturer, so far, at an end, that he receives his wages in cash, than he is set upon by the other portions of the bourgeoisie, the landlord, the shopkeeper, the pawnbroker, etc.

The lower strata of the middle class—the small tradespeople, shopkeepers, and retired tradesmen generally, the handicraftsmen and peasants—all these sink gradually into the proletariat, partly because their diminutive capital does not suffice for the scale on which Modern Industry is carried on, and is swamped in the competition with the large capitalists, partly because their specialised skill is rendered worthless by new methods of production. Thus the proletariat is recruited from all classes of the population.

The proletariat goes through various stages of development. With its birth begins its struggle with the bourgeoisie. At first the contest is carried on by individual labourers, then by the workpeople of a factory, then by the operatives of one trade, in one locality, against the individual bourgeois who directly exploits them. They direct their attacks not against the bourgeois conditions of production, but against the instruments of production themselves; they destroy imported wares that compete with their labour, they smash to pieces machinery, they set factories ablaze, they seek to restore by force the vanished status of the workman in the Middle Ages.

At this stage the labourers still form an incoherent mass scattered over the whole country, and broken up by their mutual competition. If anywhere they unite to form more compact bodies, this is not yet the consequence of their own active union, but of the union of the bourgeoisie, which class, in order to attain its own political ends, is compelled to set the whole proletariat in motion, and is moreover yet, for a time, able to do so. At this stage, therefore, the proletarians do not fight their enemies, but the enemies of their enemies, the remnants of absolute monarchy, the landowners, the non-industrial bourgeois, the petty bourgeoisie. Thus the whole historical movement is concentrated in the hands of the bourgeoisie; every victory so obtained is a victory for the bourgeoisie.

But with the development of industry the proletariat not only increases in number; it becomes concentrated in greater masses, its strength grows, and it feels that strength more. The various interests and conditions of life within the ranks of the proletariat are more and more equalised, in proportion as machinery obliterates all distinctions of labour, and nearly everywhere reduces wages to the same low level. The growing competition among the bourgeois, and the resulting commercial crises, make the wages of the workers ever more fluctuating. The unceasing improvement of machinery, ever more rapidly developing, makes their livelihood more and more precarious; the collisions between individual workmen and individual bourgeois take more and more the character of collisions between two classes. Thereupon the workers begin to form combinations (Trades Unions) against the bourgeois; they club together in order to keep up the rate of wages; they found permanent associations in order to make provision beforehand for these occasional revolts. Here and there the contest breaks out into riots.

Now and then the workers are victorious, but only for a time. The real fruit of their battles lies, not in the immediate result, but in the ever-expanding union of the workers. This union is helped on by the improved means of communication that are created by modern industry and that place the workers of different localities in contact with one another. It was just this contact that was needed to centralised the numerous local struggles, all of the same character, into one national struggle between classes. But every class struggle is a political struggle. And that union, to attain which the burghers of the Middle Ages, with their miserable highways, required centuries, the modern proletarians, thanks to railways, achieve in a few years.

This organisation of the proletarians into a class, and consequently into a political party, is continually being upset again by the competition between the workers themselves. But it ever rises up again, stronger, firmer, mightier. It compels legislative recognition of particular interests of the workers, by taking advantage of the divisions among the bourgeoisie itself. Thus the ten-hours' bill in England was carried.

Altogether collisions between the classes of the old society further, in many ways, the course of development of the proletariat. The bourgeoisie finds itself involved in a constant battle. At first with the aristocracy; later on, with those portions of the bourgeoisie itself, whose interests have become antagonistic to the progress of industry; at all times, with the bourgeoisie of foreign countries. In all these battles it sees itself compelled to appeal to the proletariat, to ask for its help, and thus, to drag it into the political arena. The bourgeoisie itself, therefore, supplies the proletariat with its own elements of political and general education, in other words, it furnishes the proletariat with weapons for fighting the bourgeoisie.

Further, as we have already seen, entire sections of the ruling classes are, by the advance of industry, precipitated into the proletariat, or are at least threatened in their conditions of existence. These also supply the proletariat with fresh elements of enlightenment and progress.

Finally, in times when the class struggle nears the decisive hour, the process of dissolution going on within the ruling class, in fact within the whole range of society, assumes such a violent, glaring character, that a small section of the ruling class cuts itself adrift, and joins the revolutionary class, the class that holds the future in its hands. Just as, therefore, at an earlier period, a section of the nobility went over to the bourgeoisie, so now a portion of the bourgeoisie goes over to the proletariat, and in particular, a portion of the bourgeois ideologists, who have raised themselves to the level of comprehending theoretically the historical movement as a whole.

Of all the classes that stand face to face with the bourgeoisie today, the proletariat alone is a really revolutionary class. The other classes decay and finally disappear in the face of Modern Industry; the proletariat is its special and essential product.

The lower middle class, the small manufacturer, the shopkeeper, the artisan, the peasant, all these fight against the bourgeoisie, to save from extinction their existence as fractions of the middle class. They are therefore not revolutionary, but conservative. Nay more, they are reactionary, for they try to roll back the wheel of history. If by chance they are revolutionary, they are so only in view of their impending transfer into the proletariat, they thus defend not their present, but their future interests, they desert their own standpoint to place themselves at that of the proletariat.

The "dangerous class," the social scum, that passively rotting mass thrown off by the lowest layers of old society, may, here and there, be swept into the movement by a proletarian revolution; its conditions of life, however, prepare it far more for the part of a bribed tool of reactionary intrigue.

In the conditions of the proletariat, those of old society at large are already virtually swamped. The proletarian is without property; his relation to his wife and children has no longer anything in common with the bourgeois family-relations; modern industrial labour, modern subjection to capital, the same in England as in France, in America as in Germany, has stripped him of every trace of national character. Law, morality, religion, are to him so many bourgeois prejudices, behind which lurk in ambush just as many bourgeois interests.

All the preceding classes that got the upper hand, sought to fortify their already acquired status by subjecting society at large to their conditions of appropriation. The proletarians cannot become masters of the productive forces of society, except by abolishing their own previous mode of appropriation, and thereby also every other previous mode of appropriation.

They have nothing of their own to secure and to fortify; their mission is to destroy all previous securities for, and insurances of, individual property.

All previous historical movements were movements of minorities, or in the interest of minorities. The proletarian movement is the self-conscious, independent movement of the immense majority, in the interest of the immense majority. The proletariat, the lowest stratum of our present society, cannot stir, cannot raise itself up, without the whole superincumbent strata of official society being sprung into the air.

Though not in substance, yet in form, the struggle of the proletariat with the bourgeoisie is at first a national struggle. The proletariat of each country must, of course, first of all settle matters with its own bourgeoisie.

In depicting the most general phases of the development of the proletariat, we traced the more or less veiled civil war, raging within existing society, up to the point where that war breaks out into open revolution, and where the violent overthrow of the bourgeoisie lays the foundation for the sway of the proletariat.

Hitherto, every form of society has been based, as we have already seen, on the antagonism of oppressing and oppressed classes. But in order to oppress a class, certain conditions must be assured to it under which it can, at least, continue its slavish existence. The serf, in the period of serfdom, raised himself to membership in the commune, just as the petty bourgeois, under the yoke of feudal absolutism, managed to develop into a bourgeois. The modern labourer, on the contrary, instead of rising with the progress of industry, sinks deeper and deeper below the conditions of existence of his own class. He becomes a pauper, and pauperism develops more rapidly than population and wealth. And here it becomes evident, that the bourgeoisie is unfit any longer to be the ruling class in society, and to impose its conditions of existence upon society as an over-riding law. It is unfit to rule because it is incompetent to assure an existence to its slave within his slavery, because it cannot help letting him sink into such a state, that it has to feed him, instead of being fed by him. Society can no longer live under this bourgeoisie, in other words, its existence is no longer compatible with society.

The essential condition for the existence, and for the sway of the bourgeois class, is the formation and augmentation of capital; the condition for capital is wage-labour. Wage-labour rests exclusively on competition between the labourers. The advance of industry, whose involuntary promoter is the bourgeoisie, replaces the isolation of the labourers, due to competition, by their revolutionary combination, due to association. The development of Modern Industry, therefore, cuts from under its feet the very foundation on which the bourgeoisie produces and appropriates products. What the bourgeoisie, therefore, produces, above all, is its own grave-diggers. Its fall and the victory of the proletariat are equally inevitable.

II PROLETARIANS AND COMMUNISTS

In what relation do the Communists stand to the proletarians as a whole?

The Communists do not form a separate party opposed to other working-class parties.

They have no interests separate and apart from those of the proletariat as a whole.

They do not set up any sectarian principles of their own, by which to shape and mould the proletarian movement.

The Communists are distinguished from the other working-class parties by this only: (1) In the national struggles of the proletarians of the different countries, they point out and bring to the front the common interests of the entire proletariat, independently of all nationality. (2) In the various stages of development which the struggle of the working class against the bourgeoisie has to pass through, they always and everywhere represent the interests of the movement as a whole.

The Communists, therefore, are on the one hand, practically, the most advanced and resolute section of the working-class parties of every country, that section which pushes forward all others; on the other hand, theoretically, they have over the great mass of the proletariat the advantage of clearly understanding the line of march, the conditions, and the ultimate general results of the proletarian movement.

The immediate aim of the Communists is the same as that of all the other proletarian parties: formation of the proletariat into a class, overthrow of the bourgeois supremacy, conquest of political power by the proletariat.

The theoretical conclusions of the Communists are in no way based on ideas or principles that have been invented, or discovered, by this or that would-be universal reformer.

They merely express, in general terms, actual relations springing from an existing class struggle, from a historical movement going on under our very eyes. The abolition of existing property relations is not at all a distinctive feature of Communism.

All property relations in the past have continually been subject to historical change consequent upon the change in historical conditions.

The French Revolution, for example, abolished feudal property in favour of bourgeois property.

The distinguishing feature of Communism is not the abolition of property generally, but the abolition of bourgeois property. But modern bourgeois private property is the final and most complete expression of the system of producing and appropriating products, that is based on class antagonisms, on the exploitation of the many by the few.

In this sense, the theory of the Communists may be summed up in the single sentence: Abolition of private property.

We Communists have been reproached with the desire of abolishing the right of personally acquiring property as the fruit of a man's own labour, which property is alleged to be the groundwork of all personal freedom, activity and independence.

Hard-won, self-acquired, self-earned property! Do you mean the property of the petty artisan and of the small peasant, a form of property that preceded the bourgeois form? There is no need to abolish that; the development of industry has to a great extent already destroyed it, and is still destroying it daily.

Or do you mean modern bourgeois private property?

But does wage-labour create any property for the labourer? Not a bit. It creates capital, i.e., that kind of property which exploits wage-labour, and which cannot increase except upon condition of begetting a new supply of wage-labour for fresh exploitation. Property, in its present form, is based on the antagonism of capital and wage-labour. Let us examine both sides of this antagonism.

To be a capitalist, is to have not only a purely personal, but a social *status* in production. Capital is collective product, and only by the united action of many members, nay, in the last resort, only by the united action of all members of society, can it be set in motion.

Capital is, therefore, not a personal, it is a social power.

When, therefore, capital is converted into common property, into the property of all members of society, personal property is not thereby transformed into social property. It is only the social character of the property that is changed. It loses its class-character.

Let us now take wage-labour.

The average price of wage-labour is the minimum wage, i.e., that quantum of the means of subsistence, which is absolutely requisite to keep the labourer in bare existence as a labourer. What, therefore, the wage-labourer appropriates by means of his labour, merely suffices to prolong and reproduce a bare existence. We by no means intend to abolish this personal appropriation of the products of labour, an appropriation that is made for the maintenance and reproduction of human life, and that leaves no surplus wherewith to command the labour of others. All that we want to do away with, is the miserable character of this appropriation, under which the labourer lives merely to increase capital, and is allowed to live only in so far as the interest of the ruling class requires it.

In bourgeois society, living labour is but a means to increase accumulated labour. In Communist society, accumulated labour is but a means to widen, to enrich, to promote the existence of the labourer.

In bourgeois society, therefore, the past dominates the present; in Communist society, the present dominates the past. In bourgeois society capital is independent and has individuality, while the living person is dependent and has no individuality.

And the abolition of this state of things is called by the bourgeois, abolition of individuality and freedom! And rightly so. The abolition of bourgeois individuality, bourgeois independence, and bourgeois freedom is undoubtedly aimed at.

By freedom is meant, under the present bourgeois conditions of production, free trade, free selling and buying.

But if selling and buying disappears, free selling and buying disappears also. This talk about free selling and buying, and all the other "brave words" of our bourgeoisie about freedom in general, have a meaning, if any, only in contrast with restricted selling and buying, with the fettered traders of the Middle Ages, but have no meaning when opposed to the Communistic abolition of buying and selling, of the bourgeois conditions of production, and of the bourgeoisie itself.

You are horrified at our intending to do away with private property. But in your existing society, private property is already done away with for nine-tenths of the population; its existence for the few is solely due to its non-existence in the hands of those nine-tenths. You reproach us, therefore, with intending to do away with a form of property, the necessary condition for whose existence is the non-existence of any property for the immense majority of society.

In one word, you reproach us with intending to do away with your property. Precisely so; that is just what we intend.

From the moment when labour can no longer be converted into capital, money, or rent, into a social power capable of being monopolized, i.e., from the moment when individual property can no longer be transformed into bourgeois property, into capital from that moment, you say, individuality vanishes.

You must, therefore, confess that by "individual" you mean no other person than the bourgeois, than the middle-class owner of property. This person must, indeed, be swept out of the way, and made impossible.

Communism deprives no man of the power to appropriate the products of society; all that it does is to deprive him of the power to subjugate the labour of others by means of such appropriation.

It has been objected that upon the abolition of private property all work will cease, and universal laziness will overtake us.

According to this, bourgeois society ought long ago to have gone to the dogs through sheer idleness; for those of its members who work, acquire nothing, and those who acquire anything, do not work. The whole of this objection is but another expression of the tautology: that there can no longer be any wage-labour when there is no longer any capital.

All objections urged against the Communistic mode of producing and appropriating material products, have, in the same way, been urged against the Communistic modes of producing and appropriating intellectual products. Just as, to the bourgeois, the disappearance of class property is the disappearance of production itself, so the disappearance of class culture is to him identical with the disappearance of all culture.

That culture, the loss of which he laments, is, for the enormous majority, a mere training to act as a machine.

But don't wrangle with us so long as you apply, to our intended abolition of bourgeois property, the standard of your bourgeois notions of freedom, culture, law, &c. Your very ideas are but the outgrowth of the conditions of your bourgeois production and bourgeois property, just as your jurisprudence is but the will of your class made into a law for all, a will, whose essential character and direction are determined by the economical conditions of existence of your class.

The selfish misconception that induces you to transform into eternal laws of nature and of reason, the social forms springing from your present mode of production and form of property—historical relations that rise and disappear in the progress of production—this misconception you share with every ruling class that has preceded you. What you see clearly in the case of ancient property, what you admit in the case of feudal property, you are of course forbidden to admit in the case of your own bourgeois form of property.

Abolition of the family! Even the most radical flare up at this infamous proposal of the Communists.

On what foundation is the present family, the bourgeois family, based? On capital, on private gain. In its completely developed form this family exists only among the bourgeoisie. But this state of things finds its complement in the practical absence of the family among the proletarians, and in public prostitution.

The bourgeois family will vanish as a matter of course when its complement vanishes, and both will vanish with the vanishing of capital.

Do you charge us with wanting to stop the exploitation of children by their parents? To this crime we plead guilty.

But, you will say, we destroy the most hallowed of relations, when we replace home education by social.

And your education! Is not that also social, and determined by the social conditions under which you educate, by the intervention, direct or indirect, of society, by means of schools, &c.? The Communists have not invented the intervention of society in education; they do but seek to alter the character of that intervention, and to rescue education from the influence of the ruling class.

The bourgeois clap-trap about the family and education, about the hallowed co-relation of parent and child, becomes all the more disgusting, the more, by the action of Modern Industry, all family ties among the proletarians are torn asunder, and their children transformed into simple articles of commerce and instruments of labour.

But you Communists would introduce community of women, screams the whole bourgeoisie in chorus.

The bourgeois sees in his wife a mere instrument of production. He hears that the instruments of production are to be exploited in common, and, naturally, can come to no other conclusion than that the lot of being common to all will likewise fall to the women.

He has not even a suspicion that the real point aimed at is to do away with the status of women as mere instruments of production.

For the rest, nothing is more ridiculous than the virtuous indignation of our bourgeois at the community of women which, they pretend, is to be openly and officially established by the Communists. The Communists have no need to introduce community of women; it has existed almost from time immemorial.

Our bourgeois, not content with having the wives and daughters of their proletarians at their disposal, not to speak of common prostitutes, take the greatest pleasure in seducing each other's wives.

Bourgeois marriage is in reality a system of wives in common and thus, at the most, what the Communists might possibly be reproached with, is that they desire to introduce, in substitution for a hypocritically concealed, an openly legalised community of women. For the rest, it is self-evident that the abolition of the present system of production must bring with it the abolition of the community of women springing from that system, i.e., of prostitution both public and private.

The Communists are further reproached with desiring to abolish countries and nationality.

The working men have no country. We cannot take from them what they have not got. Since the proletariat must first of all acquire political supremacy, must rise to be the leading class of the nation, must constitute itself *the* nation, it is, so far, itself national, though not in the bourgeois sense of the word.

National differences and antagonisms between peoples are daily more and more vanishing, owing to the development of the bourgeoisie, to freedom of commerce, to the world-market, to uniformity in the mode of production and in the conditions of life corresponding thereto.

The supremacy of the proletariat will cause them to vanish still faster. United action, of the leading civilised countries at least, is one of the first conditions for the emancipation of the proletariat.

In proportion as the exploitation of one individual by another is put an end to, the exploitation of one nation by another will also be put an end to. In proportion as the antagonism between classes within the nation vanishes, the hostility of one nation to another will come to an end.

The charges against Communism made from a religious, a philosophical, and, generally, from an ideological standpoint, are not deserving of serious examination.

Does it require deep intuition to comprehend that man's ideas, views and conceptions, in one word, man's consciousness, changes with every change in the conditions of his material existence, in his social relations and in his social life?

What else does the history of ideas prove, than that intellectual production changes its character in proportion as material production is changed? The ruling ideas of each age have ever been the ideas of its ruling class.

When people speak of ideas that revolutionise society, they do but express the fact, that within the old society, the elements of a new one have been created, and that the dissolution of the old ideas keeps even pace with the dissolution of the old conditions of existence.

When the ancient world was in its last throes, the ancient religions were overcome by Christianity. When Christian ideas succumbed in the 18th century to rationalist ideas, feudal society fought its death battle with the then revolutionary bourgeoisie. The ideas of religious liberty and freedom of conscience merely gave expression to the sway of free competition within the domain of knowledge.

"Undoubtedly," it will be said, "religious, moral, philosophical and juridical ideas have been modified in the course of historical development. But religion, morality, philosophy, political science, and law, constantly survived this change."

"There are, besides, eternal truths, such as Freedom, Justice, etc., that are common to all states of society. But Communism abolishes eternal truths, it abolishes all religion, and all morality, instead of constituting them on a new basis; it therefore acts in contradiction to all past historical experience."

What does this accusation reduce itself to? The history of all past society has consisted in the development of class antagonisms, antagonisms that assumed different forms at different epochs.

But whatever form they may have taken, one fact is common to all past ages, *viz*., the exploitation of one part of society by the other. No wonder, then, that the social consciousness of past ages, despite all the multiplicity and variety it displays, moves within certain common forms, or general ideas, which cannot completely vanish except with the total disappearance of class antagonisms.

The Communist revolution is the most radical rupture with traditional property relations; no wonder that its development involves the most radical rupture with traditional ideas.

But let us have done with the bourgeois objections to Communism.

We have seen above, that the first step in the revolution by the working class, is to raise the proletariat to the position of ruling class, to win the battle of democracy.

The proletariat will use its political supremacy to wrest, by degrees, all capital from the bourgeoisie, to centralise all instruments of production in the hands of the State, i.e., of the proletariat organised as the ruling class; and to increase the total of productive forces as rapidly as possible.

Of course, in the beginning, this cannot be effected except by means of despotic inroads on the rights of property, and on the conditions of bourgeois production; by means of measures, therefore, which appear economically insufficient and untenable, but which, in the course of the movement, outstrip themselves, necessitate further inroads upon the old social order, and are unavoidable as a means of entirely revolutionizing the mode of production.

These measures will of course be different in different countries.

Nevertheless, in the most advanced countries, the following will be pretty generally applicable.

1. Abolition of property in land and application of all rents of land to public purposes.
2. A heavy progressive or graduated income tax.
3. Abolition of all right of inheritance.
4. Confiscation of the property of all emigrants and rebels.
5. Centralisation of credit in the hands of the State, by means of a national bank with State capital and an exclusive monopoly.
6. Centralisation of the means of communication and transport in the hands of the State.
7. Extension of factories and instruments of production owned by the State; the bringing into cultivation of waste-lands, and the improvement of the soil generally in accordance with a common plan.

8. Equal liability of all to labour. Establishment of industrial armies, especially for agriculture.
9. Combination of agriculture with manufacturing industries; gradual abolition of the distinction between town and country, by a more equable distribution of the population over the country.
10. Free education for all children in public schools. Abolition of children's factory labour in its present form. Combination of education with industrial production, &c., &c.

When, in the course of development, class distinctions have disappeared, and all production has been concentrated in the hands of a vast association of the whole nation, the public power will lose its political character. Political power, properly so called, is merely the organised power of one class for oppressing another. If the proletariat during its contest with the bourgeoisie is compelled, by the force of circumstances, to organise itself as a class, if, by means of a revolution, it makes itself the ruling class, and, as such, sweeps away by force the old conditions of production, then it will, along with these conditions, have swept away the conditions for the existence of class antagonisms and of classes generally, and will thereby have abolished its own supremacy as a class.

In place of the old bourgeois society, with its classes and class antagonisms, we shall have an association, in which the free development of each is the condition for the free development of all.

. . .

IV POSITION OF THE COMMUNISTS IN RELATION TO THE VARIOUS EXISTING OPPOSITION PARTIES

Section II has made clear the relations of the Communists to the existing working-class parties, such as the Chartists in England and the Agrarian Reformers of America.

The Communists fight for the attainment of the immediate aims, for the enforcement of the momentary interests of the working class; but in the movement of the present, they also represent and take care of the future of that movement. In France the Communists ally themselves with the Social-Democrats, against the conservative and radical bourgeoisie, reserving, however, the right to take up a critical position in regard to phrases and illusions traditionally handed down from the great Revolution.

In Switzerland they support the Radicals, without losing sight of the fact that this party consists of antagonistic elements, partly of Democratic Socialists, in the French sense, partly of radical bourgeois.

In Poland they support the party that insists on an agrarian revolution as the prime condition for national emancipation, that party which fomented the insurrection of Cracow in 1846.

In Germany they fight with the bourgeoisie whenever it acts in a revolutionary way, against the absolute monarchy, the feudal squirearchy, and the petty bourgeoisie.

But they never cease, for a single instant, to instil into the working class the clearest possible recognition of the hostile antagonism between bourgeoisie and proletariat, in order that the German workers may straightway use, as so many weapons against the bourgeoisie, the social and political conditions that the bourgeoisie must necessarily introduced along with its supremacy, and in order that, after the fall of the reactionary classes in Germany, the fight against the bourgeoisie itself may immediately begin.

The Communists turn their attention chiefly to Germany, because that country is on the eve of a bourgeois revolution that is bound to be carried out under more advanced conditions of European civilisation, and with a much more developed proletariat, than that of England was in the seventeenth, and of France in the eighteenth century, and because the bourgeois revolution in Germany will be but the prelude to an immediately following proletarian revolution.

In short, the Communists everywhere support every revolutionary movement against the existing social and political order of things.

In all these movements they bring to the front, as the leading question in each, the property question, no matter what its degree of development at the time.

Finally, they labour everywhere for the union and agreement of the democratic parties of all countries.

The Communists disdain to conceal their views and aims. They openly declare that their ends can be attained only by the forcible overthrow of all existing social conditions. Let the ruling classes tremble at a Communistic revolution. The proletarians have nothing to lose but their chains. They have a world to win.

WORKING MEN OF ALL COUNTRIES, UNITE!

WAGE LABOUR AND CAPITAL

1849

I

From various quarters we have been reproached with not having presented the *economic relations* which constitute the material foundation of the present class struggles and national struggles. We have designedly touched upon these relations only where they directly forced themselves to the front in political conflicts.

The point was, above all, to trace the class struggle in current history, and to prove empirically by means of the historical material already at hand and which is being newly created daily, that, with the subjugation of the working class that February and March had wrought, its opponents were simultaneously defeated—the bourgeois republicans in France and the bourgeois and peasant classes which were fighting feudal absolutism throughout the continent of Europe; that the victory of the "honest republic" in France was at the same time the downfall of the nations that had responded to the February Revolution by heroic wars of independence; finally, that Europe, with the defeat of the revolutionary workers, had relapsed into its old double slavery, the *Anglo-Russian* slavery. The June struggle in Paris, the fall of Vienna, the tragicomedy of Berlin's November, 1848, the desperate exertions of Poland, Italy and Hungary, the starving of Ireland into submission—these were the chief factors which characterised the European class struggle between bourgeoisie and working class and by means of which we proved that every revolutionary upheaval, however remote from the class struggle its goal may appear to be, must fail until the revolutionary working class is victorious, that every social reform remains a utopia until the proletarian revolution and the feudalistic counter-revolution measure swords in a *world war*. In our presentation, as in reality, *Belgium* and *Switzerland* were tragicomic genre-pictures akin to caricature in the great historical tableau, the one being the model state of the bourgeois monarchy, the other the model state of the bourgeois republic, both of them states which imagine themselves to be as independent of the class struggle as of the European revolution.

Now, after our readers have seen the class struggle develop in colossal political forms in 1848, the time has come to deal more closely with the economic relations themselves on which the existence of the bourgeoisie and its class rule, as well as the slavery of the workers, are founded.

We shall present in three large sections: (1) the relation of *wage labour to capital*, the slavery of the worker, the domination of the capitalist; (2) *the inevitable destruction of the middle bourgeois and of the so-called peasant estate under the present system*; (3) *the commercial subjugation and exploitation of the bourgeois classes of the various European nations* by the despot of the world market—*England.*

We shall try to make our presentation as simple and popular as possible and shall not presuppose even the most elementary notions of political economy. We wish to be understood by the workers. Moreover, the most remarkable ignorance and confusion of ideas prevails in Germany in regard to the simplest economic relations, from the accredited defenders of the existing state of things to the *socialist miracle workers* and the *unrecognised political geniuses* in which fragmented Germany is even richer than in sovereign princes.

Now, therefore, for the first question: *What are wages? How are they determined?*

If workers were asked: "How much are your wages?" one would reply: "I get a mark a day from my employer"; another, "I get two marks," and so on. According to the different trades to which they belong, they would mention different sums of money which they receive from their respective employers for the performance of a particular piece of work, for example, weaving a yard of linen or typesetting a printed sheet. In spite of the variety of their statements, they would all agree on one point: wages are the sum of money paid by the capitalist for a particular labour time or for a particular output of labour.

The capitalist, it seems, therefore, *buys* their labour with money. They *sell* him their labour for money. But this is merely the appearance. In reality what they sell to the capitalist for money is their labour *power*. The capitalist buys this labour power for a day, a week, a month, etc. And after he has bought it, he uses it by having the workers work for the stipulated time. For the same sum with which the capitalist has bought their labour power, for example, two marks, he could have bought two pounds of sugar or a definite amount of any other commodity. The two marks, with which he bought two pounds of sugar, are the *price* of the two pounds of sugar. The two marks, with which he bought twelve hours' use of labour power, are the price of twelve hours' labour. Labour power, therefore, is a commodity, neither more nor less than sugar. The former is measured by the clock, the latter by the scales.

The workers exchange their commodity, labour power, for the commodity of the capitalist, for money, and this exchange takes place in a definite ratio. So much money for so long a use of labour power. For twelve hours' weaving, two marks. And do not the two marks represent all the other commodities which I can buy for two marks? In fact, therefore, the worker has exchanged his commodity, labour power, for other commodities of all kinds and that in a definite ratio. By giving him two marks, the capitalist has given him so much meat, so much clothing, so much fuel, light, etc., in exchange for his day's labour. Accordingly, the two marks express the ratio in which labour power is exchanged for other commodities, the *exchange value* of his labour power. The exchange value of a commodity, reckoned in *money*, is what is called its *price. Wages* are only a special name for the price of labour power, commonly called the *price of labour*, for the price of this peculiar commodity which has no other repository than human flesh and blood.

Let us take any worker, say, a weaver. The capitalist supplies him with the loom and yarn. The weaver sets to work and the yarn is converted into linen. The capitalist takes possession of the linen and sells it, say, for twenty marks. Now are the wages of the weaver a *share* in the linen, in the twenty marks, in the product of his labour? By no means. Long before the linen is sold, perhaps long before its weaving is finished, the weaver has received his wages. The capitalist, therefore, does not pay these wages with the money which he will obtain from the linen, but with money already in reserve. Just as the loom and the yarn are not the product of the weaver to whom they are supplied by his employer, so likewise with the commodities which the weaver receives in exchange for his commodity, labour power. It was possible that his employer found no purchaser at all for his linen. It was possible that be did not get even the amount of the wages by its sale. It is possible that he sells it very profitably in comparison with the weaver's wages. All that has nothing to do with the weaver. The capitalist buys the labour power of the weaver with a part of his available wealth, of his capital, just as he has bought the raw material—the yarn—and the instrument of labour—the loom—with another part of his wealth. After he has made these purchases, and these purchases include the labour power necessary for the production of linen, he produces only with the *raw materials and instruments of labour belonging to him*. For the latter include now, true enough, our good weaver as well, who has as little share in the product or the price of the product as the loom has.

Wages are, therefore, not the worker's share in the commodity produced by him. Wages are the part of already existing commodities with which the capitalist buys for himself definite amount of productive labour power.

Labour power is, therefore, a commodity which its possessor, the wage-worker, sells to capital. Why does he sell it? In order to live.

But the exercise of labour power, labour, is the worker's own life-activity, the manifestation of his own life. And this, *life-activity* he sells to another person in order to secure the necessary *means of subsistence*. Thus his life-activity is for him only a means to enable him to exist. He works in order to live. He does not even reckon labour as part of his life, it is rather a sacrifice of his life. It is a commodity which he has made over to another. Hence, also, the product of his activity is not the object of his activity. What he produces for himself is not the silk that he weaves, not the gold that he draws from the mine, not the palace that he builds. What he produces for himself is *wages*, and silk, gold, palace resolve themselves for him into a definite quantity of the means of subsistence, perhaps into a cotton jacket, some copper coins and a lodging in a cellar. And the worker, who for twelve hours weaves, spins, drills, turns, builds, shovels, breaks stones, carries loads, etc.—does he consider this twelve hours' weaving, spinning, drilling, turning, building, shovelling, stone breaking as a manifestation of his life, as life? On the contrary, life begins for him where this activity ceases, at table, in the public house, in bed. The twelve hours' labour, on the other hand, has no meaning for him as weaving, spinning, drilling, etc., but as *earnings*, which bring him to the table, to the public house, into bed. If the silk worm were to spin in order to continue its existence as a caterpillar, it would be a complete wage-worker. Labour power was not always a *commodity*. Labour was not always wage labour, that is, *free labour*. The *slave* did not sell his labour power to the slave owner, any more than the ox sells its services to the peasant. The slave, together with his labour power, is sold once and for all to his owner. He is a commodity which can pass from the hand of one owner to that of another He is *himself* a commodity, but the labour power is not *his* commodity. The *serf* sells only a part of his labour power. He does not receive a wage from the owner of the land; rather the owner of the land receives a tribute from him.

The serf belongs to the land and turns over to the owner of the land the fruits thereof. The *free labourer*, on the other hand, sells himself and, indeed, sells himself piecemeal. He sells at auction eight, ten, twelve, fifteen hours of his life, day after day, to the highest bidder, to the owner of the raw materials, instruments of labour and means of subsistence, that is, to the capitalist. The worker belongs neither to an owner nor to the land, but eight, ten, twelve, fifteen hours of his daily life belong to him who buys them. The worker leaves the capitalist to whom he hires himself whenever he likes, and the capitalist discharges him whenever he thinks fit, as soon as he no longer gets any profit out of him, or not the anticipated profit. But the worker, whose sole source of livelihood is the sale of his labour power, cannot leave the *whole class of purchasers, that is, the capitalist class*, without renouncing his existence. He belongs not to this or that capitalist but to the *capitalist class*, and, moreover, it is his business to dispose of himself, that is, to find a purchaser within this capitalist class.

Now, before going more closely into the relation between capital and wage labour, we shall present briefly the most general relations which come into consideration in the determination of wages.

Wages, as we have seen, are the *price* of a definite commodity, of labour power. Wages are, therefore, determined by the same laws that determine the price of every other commodity. The question, therefore, is, *how is the price of a commodity determined?*

II

By what is the *price* of a commodity determined?

By competition between buyers and sellers, by the relation of inquiry to delivery, of demand to supply. Competition, by which the price of a commodity is determined, is *three-sided.*

The same commodity is offered by various sellers. With goods of the same quality, the one who sells most cheaply is certain of driving the others out of the field and securing the greatest sale for himself. Thus, the sellers mutually contend among themselves for sales, for the market. Each of them desires to sell, to sell as much as possible and, if possible, to sell alone, to the exclusion of the other sellers. Hence, one sells cheaper than another. Consequently, *competition* takes place *among the sellers*, which *depresses* the price of the *commodities* offered by them.

But *competition* also takes place *among the buyers*, which in its turn *causes* the commodities offered to *rise* in price.

Finally *competition* occurs *between buyers and sellers*; the former desire to buy as cheaply as possible, the latter to sell as dearly as possible. The result of this competition between buyers and sellers will depend upon how the two above-mentioned sides of the competition are related, that is, whether the competition is stronger in the army of buyers or in the army of sellers. Industry leads two armies into the field against each other, each of which again carries on a battle within its own ranks, among its own troops. The army whose troops beat each other up the least gains the victory over the opposing host.

Let us suppose there are 100 bales of cotton on the market and at the same time buyers for 1,000 bales of cotton. In this case, therefore, the demand is ten times as great as the supply. Competition will be very strong among the buyers, each of whom desires to get one, and if possible all, of the hundred bales for himself. This example is no arbitrary assumption. We have experienced periods of cotton crop failure in the history of the trade when a few capitalists in alliance have tried to buy, not one hundred bales, but all the cotton stocks in the world. Hence, in the example mentioned, one buyer will seek to drive the other from the field by offering a relatively higher price per bale of cotton. The cotton sellers, who see that the troops of the enemy army are engaged in the most violent struggle among themselves and that the sale of all their hundred bales is absolutely certain, will take good care not to fall out among themselves and depress the price of cotton at the moment when their adversaries are competing with one another to force it up. Thus, peace suddenly descends on the army of the sellers. They stand facing the buyers as one man, fold their arms philosophically, and there would be no bounds to their demands were it not that the offers of even the most persistent and eager buyers have very definite limits.

If, therefore, the supply of a commodity is lower than the demand for it, then only slight competition, or none at all, takes place among the sellers. In the same proportion as this competition decreases, competition increases among the buyers. The result is a more or less considerable rise in commodity prices.

It is well known that the reverse case with a reverse result occurs more frequently. Considerable surplus of supply over demand; desperate competition among the sellers; lack of buyers; disposal of goods at ridiculously low prices.

But what is the meaning of a rise, a fall in prices; what is the meaning of high price, low price? A grain of sand is high when examined through a microscope, and a tower is low when compared with a mountain. And if price is determined by the relation between supply and demand, what determines the relation between supply and demand?

Let us turn to the first bourgeois we meet. He will not reflect for an instant but, like another Alexander the Great, will cut this metaphysical knot with the multiplication table. If the production of the goods which I sell has cost me 100 marks, he will tell us, and if I get 110 marks from the sale of these goods, within the year of course—then that is sound, honest, legitimate profit. But if I get in exchange 120 or 130 marks, that is a high profit; and if I get as much as 200 marks, that would be an extraordinary, an enormous profit. What, therefore, serves the bourgeois as his *measure* of profit? The *cost of production* of his commodity. If he receives in exchange for this commodity an amount of other commodities which it has cost less to produce, he has lost. If he receives in exchange for his commodity an amount of other commodities the production of which has cost more, he has gained. And he calculates the rise or fall of the profit according to the degree in which the exchange value of his commodity stands above or below zero—the *cost of production*.

We have thus seen how the changing relation of supply and demand causes now a rise and now a fall of prices, now high, now low prices. If the price of a commodity rises considerably because of inadequate supply or disproportionate increase of the demand, the price of some other commodity must necessarily have fallen proportionately, for the price of a commodity only expresses in money the ratio in which other commodities are given in exchange for it. If, for example, the price of a yard of silk material rises from five marks to six marks, the price of silver in relation to silk material has fallen and likewise the prices of all other commodities that have remained at their old prices have fallen in relation to the silk. One has to give a larger amount of them in exchange to get the same amount of silks. What will be the consequence of the rising price of a commodity? A mass of capital will be thrown into that flourishing branch of industry and this influx of capital into the domain of the favoured industry will continue until it yields the ordinary profits or, rather, until the price of its products, through overproduction, sinks below the cost of production.

Conversely, if the price of a commodity falls below its cost of production, capital will be withdrawn from the production of this commodity. Except in the case of a branch of industry which has become obsolete and must, therefore, perish, the production of such a commodity, that is, its supply, will go on decreasing owing to this flight of capital until it corresponds to the demand, and consequently its price is again on a level with its cost of production or, rather, until the supply has sunk below the demand, that is, until its price rises again above its cost of production, *for the current price of a commodity is always either above or below its cost of production*.

We see how capital continually migrates in and out, out of the domain of one industry into that of another. High prices bring too great an immigration and low prices too great an emigration.

We could show from another point of view how not only supply but also demand is determined by the cost of production. But this would take us too far away from our subject.

We have just seen how the fluctuations of supply and demand continually bring the price of a commodity back to the cost of production. *The real price of a commodity, it is true, is always above or below its cost of production; but rise and fall reciprocally balance each other*, so that within a certain period of time, taking the ebb and flow of the industry together, commodities are exchanged for one another in accordance with their cost of production, their price, therefore, being determined by their cost of production.

This determination of price by cost of production is not to be understood in the sense of the economists. The economists say that the *average price* of commodities is equal to the cost of production; that this is a *law*. The anarchical movement, in which rise is compensated by fall and fall by rise, is regarded by them as chance. With just as much right one could regard the fluctuations as the law and the determination by the cost of production as chance, as has actually been done by other economists. But it is solely these fluctuations which, looked at more closely, bring with them the most fearful devastations and, like earthquakes, cause bourgeois society to tremble to its foundations—it is solely in the course of these fluctuations that prices are determined by the cost of production. The total movement of this disorder is its order. In the course of this industrial anarchy, in this movement in a circle, competition compensates, so to speak, for one excess by means of another.

We see, therefore, that the price of a commodity is determined by its cost of production in such manner that the periods in which the price of this commodity rises above its cost of production are compensated by the periods in which it sinks below the cost of production, and vice versa. This does not hold good, of course, for separate, particular industrial products but only for the whole branch of industry. Consequently, it also does not hold good for the individual industrialist but only for the whole class of industrialists.

The determination of price by the cost of production is equivalent to the determination of price by the labour time necessary for the manufacture of a commodity, for the cost of production consists of (1) raw materials and depreciation of instruments, that is, of industrial products the production of which has cost a certain amount of labour days and which, therefore, represent a certain amount of labour time, and (2) of direct labour, the measure of which is, precisely, time.

Now, the same general laws that regulate the price of commodities in general of course also regulate *wages*, the *price of labour*.

Wages will rise and fall according to the relation of supply and demand, according to the turn taken by the competition between the buyers of labour power, the capitalists, and the sellers of labour power, the workers. The fluctuations in wages correspond in general to the fluctuations in prices of commodities. *Within these fluctuations, however, the price of labour will be determined by the cost of production, by the labour time necessary to produce this commodity—labour power.*

What, then, is the cost of production of labour power?

It is the cost required for maintaining the worker as a worker and of developing him into a worker.

The less the period of training, therefore, that any work requires the smaller is the cost of production of the worker and the lower is the price of his labour, his wages. In those branches of industry in which hardly any period of apprenticeship is required and where the mere bodily existence of the worker suffices, the cost necessary for his production is almost confined to the commodities necessary for keeping him alive and capable of working. The *price of his labour* will, therefore, be determined by the *price of the necessary means of subsistence.*

Another consideration, however, also comes in. The manufacturer in calculating his cost of production and, accordingly, the price of the products takes into account the wear and tear of the instruments of labour. If, for example, a machine costs him 1,000 marks and wears out in ten years, he adds 100 marks annually to the price of the commodities so as to be able to replace the worn-out machine by a new one at the end of ten years. In the same way, in calculating the cost of production of simple labour power, there must be included the cost of reproduction, whereby the race of workers is enabled to multiply and to replace worn-out workers by new ones. Thus the depreciation of the worker is taken into account in the same way as the depreciation of the machine.

The cost of production of simple labour power, therefore, amounts to the *cost of existence and reproduction of the worker*. The price of this cost of existence and reproduction constitutes wages. Wages so determined are called the *wage minimum*. This wage minimum, like the determination of the price of commodities by the cost of production in general, does not hold good for the *single individual* but for the *species*. Individual workers, millions of workers, do not get enough to be able to exist and reproduce themselves; *but the wages of the whole working class* level down, within their fluctuations, to this minimum.

Now that we have arrived at an understanding of the most general laws which regulate wages like the price of any other commodity, we can go into our subject more specifically.

III

Capital consists of raw materials, instruments of labour and means of subsistence of all kinds, which are utilised in order to produce new raw materials, new instruments of labour and new means of subsistence. All these component parts of capital are creations of labour, products of labour, *accumulated labour*. Accumulated labour which serves as a means of new production is capital.

So say the economists.

What is a Negro slave? A man of the black race. The one explanation is as good as the other.

A Negro is a Negro. He only becomes a slave in certain relations. A cotton-spinning jenny is a machine for spinning cotton. It becomes *capital* only in certain relations. Torn from these relationships it is no more capital than gold in itself is *money* or sugar the price of sugar.

In production, men not only act on nature but also on one another. They produce only by cooperating in a certain way and mutually exchanging their activities. In order to produce, they enter into definite connections and relations with one another and only within these social connections and relations does their action on nature, does production, take place.

These social relations into which the producers enter with one another, the conditions under which they exchange their activities and participate in the whole act of production, will naturally vary according to the character of the means of production. With the invention of a new instrument of warfare, firearms, the whole internal organisation of the army necessarily changed; the relationships within which individuals can constitute an army and act as an army were transformed and the relations of different armies to one another also changed.

Thus the social relations within which individuals produce, *the social relations of production, change, are transformed, with the change and development of the material means of production, the productive forces. The relations of production in their totality constitute what are called the social relations, society, and, specifically, a society at a definite stage of historical development*, a society with a peculiar, distinctive character. *Ancient* society, *feudal* society, *bourgeois* society are such totalities of production relations, each of which at the same time denotes a special stage of development in the history of mankind.

Capital, also, is a social relation of production. *It is a bourgeois production relation*, a production relation of bourgeois society. Are not the means of subsistence, the instruments of labour, the raw materials of which capital consists, produced and accumulated under given social conditions, in definite social relations? Are they not utilised for new production under given social conditions, in definite social relations? And is it not just this definite social character which turns the products serving for new production into *capital*?

Capital consists not only of means of subsistence, instruments of labour and raw materials, not only of material products; it consists just as much of *exchange values*. All the products of which it consists are *commodities*. Capital is, therefore, not only a sum of material products; it is a sum of commodities, of exchange values, *of social magnitudes*.

Capital remains the same, whether we put cotton in place of wool, rice in place of wheat or steamships in place of railways, provided only that the cotton, the rice, the steamships—the body of capital—have the same exchange value, the same price as the wool, the wheat, the railways in which it was previously incorporated. The body of capital can change continually without the capital suffering the slightest alteration.

But while all capital is a sum of commodities, that is, of exchange values, not every sum of commodities, of exchange values, is capital.

Every sum of exchange values is an exchange value. Every separate exchange value is a sum of exchange values. For instance, a house that is worth 1,000 marks is an exchange value of 1,000 marks. A piece of paper worth a pfennig is a sum of exchange values of one-hundred hundredths of a pfennig. Products which are exchangeable for others are commodities. The particular ratio in which they are exchangeable constitutes their *exchange value* or, expressed in money, their *price*. The quantity of these products can change nothing in their quality of being *commodities* or representing an *exchange value* or having a definite price. Whether a tree is large or small it is a tree. Whether we exchange iron for other products in ounces or in hundred-weights, does this make any difference in its character as commodity, as exchange value? It is a commodity of greater or lesser value, of higher or lower price, depending upon the quantity.

How, then, does any amount of commodities, of exchange value, become capital?

By maintaining and multiplying itself as an independent social *power*, that is, as the power *of a portion of society*, by means of its *exchange for direct, living labour power*. The existence of a class which possesses nothing but its capacity to labour is a necessary prerequisite of capital.

It is only the domination of accumulated, past, materialised labour over direct, living labour that turns accumulated labour into capital.

Capital does not consist in accumulated labour serving living labour as a means for new production. It consists in living labour serving accumulated labour as a means of maintaining and multiplying the exchange value of the latter.

What takes place in the exchange between capitalist and wageworker?

The worker receives means of subsistence in exchange for his labour power, but the capitalist receives in exchange for his means of subsistence labour, the productive activity of the worker, the creative power whereby the worker not only replaces what he consumes but *gives to the accumulated labour a greater value than it previously possessed.* The worker receives a part of the available means of subsistence from the capitalist. For what purpose do these means of subsistence serve him? For immediate consumption. As soon, however, as I consume the means of subsistence, they are irretrievably lost to me unless I use the time during which I am kept alive by them in order to produce new means of subsistence, in order during consumption to create by my labour new values in place of the values which perish in being consumed. But it is just this noble reproductive power that the worker surrenders to the capitalist in exchange for means of subsistence received. He has, therefore, lost it for himself.

Let us take an example: a tenant farmer gives his day labourer five silver groschen a day. For these five silver groschen the labourer works all day on the farmer's field and thus secures him a return of ten silver groschen. The farmer not only gets the value replaced that he has to give the day labourer; he doubles it. He has therefore employed, consumed, the five silver groschen that he gave to the labourer in a fruitful, productive manner. He has bought with the five silver groschen just that labour and power of the labourer which produces agricultural products of double value and makes ten silver groschen out of five. The day labourer, on the other hand, receives in place of his productive power, the effect of which he has bargained away to the farmer, five silver groschen, which he exchanges for means of subsistence, and these he consumes with greater or less rapidity. The five silver groschen have, therefore, been consumed in a double way, *reproductively* for capital, for they have been exchanged for labour power which produced ten silver groschen, *unproductively* for the worker, for they have been exchanged for means of subsistence which have disappeared forever and the value of which he can only recover by repeating the same exchange with the farmer. *Thus capital presupposes wage labour; wage labour presupposes capital. They reciprocally condition the existence of each other; they reciprocally bring forth each other.*

Does a worker in a cotton factory produce merely cotton textiles? No, he produces capital. He produces values which serve afresh to command his labour and by means of it to create new values.

Capital can only increase by exchanging itself for labour power, by calling wage labour to life. The labour power of the wage-worker can only be exchanged for capital by increasing capital, by strengthening the power whose slave it is. *Hence, increase of capital is increase of the proletariat, that is, of the working class.*

The interests of the capitalist and those of the worker are, therefore, *one and the same*, assert the bourgeois and their economists. Indeed! The worker perishes if capital does not employ him. Capital perishes if it does not exploit labour power, and in order to exploit it, it must buy it. The faster capital intended for production, productive capital, increases, the more, therefore, industry prospers, the more the bourgeoisie enriches itself and the better business is, the more workers does the capitalist need, the more dearly does the worker sell himself.

The indispensable condition for a tolerable situation of the worker is, *therefore, the fastest possible growth of productive capital.*

But what is the growth of productive capital? Growth of the power of accumulated labour over living labour. Growth of the domination of the bourgeoisie over the working class. If wage labour produces the wealth of others that rules over it, the power that is hostile to it, capital, then the means of employment, the means of subsistence, flow back to it from this hostile power, on condition that it makes itself afresh into a part of capital, into the lever which hurls capital anew into an accelerated movement of growth.

To say that the interests of capital and those of the workers are one and the same is only to say that capital and wage labour are two sides of one and the same relation. The one conditions the other, just as usurer and squanderer condition each other.

As long as the wage-worker is a wage-worker his lot depends upon capital. That is the much-vaunted community of interests between worker and capitalist.

IV

If capital grows, the mass of wage labour grows, the number of wage-workers grows; in a word, the domination of capital extends over a greater number of individuals. Let us assume the most favourable case: when productive capital grows, the demand for labour grows; consequently, the price of labour, wages, goes up.

A house may be large or small; as long as the surrounding houses are equally small it satisfies all social demands for a dwelling. But let a palace arise beside the little house, and it shrinks from a little house to a hut. The little house shows now that its owner has only very slight or no demands to make; and however high it may shoot up in the course of civilisation, if the neighbouring palace grows to an equal or even greater extent, the occupant of the relatively small house will feel more and more uncomfortable, dissatisfied and cramped within its four walls.

A noticeable increase in wages presupposes a rapid growth of productive capital. The rapid growth of productive capital brings about an equally rapid growth of wealth, luxury, social wants, social enjoyments. Thus, although the enjoyments of the worker have risen, the social satisfaction that they give has fallen in comparison with the increased enjoyments of the capitalist, which are inaccessible to the worker, in comparison with the state of development of society in general. Our desires and pleasures spring from society; we measure them, therefore, by society and not by the objects which serve for their satisfaction. Because they are of a social nature, they are of a relative nature.

In general, wages are determined not only by the amount of commodities for which I can exchange them. They embody various relations.

What the workers receive for their labour power is, in the first place, a definite sum of money. Are wages determined only by this money price?

In the sixteenth century, the gold and silver circulating in Europe increased as a result of the discovery of richer and more easily worked mines in America. Hence, the value of gold and silver fell in relation to other commodities. The workers received the same amount of coined silver for their labour power as before. The money price of their labour remained the same, and yet their wages had fallen, for in exchange for the same quantity of silver they received a smaller amount of other commodities. This was one of the circumstances which furthered the growth of capital and the rise of the bourgeoisie in the sixteenth century.

Let us take another case. In the winter of 1847, as a result of a crop failure, the most indispensable means of subsistence, cereals, meat, butter, cheese, etc., rose considerably in price. Assume that the workers received the same sum of money for their labour power as before. Had not their wages fallen? Of course. For the same money they received less bread, meat, etc., in exchange. Their wages had fallen, not because the value of silver had diminished, but because the value of the means of subsistence had increased.

Assume, finally, that the money price of labour remains the same while all agricultural and manufactured goods have fallen in price owing to the employment of new machinery, a favorable season, etc. For the same money the workers can now buy more commodities of all kinds. Their wages, therefore, have risen, just because the money value of their wages has not changed.

Thus, the money price of labour, nominal wages, do not coincide with real wages, that is, with the sum of commodities which is actually given in exchange for the wages. If, therefore, we speak of a rise or fall of wages, we must keep in mind not only the money price of labour, the nominal wages.

But neither nominal wages, that is, the sum of money for which the worker sells himself to the capitalist, nor real wages, that is, the sum of commodities which he can buy for this money, exhaust the relations contained in wages.

Wages are, above all, also determined by their relation to the gain, to the profit of the capitalist—comparative, relative wages.

Real wages express the price of labour in relation to the price of other commodities; relative wages, on the other hand, express the share of direct labour in the new value it has created in relation to the share which falls to accumulated labour, to capital.

We said above: "Wages are not the worker's share in the commodity produced by him. Wages are the part of already existing commodities with which the capitalist buys for himself a definite amount of productive labour power." But the capitalist must replace these wages out of the price at which he sells the product produced by the worker; he must replace it in such a way that there remains to him, as a rule, a surplus over the cost of production expended by him, a profit. For the capitalist, the selling price of the commodities produced by the worker is divided into three parts: *first*, the replacement of the price of the raw materials advanced by him together with replacement of the depreciation of the tools, machinery and other means of labour also advanced by him; *secondly*, the replacement of the wages advanced by him, and *thirdly*, the surplus left over, the capitalist's profit. While the first part only replaces *previously existing values*, it is clear that both the replacement of the wages and also the surplus profit of the capitalist are, on the whole, taken from the *new value created by the worker's labour* and added to the raw materials. And *in this sense*, in order to compare them with one another, we can regard both wages and profit as shares in the product of the worker.

Real wages may remain the same, they may even rise, and yet relative wages may fall. Let us suppose, for example, that all means of subsistence have gone down in price by two-thirds while wages per day have only fallen by one-third, that is to say, for example, from three marks to two marks. Although the worker can command a greater amount of commodities with these two marks than he previously could with three marks, yet his wages have gone down in relation to the profit of the capitalist. The profit of the capitalist (for example, the manufacturer) has increased by one mark; that is, for a smaller sum of exchange values which he pays to the worker, the latter must produce a greater amount of exchange values than before. The share of capital relative to the share of labour has risen. The division of social wealth between capital and labour has become still more unequal. With the same capital, the capitalist commands a greater quantity of labour. The power of the capitalist class over the working class has grown, the social position of the worker has deteriorated, has been depressed one step further below that of the capitalist.

What, then, is the general law which determines the rise and fall of wages and profit in their reciprocal relation?

They stand in inverse ratio to each other. Capital's share, profit, rises in the proportion as labour's share, wages, falls, and vice versa. Profit rises to the extent that wages fall; it falls to the extent that wages rise.

The objection will, perhaps, be made that the capitalist can profit by a favourable exchange of his products with other capitalists, by increase of the demand for his commodities, whether as a result of the opening of new markets, or as a result of a momentarily increased demand in the old markets, etc.; that the capitalist's profit can, therefore, increase by overreaching other capitalists, independently of the rise and fall of wages, of the exchange value of labour power; or that the capitalist's profit may also rise owing to the improvement of the instruments of labour, a new application of natural forces, etc.

First of all, it will have to be admitted that the result remains the same, although it is brought about in reverse fashion. True, the profit has not risen because wages have fallen, but wages have fallen because the profit has risen. With the same amount of other people's labour, the capitalist has acquired a greater amount of exchange values, without having paid more for the labour on that account; that is, therefore, labour is paid less in proportion to the net profit which it yields the capitalist.

In addition, we recall that, in spite of the fluctuations in prices of commodities, the average price of every commodity, the ratio in which it is exchanged for other commodities, is determined by its *cost of production.* Hence the overreachings within the capitalist class necessarily balance one another. The improvement of machinery, new application of natural forces in the service of production, enable a larger amount of products to be created in a given period of time with the same amount of labour and capital, but not by any means a larger amount of exchange values. If, by the use of the spinning jenny, I can turn out twice as much yarn in an hour as before its invention, say, one hundred pounds instead of fifty, then in the long run I will receive for these hundred pounds no more commodities in exchange than formerly for the fifty pounds, because the cost of production has fallen by one-half, or because I can deliver double the product at the same cost.

Finally, in whatever proportion the capitalist class, the bourgeoisie, whether of one country or of the whole world market, shares the net profit of production within itself, the total amount of this net profit always consists only of the amount by which, on the whole, accumulated labour has been increased by direct labour. This total amount grows, therefore, in the proportion in which labour augments capital, that is, in the proportion in which profit rises in comparison with wages.

We see, therefore, that even if we remain *within the relation of capital and wage labour, the interests of capital and the interests of wage labour are diametrically opposed.*

A rapid increase of capital is equivalent to a rapid increase of profit. Profit can only increase rapidly if the price of labour, if relative wages, decrease just as rapidly. Relative wages can fall although real wages rise simultaneously with nominal wages, with the money value of labour, if they do not rise, however, in the same proportion as profit. If, for instance, in times when business is good, wages rise by five per cent, profit on the other hand by thirty per cent, then the comparative, the relative wages, have not *increased* but *decreased.*

Thus if the income of the worker increases with the rapid growth of capital, the social gulf that separates the worker from the capitalist increases at the same time, and the power of capital over labour, the dependence of labour on capital, likewise increases at the same time.

To say that the worker has an interest in the rapid growth of capital is only to say that the more rapidly the worker increases the wealth of others, the richer will be the crumbs that fall to him, the greater is the number of workers that can be employed and called into existence, the more can the mass of slaves dependent on capital be increased.

We have thus seen that:

Even the *most favourable situation* for the working class, the *most rapid possible growth of capital,* however much it may improve the material existence of the worker, does not remove the antagonism between his interests and the interests of the bourgeoisie, the interests of the capitalists. *Profit and wages* remain before in *inverse proportion.*

If capital is growing rapidly, wages may rise; the profit of capital rises incomparably more rapidly. The material position of the worker has improved, but at the cost of his social position. The social gulf that divides him from the capitalist has widened.

Finally:

To say that the most favourable condition for wage labour is the most rapid possible growth of productive capital is only to say that the more rapidly the working class increases and enlarges the power that is hostile to it, the wealth that does not belong to it and that rules over it, the more favourable will be the conditions under which it is allowed to labour anew at increasing bourgeois wealth, at enlarging the power of capital, content with forging for itself the golden chains by which the bourgeoisie drags it in its train.

V

Are *growth of productive capital and rise of wages* really so inseparably connected as the bourgeois economists maintain? We must not take their word for it. We must not even believe them when they say that the fatter capital is, the better will its slave be fed. The bourgeoisie is too enlightened, it calculates too well, to share the prejudices of the feudal lord who makes a display by the brilliance of his retinue. The conditions of existence of the bourgeoisie compel it to calculate.

We must, therefore, examine more closely:

How does the growth of productive capital affect wages?

If, on the whole, the productive capital of bourgeois society grows, a *more manifold* accumulation of labour takes place. The capitals increase in number and extent. The *numerical increase* of the capitals increases the *competition between the capitalists*. The *increasing extent* of the capitals provides the means for *bringing more powerful labour armies with more gigantic instruments of war into the industrial battlefield.*

One capitalist can drive another from the field and capture his capital only by selling more cheaply. In order to be able to sell more cheaply without ruining himself, he must produce more cheaply, that is, raise the productive power of labour as much as possible. But the productive power of labour is raised, above all, by a *greater division of labour*, by a more universal introduction and continual improvement of *machinery*. The greater the labour army among whom labour is divided, the more gigantic the scale on which machinery is introduced, the more does the cost of production proportionately decrease, the more fruitful is labour. Hence, a general rivalry arises among the capitalists to increase the division of labour and machinery and to exploit them on the greatest possible scale.

If, now, by a greater division of labour, by the utilisation of new machines and their improvement, by more profitable and extensive exploitation of natural forces, one capitalist has found the means of producing with the same amount of labour or of accumulated labour a greater amount of products, of commodities, than his competitors, if he can, for example, produce a whole yard of linen in the same labour time in which his competitors weave half a yard, how will this capitalist operate?

He could continue to sell half a yard of linen at the old market price; this would, however, be no means of driving his opponents from the field and of enlarging his own sales. But in the same measure in which his production has expanded, his need to sell has also increased. The more powerful and costly means of production that he has called into life enable him, indeed, to sell his commodities more cheaply, they *compel* him, however, at the same time *to sell more commodities*, to conquer a much *larger* market for his commodities; consequently, our capitalist will sell his half yard of linen more cheaply than his competitors.

The capitalist will not, however, sell a whole yard as cheaply as his competitors sell half a yard, although the production of the whole yard does not cost him more than the half yard costs the others. Otherwise he would not gain anything extra but only get back the cost of production by the exchange. His possibly greater income would be derived from the fact of having set a larger capital into motion, but not from having made more of his capital than the others. Moreover, he attains the object he wishes to attain, if he puts the price of his goods only a small percentage lower than that of his competitors. He drives them from the field, he wrests from them at least a part of their sales, by *underselling* them. And, finally, it will be remembered that the current price always stands *above or below the cost of production*, according to whether the sale of the commodity occurs in a favourable or unfavourable industrial season. The percentage at which the capitalist who has employed new, and more fruitful means of production sells above his real cost of production will vary, depending upon whether the market price of a yard of linen stands below or above its hitherto customary cost of production.

However, the *privileged position* of our capitalist is not of long duration; other competing capitalists introduce the same machines, the same division of labour, introduce them on the same or on a larger scale, and this introduction will become so general that the price of linen is *reduced* not only *below its old*, but *below its new cost of production.*

The capitalists find themselves, therefore, in the same position relative to one another as *before* the introduction of the new means of production, and if they are able to supply by these means double the production at the same price, they are *now* forced to supply the double product *below* the old price. On the basis of this new cost of production, the same game begins again. More division of labour, more machinery, enlarged scale of exploitation of machinery and division of labour. And again competition brings the same counteraction against this result.

We see how in this way the mode of production and the means of production are continually transformed, revolutionised, *how the division of labour is necessarily followed by greater division of labour, the application of machinery by still greater application of machinery, work on a large scale by work on a still larger scale.*

That is the law which again and again throws bourgeois production out of its old course and which compels capital to intensify the productive forces of labour, *because* it has intensified them, it, the law which gives capital no rest and continually whispers in its ear: "Go on! Go on!"

This law is none other than that which, within the fluctuations of trade periods, necessarily *levels out* the price of a commodity to its *cost of production.*

However powerful the means of production which a capitalist brings into the field, competition will make these means of production universal and from the moment when it has made them universal, the only result of the greater fruitfulness of his capital is that he must now supply *for the same price* ten, twenty, a hundred times as much as before. But, as he must sell perhaps a thousand times as much as before in order to outweigh the lower selling price by the greater amount of the product sold, because a more extensive sale is now necessary, not only in order to make more profit but in order to replace the cost of production—the instrument of production itself, as we have seen, becomes more and more expensive—and because this mass sale becomes a question of life and death not only for him but also for his rivals, the old struggle begins again *all the more violently the more fruitful the already discovered means of production are. The division of labour and the application of machinery, therefore, will go on anew on an incomparably greater scale.*

Whatever the power of the means of production employed may be, competition seeks to rob capital of the golden fruits of this power by bringing the price of the commodities back to the cost of production, by thus making cheaper production—the supply of ever greater amounts of products for the same total price—an imperative law to the same extent as production can be cheapened, that is, as more can be produced with the same amount of labour. Thus the capitalist would have won nothing by his own exertions but the obligation to supply more in the same labour time, in a word, *more difficult conditions for the augmentation of the value of his capital.* While, therefore, competition continually pursues him with its law of the cost of production and every weapon that he forges against his rivals recoils against himself, the capitalist continually tries to get the better of competition by incessantly introducing new machines, more expensive, it is true, but producing more cheaply, and new division of labour in place of the old, and by not waiting until competition has rendered the new ones obsolete.

If now we picture to ourselves this feverish simultaneous agitation on the *whole world market*, it will be comprehensible how the growth, accumulation and concentration of capital results in an uninterrupted division of labour, and in the application of new and the perfecting of old machinery precipitately and on an ever more gigantic scale.

But how do these circumstances, which are inseparable from the growth of productive capital, affect the determination of wages?

The greater *division of labour* enables *one* worker to do the work of five, ten or twenty; it therefore multiplies competition among the workers fivefold, tenfold and twentyfold. The workers do not only compete by one selling himself cheaper than another; they compete by *one* doing the work of five, ten, twenty; and the *division of labour*, introduced by capital and continually increased, compels the workers to compete among themselves in this way.

Further, as the *division of labour* increases, labour *is simplified*. The special skill of the worker becomes worthless. He becomes transformed into a simple, monotonous productive force that does not have to use intense bodily or intellectual faculties. His labour becomes a labour that anyone can perform. Hence, competitors crowd upon him on all side, and besides we remind the reader that the more simple and easily learned the labour is, the lower the cost of production needed to master it, the lower do wages sink, for, like the price of every other commodity, they are determined by the cost of production.

Therefore, as labour becomes more unsatisfying, more repulsive, competition increases and wages decrease. The worker tries to keep up the amount of his wages by working more, whether by working longer hours or by producing more in one hour. Driven by want, therefore, he still further increases the evil effects of the division of labour. The result is that *the more he works the less wages he receives* and for the simple reason that he competes to that extent with his fellow workers, hence makes them into so many competitors who offer themselves on just the same bad terms as he does himself, and that, therefore, in the last resort he *competes with himself, with himself as a member of the working class.*

Machinery brings about the same results on a much greater scale, by replacing skilled workers by unskilled, men by women, adults by children. It brings about the same results, where it is newly introduced, by throwing the hand workers on to the streets in masses, and, where it is developed, improved and replaced by more productive machinery, by discharging workers in smaller batches. We have portrayed above, in a hasty sketch, the industrial war of the capitalists among themselves; *this war has the peculiarity that its battles are won less by recruiting than by discharging the army of labour. The generals, the capitalists, compete with one another as to who can discharge most soldiers of industry.*

The economists tell us, it is true, that the workers rendered superfluous by machinery find *new* branches of employment.

They dare not assert directly that the same workers who are discharged find places in the new branches of labour. The facts cry out too loudly against this lie. They really only assert that new means of employment will open up for *other component sections of the working class*, for instance, for the portion of the young generation of workers that was ready to enter the branch of industry which has gone under. That is, of course, a great consolation for the disinherited workers. The worshipful capitalists will never want for fresh exploitable flesh and blood, and will let the dead bury their dead. This is a consolation which the bourgeois give themselves rather than one which they give the workers. If the whole class of wage-workers were to be abolished owing to machinery, how dreadful that would be for capital which, without wage labour, ceases to be capital!

Let us suppose, however, that those directly driven out of their jobs by machinery, and the entire section of the new generation that was already on the watch for this employment, *find a new occupation.* Does any one imagine that it will be as highly paid as that which has been lost? *That would contradict all the laws of economics.* We have seen how modern industry always brings with it the substitution of a more simple, subordinate occupation for the more complex and higher one.

How, then, could a mass of workers who have been thrown out of one branch of industry owing to machinery find refuge in another, unless the latter *is lower, worse paid?*

The workers who work in the manufacture of machinery itself have been cited as an exception. As soon as more machinery is demanded and used in industry, it is said, there must necessarily be an increase of machines, consequently of the manufacture of machines, and consequently of the employment of workers in the manufacture of machines; and the workers engaged in this branch of industry are claimed to be skilled, even educated workers.

Since the year 1840 this assertion, which even before was only half true, has lost all semblance of truth because ever more versatile machines have been employed in the manufacture of machinery, no more and no less than in the manufacture of cotton yarn, and the workers employed in the machine factories, confronted by highly elaborate machines, can only play the part of highly unelaborate machines.

But in place of the man who has been discharged owing to the machine, the factory employs maybe *three* children and *one* woman. And did not the man's wages have to suffice for the three children and a woman? Did not the minimum of wages have to suffice to maintain and to propagate the race? What, then, does this favourite bourgeois phrase prove? Nothing more than that now four times as many workers' lives are used up in order to gain a livelihood for *one* worker's family.

Let us sum up: *The more productive capital grows, the more the division of labour and the application of machinery expands. The more the division of labour and the application of machinery expands, the more competition among the workers expands and the more their wages contract.*

In addition, the working class gains recruits from the *higher strata of society* also; a mass of petty industrialists and small rentiers are hurled down into its ranks and have nothing better to do than urgently stretch out their arms alongside those of the workers. Thus the forest of uplifted arms demanding work becomes ever thicker, while the arms themselves become ever thinner.

That the small industrialist cannot survive in a contest one of the first conditions of which is to produce on an ever greater scale, that is, precisely to be a large and not a small industrialist, is self-evident.

That the interest on capital decreases in the same measure as the mass and number of capitals increase, as capital grows; that, therefore, the small rentier can no longer live on his interest but must throw himself into industry, and, consequently, help to swell the ranks of the small industrialists and thereby of candidates for the proletariat—all this surely requires no further explanation.

Finally, as the capitalists are compelled, by the movement described above, to exploit the already existing gigantic means of production on a larger scale and to set in motion all the mainsprings of credit to this end, there is a corresponding increase in industrial earthquakes, in which the trading world can only maintain itself by sacrificing a part of wealth, of products and even of productive forces to the gods of the nether world—in a word, *crises* increase. They become more frequent and more violent, if only because, as the mass of production, and consequently the need for extended markets, grows, the world market becomes more and more contracted, fewer and fewer new markets remain available for exploitation, since every preceding crisis has subjected to world trade a market hitherto unconquered or only superficially exploited. But capital does not *live* only on labour. A lord, at once aristocratic and barbarous, it drags with it into the grave the corpses of its slaves, whole hecatombs of workers who perish in the crises. Thus we see: *if capital grows rapidly, competition among the workers grows incomparably more rapidly, that is, the means of employment, the means of subsistence, of the working class decrease proportionately so much the more, and, nevertheless, the rapid growth of capital is the most favourable condition for wage labour.*

Matilda Joslyn Gage

Matilda Joslyn Gage (1826–1898) was a woman whose disappearance from the records exemplifies feminists' claim that, in every generation, women must rediscover their history all over again. Over one hundred years ago Gage developed a radical critique of the "Patriarchate," as she called it; her insights remain stimulating today. As a historian she rummaged through the archives, reviving the lives and work of other women to show that her sex had already proved its worth in science, government, literature, and the arts. In the course of her research, Gage reconceptualized society itself

How ironic, then, that Matilda Gage, who spent much of her life recovering women's intellectual traditions, should herself now be the object of the same process. Contemporary feminists, such as Mary Daly and Sally Roesch Wagner, have "rediscovered" Gage after a long period of neglect and active suppression of her more radical critiques of male authority. Information about her is hard to obtain, in part because she eschewed personal recognition, but perhaps also due to the censure she attracted for her witty and unflinching attacks on the politicians and reverends of her day. In response to Susan B. Anthony's arrest and trial for voting illegally, for example, Gage prepared a petition to Congress that demanded for Anthony the same relief of political disabilities that had been granted to convicted criminals who had regained the right to vote.

Matilda Gage was part of the suffragist triumvirate that included Elizabeth Cady Stanton and Susan B. Anthony. Like her two comrades, she was an activist as well as a theoretician, and a writer of scholarly as well as popular works. But Gage stood apart both in the sweep of her interests and in her desire to cut beneath particular problems to reveal their foundations in the structure of patriarchal society. Most of all, she reversed the conventional wisdom regarding women's position in society: Women's rights were necessary not because by gaining them could women contribute to society, but rather because women had already contributed to society in the past and men denied their contribution. Likewise, church and state were not the *cause* of women's subjection but rather its manifestation, and thus neither church nor state could be counted on to improve women's position in society.

Gage's criticism targets cultural domination and the rewriting of history in her major work, *Women, Church and State* (1893). This magisterial study compiles the results of her research on ancient goddess religions, prehistoric matriarchies, and the persecution of witches as a misogynist practice—all of it synthesized by her powerful, ordering imagination.

WOMAN, CHURCH AND STATE

1893

CHAPTER VIII WOMAN AND WORK

And unto Adam the Lord said; "Cursed be the ground for thy sake; in sorrow shalt thou eat of it all the days of thy life; thorns and thistles shall it bring forth to thee; and thou shalt eat the herbs of the field; in the sweat of thy face shalt thou eat bread, till thou return unto the ground, for dust thou art and into dust thou shalt return." Gen. 3: 17–19.

Upon man was pronounced the curse of the world's work. The Bible declares it was because of *his* sinfulness that the earth was to be cursed; for *his* punishment that he was to eat of it in sorrow all the days of his life; because of *his* wickedness that it was to bear thorns and thistles; and in consequence of *his* disobedience that he was to eat the herb of the field in the sweat of his face until he returned unto the ground from whence he came. No curse of work was pronounced upon woman; her "curse" was of an entirely different character. It was a positive command of the Lord God Almighty, that upon man alone the work of the world should fall and this work he was to perform in sorrow and the sweat of his brow.

Thus far this book has been devoted to a consideration of the doctrines taught by christian men in regard to "woman's curse," and so earnestly has this doctrine been proclaimed that man seems to have entirely forgotten the "curse," also pronounced upon himself or if he has not forgotten, he has neglected to see its full import, and in his anxiety to keep woman in subordination he has placed *his* "curse" also upon her thus thwarting the express command of God. It is therefore but just to now devote a few pages to the consideration of man's "curse" and an investigation of the spirit in which he has accepted the penalty imposed upon him for his share in the transgression which cost him Paradise. At the commencement of this investigation, it will be well to remember that Eve was not banished from the Garden of Eden. Adam alone was cast out and to prohibit *his* re-entrance, not hers, the angel with the flaming sword was set as guardian at its gates.

We must also recall the opposition of the church through the ages to all attempts made towards the amelioration of woman's suffering at time of her bringing forth children, upon the plea that such mitigation was a direct interference with the mandate of the Almighty and an inexcusable sin. It will be recalled that in the chapter upon witchcraft, the bitter hostility of the church to the use of anæsthetics by the women physicians of that period was shown, and its opposing sermons, its charges of heresy, its burnings at the stake as methods of enforcing that opposition. Man, ever unjust to woman, has been no less so in the field of work. He has not taken upon himself the entire work of the world, as commanded, but has ever imposed a large portion of it upon woman. Neither do all men labor; but thousands in idleness evade the "curse" of work pronounced upon all men alike. The church in its teachings and through its non-preaching the duty of man in this respect, is guilty of that defiance of the Lord God it has ever been so ready to attribute to woman. . . .

From *Woman, Church, and State: A Historical Account of the Status of Women through the Christian Ages: With Reminiscences of the Matriarchate* by Matilda Gage, 2nd ed. (New York: Truth Seeker Company, 1893; reprint, Salem, N. H.: Ayer Company Publishers, Inc., 1985).

. . . Man, hereditarily unjust to woman under the principles of the Patriarchate and the lessons of Christianity, is even more unjust in the fields of work he has compelled her to enter, than in those of education and the ballot which she is seeking for herself. Organizations, strikes, the eight hour law demand, are largely conducted by men for men. The grim humor originating the proverb "a man's work is from sun to sun, a woman's work is never done," still clings with all its old force to women in most employments. To such small extent has man made the woman worker's cause his own, that instances are to be found even in the United States, where men and women working together and together going out upon a strike, the men have been reinstated at the increase demanded, the women forced to return at the old wages. Nor is our own country the chief sinner in this respect. It was found imperative many years since, among the women of England to organize leagues of their own sex alone, if they desired their own interest in labor to be protected; the male Trades Unions of that country excluding women from some of the best paid branches of industry, as carpet making, cloth weaving, letter press printing. In self defense, the Woman's Protective and Provident League, and a "Woman's Union Labor Journal" were founded. The principle of exclusion has not alone been shown against woman's entrance into well paid branches of work, but in those they have been permitted to enter they have found themselves subjected to much petty annoyance. Among the male painters of pottery a combination was formed to prevent the use by woman of the arm-rests required in this work. Tram-way trains carry London workmen at reduced rates, but a combination was entered into by male laborers to prevent women workers from using the low-priced trains. Nor in many instances are employers less the enemies of women, unions having been found necessary for the purpose of moral protection. A most deplorable evidence of the low respect in which woman is held and the slavery that work and cheap wages mean for her, is the suggestion often made by employers that she shall supplement her wages by the sale of her body. The manager of an industrial league in New York City a few years since found that no young girl escaped such temptation. Neither extreme youth nor friendliness afforded security or protection but were rather additional inducements for betrayal, most of the victims numbering but fourteen short years. . . .

. . .

The terrible condition of working women in Paris, has attracted the attention of the French government. In but three or four trades are they even fairly well paid, and these few require a peculiar adaptation, as well as an expensive training out of reach of most women laborers. And even in these best paid kinds of work, a discrimination in favor of man exists; at the China manufactory at Sévres where the men employed receive a retiring pension, the women do not. From fifteen to eighteen pence represents the daily earnings of the Parisian working girl, upon which sum it is impossible for her to properly support life. Many of these girls die of slow starvation, others are driven into prostitution, still others seek relief in the Seine. French women perform the most repulsive labors of the docks; they work in the mines dragging or pushing heavy trucks of coal like their English sisters, through narrow tunnels that run from the seams to the shaft; eating food of such poor quality that the lessening stature of the population daily shows the result. This decreasing size of Frenchmen especially among the peasantry, the majority not coming up to the regulation army height, has within the last fifteen or twenty years called attention of the government during conscription, yet without seeming to teach its cause as lying in the poor food and hard labor of women, the mothers of these men. The heaviest burdens of porters, the most offensive sanitary work, the severest agricultural labor in that country falls upon woman. "I pity the women, the donkeys, and the boys," wrote Mrs. Stanton when traveling in the south of France. It is the poor nourishment and excessive labor of woman which makes France to-day a country of rapidly decreasing birth-rate, seriously affecting its population and calling the earnest attention of statistical bureaus and physicians to this vital question; a question which affects the standing of France among the nations of the earth. According to the report of the chief of the statistical bureau, 1890, there were fewer births than deaths that year, the births amounting to 838,059, the deaths to 876,505, an excess of 38,446 deaths. Commenting upon these returns, "Der Reichsbote" of Berlin, attributed the cause to a wide-spread aversion to large families; acknowledging, however, that the lower classes had become weakened and dwarfed by the tasks imposed upon them. What neither the statistical bureau, the press, or the church yet comprehend is the fact that the work imposed upon its Christian women, the "curse" of man thrust upon her, is the chief cause of the lessening size and lessening population of that country. A French gentleman employing a large number of women in a flax factory was appalled at the great amount of infant mortality among the children of his employees. Believing the excessive death rate to be in consequence of the continued labor of women, he released expectant mothers for a month previous, and two months after the birth of a child, with a marked diminution of the death rate. The ordinary food of the peasantry is of poor quality and meager quantity. Those employed in the manufacture of silk largely subsist upon a species of black broth proverbial for its lack of nutritive qualities. The absence of certain elements in food both creates specific diseases and inability to combat disease. . . .

. . .

Germany, whose women were revered in the centuries before Christianity, now degrades them to the level of beasts. Women and dogs harnessed together are found drawing milk carts in the streets; women and cows yoked draw the plough in the fields; the German peasant wife works on the roads or carries mortar to the top of the highest buildings, while her husband smokes his pipe at the foot of the ladder until she descends for him to again fill the hod. To such extent is woman a laborer that she comes in competition with the railroad and all public methods of traffic. Eight-tenths of the agricultural laborers are women; they plow and sow, and reap the grain and carry immense loads of offal for fertilizing the land. As street cleaners they collect the garbage of towns, work with brooms and shovels to cleanse roadways; and harnessed alone, or with cows or dogs, perform all the most repulsive labors of the fields and streets. Nor for a knowledge of their work are we dependent upon the statements of travelers, but official documents corroborate the worst. An American consul says of a Circular Upon Labor recently issued by the German government:

> An important factor in the labor of Germany is not enquired of in the circular, viz, the labor of dogs. I have heard it estimated that women and dogs harnessed together do more hauling than the railroads and all other modes of conveyance of goods united. Hundreds of small wagons can be seen every day on all the roads leading to and from Dresden, each having a dog for the "near horse" harnessed, while the "off horse" is a woman with her left hand grasping the wagon tongue to give it direction, and the right hand passed through a loop in the rope which is attached to the axle, binding the shoulder; the harnessed woman and dog trudge along together, pulling miraculous loads in all sorts of weather.

The pay of woman for this strange, degrading labor is from ten to twenty-five cents a day. Nor is that of sewing more remunerative. In March, 1892, a libel suit against an embroidery manufacturer brought to light the fact that women in his employ received but five cents a day. No burden in Germany is considered too heavy for woman until the failing strength of old age necessitates a change of occupation, when amid all varities of weather they take the place of the newsboys of our own country, selling papers upon the streets. Munich, the capital of Bavarian Germany, is famed for its treasury of art; paintings, ancient and modern sculptures, old manuscripts of inestimable value, large libraries and splendid architecture make it the seat of the fine arts. But its women are still victims of Christian civilization. Dresden is another city whose art treasures and architectural beauty has rendered it famous among European cities as the "German Florence." Yet both of these cities employ women in the same kinds of work under the same repulsive conditions that are found in other portions of that empire.

Bavarian men wearing heavy wooden shoes drive their bare-footed wives and daughters before the plough in the field, or harnessed with dogs send them as carriers of immense loads of merchandise through the cities. Says a writer:

> Women become beasts of burden; still they do not grumble; they do not smile either—they simply exist. The only liberty they have is liberty to work; the only rest they have is sleep. The existence of a cow or a sheep is a perpetual heaven, while theirs is a perpetual hell.

In addition to all this out-of-door labor performed by the German women, they have that of the house and the preparation of clothing for the family. They industriously knit upon the street while doing errands; they cook, they spin and make clothing which takes them afar into the night, rearing their children amid labor so severe as forever to drive smiles from their faces, bringing the wrinkles of premature old age in their place. Switzerland, whose six hundredth anniversary was celebrated in 1888, the oldest republic, sees its women carrying luggage and blacking boots as porters at inns; propelling heavily laden barges down its romantic lakes; swinging the scythe by the side of men in the fields; bringing great baskets of hay strapped to their shoulders down the mountain side; carrying litters containing travelers up the same steep mountain top; bringing heavy baskets of fagots from the forests, and carrying in the more pleasant cutting of grapes at the vineyard harvest. From five o'clock in the morning till eight in the evening is the peasant woman's day of work. A stolid expressionless face, eyes from which no soul seems to look, a magnificent body as strong as that of the man by her side, is the result of the Swiss woman's hardships and work. It is but a few years since the laws of Switzerland compelled division of the paternal estate with sisters as well as brothers, this change provoking intense opposition from the men. On the Alps, husbands borrow and lend their wives, one neighbor not scrupling to ask the loan of another's wife to complete some farming task, which loan is readily granted with the under standing that the favor is to be returned in kind. Says one writer:

> The farmers in the Upper Alps, though by no means wealthy, live like lords in their houses, while the heaviest portion of agricultural labors devolves upon the wife. It is no uncommon thing to see a woman yoked to a plough with an ass, while her husband guides it. An Alpine farmer counts it an act of politeness to lend his wife to a neighbor who has too much work, and the neighbor in return lends his wife for a few days labor whenever requested.

In Vienna, women lay the brick in building, while throughout Austria young girls carry mortar for such work. They also work in the fields, in the mines, pave and clean the streets, or like their German sisters, harnessed with dogs, drag sprinklers for the street or serve milk at the customer's door. Prussian women are also to be found working the mines, in quarries in foundries, building railroads, acting as sailors and boatmen, or like those of Holland, dragging barges in place of horses on the canals, or like those of other European countries, performing the most severe and repulsive agricultural labors. A correspondent of the "Cincinnati Commercial" traveling through Belgium, said: "No work seems to be done except by woman and dogs. With few exceptions women do the harvesting, working like oxen." The physiological fact that the kind of labor and the kind of food affect the physical frame is noticeable in Belgium the same as in France and England. Women of all ages from fourteen to sixty, work in the coal mines, married women sometimes carrying babies strapped to their backs into the pit, laying the infants near them while digging coal, some mine owners refusing to employ a miner unless he ran bring one or more members of his family into the pit with him. Employers prefer girls and women because of their lower wages and greater docility; for twelve hours work a woman receives but thirty cents. Even in little Montenegro, husbands lend their wives to each other during the harvest season, and an exceptionally strong or quick-moving wife finds exceptional demand for her services. This little state degrades woman to still greater extent than her sister countries, as they there form the beasts of burden in war, and are counted among the "animals" belonging to the prince.

The Russian peasant woman under the Greek church, finds life equally a burden, and is even to greater extent than in most countries the slave of her husband and the priest, no form of labor or torture being looked upon as too severe to impose upon her.

The women are much more industrious than the men and the hardest work is done by them. As Russia is primarily an agricultural country it possesses immense fields of hay, oats and wheat, the work largely performed by women. The wheat sown broadcast is either harvested with sickles or the old-fashioned scythe with a broad blade. Women do the entire work of gathering up, binding and stacking the wheat, neighbors during harvest helping each other. Women of every age from the young girl to the aged grandmother, take part, assembling at daybreak. Horses are also there in number for carrying food, water, extra implements, and the men and boys of the conclave. The women, however aged, walk; the day's work lasting over eighteen hours or from daybreak until dark; in that northern land at harvest time it continues light from 3 a.m. to 9:30 p.m. Nor are mothers with young infants excused from this toil. Babies are carried into the fields where they lie all day under trees, or partially sheltered by a bough over them, covered with insects from which the mother can find no time to relieve them. Under such circumstances of neglect, it is not surprising that infant mortality is excessive. Nor do the children of a slightly larger growth receive the care requisite for their tender years, and it is estimated that eight out of every ten children in Russia die under ten years of age. But no one form of Christianity monopolizes the wrong. Everywhere, under every name and sect, man has thrown the carrying out of his "curse" on to woman. Italy, the center of Catholicism, under a careful analysis of statistics, showing that the wages of the Italian working woman do not exceed four pence a day. In Venice a traveler was recently shown some wonderfully beautiful articles of clothing; scarfs, shawls, mantles, handkerchiefs, many of them requiring six months' for the production; expressing amazement at the astonishingly low price demanded for such exquisite fabrics was told, "we pay our young girls but seven cents a day." A correspondent of the Philadelphia "Press," writing from abroad in 1885, declared the debasement of woman to be more thorough and complete in Protestant Stockholm than in any city of northern Europe, as there she supplanted the beasts of burden. He spoke of her as doing all the heavy work on buildings and paid only one kronor (equivalent to a trifle over twenty-six cents) for a hard day of this toil. He found women sweeping the streets, hauling rubbish, dragging hand-carts up the hills and over the cobble-stones, unloading bricks at the quays, attending to the parks, doing the gardening and rowing the numerous ferries which abound in that city . . . .

. . .

Max Weber

Max Weber (1864–1920) was an encyclopedic scholar whose expertise left hardly a field untouched: politics, economics, legal history, urbanism, classical studies, music, and world religions are all areas in which he made important contributions. Unlike most of his contemporaries, however, Weber amassed this astonishing erudition not for its own sake but to fashion the intellectual tools necessary for understanding modern societies—above all, the peculiar importance of "rationality" in the modern world.

To achieve this, Weber developed a sociology that was both interpretive and value free. Weber's interpretive sociology comprehends social relationships by showing the sense they make to those who participate in them. At the same time, meaningful actions tend to form recurrent patterns, raising the possibility of causal connections that can be tested empirically. The result, then, is a compromise between the scientist's concern with causal generalizations and the historian's emphasis on the irreducible uniqueness of events. As for *value freedom*, Weber meant that experts must separate their personal evaluations from their scientific pronouncements because such value judgments cannot be logically deduced from facts. By protecting science from the taint of ideology, Weber hoped also to protect political debate from the unwarranted claims of experts. Value freedom does not mean that the theorist lacks commitments; on the contrary, he or she must use value judgments to select subjects deemed worthy of research, and must engage with the minds and feelings of the social actors being studied.

Max Weber struggled as a person as well as a scholar to resolve the great dualities: to weigh the strength of human intentions, such as religious or political ideals, against the power of impersonal forces in history; to weigh the import of the subject versus the object in intellectual and scientific life; and to respect with utmost seriousness rival answers to the question of whether history has meaning and direction or is rather just the immense but aimless treasure of unique cultures and events, each of them "equally close to God." Wrestling with these dualities, Weber took on every intellectual tradition of his day: English utilitarianism in the spirit of Hobbes, Locke, and Smith; German idealism and its transformation into Marxism, on the one hand, and into historicism on the other; the French positivism of Comte and Durkheim; and the various biological or racial theories of the era. The result is a body of work as sophisticated in method as it is monumental in scope.

Max Weber was born into a middle-class family in Erfurt, Germany, in 1864. His father was an active politician serving at various levels of local and national government, while his mother was a cultured and liberal Protestant who tended to the household and was devoted to her son. In 1869 the Webers moved to Berlin, soon to become the booming capital of Bismarck's Reich, where they mingled with the academic and political elite.

Weber studied law at the universities in Berlin and Göttingen and went on to earn a Ph.D. in economic and legal history in 1889. Along the way, he studied a variety of cultural subjects, including history and philosophy, and served a stultifying year in the army. He married Marianne Schnitger in 1893, and her devotion to him is evident throughout her insightful biography, *Max Weber: A Life*. For the next several years he lived as a successful young scholar in Berlin, becoming the colleague of his former teachers, and many nights working until one o'clock a.m.

The death of Weber's father in 1897, following a terrible quarrel between the two, had a profound impact. Weber collapsed from anxiety, exhaustion, and remorse, and for the rest of his life was to suffer intermittently from severe depression followed by almost manic bursts of productivity and travel. After a long leave of absence, including a brief stay at a mental hospital, Weber resumed his academic duties at Heidelberg in 1902. As if to make up for his years of intellectual loss, he then threw himself into the exploration of a vast literature that included art history, economics, politics, and the history of monastic orders. In 1903 he joined with Werner Sombart to edit Germany's leading social science journal until it was suppressed by the Nazis. The following year he published essays on the social problems on Junker estates and on objectivity in the social sciences, and made a stimulating trip to the United States.

The greatest fruit of these years was the first section of Weber's most famous work, *The Protestant Ethic and the Spirit of Capitalism* (1905), a study of the relationship of religious ideas to economic activity. The book ends with his famous image of the "iron cage" of rationality, Weber's indictment of the dehumanizing effects of the modern world's overly controlled social order. In later writings Weber was to argue that the characteristic form of modern organization—whether in the state, the corporation, the military, the university, or the church—is bureaucratic. Whereas Marx predicted a proletarian revolution that would shatter the capitalist order, and Durkheim foresaw new social movements that would revivify politics, Weber saw no such future. Socialism, he believed, would fulfill, not annul, the rationalization process, and by abolishing the opposing spheres of economy and state, would lead to an even greater threat to individual freedom.

During the years 1906 to 1910, Weber was at the center of Heidelberg's intense intellectual life, participating in discussions with social scientists, philosophers, artists, and several disciples of Freud. In 1908 he founded a sociological society and stimulated a number of research enterprises. When World War I began, he was made a captain and charged with running several Heidelberg hospitals, where he experienced from the inside what had become a central concept in his sociology—bureaucracy. Weber returned to the university in the fall of 1916, working on various sections of his major study, *Economy and Society*, many chapters of which were not published until after his death. During the last few years of his life, Weber began lecturing again, delivering his famous remarks on "Science as a Vocation" and "Politics as a Vocation" in Munich in 1918, and presenting his sociology of world religions and politics under the title "A Positive Critique of the Materialist Conception of History." His lectures filled the largest halls available, attracting professors, state officials, and politicians. In 1918 he welcomed the new German Republic, but refused any political position in the regime. Weber died in the great influenza epidemic in 1920.

"CLASS, STATUS, PARTY"*

1922

I ECONOMICALLY DETERMINED POWER AND THE SOCIAL ORDER

Law exists when there is a probability that an order will be upheld by a specific staff of men who will use physical or psychical compulsion with the intention of obtaining conformity with the order, or of inflicting sanctions for infringement of it.† The structure of every legal order directly influences the distribution of power, economic or otherwise, within its respective community. This is true of all legal orders and not only that of the state. In general, we understand by "power" the chance of a man or of a number of men to realize their own will in a communal action even against the resistance of others who are participating in the action.

"Economically conditioned" power is not, of course, identical with "power" as such. On the contrary, the emergence of economic power may be the consequence of power existing on other grounds. Man does not strive for power only in order to enrich himself economically. Power, including economic power, may be valued "for its own sake." Very frequently the striving for power is also conditioned by the social "honor" it entails. Not all power, however, entails social honor: The typical American Boss, as well as the typical big speculator, deliberately relinquishes social honor. Quite generally, "mere economic" power, and especially "naked" money power, is by no means a recognized basis of social honor. Nor is power the only basis of social honor. Indeed, social honor, or prestige, may even be the basis of political or economic power, and very frequently has been. Power, as well as honor, may be guaranteed by the legal order, but, at least normally, it is not their primary source. The legal order is rather an additional factor that enhances the chance to hold power or honor; but it cannot always secure them.

The way in which social honor is distributed in a community between typical groups participating in this distribution we may call the "social order." The social order and the economic order are, of course, similarly related to the "legal order." However, the social and the economic order are not identical. The economic order is for us merely the way in which economic goods and services are distributed and used. The social order is of course conditioned by the economic order to a high degree, and in its turn reacts upon it.

Now: "classes," "status groups," and "parties" are phenomena of the distribution of power within a community.

II DETERMINATION OF CLASS-SITUATION BY MARKET-SITUATION

In our terminology, "classes" are not communities; they merely represent possible, and frequent, bases

* All Weber selections are from *Max Weber: Essays in Sociology* by Max Weber, edited by H. H. Gerth & C. Wright Mills, translated by H. H. Gerth & C. Wright Mills, copyright 1946, 1958, 1973, by H. H. Gerth and C. Wright Mills. Used by permission of Oxford University Press, Inc.

† *Wirtschaft und Gesellschaft*, part III, chap. 4, pp. 631–640. The first sentence in paragraph one and the several definitions in this chapter that are in brackets do not appear in the original text. They have been taken from other contexts of *Wirtschaft und Gesellschaft*.

for communal action. We may speak of a "class" when (1) a number of people have in common a specific causal component of their life chances, in so far as (2) this component is represented exclusively by economic interests in the possession of goods and opportunities for income, and (3) is represented under the conditions of the commodity or labor markets. [These points refer to "class situation," which we may express more briefly as the typical chance for a supply of goods, external living conditions, and personal life experiences, in so far as this chance is determined by the amount and kind of power, or lack of such, to dispose of goods or skills for the sake of income in a given economic order. The term "class" refers to any group of people that is found in the same class situation.]

It is the most elemental economic fact that the way in which the disposition over material property is distributed among a plurality of people, meeting competitively in the market for the purpose of exchange, in itself creates specific life chances. According to the law of marginal utility this mode of distribution excludes the non-owners from competing for highly valued goods; it favors the owners and, in fact, gives to them a monopoly to acquire such goods. Other things being equal, this mode of distribution monopolizes the opportunities for profitable deals for all those who, provided with goods, do not necessarily have to exchange them. It increases, at least generally, their power in price wars with those who, being propertyless, have nothing to offer but their services in native form or goods in a form constituted through their own labor, and who above all are compelled to get rid of these products in order barely to subsist. This mode of distribution gives to the propertied a monopoly on the possibility of transferring property from the sphere of use as a "fortune," to the sphere of "capital goods"; that is, it gives them the entrepreneurial function and all chances to share directly or indirectly in returns on capital. All this holds true within the area in which pure market conditions prevail. "Property" and "lack of property" are, therefore, the basic categories of all class situations. It does not matter whether these two categories become effective in price wars or in competitive struggles.

Within these categories, however, class situations are further differentiated: on the one hand, according to the kind of property that is usable for returns; and, on the other hand, according to the kind of services that can be offered in the market. Ownership of domestic buildings; productive establishments; warehouses; stores; agriculturally usable land, large and small holdings—quantitative differences with possibly qualitative consequences—; ownership of mines; cattle; men (slaves); disposition over mobile instruments of production, or capital goods of all sorts, especially money or objects that can be exchanged for money easily and at any time; disposition over products of one's own labor or of others' labor differing according to their various distances from consumability; disposition over transferable monopolies of any kind—all these distinctions differentiate the class situations of the propertied just as does the "meaning" which they can and do give to the utilization of property, especially to property which has money equivalence. Accordingly, the propertied, for instance, may belong to the class of rentiers or to the class of entrepreneurs.

Those who have no property but who offer services are differentiated just as much according to their kinds of services as according to the way in which they make use of these services, in a continuous or discontinuous relation to a recipient. But always this is the generic connotation of the concept of class: that the kind of chance in the *market* is the decisive moment which presents a common condition for the individual's fate. "Class situation" is, in this sense, ultimately "market situation." The effect of naked possession per se, which among cattle breeders gives the nonowning slave or serf into the power of the cattle owner, is only a forerunner of real "class" formation. However, in the cattle loan and in the naked severity of the law of debts in such communities, for the first time mere "possession" as such emerges as decisive for the fate of the individual. This is very much in contrast to the agricultural communities based on labor. The creditor-debtor relation becomes the basis of "class situations" only in those cities were a "credit market," however primitive, with rates of interest increasing according to the extent of dearth and a factual monopolization of credits, is developed by a plutocracy. Therewith "class struggles" begin.

Those men whose fate is not determined by the chance of using goods or services for themselves on the market, e.g. slaves, are not, however, a "class" in the technical sense of the term. They are, rather, a "status group."

III COMMUNAL ACTION FLOWING FROM CLASS INTEREST

According to our terminology, the factor that creates "class" is unambiguously economic interest, and indeed, only those interests involved in the existence of the "market." Nevertheless, the concept of "class-interest" is an ambiguous one: even as an empirical concept it is ambiguous as soon as one understands by it something other than the factual direction of interests following with a certain probability from the class situation for a certain "average" of those people subjected to the class situation. The class situation and other circumstances remaining the same, the direction in which the individual worker, for instance, is likely to pursue his interests may vary widely, according to whether he is constitutionally qualified for the task at hand to a high, to an average, or to a low degree. In the same way, the direction of interests may vary according to whether or not a *communal* action of a larger or smaller portion of those commonly affected by the "class situation," or even an association among them, e.g. a "trade union," has grown out of the class situation from which the individual may or may not expect promising results. [Communal action refers to that action which is oriented to the feeling of the actors that they belong together. Societal action, on the other hand, is oriented to a rationally motivated adjustment of interests.] The rise of societal or even of communal action from a common class situation is by no means a universal phenomenon.

The class situation may be restricted in its effects to the generation of essentially *similar* reactions, that is to say, within our terminology, of "mass actions." However, it may not have even this result. Furthermore, often merely an amorphous communal action emerges. For example, the "murmuring" of the workers known in ancient oriental ethics: the moral disapproval of the workmaster's conduct, which in its practical significance was probably equivalent to an increasingly typical phenomenon of precisely the latest industrial development, namely, the "slow down" (the deliberate limiting of work effort) of laborers by virtue of tacit agreement. The degree in which "communal action" and possibly "societal action," emerges from the "mass actions" of the members of a class is linked to general cultural conditions, especially to those of an intellectual sort. It is also linked to the extent of the contrasts that have already evolved, and is especially linked to the *transparency* of the connections between the causes and the consequences of the "class situation." For however different life chances may be, this fact in itself, according to all experience, by no means gives birth to "class action" (communal action by the members of a class). The fact of being conditioned and the results of the class situation must be distinctly recognizable. For only then the contrast of life chances can be felt not as an absolutely given fact to be accepted, but as a resultant from either (1) the given distribution of property, or (2) the structure of the concrete economic order. It is only then that people may react against the class structure not only through acts of an intermittent and irrational protest, but in the form of rational association. There have been "class situations" of the first category (1), of a specifically naked and transparent sort, in the urban centers of Antiquity and during the Middle Ages; especially then, when great fortunes were accumulated by factually monopolized trading in industrial products of these localities or in foodstuffs. Furthermore, under certain circumstances, in the rural economy of the most diverse periods, when agriculture was increasingly exploited in a profit-making manner. The most important historical example of the second category (2) is the class situation of the modern "proletariat."

IV TYPES OF "CLASS STRUGGLE"

Thus every class may be the carrier of any one of the possibly innumerable forms of "class action," but this is not necessarily so. In any case, a class does not in itself constitute a community. To treat "class" conceptually as having the same value as "community" leads to distortion. That men in the same class situation regularly react in mass actions to such tangible situations as economic ones in the direction of those interests that are most adequate to their average number is an important and after all simple fact for the understanding of historical events. Above all, this fact must not lead to that kind of pseudo-scientific operation with the concepts of "class" and "class interests" so frequently found these days, and which has found its most classic expression in the statement of a talented author, that the individual may be in error concerning his interests but that the "class" is "infallible" about its interests. Yet, if classes as such are not communities, nevertheless class situations emerge only on the basis of communalization. The communal action that brings forth class situations, however, is not basically action between members of the identical class; it is an action between members of different classes. Communal actions that directly determine the class situation of the worker and the entrepreneur are: the labor market, the commodities market, and the capitalistic enterprise. But, in its turn, the existence of a capitalistic enterprise presupposes that a very specific communal action exists and that it is specifically structured to protect the possession of goods *per se*, and especially the power of individuals to dispose, in principle freely, over the means of production. The existence of a capitalistic enterprise is preconditioned by a specific kind of "legal order." Each kind of class situation, and above all when it rests upon the power of property *per se*, will become most clearly efficacious when all other determinants of reciprocal relations are, as far as possible, eliminated in their significance. It is in this way that the utilization of the power of property in the market obtains its most sovereign importance.

Now "status groups" hinder the strict carrying through of the sheer market principle. In the present context they are of interest to us only from this one point of view. Before we briefly consider them, note that not much of a general nature can be said about the more specific kinds of antagonism between "classes" (in our meaning of the term). The great shift, which has been going on continuously in the past, and up to our times, may be summarized, although at the cost of some precision: the struggle in which class situations are effective has progressively shifted from consumption credit toward, first, competitive struggles in the commodity market and, then, toward price wars on the labor market. The "class struggles" of antiquity—to the extent that they were genuine class struggles and not struggles between status groups—were initially carried on by indebted peasants, and perhaps also by artisans threatened by debt bondage and struggling against urban creditors. For debt bondage is the normal result of the differentiation of wealth in commercial cities, especially in seaport cities. A similar situation has existed among cattle breeders. Debt relationships as such produced class action up to the time of Cataline. Along with this, and with an increase in provision of grain for the city by transporting it from the outside, the struggle over the means of sustenance emerged. It centered in the first place around the provision of bread and the determination of the price of bread. It lasted throughout antiquity and the entire Middle Ages. The propertyless as such flocked together against those who actually and supposedly were interested in the dearth of bread. This fight spread until it involved all those commodities essential to the way of life and to handicraft production. There were only incipient discussions of wage disputes in antiquity and in the Middle Ages. But they have been slowly increasing up into modern times. In the earlier periods they were completely secondary to slave rebellions as well as to fights in the commodity market.

The propertyless of antiquity and of the Middle Ages protested against monopolies, pre-emption, forestalling, and the withholding of goods from the market in order to raise prices. Today the central issue is the determination of the price of labor.

This transition is represented by the fight for access to the market and for the determination of the price of products. Such fights went on between merchants and workers in the putting-out system of domestic handicraft during the transition to modern times. Since it is quite a general phenomenon we must mention here that the class antagonisms that are conditioned through the market situation are usually most bitter between those who actually and directly participate as opponents in price wars. It is not the rentier, the share-holder, and the banker who suffer the ill will of the worker, but almost exclusively the manufacturer and the business executives who are the direct opponents of workers in price wars. This is so in spite of the fact that it is precisely the cash boxes of the rentier, the share-holder, and the banker into which the more or less "unearned" gains flow, rather than into the pockets of the manufacturers or of the business executives. This simple state of affairs has very frequently been decisive for the role the class situation has played in the formation of political parties. For example, it has made possible the varieties of patriarchal socialism and the frequent attempts—formerly, at least—of threatened status groups to form alliances with the proletariat against the "bourgeoisie."

V STATUS HONOR

In contrast to classes, *status groups* are normally communities. They are, however, often of an amorphous kind. In contrast to the purely economically determined "class situation" we wish to designate as "status situation" every typical component of the life fate of men that is determined by a specific, positive or negative, social estimation of *honor*. This honor may be connected with any quality shared by a plurality, and, of course, it can be knit to a class situation: class distinctions are linked in the most varied ways with status distinctions. Property as such is not always recognized as a status qualification, but in the long run it is, and with extraordinary regularity. In the subsistence economy of the organized neighborhood, very often the richest man is simply the chieftain. However, this often means only an honorific preference. For example, in the so-called pure modern "democracy," that is, one devoid of any expressly ordered status privileges for individuals, it may be that only the families coming under approximately the same tax class dance with one another. This example is reported of certain smaller Swiss cities. But status honor need not necessarily be linked with a "class situation." On the contrary, it normally stands in sharp opposition to the pretensions of sheer property.

Both propertied and propertyless people can belong to the same status group, and frequently they do with very tangible consequences. This "equality" of social esteem may, however, in the long run become quite precarious. The "equality" of status among the American "gentlemen," for instance, is expressed by the fact that outside the subordination determined by the different functions of "business," it would be considered strictly repugnant—wherever the old tradition still prevails—if even the richest "chief," while playing billiards or cards in his club in the evening, would not treat his "clerk" as in every sense fully his equal in birthright. It would be repugnant if the American "chief" would bestow upon his "clerk" the condescending "benevolence" marking a distinction of "position," which the German chief can never dissever from his attitude. This is one of the most important reasons why in America the German "clubby-ness" has never been able to attain the attraction that the American clubs have.

VI GUARANTEES OF STATUS STRATIFICATION

In content, status honor is normally expressed by the fact that above all else a specific *style of life* can be expected from all those who wish to belong to the circle. Linked with this expectation are restrictions on "social" intercourse (that is, intercourse which is not subservient to economic or any other of business's "functional" purposes). These restrictions may confine normal marriages to within the status circle and may lead to complete endogamous closure. As soon as there is not a mere individual and socially irrelevant imitation of another style of life, but an agreed-upon communal action of this closing character, the "status" development is under way.

In its characteristic form, stratification by "status groups" on the basis of conventional styles of life evolves at the present time in the United States out of the traditional democracy. For example, only the resident of a certain street ("the street") is considered as belonging to "society," is qualified for social intercourse, and is visited and invited. Above all, this differentiation evolves in such a way as to make for strict submission to the fashion that is dominant at a given time in society. This submission to fashion also exists among men in America to a degree unknown in Germany. Such submission is considered to be an indication of the fact that a given man *pretends* to qualify as a gentleman. This submission decides, at least prima facie, that he will be treated as such. And this recognition becomes just as important for his employment chances in "swank" establishments, and above all, for social intercourse and marriage with "esteemed" families, as the qualification for dueling among Germans in the Kaiser's day. As for the rest: certain families resident for a long time, and, of course, correspondingly wealthy, e.g. "F.F.V., i.e. First Families of Virginia," or the actual or alleged descendants of the "Indian Princess" Pocahontas, of the Pilgrim fathers, or of the Knickerbockers, the members of almost inaccessible sects and all sorts of circles setting themselves apart by means of any other characteristics and badges . . . all these elements usurp "status" honor. The development of status is essentially a question of stratification resting upon usurpation. Such usurpation is the normal origin of almost all status honor. But the road from this purely conventional situation to legal privilege, positive or negative, is easily traveled as soon as a certain stratification of the social order has in fact been "lived in" and has achieved stability by virtue of a stable distribution of economic power.

VII "ETHNIC" SEGREGATION AND "CASTE"

Where the consequences have been realized to their full extent, the status group evolves into a closed "caste." Status distinctions are then guaranteed not merely by conventions and laws, but also by *rituals*. This occurs in such a way that every physical contact with a member of any caste that is considered to be "lower" by the members of a "higher" caste is considered as making for a ritualistic impurity and to be a stigma which must be expiated by a religious act. Individual castes develop quite distinct cults and gods.

In general, however, the status structure reaches such extreme consequences only where there are underlying differences which are held to be "ethnic." The "caste" is, indeed, the normal form in which ethnic communities usually live side by side in a "societalized" manner. These ethnic communities believe in blood relationship and exclude exogamous marriage and social intercourse. Such a caste situation is part of the phenomenon of "pariah" peoples and is found all over the world. These people form communities, acquire specific occupational traditions of handicrafts or of other arts, and cultivate a belief in their ethnic community. They live in a "diaspora" strictly segregated from all personal intercourse, except that of an unavoidable sort, and their situation is legally precarious. Yet, by virtue of their economic indispensability, they are tolerated, indeed, frequently privileged, and they live in interspersed political communities. The Jews are the most impressive historical example.

A "status" segregation grown into a "caste" differs in its structure from a mere "ethnic" segregation: the caste structure transforms the horizontal and unconnected coexistences of ethnically segregated groups into a vertical social system of super and subordination. Correctly formulated: a comprehensive societalization integrates the ethnically divided communities into specific political and communal action. In their consequences they differ precisely in this way: ethnic coexistences condition a mutual repulsion and disdain but allow each ethnic community to consider its own honor as the highest one; the caste structure brings about a social subordination and an acknowledgment of "more honor" in favor of the privileged caste and status groups. This is due to the fact that in the caste structure ethnic distinctions as such have become "functional" distinctions within the political societalization (warriors, priests, artisans that are politically important for war and for building, and so on). But even pariah people who are most despised are usually apt to continue cultivating in some manner that which is equally peculiar to ethnic and to status communities: the belief in their own specific "honor." This is the case with the Jews.

Only with the negatively privileged status groups does the "sense of dignity" take a specific deviation.

A sense of dignity is the precipitation in individuals of social honor and of conventional demands which a positively privileged status group raises for the deportment of its members. The sense of dignity that characterizes positively privileged status groups is naturally related to their "being" which does not transcend itself, that is, it is to their "beauty and excellence" (χαλο-χάγαθια). Their kingdom is "of this world." They live for the present and by exploiting their great past. The sense of dignity of the negatively privileged strata naturally refers to a future lying beyond the present, whether it is of this life or of another. In other words, it must be nurtured by the belief in a providential "mission" and by a belief in a specific honor before God. The "chosen people's" dignity is nurtured by a belief either that in the beyond "the last will be the first," or that in this life a Messiah will appear to bring forth into the light of the world which has cast them out the hidden honor of the pariah people. This simple state of affairs, and not the "resentment" which is so strongly emphasized in Nietzsche's much admired construction in the *Genealogy of Morals*, is the source of the religiosity cultivated by pariah status groups. In passing, we may note that resentment may be accurately applied only to a limited extent; for one of Nietzsche's main examples, Buddhism, it is not at all applicable.

Incidentally, the development of status groups from ethnic segregations is by no means the normal phenomenon. On the contrary, since objective "racial differences" are by no means basic to every subjective sentiment of an ethnic community, the ultimately racial foundation of status structure is rightly and absolutely a question of the concrete individual case. Very frequently a status group is instrumental in the production of a thoroughbred anthropological type. Certainly a status group is to a high degree effective in producing extreme types, for they select personally qualified individuals (e.g., the Knighthood selects those who are fit for warfare, physically and psychically). But selection is far from being the only, or the predominant, way in which status groups are formed: Political membership or class situation has at all times been it least as frequently decisive. And today the class situation is by far the predominant factor, for of course the possibility of a style of life expected for members of a status group is usually conditioned economically.

VIII STATUS PRIVILEGES

For all practical purposes, stratification by status goes hand in hand with a monopolization of ideal and material goods or opportunities, in a manner we have come to know as typical. Besides the specific status honor, which always rests upon distance and exclusiveness, we find all sorts of material monopolies. Such honorific preferences may consist of the privilege of wearing special costumes, of eating special dishes taboo to others, of carrying arms—which is most obvious in its consequences—the right to pursue certain nonprofessional dilettante artistic practices, e.g. to play certain musical instruments. Of course, material monopolies provide the most effective motives for the exclusiveness of a status group; although, in themselves, they are rarely sufficient, almost always they come into play to some extent. Within a status circle there is the question of intermarriage: the interest of the families in the monopolization of potential bridegrooms is at least of equal importance and is parallel to the interest in the monopolization of daughters. The daughters of the circle must be provided for. With an increased inclosure of the status group, the conventional preferential opportunities for special employment grow into a legal monopoly of special offices for the members. Certain goods become objects for monopolization by status groups. In the typical fashion these include "entailed estates" and frequently also the possessions of serfs or bondsmen and, finally, special trades. This monopolization occurs positively when the status group is exclusively entitled to own and to manage them; and negatively when, in order to maintain its specific way of life, the status group must *not* own and manage them.

The decisive role of a "style of life" in status "honor" means that status groups are the specific bearers of all "conventions." In whatever way it may be manifest, all "stylization" of life either originates in status groups or is at least conserved by them.

Even if the principles of status conventions differ greatly, they reveal certain typical traits, especially among those strata which are most privileged. Quite generally, among privileged status groups there is a status disqualification that operates against the performance of common physical labor. This disqualification is now "setting in" in America against the old tradition of esteem for labor. Very frequently every rational economic pursuit, and especially "entrepreneurial activity," is looked upon as a disqualification of status. Artistic and literary activity is also considered as degrading work as soon as it is exploited for income, or at least when it is connected with hard physical exertion. An example is the sculptor working like a mason in his dusty smock is over against the painter in his salon-like "studio" and those forms of musical practice that are acceptable to the status group.

IX ECONOMIC CONDITIONS AND EFFECTS OF STATUS STRATIFICATION

The frequent disqualification of the gainfully employed as such is a direct result of the principle of status stratification peculiar to the social order, and of course, of this principle's opposition to a distribution of power which is regulated exclusively through the market. These two factors operate along with various individual ones, which will be touched upon below.

We have seen above that the market and its processes "knows no personal distinctions": "functional" interests dominate it. It knows nothing of "honor." The status order means precisely the reverse, viz.: stratification in terms of "honor" and of styles of life peculiar to status groups as such. If mere economic acquisition and naked economic power still bearing the stigma of its extra-status origin could bestow upon anyone who has won it the same honor as those who are interested in status by virtue of style of life claim for themselves, the status order would be threatened at its very root. This is the more so as, given equality of status honor, property *per se* represents an addition even if it is not overtly acknowledged to be such. Yet if such economic acquisition and power gave the agent any honor at all, his wealth would result in his attaining more honor than those who successfully claim honor by virtue of style of life. Therefore all groups having interests in the status order react with special sharpness precisely against the pretensions of purely economic acquisition. In most cases they react the more vigorously the more they feel themselves threatened. Calderon's respectful treatment of the peasant, for instance, as opposed to Shakespeare's simultaneous and ostensible disdain of the *canaille* illustrates the different way in which a firmly structured status order reacts as compared with a status order that has become economically precarious. This is an example of a state of affairs that recurs everywhere. Precisely because of the rigorous reactions against the claims of property per se, the "parvenu" is never accepted, personally and without reservation, by the privileged status groups, no matter how completely his style of life has been adjusted to theirs. They will only accept his descendants who have been educated in the conventions of their status group and who have never besmirched its honor by their own economic labor.

As to the general *effect* of the status order, only one consequence can be stated, but it is a very important one: the hindrance of the free development of the market occurs first for those goods which status groups directly withheld from free exchange by monopolization. This monopolization may be effected either legally or conventionally. For example, in many Hellenic cities during the epoch of status groups, and also originally in Rome, the inherited estate (as is shown by the old formula for indiction against spendthrifts) was monopolized just as were the estates of knights, peasants, priests, and especially the clientele of the craft and merchant guilds. The market is restricted, and the power of naked property per se, which gives its stamp to "class formation," is pushed into the background. The results of this process can be most varied. Of course, they do not necessarily weaken the contrasts in the economic situation. Frequently they strengthen these contrasts, and in any case, where stratification by status permeates a community as strongly as was the case in all political communities of antiquity and of the

Middle Ages, one can never speak of a genuinely free market competition as we understand it today. There are wider effects than this direct exclusion of special goods from the market. From the contrariety between the status order and the purely economic order mentioned above, it follows that in most instances the notion of honor peculiar to status absolutely abhors that which is essential to the market: higgling. Honor abhors higgling among peers and occasionally it taboos higgling for the members of a status group in general. Therefore, everywhere some status groups, and usually the most influential, consider almost any kind of overt participation in economic acquisition as absolutely stigmatizing.

With some over-simplification, one might thus say that "classes" are stratified according to their relations to the production and acquisition of goods; whereas "status groups" are stratified according to the principles of their *consumption* of goods as represented by special "styles of life."

An "occupational group" is also a status group. For normally, it successfully claims social honor only by virtue of the special style of life which may be determined by it. The differences between classes and status groups frequently overlap. It is precisely those status communities most strictly segregated in terms of honor (viz. the Indian castes) who today show, although within very rigid limits, a relatively high degree of indifference to pecuniary income. However, the Brahmins seek such income in many different ways.

As to the general economic conditions making for the predominance of stratification by "status," only very little can be said. When the bases of the acquisition and distribution of goods are relatively stable, stratification by status is favored. Every technological repercussion and economic transformation threatens stratification by status and pushes the class situation into the foreground. Epochs and countries in which the naked class situation is of predominant significance are regularly the periods of technical and economic transformations. And every slowing down of the shifting of economic stratifications leads, in due course, to the growth of status structures and makes for a resuscitation of the important role of social honor.

X PARTIES

Whereas the genuine place of "classes" is within the economic order, the place of "status groups" is within the social order, that is, within the sphere of the distribution of "honor." From within these spheres, classes and status groups influence one another and they influence the legal order and are in turn influenced by it. But "parties" live in a house of "power."

Their action is oriented toward the acquisition of social "power," that is to say, toward influencing a communal action no matter what its content may be. In principle, parties may exist in a social "club" as well as in a "state." As over against the actions of classes and status groups, for which this is not necessarily the case, the communal actions of "parties" always mean a societalization. For party actions are always directed toward a goal which is striven for in planned manner. This goal may be a "cause" (the party may aim at realizing a program for ideal or material purposes), or the goal may be "personal" (sinecures, power, and from these, honor for the leader and the followers of the party). Usually the party action aims at all these simultaneously. Parties are, therefore, only possible within communities that are societalized, that is, which have some rational order and a staff of persons available who are ready to enforce it. For parties aim precisely at influencing this staff, and if possible, to recruit it from party followers.

In any individual case, parties may represent interests determined through "class situation" or "status situation," and they may recruit their following respectively from one or the other. But they need be neither purely "class" nor purely "status" parties. In most cases they are partly class parties and partly status parties, but sometimes they are neither. They may represent ephemeral or enduring structures. Their means of attaining power may be quite varied, ranging from naked violence of any sort to canvassing for votes with coarse or subtle means: money, social influence, the force of speech, suggestion, clumsy hoax, and so on to the rougher or more artful tactics of obstruction in parliamentary bodies.

The sociological structure of parties differs in a basic way according to the kind of communal action which they struggle to influence. Parties also differ according to whether or not the community is stratified by status or by classes. Above all else, they vary according to the structure of domination within the community. For their leaders normally deal with the conquest of a community. They are, in the general concept which is maintained here, not only products of specially modern forms of domination. We shall also designate as parties the ancient and medieval "parties," despite the fact that their structure differs basically from the structure of modern parties. By virtue of these structural differences of domination it is impossible to say anything about the structure of parties without discussing the structural forms of social domination, per se. Parties, which are always structures struggling for domination, are very frequently organized in a very strict "authoritarian" fashion . . .

Concerning "classes," "status groups," and "parties," it must be said in general that they necessarily presuppose a comprehensive societalization, and especially a political framework of communal action, within which they operate. This does not mean that parties would be confined by the frontiers of any individual political community. On the contrary, at all times it has been the order of the day that the societalization (even when it aims at the use of military force in common) reaches beyond the frontiers of politics. This has been the case in the solidarity of interests among the Oligarchs and among the democrats in Hellas, among the Guelfs and among Ghibellines in the Middle Ages, and within the Calvinist party during the period of religious struggles. It has been the case up to the solidarity of the landlords (international congress of agrarian landlords), and has continued among princes (holy alliance, Karlsbad decrees), socialist workers, conservatives (the longing of Prussian conservatives for Russian intervention in 1850). But their aim is not necessarily the establishment of new international political, i.e. *territorial*, dominion. In the main they aim to influence the existing dominion.

"BUREAUCRACY"

1922

I CHARACTERISTICS OF BUREAUCRACY

Modern officialdom functions in the following specific manner:

I. There is the principle of fixed and official jurisdictional areas, which are generally ordered by rules, that is, by laws or administrative regulations.
    1. The regular activities required for the purposes of the bureaucratically governed structure are distributed in a fixed way as official, duties.
    2. The authority to give the commands required for the discharge of these duties is distributed in a stable way and is strictly delimited by rules concerning the coercive means, physical, sacerdotal, or otherwise, which may be placed at the disposal of officials.
    3. Methodical provision is made for the regular and continuous fulfilment of these duties and for the execution of the corresponding rights; only persons who have the generally regulated qualifications to serve are employed.

In public and lawful government these three elements constitute "bureaucratic authority." In private economic domination, they constitute bureaucratic "management." Bureaucracy, thus understood, is fully developed in political and ecclesiastical communities only in the modern state, and, in the private economy, only in the most advanced institutions of capitalism. Permanent and public office authority, with fixed jurisdiction, is not the historical rule but rather the exception. This is so even in large political structures such as those of the ancient Orient, the Germanic and Mongolian empires of conquest, or of many feudal structures of state. In all these cases, the ruler executes the most important measures through personal trustees, table-companions, or court-servants. Their commissions and authority are not precisely delimited and are temporarily called into being for each case.

II. The principles of office hierarchy and of levels of graded authority mean a firmly ordered system of super- and subordination in which there is a supervision of the lower offices by the higher ones. Such a system offers the governed the possibility of appealing the decision of a lower office to its higher authority, in a definitely regulated manner. With the full development of the bureaucratic type, the office hierarchy is monocratically organized. The principle of hierarchical office authority is found in all bureaucratic structures: in state and ecclesiastical structures as well as in large party organizations and private enterprises. It does not matter for the character of bureaucracy whether its authority is called "private" or "public."

When the principle of jurisdictional "competency" is fully carried through, hierarchical subordination—at least in public office—does not mean that the "higher" authority is simply authorized to take over the business of the "lower." Indeed, the opposite is the rule. Once established and having fulfilled its task, an office tends to continue in existence and be held by another incumbent.

III. The management of the modern office is based upon written documents ("the files"), which are preserved in their original or draught form. There is, therefore, a staff of subaltern officials and scribes of all sorts. The body of officials actively engaged in a "public" office, along with the respective apparatus of material implements and the files, make up a "bureau." In private enterprise, "the bureau" is often called "the office."

In principle, the modern organization of the civil service separates the bureau from the private domicile of the official, and, in general, bureaucracy segregates official activity as something distinct from the sphere of private life. Public monies and equipment are divorced from the private property of the official. This condition is everywhere the product of a long development. Nowadays, it is found in public as well as in private enterprises; in the latter, the principle extends even to the leading entrepreneur. In principle, the executive office is separated from the household, business from private correspondence, and business assets from private fortunes. The more consistently the modern type of business management has been carried through the more are these separations the case. The beginnings of this process are to be found as early as the Middle Ages.

It is the peculiarity of the modern entrepreneur that he conducts himself as the "first official" of his enterprise, in the very same way in which the ruler of a specifically modern bureaucratic state spoke of himself as "the first servant" of the state. The idea that the bureau activities of the state are intrinsically different in character from the management of private economic offices is a continental European notion and, by way of contrast, is totally foreign to the American way.

IV. Office management, at least all specialized office management—and such management is distinctly modern—usually presupposes thorough and expert training. This increasingly holds for the modern executive and employee of private enterprises, in the same manner as it holds for the state official.

V. When the office is fully developed, official activity demands the full working capacity of the official, irrespective of the fact that his obligatory time in the bureau may be firmly delimited. In the normal case, this is only the product of a long development, in the public as well as in the private office. Formerly, in all cases, the normal state of affairs was reversed: official business was discharged as a secondary activity.

VI. The management of the office follows general rules, which are more or less stable, more or less exhaustive, and which can be learned. Knowledge of these rules represents a special technical learning which the officials possess. It involves jurisprudence, or administrative or business management.

The reduction of modern office management to rules is deeply embedded in its very nature. The theory of modern public administration, for instance, assumes that the authority to order certain matters by decree—which has been legally granted to public authorities—does not entitle the bureau to regulate the matter by commands given for each case, but only to regulate the matter abstractly. This stands in extreme contrast to the regulation of all relationships through individual privileges and bestowals of favor, which is absolutely dominant in patrimonialism, at least in so far as such relationships are not fixed by sacred tradition.

II THE POSITION OF THE OFFICIAL

All this results in the following for the internal and external position of the official:

I. Office holding is a "vocation." This is shown, first, in the requirement of a firmly prescribed course of training, which demands the entire capacity for work for a long period of time, and in the generally prescribed and special examinations which are prerequisites of employment. Furthermore, the position of the official is in the nature of a duty. This determines the internal structure of his relations, in the following manner: Legally and actually, office holding is not considered a source to be exploited for rents or emoluments, as was normally the case during the Middle Ages and frequently up to the threshold of recent times. Nor is office holding considered a usual exchange of services for equivalents, as is the case with free labor contracts. Entrance into an office, including one in the private economy, is considered an acceptance of a specific obligation of faithful management in return for a secure existence. It is decisive for the specific nature of modern loyalty to an office that, in the pure type, it does not establish a relationship to a *person*, like the vassal's or disciple's faith in feudal or in patrimonial relations of authority. Modern loyalty is devoted to impersonal and functional purposes. Behind the functional purposes, of course, "ideas of culture-values" usually stand. These are *ersatz* for the earthly or supramundane personal master: ideas such as "state," "church," "community," "party," or "enterprise" are thought of as being realized in a community; they provide an ideological halo for the master.

The political official—at least in the fully developed modern state—is not considered the personal servant of a ruler. Today, the bishop, the priest, and the preacher are in fact no longer, as in early Christian times, holders of purely personal charisma. The supra-mundane and sacred values which they offer are given to everybody who seems to be worthy of them and who asks for them. In former times, such leaders acted upon the personal command of their master; in principle, they were responsible only to him. Nowadays, in spite of the partial survival of the old theory, such religious leaders are officials in the service of a functional purpose, which in the present-day "church" has become routinized and, in turn, ideologically hallowed.

II. The personal position of the official is patterned in the following way:

1. Whether he is in a private office or a public bureau, the modern official always strives and usually enjoys a distinct *social esteem* as compared with the governed. His social position is guaranteed by the prescriptive

rules of rank order and, for the political official, by special definitions of the criminal code against "insults of officials" and "contempt" of state and church authorities.

The actual social position of the official is normally highest where, as in old civilized countries, the following conditions prevail: a strong demand for administration by trained experts; a strong and stable social differentiation, where the official predominantly derives from socially and economically privileged strata because of the social distribution of power; or where the costliness of the required training and status conventions are binding upon him. The possession of educational certificates—to be discussed elsewhere—are usually linked with qualification for office. Naturally, such certificates or patents enhance the "status element" in the social position of the official. For the rest this status factor in individual cases is explicitly and impassively acknowledged; for example, in the prescription that the acceptance or rejection of an aspirant to an official career depends upon the consent ("election") of the members of the official body. This is the case in the German army with the officer corps. Similar phenomena, which promote this guild-like closure of officialdom, are typically found in patrimonial and, particularly, in prebendal officialdoms of the past. The desire to resurrect such phenomena in changed forms is by no means infrequent among modern bureaucrats. For instance, they have played a role among the demands of the quite proletarian and expert officials (the *tretyj* element) during the Russian revolution.

Usually the social esteem of the officials as such is especially low where the demand for expert administration and the dominance of status conventions are weak. This is especially the case in the United States; it is often the case in new settlements by virtue of their wide fields for profit-making and the great instability of their social stratification.

2. The pure type of bureaucratic official is *appointed* by a superior authority. An official elected by the governed is not a purely bureaucratic figure. Of course, the formal existence of an election does not by itself mean that no appointment hides behind the election—in the state, especially, appointment by party chiefs. Whether or not this is the case does not depend upon legal statutes but upon the way in which the party mechanism functions. Once firmly organized, the parties can turn a formally free election into the mere acclamation of a candidate designated by the party chief. As a rule, however, a formally free election is turned into a fight, conducted according to definite rules, for votes in favor of one of two designated candidates.

In all circumstances, the designation of officials by means of an election among the governed modifies the strictness of hierarchical subordination. In principle an official who is so elected has an autonomous position opposite the superordinate official. The elected official does not derive his position "from above" but "from below," or at least not from a superior authority of the official hierarchy but from powerful party men ("bosses"), who also determine his further career. The career of the elected official is not, or at least not primarily, dependent upon his chief in the administration. The official who is not elected but appointed by a chief normally functions more exactly, from a technical point of view, because, all other circumstances being equal, it is more likely that purely functional points of consideration and qualities will determine his selection and career. As laymen, the governed can become acquainted with the extent to which a candidate is expertly qualified for office only in terms of experience, and hence only after his service. Moreover, in every sort of selection of officials by election, parties quite naturally give decisive weight not to expert considerations but to the services a follower renders to the party boss. This holds for all kinds of procurement of officials by elections, for the designation of formally free, elected officials by party bosses when they determine the slate of candidates, or the free appointment by a chief who has himself been elected. The contrast, however, is relative: substantially similar conditions hold where legitimate monarchs and their subordinates appoint officials, except that the influence of the followings are then less controllable.

Where the demand for administration by trained experts is considerable, and the party followings have to recognize an intellectually developed, educated, and freely moving "public opinion," the use of unqualified officials falls back upon the party in power at the next election. Naturally, this is more likely to happen when the officials are appointed by the chief. The demand for a trained administration now exists in the United States, but in the large cities, where immigrant votes are "corraled," there is, of course, no educated public opinion. Therefore, popular elections of the administrative chief and also of his subordinate officials usually endanger the expert qualification of the official as well as the precise functioning of the bureaucratic mechanism. It also weakens the dependence of the officials upon the hierarchy. This holds at least for the large administrative bodies that are difficult to supervise. The superior qualification and integrity of federal judges, appointed by the President, as over against elected judges in the United States is well known, although both types of officials have been selected primarily in terms of party considerations. The great changes in American metropolitan administrations demanded by reformers have proceeded essentially from elected mayors working with an apparatus of officials who were appointed by them. These reforms have thus come about in a "Caesarist" fashion. Viewed technically, as an organized form of authority, the efficiency of "Caesarism," which often grows out of democracy, rests in general upon the position of the "Caesar" as a free trustee of the masses (of the army or of the citizenry), who is unfettered by tradition. The "Caesar" is thus the unrestrained master of a body of highly qualified military officers and officials whom he selects freely and personally without regard to tradition or to any other considerations. This "rule of the personal genius," however, stands in contradiction to the formally "democratic" principle of a universally elected officialdom.

3. Normally, the position of the official is held for life, at least in public bureaucracies; and this is increasingly the case for all similar structures. As a factual rule, *tenure for life* is presupposed, even where the giving of notice or periodic reappointment occurs. In contrast to the worker in a private enterprise, the official normally holds tenure. Legal or actual life-tenure, however, is not recognized as the official's right to the possession of office, as was the case with many structures of authority in the past. Where legal guarantees against arbitrary dismissal or transfer are developed, they merely serve to guarantee a strictly objective discharge of specific office duties free from all personal considerations. In Germany, this is the case for all juridical and, increasingly, for all administrative officials.

Within the bureaucracy, therefore, the measure of "independence," legally guaranteed by tenure, is not always a source of increased status for the official whose position is thus secured. Indeed, often the reverse holds, especially in old cultures and communities that are highly differentiated. In such communities, the stricter the subordination under the arbitrary rule of the master, the more it guarantees the maintenance of the conventional seigneurial style of living for the official. Because of the very absence of these legal guarantees of tenure, the conventional esteem for the official may rise in the same way as, during the Middle Ages the esteem of the nobility of office rose at the expense of esteem for the freemen, and as the king's judge surpassed that of the people's judge. In Germany, the military officer or the administrative official can be removed from office at any time, or at least far more readily than the "independent judge," who never pays with loss of his office for even the grossest offense against the "code of honor" or against social conventions of the salon. For this very reason, if other things are equal, in the eyes of the master stratum the judge is considered less qualified for social intercourse than are officers and administrative officials, whose greater dependence on the master is a greater guarantee of their conformity with status conventions. Of course, the average official strives for a civil-service law, which would materially secure his old age and provide increased guarantees against his arbitrary removal from office. This striving, however, has its limits. A very strong development of the "right to the office" naturally makes it more difficult to staff them with regard to technical efficiency, for such a development decreases the career-opportunities of ambitious candidates for office. This makes for the fact that officials, on the whole, do not feel their dependency upon those at the top. This lack of a feeling of dependency, however, rests primarily upon the inclination to depend upon one's equals rather than upon the socially inferior and governed strata. The present conservative movement among the Badenia clergy, occasioned by the anxiety of a presumably threatening separation of church and state, has been expressly determined by the desire not to be turned "from a master into a servant of the parish."

4. The official receives the regular *pecuniary* compensation of a normally fixed *salary* and the old age security provided by a pension. The salary is not measured like a wage in terms of work done, but according to "status," that is, according to the kind of function (the "rank") and, in addition, possibly, according to the length of service. The relatively great security of the official's income, as well as the rewards of social esteem, make the office a sought-after position, especially in countries which no longer provide opportunities for colonial profits. In such countries, this situation permits relatively low salaries for officials.
5. The official is set for a "*career*" within the hierarchical order of the public service. He moves from the lower, less important, and lower paid to the higher positions. The average official naturally desires a mechanical fixing of the conditions of promotion: if not of the offices, at least of the salary levels. He wants these conditions fixed in terms of "seniority," or possibly according to grades achieved in a developed system of expert examinations. Here and there, such examinations actually form a character *indelebilis* of the official and have lifelong effects on his career. To this is joined the desire to qualify the right to office and the increasing tendency toward status group closure and economic security. All of this makes for a tendency to consider the offices as "prebends" of those who are qualified by educational certificates. The necessity of taking general personal and intellectual qualifications into consideration, irrespective of the often subaltern character of the educational certificate, has led to a condition in which the highest political offices, especially the positions of "ministers," are principally filled without reference to such certificates.

III THE PRESUPPOSITIONS AND CAUSES OF BUREAUCRACY

The social and economic presuppositions of the modern structure of the office are as follows:

The development of the *money economy*, in so far as a pecuniary compensation of the officials is concerned, is a presupposition of bureaucracy. Today it not only prevails but is predominant. This fact is of very great importance for the whole bearing of bureaucracy, yet by itself it is by no means decisive for the existence of bureaucracy.

Historical examples of rather distinctly developed and quantitatively large bureaucracies are: (a) Egypt, during the period of the new Empire which, however, contained strong patrimonial elements; (b) the later Roman Principate, and especially the Diocletian monarchy and the Byzantine polity which developed out of it and yet retained strong feudal and patrimonial elements; (c) the Roman Catholic Church, increasingly so since the end of the thirteenth century; (d) China, from the time of Shi Hwangti until the present, but with strong patrimonial and prebendal elements; (e) in ever purer forms, the modern European states and, increasingly, all public corporations since the time of princely absolutism; (f) the large modern capitalist enterprise, the more so as it becomes greater and more complicated.

To a very great extent, partly even predominantly, cases (a) to (d) have rested upon compensation of the officials in kind. Yet they have displayed many other traits and effects characteristic of bureaucracy. The historical model of all later bureaucracies—the new Empire of Egypt—is at the same time one of the most grandiose examples of an organized subsistence economy. Yet this coincidence of bureaucracy and subsistence economy is understandable in view of the quite unique conditions that existed in Egypt. And the reservations—and they are quite considerable—which one must make in classifying this Egyptian structure as a bureaucracy are conditioned by the subsistence economy. A certain measure of a developed money economy is the normal precondition for the unchanged and continued existence, if not for the establishment, of pure bureaucratic administrations.

According to historical experience, without a money economy the bureaucratic structure can hardly avoid undergoing substantial internal changes, or indeed, turning into another type of structure. The allocation of fixed income in kind, from the magazines of the lord or from his current intake, to the officials easily means a first step toward appropriation of the sources of taxation and their exploitation as private property. This kind of allocation has been the rule in Egypt and China for thousands of years and played an important part in the later Roman monarchy as well as elsewhere. The income in kind has protected the official against the often sharp fluctuations in the purchasing power of money. Whenever the lord's prerogatives have relaxed, the taxes in kind, as a rule, have been irregular. In this case, the official has direct recourse to the tributaries of his bailiwick, whether or not he is authorized. Close at hand is the idea of securing the official against such oscillations by mortgaging or transferring the levies and therewith the power to tax, or by leasing profitable lands of the lord to the official for his own use. Every central authority which is not strictly organized is tempted to take this course either voluntarily or because the officials compel it to do so. The official may satisfy himself with the use of these levies or loans up to the level of his salary claim and then hand over the surplus. This implies strong temptation and therefore yields results chiefly unsatisfactory to the lord. Another process involves fixing the official's salary: This often occurred in the early history of German officialdom; and it happened on the largest scale in all Eastern Satrap administrations: the official hands over a stipulated amount and retains the surplus.

In such cases the official is economically in a position rather similar to that of the entrepreneurial tax-farmer. Indeed, office-farming including even the leasing of offices to the highest bidder is regularly found. On the soil of a private economy, the transformation of the statutes of villenage into tenancy relations is one of the most important among numerous examples. By tenancy arrangements the lord can transfer the trouble of changing his income-in-kind into money-income to the office tenant or to the official who is to be given a fixed sum. This was plainly the case with some Oriental regents in Antiquity. And above all, the farming out of public collection of taxes in lieu of the lord's own management of taxgathering served this purpose. From this procedure there develops the possibility for the lord to progress in the ordering of his finances into a systematic budget. This is a very important advance, for it means that a fixed estimate of the income, and correspondingly of the expenses, can take the place of a hand-to-mouth living from incalculable incomes in kind, a condition typical of all the early states of public households. On the other hand, in systematizing his budget in this way, the lord renounces the control and full exploitation of his capacity to tax for his own use. According to the measure of freedom left to the official, to the office, or to the tax-farmer, the lasting capacity to pay taxes is endangered by inconsiderate exploitation. For, unlike the political overlord, the capitalist is not in the same way permanently interested in the subject's ability to pay.

The lord seeks to safeguard himself against this loss of control by regulations. The mode of tax-farming or the transfer of taxes can thus vary widely, according to the distribution of power between the lord and the tenant. Either the tenant's interest in the free exploitation of capacity to pay taxes or the lord's interest in the permanence of this capacity prevails. The nature of the tax-farming system rests essentially upon the joint or the opposing influence of these motives: the elimination of oscillations in the yields, the possibility of a budget, the safeguarding of the subjects' capacity to pay by protecting them against uneconomical exploitation, and a state control of the tax-farmer's yields for the sake of appropriating the maximum possible. In the Ptolemaic empire, as in Hellas and in Rome, the tax-farmer was still a private capitalist. The raising of taxes, however, was bureaucratically executed and controlled by the Ptolemaic state. The tenant's profit consisted in only a share of the respective surplus over and above the tax-farmer's fee, which was, in fact, only a guarantee. The tax-farmer's risk consisted in the possibility of yields that were lower than this sum.

The purely economic conception of the office as a source of the official's private income can also lead to the direct purchase of offices. This occurs when the lord finds himself in a position in which he requires not only a current income but money capital—for instance, for warfare or for debt payments. The purchase of office as a regular institution has existed in modern states, in the church state as well as in that of France and England; it has existed in the cases of sinecures as well as of very serious offices; and, in the case of officers' commissions, it lagged over until the early nineteenth century. In individual cases, the economic meaning of such a purchase of office can be altered so that the purchasing sum is partly or wholly in the nature of bail deposited for faithful service, but this has not been the rule.

Every sort of assignment of usufructs, tributes and services which are due to the lord himself or to the official for personal exploitation, always means a surrender of the pure type of bureaucratic organization. The official in such positions has a personal right to the possession of his office. This is the case to a still higher degree when official duty and compensation are interrelated in such a way that the official does not transfer to the lord any yields gained from the objects left to him, but handles these objects for his private ends and in rurn renders to the lord services of a personal or a military, political, or ecclesiastical character.

We wish to speak of "*prebends*" and of a "prebendal" organization of office, wherever the lord assigns to the official rent payments for life, payments which are somehow fixed to objects or which are essentially *economic* usufruct from lands or other sources. They must be compensations for the fulfilment of actual or fictitious office duties; they are goods permanently set aside for the economic assurance of the office.

The transition from such prebendal organization of office to salaried officialdom is quite fluid. Very often the economic endowment of priesthoods has been "prebendal," as in Antiquity and the Middle Ages, and even up to the modern period. But in almost all periods the same form has been found in other areas. In Chinese sacerdotal law, the prebendal character of all offices forced the mourning official to resign his office. For during the ritual mourning period for the father or other household authorities abstention from the enjoyment of possessions was prescribed. Originally this prescription was aimed at avoiding the ill-will of the deceased master of the house, for the house belonged to this master and the office was considered purely as a prebend, a source for rent.

When not only economic rights but also lordly prerogatives are leased for personal execution with the stipulation of *personal* services to the lord, a further step away from salaried bureaucracy is taken. These leased prerogatives vary; for instance, with the political official, they may be in the nature of landlordism or in the nature of office authority. In both instances, and certainly in the latter, the specific nature of bureaucratic organization is completely destroyed and we enter the organizational realm of *feudal* dominion. All kinds of assignments of services and usufructs in kind as endowments for officials tend to loosen the bureaucratic mechanism, and especially to weaken hierarchic subordination. This subordination is most strictly developed in the discipline of modern officialdom. A precision similar to the precision of the contractually employed official of the modern Occident can only be attained—at least under very energetic leadership—where the subjection of the officials to the lord is personally absolute, where slaves, or employees treated like slaves, are used for administration.

The Egyptian officials were slaves of the Pharaoh, if not legally, at least in fact. The Roman latifundia owners liked to commission slaves with the direct management of money matters, because of the possibility of subjecting them to torture. In China, similar results have been sought by the prodigial use of the bamboo as a disciplinary instrument. The chances, however, for such direct means of coercion to function with *steadiness* are extremely unfavorable. According to experience, the relative optimum for the success and maintenance of a strict mechanization of the bureaucratic apparatus is offered by a secured money salary connected with the opportunity of a career that is not dependent upon mere accident and arbitrariness. Strict discipline and control, which at the same time has consideration for the official's sense of honor, and the development of prestige sentiments of the status group, as well as the possibility of public criticism, work in the direction of strict mechanization. With all this, the bureaucratic apparatus functions more assuredly than does any legal enslavement of functionaries. A strong status sentiment among officials not only agrees with the official's readiness to subordinate himself to the chief without any will of his own, but—just as is the case with the officer—status sentiments are the consequence of such subordination for internally they balance the official's self-feeling. The purely impersonal character of office work, with its principled separation of the private sphere of the official from that of the office, facilitates the official's integration into the given functional conditions of a fixed mechanism based upon discipline.

Even though the full development of a money economy is not an indispensable precondition for bureaucratization, bureaucracy as a permanent structure is knit to the one presupposition of a constant income for maintaining it. Where such an income cannot be derived from private profits, as is the case with the bureaucratic organization of large modern enterprises, or from fixed land rents, as with the manor, a stable system of *taxation* is the precondition for the permanent existence of bureaucratic administration. For well-known and general reasons, only a fully developed money economy offers a secure basis for such a taxation system. The degree of administrative bureaucratization in urban communities with fully developed money economies has not infrequently been relatively greater in the contemporary far larger states of plains. Yet as soon as these plain states have been able to develop orderly systems of tribute, bureaucracy has developed more comprehensively than in city states. Whenever the size of the city states has remained confined to moderate limits, the tendency for a plutocratic and collegial administration by notables has corresponded most adequately to their structure.

. . .

V QUALITATIVE CHANGES OF ADMINISTRATIVE TASKS

Bureaucratization is occasioned more by intensive and qualitative enlargement and internal deployment of the scope of administrative tasks than by their extensive and quantitative increase. But the direction bureaucratization takes and the reasons that occasion it vary widely.

In Egypt, the oldest country of bureaucratic state administration, the public and collective regulation of waterways for the whole country and from the top could not be avoided because of technical economic factors. This regulation created the mechanism of scribes and officials. Once established, this mechanism, even in early times, found its second realm of business in the extraordinary construction activities which were organized militarily. As mentioned before, the bureaucratic tendency has chiefly been influenced by needs arising from the creation of standing armies as determined by power politics and by the development of public finance connected with the military establishment. In the modern state, the increasing demands for administration rest on the increasing complexity of civilization and push towards bureaucratization.

Very considerable expansions, especially overseas, have, of course, been managed by states ruled by notables (Rome, England, Venice), as will become evident in the appropriate context. Yet the "intensity" of the administration, that is, the transfer of as many tasks as possible to the organization of the state proper for continuous management and discharge, has been only slightly developed among the great states ruled by notables, especially Rome and England, if we compare them with bureaucratic politics.

Both in notable and bureaucratic administrations the *structure* of state power has influenced culture very strongly. But it has done so relatively slightly in the form of management and control by the state. This holds from justice down to education. The growing demands on culture, in turn, are determined, though to a varying extent, by the growing wealth of the most influential strata in the state. To this extent increasing bureaucratization is a function of the increasing possession of goods used for consumption, and of an increasingly sophisticated technique of fashioning external life—a technique which corresponds to the opportunities provided by such wealth. This reacts upon the standard of living and makes for an increasing subjective indispensability of organized, collective, inter-local, and thus bureaucratic, provision for the most varied wants, which previously were either unknown, or were satisfied locally or by a private economy.

Among purely political factors, the increasing demand of a society, accustomed to absolute pacification, for order and protection ("police") in all fields exerts an especially persevering influence in the direction of bureaucratization. A steady road leads from modifications of the blood feud, sacerdotally, or by means of arbitration, to the present position of the policeman as the "representative of God on earth." The former means placed the guarantees for the individual's rights and security squarely upon the members of his sib, who are obligated, to assist him with oath and vengeance. Among other factors, primarily the manifold tasks of the so-called "policy of social welfare" operate in the direction of bureaucratization, for these tasks are, in part, saddled upon the state by interest groups and, in part, the state usurps them, either for reasons of power policy or for ideological motives. Of course, these tasks are to a large extent economically determined.

Among essentially technical factors, the specifically modern means of communication enter the picture as pacemakers of bureaucratization. Public land and water-ways, railroads, the telegraph, et cetera—they must, in part, necessarily be administered in a public and collective way; in part, such administration is technically expedient. In this respect, the contemporary means of communication frequently play a role similar to that of the canals of Mesopotamia and the regulation of the Nile in the ancient Orient. The degree to which the means of communication have been developed is a condition of decisive importance for the possibility of bureaucratic administration, although it is not the only decisive condition. Certainly in Egypt, bureaucratic centralization, on the basis of an almost pure subsistence economy, could never have reached the actual degree which it did without the natural trade route of the Nile. In order to promote bureaucratic centralization in modern Persia, the telegraph officials were officially commissioned with reporting all occurrences in the provinces to the Shah, over the heads of the local authorities. In addition, everyone received the right to remonstrate directly by telegraph. The modern Occidental state can be administered the way it actually is only because the state controls the telegraph network and has the mails and railroads at its disposal.

Railroads, in turn, are intimately connected with the development of an inter-local traffic of mass goods. This traffic is among the causal factors in the formation of the modern state. As we have already seen, this does not hold unconditionally for the past.

VI TECHNICAL ADVANTAGES OF BUREAUCRATIC ORGANIZATION

The decisive reason for the advance of bureaucratic organization has always been its purely technical superiority over any other form of organization. The fully developed bureaucratic mechanism compares with other organizations exactly as does the machine with the nonmechanical modes of production.

Precision, speed, unambiguity, knowledge of the files, continuity, discretion, unity, strict subordination, reduction of friction and of material and personal costs—these are raised to the optimum point in the strictly bureaucratic administration, and especially in its monocratic form. As compared with all collegiate, honorific, and avocational forms of administration, trained bureaucracy is superior on all these points. And as far as complicated tasks are concerned, paid bureaucratic work is not only more precise but, in the last analysis, it is often cheaper than even formally unremunerated honorific service.

Honorific arrangements make administrative work an avocation and, for this reason alone, honorific service normally functions more slowly; being less bound to schemata and being more formless. Hence it is less precise and less unified than bureaucratic work because it is less dependent upon superiors and because the establishment and exploitation of the apparatus of subordinate officials and filing services are almost unavoidably less economical. Honorific service is less continuous than bureaucratic and frequently quite expensive. This is especially the case if one thinks not only of the money costs to the public treasury—costs which bureaucratic administration, in comparison with administration by notables, usually substantially increases—but also of the frequent economic losses of the governed caused by delays and lack of precision. The possibility of administration by notables normally and permanently exists only where official management can be satisfactorily discharged as an avocation. With the qualitative increase of tasks the administration has to face, administration by notables reaches its limits—today, even in England. Work organized by collegiate bodies causes friction and delay and requires compromises between colliding interests and views. The administration, therefore, runs less precisely and is more independent of superiors; hence, it is less unified and slower. All advances of the Prussian administrative organization have been and will in the future be advances of the bureaucratic, and especially of the monocratic, principle.

Today, it is primarily the capitalist market economy which demands that the official business of the administration be discharged precisely, unambiguously, continuously, and with as much speed as possible. Normally, the very large, modern capitalist enterprises are themselves unequalled models of strict bureaucratic organization. Business management throughout rests on increasing precision, steadiness, and, above all, the speed of operations. This, in turn, is determined by the peculiar nature of the modern means of communication, including, among other things, the news service of the press. The extraordinary increase in the speed by which public announcements, as well as economic and political facts, are transmitted exerts a steady and sharp pressure in the direction of speeding up the tempo of administrative reaction towards various situations. The optimum of such reaction time is normally attained only by a strictly bureaucratic organization.

Bureaucratization offers above all the optimum possibility for carrying through the principle of specializing administrative functions according to purely objective considerations. Individual performances are allocated to functionaries who have specialized training and who by constant practice learn more and more. The "objective" discharge of business primarily means a discharge of business according to *calculable rules* and "without regard for persons."

"Without regard for persons" is also the watchword of the "market" and, in general, of all pursuits of naked economic interests. A consistent execution of bureaucratic domination means the leveling of status "honor." Hence, if the principle of the free-market is not at the same time restricted, it means the universal domination of the "class situation." That this consequence of bureaucratic domination has not set in everywhere, parallel to the extent of bureaucratization, is due to the differences among possible principles by which polities may meet their demands.

The second element mentioned, "calculable rules," also is of paramount importance for modern bureaucracy. The peculiarity of modern culture, and specifically of its technical and economic basis, demands this very "calculability" of results. When fully developed, bureaucracy also stands, in a specific sense, under the principle of *sine ira ac studio*. Its specific nature, which is welcomed by capitalism, develops the more perfectly the more the bureaucracy is "dehumanized," the more completely it succeeds in eliminating from official business love, hatred, and all purely personal, irrational, and emotional elements which escape calculation. This is the specific nature of bureaucracy and it is appraised as its special virtue.

The more complicated and specialized modern culture becomes, the more its external supporting apparatus demands the personally detached and strictly "objective" *expert*, in lieu of the master of older social structures, who was moved by personal sympathy and favor, by grace and gratitude. Bureaucracy offers the attitudes demanded by the external apparatus of modern culture in the most favorable combination. As a rule, only bureaucracy has established the foundation for the administration of a rational law conceptually systematized on the basis of such enactments as the latter Roman imperial period first created with a high degree of technical perfection. During the Middle Ages, this law was received along with the bureaucratization of legal administration, that is to say, with the displacement of the old trial procedure which was bound to tradition or to irrational presuppositions, by the rationally trained and specialized expert.

VII BUREAUCRACY AND LAW

The "rational" interpretation of law on the basis of strictly formal conceptions stands opposite the kind of adjudication that is primarily bound to sacred traditions. The single case that cannot be unambiguously decided by tradition is either settled by concrete "revelation" (oracle, prophetic dicta, or ordeal—that is, by "charismatic" justice) or—and only these cases interest us here—by informal judgments rendered in terms of concrete ethical or other practical valuations. This is "Kadi-justice," as R. Schmidt has fittingly called it. Or, formal judgments are rendered, though not by subsumption under rational concepts, but by drawing on "analogies" and by depending upon and interpreting concrete "precedents." This is "empirical justice."

Kadi-justice knows no reasoned judgment whatever. Nor does empirical justice of the pure type give any reasons which in our sense could be called rational. The concrete valuational character of Kadi-justice can advance to a prophetic break with all tradition. Empirical justice, on the other hand, can be sublimated and rationalized into a "technology." All non-bureaucratic forms of domination display a peculiar coexistence: on the one hand, there is a sphere of strict traditionalism, and, on the other, a sphere of free arbitrariness and lordly grace. Therefore, combinations and transitional forms between these two principles are very frequent; they will be discussed in another context.

Even today in England, as Mendelssohn has demonstrated, a broad substratum of justice is actually Kadi-justice to an extent that is hardly conceivable on the Continent. The justice of German juries which preclude a statement of the reasons for their verdict often functions in practice in the same way as this English justice. In general, one has to beware of believing that "democratic" principles of justice are identical with "rational" adjudication (in the sense of formal rationality). Indeed, the contrary holds, as will be shown in another context. The English and American adjudication of the highest courts is still to a great extent empirical; and especially is it adjudication by precedents. In England, the reason for the failure of all efforts at a rational codification of law, as well as the failure to borrow Roman law, was due to the successful resistance against such rationalization offered by the great and centrally organized lawyers' guilds. These guilds formed a monopolistic stratum of notables from whose midst the judges of the high courts of the realm were recruited. They retained in their hands juristic training as an empirical and highly developed technology, and they successfully fought all moves towards rational law that threatened their social and material position. Such moves came especially from the ecclesiastical courts and, for a time, also from the universities.

The fight of the common law advocates against the Roman and ecclesiastical law and the power of the church in general was to a considerable degree economically caused by the lawyer's interest in fees; this is distinctly evidenced by the way in which the king intervened in this struggle. But the power position of the lawyers, who emerged victoriously from this struggle, was conditioned by political centralization. In Germany, primarily for political reasons, a socially powerful estate of notables was lacking. There was no estate which, like the English lawyers, could have been the carriers of a national administration of law, which could have raised national law to the level of a technology with regulated apprenticeship, and which could have offered resistance to the intrusion of the technically superior training of jurists in Roman law.

That fact that Roman law was substantively better adjusted to the needs of emerging capitalism did not decide its victory on the Continent. . . .

. . .

X THE PERMANENT CHARACTER OF THE BUREAUCRATIC MACHINE

Once it is fully established, bureaucracy is among those social structures which are the hardest to destroy. Bureaucracy is *the* means of carrying "community action" over into rationally ordered "societal action." Therefore, as an instrument for "societalizing" relations of power, bureaucracy has been and is a power instrument of the first order—for the one who controls the bureaucratic apparatus.

Under otherwise equal conditions, a "societal action," which is methodically ordered and led, is superior to every resistance of "mass" or even of "communal action." And where the bureaucratization of administration has been completely carried through, a form of power relation is established that is practically unshatterable.

The individual bureaucrat cannot squirm out of the apparatus in which he is harnessed. In contrast to the honorific or avocational "notable," the professional bureaucrat is chained to his activity by his entire material and ideal existence. In the great majority of cases, he is only a single cog in an ever-moving mechanism which prescribes to him an essentially fixed route of march. The official is entrusted with specialized tasks and normally the mechanism cannot be put into motion or arrested by him, but only from the very top. The individual bureaucrat is thus forged to the community of all the functionaries who are integrated into the mechanism. They have a common interest in seeing that the mechanism continues its functions and that the societally exercised authority carries on.

The ruled, for their part, cannot dispense with or replace the bureaucratic apparatus of authority once it exists. For this bureaucracy rests upon expert training, a functional specialization of work, and an attitude set for habitual and virtuoso-like mastery of single yet methodically integrated functions. If the official stops working, or if his work is forcefully interrupted, chaos results, and it is difficult to improvise replacements from among the governed who are fit to master such chaos. This holds for public administration as well as for private economic management. More and more the material fate of the masses depends upon the steady and correct functioning of the increasingly bureaucratic organizations of private capitalism. The idea of eliminating these organizations becomes more and more utopian.

The discipline of officialdom refers to the attitude-set of the official for precise obedience within his *habitual* activity, in public as well as in private organizations. This discipline increasingly becomes the basis of all order, however great the practical importance of administration on the basis of the filed documents may be. The naive idea of Bakuninism of destroying the basis of "acquired rights" and "domination" by destroying public documents overlooks the settled orientation of *man* for keeping to the habitual rules and regulations that continue to exist independently of the documents. Every reorganization of beaten or dissolved troops, as well as the restoration of administrative orders destroyed by revolt, panic, or other catastrophes, is realized by appealing to the trained orientation of obedient compliance to such orders. Such compliance has been conditioned into the officials, on the one hand, and, on the other hand, into the governed. If such an appeal is successful it brings, as it were, the disturbed mechanism into gear again.

The objective indispensability of the once-existing apparatus, with its peculiar, "impersonal" character, means that the mechanism—in contrast to feudal orders based upon personal piety—is easily made to work for anybody who knows how to gain control over it. A rationally ordered system of officials continues to function smoothly after the enemy has occupied the area; he merely needs to change the top officials. This body of officials continues to operate because it is to the vital interest of everyone concerned, including above all the enemy.

During the course of his long years in power, Bismarck brought his ministerial colleagues into unconditional bureaucratic dependence by eliminating all independent statesmen. Upon his retirement, he saw to his surprise that they continued to manage their offices unconcerned and undismayed, as if he had not been the master mind and creator of these creatures, but rather as if some single figure had been exchanged for some other figure in the bureaucratic machine. With all the changes of masters in France since the time of the First Empire, the power machine has remained essentially the same. Such a machine makes "revolution," in the sense of the forceful creation of entirely new formations of authority, technically more and more impossible, especially when the apparatus controls the modern means of communication (telegraph, et cetera) and also by virtue of its internal rationalized structure. In classic fashion, France has demonstrated how this process has substituted coups d'état for "revolutions": all successful transformations in France have amounted to coups d'état.

XI ECONOMIC AND SOCIAL CONSEQUENCES OF BUREAUCRACY

It is clear that the bureaucratic organization of a social structure, and especially of a political one, can and regularly does have far-reaching economic consequences. But what sort of consequences? Of course in any individual case it depends upon the distribution of economic and social power, and especially upon the sphere that is occupied by the emerging bureaucratic mechanism. The consequences of bureaucracy depend therefore upon the direction which the powers using the apparatus give to it. And very frequently a crypto-plutocratic distribution of power has been the result.

In England, but especially in the United States, party donors regularly stand behind the bureaucratic party organizations. They have financed these parties and have been able to influence them to a large extent. The breweries in England, the so-called "heavy industry," and in Germany the Hansa League with their voting funds are well enough known as political donors to parties. In modern times bureaucratization and social leveling within political, and particularly within state organizations in connection with the destruction of feudal and local privileges, have very frequently benefited the interests of capitalism. Often bureaucratization has been carried out in direct alliance with capitalist interests, for example, the great historical alliance of the power of the absolute prince with capitalist interests. In general, a legal leveling and destruction of firmly established local structures ruled by notables has usually made for a wider range of capitalist activity. Yet one may expect as an effect of bureaucratization, a policy that meets the petty bourgeois interest in a secured traditional "subsistence," or even a state socialist policy that strangles opportunities for private profit. This has occurred in several cases of historical and far-reaching importance, specifically during antiquity; it is undoubtedly to be expected as a future development. Perhaps it will occur in Germany.

The very different effects of political organizations which were, at least in principle, quite similar —in Egypt under the Pharaohs and in Hellenic and Roman times—show the very different economic significances of bureaucratization which are possible according to the direction of other factors. The mere fact of bureaucratic organization does not unambiguously tell us about the concrete direction of its economic effects, which are always in some manner present. At least it does not tell us as much as can be told about its relatively leveling effect socially. In this respect, one has to remember that bureaucracy as such is a precision instrument which can put itself at the disposal of quite varied—purely political as well as purely economic, or any other sort—of interests in domination. Therefore, the measure of its parallelism with democratization must not be exaggerated, however typical it may be. Under certain conditions, strata of feudal lords have also put bureaucracy into their service. There is also the possibility—and often it has become a fact, for instance, in the Roman principate and in some forms of absolutist state structures—that a bureaucratization of administration is deliberately connected with the formation of *estates*, or is entangled with them by the force of the existing groupings of social power.

The express reservation of offices for certain status groups is very frequent, and actual reservations are even more frequent. The democratization of society in its totality, and in the *modern* sense of the term, whether actual or perhaps merely formal, is an especially favorable basis of bureaucratization, but by no means the only possible one. After all, bureaucracy strives merely to level those powers that stand in its way and in those areas that, in the individual case, it seeks to occupy. We must remember this fact—which we have encountered several times and which we shall have to discuss repeatedly: that "democracy" as such is opposed to the rule of bureaucracy, in spite and perhaps because of its unavoidable yet unintended promotion of bureaucratization. Under certain conditions, democracy creates obvious ruptures and blockages to bureaucratic organization. Hence, in every individual historical case, one must observe in what special direction bureaucratization has developed.

XII THE POWER POSITION OF BUREAUCRACY

Everywhere the modern state is undergoing bureaucratization. But whether the *power* of bureaucracy within the polity is universally increasing must here remain an open question.

The fact that bureaucratic organization is technically the most highly developed means of power in the hands of the man who controls it does not determine the weight that bureaucracy as such is capable of having in a particular social structure. The ever-increasing "indispensability" of the officialdom, swollen to millions, is no more decisive for this question than is the view of some representatives of the proletarian movement that the economic indispensability of the proletarians is decisive for the measure of their social and political power position. If "indispensability" were decisive, then where slave labor prevailed and where freemen usually abhor work as a dishonor, the "indispensable" slaves ought to have held the positions of power, for they were at least as indispensable as officials and proletarians are today. Whether the power of bureaucracy as such increases cannot be decided a priori from such reasons. The drawing in of economic interest groups or other non-official experts, or the drawing in of non-expert lay representatives, the establishment of local, inter-local, or central parliamentary or other representative bodies, or of occupational associations—these *seem* to run directly against the bureaucratic tendency. How far this appearance is the truth must be discussed in another chapter rather than in this purely formal and typological discussion. In general, only the following can be said here:

Under normal conditions, the power position of a fully developed bureaucracy is always overtowering. The "political master" finds himself in the position of the "dilettante" who stands opposite the "expert," facing the trained official who stands within the management of administration. This holds whether the "master" whom the bureaucracy serves is a "people," equipped with the weapons of "legislative initiative," the "referendum," and the right to remove officials, or a parliament, elected on a more aristocratic or more "democratic" basis and equipped with the right to vote a lack of confidence, or with the actual authority to vote it. It holds whether the master is an aristocratic, collegiate body, legally or actually based on self-recruitment, or whether he is a popularly elected president, a hereditary and "absolute" or a "constitutional" monarch.

Every bureaucracy seeks to increase the superiority of the professionally informed by keeping their knowledge and intentions secret. Bureaucratic administration always tends to be an administration of "secret sessions": in so far as it can, it hides its knowledge and action from criticism. Prussian church authorities now threaten to use disciplinary measures against pastors who make reprimands or other admonitory measures in any way accessible to third parties. They do this because the pastor, in making such criticism available, is "guilty" of facilitating a possible criticism of the church authorities. The treasury officials of the Persian shah have made a secret doctrine of their budgetary art and even use secret script. The official statistics of Prussia, in general, make public only what cannot do any harm to the intentions of the power-wielding bureaucracy. The tendency toward secrecy in certain administrative fields follows their material nature: everywhere that the power interests of the domination structure toward *the outside* are at stake, whether it is an economic competitor of a private enterprise, or a foreign, potentially hostile polity, we find secrecy. If it is to be successful, the management of diplomacy can only be publicly controlled to a very limited extent. The military administration must insist on the concealment of its most important measures; with the increasing significance of purely technical aspects, this is all the more the case. Political parties do not proceed differently, in spite of all the ostensible publicity of Catholic congresses and party conventions. With the increasing bureaucratization of party organizations, this secrecy will prevail even more. Commercial policy, in Germany for instance, brings about a concealment of production statistics. Every fighting posture of a social structure toward the outside tends to buttress the position of the group in power.

The pure interest of the bureaucracy in power, however, is efficacious far beyond those areas where purely functional interests make for secrecy. The concept of the "official secret" is the specific invention of bureaucracy, and nothing is so fanatically defended by the bureaucracy as this attitude, which cannot be substantially justified beyond these specifically qualified areas. In facing a parliament, the bureaucracy, out of a sure power instinct, fights every attempt of the parliament to gain knowledge by means of its own experts or from interest groups. The so-called right of parliamentary investigation is one of the means by which parliament seeks such knowledge. Bureaucracy naturally welcomes a poorly informed and hence a powerless parliament —at least in so far as ignorance somehow agrees with the bureaucracy's interests.

The absolute monarch is powerless opposite the superior knowledge of the bureaucratic expert—in a certain sense more powerless than any other political head. All the scornful decrees of Frederick the Great concerning the "abolition of serfdom" were derailed, as it were, in the course of their realization because the official mechanism simply ignored them as the occasional ideas of a dilettante. When a constitutional king agrees with a socially important part of the governed, he very frequently exerts a greater influence upon the course of administration than does the absolute monarch. The constitutional king can control these experts better because of what is, at least relatively, the public character of criticism, whereas the absolute monarch is dependent for information solely upon the bureaucracy. The Russian czar of the old regime was seldom able to accomplish permanently anything that displeased his bureaucracy and hurt the power interests of the bureaucrats. His ministerial departments, placed directly under him as the autocrat, represented a conglomerate of satrapies, as was correctly noted by Leroy-Beaulieu. These satrapies constantly fought against one another by all the means of personal intrigue, and, especially, they bombarded one another with voluminous "memorials," in the face of which, the monarch, as a dilettante, was helpless.

With the transition to constitutional government, the concentration of the power of the central bureaucracy in one head became unavoidable. Officialdom was placed under a monocratic head, the prime minister, through whose hands everything had to go before it got to the monarch. This put the latter, to a large extent, under the tutelage of the chief of the bureaucracy. Wilhelm II, in his well-known conflict with Bismarck, fought against this principle, but he had to withdraw his attack very soon. Under the rule of expert knowledge, the actual influence of the monarch can attain steadiness only by a continuous communication with the bureaucratic chiefs; this intercourse must be methodically planned and directed by the head of the bureaucracy.

At the same time, constitutionalism binds the bureaucracy and the ruler into a community of interests against the desires of party chiefs for power in the parliamentary bodies. And if he cannot find support in parliament the constitutional monarch is powerless against the bureaucracy. The desertion of the "Great of the Reich," the Prussian ministers and top officials of the Reich in November 1918, brought a monarch into approximately the same situation as existed in the feudal state in 1056. However, this is an exception, for, on the whole, the power position of a monarch opposite bureaucratic officials is far stronger than it was in any feudal state or in the "stereotyped" patrimonial state. This is because of the constant presence of aspirants for promotion, with whom the monarch can easily replace inconvenient and independent officials. Other circumstances being equal, only economically independent officials, that is, officials who belong to the propertied strata, can permit themselves to risk the loss of their offices. Today as always, the recruitment of officials from among propertyless strata increases the power of the rulers. Only officials who belong to a socially influential stratum, whom the monarch believes he must take into account as personal supporters, like the so-called *Kanalrebellen* in Prussia, can permanently and completely paralyse the substance of his will.

Only the expert knowledge of private economic interest groups in the field of "business" is superior to the expert knowledge of the bureaucracy. This is so because the exact knowledge of facts in their field is vital to the economic existence of businessmen. Errors in official statistics do not have direct economic consequences for the guilty official, but errors in the calculation of a capitalist enterprise are paid for by losses, perhaps by its existence. The "secret," as a means of power, is, after all, more safely hidden in the books of an enterpriser than it is in the files of public authorities. For this reason alone authorities are held within narrow barriers when they seek to influence economic life in the capitalist epoch. Very frequently the measures of the state in the field of capitalism take unforeseen and unintended courses, or they are made illusory by the superior expert knowledge of interest groups.

. . .

XIV THE "RATIONALIZATION" OF EDUCATION AND TRAINING

We cannot here analyze the far-reaching and general cultural effects that the advance of the rational bureaucratic structure of domination, as such, develops quite independently of the areas in which it takes hold. Naturally, bureaucracy promotes a "rationalist" way of life, but the concept of rationalism allows for widely differing contents. Quite generally, one can only say that the bureaucratization of all domination very strongly furthers the development of "rational matter-of-factness" and the personality type of the professional expert. This has far-reaching ramifications, but only one important element of the process can be briefly indicated here: its effect upon the nature of training and education.

Educational institutions on the European continent, especially the institutions of higher learning —the universities, as well as technical academies, business colleges, gymnasiums, and other middle schools—are dominated and influenced by the need for the kind of "education" that produces a system of special examinations and the trained expertness that is increasingly indispensable for modern bureaucracy.

The "special examination," in the present sense, was and is found also outside of bureaucratic structures proper; thus, today it is found in the "free" professions of medicine and law and in the guild-organized trades. Expert examinations are neither indispensable to nor concomitant phenomena of bureaucratization. The French, English, and American bureaucracies have for a long time foregone such examinations entirely or to a large extent, for training and service in party organizations have made up for them.

"Democracy" also takes an ambivalent stand in the face of specialized examinations, as it does in the face of all the phenomena of bureaucracy—although democracy itself promotes these developments. Special examinations, on the one hand, mean or appear to mean a "selection" of those who qualify from all social strata rather than a rule by notables. On the other hand, democracy fears that a merit system and educational certificates will result in a privileged "caste." Hence, democracy fights against the special-examination system.

The special examination is found even in pre-bureaucratic or semi-bureaucratic epochs. Indeed, the regular and earliest locus of special examinations is among prebendally organized dominions. Expectancies of prebends, first of church prebends—as in the Islamite Orient and in the Occidental Middle

Ages—then, as was especially the case in China, secular prebends, are the typical prizes for which people study and are examined. These examinations, however, have in truth only a partially specialized and expert character.

The modern development of full bureaucratization brings the system of rational, specialized, and expert examinations irresistibly to the fore. The civil-service reform gradually imports expert training and specialized examinations into the United States. In all other countries this system also advances, stemming from its main breeding place, Germany. The increasing bureaucratization of administration enhances the importance of the specialized examination in England. In China, the attempt to replace the semi-patrimonial and ancient bureaucracy by a modern bureaucracy brought the expert examination; it took the place of a former and quite differently structured system of examinations. The bureaucratization of capitalism, with its demand for expertly trained technicians, clerks, et cetera, carries such examinations all over the world. Above all, the development is greatly furthered by the social prestige of the educational certificates acquired through such specialized examinations. This is all the more the case as the educational patent is turned to economic advantage. Today, the certificate of education becomes what the test for ancestors has been in the past, at least where the nobility has remained powerful: a prerequisite for equality of birth, a qualification for a canonship, and for state office.

The development of the diploma from universities, and business and engineering colleges, and the universal clamor for the creation of educational certificates in all fields make for the formation of a privileged stratum in bureaus and in offices. Such certificates support their holders' claims for intermarriages with notable families (in business offices people naturally hope for preferment with regard to the chief's daughter), claims to be admitted into the circles that adhere to "codes of honor," claims for a "respectable" remuneration rather than remuneration for work done, claims for assured advancement and old-age insurance, and, above all, claims to monopolize socially and economically advantageous positions. When we hear from all sides the demand for an introduction of regular curricula and special examinations, the reason behind it is, of course, not a suddenly awakened "thirst for education" but the desire for restricting the supply for these positions and their monopolization by the owners of educational certificates. Today, the "examination" is the universal means of this monopolization, and therefore examinations irresistibly advance. As the education prerequisite to the acquisition of the educational certificate requires considerable expense and a period of waiting for full remuneration, this striving means a setback for talent (charisma) in favor of property. For the "intellectual" costs of educational certificates are always low, and with the increasing volume of such certificates, their intellectual costs do not increase, but rather decrease.

The requirement of a chivalrous style of life in the old qualification for fiefs in Germany is replaced by the necessity of participating in its present rudimental form as represented by the dueling corps of the universities which also distribute the educational certificates. In Anglo-Saxon countries, athletic and social clubs fulfil the same function. The bureaucracy, on the other hand, strives everywhere for a "right to the office" by the establishment of a regular disciplinary procedure and by removal of the completely arbitrary disposition of the "chief" over the subordinate official. The bureaucracy seeks to secure the official position, the orderly advancement, and the provision for old age. In this, the bureaucracy is supported by the "democratic" sentiment of the governed, which demands that domination be minimized. Those who hold this attitude believe themselves able to discern a weakening of the master's prerogatives in every weakening of the arbitrary disposition of the master over the officials. To this extent, bureaucracy, both in business offices and in public service, is a carrier of a specific "status" development, as have been the quite differently structured officeholders of the past. We have already pointed out that these status characteristics are usually also exploited, and that by their nature they contribute to the technical usefulness of the bureaucracy in fulfilling its specific tasks.

"Democracy" reacts precisely against the unavoidable "status" character of bureaucracy. Democracy seeks to put the election of officials for short terms in the place of appointed officials; it seeks to substitute the removal of officials by election for a regulated procedure of discipline. Thus, democracy seeks to replace the arbitrary disposition of the hierarchically superordinate "master" by the equally arbitrary disposition of the governed and the party chiefs dominating them.

Social prestige based upon the advantage of special education and training as such is by no means specific to bureaucracy. On the contrary! But educational prestige in other structures of domination rests upon substantially different foundations.

Expressed in slogan-like fashion, the "cultivated man," rather that the "specialist," has been the end sought by education and has formed the basis of social esteem in such various systems as the feudal, theocratic, and patrimonial structures of dominion: in the English notable administration, in the old Chinese patrimonial bureaucracy, as well as under the rule of demagogues in the so-called Hellenic democracy.

The term "cultivated man" is used here in a completely value-neutral sense; it is understood to mean solely that the goal of education consists in the quality of a man's bearing in life which was *considered* "cultivated," rather than in a specialized training for expertness. The "cultivated" personality formed the educational ideal, which was stamped by the structure of domination and by the social condition for membership in the ruling stratum. Such education aimed at a chivalrous or an ascetic type; or, at a literary type, as in China; a gymnastic-humanist type, as in Hellas; or it aimed at a conventional type, as in the case of the Anglo-Saxon gentleman. The qualification of the ruling stratum as such rested upon the possession of "more" cultural quality (in the absolutely changeable, value-neutral sense in which we use the term here), rather than upon "more" expert knowledge. Special military, theological, and juridical ability was of course intensely practiced; but the point of gravity in Hellenic, in medieval, as well as in Chinese education, has rested upon educational elements that were entirely different from what was "useful" in one's specialty.

Behind all the present discussions of the foundations of the educational system, the struggle of the "specialist type of man" against the older type of "cultivated man" is hidden at some decisive point. This fight is determined by the irresistibly expanding bureaucratization of all public and private relations of authority and by the ever-increasing importance of expert and specialized knowledge. This fight intrudes into all intimate cultural questions.

During its advance, bureaucratic organization has had to overcome those essentially negative obstacles that have stood in the way of the leveling process necessary for bureaucracy. In addition, administrative structures based on different principles intersect with bureaucratic organizations. Since these have been touched upon above, only some especially important structural *principles* will be briefly discussed here in a very simplified schema. We would be led too far afield were we to discuss all the actually existing types. We shall proceed by asking the following questions:

1. How far are administrative structures subject to economic determination? Or, how far are opportunities for development created by other circumstances, for instance, the purely political? Or, finally, how far are developments created by an "autonomous" logic that is solely of the technical structure as such?
2. We shall ask whether or not these structural principles, in turn, release specific economic effects, and if so, what effects. In doing this, one of course from the beginning has to keep his eye on the fluidity and the overlapping transitions of all these organizational principles. Their "pure" types, after all, are to be considered merely as border cases which are especially valuable and indispensable for analysis. Historical realities, which almost always appear in mixed forms, have moved and still move between such pure types.

The bureaucratic structure is everywhere a late product of development. The further back we trace our steps, the more typical is the absence of bureaucracy and officialdom in the structure of domination. Bureaucracy has a "rational" character: rules, means, ends, and matter-of-factness dominate its bearing. Everywhere its origin and its diffusion have therefore had "revolutionary" results, in a special sense, which has still to be discussed. This is the same influence which the advance of *rationalism* in general has had. The march of bureaucracy has destroyed structures of domination which had no rational character, in the special sense of the term. Hence, we may ask: What were these structures?

"THE SOCIOLOGY OF CHARISMATIC AUTHORITY"

1922

I THE GENERAL CHARACTER OF CHARISMA

Bureaucratic and patriarchal structures are antagonistic in many ways, yet they have in common a most important peculiarity: permanence. In this respect they are both institutions of daily routine. Patriarchal power especially is rooted in the provisioning of recurrent and normal needs of the workaday life. Patriarchal authority thus has its original locus in the economy, that is, in those branches of the economy that can be satisfied by means of normal routine. The patriarch is the "natural leader" of the daily routine. And in this respect, the bureaucratic structure is only the counter-image of patriarchalism transposed into rationality. As a permanent structure with a system of rational rules, bureaucracy is fashioned to meet calculable and recurrent needs by means of a normal routine.

The provisioning of all demands that go beyond those of everyday routine has had, in principle, an entirely heterogeneous, namely, a *charismatic*, foundation; the further back we look in history, the more we find this to be the case. This means that the "natural" leaders—in times of psychic, physical, economic, ethical, religious, political distress—have been neither officeholders nor incumbents of an "occupation" in the present sense of the word, that is, men who have acquired expert knowledge and who serve for remuneration. The natural leaders in distress have been holders of specific gifts of the body and spirit; and these gifts have been believed to be supernatural, not accessible to everybody. The concept of "charisma" is here used in a completely "value-neutral" sense.

The capacity of the Irish culture hero, Cuchulain, or of the Homeric Achilles for heroic frenzy is a manic seizure, just as is that of the Arabian berserk who bites his shield like a mad dog—biting around until he darts off in raving bloodthirstiness. For a long time it has been maintained that the seizure of the berserk is artificially produced through acute poisoning. In Byzantium, a number of "blond beasts," disposed to such seizures, were kept about, just as war elephants were formerly kept. Shamanist ecstasy is linked to constitutional epilepsy, the possession and the testing of which represents a charismatic qualification. Hence neither is "edifying" to our minds. They are just as little edifying to us as is the kind of "revelation," for instance, of the

Sacred Book of the Mormons, which, at least from an evaluative standpoint, perhaps would have to be called a "hoax." But sociology is not concerned with such questions. In the faith of their followers, the chief of the Mormons has proved himself to be charismatically qualified, as have "heroes" and "sorcerers." All of them have practiced their arts and ruled by virtue of this gift (charisma) and, where the idea of God has already been clearly conceived, by virtue of the divine mission lying therein. This holds for doctors and prophets, just as for judges and military leaders, or for leaders of big hunting expeditions.

It is to his credit that Rudolf Sohm brought out the sociological peculiarity of this category of domination-structure for a historically important special case, namely, the historical development of the authority of the early Christian church. Sohm performed this task with logical consistency, and hence, by necessity, he was one-sided from a purely historical point of view. In principle, however, the very same state of affairs recurs universally, although often it is most clearly developed in the field of religion.

In contrast to any kind of bureaucratic organization of offices, the charismatic structure knows nothing of a form or of an ordered procedure of appointment or dismissal. It knows no regulated "career," "advancement," "salary," or regulated and expert training of the holder of charisma or of his aids. It knows no agency of control or appeal, no local bailiwicks or exclusive functional jurisdictions; nor does it embrace permanent institutions like our bureaucratic "departments," which are independent of persons and of purely personal charisma.

Charisma knows only inner determination and inner restraint. The holder of charisma seizes the task that is adequate for him and demands obedience and a following by virtue of his mission. His success determines whether he finds them. His charismatic claim breaks down if his mission is not recognized by those to whom he feels he has been sent. If they recognize him, he is their master—so long as he knows how to maintain recognition through "proving" himself. But he does not derive his "right" from their will, in the manner of an election. Rather, the reverse holds: it is the *duty* of those to whom he addresses his mission to recognize him as their charismatically qualified leader.

In Chinese theory, the emperor's prerogatives are made dependent upon the recognition of the people. But this does not mean recognition of the sovereignty of the people any more than did the prophet's necessity of getting recognition from the believers in the early Christian community. The Chinese theory, rather, characterizes the charismatic nature of the *monarch's position*, which adheres to his *personal* qualification and to his *proved* worth.

Charisma can be, and of course regularly is, qualitatively particularized. This is an internal rather than an external affair, and results in the qualitative barrier of the charisma holder's mission and power. In meaning and in content the mission may be addressed to a group of men who are delimited locally, ethnically, socially, politically, occupationally, or in some other way. If the mission is thus addressed to a limited group of men, as is the rule, it finds its limits within their circle.

In its economic sub-structure, as in everything else, charismatic domination is the very opposite of bureaucratic domination. If bureaucratic domination depends upon regular income, and hence at least *a priori* on a money economy and money taxes, charisma lives in, though not off, this world. This has to be property understood. Frequently charisma quite deliberately shuns the possession of money and of pecuniary income per se, as did Saint Francis and many of his like; but this is of course not the rule. Even a pirate genius may exercise a "charismatic" domination, in the value-neutral sense intended here. Charismatic political heroes seek booty and, above all, gold. But charisma, and this is decisive, always rejects as undignified any pecuniary gain that is methodical and rational. In general, charisma rejects all rational economic conduct.

The sharp contrast between charisma and any "patriarchal" structure that rests upon the ordered base of the "household" lies in this rejection of rational economic conduct. In its "pure" form, charisma is never a source of private gain for its holders in the sense of economic exploitation by the making of a deal. Nor is it a source of income in the form of pecuniary compensation, and just as little does it involve an orderly taxation for the material requirements of its mission. If the mission is one of peace, individual patrons provide the necessary means for charismatic structures; or those to whom the charisma is addressed provide honorific gifts, donations, or other voluntary contributions. In the case of charismatic warrior heroes, booty represents one of the ends as well as the material means of the mission. "Pure" charisma is contrary to all patriarchal domination (in the sense of the term used here). It is the opposite of all ordered economy. It is the very force that disregards economy. This also holds, indeed precisely, where the charismatic leader is after the acquisition of goods, as is the case with the charismatic warrior hero. Charisma can do this because by its very nature it is not an "institutional" and permanent structure, but rather, where its "pure" type is at work, it is the very opposite of the institutionally permanent.

In order to do justice to their mission, the holders of charisma, the master as well as his disciples and followers, must stand outside the ties of this world, outside of routine occupations, as well as outside the routine obligations of family life. The statutes of the Jesuit order preclude the acceptance of church offices; the members of orders are forbidden to own property or, according to the original rule of St. Francis, the order as such is forbidden to do so. The priest and the knight of an order have to live in celibacy, and numerous holders of a prophetic or artistic charisma are actually single. All this is indicative of the unavoidable separation from this world of those who partake ("χλῆροξ") of charisma. In these respects, the economic conditions of participation in charisma may have an (apparently) antagonistic appearance, depending upon the type of charisma—artistic or religious, for instance—and the way of life flowing from its meaning. Modern charismatic movements of artistic origin represent "independents without gainful employment" (in everyday language, rentiers). Normally such persons are the best qualified to follow a charismatic leader. This is just as logically consistent as was the medieval friar's vow of poverty, which demanded the very opposite.

II FOUNDATIONS AND INSTABILITY OF CHARISMATIC AUTHORITY

By its very nature, the existence of charismatic authority is specifically unstable. The holder may forego his charisma; he may feel "forsaken by his God," as Jesus did on the cross; he may prove to his followers that "virtue is gone out of him." It is then that his mission is extinguished, and hope waits and searches for a new holder of charisma. The charismatic holder is deserted by his following, however, (only) because pure charisma does not know any "legitimacy" other than that flowing from personal strength, that is, one which is constantly being proved. The charismatic hero does not deduce his authority from codes and statutes, as is the case with the jurisdiction of office; nor does he deduce his authority from traditional custom or feudal vows of faith, as is the case with patrimonial power.

The charismatic leader gains and maintains authority solely by proving his strength in life. If he wants to be a prophet, he must perform miracles; if he wants to be a war lord, he must perform heroic deeds. Above all, however, his divine mission must "prove" itself in that those who faithfully surrender to him must fare well. If they do not fare well, he is obviously not the master sent by the gods.

This very serious meaning of genuine charisma evidently stands in radical contrast to the convenient pretensions of present rulers to a "divine right of kings," with its reference to the "inscrutable" will of the Lord, "to whom alone the monarch is responsible." The genuinely charismatic ruler is responsible precisely to those whom he rules. He is responsible for but one thing, that he personally and actually be the God-willed master.

During these last decades we have witnessed how the Chinese monarch impeaches himself before all the people because of his sins and insufficiencies if his administration does not succeed in warding off some distress from the governed, whether it is inundations or unsuccessful wars. Thus does a ruler whose power, even in vestiges and theoretically, is genuinely charismatic deport himself. And if even this penitence does not reconcile the deities, the charismatic emperor faces dispossession and death, which often enough is consummated as a propitiatory sacrifice.

Meng-tse's (Mencius') thesis that the people's voice is "God's voice" (according to him the *only* way in which God speaks!) has a very specific meaning: if the people cease to recognize the ruler, it is expressly stated that he simply becomes a private citizen; and if he then wishes to be more, he becomes a usurper deserving of punishment. The state of affairs that corresponds to these phrases, which sound highly revolutionary, recurs under primitive conditions without any such pathos. The charismatic character adheres to almost all primitive authorities with the exception of domestic power in the narrowest sense, and the chieftain is often enough simply deserted if success does not remain faithful to him.

The subjects may extend a more active or passive "recognition" to the personal mission of the charismatic master. His power rests upon this purely factual recognition and springs from faithful devotion. It is devotion to the extraordinary and unheard-of, to what is strange to all rule and tradition and which therefore is viewed as divine. It is a devotion born of distress and enthusiasm.

Genuine charismatic domination therefore knows of no abstract legal codes and statutes and of no "formal" way of adjudication. Its "objective" law emanates concretely from the highly personal experience of heavenly grace and from the god-like strength of the hero. Charismatic domination means a rejection of all ties to any external order in favor of the exclusive glorification of the genuine mentality of the prophet and hero. Hence, its attitude is revolutionary and transvalues everything; it makes a sovereign break with all traditional or rational norms; "It is written, but I say unto you."

The specifically charismatic form of settling disputes is by way of the prophet's revelation, by way of the oracle, or by way of "Solomonic" arbitration by a charismatically qualified sage. This arbitration is determined by means of strictly concrete and individual evaluations, which, however, claim absolute validity. Here lies the proper locus of "Kadi-justice" in the proverbial—not the historical—sense of the phrase. In its actual historical appearance the jurisdiction of the Islamic Kadi is, of course, bound to sacred tradition and is often a highly formalistic interpretation.

Only where these intellectual tools fail does jurisdiction rise to an unfettered individual act valuing the particular case; but then it does indeed. Genuinely charismatic justice always acts in this manner. In its pure form it is the polar opposite of formal and traditional bonds, and it is just as free in the face of the sanctity of tradition as it is in the face of any rationalist deductions from abstract concepts.

This is not the place to discuss how the reference to the *aegum et bonum* in the Roman administration of justice and the original meaning of English "equity" are related to charismatic justice in general and to the theocratic Kadi-justice of Islamism in particular. Both the *aegum et bonum* and "equity" are partly the products of a strongly rationalized administration of justice and partly the product of abstract conceptions of natural law. In any case the *ex bona fide* contains a reference to the "mores" of business life and thus retains just as little of a genuine irrational justice as does, for instance, the German judge's "free discretion."

Any kind of ordeal as a means of evidence is, of course, a derivative of charismatic justice. But the ordeal displaces the personal authority of the holder of charisma by a mechanism of rules for formally ascertaining the divine will. This falls in the sphere of the "routinization" of charisma, with which we shall deal below.

III CHARISMATIC KINGSHIP

In the evolution of political charisma, kingship represents a particularly important case in the historical development of the charismatic legitimization of institutions. The king is everywhere primarily a war lord, and kingship evolves from charismatic heroism.

In the form it displays in the history of civilized peoples, kingship is not the oldest evolutionary form of "political" domination. By "political" domination is meant a power that reaches beyond and which is, in principle, distinct from domestic authority. It is distinct because, in the first place, it is not devoted to leading the peaceful struggle of man with nature; it is, rather, devoted to leading in the violent conflict of one human community with another.

The predecessors of kingship were the holders of all those charismatic powers that guaranteed to remedy extraordinary external and internal distress, or guaranteed the success of extraordinary ventures. The chieftain of early history, the predecessor of kingship, is still a dual figure. On the one hand, he is the patriarchal head of the family or sib, and on the other, he is the charismatic leader of the hunt and war, the sorcerer, the rainmaker, the medicine man—and thus the priest and the doctor—and finally, the arbiter, Often, yet not always, such charismatic functions are split into as many special holders of charisma. Rather frequently the chieftain of the hunt and of war stands beside the chieftain of peace, who has essentially economic functions. In contrast to the latter, the chieftain of war acquires his charisma by proving his heroism to a voluntary following in successful raids leading to victory and booty. Even the royal Assyrian inscriptions enumerate booties of the hunt and cedars from Lebanon—dragged along for building purposes—alongside figures of the slain enemies and the size of the walls of conquered cities, which are covered with skins peeled off the enemies.

The charismatic position (among primitives) is thus acquired without regard to position in the sibs or domestic communities and without any rules whatsoever. This dualism of charisma and everyday routine is very frequently found among the American Indians, for instance, among the Confederacy of the Iroquois, as well as in Africa and elsewhere.

Where war and the big game hunt are absent, the charismatic chieftain—the "war lord" as we wish to call him, in contrast to the chieftain of peace—is absent as well. In peacetime, especially if elemental calamities, particularly drought and diseases, are frequent, a charismatic sorcerer may have an essentially similar power in his hands. He is a priestly lord. The charisma of the war lord may or may not be unstable in nature according to whether or not he proves himself and whether or not there is any need for a war lord. He becomes a permanent figure when warfare becomes a chronic state of affairs. It is a mere terminological question whether one wishes to let kingship, and with it the state, begin only when strangers are affiliated with and integrated into the community as subjects. For our purposes it will be expedient to continue delimiting the term "state" far more narrowly.

The existence of the war lord as a regular figure certainly does not depend upon a tribal rule over subjects of other tribes or upon individual slaves. His existence depends solely upon a chronic state of war and upon a comprehensive organization set for warfare. On the other hand, the development of kingship into a regular royal administration does emerge only at the stage when a following of royal professional warriors rules over the working or paying masses; at least, that is often the case. The forceful subjection of strange tribes, however, is not an absolutely indispensable link in this development. Internal class stratification may bring about the very same social differentiation: the charismatic following of warriors develops into a ruling caste. But in every case, princely power and those groups having interests vested in it—that is, the war lord's following—strive for legitimacy as soon as the rule has become stable. They crave for a characteristic which would define the charismatically qualified ruler.

"THE MEANING OF DISCIPLINE"

1922

It is the fate of charisma, whenever it comes into the permanent institutions of a community, to give way to powers of tradition or of rational socialization. This waning of charisma generally indicates the diminishing importance of individual action. And of all those powers that lessen the importance of individual action, the most irresistible is *rational discipline*.

The force of discipline not only eradicates personal charisma but also stratification by status groups; at least one of its results is the rational transformation of status stratification.

The content of discipline is nothing but the consistently rationalized, methodically trained and exact execution of the received order, in which all personal criticism is unconditionally suspended and the actor is unswervingly and exclusively set for carrying out the command. In addition, this conduct under orders is uniform. Its quality as the communal action of a *mass* organization conditions the specific effects of such uniformity. Those who obey are not necessarily a simultaneously obedient or an especially large mass, nor are they necessarily united in a specific locality. What is decisive for discipline is that the obedience of a plurality of men is rationally uniform.

Discipline as such is certainly not hostile to charisma or to status group honor. On the contrary, status groups that are attempting to rule over large territories or large organizations—the Venetian aristocratic counselors, the Spartans, the Jesuits in Paraguay, or a modern officer corps with a prince at its head—can maintain their alertness and their superiority over their subjects only by means of a very strict discipline. This discipline is enforced within their own group, for the blind obedience of subjects can be secured only by training them exclusively for submission under the disciplinary code. The cultivation of a stereotyped prestige and style of life of a status group, only for reasons of discipline, will have a strongly conscious and rationally intended character. This factor affects all culture in any way influenced by these status communities; we shall not discuss these effects here. A charismatic hero may make use of discipline in the same way; indeed, he must do so if he wishes to expand his sphere of domination. Thus Napoleon created a strict disciplinary organization for France, which is still effective today.

Discipline in general, like its most rational offspring, bureaucracy, is impersonal. Unfailingly neutral, it places itself at the disposal of every power that claims its service and knows how to promote it. This does not prevent bureaucracy from being intrinsically alien and opposed to charisma, as well as to honor, especially of a feudal sort. The berserk with maniac seizures of frenzy and the feudal knight who measures swords with an equal adversary in order to gain personal honor are equally alien to discipline. The berserk is alien to it because his action is irrational; the knight because his subjective attitude lacks matter-of-factness. In place of individual hero-ecstasy or piety, of spirited enthusiasm or devotion to a leader as a person, of the cult of "honor," or the exercise of personal ability as an "art"—discipline substitutes habituation to routinized skill. In so far as discipline appeals to firm motives of an "ethical" character, it presupposes a "sense of duty" and "conscientiousness." ("Men of Conscience" *versus* "Men of Honor," in Cromwell's terms.)

The masses are uniformly conditioned and trained for discipline in order that their optimum of physical and psychic power in attack may be rationally calculated. Enthusiasm and unreserved devotion may, of course, have a place in discipline;

every modern conduct of war weighs, frequently above everything else, precisely the "moral" elements of a troop's endurance. Military leadership uses emotional means of all sorts—just as the most sophisticated techniques of religious discipline, the *exercitia spiritualia* of Ignatius Loyola, do in their way. In combat, military leadership seeks to influence followers through "inspiration" and, even more, to train them in "emphatic understanding" of the leader's will. The sociologically decisive points, however, are, first, that everything, and especially these "imponderable" and irrational emotional factors, are rationally calculated—in principle, at least, in the same manner as one calculates the yields of coal and iron deposits. Secondly, devotion, in its purposefulness and according to its normal content, is of an objective character. It is devotion to a common "cause," to a rationally intended "success"; it does not mean devotion to a person as such—however "personally" tinged it may be in the concrete instance of a fascinating leader.

The case is different only when the prerogatives of a slaveholder create a situation of discipline—on a plantation or in a slave army of the ancient Orient, on galleys manned by slaves or among prisoners in Antiquity and the Middle Ages. Indeed, the individual cannot escape from such a mechanized organization, for routinized training puts him in his place and compels him to "travel along." Those who are enlisted in the ranks are forcibly integrated into the whole. This integration is a strong element in the efficacy of all discipline, and especially in every war conducted in a disciplined fashion. It is the only efficacious element and—as *caput mortuum*—it always remains after the "ethical" qualities of duty and conscientiousness have failed.

I THE ORIGINS OF DISCIPLINE IN WAR

The conflict between discipline and individual charisma has been full of vicissitudes. It has its classic seat in the development of the structure of warfare, in which sphere the conflict is, of course, to some extent determined by the technique of warfare. The kind of weapons—pike, sword, bow—are not necessarily decisive; for all of them allow disciplined as well as individual combat. At the beginning of the known history of the Near East and of the Occident, however, the importation of the horse and probably, to some uncertain degree, the beginning of the predominance of iron for tools have played parts which have been epoch-making in every way.

The horse brought the war chariot and with it the hero driving into combat and possibly fighting from his chariot. The hero has been dominant in the warfare of the Oriental, Indian, and ancient Chinese kings, as well as throughout Occidental societies, including the Celtic. In Ireland "hero combat" prevailed until late times. Horseback riding came after the war chariot, but persisted longer. From such horseback riding the "knight" emerged—the Persian, as well as the Thessalian, Athenian, Roman, Celtic, and Germanic. The footman, who certainly played some part earlier in the development of discipline, receded in importance for quite some time.

The substitution of iron side-arms for bronze javelins was probably among the factors that again pushed development in the opposite direction, toward discipline. Yet, just as in the Middle Ages gun powder can scarcely be said to have brought about the transition from undisciplined to disciplined fighting, so iron, as such, did not bring about the change—for long-range and knightly weapons were made of iron.

It was the discipline of the Hellenic and Roman Hoplites which brought about the change. Even Homer, as an oft-quoted passage indicates, knew of the beginnings of discipline with its prohibition of fighting out of line. For Rome, the important turning-point is symbolized by the legend of the execution of the consul's son, who, in accordance with the ancient fashion of heroes, had slain the opposing war lord in individual combat. At first, the well-trained army of the Spartan professional soldier, the holy Lochos of the Boeotians, the well-trained *sarissa*-equipped phalanx of the Macedonians, and then the tactic of the highly trained, more mobile maniple of the Romans, gained supremacy over the Persian knight, the militias of the Hellenic and Italic citizenry, and the people's armies of the Barbarians.

In the early period of the Hellenic Hoplites, incipient attempts were made to exclude long range weapons by "international law" as unchivalrous, just as during the Middle Ages there were attempts to forbid the cross-bow.

The kind of weapon has been the result and not the cause of discipline. Exclusive use of the infantry tactic of close combat during antiquity brought about the decay of cavalry, and in Rome the "census of knights" became practically equivalent to exemption from military service.

At the close of the Middle Ages it was the massed force of the Swiss, with its parallel and ensuing developments, which first broke the monopoly of knighthood to wage war. And even then, the Swiss still allowed the Halberdiers to break forth from the main force for hero combat, after the main force had advanced in closed formation—the pike-men occupying the outside positions. At first these massed forces of the Swiss only succeeded in dispersing the knights. And in the battles of the sixteenth and seventeenth centuries, cavalry, as such, increasingly disciplined, still played a completely decisive role. Without cavalry it was still impossible to wage offensive wars and actually to overpower the enemy, as the course of the English Civil War demonstrated.

It was discipline and not gun powder which initiated the transformation. The Dutch army under Maurice of the House of Orange was one of the first modern disciplined armies. It was shorn of all status privileges; and thus, for example, the previously effective refusal of the mercenaries to do rampart work (*opera servitia*) became ineffective. Cromwell's victories—despite the fierce bravery of the Cavaliers—were due to sober and rational Puritan discipline. His "Ironsides"—the "men of conscience"—trotted forward in firmly closed formation, at the same time calmly firing, and then, thrusting, brought about a successful attack. The major contrast lies in the fact that after the attack they remained in closed formation or immediately re-aligned themselves. It was this disciplined cavalry attack which was technically superior to the Cavaliers' ardor. For it was the habit of the Cavaliers to gallop enthusiastically into the attack and then, without discipline, to disperse, either to plunder the camp of the enemy or prematurely and individually to pursue single opponents in order to capture them for ransom. All successes were forfeited by such habits, as was typically and often the case in Antiquity and the Middle Ages (for example, at Tagliacozzo). Gun powder and all the war techniques associated with it became significant only with the existence of discipline—and to the full extent only with the use of war machinery, which presupposes discipline.

The economic bases upon which army organizations have been founded are not the only agent determining the development of discipline, yet they have been of considerable importance. The discipline of well-trained armies and the major or minor role they have played in warfare reacted still more, and with more lasting effects, upon the political and social order. This influence, however, has been ambiguous. Discipline, as the basis of warfare, gave birth to patriarchal kingship among the Zulus, where the monarch is constitutionally limited by the power of the army leaders (like the Spartan Ephors). Similarly, discipline gave birth to the Hellenic polis with its gymnasiums.

When infantry drill is perfected to the point of virtuosity (Sparta), the polis has an inevitably "aristocratic" structure. When cities are based upon naval discipline, they have "democratic" structures (Athens). Discipline gave rise to Swiss "democracy," which is quite different in nature. It involved a dominance (in Hellenic terms) over metics as well as territorial helots, during the time when Swiss mercenaries enlisted in foreign armies. The rule of the Roman particiate, of the Egyptian, Assyrian, and finally of the modern European bureaucratic state organizations—all have their origin in discipline.

War discipline may go hand in hand with totally different economic conditions, as these examples show. However, discipline has always affected the structure of the state, the economy, and possibly the family. For in the past a fully disciplined army has necessarily been a professional army, and therefore the basic problem has always been how to provide for the sustenance of the warriors.

The primeval way of creating trained troops—ever ready to strike, and allowing themselves to be disciplined—was *warrior communism*, which we have already mentioned. It may take the form of the bachelor house as a kind of barracks or casino of the professional warriors; in this form it is spread over the largest part of the earth. Or, it may follow the pattern of the communist community of the Ligurian pirates, or of the Spartan syssitia organized according to the "picnic" principle; or it may follow Caliph Omar's organization, or the religious knight orders of the Middle Ages. The warrior community may constitute, as we have noticed above, either a completely autonomous society closed against the outside, or, as is the rule, it may be incorporated into a political association whose territory is fixed by boundaries. As a part of such a corporate group, the warrior community may decisively determine its order. Thus, the recruitment of the warrior community is linked to the order of the corporate group. But this linkage is largely relative. Even the Spartans, for example, did not insist upon a strict "purity of blood." Military education was decisive for membership in its warrior community.

Under warrior communism, the existence of the warrior is the perfect counterpart to the existence of the monk, whose garrisoned communist life in the monastery also serves the purpose of disciplining him in the service of his master in the hereafter (and possibly also resulting in service to a this-worldly master). The dissociation from the family and from all private economic interests also occurs outside the celibate knight orders, which were created in direct analogy to the monk orders.

When the institution of the bachelor house is fully developed, familial relations are often completely excluded. The inmates of the house purchase or capture girls, or they claim that the girls of the subject community be at their disposal so long as they have not been sold in marriage. The children of the Ariloi—the ruling estate in Melanesia—are killed. Men can join enduring sexual communities with a separate economy only after having completed their "service" in the bachelor house—often only at an advanced age. Stratification according to age groups, which with some peoples is also important for the regulation of sexual relationship; the alleged survivals from primitive "endogenous sexual promiscuity"; the alleged survivals of a supposedly "primeval right" of all comrades to all girls not yet appropriated by an individual; as well as "marriage by capture"—allegedly the earliest form of marriage; and, above all, the "matriarchate"—all of these might be in most cases survivals of such military organizations as we are discussing. These military organizations split the life of the warrior from the household and family, and, under conditions of chronic warfare, such organizations have been widely diffused.

Almost everywhere the communistic warrior community may be the *caput mortuum* of the followers of charismatic war lords. Such a following has usually been societalized into a chronic institution and, once existing in peacetime, has led to the decline of warrior chieftainship. Yet under favorable conditions, the warrior chief may well rise to absolute lordship over the disciplined warrior formations. Accordingly, the *oikos*, as the basis of a military structure, offers an extreme contrast to this communism of warriors who live on accumulated stores, as well as contributions of the women, of those unfit to bear arms, and possibly of serfs. The patrimonial army is sustained and equipped from the stores of a commanding overlord. It was known especially in Egypt, but its fragments are widely dispersed in military organizations of different natures, and they form the bases of princely despotisms.

The reverse phenomenon, the emancipation of the warrior community from the unlimited power of the overlord, as evidenced in Sparta through the institution of the Ephors, has proceeded only so far as the interest in discipline has permitted, in the polis, therefore, the weakening of the king's power—which meant the weakening of discipline—prevailed only in peace and in the homeland (*domi* in contrast to *militiae*, according to the technical terms of Roman administrative law). The Spartan king's prerogatives approached the zero point only in peacetime. In the interests of discipline, the king was omnipotent in the field.

An all-around weakening of discipline usually accompanies any kind of decentralized military establishment—whether it is of prebendal or of feudal type. This weakening of discipline may vary greatly in degree. The well-trained Spartan army, the *δχλῆροι* of the other Hellenic and

Macedonian and of several Oriental military establishments, the Turkish quasi-prebendal fiefs, and finally the feudal fiefs of the Japanese and Occidental Middle Ages—all of these were phases of economic decentralization, usually going hand in hand with the weakening of discipline and the rising importance of individual heroism.

From the disciplinary aspect, just as from the economic, the feudal lord and vassal represents an extreme contrast to the patrimonial or bureaucratic soldier. And the disciplinary aspect is a consequence of the economic aspect. The feudal vassal and lord not only cares for his own equipment and provisions, directs his own baggage-train, but he summons and leads sub-vassals who, in turn, also equip themselves.

Discipline has grown on the basis of an increased concentration of the means of warfare in the hands of the war lord. This has been achieved by having a condottiere recruit mercenary armies, in part or wholly, in the manner of a private capitalist. Such an arrangement was dominant in the late Middle Ages and the beginning of the modern era. It was followed by the raising and equipping of standing armies by means of political authority and a collective economy. We shall not describe here in detail the increasing rationalization of procurement for the armies. It began with Maurice of the House of Orange, proceeded to Wallenstein, Gustav Adolf, Cromwell, the armies of the French, of Frederick the Great, and of Maria Theresa; it passed through a transition from the professional army to the people's army of the French Revolution, and from the disciplining of the people's army by Napoleon into a partly professional army. Finally universal conscription was introduced during the nineteenth century. The whole development meant, in effect, the clearly increasing importance of discipline and, just as clearly, the consistent execution of the economic process through which a public and collective economy was substituted for private capitalism as the basis for military organization.

Whether the exclusive dominance of universal conscription will be the last word in the age of machine warfare remains to be seen. The shooting records of the British navy, for instance, seem to be affected by ensembling gun crews of professional soldiers, which allows for their continuation as a team through the years. The belief in the technical superiority of the professional soldier for certain categories of troops is almost sure to gain in influence, especially if the process of shortening the term of service—stagnating in Europe at the moment—should continue. In several officers' circles, this view is already esoterically held. The introduction of a three-year period of compulsory service by the French army (1913) was motivated here and there by the slogan of "professional army"—a somewhat inappropriate slogan, since all differentiation of the troops into categories was absent. These still ambiguous possibilities, and also their possible political consequences, are not to be discussed here. In any case, none of them will alter the exclusive importance of mass discipline. What has concerned us here has been to show that the separation of the warrior from the means of warfare, and the concentration of the means of warfare in the hands of the war lord have everywhere been one of the typical bases of mass discipline. And this has been the case whether the process of separation and of concentration was executed in the form of oikos, capitalist enterprise, or bureaucratic organization.

II THE DISCIPLINE OF LARGE-SCALE ECONOMIC ORGANIZATIONS

The discipline of the army gives birth to all discipline. The large-scale economic organization is the second great agency which trains men for discipline. No direct historical and transitional organizations link the Pharaonic workshops and construction work (however little detail about their organization is known) with the Carthaginian Roman plantation, the mines of the late Middle Ages, the slave plantation of colonial economics, and finally the modern factory. However, all of these have in common the one element of discipline.

The slaves of the ancient plantations slept in barracks, living without family and without property. Only the managers—especially the *villicus*—had individual domiciles, somewhat comparable to the lieutenant's domicile or the residence of a manager of a modern, large-scale agricultural enterprise. The *villicus* alone usually had quasi-property (*peculium*, i.e. originally property in cattle) and quasi-marriage (*contubernium*). In the morning the work-slaves lined up in "squads" (in *decuriae*) and were led to work by overseers (*monitores*); their personal equipment (to use a barrack term) was stored away and handed out according to need. And hospitals and prison cells were not absent. The discipline of the manor of the Middle Ages and the modern era was considerably less strict because it was traditionally stereotyped, and therefore it somewhat limited the lord's power.

No special proof is necessary to show that military discipline is the ideal model for the modern capitalist factory, as it was for the ancient plantation. In contrast to the plantation, organizational discipline in the factory is founded upon a completely rational basis. With the help of appropriate methods of measurement, the optimum profitability of the individual worker is calculated like that of any material means of production. On the basis of this calculation, the American system of "scientific management" enjoys the greatest triumphs in the rational conditioning and training of work performances. The final consequences are drawn from the mechanization and discipline of the plant, and the psycho-physical apparatus of man is completely adjusted to the demands of the outer world, the tools, the machines—in short, to an individual "function." The individual is shorn of his natural rhythm as determined by the structure of his organism; his psycho-physical apparatus is atuned to a new rhythm through a methodical specialization of separately functioning muscles, and an optimal economy of forces is established corresponding to the conditions of work. This whole process of rationalization, in the factory as elsewhere, and especially in the bureaucratic state machine, parallels the centralization of the material implements of organization in the discretionary power of the overlord.

The ever-widening grasp of discipline irresistibly proceeds with the rationalization of the supply of economic and political demands. This universal phenomenon increasingly restricts the importance of charisma and of individually differentiated conduct.

III DISCIPLINE AND CHARISMA

Charisma, as a creative power, recedes in the face of domination, which hardens into lasting institutions, and becomes efficacious only in short-lived mass emotions of incalculable effects, as on elections and similar occasions. Nevertheless charisma remains a highly important element of the social structure, although of course in a greatly changed sense.

We must now return to the economic factors, already mentioned above, which predominantly determine the routinization of charisma: the need of social strata, privileged through existing political, social, and economic orders, to have their social and economic positions "legitimized." They wish to see their positions transformed from purely factual power relations into a cosmos of acquired rights, and to know that they are thus sanctified. These interests comprise by far the strongest motive for the conservation of charismatic elements of an objectified nature within the structure of domination. Genuine charisma is absolutely opposed to this objectified form. It does not appeal to an enacted or traditional order, nor does it base its claims upon acquired rights. Genuine charisma rests upon the legitimation of personal heroism or personal revelation. Yet precisely this quality of charisma as an extraordinary, supernatural, divine power transforms it, after its routinization, into a suitable source for the legitimate acquisition of sovereign power by the successors of the charismatic hero. Routinized charisma thus continues to work in favor of all those whose power and possession is guaranteed by that sovereign power, and who thus depend upon the continued existence of such power.

The forms in which a ruler's charismatic legitimation may express itself vary according to the relation of the original charismatic power-holder with the supernatural powers. If the ruler's legitimation cannot be determined, according to unambiguous rules, through hereditary charisma, he is in need of legitimation through some other charismatic power. Normally, this can only be hierocratic power. This holds expressly for the sovereign who represents a divine incarnation, and who thus possesses the highest "personal charisma." Unless it is supported and proved by personal deeds, his claim of charisma requires the acknowledgment of professional experts in divinity. Incarnated monarchs are indeed exposed to the peculiar process of interment by close court officials and priests, who are materially and ideally interested in legitimacy. This seclusion may proceed to a permanent palace arrest and even to killing upon maturity, lest the god have occasion to compromise divinity or to free himself from tutelage. Yet generally, according to the genuine view as well as in practice, the weight of responsibility which the charismatic ruler must carry before his subjects works very definitely in the direction of the need for his tutelage.

It is because of their high charismatic qualifications that such rulers as the Oriental Caliph, Sultan, and Shah urgently need, even nowadays (1913), a single personality to assume responsibility for governmental actions, especially for failures and unpopular actions. This is the basis for the traditional and specific position of the "Grand Vizier" in all those realms. The attempt to abolish and replace the office of the Grand Vizier by bureaucratic departments under ministers with the Shah's personal chairmanship failed in Persia during the last generation. This change would have placed the Shah in the role of a leader of the administration, personally responsible for all its abuses and for all the sufferings of the people. This role not only would have continuously jeopardized him, but would have shaken the belief in his very "charismatic" legitimacy. The office of Grand Vizier with its responsibilities had to be restored in order to protect the Shah and his charisma.

The Grand Vizier is the Oriental counterpart of the position of the responsible prime minister of the Occident, especially in parliamentary states. The formula, *le roi règne mais il ne gouverne pas*, and the theory that, in the interest of the dignity of his position, the king must not "figure without ministerial decorations," or, that he must abstain entirely from intervening in the normal administration directed by bureaucratic experts and specialists, or that he must abstain from administration in favor of the political party leaders occupying ministerial positions—all these theories correspond entirely to the enshrinement of the deified, patrimonial sovereign by the experts in tradition and ceremony: priests, court officers, and high dignitaries. In all these cases the sociological nature of charisma plays just as great a part as that of court officials or party leaders and their followings. Despite his lack of parliamentary power, the constitutional monarch is preserved, and above all, his mere existence and his charisma guarantee the *legitimacy* of the existing social and property order, since decisions are carried out "in his name." Besides, all those interested in the social order must fear for the belief in "legality" lest it be shaken by doubts of its legitimacy.

A president elected according to fixed rules can formally legitimize the governmental actions of the respective victorious party as "lawful," just as well as a parliamentary monarch. But the monarch, in addition to such legitimation, can perform a function which an elected president can not fulfil: a parliamentary monarch formally delimits the politicians' quest for power, because the highest position in the state is occupied once and for all. From a political point of view this essentially negative function, associated with the mere existence of a king enthroned according to fixed rules, is of the greatest practical importance. Formulated positively it means, for the archetype of the species, that the king cannot gain an actual share in political power by prerogative (kingdom of prerogative). He can share power only by virtue of outstanding personal ability or social influence (kingdom of influence). Yet he is in position to exert this influence in spite of all parliamentary government, as events and personalities of recent times have shown.

"Parliamentary" kingship in England means a selective admission to actual power for that monarch who qualifies as a statesman. But a misstep at home or in foreign affairs, or the raising of pretensions that do not correspond with his personal abilities and prestige, may cost him his crown. Thus English parliamentary kingship is formed in a more genuinely charismatic fashion than kingships on the Continent. On the Continent, mere birth-right equally endows the fool and the political genius with the pretensions of a sovereign.

Émile Durkheim

Émile Durkheim (1858–1917) was born in Lorraine in eastern France, the descendant of a long line of rabbis. Although Durkheim relinquished his roots in this provincial religious community, he devoted his intellectual life to studying, teaching, and making practical contributions to the sociology of moral life.

After a brilliant student career at the École Normale Supérieure in Paris, Durkheim spent five years teaching philosophy at high schools, then studied for a year in Germany, where he was impressed by the work of the psychologist Wilhelm Wundt. In 1887 a professorship of sociology (combined with education), the first in France, was created for him at Bordeaux. There he remained until 1902, when he received a professorship at the Sorbonne in Paris. At the Sorbonne, Durkheim gathered around himself a famed circle of younger men, including Marcel Granet; Maurice Halbwachs; and, not the least, his own nephew Marcel Mauss, and in close relation to his own work, founded and edited the influential journal, *L'anne sociologique*. In its pages the Durkheimians showed how social questions could be studied empirically, not simply discussed speculatively, so that reforms might be put on a solid footing and lifted out of the realm of interminable ideological dispute.

Durkheim became a prominent figure in Third Republic France. He participated in the Dreyfus controversy and was a tireless advocate of applied sociology, particularly in the field of education. Deeply attached to the new republican society yet conscious of the weak foundation on which it rested, Durkheim made it his mission to contribute to the development of a new French republican moral order that was neither capitalist, socialist, nor Catholic but that transcended all of these. A science of society, he wrote, "would have no worth at all" if it did not lend itself to practical application. Durkheim's commitment to republican ideals had a tragic aspect, however; the outbreak of the First World War shocked him severely, and in the next three years the war was to claim the lives of over half his students at the École Normale, including his own son. Durkheim died from a heart attack in 1917.

Suicide (1897) is a classic example of Durkheim's empirical method. On the surface, suicide appears to be the ultimate individual act. Yet Durkheim shifts attention away from psychological motives and shows that larger social conditions account for suicide. Put in the simplest terms, the freer the individual is from external restraints and the more isolated from group life, the more prone he or she is to suicide. Rates of suicide vary according to many characteristics of the populations involved—their nationality, religion, age, sex, social class, and so on. *In The Rules of Sociological Method* (1895) Durkheim calls these "social facts" because like physical things, they are external to the individual and constrain him. Unlike physical reality, however, society is powerful because it exists partly inside the individual, where as conscience it exerts moral authority over the self.

Durkheim's sensitivity to the problem of suicide dated back to his doctoral thesis, *The Division of Labor in Society* (1893). Here he laid out his famous thesis that social order cannot be accounted for by the utilitarian pursuit of self-interest but instead rests on an underlying solidarity that defines how people are to treat one another. Rousseau had called this solidarity "the general will," and Comte called it "consensus," but neither had attempted to study it empirically. In traditional societies, solidarity is relatively obvious; life is uniform and members share a common culture, a common sense of morality that Durkheim characterizes as "mechanical solidarity." In modern societies, with their intricate division of labor and their diverse and conflicting interests, common values are less obvious but present nevertheless. They exist at a more general level, are contestable, and must be applied to a myriad of new and unforeseen situations. This solidarity based upon differences Durkheim calls "organic." In his early work he equates it with people's sheer economic interdependence, which is said to endow them with feelings of purpose and mutual need and so can replace the intense and far more specific moral codes of the past. Over time, however, Durkheim became more pessimistic. Like a modern Rousseau, he warned that the "master institutions" of modern society—the capitalist economy and the bureaucratic state—threatened order more than they fostered it, destroying stable beliefs and afflicting persons with a sense of meaninglessness that he labeled "anomie." For the rest of his life Durkheim was to search for a moral foundation, for a "religion of individualism," that would be appropriate to a modern, highly differentiated, and individualistic society.

In the last phase of his career, this increasing emphasis on the moral needs of society led Durkheim to a fruitful study of religion and religious evolution. *In The Elementary Forms of Religious Life* (1912) he shows how closely integrated religious beliefs and practices are with the structure of society itself, not only in primitive societies but elsewhere as well. All religious symbols are actually symbols of society, that is, of moral unity, and the feelings of awe or reverence that we associate with the realm of the sacred are feelings of moral respect for society. Religious or cultural creativity is also a factor in change, Durkheim contends. The "effervescence" of collective celebrations and rites gives birth to ideas and symbols that redirect people's energies and provide new interpretations of the world.

Durkheim's influence has been immense, not only in sociology, where he ranks with Marx and Weber as one of the founders of the discipline, but in anthropology, social psychology, and history. In addition to the works already mentioned, he published a critique of socialism, *Socialism and Saint Simon* (1896); a political sociology, *Professional Ethics and Civic Morals* (1900); *Moral Education* (1906); and many essays on philosophy, including *Sociology and Pragmatism* (1914). Durkheim's use of statistics was pioneering for his time, and his concept of the *social fact*, his rigorous comparative method, and his functional style of analysis have been widely adopted. In more general terms, Durkheim's emphasis on society as a moral reality has served as a powerful critique of the reifying tendencies at work both within modern societies and in the social sciences that purport to describe them. With this emphasis, he rescued the crucial insights of traditional social philosophy and gave them empirical footing in an age of widespread cynicism and economic or psychological reductionism.

THE DIVISION OF LABOR IN SOCIETY

1893

VII ORGANIC SOLIDARITY AND CONTRACTUAL SOLIDARITY

I

It is true that in the industrial societies that Spencer speaks of, just as in organized societies, social harmony comes essentially from the division of labor. It is characterized by a co-operation which is automatically produced through the pursuit by each individual of his own interests. It suffices that each individual consecrate himself to a special function in order, by the force of events, to make himself solidary with others. Is this not the distinctive sign of organized societies?

But if Spencer has justly noted what the principal cause of social solidarity in higher societies is, he has misunderstood the manner in which this cause produces its effect, and, accordingly, misunderstood the nature of the latter.

In short, for him, industrial solidarity, as he calls it, presents the two following characters:

Since it is spontaneous, it does not require any coercive force either to produce or to maintain it. Society does not have to intervene to assure the harmony which is self-established. Spencer says that each man can maintain himself through his work, can exchange his produce for the goods of another, can lend assistance and receive payment, can enter into some association for pursuing some enterprise, small or large, without obeying the direction of society in its totality. The sphere of social action would thus grow narrower and narrower, for it would have no other object than that of keeping individuals from disturbing and harming one another. That is to say, it would have only a negative regulative force.

Under these conditions, the only remaining link between men would be that of an absolutely free exchange. As Spencer says, all industrial affairs take place through the medium of free exchange, and this relation becomes predominant in society in so far as individual activity becomes dominant. But the normal form of exchange is the contract. That is why in proportion to the decline of militarism and the ascendancy of industrialism, power as the gateway to authority becomes of less importance and free activity increases, and the relationship of contract becomes general. Finally, in the fully developed industrial type, this relationship becomes universal.

By that, Spencer does not mean that society always rests on an implicit or formal contract. The hypothesis of a social contract is irreconcilable with the notion of the division of labor. The greater the part taken by the latter, the more completely must Rousseau's postulate be renounced. For in order for such a contract to be possible, it is necessary that, at a given moment, all individual wills direct themselves toward the common bases of the social organization, and, consequently, that each particular conscience pose the political problem for itself in all its generality. But that would make it necessary for each individual to leave his special sphere, so that all might equally play the same role, that of statesman and constituents. Thus, this is the situation when society makes a contract: if adhesion is unanimous, the content of all consciences is identical. Then, in the measure that social solidarity proceeds from such a cause, it has no relation with the division of labor.

Nothing, however, less resembles the spontaneous, automatic solidarity which, according to Spencer, distinguishes industrial societies, for he sees, on the contrary, in this conscious pursuit of social ends the characteristic of military societies. Such a contract supposes that all individuals are able to represent in themselves the general conditions of the collective life in order to make a choice with knowledge. But Spencer understands that such a representation goes beyond the bounds of science in its actual state, and, consequently, beyond the bounds of conscience. He is so convinced of the vanity of reflection when it is applied to such matters that he wishes to take them away even from the legislator, to say nothing of submitting them to public opinion. He believes that social life, just as all life in general, can naturally organize itself only by an unconscious, spontaneous adaptation under the immediate pressure of needs, and not according to a rational plan of reflective intelligence. He does not believe that higher societies can be built according to a rigidly drawn program.

Thus, the conception of a social contract is today difficult to defend, for it has no relation to the facts. The observer does not meet it along his road, so to speak. Not only are there no societies which have such an origin, but there is none whose structure presents the least trace of a contractual organization. It is neither a fact acquired through history nor a tendency which grows out of historical development. Hence, to rejuvenate this doctrine and accredit it, it would be necessary to qualify as a contract the adhesion which each individual, as adult, gave to the society when he was born, solely by reason of which he continues to live. But then we would have to term contractual every action of man which is not determined by constraint. In this light, there is no society, neither present nor past, which is not or has not been contractual, for there is none which could exist solely through pressure. We have given the reason for this above. If it has sometimes been thought that force was greater previously than it is today, that is because of the illusion which attributes to a coercive regime the small place given over to individual liberty in lower societies. In reality, social life, wherever it is normal, is spontaneous, and if it is abnormal, it cannot endure. The individual abdicates spontaneously. In fact, it is unjust to speak of abdication where there is nothing to abdicate. If this large and somewhat warped interpretation is given to this word, no distinction can be made between different social types, and if we understand by type only the very defined juridical tie which the word designates, we can be sure that no tie of this kind has ever existed between individuals and society.

But if higher societies do not rest upon a fundamental contract which sets forth the general principles of political life, they would have, or would be considered to have, according to Spencer, the vast system of particular contracts which link individuals as a unique basis. They would depend upon the group only in proportion to their dependence upon one another, and they would depend upon one another only in proportion to conventions privately entered into and freely concluded. Social solidarity would then be nothing else than the spontaneous accord of individual interests, an accord of which contracts are the natural expression. The typical social relation would be the economic, stripped of all regulation and resulting from the entirely free initiative of the parties. In short, society would be solely the stage where individuals exchanged the products of their labor, without any action properly social coming to regulate this exchange.

Is this the character of societies whose unity is produced by the division of labor? If this were so, we could with justice doubt their stability. For if interest relates men, it is never for more than some few moments. It can create only an external link between them. In the fact of exchange, the various agents remain outside of each other, and when the business has been completed, each one retires and is left entirely on his own. Consciences are only superficially in contact; they neither penetrate each other, nor do they adhere. If we look further into the matter, we shall see that this total harmony of interests conceals a latent or deferred conflict. For where interest is the only ruling force each individual finds himself in a state of war with every other since nothing comes to mollify the egos, and any truce in this eternal antagonism would not be of long duration. There is nothing less constant than interest. Today, it unites me to you; tomorrow, it will make me your enemy. Such a cause can only give rise to transient relations and passing associations. We now understand how necessary it is to see if this is really the nature of organic solidarity.

In no respect, according to Spencer, does industrial society exist in a pure state. It is a partially ideal type which slowly disengages itself in the evolutionary process, but it has not yet been completely realized. Consequently, to rightly attribute to it the qualities we have just been discussing, we would have to establish systematically that societies appear in a fashion as complete as they are elevated, discounting cases of regression.

It is first affirmed that the sphere of social activity grows smaller and smaller, to the great advantage of the individual. But to prove this proposition by real instances, it is not enough to cite, as Spencer does, some cases where the individual has been effectively emancipated from collective influence. These examples, numerous as they may be, can serve only as illustrations, and are, by themselves, devoid of any demonstrative force. It is very possible that, in this respect, social action has regressed, but that, in other respects, it has been extended, and that, ultimately, we are mistaking a transformation for a disappearance. The only way of giving objective proof is not to cite some facts taken at random, but to follow historically, from its origins until recent times, the way in which social action has essentially manifested itself, and to see whether, in time, it has added or lost volume. We know that this is law. The obligations that society imposes upon its members, as inconsequential and unenduring as they may be, take on a juridical form. Consequently, the relative dimensions of this system permit us to measure with exactitude the relative extent of social action.

But it is very evident that, far from diminishing, it grows greater and greater and becomes more and more complex. The more primitive a code is, the smaller its volume. On the contrary, it is as large as it is more recent. There can be no doubt about this. To be sure, it does not result in making the sphere of individual activity smaller. We must not forget that if there is more regulation in life, there is more life in general. This is sufficient proof that social discipline has not been relaxing. One of its forms tends, it is true, to regress, as we have already seen, but others, much richer and much more complex, develop in its place. If repressive law loses ground, restitutive law, which originally did not exist at all, keeps growing. If society no longer imposes upon everybody certain uniform practices, it takes greater care to define and regulate the special relations between different social functions, and this activity is not smaller because it is different.

Spencer would reply that he had not insisted upon the diminution of every kind of control, but only of positive control. Let us admit this distinction. Whether it be positive or negative, the control is none the less social, and the principal question is to understand whether it has extended itself or contracted. Whether it be to command or to deny, to say *Do this* or *Do not do that*, if society intervenes more, we have not the right to say that individual spontaneity suffices more and more in all spheres. If the rules determining conduct have multiplied, whether they be imperative or prohibitive, it is not true that it depends more and more completely on private initiative.

But has this distinction itself any foundation? By positive control, Spencer means that which commands action, while negative control commands only abstention. As he says: A man has a piece of land; I cultivate it for him either wholly or in part, or else I impose upon him either wholly or in part the way in which he should cultivate it. This is a positive control. On the other hand, I give him neither aid nor advice about its cultivation; I simply do not molest my neighbor's crop, or trespass upon my neighbor's land, or put rubbish on his clearing. This is a negative control. The difference is very marked between ordering him to follow, as a citizen, a certain course, or suggesting means for the citizen to employ, and, on the other hand, not disturbing the course which some citizen is pursuing. If such is the meaning of these terms, then positive control is not disappearing.

We know, of course, that restitutive law is growing. But, in the large majority of cases, it either points out to a citizen the course he ought to pursue, or it interests itself in the means that this citizen is employing to attain his end. It answers the two following questions for each juridical relation: (1) Under what conditions and in what form does it normally exist? (2) What are the obligations it entails? The determination of the form and the conditions is essentially positive, since it forces the individual to follow a certain procedure in order to attain his end. As for the obligations, if they only forbid, in principle, our troubling another person in the exercise of his functions, Spencer's thesis would be true, at least in part. But they consist most often in the statement of services of a positive nature.

On this point we must go into some detail.

II

It is quite true that contractual relations, which originally were rare or completely absent, multiply as social labor becomes divided. But what Spencer seems to have failed to see is that non-contractual relations develop at the same time.

First, let us examine that part of law which is improperly termed private, and which, in reality, regulates diffuse social functions, or what may be called the visceral life of the social organism.

In the first place, we know that domestic law, as simple as it was in the beginning, has become more and more complex. That is to say, that the different species of juridical relations to which family life gives rise are much more numerous than heretofore. But the obligations which result from this are of an eminently positive nature; they constitute a reciprocity of rights and duties. Moreover, they are not contractual, at least in their typical form. The conditions upon which they are dependent are related to our personal status which, in turn, depends upon birth, on our consanguineous relations, and, consequently, upon facts which are beyond volition.

Marriage and adoption, however, are sources of domestic relations and they are contracts. But it rightly happens that the closer we get to the most elevated social types, the more also do these two juridical operations lose their properly contractual character.

Not only in lower societies, but in Rome itself until the end of the Empire, marriage remains an entirely private affair. It generally is a sale, real among primitive people, later fictive, but valid only through the consent of the parties duly attested. Neither solemn formalities of any kind nor intervention by some authority were then necessary. It is only with Christianity that marriage took on another character. The Christians early got into the habit of having their union consecrated by a priest. An act of the emperor Leo the Philosopher converted this usage into a law for the East. The Council of Trent sanctioned it likewise for the West. From then on, marriage ceased to be freely contracted, and was concluded through the intermediary of a public power, the Church, and the role that the Church played was not only that of a witness, but it was she and she alone who created the juridical tie which until then the wills of the participants sufficed to establish. We know how, later, the civil authority was substituted in this function for the religious authority, and how at the same time the part played by society and its necessary formalities was extended.

The history of the contract of adoption is still more instructive.

We have already seen with what facility and on what a large scale adoption was practiced among the Indian tribes of North America. It could give rise to all the forms of kinship. If the adopted was of the same age as the adopting, they became brothers and sisters; if the adopted was already a mother, she became the mother of the one who adopted her.

Among the Arabs, before Mohammed, adoption often served to establish real families. It frequently happened that several persons would mutually adopt one another. They then became brothers and sisters, and the kinship which united them was just as strong as if they had been descended from a common origin. We find the same type of adoption among the Slavs. Very often, the members of different families became brothers and sisters and formed what is called a confraternity (*pro-batinstvo*). These societies were contracted for freely and without formality; agreement was enough to establish them. Moreover, the tie which binds these elective brothers is even stronger than that which results from natural fraternity.

Among the Germans, adoption was probably quite as easy and frequent. Very simple ceremonies were enough to establish it. But in India, Greece, and Rome, it was already subordinated to determined conditions. The one adopting had to be of a certain age, could not stand in such relation to the age of the adopted that it would be impossible to be his natural father. Ultimately, this change of family became a highly complex juridical operation which necessitated the intervention of a magistrate. At the same time, the number of those who could enjoy the right of adoption became more restricted. Only the father of a family or a bachelor *sui juris* could adopt, and the first could, only if he had no legitimate children.

In our current law the restrictive conditions have been even more multiplied. The adopted must be of age, the adopting must be more than fifty years of age, and have long treated the adopted as his child. We must notice that, thus limited, it has become a very rare event. Before the appearance of the French Code, the whole procedure had almost completely fallen into disuse, and today it is, in certain countries such as Holland and lower Canada, not permitted at all.

At the same time, that it became more rare, adoption lost its efficacy. In the beginning, adoptive kinship was in all respects similar to natural kinship. In Rome, the similarity was still very great. It was no longer, however, a perfect identity. In the sixteenth century, the adopted no longer has the right of succession if the adoptive father dies intestate. The French Code has re-established this right, but the kinship to which the adoption gives rise does not extend beyond the adopting and the adopted.

We see how insufficient the traditional explanation is, which attributes this custom of adoption among ancient societies to the need of assuring the perpetuity of the ancestral cult. The peoples who have practiced it in the greatest and freest manner, as the Indians of America, the Arabs, the Slavs, had no such cult, and, furthermore, at Rome and Athens, where domestic religion was at its height, this law is for the first time submitted to control and restrictions. If it was able to satisfy these needs, it was not established to satisfy them, and, inversely, if it tends to disappear, it is not because we have less desire to perpetuate our name and our race. It is in the structure of actual societies and in the place which the family occupies that we must seek the determining cause for this change.

Another proof of the truth of this is that it has become even more impossible to leave a family by an act of private authority than to enter into it. As the kinship-tie does not result from a contract, it cannot be broken as a contract can. Among the Iroquois, we sometimes see a part of a clan leave to go to join a neighboring clan. Among the Slavs, a member of the Zadruga who is tired of the common life can separate himself from the rest of the family and become a juridical stranger to it, even as he can be excluded by it. Among the Germans, a ceremony of some slight complexity permitted every Frank who so desired to completely drop off all kinship-obligations. In Rome, the son could not leave the family of his own will, and by this sign we recognize a more elevated social type. But the tie that the son could not break could be broken by the father. Thus was emancipation possible. Today neither the father nor the son can alter the natural state of domestic relations. They remain as birth determines them.

In short, at the same time that domestic obligations become more numerous, they take on, as is said, a public character. Not only in early times do they not have a contractual origin, but the role which contract plays in them becomes ever smaller. On the contrary, social control over the manner in which they form, break down, and are modified, becomes greater. The reason lies in the progressive effacement of segmental organization. The family, in truth, is for a long time a veritable social segment. In origin, it confounds itself with the clan. If, later, it becomes distinguished from the clan, it is as a part of the whole. It is a product of a secondary segmentation of the clan, identical with that which has given birth to the clan itself, and when the latter has disappeared, it still keeps the same quality. But everything segmental tends to be more and more reabsorbed into the social mass. That is why the family is forced to transform itself. Instead of remaining an autonomous society along side of the great society, it becomes more and more involved in the system of social organs. It even becomes one of the organs, charged with special functions, and, accordingly, everything that happens within it is capable of general repercussions. That is what brings it about that the regulative organs of society are forced to intervene in order to exercise a moderating influence over the functioning of the family, or even, in certain cases, a positively arousing influence.

But it is not only outside of contractual relations, it is in the play of these relations themselves that social action makes itself felt. For everything in the contract is not contractual. The only engagements which deserve this name are those which have been desired by the individuals and which have no other origin except in this manifestation of free will. Inversely, every obligation which has not been mutually consented to has nothing contractual about it. But wherever a contract exists, it is submitted to regulation which is the work of society and not that of individuals, and which becomes ever more voluminous and more complicated.

It is true that the contracting parties can, in certain respects, arrange to act contrary to the dispositions of the law. But, of course, their rights in this regard are not unlimited. For example, the agreement of the parties cannot make a contract valid if it does not satisfy the conditions of validity required by law. To be sure, in the great majority of cases, a contract is no longer restricted to determined forms. Still it must not be forgotten that there are in our Codes solemn contracts. But if law no longer has the formal exigencies of yesterday, it subjects contracts to obligations of a different sort. It refuses all obligatory force to engagements contracted by an incompetent, or without object, or with illicit purpose, or made by a person who cannot sell, or transacted over an article which cannot be sold. Among the obligations which it attaches to various contracts, there are some which cannot be changed by any stipulation. Thus, a vendor cannot fail in his obligation to guarantee the purchaser against any eviction which results from something personal to the vendor (art. 1628); he cannot fail to repay the purchase-price in case of eviction, whatever its origin, provided that the buyer has not known of the danger (art. 1629), nor to set forth clearly what is being contracted for (art. 1602). Indeed, in a certain measure, he cannot be exempt from guaranteeing against hidden defects (arts. 1641 and 1643), particularly when known. If it is a question of fixtures, it is the buyer who must not profit from the situation by imposing a price too obviously below the real value of the thing (art. 1674), etc. Moreover, everything that relates to proof, the nature of the actions to which the contract gives a right, the time in which they must be begun, is absolutely independent of individual transactions.

In other cases social action does not manifest itself only by the refusal to recognize a contract formed in violation of the law, but by a positive intervention. Thus, the judge can, whatever the terms of the agreement, grant a delay to a debtor (arts. 1184, 1244, 1655, 1900), or even oblige the borrower to restore the article to the lender before the term agreed upon, if the latter has pressing need of it (art. 1189). But what shows better than anything else that contracts give rise to obligations which have not been contracted for is that they "make obligatory not only what there is expressed in them, but also all consequences which equity, usage, or the law imputes from the nature of the obligation" (art. 1135). In virtue of this principle, there must be supplied in the contract "clauses pertaining to usage, although they may not be expressed therein" (art. 1160).

But even if social action should not express itself in this way, it would not cease to be real. This possibility of derogating the law, which seems to reduce the contractual right to the role of eventual substitute for contracts properly called, is, in the very great majority of cases, purely theoretical. We can convince ourselves of this by showing what it consists in.

To be sure, when men unite in a contract, it is because, through the division of labor, either simple or complex, they need each other. But in order for them to co-operate harmoniously, it is not enough that they enter into a relationship, nor even that they feel the state of mutual dependence in which they find themselves. It is still necessary that the conditions of this co-operation be fixed for the duration of their relations. The rights and duties of each must be defined, not only in view of the situation such as it presents itself at the moment when the contract is made, but with foresight for the circumstances which may arise to modify it. Otherwise, at every instant, there would be conflicts and endless difficulties. We must not forget that, if the division of labor makes interests solidary, it does not confound them; it keeps them distinct and opposite. Even as in the internal workings of the individual organism each organ is in conflict with others while co-operating with them, each of the contractants, while needing the other, seeks to obtain what he needs at the least expense; that is to say, to acquire as many rights as possible in exchange for the smallest possible obligations.

It is necessary therefore to pre-determine the share of each, but this cannot be done according to a preconceived plan. There is nothing in the nature of things from which one can deduce what the obligations of one or the other ought to be until a certain limit is reached. Every determination of this kind can only result in compromise. It is a compromise between the rivalry of interests present and their solidarity. It is a position of equilibrium which can be found only after more or less laborious experiments. But it is quite evident that we can neither begin these experiments over again nor restore this equilibrium at fresh expense every time that we engage in some contractual relation. We lack all ability to do that. It is not at the moment when difficulties surge upon us that we must resolve them, and, moreover, we can neither foresee the variety of possible circumstances in which our contract will involve itself, nor fix in advance with the aid of simple mental calculus what will be in each case the rights and duties of each, save in matters in which we have a very definite experience. Moreover, the material conditions of life oppose themselves to the repetition of such operations. For, at each instant, and often at the most inopportune, we find ourselves contracting, either for something we have bought, or sold, somewhere we are traveling, our hiring of one's services, some acceptance of hostelry, etc. The greater part of our relations with others is of a contractual nature. If, then, it were necessary each time to begin the struggles anew, to again go through the conferences necessary to establish firmly all the conditions of agreement for the present and the future, we would be put to rout. For all these reasons, if we were linked only by the terms of our contracts, as they are agreed upon, only a precarious solidarity would result.

But contract-law is that which determines the juridical consequences of our acts that we have not determined. It expresses the normal conditions of equilibrium, as they arise from themselves or from the average. A résumé of numerous, varied experiences, what we cannot foresee individually is there provided for, what we cannot regulate is there regulated, and this regulation imposes itself upon us, although it may not be our handiwork, but that of society and tradition. It forces us to assume obligations that we have not contracted for, in the exact sense of the word, since we have not deliberated upon them, nor even, occasionally, had any knowledge about them in advance. Of course, the initial act is always contractual, but there are consequences, sometimes immediate, which run over the limits of the contract. We co-operate because we wish to, but our voluntary co-operation creates duties for us that we did not desire.

From this point of view, the law of contracts appears in an entirely different light. It is no longer simply a useful complement of individual conventions; it is their fundamental norm. Imposing itself upon us with the authority of traditional experience, it constitutes the foundation of our contractual relations. We cannot evade it, except partially and accidentally. The law confers its rights upon us and subjects us to duties deriving from such acts of our will. We can, in certain cases, abandon them or change them for others. But both are none the less the normal type of rights and duties which circumstance lays upon us, and an express act is necessary for their modification. Thus, modifications are relatively rare. In principle, the rule applies; innovations are exceptional. The law of contracts exercises over us a regulative force of the greatest importance, since it determines what we ought, to do and what we can require. It is a law which can be changed only by the consent of the parties, but so long as it is not abrogated or replaced, it guards its authority, and, moreover, a legislative act can be passed only in rare cases, There is, then, only a difference of degree between the law which regulates the obligations which that contract engenders and those which fix the other duties of citizens.

Finally, besides this organized, defined pressure which law exercises, there is one which comes from custom. In the way in which we make our contracts and in which we execute them, we are held to conform to rules which, though not sanctioned either directly or indirectly by any code, are none the less imperative. There are professional obligations, purely moral, which are, however, very strict. They are particularly apparent in the so-called liberal professions, and if they are perhaps less numerous in others, there is place for demanding them, as we shall see, if such demand is not the result of a morbid condition. But if this action is more diffuse than the preceding, it is just, as social. Moreover, it is necessarily as much more extended as the contractual relations are more developed, for it is diversified like contracts.

In sum, a contract is not sufficient unto itself, but is possible only thanks to a regulation of the contract which is originally social. It is implied, first, because it has for its function much less the creation of new rules than the diversification in particular cases of pre-established rules; then, because it has and can have the power to bind only under certain conditions which it is necessary to define. If, in principle, society lends it an obligatory force, it is because, in general, the accord of particular wills suffices to assure, with the preceding reservations, the harmonious coming together of diffuse social functions. But if it conflicts with social purposes, if it tends to trouble the regular operation of organs, if, as is said, it is not just, it, is necessary, while depriving it of all social value, to strip it of all authority as well. The role of society is not, then, in any case, simply to see passively that contracts are carried out. It is also to determine under what conditions they are executable, and if it is necessary, to restore them to their normal form. The agreement of parties cannot render a clause just which by itself is unjust, and there are rules of justice whose violation social justice prevents, even if it has been consented to by the interested parties.

A regulation whose extent cannot be limited in advance is thus necessary. A contract, says Spencer, has for its object assuring the worker the equivalent of the expense which his work has cost him. If such is truly the role of a contract, it will never be able to fulfill it unless it is more minutely regulated than it is today, for it surely would be a miracle if it succeeded in bringing about this equivalence. In fact, it is as much the gain which exceeds the expense, as the expense which exceeds the gain, and the disproportion is often striking. But, replies a whole school, if the gains are too small, the function will be abandoned for others. If they are too high, they will be sought after and this will diminish the profits. It is forgotten that one whole part of the population cannot thus quit its task, because no other is accessible to it. The very ones who have more liberty of movement cannot replace it in an instant. Such revolutions always take long to accomplish. While waiting, unjust contracts, unsocial by definition, have been executed with the agreement of society, and when the equilibrium in this respect has been reestablished, there is no reason for not breaking it for another.

There is no need for showing that this intervention, under its different forms, is of an eminently positive nature, since it has for its purpose the determination of the way in which we ought to co-operate. It is not it, it is true, which gives the impulse to the functions concurring, but once the concourse has begun, it rules it. As soon as we have made the first step towards co-operation, we are involved in the regulative action which society exercises over us. If Spencer qualified this as negative, it is because, for him, contract consists only in exchange. But, even from this point of view, the expression he employs is not exact. No doubt, when, after having an object delivered, or profiting from a service, I refuse to furnish a suitable equivalent, I take from another what belongs to him, and we can say that society, by obliging me to keep my promise, is only preventing an injury, an indirect aggression. But if I have simply promised a service without having previously received remuneration, I am not less held to keep my engagement. In this case, however, I do not enrich myself at the expense of another; I only refuse to be useful to him. Moreover, exchange, as we have seen, is not all there is to a contract. There is also the proper harmony of functions concurring. They are not only in contact for the short time during which things pass from one hand to another; but more extensive relations necessarily result from them, in the course of which it is important that their solidarity be not troubled.

Even the biological comparisons on which Spencer willingly bases his theory of free contract are rather the refutation of it. He compares, as we have done, economic functions to the visceral life of the individual organism, and remarks that the latter does not directly depend upon the cerebrospinal system, but upon a special system whose principal branches are the great sympathetic and the pneumogastric. But if from this comparison he is permitted to induce, with some probability, that economic functions are not of a kind to be placed under the immediate influence of the social brain, it does not follow that they can be freed of all regulative influences, for, if the great sympathetic is, in certain measure, independent of the brain, it dominates the movements of the visceral system just as the brain does those of the muscles. If, then, there is in society a system of the same kind, it must have an analogous action over the organs subject to it.

What corresponds to it, according to Spencer, is this exchange of information which takes place unceasingly from one place to another through supply and demand, and which, accordingly, stops or stimulates production. But there is nothing here which resembles a regulatory action. To transmit a new movement is not to command movements. This function pertains to the afferent nerves, but it has nothing in common with that of the nerve-ganglia. It is the latter which exercise the domination of which we have been speaking. Interposed in the path of sensations, it is exclusively through their mediation that the latter reflect themselves in movements. Very probably, if the study were more advanced, we would see that their role, whether they are central or not, is to assure the harmonious concourse of the functions that they govern, which would at every instant be disorganized if it had to vary with each variation of the excitatory impressions. The great social sympathetic must, then, comprise, besides a system of roads for transmission, organs truly regulative which, charged to combine the intestinal acts as the cerebral ganglion combines the external acts, would have the power either to stop the excitations, or to amplify them, or to moderate them according to need.

This comparison induces us to think that the regulative action to which economic life is actually submitted is not what it should normally be. Of course, it is not nil; we have just shown that. Either it is diffuse, or else it comes directly from the State. We will with difficulty find in contemporary societies regulative centres analogous to the ganglia of the great sympathetic. Assuredly, if this doubt had no other basis than the lack of symmetry between the individual and society, it would not merit any attention. But it must not be forgotten that up until recent times these intermediary organizations existed; they were the bodies of workers. We do not have to discuss here their advantages or disadvantages. Moreover, it is difficult to be objective about such discussion, for we cannot settle questions of practical utility without regard to personal feelings. But because of this fact alone, that an institution has been necessary to societies for centuries, it appears improbable that it should all at once fall away. No doubt, societies have changed, but it is legitimate to presume a priori that the changes through which they have passed demand less a radical destruction of this type of organization than a transformation. In any case, we have not lived under present conditions long enough to know if this state is normal and definitive or simply accidental and morbid. Even the uneasiness which is felt during this epoch in this sphere of social life does not seem to prejudge a favorable reply. We shall find in the rest of this work other facts which confirm this presumption.

. . .

IV

The following propositions sum up the first part of our work.

Social life comes from a double source, the likeness of consciences and the division of social labor.

The individual is socialized in the first case, because, not having any real individuality, he becomes, with those whom he resembles, part of the same collective type; in the second case, because, while having a physiognomy and a personal activity which distinguishes him from others, he depends upon them in the same measure that he is distinguished from them, and consequently upon the society which results from their union.

The similitude of consciences gives rise to juridical rules which, with the threat of repressive measures, impose uniform beliefs and practices upon all. The more pronounced this is, the more completely is social life confounded with religious life, and the nearer to communism are economic institutions.

The division of labor gives rise to juridical rules which determine the nature and the relations of divided functions, but whose violation calls forth only restitutive measures without any expiatory character.

Each of these bodies of juridical rules is, moreover, accompanied by a body of purely moral rules. Where penal law is very voluminous, common morality is very extensive; that is to say, there is a multitude of collective practices placed under the protection of public opinion. Where restitutive law is highly developed, there is an occupational morality for each profession. In the interior of the same group of workers, there exists an opinion, diffuse in the entire extent of this circumscribed aggregate, which, without being furnished with legal sanctions, is rendered obedience. There are usages and customs common to the same order of functionaries which no one of them can break without incurring the censure of the corporation. This morality is distinguished from the preceding by differences analogous to those which separate the two corresponding types of law. It is localized in a limited region of society. Moreover, the repressive character of the sanctions attaching to it is much less accentuated. Professional misdeeds call forth reprobation much more feeble than attacks against public morality.

The rules of occupational morality and justice, however, are as imperative as the others. They force the individual to act in view of ends which are not strictly his own, to make concessions, to consent to compromises, to take into account interests higher than his own. Consequently, even where society relies most completely upon the division of labor, it does not become a jumble of juxtaposed atoms, between which it can establish only external, transient contacts. Rather the members are united by ties which extend deeper and far beyond the short moments during which the exchange is made. Each of the functions that they exercise is, in a fixed way, dependent upon others, and with them forms a solidary system. Accordingly, from the nature of the chosen task permanent duties arise. Because we fill some certain domestic or social function, we are involved in a complex of obligations from which we have no right to free ourselves. There is, above all, an organ upon which we are tending to depend more and more; this is the State. The points at which we are in contact with it multiply as do the occasions when it is entrusted with the duty of reminding us of the sentiment of common solidarity.

Thus, altruism is not destined to become, as Spencer desires, a sort of agreeable ornament to social life, but it will forever be its fundamental basis. How can we ever really dispense with it? Men cannot live together without acknowledging, and, consequently, making mutual sacrifices, without tying themselves to one another with strong, durable bonds. Every society is a moral society. In certain respects, this character is even more pronounced in organized societies. Because the individual is not sufficient unto himself, it is from society that he receives everything necessary to him, as it is for society that he works. Thus is formed a very strong sentiment of the state of dependence in which he finds himself. He becomes accustomed to estimating it at its just value, that is to say, in regarding himself as part of a whole, the organ of an organism. Such sentiments naturally inspire not only mundane sacrifices which assure the regular development of daily social life, but even, on occasion, acts of complete self-renunciation and wholesale abnegation. On its side, society learns to regard its members no longer as things over which it has rights, but as co-operators whom it cannot neglect and towards whom it owes duties. Thus, it is wrong to oppose a society which comes from a community of beliefs to one which has a co-operative basis, according only to the first a moral character, and seeing in the latter only an economic grouping. In reality, co-operation also has its intrinsic morality. There is, however, reason to believe, as we shall see later, that in contemporary societies this morality has not yet reached the high development which would now seem necessary to it.

But it is not of the same nature as the other. The other is strong only if the individual is not. Made up of rules which are practiced by all indistinctly, it receives from this universal, uniform practice an authority which bestows something superhuman upon it, and which puts it beyond the pale of discussion. The co-operative society, on the contrary, develops in the measure that individual personality becomes stronger. As regulated as a function may be, there is a large place always left for personal initiative. A great many of the obligations thus sanctioned have their origin in a choice of the will. It is we who choose our professions, and even certain of our domestic functions. Of course, once our resolution has ceased to be internal and has been externally translated by social consequences, we are tied down. Duties are imposed upon us that we have not expressly desired. It is, however, through a voluntary act that this has taken place. Finally, because these rules of conduct relate, not to the conditions of common life, but to the different forms of professional activity, they have a more temporal character, which, while lessening their obligatory force, renders them more accessible to the action of men.

There are, then, two great currents of social life to which two types of structure, not less different, correspond.

Of these currents, that which his its origin in social similitudes first runs on alone and without a rival. At this moment, it confounds itself with the very life of society; then, little by little, it canalizes, rarefies, while the second is always growing. Indeed, the segmental structure is more and more covered over by the other, but without ever completely disappearing.

We have just established the reality of this relation of inverse variation. We shall find the causes for it in the following book.

. . .

CONCLUSION

I

We are now in a position to solve the practical problem that we posed for ourselves at the beginning of this work.

If there is one rule of conduct which is incontestable, it is that which orders us to realize in ourselves the essential traits of the collective type. Among lower peoples, this reaches its greatest rigor. There, one's first duty is to resemble everybody else, not to have anything personal about one's beliefs or actions. In more advanced societies, required likenesses are less numerous; the absences of some likenesses, however, is still a sign of moral failure. Of course, crime falls into fewer different categories; but today, as heretofore, if a criminal is the object of reprobation, it is because he is unlike us. Likewise, in lesser degree, acts simply immoral and prohibited as such are those which evince dissemblances less profound but nevertheless considered serious. Is this not the case with the rule which common morality expresses when it orders a man to be a man in every sense of the word, which is to say, to have all the ideas and sentiments which go to make up a human conscience? No doubt, if this formula is taken literally, the man prescribed would be man in general and not one of some particular social species. But, in reality, this human conscience that we must integrally realize is nothing else than the collective conscience of the group of which we are a part. For what can it be composed of, if not the ideas and sentiments to which we are most attached? Where can we find the traits of our model, if not within us and around us? If we believe that this collective ideal is that of all humanity, that is because it has become so abstract and general that it appears fitting for all men indiscriminately. But, really, every people makes for itself some particular conception of this type which pertains to its personal temperament. Each represents it in its own image. Even the moralist who thinks he can, through thought, overcome the influence of transient ideas, cannot do so, for he is impregnated with them, and no matter what he does, he finds these precepts in the body of his deductions. That is why each nation has its own school of moral philosophy conforming to its character.

On the other hand, we have shown that this rule had as its function the prevention of all agitation of the common conscience, and, consequently, of social solidarity, and that it could accomplish this role only by having a moral character. It is impossible for offenses against the most fundamental collective sentiments to be tolerated without the disintegration of society, and it is necessary to combat them with the aid of the particularly energetic reaction which attaches to moral rules.

But the contrary rule, which orders us to specialize, has exactly the same function. It also is necessary for the cohesion of societies, at least at a certain period in their evolution. Of course, its solidarity is different from the preceding, but though it is different, it is no less indispensable. Higher societies can maintain themselves in equilibrium only if labor is divided; the attraction of like for like less and less suffices to produce this result. If, then, the moral character of the first of these rules is necessary to the playing of its role, it is no less necessary to the second. They both correspond to the same social need, but satisfy the need differently, because the conditions of existence in the societies themselves differ. Consequently, without speculating concerning the first principle of ethics, we can induce the moral value of one from the moral value of the other. If, from certain points of view, there is a real antagonism between them, that is not because they serve different ends. On the contrary, it is because they lead to the same end, but through opposed means. Accordingly, there is no necessity for choosing between them once for all nor of condemning one in the name of the other. What is necessary is to give each, at each moment in history, the place that is fitting to it.

Perhaps we can even generalize further in this matter.

The requirements of our subject have obliged us to classify moral rules and to review the principal types. We are thus in a better position than we were in the beginning to see, or at least to conjecture, not only upon the external sign, but also upon the internal character which is common to all of them and which can serve to define them. We have put them into two groups: rules with repressive sanctions, which may be diffuse or organized, and rules with restitutive sanctions. We have seen that the first of these express the conditions of the solidarity, *sui generis*, which comes from resemblances, and to which we have given the name mechanical; the second, the conditions of negative solidarity and organic solidarity. We can thus say that, in general, the characteristic of moral rules is that they enunciate the fundamental conditions of social solidarity. Law and morality are the totality of ties which bind each of us to society, which make a unitary, coherent aggregate of the mass of individuals. Everything which is a source of solidarity is moral, everything which forces man to take account of other men is moral, everything which forces him to regulate his conduct through something other than the striving of his ego is moral, and morality is as solid as these ties are numerous and strong. We can see how inexact it is to define it, as is often done, through liberty. It rather consists in a state of dependence. Far from serving to emancipate the individual, or disengaging him from the environment which surrounds him, it has, on the contrary, the function of making him an integral part of a whole, and, consequently, of depriving him of some liberty of movement. We sometimes, it is true, come across people not without nobility who find the idea of such dependence intolerable. But that is because they do not perceive the source from which their own morality flows, since these sources are very deep. Conscience is a bad judge of what goes on in the depths of a person, because it does not penetrate to them.

Society is not, then, as has often been thought, a stranger to the moral world, or something which has only secondary repercussions upon it. It is, on the contrary, the necessary condition of its existence. It is not a simple juxtaposition of individuals who bring an intrinsic morality with them, but rather man is a moral being only because he lives in society, since morality consists in being solidary with a group and varying with this solidarity. Let all social life disappear, and moral life will disappear with it, since it would no longer have any objective. The state of nature of the philosophers of the eighteenth century, if not immoral, is, at least, *amoral*. Rousseau himself recognized this. Through this, however, we do not come upon the formula which expresses morality as a function of social interest. To be sure, society cannot exist if its parts are not solidary, but solidarity is only one of its conditions of existence. There are many others which are no less necessary and which are not moral. Moreover, it can happen that, in the system of ties which make up morality, there are some which are not useful in themselves or which have power without any relation to their degree of utility. The idea of utility does not enter as an essential element in our definition.

As for what is called individual morality, if we understand by that a totality of duties of which the individual would, at the same time, be subject and object, and which would link him only to himself, and which would, consequently, exist even if he were solitary, —that is an abstract conception which has no relation to reality. Morality, in all its forms, is never met with except in society. It never varies except in relation to social conditions. To ask what it would be if societies did not exist is thus to depart from facts and enter the domain of gratuitous hypotheses and unverifiable flights of the imagination. The duties of the individual towards himself are, in reality, duties towards society. They correspond to certain collective sentiments which he cannot offend, whether the offended and the offender are one and the same person, or whether they are distinct. Today, for example, there is in all healthy consciences a very lively sense of respect for human dignity, to which we are supposed to conform as much in our relations with ourselves as in our relations with others, and this constitutes the essential quality of what is called individual morality. Every act which contravenes this is censured, even when the agent and the sufferer are the same person. That is why, according to the Kantian formula, we ought to respect human personality wherever we find it, which is to say, in ourselves as in those like us. The sentiment of which it is the object is not less offended in one case than in the other.

But not only does the division of labor present the character by which we have defined morality; it more and more tends to become the essential condition of social solidarity. As we advance in the evolutionary scale, the ties which bind the individual to his family, to his native soil, to traditions which the past has given to him, to collective group usages, become loose. More mobile, he changes his environment more easily, leaves his people to go elsewhere to live a more autonomous existence, to a greater extent forms his own ideas and sentiments. Of course, the whole common conscience does not, on this account, pass out of existence. At least there will always remain this cult of personality, of individual dignity of which we have just been speaking, and which, today, is the rallying-point of so many people. But how little a thing it is when one contemplates the ever increasing extent of social life, and, consequently, of individual consciences! For, as they become more voluminous, as intelligence becomes richer, activity more varied, in order for morality to remain constant, that is to say, in order for the individual to remain attached to the group with a force equal to that of yesterday, the ties which bind him to it must become stronger and more numerous. If, then, he formed no others than those which come from resemblances, the effacement of the segmental type would be accompanied by a systematic debasement of morality. Man would no longer be sufficiently obligated; he would no longer feel about and above him this salutary pressure of society which moderates his egoism and makes him a moral being. This is what gives moral value to the division of labor. Through it, the individual becomes cognizant of his dependence upon society; from it come the forces which keep him in check and restrain him. In short, since the division of labor becomes the chief source of social solidarity, it becomes, at the same time, the foundation of the moral order.

We can then say that, in higher societies, our duty is not to spread our activity over a large surface, but to concentrate and specialize it. We must contract our horizon, choose a definite task and immerse ourselves in it completely, instead of trying to make ourselves a sort of creative masterpiece, quite complete, which contains its worth in itself and not in the services that it renders. Finally, this specialization ought to be pushed as far as the elevation of the social type, without assigning any other limit to it. No doubt, we ought so to work as to realize in ourselves the collective type as it exists. There are common sentiments, common ideas, without which, as has been said, one is not a man. The rule which orders us to specialize remains limited by the contrary rule. Our conclusion is not that it is good to press specialization as far as possible, but as far as necessary. As for the part that is to be played by these two opposing necessities, that is determined by experience and cannot be calculated a priori. It is enough for us to have shown that the second is not of a different nature from the first, but that it also is moral, and that, moreover, this duty becomes ever more important and pressing, because the general qualities which are in question suffice less and less to socialize the individual.

It is not without reason that public sentiment reproves an ever more pronounced tendency on the part of dilettantes and even others to be taken up with an exclusively general culture and refuse to take any part in occupational organization. That is because they are not sufficiently attached to society, or, if one wishes, society is not sufficiently attached to them, and they escape it. Precisely because they feel its effect neither with vivacity nor with the continuity that is necessary, they have no cognizance of all the obligations their positions, as social beings demand of them. The general ideal to which they are attached being, for the reasons we have spoken of, formal and shifting, it cannot take them out of themselves. We do not cling to very much when we have no very determined objective, and, consequently, we cannot very well elevate ourselves beyond a more or less refined egotism. On the contrary, he who gives himself over to a definite task is, at every moment, struck by the sentiment of common solidarity in the thousand duties of occupational morality.

II

But does not the division of labor by making each of us an incomplete being bring on a diminution of individual personality? That is a reproach which has often been levelled at it.

Let us first of all remark that it is difficult to see why it would be more in keeping with the logic of human nature to develop superficially rather than profoundly. Why would a more extensive activity, but more dispersed, be superior to a more concentrated, but circumscribed, activity? Why would there be more dignity in being complete and mediocre, rather than in living a more specialized, but more intense life, particularly if it is thus possible for us to find what we have lost in this specialization, through our association with other beings who have what we lack and who complete us? We take off from the principle that man ought to realize his nature as man, to accomplish his *ὀικεῖον ἔργον*, as Aristotle said. But this nature does not remain constant throughout history; it is modified with societies. Among lower peoples, the proper duty of man is to resemble his companions, to realize in himself all the traits of the collective type which are then confounded, much more than today, with the human type. But, in more advanced societies, his nature is, in large part, to be an organ of society, and his proper duty, consequently, is to play his role as an organ.

Moreover, far from being trammelled by the progress of specialization, individual personality develops with the division of labor.

To be a person is to be an autonomous source of action. Man acquires this quality only in so far as there is something in him which is his alone and which individualizes him, as he is something more than a simple incarnation of the generic type of his race and his group. It will be said that he is endowed with free will and that is enough to establish his personality. But although there may be some of this liberty in him, an object of so many discussions, it is not this metaphysical, impersonal, invariable attribute which can serve as the unique basis for concrete personality, which is empirical and variable with individuals. That could not be constituted by the wholly abstract power of choice between two opposites, but it is still necessary for this faculty to be exercised towards ends and aims which are proper to the agent. In other words, the very materials of conscience must have a personal character. But we have seen in the second book of this work that this result is progressively produced as the division of labor progresses. The effacement of the segmental type, at the same time that it necessitates a very great specialization, partially lifts the individual conscience from the organic environment which supports it, as from the social environment which envelops it, and, accordingly, because of this double emancipation, the individual becomes more of an independent factor in his own conduct. The division of labor itself contributes to this enfranchisement, for individual natures, while specializing, become more complex, and by that are in part freed from collective action and hereditary influences which can only enforce themselves upon simple, general things.

It is, accordingly, a real illusion which makes us believe that personality was so much more complete when the division of labor had penetrated less. No doubt, in looking from without at the diversity of occupations which the individual then embraces, it may seem that he is developing in a very free and complete manner. But, in reality, this activity which he manifests is not really his. It is society, it is the race acting in and through him; he is only the intermediary through which they realize themselves. His liberty is only apparent and his personality borrowed. Because the life of these societies is, in certain respects, less regular, we imagine that original talents have more opportunity for free play, that it is easier for each one to pursue his own tastes, that a very large place is left to free fantasy. But this is to forget that personal sentiments are then very rare. If the motives which govern conduct do not appear as periodically as they do today, they do not leave off being collective, and, consequently, impersonal, and it is the same with the actions that they inspire. Moreover, we have shown above how activity becomes richer and more intense as it becomes more specialized.

Thus, the progress of individual personality and that of the division of labor depend upon one and the same cause. It is thus impossible to desire one without desiring the other. But no one today contests the obligatory character of the rule which orders us to be more and more of a person.

One last consideration will make us see to what extent the division of labor is linked with our whole moral life.

Men have long dreamt of finally realizing in fact the ideal of human fraternity. People pray for a state where war will no longer be the law of international relations, where relations between societies will be pacifically regulated, as those between individuals already are, where all men will collaborate in the same work and live the same life. Although these aspirations are in part neutralized by those which have as their object the particular society of which we are a part, they have not left off being active and are even gaining in force. But they can be satisfied only if all men form one society, subject to the same laws. For, just as private conflicts can be regulated only by the action of the society in which the individuals live, so intersocial conflicts can be regulated only by a society which comprises in its scope all others. The only power which can serve to moderate individual egotism is the power of the group; the only power which can serve to moderate the egotism of groups is that of some other group which embraces them.

Truly, when the problem has been posed in these terms, we must recognize that this ideal is not on the verge of being integrally realized, for there are too many intellectual and moral diversities between different social types existing together on the earth to admit of fraternalization in the same society. But what is possible is that societies of the same type may come together, and it is, indeed, in this direction that evolution appears to move. We have already seen that among European peoples there is a tendency to form, by spontaneous movement, a European society which has, at present, some idea of itself and the beginning of organization. If the formation of a single human society is forever impossible, a fact which has not been proved, at least the formation of continually larger societies brings us vaguely near the goal. These facts, moreover, in no wise contradict the definition of morality that we have given, for if we cling to humanity and if we ought to cling to it, it is because it is a society which is in process of realizing itself in this way, and with which we are solidary.

But we know that greater societies cannot be formed except through the development of the division of labor, for not only could they not maintain themselves in equilibrium without a greater specialization of functions, but even the increase in the number of those competing would suffice to produce this result mechanically; and that, so much the more, since the growth of volume is generally accompanied by a growth in density. We can then formulate the following proposition: the ideal of human fraternity can be realized only in proportion to the progress of the division of labor. We must choose: either to renounce our dream; if we refuse further to circumscribe our activity, or else to push forward its accomplishment under the condition we have just set forth.

III

But if the division of labor produces solidarity, it is not only because it makes each individual an *exchangist*, as the economists say; it is because it creates among men an entire system of rights and duties which link them together in a durable way. Just as social similitudes give rise to a law and a morality which protect them, so the division of labor gives rise to rules which assure pacific and regular concourse of divided functions. If economists have believed that it would bring forth an abiding solidarity, in some manner of its own making, and if, accordingly, they have held that human societies could and would resolve themselves into purely economic associations, that is because they believed that it affected only individual, temporary interests. Consequently, to estimate the interests in conflict and the way in which they ought to equilibrate, that is to say, to determine the conditions under which exchange ought to take place, is solely a matter of individual competence; and, since these interests are in a perpetual state of becoming, there is no place for any permanent regulation. But such a conception is, in all ways, inadequate for the facts. The division of labor does not present individuals to one another, but social functions. And society is interested in the play of the latter; in so far as they regularly concur, or do not concur, it will be healthy or ill. Its existence thus depends upon them, and the more they are divided the greater its dependence. That is why it cannot leave them in a state of indetermination. In addition to this, they are determined by themselves. Thus are formed those rules whose number grows as labor is divided, and whose absence makes organic solidarity either impossible or imperfect.

But it is not enough that there be rules; they must be just, and for that it is necessary for the external conditions of competition to be equal. If, moreover, we remember that the collective conscience is becoming more and more a cult of the individual, we shall see that what characterizes the morality of organized societies, compared to that of segmental societies, is that there is something more human, therefore more rational, about them. It does not direct our activities to ends which do not immediately concern us; it does not make us servants of ideal powers of a nature other than our own, which follow their directions without occupying themselves with the interests of men. It only asks that we be thoughtful of our fellows and that we be just, that we fulfill our duty, that we work at the function we can best execute, and receive the just reward for our services. The rules which constitute it do not have a constraining force which snuffs out free thought; but, because they are rather made for us and, in a certain sense, by us, we are free. We wish to understand them; we do not fear to change them. We must, however, guard against finding such an ideal inadequate on the pretext that it is too earthly and too much to our liking. An ideal is not more elevated because more transcendent, but because it leads us to vaster perspectives. What is important is not that it tower high above us, until it becomes a stranger to our lives, but that it open to our activity a large enough field. This is far from being on the verge of realization. We know only too well what a laborious work it is to erect this society where each individual will have the place he merits, will be rewarded as he deserves, where everybody, accordingly, will spontaneously work for the good of all and of each. Indeed, a moral code is not above another because it commands in a drier and more authoritarian manner, or because it is more sheltered from reflection. Of course, it must attach us to something besides ourselves but it is not necessary for it to chain us to it with impregnable bonds.

It has been said with justice that morality—and by that must be understood, not only moral doctrines, but customs—is going through a real crisis. What precedes can help us to understand the nature and causes of this sick condition. Profound changes have been produced in the structure of our societies in a very short time; they have been freed from the segmental type with a rapidity and in proportions such as have never before been seen in history. Accordingly, the morality which corresponds to this social type has regressed, but without another developing quickly enough to fill the ground that the first left vacant in our consciences. Our faith has been troubled; tradition has lost its sway; individual judgment has been freed from collective judgment. But, on the other hand, the functions which have been disrupted in the course of the upheaval have not had the time to adjust themselves to one another; the new life which has emerged so suddenly has not been able to be completely organized, and above all, it has not been organized in a way to satisfy the need for justice which has grown more ardent in our hearts. If this be so, the remedy for the evil is not to seek to resuscitate traditions and practices which, no longer responding to present conditions of society, can only live an artificial, false existence. What we must do to relieve this anomy is to discover the means for making the organs which are still wasting themselves in discordant movements harmoniously concur by introducing into their relations more justice by more and more extenuating the external inequalities which are the source of the evil. Our illness is not, then, as has often been believed, of an intellectual sort; it has more profound causes. We shall not suffer because we no longer know on what theoretical notion to base the morality we have been practicing, but because, in certain of its parts, this morality is irremediably shattered, and that which is necessary to us is only in process of formation. Our anxiety does not arise because the criticism of scholars has broken down the traditional explanation we use to give to our duties; consequently, it is not a new philosophical system which will relieve the situation. Because certain of our duties are no longer founded in the reality of things, a breakdown has resulted which will be repaired only in so far as a new discipline is established and consolidated. In short, our first duty is to make a moral code for ourselves. Such a work cannot be improvised in the silence of the study; it can arise only through itself, little by little, under the pressure of internal causes which make it necessary. But the service that thought can and must render is in fixing the goal that we must attain. That is what we have tried to do.

THE ELEMENTARY FORMS OF THE RELIGIOUS LIFE

1912

CONCLUSION

At the beginning of this work we announced that the religion whose study we were taking up contained within it the most characteristic elements of the religious life. The exactness of this proposition may now be verified. Howsoever simple the system which we have studied may be, we have found within it all the great ideas and the principal ritual attitudes which are at the basis of even the most advanced religions; the division of things into sacred and profane, the notions of the soul, of spirits, of mythical personalities, and of a national and even international divinity, a negative cult with ascetic practices which are its exaggerated form, rites of oblation and communion, imitative rites, commemorative rites and expiatory rites; nothing essential is lacking. We are thus in a position to hope that the results at which we have arrived are not peculiar to totemism alone, but can aid us in an understanding of what religion in general is.

It may be objected that one single religion, whatever its field of extension may be, is too narrow a base for such an induction. We have not dreamed for a moment of ignoring the fact that an extended verification may add to the authority of a theory, but it is equally true that when a law has been proven by one well-made experiment, this proof is valid universally. If in one single case a scientist succeeded in finding out the secret of the life of even the most protoplasmic creature that can be imagined, the truths thus obtained would be applicable to all living beings, even the most advanced. Then if, in our studies of these very humble societies, we have really succeeded in discovering some of the elements out of which the most fundamental religious notions are made up, there is no reason for not extending the most general results of our researches to other religions. In fact, it is inconceivable that the same effect may be due now to one cause, now to another, according to the circumstances, unless the two causes are at bottom only one. A single idea cannot express one reality here and another one there, unless the duality is only apparent. If among certain peoples the ideas of sacredness, the soul and God are to be explained sociologically, it should be presumed scientifically that, in principle, the same explanation is valid for all the peoples among whom these same ideas are found with the same essential characteristics. Therefore, supposing that we have not been deceived, certain at least of our conclusions can be legitimately generalized. The moment has come to disengage these. And an induction of this sort, having at its foundation a clearly defined experiment, is less adventurous than many summary generalizations which, while attempting to reach the essence of religion at once, without resting upon the careful analysis of any religion in particular, greatly risk losing themselves in space.

I

The theorists who have undertaken to explain religion in rational terms have generally seen in it before all else a system of ideas, corresponding to some determined object. This object has been conceived in a multitude of ways: nature, the infinite, the unknowable, the ideal, etc.; but these differences matter but little. In any case, it was the conceptions and beliefs which were considered as the essential elements of religion. As for the rites, from this point of view they appear to be only an external translation, contingent and material, of these internal states which alone pass as having any intrinsic value. This conception is so commonly held that generally the disputes of which religion is the theme turn about the question whether it can conciliate itself with science or not, that is to say, whether or not there is a place beside our scientific knowledge for another form of thought which would be specifically religious.

But the believers, the men who lead the religious life and have a direct sensation of what it really is, object to this way of regarding it, saying that it does not correspond to their daily experience. In fact, they feel that the real function of religion is not to make us think, to enrich our knowledge, nor to add to the conceptions which we owe to science others of another origin and another character, but rather, it is to make us act, to aid us to live. The believer who has communicated with his god is not merely a man who sees new truths of which the unbeliever is ignorant; he is a man who is *stronger*. He feels within him more force, either to endure the trials of existence, or to conquer them. It is as though he were raised above the miseries of the world, because he is raised above his condition as a mere man; he believes that he is saved from evil, under whatever form he may conceive this evil. The first article in every creed is the belief in salvation by faith. But it is hard to see how a mere idea could have this efficacy. An idea is in reality only a part of ourselves; then how could it confer upon us powers superior to those which we have of our own nature? Howsoever rich it might be in affective virtues, it could add nothing to our natural vitality; for it could only release the motive powers which are within us, neither creating them nor increasing them. From the mere fact that we consider an object worthy of being loved and sought after, it does not follow that we feel ourselves stronger afterwards; it is also necessary that this object set free energies superior to these which we ordinarily have at our command and also that we have some means of making these enter into us and unite themselves to our interior lives. Now for that, it is not enough that we think of them; it is also indispensable that we place ourselves within their sphere of action, and that we set ourselves where we may best feel their influence; in a word, it is necessary that we act, and that we repeat the acts thus necessary every time we feel the need of renewing their effects. From this point of view, it is readily seen how that group of regularly repeated acts which form the cult get their importance. In fact, whoever has really practised a religion knows very well that it is the cult which gives rise to these impressions of joy, of interior peace, of serenity, of enthusiasm which are, for the believer, an experimental proof of his beliefs. The cult is not simply a system of signs by which the faith is outwardly translated; it is a collection of the means by which this is created and recreated periodically. Whether it consists in material acts or mental operations, it is always this which is efficacious.

Our entire study rests upon this postulate that the unanimous sentiment of the believers of all times cannot be purely illusory. Together with a recent apologist of the faith we admit that these religious beliefs rest upon a specific experience whose demonstrative value is, in one sense, not one bit inferior to that of scientific experiments, though different from them. We, too, think that "a tree is known by its fruits," and that fertility is the best proof of what the roots are worth. But from the fact that a "religious experience," if we choose to call it this, does exist and that it has a certain foundation —and, by the way, is there any experience which has none?—it does not follow that the reality which is its foundation conforms objectively to the idea which believers have of it. The very fact that the fashion in which it has been conceived has varied infinitely in different times is enough to prove that none of these conceptions express it adequately. If a scientist states it as an axiom that the sensations of heat and light which we feel correspond to some objective cause, he does not conclude that this is what it appears to the senses to be. Likewise, even if the impressions which the faithful feel are not imaginary, still they are in no way privileged intuitions; there is no reason for believing that they inform us better upon the nature of their object than do ordinary sensations upon the nature of bodies and their properties. In order to discover what this object consists of, we must submit them to an examination and elaboration analogous to that which has susbstituted for the sensuous idea of the world another which is scientific and conceptual.

This is precisely what we have tried to do, and we have seen that this reality, which mythologies have represented under so many different forms, but which is the universal and eternal objective cause of these sensations *sui generis* out of which religious experience is made, is society. We have shown what moral forces it develops and how it awakens this sentiment of a refuge, of a shield and of a guardian support which attaches the believer to his cult. It is that which raises him outside himself; it is even that which made him. For that which makes a man is the totality of the intellectual property which constitutes civilization, and civilization is the work of society. This is explained the preponderating rôle of the cult in all religions, whichever they may be. This is because society cannot make its influence felt unless it is in action, and it is not in action unless the individuals who compose it are assembled together and act in common. It is by common action that it takes consciousness of itself and realizes its position; it is before all else an active co-operation. The collective ideas and sentiments are even possible only owing to these exterior movements which symbolize them, as we have established. Then it is action which dominates the religious life, because of the mere fact that it is society which is its source.

In addition to all the reasons which have been given to justify this conception, a final one may be added here, which is the result of our whole work. As we have progressed, we have established the fact that the fundamental categories of thought, and consequently of science, are of religious origin. We have seen that the same is true for magic and consequently for the different processes which have issued from it. On the other hand, it has long been known that up until a relatively advanced moment of evolution, moral and legal rules have been indistinguishable from ritual prescriptions. In summing up, then, it may be said that nearly all the great social institutions have been born in religion. Now in order that these principal aspects of the collective life may have commenced by being only varied aspects of the religious life, it is obviously necessary that the religious life be the eminent form and, as it were, the concentrated expression of the whole collective life. If religion has given birth to all that is essential in society, it is because the idea of society is the soul of religion.

Religious forces are therefore human forces, moral forces. It is true that since collective sentiments can become conscious of themselves only by fixing themselves upon external objects, they have not been able to take form without adopting some of their characteristics from other things: they have thus acquired a sort of physical nature; in this way they have come to mix themselves with the life of the material world, and then have considered themselves capable of explaining what passes there. But when they are considered only from this point of view and in this rôle, only their most superficial aspect is seen. In reality, the essential elements of which these collective sentiments are made have been borrowed by the understanding. It ordinarily seems that they should have a human character only when they are conceived under human forms; but even the most impersonal and the most anonymous are nothing else than objectified sentiments.

It is only by regarding religion from this angle that it is possible to see its real significance. If we stick closely to appearances, rites often give the effect of purely manual operations: they are anointings, washings, meals. To consecrate something, it is put in contact with a source of religious energy, just as to-day a body is put in contact with a source of heat or electricity to warm or electrize it; the two processes employed are not essentially different. Thus understood, religious technique seems to be a sort of mystic mechanics. But these material manœuvres are only the external envelope under which the mental operations are hidden. Finally, there is no question of exercising a physical constraint upon blind and, incidentally, imaginary forces, but rather of reaching individual consciousnesses of giving them a direction and of disciplining them. It is sometimes said that inferior religions are materialistic. Such an expression is inexact. All religions, even the crudest, are in a sense spiritualistic: for the powers they put in play are before all spiritual, and also their principal object is to act upon the moral life. Thus it is seen that whatever has been done in the name of religion cannot have been done in vain: for it is necessarily the society that did it, and it is humanity that has reaped the fruits.

But, it is said, what society is it that has thus made the basis of religion? Is it the real society, such as it is and acts before our very eyes, with the legal and moral organization which it has laboriously fashioned during the course of history? This is full of defects and imperfections. In it, evil goes beside the good, injustice often reigns supreme, and the truth is often obscured by error. How could anything so crudely organized inspire the sentiments of love, the ardent enthusiasm and the spirit of abnegation which all religions claim of their followers? These perfect beings which are gods could not have taken their traits from so mediocre, and sometimes even so base a reality.

But, on the other hand, does someone think of a perfect society, where justice and truth would be sovereign, and from which evil in all its forms would be banished for ever? No one would deny that this is in close relations with the religious sentiment; for, they would say, it is towards the realization of this that all religions strive. But that society is not an empirical fact, definite and observable; it is a fancy, a dream with which men have lightened their sufferings, but in which they have never really lived. It is merely an idea which comes to express our more or less obscure aspirations towards the good, the beautiful and the ideal. Now these aspirations have their roots in us; they come from the very depths of our being; then there is nothing outside of us which can account for them. Moreover, they are already religious in themselves; thus it would seem that the ideal society presupposes religion, far from being able to explain it.

But, in the first place, things are arbitrarily simplified when religion is seen only on its idealistic side: in its way, it is realistic. There is no physical or moral ugliness, there are no vices or evils which do not have a special divinity. There are gods of theft and trickery, of lust and war, of sickness and of death. Christianity itself, howsoever high the idea which it has made of the divinity may be, has been obliged to give the spirit of evil a place in its mythology. Satan is an essential piece of the Christian system; even if he is an impure being, he is not a profane one. The anti-god is a god, inferior and subordinated, it is true, but nevertheless endowed with extended powers; he is even the object of rites, at least of negative ones. Thus religion, far from ignoring the real society and making abstraction of it, is in its image; it reflects all its aspects, even the most vulgar and the most repulsive. All is to be found there, and if in the majority of cases we see the good victorious over evil, life over death, the powers of light over the powers of darkness, it is because reality is not otherwise. If the relation between these two contrary forces were reversed, life would be impossible; but, as a matter of fact, it maintains itself and even tends to develop.

But if, in the midst of these mythologies and theologies we see reality clearly appearing, it is none the less true that it is found there only in an enlarged, transformed and idealized form. In this respect, the most primitive religions do not differ from the most recent and the most refined. For example, we have seen how the Arunta place at the beginning of time a mythical society whose organization exactly reproduces that which still exists to-day; it includes the same clans and phratries, it is under the same matrimonial rules and it practises the same rites. But the personages who compose it are ideal beings, gifted with powers and virtues to which common mortals cannot pretend. Their nature is not only higher, but it is different, since it is at once animal and human. The evil powers there undergo a similar metamorphosis: evil itself is, as it were, made sublime and idealized. The question now raises itself of whence this idealization comes.

Some reply that men have a natural faculty for idealizing, that is to say, of substituting for the real world another different one, to which they transport themselves by thought. But that is merely changing the terms of the problem; it is not resolving it or even advancing it. This systematic idealization is an essential characteristic of religions. Explaining them by an innate power of idealization is simply replacing one word by another which is the equivalent of the first; it is as if they said that men have made religions because they have a religious nature. Animals know only one world, the one which they perceive by experience, internal as well as external. Men alone have the faculty of conceiving the ideal, of adding something to the real. Now where does this singular privilege come from? Before making it an initial fact or a mysterious virtue which escapes science, we must be sure that it does not depend upon empirically determinable conditions.

The explanation of religion which we have proposed has precisely this advantage, that it gives an answer to this question. For our definition of the sacred is that it is something added to and above the real: now the ideal answers to this same definition; we cannot explain one without explaining the other. In fact, we have seen that if collective life awakens religious thought on reaching a certain degree of intensity, it is because it brings about a state of effervescence which changes the conditions of psychic activity. Vital energies are over-excited, passions more active, sensations stronger; there are even some which are produced only at this moment. A man does not recognize himself; he feels himself transformed and consequently he transforms the environment which surrounds him. In order to account for the very particular impressions which he receives, he attributes to the things with which he is in most direct contact properties which they have not, exceptional powers and virtues which the objects of every-day experience do not possess. In a word, above the real world where his profane life passes he has placed another which, in one sense, does not exist except in thought, but to which he attributes a higher sort of dignity than to the first. Thus, from a double point of view it is an ideal world.

The formation of the ideal world is therefore not an irreducible fact which escapes science; it depends upon conditions which observation can touch; it is a natural product of social life. For a society to become conscious of itself and maintain at the necessary degree of intensity the sentiments which it thus attains, it must assemble and concentrate itself. Now this concentration brings about an exaltation of the mental life which takes form in a group of ideal conceptions where is portrayed the new life thus awakened; they correspond to this new set of psychical forces which is added to those which we have at our disposition for the daily tasks of existence. A society can neither create itself nor recreate itself without at the same time creating an ideal. This creation is not a sort of work of supererogation for it, by which it would complete itself, being already formed; it is the act by which it is periodically made and remade. Therefore when some oppose the ideal society to the real society, like two antagonists which would lead us in opposite directions, they materialize and oppose abstractions. The ideal society is not outside of the real society; it is a part of it. Far from being divided between them as between two poles which mutually repel each other, we cannot hold to one without holding to the other. For a society is not made up merely of the mass of individuals who compose it, the ground which they occupy, the things which they use and the movements which they perform, but above all is the idea which it forms of itself. It is undoubtedly true that it hesitates over the manner in which it ought to conceive itself; it feels itself drawn in divergent directions. But these conflicts which break forth are not between the ideal and reality, but between two different ideals, that of yesterday and that of to-day, that which has the authority of tradition and that which has the hope of the future. There is surely a place for investigating whence these ideals evolve; but whatever solution may be given to this problem, it still remains that all passes in the world of the ideal.

Thus the collective ideal which religion expresses is far from being due to a vague innate power of the individual, but it is rather at the school of collective life that the individual has learned to idealize. It is in assimilating the ideals elaborated by society that he has become capable of conceiving the ideal. It is society which, by leading him within its sphere of action, has made him acquire the need of raising himself above the world of experience and has at the same time furnished him with the means of conceiving another. For society has constructed this new world in constructing itself, since it is society which this expresses. Thus both with the individual and in the group, the faculty of idealizing has nothing mysterious about it. It is not a sort of luxury which a man could get along without, but a condition of his very existence. He could not be a social being, that is to say, he could not be a man, if he had not acquired it. It is true that in incarnating themselves in individuals, collective ideals tend to individualize themselves. Each understands them after his own fashion and marks them with his own stamp; he suppresses certain elements and adds others. Thus the personal ideal disengages itself from the social ideal in proportion as the individual personality develops itself and becomes an autonomous source of action. But if we wish to understand this aptitude, so singular in appearance, of living outside of reality, it is enough to connect it with the social conditions upon which it depends.

Therefore it is necessary to avoid seeing in this theory of religion a simple restatement of historical materialism: that would be misunderstanding our thought to an extreme degree. In showing that religion is something essentially social, we do not mean to say that it confines itself to translating into another language the material forms of society and its immediate vital necessities. It is true that we take it as evident that social life depends upon its material foundation and bears its mark, just as the mental life of an individual depends upon his nervous system and in fact his whole organism. But collective consciousness is something more than a mere epiphenomenon of its morphological basis, just as individual consciousness is something more than a simple efflorescence of the nervous system. In order that the former may appear, a synthesis *sui generis* of particular consciousnesses is required. Now this synthesis has the effect of disengaging a whole world of sentiments, ideas and images which, once born, obey laws all their own. They attract each other, repel each other, unite, divide themselves, and multiply, though these combinations are not commanded and necessitated by the condition of the underlying reality. The life thus brought into being even enjoys so great an independence that it sometimes indulges in manifestations with no purpose or utility of any sort, for the mere pleasure of affirming itself. We have shown that this is often precisely the case with ritual activity and mythological thought.

But if religion is the product of social causes, how can we explain the individual cult and the universalistic character of certain religions? If it is born *in foro externo*, how has it been able to pass into the inner conscience of the individual and penetrate there ever more and more profoundly? If it is the work of definite and individualized societies, how has it been able to detach itself from them, even to the point of being conceived as something common to all humanity?

In the course of our studies, we have met with the germs of individual religion and of religious cosmopolitanism, and we have seen how they were formed; thus we possess the more general elements of the reply which is to be given to this double question.

We have shown how the religious force which animates the clan particularizes itself, by incarnating itself in particular consciousnesses. Thus secondary sacred beings are formed; each individual has his own, made in his own image, associated to his own intimate life, bound up with his own destiny; it is the soul, the individual totem, the protecting ancestor, etc. These beings are the object of rites which the individual can celebrate by himself, outside of any group; this is the first form of the individual cult. To be sure, it is only a very rudimentary cult; but since the personality of the individual is still only slightly marked, and but little value is attributed to it, the cult which expresses it could hardly be expected to be very highly developed as yet. But as individuals have differentiated themselves more and more and the value of an individual has increased, the corresponding cult has taken a relatively greater place in the totality of the religious life and at the same time it is more fully closed to outside influences.

Thus the existence of individual cults implies nothing which contradicts or embarrasses the sociological interpretation of religion; for the religious forces to which it addresses itself are only the individualized forms of collective forces. Therefore, even when religion seems to be entirely within the individual conscience, it is still in society that it finds the living source from which it is nourished. We are now able to appreciate the value of the radical individualism which would make religion something purely individual: it misunderstands the fundamental conditions of the religious life. If up to the present it has remained in the stage of theoretical aspirations which have never been realized, it is because it is unrealizable. A philosophy may well be elaborated in the silence of the interior imagination, but not so a faith. For before all else, a faith is warmth, life, enthusiasm, the exaltation of the whole mental life, the raising of the individual above himself. Now how could he add to the energies which he possesses without going outside himself? How could he surpass himself merely by his own forces? The only source of life at which we can morally reanimate ourselves is that formed by the society of our fellow beings; the only moral forces with which we can sustain and increase our own are those which we get from others. Let us even admit that there really are beings more or less analogous to those which the mythologies represent. In order that they may exercise over souls the useful direction which is their reason for existence, it is necessary that men believe in them. Now these beliefs are active only when they are partaken by many. A man cannot retain them any length of time by a purely personal effort; it is not thus that they are born or that they are acquired; it is even doubtful if they can be kept under these conditions. In fact, a man who has a veritable faith feels an invincible need of spreading it: therefore he leaves his isolation, approaches others and seeks to convince them, and it is the ardour of the convictions which he arouses that strengthens his own. It would quickly weaken if it remained alone.

It is the same with religious universalism as with this individualism. Far from being an exclusive attribute of certain very great religions, we have found it, not at the base, it is true, but at the summit of the Australian system. Bunjil, Daramulun or Baiame are not simple tribal gods; each of them is recognized by a number of different tribes. In a sense, their cult is international. This conception is therefore very near to that found in the most recent theologies. So certain writers have felt it their duty to deny its authenticity, howsoever incontestable this may be.

And we have been able to show how this has been formed.

Neighboring tribes of a similar civilization cannot fail to be in constant relations with each other. All sorts of circumstances give an occasion for it: besides commerce, which is still rudimentary, there are marriages; these international marriages are very common in Australia. In the course of these meetings, men naturally become conscious of the moral relationship which united them. They have the same social organization, the same division into phratries, clans and matrimonial classes; they practise the same rites of initiation, or wholly similar ones. Mutual loans and treaties result in reinforcing these spontaneous resemblances. The gods to which these manifestly identical institutions were attached could hardly have remained distinct in their minds. Everything tended to bring them together and consequently, even supposing that each tribe elaborated the notion independently, they must necessarily have tended to confound themselves with each other. Also, it is probable that it was in inter-tribal assemblies that they were first conceived. For they are chiefly the gods of initiation, and in the initiation ceremonies, the different tribes are usually represented. So if sacred beings are formed which are connected with no geographically determined society, that is not because they have an extra-social origin. It is because there are other groups above these geographically determined ones, whose contours are less clearly marked: they have no fixed frontiers, but include all sorts of more or less neighbouring and related tribes. The particular social life thus created tends to spread itself over an area with no definite limits. Naturally the mythological personages who correspond to it have the same character; their sphere of influence is not limited; they go beyond the particular tribes and their territory. They are the great international gods.

Now there is nothing in this situation which is peculiar to Australian societies. There is no people and no state which is not a part of another society, more or less unlimited, which embraces all the peoples and all the States with which the first comes in contact, either directly or indirectly; there is no national life which is not dominated by a collective life of an international nature. In proportion as we advance in history, these international groups acquire a greater importance and extent. Thus we see how, in certain cases, this universalistic tendency has been able to develop itself to the point of affecting not only the higher ideas of the religious system, but even the principles upon which it rests.

II

Thus there is something eternal in religion which is destined to survive all the particular symbols in which religious thought has successively enveloped itself. There can be no society which does not feel the need of upholding and reaffirming at regular intervals the collective sentiments and the collective ideas which make its unity and its personality. Now this moral remaking cannot be achieved except by the means of reunions, assemblies and meetings where the individuals, being closely united to one another, reaffirm in common their common sentiments; hence come ceremonies which do not differ from regular religious ceremonies, either in their object, the results which they produce, or the processes employed to attain these results. What essential difference is there between an assembly of Christians celebrating the principal dates of the life of Christ, or of Jews remembering the exodus from Egypt or the promulgation of the decalogue, and a reunion of citizens commemorating the promulgation of a new moral or legal system or some great event in the national life?

If we find a little difficulty to-day in imagining what these feasts and ceremonies of the future could consist in, it is because we are going through a stage of transition and moral mediocrity. The great things of the past which filled our fathers with enthusiasm do not excite the same ardour in us, either because they have come into common usage to such an extent that we are unconscious of them, or else because they no longer answer to our actual aspirations; but as yet there is nothing to replace them. We can no longer impassionate ourselves for the principles in the name of which Christianity recommended to masters that they treat their slaves humanely, and, on the other hand, the idea which it has formed of human equality and fraternity seems to us to-day to leave too large a place for unjust inequalities. Its pity for the outcast seems to us too Platonic; we desire another which would be more practicable; but as yet we cannot clearly see what it should be nor how it could be realized in facts. In a word, the old gods are growing old or already dead, and others are not yet born. This is what rendered vain the attempt of Comte with the old historic souvenirs artificially revived: it is life itself, and not a dead past which can produce a living cult. But this state of incertitude and confused agitation cannot last for ever. A day will come when our societies will know again those hours of creative effervescence, in the course of which new ideas arise and new formulæ are found which serve for a while as a guide to humanity; and when these hours shall have been passed through once, men will spontaneously feel the need of reliving them from time to time in thought, that is to say, of keeping alive their memory by means of celebrations which regularly reproduce their fruits. We have already seen how the French Revolution established a whole cycle of holidays to keep the principles with which it was inspired in a state of perpetual youth. If this institution quickly fell away, it was because the revolutionary faith lasted but a moment, and deceptions and discouragements rapidly succeeded the first moments of enthusiasm. But though the work may have miscarried, it enables us to imagine what might have happened in other conditions; and everything leads us to believe that it will be taken up again sooner or later. There are no gospels which are immortal, but neither is there any reason for believing that humanity is incapable of inventing new ones. As to the question of what symbols this new faith will express itself with, whether they will resemble those of the past or not, and whether or not they will be more adequate for the reality which they seek to translate, that is something which surpasses the human faculty of foresight and which does not appertain to the principal question.

But feasts and rites, in a word, the cult, are not the whole religion. This is not merely a system of practices, but also a system of ideas whose object is to explain the world; we have seen that even the humblest have their cosmology. Whatever connection there may be between these two elements of the religious life, they are still quite different. The one is turned towards action, which it demands and regulates; the other is turned towards thought, which it enriches and organizes. Then they do not depend upon the same conditions, and consequently it may be asked if the second answers to necessities as universal and as permanent as the first.

When specific characteristics are attributed to religious thought, and when it is believed that its function is to express, by means peculiar to itself, an aspect of reality which evades ordinary knowledge as well as science, one naturally refuses to admit that religion can ever abandon its speculative rôle. But our analysis of the facts does not seem to have shown this specific quality of religion. The religion which we have just studied is one of those whose symbols are the most disconcerting for the reason. There all appears mysterious. These beings which belong to the most heterogeneous groups at the same time, who multiply without ceasing to be one, who divide without diminishing, all seem, at first view, to belong to an entirely different world from the one where we live; some have even gone so far as to say that the mind which constructed them ignored the laws of logic completely. Perhaps the contrast between reason and faith has never been more thorough. Then if there has ever been a moment in history when their heterogeneousness should have stood out clearly, it is here. But contrary to all appearances, as we have pointed out, the realities to which religious speculation is then applied are the same as those which later serve as the subject of reflection for philosophers: they are nature, man, society. The mystery which appears to surround them is wholly superficial and disappears before a more painstaking observation: it is enough merely to set aside the veil with which mythological imagination has covered them for them to appear such as they really are. Religion sets itself to translate these realities into an intelligible language which does not differ in nature from that employed by science; the attempt is made by both to connect things with each other, to establish internal relations between them, to classify them and to systematize them. We have even seen that the essential ideas of scientific logic are of religious origin. It is true that in order to utilize them, science gives them a new elaboration; it purges them of all accidental elements; in a general way, it brings a spirit of criticism into all its doings, which religion ignores; it surrounds itself with precautions to "escape precipitation and bias," and to hold aside the passions, prejudices and all subjective influences. But these perfectionings of method are not enough to differentiate it from religion. In this regard, both pursue the same end; scientific thought is only a more perfect form of religious thought. Thus it seems natural that the second should progressively retire before the first, as this becomes better fitted to perform the task.

And there is no doubt that this regression has taken place in the course of history. Having left religion, science tends to substitute itself for this latter in all that which concerns the cognitive and intellectual functions. Christianity has already definitely consecrated this substitution in the order of material things. Seeing in matter that which is profane before all else, it readily left the knowledge of this to another discipline, *tradidit mundum hominum disputationi*, "He gave the world over to the disputes of men"; it is thus that the natural sciences have been able to establish themselves and make their authority recognized without very great difficulty. But it could not give up the world of souls so easily; for it is before all over souls that the god of the Christians aspires to reign. That is why the idea of submitting the psychic life to science produced the effect of a sort of profanation for a long time; even to-day it is repugnant to many minds. However, experimental and comparative psychology is founded and to-day we must reckon with it. But the world of the religious and moral life is still forbidden. The great majority of men continue to believe that here there is an order of things which the mind cannot penetrate except by very special ways. Hence comes the active resistance which is met with every time that someone tries to treat religious and moral phenomena scientifically. But in spite of these oppositions, these attempts are constantly repeated and this persistence even allows us to foresee that this final barrier will finally give way and that science will establish herself as mistress even in this reserved region.

That is what the conflict between science and religion really amounts to. It is said that science denies religion in principle. But religion exists; it is a system of given facts; in a word, it is a reality. How could science deny this reality? Also, in so far as religion is action, and in so far as it is a means of making men live, science could not take its place, for even if this expresses life, it does not create it; it may well seek to explain the faith, but by that very act it presupposes it. Thus there is no conflict except upon one limited point. Of the two functions which religion originally fulfilled, there is one, and only one, which tends to escape it more and more: that is its speculative function. That which science refuses to grant to religion is not its right to exist, but its right to dogmatize upon the nature of things and the special competence which it claims for itself for knowing man and the world. As a matter of fact, it does not know itself. It does not even know what it is made of, nor to what need it answers. It is itself a subject for science, so far is it from being able to make the law for science! And from another point of view, since there is no proper subject for religious speculation outside that reality to which scientific reflection is applied, it is evident that this former cannot play the same rôle in the future that it has played in the past.

However, it seems destined to transform itself rather than to disappear.

We have said that there is something eternal in religion: it is the cult and the faith. Men cannot celebrate ceremonies for which they see no reason, nor can they accept a faith which they in no way understand. To spread itself or merely to maintain itself, it must be justified, that is to say, a theory must be made of it. A theory of this sort must undoubtedly be founded upon the different sciences, from the moment when these exist; first of all, upon the social sciences, for religious faith has its origin in society; then upon psychology, for society is a sythesis of human consciousnesses; and finally upon the sciences of nature, for man and society are a part of the universe and can be abstracted from it only artificially. But howsoever important these facts taken from the constituted sciences may be, they are not enough; for faith is before all else an impetus to action, while science, no matter how far it may be pushed, always remains at a distance from this. Science is fragmentary and incomplete; it advances but slowly and is never finished; but life cannot wait. The theories which are destined to make men live and act are therefore obliged to pass science and complete it prematurely. They are possible only when the practical exigencies and the vital necessities which we feel without distinctly conceiving them push thought in advance, beyond that which science permits us to affirm. Thus religions, even the most rational and laicized, cannot and never will be able to dispense with a particular form of speculation which, though having the same subjects as science itself, cannot be really scientific: the obscure intuitions of sensation and sentiment too often take the place of logical reasons. On one side, this speculation resembles that which we meet with in the religions of the past; but on another, it is different. While claiming and exercising the right of going beyond science, it must commence by knowing this and by inspiring itself with it. Ever since the authority of science was established, it must be reckoned with; one can go farther than it under the pressure of necessity, but he must take his direction from it. He can affirm nothing that it denies, deny nothing that it affirms, and establish nothing that is not directly or indirectly founded upon principles taken from it. From now on, the faith no longer exercises the same hegemony as formerly over the system of ideas that we may continue to call religion. A rival power rises up before it which, being born of it, ever after submits it to its criticism and control. And everything makes us foresee that this control will constantly become more extended and efficient, while no limit can be assigned to its future influence.

III

But if the fundamental notions of science are of a religious origin, how has religion been able to bring them forth? At first sight, one does not see what relations there can be between religion and logic. Or, since the reality which religious thought expresses is society, the question can be stated in the following terms, which make the entire difficulty appear even better: what has been able to make social life so important a source for the logical life? It seems as though nothing could have predestined it to this rôle, for it certainly was not to satisfy their speculative needs that men associated themselves together.

Perhaps we shall be found over bold in attempting so complex a question here. To treat it as it should be treated, the sociological conditions of knowledge should be known much better than they actually are; we are only beginning to catch glimpses of some of them. However, the question is so grave, and so directly implied in all that has preceded, that we must make an effort not to leave it without an answer. Perhaps it is not impossible, even at present, to state some general principles which may at least aid in the solution.

Logical thought is made up of concepts. Seeking how society can have played a rôle in the genesis of logical thought thus reduces itself to seeking how it can have taken a part in the formation of concepts.

If, as is ordinarily the case, we see in the concept only a general idea, the problem appears insoluble. By his own power, the individual can compare his conceptions and images, disengage that which they have in common, and thus, in a word, generalize. Then it is hard to see why this generalization should be possible only in and through society. But, in the first place, it is inadmissible that logical thought is characterized only by the greater extension of the conceptions of which it is made up. If particular ideas have nothing logical about them, why should it be different with general ones? The general exists only in the particular; it is the particular simplified and impoverished. Then the first could have no virtues or privileges which the second has not. Inversely, if conceptual thought can be applied to the class, species or variety, howsoever restricted these may be, why can it not be extended to the individual, that is to say, to the limit towards which the conception tends, proportionately as its extension diminishes? As a matter of fact, there are many concepts which have only individuals as their object. In every sort of religion, gods are individualities distinct from each other; however, they are conceived, not perceived. Each people represents its historic or legendary heroes in fashions which vary with the time. Finally, every one of us forms an idea of the individuals with whom he comes in contact, of their character, of their appearance, their distinctive traits and their moral and physical temperaments: these notions, too, are real concepts. It is true that in general they are formed crudely enough; but even among scientific concepts, are there a great many that are perfectly adequate for their object? In this direction, there are only differences of degree between them.

Therefore the concept must be defined by other characteristics. It is opposed to sensual representations of every order—sensations, perceptions or images—by the following properties.

Sensual representations are in a perpetual flux; they come after each other like the waves of a river, and even during the time that they last, they do not remain the same thing. Each of them is an integral part of the precise instant when it takes place. We are never sure of again finding a perception such as we experienced it the first time; for if the thing perceived has not changed, it is we who are no longer the same. On the contrary, the concept is, as it were, outside of time and change; it is in the depths below all this agitation; it might be said that it is in a different portion of the mind, which is serener and calmer. It does not move of itself, by an internal and spontaneous evolution, but, on the contrary, it resists change. It is a manner of thinking that, at every moment of time, is fixed and crystallized. In so far as it is what it ought to be, it is immutable. If it changes, it is not because it is its nature to do so, but because we have discovered some imperfection in it; it is because it had to be rectified. The system of concepts with which we think in everyday life is that expressed by the vocabulary of our mother tongue; for every word translates a concept. Now language is something fixed; it changes but very slowly, and consequently it is the same with the conceptual system which it expresses. The scholar finds himself in the same situation in regard to the special terminology employed by the science to which he has consecrated himself, and hence in regard to the special scheme of concepts to which this terminology corresponds. It is true that he can make innovations, but these are always a sort of violence done to the established ways of thinking.

And at the same time that it is relatively immutable, the concept is universal, or at least capable of becoming so. A concept is not my concept; I hold it in common with other men, or, in any case, can communicate it to them. It is impossible for me to make a sensation pass from my consciousness into that of another; it holds closely to my organism and personality and cannot be detached from them. All that I can do is to invite others to place themselves before the same object as myself and to leave themselves to its action. On the other hand, conversation and all intellectual communication between men is an exchange of concepts. The concept is an essentially impersonal representation; it is through it that human intelligences communicate.

The nature of the concept, thus defined, bespeaks its origin. If it is common to all, it is the work of the community. Since it bears the mark of no particular mind, it is clear that it was elaborated by a unique intelligence, where all others meet each other, and after a fashion, come to nourish themselves. If it has more stability than sensations or images, it is because the collective representations are more stable than the individual ones; for while an individual is conscious even of the slight changes which take place in his environment, only events of a greater gravity can succeed in affecting the mental status of a society. Every time that we are in the presence of a *type* of thought or action which is imposed uniformly upon particular wills or intelligences, this pressure exercised over the individual betrays the intervention of the group. Also, as we have already said, the concepts with which we ordinarily think are those of our vocabulary. Now it is unquestionable that language, and consequently the system of concepts which it translates, is the product of a collective elaboration. What it expresses is the manner in which society as a whole represents the facts of experience. The ideas which correspond to the diverse elements of language are thus collective representations.

Even their contents bear witness to the same fact. In fact, there are scarcely any words among those which we usually employ whose meaning does not pass, to a greater or less extent, the limits of our personal experience. Very frequently a term expresses things which we have never perceived or experiences which we have never had or of which we have never been the witnesses. Even when we know some of the objects which it concerns, it is only as particular examples that they serve to illustrate the idea which they would never have been able to form by themselves. Thus there is a great deal of knowledge condensed in the word which I never collected, and which is not individual; it even surpasses me to such an extent that I cannot even completely appropriate all its results. Which of us knows all the words of the language he speaks and the entire signification of each?

This remark enables us to determine the sense in which we mean to say that concepts are collective representations. If they belong to a whole social group, it is not because they represent the average of the corresponding individual representations; for in that case they would be poorer than the latter in intellectual content, while, as a matter of fact, they contain much that surpasses the knowledge of the average individual. They are not abstractions which have a reality only in particular consciousnesses, but they are as concrete representations as an individual could form of his own personal environment: they correspond to the way in which this very special being, society, considers the things of its own proper experience. If, as a matter of fact, the concepts are nearly always general ideas, and if they express categories and classes rather than particular objects, it is because the unique and variable characteristics of things interest society but rarely; because of its very extent, it can scarcely be affected by more than their general and permanent qualities. Therefore it is to this aspect of affairs that it gives its attention: it is a part of its nature to see things in large and under the aspect which they ordinarily have. But this generality is not necessary for them, and, in any case, even when these representations have the generic character which they ordinarily have, they are the work of society and are enriched by its experience.

That is what makes conceptual thought so valuable for us. If concepts were only general ideas, they would not enrich knowledge a great deal, for, as we have already pointed out, the general contains nothing more than the particular. But if before all else they are collective representations, they add to that which we can learn by our own personal experience all that wisdom and science which the group has accumulated in the course of centuries. Thinking by concepts is not merely seeing reality on its most general side, but is projecting a light upon the sensation which illuminates it, penetrates it and transforms it. Conceiving something is both learning its essential elements better and also locating it in its place; for each civilization has its organized system of concepts which characterizes it. Before this scheme of ideas, the individual is in the same situation as the *νοῦς* of Plato before the world of Ideas. He must assimilate them to himself, for he must have them to hold intercourse with others; but the assimilation is always imperfect. Each of us sees them after his own fashion. There are some which escape us completely and remain outside of our circle of vision; there are others of which we perceive certain aspects only. There are even a great many which we pervert in holding, for as they are collective by nature, they cannot become individualized without being retouched, modified, and consequently falsified. Hence comes the great trouble we have in understanding each other, and the fact that we even lie to each other without wishing to: it is because we all use the same words without giving them the same meaning.

We are now able to see what the part of society in the genesis of logical thought is. This is possible only from the moment when, above the fugitive conceptions which they owe to sensuous experience, men have succeeded in conceiving a whole world of stable ideas, the common ground of all intelligences. In fact, logical thinking is always impersonal thinking, and is also thought *sub species æternitatis*—as though for all time. Impersonality and stability are the two characteristics of truth. Now logical life evidently presupposes that men know, at least confusedly, that there is such a thing as truth, distinct from sensuous appearances. But how have they been able to arrive at this conception? We generally talk as though it should have spontaneously presented itself to them from the moment they opened their eyes upon the world. However, there is nothing in immediate experience which could suggest it; everything even contradicts it. Thus the child and the animal have no suspicion of it. History shows that it has taken centuries for it to disengage and establish itself. In our Western world, it was with the great thinkers of Greece that it first became clearly conscious of itself and of the consequences which it implies; when the discovery was made, it caused an amazement which Plato has translated into magnificent language. But if it is only at this epoch that the idea is expressed in philosophic formulæ, it was necessarily pre-existent in the stage of an obscure sentiment. Philosophers have sought to elucidate this sentiment, but they have not succeeded. In order that they might reflect upon it and analyse it, it was necessary that it be given them, and that they seek to know whence it came, that is to say, in what experience it was founded. This is in collective experience. It is under the form of collective thought that impersonal thought is for the first time revealed to humanity; we cannot see by what other way this revelation could have been made. From the mere fact that society exists, there is also, outside of the individual sensations and images, a whole system of representations which enjoy marvellous properties. By means of them, men understand each other and intelligences grasp each other. They have within them a sort of force or moral ascendancy, in virtue of which they impose themselves upon individual minds. Hence the individual at least obscurely takes account of the fact that above his private ideas, there is a world of absolute ideas according to which he must shape his own; he catches a glimpse of a whole intellectual kingdom in which he participates, but which is greater than he. This is the first intuition of the realm of truth. From the moment when he first becomes conscious of these higher ideas, he sets himself to scrutinizing their nature; he asks whence these pre-eminent representations hold their prerogatives and, in so far as he believes that be has discovered their causes, he undertakes to put these causes into action for himself, in order that he may draw from them by his own force the effects which they produce; that is to say, he attributes to himself the right of making concepts. Thus the faculty of conception has individualized itself. But to understand its origins and function, it must be attached to the social conditions upon which it depends.

It may be objected that we show the concept in one of its aspects only, and that its unique rôle is not the assuring of a harmony among minds, but also, and to a greater extent, their harmony with the nature of things. It seems as though it had a reason for existence only on condition of being true, that is to say, objective, and as though its impersonality were only a consequence of its objectivity. It is in regard to things, thought of as adequately as possible, that minds ought to communicate. Nor do we deny that the evolution of concepts has been partially in this direction. The concept which was first held as true because it was collective tends to be no longer collective except on condition of being held as true: we demand its credentials of it before according it our confidence. But we must not lose sight of the fact that even to-day the great majority of the concepts which we use are not methodically constituted; we get them from language, that is to say, from common experience, without submitting them to any criticism. The scientifically elaborated and criticized concepts are always in the very slight minority. Also, between them and those which draw all their authority from the fact that they are collective, there are only differences of degree. A collective representation presents guarantees of objectivity by the fact that it is collective: for it is not without sufficient reason that it has been able to generalize and maintain itself with persistence. If it were out of accord with the nature of things, it would never have been able to acquire an extended and prolonged empire over intellects. At bottom, the confidence inspired by scientific concepts is due to, the fact that they can be methodically controlled. But a collective representation is necessarily submitted to a control that is repeated indefinitely; the men who accept it verify it by their own experience. Therefore, it could not be wholly inadequate for its subject. It is true that it may express this by means of imperfect symbols; but scientific symbols themselves are never more than approximative. It is precisely this principle which is at the basis of the method which we follow in the study of religious phenomena: we take it as an axiom that religious beliefs, howsoever strange their appearance may be at times, contain a truth which must be discovered.

On the other hand, it is not at all true that concepts, even when constructed according to the rules of science, get their authority uniquely from their objective value. It is not enough that they be true to be believed. If they are not in harmony with the other beliefs and opinions, or, in a word, with the mass of the other collective representations, they will be denied; minds will be closed to them; consequently it will be as though they did not exist. To-day it is generally sufficient that they bear the stamp of science to receive a sort of privileged credit, because we have faith in science. But this faith does not differ essentially from religious faith. In the last resort, the value which we attribute to science depends upon the idea which we collectively form of its nature and rôle in life; that is as much as to say that it expresses a state of public opinion. In all social life, in fact, science rests upon opinion. It is undoubtedly true that this opinion can be taken as the object of a study and a science made of it; this is what sociology principally consists in. But the science of opinion does not make opinions; it can only observe them and make them more conscious of themselves. It is true that by this means it can lead them to change, but science continues to be dependent upon opinion at the very moment when it seems to be making its laws; for, as we have already shown, it is from opinion that it holds the force necessary to act upon opinion.

Saying that concepts express the manner in which society represents things is also saying that conceptual thought is coeval with humanity itself. We refuse to see in it the product of a more or less retarded culture. A man who did not think with concepts would not be a man, for he would not be a social being. If reduced to having only individual perceptions, he would be indistinguishable from the beasts. If it has been possible to sustain the contrary thesis, it is because concepts have been defined by characteristics which are not essential to them. They have been identified with general ideas and with clearly limited and circumscribed general ideas. In these conditions it has possibly seemed as though the inferior societies had no concepts properly so called; for they have only rudimentary processes of generalization and the ideas which they use are not generally very well defined. But the greater part of our concepts are equally indetermined; we force ourselves to define them only in discussions or when doing careful work. We have also seen that conceiving is not generalizing. Thinking conceptually is not simply isolating and grouping together the common characteristics of a certain number of objects; it is relating the variable to the permanent, the individual to the social. And since logical thought commences with the concept, it follows that it has always existed; there is no period in history when men have lived in a chronic confusion and contradiction. To be sure, we cannot insist too much upon the different characteristics which logic presents at different periods in history; it develops like the societies themselves. But howsoever real these differences may be, they should not cause us to neglect the similarities, which are no less essential.

IV

We are now in a position to take up a final question which has already been raised in our introduction and which has been taken as understood in the remainder of this work. We have seen that at least some of the categories are social things. The question is where they got this character.

Undoubtedly it will be easily understood that since they are themselves concepts, they are the work of the group. It can even be said that there are no other concepts which present to an equal degree the signs by which a collective representation is recognized. In fact, their stability and impersonality are such that they have often passed as being absolutely universal and immutable. Also, as they express the fundamental conditions for an agreement between minds, it seems evident that they have been elaborated by society.

But the problem concerning them is more complex, for they are social in another sense and, as it were, in the second degree. They not only come from society, but the things which they express are of a social nature. Not only is it society which has founded them, but their contents are the different aspects of the social being; the category of class was at first indistinct from the concept of the human group; it is the rhythm of social life which is at the basis of the category of time; the territory occupied by the society furnished the material for the category of space; it is the collective force which was the prototype of the concept of efficient force, an essential element in the category of causality. However, the categories are not made to be applied only to the social realm; they reach out to all reality. Then how is it that they have taken from society the models upon which they have been constructed?

It is because they are the pre-eminent concepts, which have a preponderating part in our knowledge. In fact, the function of the categories is to dominate and envelop all the other concepts; they are permanent moulds for the mental life. Now for them to embrace such an object, they must be founded upon a reality of equal amplitude.

Undoubtedly the relations which they express exist in an implicit way in individual consciousnesses. The individual lives in time, and, as we have said, he has a certain sense of temporal orientation. He is situated at a determined point in space, and it has even been held, and sustained with good reasons, that all sensations have something special about them. He has a feeling of resemblances; similar representations are brought together and the new representation formed by their union has a sort of generic character. We also have the sensation of a certain regularity in the order of the succession of phenomena; even an animal is not incapable of this. However, all these relations are strictly personal for the individual who recognizes them, and consequently the notion of them which he may have can in no case go beyond his own narrow horizon. The generic images which are formed in my consciousness by the fusion of similar images represent only the objects which I have perceived directly; there is nothing there which could give me the idea of a class, that is to say, of a mould including the *whole* group of all possible objects which satisfy the same condition. Also, it would be necessary to have the idea of group in the first place, and the mere observations of our interior life could never awaken that in us. But, above all, there is no individual experience, howsoever extended and prolonged it may be, which could give a suspicion of the existence of a whole class which would embrace every single being, and to which other classes are only coordinated or subordinated species. This idea of *all*, which is at the basis of the classifications which we have just cited, could not have come from the individual himself, who is only a part in relation to the whole and who never attains more than an infinitesimal fraction of reality. And yet there is perhaps no other category of greater importance; for as the rôle of the categories is to envelop all the other concepts, the category *par excellence* would seem to be this very concept of *totality*. The theorists of knowledge ordinarily postulate it is if it came of itself, while it really surpasses the contents of each individual consciousness taken alone to an infinite degree.

For the same reasons, the space which I know by my senses, of which I am the centre and where everything is disposed in relation to me, could not be space in general, which contains all extensions and where these are coordinated by personal guidelines which are common to everybody. In the same way, the concrete duration which I feel passing within me and with me could not give me the idea of time in general: the first expresses only the rhythm of my individual life; the second should correspond to the rhythm of a life which is not that of any individual in particular, but in which all participate. In the same way, finally, the regularities which I am able to conceive in the manner in which my sensations succeed one another may well have a value for me; they explain how it comes about that when I am given the first of two phenomena whose concurrence I have observed, I tend to expect the other. But this personal state of expectation could not be confounded with the conception of a universal order of succession which imposes itself upon all minds and all events.

Since the world expressed by the entire system of concepts is the one that society regards, society alone can furnish the most general notions with which it should be represented. Such an object can be embraced only by a subject which contains all the individual subjects within it. Since the universe does not exist except in so far as it is thought of, and since it is not completely thought of except by society, it takes a place in this latter; it becomes a part of society's interior life, while this is the totality, outside of which nothing exists. The concept of totality is only the abstract form of the concept of society: it is the whole which includes all things, the supreme class which embraces all other classes. Such is the final principle upon which repose all these primitive classifications where beings from every realm are placed and classified in social forms, exactly like men. But if the world is inside of society, the space which this latter occupies becomes confounded with space in general. In fact, we have seen how each thing has its assigned place in social space, and the degree to which this space in general differs from the concrete expanses which we perceive is well shown by the fact that this localization is wholly ideal and in no way resembles what it would have been if it had been dictated to us by sensuous experience alone. For the same reason, the rhythm of collective life dominates and embraces the varied rhythms of all the elementary lives from which it results; consequently the time which it expresses dominates and embraces all particular durations. It is time in general. For a long time the history of the world has been only another aspect of the history of society. The one commences with the other; the periods of the first are determined by the periods of the second. This impersonal and total duration is measured, and the guide-lines in relation to which it is divided and organized are fixed by the movements of concentration or dispersion of society; or, more generally, the periodical necessities for a collective renewal. If these critical instants are generally attached to some material phenomenon, such as the regular recurrence of such or such a star or the alternation of the seasons, it is because objective signs are necessary to make this essentially social organization intelligible to all. In the same way, finally, the causal relation, from the moment when it is collectively stated by the group, becomes independent of every individual consciousness; it rises above all particular minds and events. It is a law whose value depends upon no person. We have already shown how it is clearly thus that it seems to have originated.

Another reason explains why the constituent elements of the categories should have been taken from social life: it is because the relations which they express could not have been learned except in and through society. If they are in a sense immanent in the life of an individual, he has neither a reason nor the means for learning them, reflecting upon them and forming them into distinct ideas. In order to orient himself personally in space and to know at what moments he should satisfy his various organic needs, he has no need of making, once and for all, a conceptual representation of time and space. Many animals are able to find the road which leads to places with which they are familiar; they come back at a proper moment without knowing any of the categories; sensations are enough to direct them automatically. They would also be enough for men, if their sensations had to satisfy only individual needs. To recognize the fact that one thing resembles another which we have already experienced, it is in no way necessary that we arrange them all in groups and species: the way in which similar images call up each other and unite is enough to give the feeling of resemblance. The impression that a certain thing has already been seen or experienced implies no classification. To recognize the things which we should seek or from which we should flee, it would not be necessary to attach the effects of the two to their causes by a logical bond, if individual conveniences were the only ones in question. Purely empirical sequences and strong connections between the concrete representations would be as sure guides for the will. Not only is it true that the animal has no others, but also our own personal conduct frequently supposes nothing more. The prudent man is the one who has a very clear sensation of what must be done, but which he would ordinarily be quite incapable of stating as a general law.

It is a different matter with society. This is possible only when the individuals and things which compose it are divided into certain groups, that is to say, classified, and when these groups are classified in relation to each other. Society supposes a self-conscious organization which is nothing other than a classification. This organization of society naturally extends itself to the place which this occupies. To avoid all collisions, it is necessary that each particular group have a determined portion of space assigned to it: in other terms, it is necessary that space in general be divided, differentiated, arranged, and that these divisions and arrangements be known to everybody. On the other hand, every summons to a celebration, a hunt or a military expedition implies fixed and established dates, and consequently that a common time is agreed upon, which everybody conceives in the same fashion. Finally, the co-operation of many persons with the same end in view is possible only when they are in agreement as to the relation which exists between this end and the means of attaining it, that is to say, when the same causal relation is admitted by all the co-operators in the enterprise. It is not surprising, therefore, that social time, social space, social classes and causality should be the basis of the corresponding categories, since it is under their social forms that these different relations were first grasped with a certain clarity by the human intellect.

In summing up, then, we must say that society is not at all the illogical or a-logical, incoherent and fantastic being which it has too often been considered. Quite on the contrary, the collective consciousness is the highest form of the psychic life, since it is the consciousness of the consciousnesses. Being placed outside of and above individual and local contingencies, it sees things only in their permanent and essential aspects, which it crystallizes into communicable ideas. At the same time that it sees from above, it sees farther; at every moment of time, it embraces all known reality; that is why it alone can furnish the mind with the moulds which are applicable to the totality of things and which make it possible to think of them. It does not create these moulds artificially; it finds them within itself; it does nothing but become conscious of them. They translate the ways of being which are found in all the stages of reality but which appear in their full clarity only at the summit, because the extreme complexity of the psychic life which passes there necessitates a greater development of consciousness. Attributing social origins to logical thought is not debasing it or diminishing its value or reducing it to nothing more than a system of artificial combinations; on the contrary, it is relating it to a cause which implies it naturally. But this is not saying that the ideas elaborated in this way are at once adequate for their object. If society is something universal in relation to the individual, it is none the less an individuality itself, which has its own personal physiognomy and its idiosyncrasies; it is a particular subject and consequently particularizes whatever it thinks of. Therefore collective representations also contain subjective elements, and these must be progressively rooted out, if we are to approach reality more closely. But howsoever crude these may have been at the beginning, the fact remains that with them the germ of a new mentality was given, to which the individual could never have raised himself by his own efforts: by them the way was opened to a stable, impersonal and organized thought which then had nothing to do except to develop its nature.

Also, the causes which have determined this development do not seem to be specifically different from those which gave it its initial impulse. If logical thought tends to rid itself more and more of the subjective and personal elements which it still retains from its origin, it is not because extrasocial factors have intervened; it is much rather because a social life of a new sort is developing. It is this international life which has already resulted in universalizing religious beliefs. As it extends, the collective horizon enlarges; the society ceases to appear as the only whole, to become a part of a much vaster one, with indetermined frontiers, which is susceptible of advancing indefinitely. Consequently things can no longer be contained in the social moulds according to which they were primitively classified; they must be organized according to principles which are their own, so logical organization differentiates itself from the social organization and becomes autonomous. Really and truly human thought is not a primitive fact; it is the product of history; it is the ideal limit towards which we are constantly approaching, but which in all probability we shall never succeed in reaching.

Thus it is not at all true that between science on the one hand, and morals and religion on the other, there exists that sort of antimony which has so frequently been admitted, for the two forms of human activity really come from one and the same source. Kant understood this very well, and therefore he made the speculative reason and the practical reason two different aspects of the same faculty. According to him, what makes their unity is the fact that the two are directed towards the universal. Rational thinking is thinking according to the laws which are imposed upon all reasonable beings; acting morally is conducting one's self according to those maxims which can be extended without contradiction to all wills. In other words, science and morals imply that the individual is capable of raising himself above his own peculiar point of view and of living an impersonal life. In fact, it cannot be doubted that this is a trait common to all the higher forms of thought and action. What Kant's system does not explain, however, is the origin of this sort of contradiction which is realized in man. Why is he forced to do violence to himself by leaving his individuality, and, inversely, why is the impersonal law obliged to be dissipated by incarnating itself in individuals? Is it answered that there are two antagonistic worlds in which we participate equally, the world of matter and sense on the one hand, and the world of pure and impersonal reason on the other? That is merely repeating the question in slightly different terms, for what we are trying to find out is why we must lead these two existences at the same time. Why do these two worlds, which seem to contradict each other, not remain outside of each other, and why must they mutually penetrate one another in spite of their antagonism? The only explanation which has ever been given of this singular necessity is the hypothesis of the Fall, with all the difficulties which it implies, and which need not be repeated here. On the other hand, all mystery disappears the moment that it is recognized that impersonal reason is only another name given to collective thought. For this is possible only through a group of individuals; it supposes them, and in their turn, they suppose it, for they can continue to exist only by grouping themselves together. The kingdom of ends and impersonal truths can realize itself only by the co-operation of particular wills, and the reasons for which these participate in it are the same as those for which they co-operate. In a word, there is something impersonal in us because there is something social in all of us, and since social life embraces at once both representations and practices, this impersonality naturally extends to ideas as well as to acts.

Perhaps some will be surprised to see us connect the most elevated forms of thought with society: the cause appears quite humble, in consideration of the value which we attribute to the effect. Between the world of the senses and appetites on the one hand, and that of reason and morals on the other, the distance is so considerable that the second would seem to have been able to add itself to the first only by a creative act. But attributing to society this preponderating rôle in the genesis of our nature is not denying this creation; for society has a creative power which no other observable being can equal. In fact, all creation, if not a mystical operation which escapes science and knowledge, is the product of a synthesis. Now if the synthesis of particular conceptions which take place in each individual consciousness are already and of themselves productive of novelties, how much more efficacious these vast synthesis of complete consciousnesses which make society must be! A society is the most powerful combination of physical and moral forces of which nature offers us an example. Nowhere else is an equal richness of different materials, carried to such a degree of concentration, to be found. Then it is not surprising that a higher life disengages itself which, by reacting upon the elements of which it is the product, raises them to a higher plane of existence and transforms them.

Thus sociology appears destined to open a new way to the science of man. Up to the present, thinkers were placed before this double alternative: either explain the superior and specific faculties of men by connecting them to the inferior forms of his being, the reason to the senses, or the mind to matter, which is equivalent to denying their uniqueness; or else attach them to some super-experimental reality which was postulated, but whose existence could be established by no observation. What put them in this difficulty was the fact that the individual passed as being the *finis naturæ*—the ultimate creation of nature; it seemed that there was nothing beyond him, or at least nothing that science could touch. But from the moment when it is recognized that above the individual there is society, and that this is not a nominal being created by reason, but a system of active forces, a new manner of explaining men becomes possible. To conserve his distinctive traits it is no longer necessary to put them outside experience. At least, before going to this last extremity, it would be well to see if that which surpasses the individual, though it is within him, does not come from this super-individual reality which we experience in society. To be sure, it cannot be said at present to what point these explanations may be able to reach, and whether or not they are of a nature to resolve all the problems. But it is equally impossible to mark in advance a limit beyond which they cannot go. What must be done is to try the hypothesis and submit it as methodically as possible to the control of facts. This is what we have tried to do.

PART THREE

The Critique of Consumption, Rationality, and Imperialism

SIGMUND FREUD

Sigmund Freud (1856–1939), the founder of psychoanalysis, was by training a research scientist and physician, yet like the other classical social theorists he was also a broadly educated individual. His literary gifts; humanistic scholarship; and, above all, his courageous self-analysis rendered him unusually sensitive to the ill-defined realm of emotional disorders that lay neglected by the medical science of his day. In later works, such as *Totem and Taboo* (1912–1913), The *Future of an Illusion* (1927), and especially *Civilization and Its Discontents* (1930), he extended his analysis of the individual psyche to society and culture. Like Durkheim and Weber, Freud was an Enlightenment figure who used science to expose the limits of reason and who respected the power of the nonrational in human affairs. Living through a world war, personal depression, and Hitler, he harbored doubts even greater than theirs about the alleged superiority of Western civilization.

Freud was born in Moravia of Jewish parents. As a medical student at the University of Vienna, he was swept up in the revolutionary physiology that conceived of human beings as energy systems to which the laws of physics and chemistry apply. For fifteen years he conducted research in neurology, and he always defined himself as a scientist endeavoring to explain the mind deterministically, in biological terms.

In 1884 Freud abandoned the laboratory and took up the practice of medicine to support his growing family. He joined Josef Breuer, a leading Viennese specialist in internal medicine, in studies on the treatment of hysteria by hypnosis. From Breuer he learned the benefits of the cathartic or "talking out" form of therapy that he would later refine as the free-association method. Freud's probings into the minds of his patients revealed dynamic forces at work that seemed responsible for their abnormal symptoms. Gradually he formed the idea that most of these forces are unconscious and that the patient represses them to defend against unacceptable wishes or drives.

In the course of this work, Freud began with characteristic doggedness an intensive self-analysis in order to check on the material provided by his patients. By analyzing his dreams, he confirmed that many mental processes never reach awareness and are isolated from the rest of experience. Comparing the manifest content of the dream with the free associations it inspired, he was able to discover the latent or unconscious content of the dream. From here Freud could describe the series of maneuvers, called "mental mechanisms," that distort the latent content and enable unacceptable wishes or impulses to find indirect gratification. *The Interpretation of Dreams* (1900), with its last chapter outlining Freud's theory of the mind, triggered a succession of brilliant books on psychoanalysis during the next ten years. *Wit and Its Relation to the Unconscious* (1905) extends the analysis of "dream work" to cultural material, such as jokes, and develops a psychoanalytic theory of art. *The Psychopathology of Everyday Life* (1904) contends that slips of the tongue, errors, accidents, and faulty memory are all due to unconscious motives.

Seeking the cause of neurosis, Freud in these years developed his most controversial doctrine—the libido theory. In one essay he showed how dream interpretation can treat neurotic symptoms by unearthing the patient's early sexual history. In *Three Essays on the Theory of Sexuality* (1904), he described infantile sexuality and outlined the stages of development of the sexual drive. Based on studies of human neuroses and perversions, Freud argued that failures in development could prevent the individual from reaching the mature, or genital, stage, forcing him or her to remain at earlier levels.

By this time Freud had defied three shibboleths of bourgeois society: the doctrine of free will, the separation of soul and body, and the cordon sanitaire between reason and madness. He eagerly sought support for his methods and conclusions. In 1906 two leading Swiss analysts, Eugen Bleuler and Carl Jung, announced their allegiance. Together with the Viennese Alfred Adler and an English physician, Ernest Jones, they helped establish psychoanalysis as an international movement and formed a barrier between Freud and an increasingly hostile world. In September 1909 Freud made his only trip to America, where he and Jung lectured at Clark University on the invitation of its president, G. Stanley Hall. In 1911 the New York Psychoanalytic Society was established.

Besides publishing an immense number of clinical papers on the detailed problems of neurosis, as well as five lengthy case histories, Freud wrote extensively on the broader implications of his discoveries. For this purpose he founded in 1912 the journal *Imago*, devoted to nonmedical applications of his work. Some of Freud's pupils, notably Sandor Ferenczi, Otto Rank, and Karl Abraham, applied his methods to the unraveling of folklore and myths. Freud's most important cultural study before World War I was *Totem and Taboo* (1913), on the origin of religion and morality in the ambivalence of feelings that he found common to both children and primitive man.

After the war Freud published the essays that were the culmination of his life's work. In *Beyond the Pleasure Principle* (1919), a book that startled even his disciples, he presented a new theory of the mind. Previously, Freud had held that the mind was ruled by the pleasure principle, with its derivative the reality principle. Now he postulated a more basic principle, repetition-compulsion, with its tendency to restore earlier states of being. This implied that there was a tendency working to reduce life to inanimate matter, a drive Freud termed the "death instinct." Only the most speculative of his followers have felt able to accept this.

In the early 1920s, two books followed that proposed a new division of the mind into *id*, *ego*, and *superego* and laid the basis for a new psychology of the ego. *Group Psychology and the Analysis of the Ego* applied this theory to two institutions, the army and the church, which are nonfamilial hierarchies and therefore distinctive in social life. *The Ego and the Id* revised Freud's theory of conscience, which is still being debated with fruitful results by critics such as Nancy Chodorow and Eli Sagan. His *New Introductory Lectures on Psychoanalysis* (1932), from which "The Dissection of the Psychical Personality" is taken, provided a summation of his psychoanalytic theories, written expressly for a lay audience.

Around the spring of 1923, Freud was stricken by cancer of the mouth and underwent surgery that removed half his upper jaw. For the final sixteen years of his life, he endured thirty-three operations, hundreds of treatments, and nearly chronic pain. Yet according to his biographer Ernest Jones, Freud is not once recorded as having uttered a word of complaint.

In 1930 there appeared *Civilization and Its Discontents*, Freud's most famous study of culture. Civilization requires that we renounce our sexual and aggressive instincts, and with this comes almost unbearable tension and guilt. Its price may be too high, Freud argues, for human psychology has become the victim of the culture that it created. Freud, like Max Weber before him, leaves unanswered the question of culture's future in the grips of this paradox, although a few of his boldest followers, notably Erich Fromm, Herbert Marcuse, and Norman Brown, have envisioned their way out.

The Nazi persecutions of Jews had a tremendous impact on Freud. His supporters were driven from Germany, his writings were burned, and his publisher's stock of books were confiscated. Freud's last book, *Moses and Monotheism*, could not be published in authoritarian Vienna and appeared only in English translation during the last months of his life. When the Nazis invaded Austria in March 1938, Freud emigrated to England. There, at the age of 82, he underwent his last operation for cancer. Although the surgery was especially severe, the disease came back a few months later and was judged inoperable. Nevertheless, Freud continued to see patients and visitors and carried on his writing, until the last month of his life. He died in September 1939.

"THE DISSECTION OF THE PSYCHICAL PERSONALITY"

1932

Ladies and Gentlemen,—I know you are aware in regard to your own relations, whether with people or things, of the importance of your starting-point. This was also the case with psycho-analysis. It has not been a matter of indifference for the course of its development or for the reception it met with that it began its work on what is, of all the contents of the mind, most foreign to the ego—on symptoms. Symptoms are derived from the repressed, they are, as it were, its representatives before the ego; but the repressed is foreign territory to the ego—internal foreign territory—just as reality (if you will forgive the unusual expression) is external foreign territory. The path led from symptoms to the unconscious, to the life of the instincts, to sexuality; and it was then that psychoanalysis was met by the brilliant objection that human beings are not merely sexual creatures but have nobler and higher impulses as well. It might have been added that, exalted by their consciousness of these higher impulses they often assume the right to think nonsense and to neglect facts.

You know better. From the very first we have said that human beings fall ill of a conflict between the claims of instinctual life and the resistance which arises within them against it; and not for a moment have we forgotten this resisting, repelling, repressing agency, which we thought of as equipped with its special forces, the ego-instincts, and which coincides with the ego of popular psychology. The truth was merely that, in view of the laborious nature of the progress made by scientific work, even psycho-analysis was not able to study every field simultaneously and to express its views on every problem in a single breath. But at last the point was reached when it was possible for us to divert our attention from the repressed to the repressing forces, and we faced this ego, which had seemed so self-evident, with the secure expectation that here once again we should find things for which we could not have been prepared. It was not easy, however, to find a first approach; and that is what I intend to talk to you about to-day.

I must, however, let you know of my suspicion that this account of mine of ego-psychology will affect you differently from the introduction into the psychical underworld which preceded it. I cannot say with certainty why this should be so. I thought first that you would discover that whereas what I reported to you previously were, in the main, facts, however strange and peculiar, now you will be listening principally to opinions—that is, to speculations. But that does not meet the position. After further consideration I must maintain that the amount of intellectual working-over of the factual material in our ego-psychology is not much greater than it was in the psychology of the neuroses. I have been obliged to reject other explanations as well of the result I anticipate: I now believe that it is somehow a question of the nature of the material itself and of our being unaccustomed to dealing with it. In any case, I shall not be surprised if you show yourselves even more reserved and cautious in your judgement than hitherto.

The situation in which we find ourselves at the beginning of our enquiry may be expected itself to point the way for us. We wish to make the ego the matter of our enquiry, our very own ego. But is that possible? After all, the ego is in its very essence a subject; how can it be made into an object? Well, there is no doubt that it can be. The ego can take itself as an object, can treat itself like other objects, can observe itself, criticize itself, and do Heaven knows what with itself. In this, one part of the ego is setting itself over against the rest. So the ego can be split; it splits itself during a number of its functions—temporarily at least. Its parts can come together again afterwards. That is not exactly a novelty, though it may perhaps be putting an unusual emphasis on what is generally known. On the other hand, we are familiar with the notion that pathology, by making things larger and coarser, can draw our attention to normal conditions which would otherwise have escaped us. Where it points to a breach or a rent, there may normally be an articulation present. If we throw a crystal to the floor, it breaks; but not into haphazard pieces. It comes apart along its lines of cleavage into fragments whose boundaries, though they were invisible, were predetermined by the crystal's structure. Mental patients are split and broken structures of this same kind. Even we cannot withhold from them something of the reverential awe which peoples of the past felt for the insane. They have turned away from external reality, but for that very reason they know more about internal, psychical reality and can reveal a number of things to us that would otherwise be inaccessible to us.

We describe one group of these patients as suffering from delusions of being observed. They complain to us that perpetually, and down to their most intimate actions, they are being molested by the observation of unknown powers—presumably persons—and that in hallucinations they hear these persons reporting the outcome of their observation: "now he's going to say this, now he's dressing to go out" and so on. Observation of this sort is not yet the same thing as persecution, but it is not far from it; it presupposes that people distrust them, and expect to catch them carrying out forbidden actions for which they would be punished. How would it be if these insane people were right, if in each of us there is present in his ego an agency like this which observes and threatens to punish, and which in them has merely become sharply divided from their ego and mistakenly displaced into external reality?

I cannot tell whether the same thing will happen to you as to me. Ever since, under the powerful impression of this clinical picture, I formed the idea that the separation of the observing agency from the rest of the ego might be a regular feature of the ego's structure, that idea has never left me, and I was driven to investigate the further characteristics and connections of the agency which was thus separated off. The next step is quickly taken. The content of the delusions of being observed already suggests that the observing is only a preparation for judging and punishing, and we accordingly guess that another function of this agency must be what we call our conscience. There is scarcely anything else in us that we so regularly separate from our ego and so easily set over against it as precisely our conscience. I feel an inclination to do something that I think will give me pleasure, but I abandon it on the ground that my conscience does not allow it. Or I have let myself be persuaded by too great an expectation of pleasure into doing something to which the voice of conscience has objected and after the deed my conscience punishes me with distressing reproaches and causes me to feel remorse for the deed. I might simply say that the special agency which I am beginning to distinguish in the ego is conscience. But it is more prudent to keep the agency as something independent and to suppose that conscience is one of its functions and that self-observation, which is an essential preliminary to the judging activity of conscience, is another of them. And since when we recognize that something has a separate existence we give it a name of its own, from this time forward I will describe this agency in the ego as the "*super-ego*."

I am now prepared to hear you ask me scornfully whether our ego-psychology comes down to nothing more than taking commonly used abstractions literally and in a crude sense, and transforming them from concepts into things—by which not much would be gained. To this I would reply that in ego-psychology it will be difficult to escape what is universally known; it will rather be a question of new ways of looking at things and new ways of arranging them than of new discoveries. So hold to your contemptuous criticism for the time being and await further explanations. The facts of pathology give our efforts a background that you would look for in vain in popular psychology. So I will proceed.

Hardly have we familiarized ourselves with the idea of a super-ego like this which enjoys a certain degree of autonomy, follows its own intentions and is independent of the ego for its supply of energy, than a clinical picture forces itself on our notice which throws a striking light on the severity of this agency and indeed its cruelty, and on its changing relations to the ego. I am thinking of the condition of melancholia, or, more precisely, of melancholic attacks, which you too will have heard plenty about, even if you are not psychiatrists. The most striking feature of this illness, of whose causation and mechanism we know much too little, is the way in which the super-ego—"conscience," you may call it, quietly—treats the ego. While a melancholic can, like other people, show a greater or lesser degree of severity to himself in his healthy periods, during a melancholic attack his super-ego becomes over-severe, abuses the poor ego, humiliates it and ill-treats it, threatens it with the direst punishments, reproaches it for actions in the remotest past which had been taken lightly at the time—as though it had spent the whole interval in collecting accusations and had only been waiting for its present access of strength in order to bring them up and make a condemnatory judgement on their basis. The super-ego applies the strictest moral standard to the helpless ego which is at its mercy; in general it represents the claims of morality, and we realize all at once that our moral sense of guilt is the expression of the tension between the ego and the super-ego. It is a most remarkable experience to see morality, which is supposed to have been given us by God and thus deeply implanted in us, functioning [in these patients] as a periodic phenomenon. For after a certain number of months the whole moral fuss is over, the criticism of the super-ego is silent, the ego is rehabilitated and again enjoys all the rights of man till the next attack. In some forms of the disease, indeed, something of a contrary sort occurs in the intervals; the ego finds itself in a blissful state of intoxication, it celebrates a triumph, as though the super-ego had lost all its strength or had melted into the ego; and this liberated, manic ego permits itself a truly uninhibited satisfaction of all its appetites. Here are happenings rich in unsolved riddles!

No doubt you will expect me to give you more than a mere illustration when I inform you that we have found out all kinds of things about the formation of the super-ego—that is to say, about the origin of conscience. Following a well-known pronouncement of Kant's which couples the conscience within us with the starry Heavens, a pious man might well be tempted to honour these two things as the masterpieces of creation. The stars are indeed magnificent, but as regards conscience God has done an uneven and careless piece of work, for a large majority of men have brought along with them only a modest amount of it or scarcely enough to be worth mentioning. We are far from overlooking the portion of psychological truth that is contained in the assertion that conscience is of divine origin; but the thesis needs interpretation. Even if conscience is something "within us," yet it is not so from the first. In this it is a real contrast to sexual life, which is in fact there from the beginning of life and not only a later addition. But, as is well known, young children are amoral and possess no internal inhibitions against their impulses striving for pleasure. The part which is later taken on by the super-ego is played to begin with by an external power, by parental authority. Parental influence governs the child by offering proofs of love and by threatening punishments which are signs to the child of loss of love and are bound to be feared on their own account. This realistic anxiety is the precursor of the later moral anxiety. So long as it is dominant there is no need to talk of a super-ego and of a conscience. It is only subsequently that the secondary situation develops (which we are all too ready to regard as the normal one), where the external restraint is internalized and the super-ego takes the place of the parental agency and observes, directs and threatens the ego in exactly the same way as earlier the parents did with the child.

The super-ego, which thus takes over the power, function and even the methods of the parental agency, is however not merely its successor but actually the legitimate heir of its body. It proceeds directly out of it, we shall learn presently by what process. First, however, we must dwell upon a discrepancy between the two. The super-ego seems to have made a one-sided choice and to have picked out only the parents' strictness and severity, their prohibiting and punitive function, whereas their loving care seems not to have been taken over and maintained. If the parents have really enforced their authority with severity we can easily understand the child's in turn developing a severe super-ego. But, contrary to our expectation, experience shows that the super-ego can acquire the same characteristic of relentless severity even if the upbringing had been mild and kindly and had so far as possible avoided threats and punishments. We shall come back later to this contradiction when we deal with the transformations of instinct during the formation of the super-ego.

I cannot tell you as much as I should like about the metamorphosis of the parental relationship into the super-ego, partly because that process is so complicated that an account of it will not fit into the framework of an introductory course of lectures such as I am trying to give you, but partly also because we ourselves do not feel sure that we understand it completely. So you must be content with the sketch that follows.

The basis of the process is what is called an "identification"—that is to say, the assimilation of one ego to another one, as a result of which the first ego behaves like the second in certain respects, imitates it and in a sense takes it up into itself. Identification has been not unsuitably compared with the oral, cannibalistic incorporation of the other person. It is a very important form of attachment to someone else, probably the very first, and not the same thing as the choice of an object. The difference between the two can be expressed in some such way as this. If a boy identifies himself with his father, he wants to *be like* his father; if he makes him the object of his choice, he wants to *have* him, to possess him. In the first case his ego is altered on the model of his father; in the second case that is not necessary. Identification and object-choice are to a large extent independent of each other; it is however possible to identify oneself with someone whom, for instance, one has taken as a sexual object, and to alter one's ego on his model. It is said that the influencing of the ego by the sexual object occurs particularly often with women and is characteristic of femininity. I must already have spoken to you in my earlier lectures of what is by far the most instructive relation between identification and object-choice. It can be observed equally easily in children and adults, in normal as in sick people. If one has lost an object or has been obliged to give it up, one often compensates oneself by identifying oneself with it and by setting it up once more in one's ego, so that here object-choice regresses, as it were, to identification.

I myself am far from satisfied with these remarks on identification; but it will be enough if you can grant me that the installation of the super-ego can be described as a successful instance of identification with the parental agency. The fact that speaks decisively for this view is that this new creation of a superior agency within the ego is most intimately linked with the destiny of the Oedipus complex, so that the super-ego appears as the heir of that emotional attachment which is of such importance for childhood. With his abandonment of the Oedipus complex a child must, as we can see, renounce the intense object-cathexes which he has deposited with his parents, and it is as a compensation for this loss of objects that there is such a strong intensification of the identifications with his parents which have probably long been present in his ego. Identifications of this kind as precipitates of object-cathexes that have been given up will be repeated often enough later in the child's life; but it is entirely in accordance with the emotional importance of this first instance of such a transformation that a special place in the ego should be found for its outcome. Close investigation has shown us, too, that the super-ego is stunted in its strength and growth if the surmounting of the Oedipus complex is only incompletely successful. In the course of development the superego also takes on the influences of those who have stepped into the place of parents—educators, teachers, people chosen as ideal models. Normally it departs more and more from the original parental figures; it becomes, so to say, more impersonal. Nor must it be forgotten that a child has a different estimate of its parents at different periods of its life. At the time at which the Oedipus complex gives place to the super-ego they are something quite magnificent; but later they lose much of this. Identifications then come about with these later parents as well, and indeed they regularly make important contributions to the formation of character; but in that case they only affect the ego, they no longer influence the super-ego, which has been determined by the earliest parental imagos.

I hope you have already formed an impression that the hypothesis of the super-ego really describes a structural relation and is not merely a personification of some such abstraction as that of conscience. One more important function remains to be mentioned which we attribute to this super-ego. It is also the vehicle of the ego ideal by which the ego measures itself, which it emulates, and whose demand for ever greater perfection it strives to fulfil. There is no doubt that this ego ideal is the precipitate of the old picture of the parents, the expression of admiration for the perfection which the child then attributed to them.

I am sure you have heard a great deal of the sense of inferiority which is supposed particularly to characterize neurotics. It especially haunts the pages of what are known as *belles lettres*. An author who uses the term "inferiority complex" thinks that by so doing he has fulfilled all the demands of psycho-analysis and has raised his composition to a higher psychological plane. In fact "inferiority complex" is a technical term that is scarcely used in psycho-analysis. For us it does not bear the meaning of anything simple, let alone elementary. To trace it back to the self-perception of possible organic defects, as the school of what are known as "Individual Psychologists" likes to do, seems to us a short-sighted error. The sense of inferiority has strong erotic roots. A child feels inferior if he notices that he is not loved, and so does an adult. The only bodily organ which is really regarded as inferior is the atrophied penis, a girl's clitoris. But the major part of the sense of inferiority derives from the ego's relation to its super-ego; like the sense of guilt it is an expression of the tension between them. Altogether, it is hard to separate the sense of inferiority and the sense of guilt. It would perhaps be right to regard the former as the erotic complement to the moral sense of inferiority. Little attention has been given in psycho-analysis to the question of the delimitation of the two concepts.

If only because the inferiority complex has become so popular, I will venture to entertain you here with a short digression. A historical personality of our own days, who is still alive though at the moment he has retired into the background, suffers from a defect in one of his limbs owing to an injury at the time of his birth. A very well-known contemporary writer who is particularly fond of compiling the biographies of celebrities has dealt, among others, with the life of the man I am speaking of. Now in writing a biography it may well be difficult to suppress a need to plumb the psychological depths. For this reason our author has ventured on an attempt to erect the whole of the development of his hero's character on the sense of inferiority which must have been called up by his physical defect. In doing so, he has overlooked one small but not insignificant fact. It is usual for mothers whom Fate has presented with a child who is sickly or otherwise at a disadvantage to try to compensate him for his unfair handicap by a superabundance of love. In the instance before us, the proud mother behaved otherwise; she withdrew her love from the child on account of his infirmity. When he had grown up into a man of great power, he proved unambiguously by his actions that he had never forgiven his mother. When you consider the importance of a mother's love for the mental life of a child, you will no doubt make a tacit correction of the biographer's inferiority theory.

But let us return to the super-ego. We have allotted it the functions of self-observation, of conscience and of [maintaining] the ideal. It follows from what we have said about its origin that it presupposes an immensely important biological fact and a fateful psychological one: namely, the human child's long dependence on its parents and the Oedipus complex, both of which, again, are intimately interconnected. The super-ego is the representative for us of every moral restriction, the advocate of a striving towards perfection—it is, in short, as much as we have been able to grasp psychologically of what is described as the higher side of human life. Since it itself goes back to the influence of parents, educators and so on, we learn still more of its significance if we turn to those who are its sources. As a rule parents and authorities analogous to them follow the precepts of their own super-egos in educating children. Whatever understanding their ego may have come to with their super-ego, they are severe and exacting in educating children. They have forgotten the difficulties of their own childhood and they are glad to be able now to identify themselves fully with their own parents who in the past laid such severe restrictions upon them. Thus a child's super-ego is in fact constructed on the model not of its parents but of its parents' super-ego; the contents which fill it are the same and it becomes the vehicle of tradition and of all the time-resisting judgements of value which have propagated themselves in this manner from generation to generation. You may easily guess what important assistance taking the super-ego into account will give us in our understanding of the social behaviour of mankind—in the problem of delinquency, for instance—and perhaps even what practical hints on education. It seems likely that what are known as materialistic views of history sin in under-estimating this factor. They brush it aside with the remark that human "ideologies" are nothing other than the product and superstructure of their contemporary economic conditions. That is true, but very probably not the whole truth. Mankind never lives entirely in the present. The past, the tradition of the race and of the people, lives on in the ideologies of the super-ego, and yields only slowly to the influences of the present and to new changes; and so long as it operates through the super-ego it plays a powerful part in human life, independently of economic conditions.

In 1921 I endeavoured to make use of the differentiation between the ego and the super-ego in a study of group psychology. I arrived at a formula such as this: a psychological group is a collection of individuals who have introduced the same person into their super-ego and, on the basis of this common element, have identified themselves with one another in their ego. This applies, of course, only to groups that have a leader. If we possessed more applications of this kind, the hypothesis of the superego would lose its last touch of strangeness for us, and we should become completely free of the embarrassment that still comes over us when, accustomed as we are to the atmosphere of the underworld, we move in the more superficial, higher strata of the mental apparatus. We do not suppose, of course, that with the separation off of the super-ego we have said the last word on the psychology of the ego. It is rather a first step; but in this case it is not only the first step that is hard.

Now, however, another problem awaits us—at the opposite end of the ego, as we might put it. It is presented to us by an observation during the work of analysis, an observation which is actually a very old one. As not infrequently happens, it has taken a long time to come to the point of appreciating its importance. The whole theory of psycho-analysis is, as you know, in fact built up on the perception of the resistance offered to us by the patient when we attempt to make his unconscious conscious to him. The objective sign of this resistance is that his associations fail or depart widely from the topic that is being dealt with. He may also recognize the resistance *subjectively* by the fact that he has distressing feelings when he approaches the topic. But this last sign may also be absent. We then say to the patient that we infer from his behaviour that he is now in a state of resistance; and he replies that he knows nothing of that, and is only aware that his associations have become more difficult. It turns out that we were right; but in that case his resistance was unconscious too, just as unconscious as the repressed, at the lifting of which we were working. We should long ago have asked the question: from what part of his mind does an unconscious resistance like this arise? The beginner in psycho-analysis will be ready at once with the answer: it is, of course, the resistance of the unconscious. An ambiguous and unserviceable answer! If it means that the resistance arises from the repressed, we must rejoin: certainly not! We must rather attribute to the repressed a strong upward drive, an impulsion to break through into consciousness. The resistance can only be a manifestation of the ego, which originally put the repression into force and now wishes to maintain it. That, moreover, is the view we always took. Since we have come to assume a special agency in the ego, the super-ego, which represents demands of a restrictive and rejecting character, we may say that repression is the work of this super-ego and that it is carried out either by itself or by the ego in obedience to its orders. If then we are met by the case of the resistance in analysis not being conscious to the patient, this means either that in quite important situations the super-ego and the ego can operate unconsciously, or—and this would be still more important—that portions of both of them, the ego and the super-ego themselves, are unconscious. In both cases we have to reckon with the disagreeable discovery that on the one hand (super-) ego and conscious and on the other hand repressed and unconscious are far from coinciding.

And here, Ladies and Gentlemen, I feel that I must make a pause to take breath—which you too will welcome as a relief—and, before I go on, to apologize to you. My intention is to give you some addenda to the introductory lectures on psycho-analysis which I began fifteen years ago, and I am obliged to behave as though you as well as I had in the interval done nothing but practise psycho-analysis. I know that that assumption is out of place; but I am helpless, I cannot do otherwise. This is no doubt related to the fact that it is in general so hard to give anyone who is not himself a psycho-analyst an insight into psycho-analysis. You can believe me when I tell you that we do not enjoy giving an impression of being members of a secret society and of practising a mystical science. Yet we have been obliged to recognize and express as our conviction that no one has a right to join in a discussion of psycho-analysis who has not had particular experiences which can only be obtained by being analysed one-self. When I gave you my lectures fifteen years ago I tried to spare you certain speculative portions of our theory; but it is precisely from them that are derived the new acquisitions of which I must speak to you to-day.

I return now to our topic. In face of the doubt whether the ego and super-ego are themselves unconscious or merely produce unconscious effects, we have, for good reasons, decided in favour of the former possibility. And it is indeed the case that large portions of the ego and super-ego can remain unconscious and are normally unconscious. That is to say, the individual knows nothing of their contents and it requires an expenditure of effort to make them conscious. It is a fact that ego and conscious, repressed and unconscious do not coincide. We feel a need to make a fundamental revision of our attitude to the problem of conscious-unconscious. At first we are inclined greatly to reduce the value of the criterion of being conscious since it has shown itself so untrustworthy. But we should be doing it an injustice. As may be said of our life, it is not worth much, but it is all we have. Without the illumination thrown by the quality of consciousness, we should be lost in the obscurity of depth-psychology; but we must attempt to find our bearings afresh.

There is no need to discuss what is to be called conscious: it is removed from all doubt. The oldest and best meaning of the word "unconscious" is the descriptive one; we call a psychical process unconscious whose existence we are obliged to assume —for some such reason as that we infer it from its effects—, but of which we know nothing. In that case we have the same relation to it as we have to a psychical process in another person, except that it is in fact one of our own. If we want to be still more correct, we shall modify our assertion by saying that we call a process unconscious if we are obliged to assume that it is being activated *at the moment*, though *at the moment* we know nothing about it. This qualification makes us reflect that the majority of conscious processes are conscious only for a short time; very soon they become *latent*, but can easily become conscious again. We might also say that they had become unconscious, if it were at all certain that in the condition of latency they are still something psychical. So far we should have learnt nothing new; nor should we have acquired the right to introduce the concept of an unconscious into psychology. But then comes the new observation that we were already able to make in parapraxes. In order to explain a slip of the tongue, for instance, we find ourselves obliged to assume that the intention to make a particular remark was present in the subject. We infer it with certainty from the interference with his remark which has occurred; but the intention did not put itself through and was thus unconscious. If, when we subsequently put it before the speaker, he recognizes it as one familiar to him, then it was only temporarily unconscious to him; but if he repudiates it as something foreign to him, then it was permanently unconscious. From this experience we retrospectively obtain the right also to pronounce as something unconscious what had been described as latent. A consideration of these dynamic relations permits us now to distinguish two kinds of unconscious—one which is easily, under frequently occurring circumstances, transformed into something conscious, and another with which this transformation is difficult and takes place only subject to a considerable expenditure of effort or possibly never at all. In order to escape the ambiguity as to whether we mean the one or the other unconscious, whether we are using the word in the descriptive or in the dynamic sense, we make use of a permissible and simple way out. We call the unconscious which is only latent, and thus easily becomes conscious, the "preconscious" and retain the term "unconscious" for the other. We now have three terms, "conscious," "preconscious" and "unconscious," with which we can get along in our description of mental phenomena. Once again: the preconscious is also unconscious in the purely descriptive sense, but we do not give it that name, except in talking loosely or when we have to make a defence of the existence in mental life of unconscious processes in general.

You will admit, I hope, that so far that is not too bad and allows of convenient handling. Yes, but unluckily the work of psycho-analysis has found itself compelled to use the word "unconscious" in yet another, third, sense, and this may, to be sure, have led to confusion. Under the new and powerful impression of there being an extensive and important field of mental life which is normally withdrawn from the ego's knowledge so that the processes occurring in it have to be regarded as unconscious in the truly dynamic sense, we have come to understand the term "unconscious" in a topographical or systematic sense as well; we have come to speak of a "system" of the preconscious and a "system" of the unconscious, of a conflict between the ego and the system *Ucs.*, and have used the word more and more to denote a mental province rather than a quality of what is mental. The discovery, actually an inconvenient one, that portions of the ego and super-ego as well are unconscious in the dynamic sense, operates at this point as a relief—it makes possible the removal of a complication. We perceive that we have no right to name the mental region that is foreign to the ego "the system *Ucs.*," since the characteristic of being unconscious is not restricted to it. Very well; we will no longer use the term "unconscious" in the systematic sense and we will give what we have hitherto so described a better name and one no longer open to misunderstanding. Following a verbal usage of Nietzsche's and taking up a suggestion by Georg Groddeck [1923], we will in future call it the "id." This impersonal pronoun seems particularly well suited for expressing the main characteristic of this province of the mind—the fact of its being alien to the ego. The super-ego, the ego and the id—these, then, are the three realms, regions, provinces, into which we divide an individual's mental apparatus, and with the mutual relations of which we shall be concerned in what follows.

But first a short interpolation. I suspect that you feel dissatisfied because the three qualities of the characteristic of consciousness and the three provinces of the mental apparatus do not fall together into three peaceable couples, and you may regard this as in some sense obscuring our findings. I do not think, however, that we should regret it, and we should tell ourselves that we had no right to expect any such smooth arrangement. Let me give you an analogy; analogies, it is true, decide nothing, but they can make one feel more at home. I am imagining a country with a landscape of varying configuration—hill-country, plains, and chains of lakes—, and with a mixed population: it is inhabited by Germans, Magyars and Slovaks, who carry on different activities. Now things might be partitioned in such a way that the Germans, who breed cattle, live in the hill-country, the Magyars, who grow cereals and wine, live in the plains, and the Slovaks, who catch fish and plait reeds, live by the lakes. If the partitioning could be neat and clear-cut like this, a Woodrow Wilson would be delighted by it; it would also be convenient for a lecture in a geography lesson. The probability is, however, that you will find less orderliness and more mixing, if you travel through the region. Germans, Magyars and Slovaks live interspersed all over it; in the hill-country there is agricultural land as well, cattle are bred in the plains too. A few things are naturally as you expected, for fish cannot be caught in the mountains and wine does not grow in the water. Indeed, the picture of the region that you brought with you may on the whole fit the facts; but you will have to put up with deviations in the details.

You will not expect me to have much to tell you that is new about the id apart from its new name. It is the dark, inaccessible part of our personality; what little we know of it we have learnt from our study of the dream-work and of the construction of neurotic symptoms, and most of that is of a negative character and can be described only as a contrast to the ego. We approach the id with analogies: we call it a chaos, a cauldron full of seething excitations. We picture it as being open at its end to somatic influences, and as there taking up into itself instinctual needs which find their psychical expression in it, but we cannot say in what substratum. It is filled with energy reaching it from the instincts, but it has no organization, produces no collective will, but only a striving to bring about the satisfaction of the instinctual needs subject to the observance of the pleasure principle. The logical laws of thought do not apply in the id, and this is true above all of the law of contradiction. Contrary impulses exist side by side, without cancelling each other out or diminishing each other: at the most they may converge to form compromises under the dominating economic pressure towards the discharge of energy. There is nothing in the id that could be compared with negation; and we perceive with surprise an exception to the philosophical theorem that space and time are necessary forms of our mental acts. There is nothing in the id that corresponds to the idea of time; there is no recognition of the passage of time, and—a thing that is most remarkable and awaits consideration in philosophical thought—no alteration in its mental processes is produced by the passage of time. Wishful impulses which have never passed beyond the id, but impressions, too, which have been sunk into the id by repression, are virtually immortal; after the passage of decades they behave as though they had just occurred. They can only be recognized as belonging to the past, can only lose their importance and be deprived of their cathexis of energy, when they have been made conscious by the work of analysis and it is on this that the therapeutic effect of analytic treatment rests to no small extent.

Again and again I have had the impression that we have made too little theoretical use of this fact, established beyond any doubt, of the unalterability by time of the repressed. This seems to offer an approach to the most profound discoveries. Nor, unfortunately, have I myself made any progress here.

The id of course knows no judgements of value: no good and evil, no morality. The economic or, if you prefer, the quantitative factor, which is intimately linked to the pleasure principle, dominates all its processes. Instinctual cathexes seeking discharge—that, in our view, is all there is in the id. It even seems that the energy of these instinctual impulses is in a state different from that in the other regions of the mind, far more mobile and capable of discharge; otherwise the displacements and condensations would not occur which are characteristic of the id and which so completely disregard the *quality* of what is cathected—what in the ego we should call an idea. We would give much to understand more about these things! You can see, incidentally, that we are in a position to attribute to the id characteristics other than that of its being unconscious, and you can recognize the possibility of portions of the ego and super-ego being unconscious without possessing the same primitive and irrational characteristics.

We can best arrive at the characteristics of the actual ego, in so far as it can be distinguished from the id and from the super-ego, by examining its relation to the outermost superficial portion of the mental apparatus, which we describe as the system *Pcpt.-Cs.* This system is turned towards the external world, it is the medium for the perceptions arising thence, and during its functioning the phenomenon of consciousness arises in it. It is the sense-organ of the entire apparatus; moreover it is receptive not only to excitations from outside but also to those arising from the interior of the mind. We need scarcely look for a justification of the view that the ego is that portion of the id which was modified by the proximity and influence of the external world, which is adapted for the reception of stimuli and as a protective shield against stimuli, comparable to the cortical layer by which a small piece of living substance is surrounded. The relation to the external world has become the decisive factor for the ego; it has taken on the task of representing the external world to the id—fortunately for the id, which could not escape destruction if, in its blind efforts for the satisfaction of its instincts, it disregarded that supreme external power. In accomplishing this function, the ego must observe the external world, must lay down an accurate picture of it in the memory-traces of its perceptions, and by its exercise of the function of "reality-testing" must put aside whatever in this picture of the external world is an addition derived from internal sources of excitation. The ego controls the approaches to motility under the id's orders; but between a need and an action it has interposed a postponement in the form of the activity of thought, during which it makes use of the mnemic residues of experience. In that way it has dethroned the pleasure principle which dominates the course of events in the id without any restriction and has replaced it by the reality principle, which promises more certainty and greater success.

The relation to time, which is so hard to describe, is also introduced into the ego by the perceptual system; it can scarcely be doubted that the mode of operation of that system is what provides the origin of the idea of time. But what distinguishes the ego from the id quite especially is a tendency to synthesis in its contents, to a combination and unification in its mental processes which are totally lacking in the id. When presently we come to deal with the instincts in mental life we shall, I hope, succeed in tracing this essential characteristic of the ego back to its source. It alone produces the high degree of organization which the ego needs for its best achievements. The ego develops from perceiving the instincts to controlling them; but this last is only achieved by the [psychical] representative of the instinct being allotted its proper place in a considerable assemblage, by its being taken up into a coherent context. To adopt a popular mode of speaking, we might say that the ego stands for reason and good sense while the id stands for the untamed passions.

So far we have allowed ourselves to be impressed by the merits and capabilities of the ego; it is now time to consider the other side as well. The ego is after all only a portion of the id, a portion that has been expediently modified by the proximity of the external world with its threat of danger. From a dynamic point of view it is weak, it has borrowed its energies from the id, and we are not entirely without insight into the methods—we might call them dodges —by which it extracts further amounts of energy from the id. One such method, for instance, is by identifying itself with actual or abandoned objects. The object-cathexes spring from the instinctual demands of the id. The ego has in the first instance to take note of them. But by identifying itself with the object it recommends itself to the id in place of the object and seeks to divert the id's libido on to itself. We have already seen that in the course of its life the ego takes into itself a large number of precipitates like this of former object-cathexes. The ego must on the whole carry out the id's intentions, it fulfils its task by finding out the circumstances in which those intentions can best be achieved. The ego's relation to the id might be compared with that of a rider to his horse. The horse supplies the locomotive energy, while the rider has the privilege of deciding on the goal and of guiding the powerful animal's movement. But only too often there arises between the ego and the id the not precisely ideal situation of the rider being obliged to guide the horse along the path by which it itself wants to go.

There is one portion of the id from which the ego has separated itself by resistances due to repression. But the repression is not carried over into the id: the repressed merges into the remainder of the id.

We are warned by a proverb against serving two masters at the same time. The poor ego has things even worse: it serves three severe masters and does what it can to bring their claims and demands into harmony with one another. These claims are always divergent and often seem incompatible. No wonder that the ego so often fails in its task. Its three tyrannical masters are the external world, the super-ego and the id. When we follow the ego's efforts to satisfy them simultaneously—or rather, to obey them simultaneously—we cannot feel any regret at having personified this ego and having set it up as a separate organism. It feels hemmed in on three sides, threatened by three kinds of danger, to which, if it is hard pressed, it reacts by generating anxiety. Owing to its origin from the experiences of the perceptual system, it is earmarked for representing the demands of the external world, but it strives too to be a loyal servant of the id, to remain on good terms with it, to recommend itself to it as an object and to attract its libido to itself. In its attempts to mediate between the id and reality, it is often obliged to cloak the *Ucs.* commands of the id with its own *Pcs.* rationalizations, to conceal the id's conflicts with reality, to profess, with diplomatic disingenuousness, to be taking notice of reality even when the id has remained rigid and unyielding. On the other hand it is observed at every step it takes by the strict super-ego, which lays down definite standards for its conduct, without taking any account of its difficulties from the direction of the id and the external world, and which, if those standards are not obeyed, punishes it with tense feelings of inferiority and of guilt. Thus the ego, driven by the id, confined by the super-ego, repulsed by reality, struggles to master its economic task of bringing about harmony among the forces and influences working in and upon it; and we can understand how it is that so often we cannot suppress a cry: "Life is not easy!" If the ego is obliged to admit its weakness, it breaks out in anxiety—realistic anxiety regarding the external world, moral anxiety regarding the super-ego and neurotic anxiety regarding the strength of the passions in the id.

I should like to portray the structural relations of the mental personality, as I have described them to you, in the unassuming sketch which I now present you with:

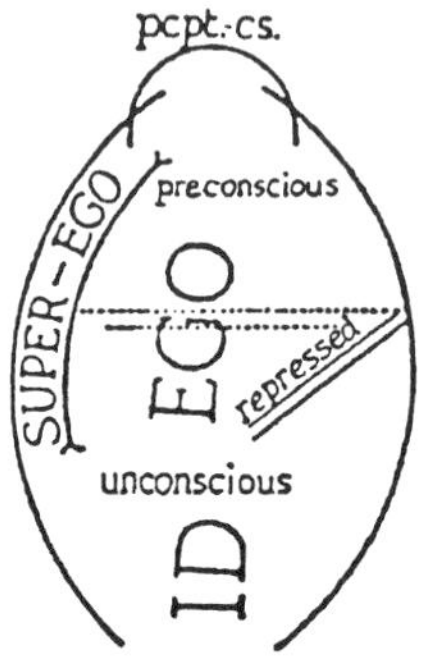

As you see here, the super-ego merges into the id; indeed, as heir to the Oedipus complex it has intimate relations with the id; it is more remote than the ego from the perceptual system. The id has intercourse with the external world only through the ego—at least, according to this diagram. It is certainly hard to say to-day how far the drawing is correct. In one respect it is undoubtedly not. The space occupied by the unconscious id ought to have been incomparably greater than that of the ego or the preconscious. I must ask you to correct it in your thoughts.

And here is another warning, to conclude these remarks, which have certainly been exacting and not, perhaps, very illuminating. In thinking of this division of the personality into an ego, a super-ego and an id, you will not, of course, have pictured sharp frontiers like the artificial ones drawn in political geography. We cannot do justice to the characteristics of the mind by linear outlines like those in a drawing or in primitive painting, but rather by areas of colour melting into one another as they are presented by modern artists. After making the separation we must allow what we have separated to merge together once more. You must not judge too harshly a first attempt at giving a pictorial representation of something so intangible as psychical processes. It is highly probable that the development of these divisions is subject to great variations in different individuals; it is possible that in the course of actual functioning they may change and go through a temporary phase of involution. Particularly in the case of what is phylogeneticary the last and most delicate of these divisions—the differentiation between the ego and the super-ego—something of the sort seems to be true. There is no question but that the same thing results from psychical illness. It is easy to imagine, too, that certain mystical practices may succeed in upsetting the normal relations between the different regions of the mind, so that, for instance, perception may be able to grasp happenings in the depths of the ego and in the id which were otherwise inaccessible to it. It may safely be doubted, however, whether this road will lead us to the ultimate truths from which salvation is to be expected. Nevertheless it may be admitted that the therapeutic efforts of psycho-analysis have chosen a similar line of approach. Its intention is, indeed, to strengthen the ego, to make it more independent of the super-ego, to widen its field of perception and enlarge its organization, so that it can appropriate fresh portions of the id. Where id was, there ego shall be. It is a work of culture—not unlike the draining of the Zuider Zee.

GROUP PSYCHOLOGY AND THE ANALYSIS OF THE EGO

1921

V TWO ARTIFICIAL GROUPS: THE CHURCH AND THE ARMY

We may recall from what we know of the morphology of groups that it is possible to distinguish very different kinds of groups and opposing lines in their development. There are very fleeting groups and extremely lasting ones; homogeneous ones; made up of the same sorts of individuals, and unhomogeneous ones; natural groups, and artificial ones, requiring an external force to keep them together; primitive groups, and highly organized ones with a definite structure. But for reasons which remain to be explained we should like to lay particular stress upon a distinction to which writers on the subject have been inclined to give too little attention; I refer to that between leaderless groups and those with leaders. And, in complete opposition to the usual practice, we shall not choose a relatively simple group formation as our point of departure, but shall begin with highly organized, lasting and artificial groups. The most interesting example of such structures are Churches—communities of believers—and armies.

A Church and an army are artificial groups—that is, a certain external force is employed to prevent them from disintegrating and to check alterations in their structure. As a rule a person is not consulted, or is given no choice, as to whether he wants to enter such a group; any attempt at leaving it is usually met with persecution or with severe punishment, or has quite definite conditions attached to it. It is quite outside our present interest to enquire why these associations need such special safeguards. We are only attracted by one circumstance, namely that certain facts, which are far more concealed in other cases, can be observed very clearly in those highly organized groups which are protected from dissolution in the manner that has been mentioned.

In a Church (and we may with advantage take the Catholic Church as a type) as well as in an army, however different the two may be in other respects, the same illusion holds good of there being a head —in the Catholic Church Christ, in an army its Commander-in-Chief—who loves all the individuals in the group with an equal love. Everything depends upon this illusion; if it were to be dropped, then both Church and army would dissolve, so far as the external force permitted them to. This equal love was expressly enunciated by Christ: "Inasmuch as ye have done it unto one of the least of these my brethren, ye have done it unto me." He stands to the individual members of the group of believers in the relation of a kind elder brother; he is their substitute father. All the demands that are made upon the individual are derived from this love of Christ's. A democratic strain runs through the Church, for the very reason that before Christ everyone is equal, and that everyone has an equal share in his love. It is not without a deep reason that the similarity between the Christian community and a family is invoked, and that believers call themselves brothers in Christ, that is, brothers through the love which Christ has for them. There is no doubt that the tie which unites each individual with Christ is also the cause of the tie which unites them with one another. The like holds good of an army. The Commander-in-Chief is a father who loves all soldiers equally, and for that reason they are comrades among themselves. The army differs structurally from the Church in being built up of a series of such groups. Every captain is, as it were, the Commander-in-Chief and the father of his company, and so is every non-commissioned officer of his section. It is true that a similar hierarchy has been constructed in the Church, but it does not play the same part in it economically; for more knowledge and care about individuals may be attributed to Christ than to a human Commander-in-Chief.

An objection will justly be raised against this conception of the libidinal structure of an army on the ground that no place has been found in it for such ideas as those of one's country, of national glory, etc., which are of such importance in holding an army together. The answer is that that is a different instance of a group tie, and no longer such a simple one; for the examples of great generals, like Caesar, Wallenstein, or Napoleon, show that such ideas are not indispensable to the existence of an army. We shall presently touch upon the possibility of a leading idea being substituted for a leader and upon the relations between the two. The neglect of this libidinal factor in an army, even when it is not the only factor operative, seems to be not merely a theoretical omission but also a practical danger. Prussian militarism, which was just as unpsychological as German science, may have had to suffer the consequences of this in the [first] World War. We know that the war neuroses which ravaged the German army have been recognized as being a protest of the individual against the part he was expected to play in the army; and according to the communication of Simmel (1918), the hard treatment of the men by their superiors may be considered as foremost among the motive forces of the disease. If the importance of the libido's claims on this score had been better appreciated, the fantastic promises of the American President's Fourteen Points would probably not have been believed so easily, and the splendid instrument would not have broken in the hands of the German leaders.

It is to be noticed that in these two artificial groups each individual is bound by libidinal ties on the one hand to the leader (Christ, the Commander-in-Chief) and on the other hand to the other members of the group. How these two ties are related to each other, whether they are of the same kind and the same value, and how they are to be described psychologically—these questions must be reserved for subsequent enquiry. But we shall venture even now upon a mild reproach against earlier writers for not having sufficiently appreciated the importance of the leader in the psychology of the group, while our own choice of this as a first subject for investigation has brought us into a more favourable position. It would appear as though we were on the right road towards an explanation of the principal phenomenon of group psychology—the individual's lack of freedom in a group. If each individual is bound in two directions by such an intense emotional tie, we shall find no difficulty in attributing to that circumstance the alteration and limitation which have been observed in his personality.

A hint to the same effect, that the essence of a group lies in the libidinal ties existing in it, is also to be found in the phenomenon of panic, which is best studied in military groups. A panic arises if a group of that kind becomes disintegrated. Its characteristics are that none of the orders given by superiors are any longer listened to, and that each individual is only solicitous on his own account, and without any consideration for the rest. The mutual ties have ceased to exist, and a gigantic and senseless fear is set free. At this point, again, the objection will naturally be made that it is rather the other way round; and that the fear has grown so great as to be able to disregard all ties and all feelings of consideration for others. McDougall (1920, 24) has even made use of panic (though not of military panic) as a typical instance of that intensification of emotion by contagion ("primary induction") on which he lays so much emphasis. But nevertheless this rational method of explanation is here quite inadequate. The very question that needs explanation is why the fear has become so gigantic. The greatness of the danger cannot be responsible, for the same army which now falls a victim to panic may previously have faced equally great or greater danger with complete success; it is of the very essence of panic that it bears no relation to the danger that threatens, and often breaks out upon the most trivial occasions. If an individual in panic fear begins to be solicitous only on his own account, he bears witness in so doing to the fact that the emotional ties, which have hitherto made the danger seem small to him, have ceased to exist. Now that he is by himself in facing the danger, he may surely think it greater. The fact is, therefore, that panic fear presupposes a relaxation in the libidinal structure of the group and reacts to that relaxation in a justifiable manner, and the contrary view—that the libidinal ties of the group are destroyed owing to fear in the face of the danger—can be refuted.

The contention that fear in a group is increased to enormous proportions through induction (contagion) is not in the least contradicted by these remarks. McDougall's view meets the case entirely when the danger is a really great one and when the group has no strong emotional ties—conditions which are fulfilled, for instance, when a fire breaks out in a theatre or a place of amusement. But the truly instructive case and the one which can be best employed for our purposes is that mentioned above, in which a body of troops breaks into a panic although the danger has not increased beyond a degree that is usual and has often been previously faced. It is not to be expected that the usage of the word "panic" should be clearly and unambiguously determined. Sometimes it is used to describe any collective fear, sometimes even fear in an individual when it exceeds all bounds, and often the name seems to be reserved for cases in which the outbreak of fear is not warranted by the occasion. If we take the word "panic" in the sense of collective fear, we can establish a far-reaching analogy. Fear in an individual is provoked either by the greatness of a danger or by the cessation of emotional ties (libidinal cathexes); the latter is the case of neurotic fear or anxiety. In just the same way panic arises either owing to an increase of the common danger or owing to the disappearance of the emotional ties which hold the group together; and the latter case is analogous to that of neurotic anxiety.

Anyone who, like McDougall (1920), describes a panic as one of the plainest functions of the "group mind," arrives at the paradoxical position that this group mind does away with itself in one of its most striking manifestations. It is impossible to doubt that panic means the disintegration of a group; it involves the cessation of all the feelings of consideration which the members of the group otherwise show one another.

The typical occasion of the outbreak of a panic is very much as it is represented in Nestroy's parody of Hebbel's play about Judith and Holofernes. A soldier cries out: "The general has lost his head!" and thereupon all the Assyrians take to flight. The loss of the leader in some sense or other, the birth of misgivings about him, brings on the outbreak of panic, though the danger remains the same; the mutual ties between the members of the group disappear, as a rule, at the same time as the tie with their leader. The group vanishes in dust, like a Prince Rupert's drop when its tail is broken off.

The dissolution of a religious group is not so easy to observe. A short time ago there came into my hands an English novel of Catholic origin, recommended by the Bishop of London, with the title *When It Was Dark*. It gave a clever and, as it seems to me, a convincing picture of such a possibility and its consequences. The novel, which is supposed to relate to the present day, tells how a conspiracy of enemies of the person of Christ and of the Christian faith succeed in arranging for a sepulchre to be discovered in Jerusalem. In this sepulchre is an inscription, in which Joseph of Arimathaea confesses that for reasons of piety he secretly removed the body of Christ from its grave on the third day after its entombment and buried it in this spot. The resurrection of Christ and his divine nature are by this means disproved, and the result of this archaeological discovery is a convulsion in European civilization and an extraordinary increase in all crimes and acts of violence, which only ceases when the forgers' plot has been revealed.

The phenomenon which accompanies the dissolution that is here supposed to overtake a religious group is not fear, for which the occasion is wanting. Instead of it ruthless and hostile impulses towards other people make their appearance, which, owing to the equal love of Christ, they had previously been unable to do. But even during the kingdom of Christ those people who do not belong to the community of believers, who do not love him, and whom he does not love, stand outside this tie. Therefore a religion, even if it calls itself the religion of love, must be hard and unloving to those who do not belong to it. Fundamentally indeed every religion is in this same way a religion of love for all those whom it embraces; while cruelty and intolerance towards those who do not belong to it are natural to every religion. However difficult we may find it personally, we ought not to reproach believers too severely on this account; people who are unbelieving or indifferent are so much better off psychologically in this matter [of cruelty and intolerance]. If to-day that intolerance no longer shows itself so violent and cruel as in former centuries, we can scarcely conclude that there has been a softening in human manners. The cause is rather to be found in the undeniable weakening of religious feelings and the libidinal ties which depend upon them. If another group tie takes the place of the religious one—and the socialistic tie seems to be succeeding in doing so—then there will be the same intolerance towards outsiders as in the age of the Wars of Religion; and if differences between scientific opinions could ever attain a similar significance for groups, the same result would again be repeated with this new motivation.

CIVILIZATION AND ITS DISCONTENTS

1930

Beauty, cleanliness and order obviously occupy a special position among the requirements of civilization. No one will maintain that they are as important for life as control over the forces of nature or as some other factors with which we shall become acquainted. And yet no one would care to put them in the background as trivialities. That civilization is not exclusively taken up with what is useful is already shown by the example of beauty, which we decline to omit from among the interests of civilization. The usefulness of order is quite evident. With regard to cleanliness, we must bear in mind that it is demanded of us by hygiene as well, and we may suspect that even before the days of scientific prophylaxis the connection between the two was not altogether strange to man. Yet utility does not entirely explain these efforts; something else must be at work besides.

No feature, however, seems better to characterize civilization than its esteem and encouragement of man's higher mental activities—his intellectual, scientific and artistic achievements—and the leading role that it assigns to ideas in human life. Foremost among those ideas are the religious systems, on whose complicated structure I have endeavoured to throw light elsewhere. Next come the speculations of philosophy; and finally what might be called man's "ideals"—his ideas of a possible perfection of individuals, or of peoples or of the whole of humanity, and the demands he sets up on the basis of such ideas. The fact that these creations of his are not independent of one another, but are on the contrary closely interwoven, increases the difficulty not only of describing them but of tracing their psychological derivation. If we assume quite generally that the motive force of all human activities is a striving towards the two confluent goals of utility and a yield of pleasure, we must suppose that this is also true of the manifestations of civilization which we have been discussing here, although this is easily visible only in scientific and aesthetic activities. But it cannot be doubted that the other activities, too, correspond to strong needs in men—perhaps to needs which are only developed in a minority. Nor must we allow ourselves to be misled by judgements of value concerning any particular religion, or philosophic system, or ideal. Whether we think to find in them the highest achievements of the human spirit, or whether we deplore them as aberrations, we cannot but recognize that where they are present, and, in especial, where they are dominant, a high level of civilization is implied.

The last, but certainly not the least important, of the characteristic features of civilization remains to be assessed: the manner in which the relationships of men to one another, their social relationships, are regulated—relationships which affect a person as a neighbour, as a source of help, as another person's sexual object, as a member of a family and of a State. Here it is especially difficult to keep clear of particular ideal demands and to see what is civilized in general. Perhaps we may begin by explaining that the element of civilization enters on the scene with the first attempt to regulate these social relationships. If the attempt were not made, the relationships would be subject to the arbitrary will of the individual: that is to say, the physically stronger man would decide them in the sense of his own interests and instinctual impulses. Nothing would be changed in this if this stronger man should in his turn meet someone even stronger than he. Human life in common is only made possible when a majority comes together which is stronger than any separate individual and which remains united against all separate individuals. The power of this community is then set up as "right" in opposition to the power of the individual, which is condemned as "brute force". This replacement of the power of the individual by the power of a community constitutes the decisive step of civilization. The essence of it lies in the fact that the members of the community restrict themselves in their possibilities of satisfaction, whereas the individual knew no such restrictions. The first requisite of civilization, therefore, is that of justice—that is, the assurance that a law once made will not be broken in favour of an individual. This implies nothing as to the ethical value of such a law. The further course of cultural development seems to tend towards making the law no longer an expression of the will of a small community—a caste or a stratum of the population or a racial group—which, in its turn, behaves like a violent individual towards other, and perhaps more numerous, collections of people. The final outcome should be a rule of law to which all—except those who are not capable of entering a community—have contributed by a sacrifice of their instincts, and which leaves no one—again with the same exception—at the mercy of brute force.

The liberty of the individual is no gift of civilization. It was greatest before there was any civilization, though then, it is true, it had for the most part no value, since the individual was scarcely in a position to defend it. The development of civilization imposes restrictions on it, and justice demands that no one shall escape those restrictions. What makes itself felt in a human community as a desire for freedom may be their revolt against some existing injustice, and so may prove favourable to a further development of civilization; it may remain compatible with civilization. But it may also spring from the remains of their original personality, which is still untamed by civilization and may thus become the basis in them of hostility to civilization. The urge for freedom, therefore, is directed against particular forms and demands of civilization or against civilization altogether. It does not seem as though any influence could induce a man to change his nature into a termite's. No doubt he will always defend his claim to individual liberty against the will of the group. A good part of the struggles of mankind centre round the single task of finding an expedient accommodation—one, that is, that will bring happiness—between this claim of the individual and the cultural claims of the group; and one of the problems that touches the fate of humanity is whether such an accommodation can be reached by means of some particular form of civilization or whether this conflict is irreconcilable.

By allowing common feeling to be our guide in deciding what features of human life are to be regarded as civilized, we have obtained a clear impression of the general picture of civilization; but it is true that so far we have discovered nothing that is not universally known. At the same time we have been careful not to fall in with the prejudice that civilization is synonymous with perfecting, that it is the road to perfection pre-ordained for men. But now a point of view presents itself which may lead in a different direction. The development of civilization appears to us as a peculiar process which mankind undergoes, and in which several things strike us as familiar. We may characterize this process with reference to the changes which it brings about in the familiar instinctual dispositions of human beings, to satisfy which is, after all, the economic task of our lives. A few of these instincts are used up in such a manner that something appears in their place which, in an individual, we describe as a character-trait. The most remarkable example of such a process is found in the anal erotism of young human beings. Their original interest in the excretory function, its organs and products, is changed in the course of their growth into a group of traits which are familiar to us as parsimony, a sense of order and cleanliness—qualities which, though valuable and welcome in themselves, may be intensified till they become markedly dominant and produce what is called the anal character. How this happens we do not know, but there is no doubt about the correctness of the finding. Now we have seen that order and cleanliness are important requirements of civilization, although their vital necessity is not very apparent, any more than their suitability as sources of enjoyment. At this point we cannot fail to be struck by the similarity between the process of civilization and the libidinal development of the individual. Other instincts [besides anal erotism] are induced to displace the conditions for their satisfaction, to lead them into other paths. In most cases this process coincides with that of the *sublimation* (of instinctual aims) with which we are familiar, but in some it can be differentiated from it. Sublimation of instinct is an especially conspicuous feature of cultural development; it is what makes it possible for higher psychical activities, scientific, artistic or ideological, to play such an important part in civilized life. If one were to yield to a first impression, one would say that sublimation is a vicissitude which has been forced upon the instincts entirely by civilization. But it would be wiser to reflect upon this a little longer. In the third place, finally, and this seems the most important of all, it is impossible to overlook the extent to which civilization is built up upon a renunciation of instinct, how much it presupposes precisely the non-satisfaction (by suppression, repression or some other means?) of powerful instincts. This "cultural frustration" dominates the large field of social relationships between human beings. As we already know, it is the cause of the hostility against which all civilizations have to struggle. It will also make severe demands on our scientific work, and we shall have much to explain here. It is not easy to understand how it can become possible to deprive an instinct of satisfaction. Nor is doing so without danger. If the loss is not compensated for economically, one can be certain that serious disorders will ensue.

But if we want to know what value can be attributed to our view that the development of civilization is a special process, comparable to the normal maturation of the individual, we must clearly attack another problem. We must ask ourselves to what influences the development of civilization owes its origin, how it arose, and by what its course has been determined.

IV

THE task seems an immense one, and it is natural to feel diffidence in the face of it. But here are such conjectures as I have been able to make.

After primal man had discovered that it lay in his own hands, literally, to improve his lot on earth by working, it cannot have been a matter of indifference to him whether another man worked with or against him. The other man acquired the value for him of a fellow-worker, with whom it was useful to live together. Even earlier, in his ape-like prehistory, man had adopted the habit of forming families, and the members of his family were probably his first helpers. One may suppose that the founding of families was connected with the fact that a moment came when the need for genital satisfaction no longer made its appearance like a guest who drops in suddenly, and after his departure, is heard of no more for a long time, but instead took up its quarters as a permanent lodger. When this happened, the male acquired a motive for keeping the female, or, speaking more generally, his sexual objects, near him; while the female, who did not want to be separated from her helpless young, was obliged, in their interests, to remain with the stronger male.[1] In this primitive family one essential feature of civilization is still lacking. The arbitrary will of its head, the father, was unrestricted. In *Totem and Taboo* [1912–13] I have tried to show how the way led from this family to the succeeding stage of communal life in

[1] The organic periodicity of the sexual process has persisted, it is true, but its effect on psychical sexual excitation has rather been reversed. This change seems most likely to be connected with the diminution of the olfactory stimuli by means of which the menstrual process produced an effect on the male psyche. Their role was taken over by visual excitations, which, in contrast to the intermittent olfactory stimuli, were able to maintain a permanent effect. The taboo on menstruation is derived from this "organic repression", as a defence against a phase of development that has been surmounted. All other motives are probably of a secondary nature. (Cf. C. D. Daly, 1927.) This process is repeated on another level when the gods of a superseded period of civilization turn into demons. The diminution of

the form of bands of brothers. In overpowering their father, the sons had made the discovery that a combination can be stronger than a single individual. The totemic culture is based on the restrictions which the sons had to impose on one another in order to keep this new state of affairs in being. The taboo-observances were the first "right" or "law". The communal life of human beings had, therefore, a two-fold foundation: the compulsion to work, which was created by external necessity, and the power of love, which made the man unwilling to be deprived of his sexual object—the woman—, and made the woman unwilling to be deprived of the part of herself which had been separated off from her—her child. Eros and Ananke [Love and Necessity] have become the parents of human civilization too. The first result of civilization was that even a fairly large number of people were now able to live together in a community. And since these two great powers were cooperating in this, one might expect that the further development of civilization would proceed smoothly towards an even better control over the external world and towards a further extension of the number of people included in the community. Nor is it easy to understand how this civilization could act upon its participants otherwise than to make them happy.

Before we go on to enquire from what quarter an interference might arise, this recognition of love as one of the foundations of civilization may serve as an excuse for a digression which will enable us to fill in a gap which we left in an earlier discussion. We said there that man's discovery that sexual (genital) love afforded him the strongest experiences of satisfaction, and in fact provided him with the prototype of all happiness, must have suggested to him that he should continue to seek the satisfaction of happiness in his life along the path of sexual relations and that he should make genital erotism the central point of his life. We went on to say that in doing so he made himself dependent in a most dangerous way on a portion of the external world, namely, his chosen love-object, and exposed himself to extreme suffering if he should be rejected by that object or should lose it through unfaithfulness

---

the olfactory stimuli seems itself to be a consequence of man's raising himself from the ground, of his assumption of an upright gait; this made his genitals, which were previously concealed, visible and in need of protection, and so provoked feelings of shame in him.

The fateful process of civilization would thus have set in with man's adoption of an erect posture. From that point the chain of events would have proceeded through the devaluation of olfactory stimuli and the isolation of the menstrual period to the time when visual stimuli were paramount and the genitals became visible, and thence to the continuity of sexual excitation, the founding of the family and so to the threshold of human civilization. This is only a theoretical speculation, but it is important enough to deserve careful checking with reference to the conditions of life which obtain among animals closely related to man.

A social factor is also unmistakably present in the cultural trend towards cleanliness, which has received *ex post facto* justification in hygienic considerations but which manifested itself before their discovery. The incitement to cleanliness originates in an urge to get rid of the excreta, which have become disagreeable to the sense perceptions. We know that in the nursery things are different. The excreta arouse no disgust in children. They seem valuable to them as being a part of their own body which has come away from it. Here upbringing insists with special energy on hastening the course of development which lies ahead, and which should make the excreta worthless, disgusting, abhorrent and abominable. Such a reversal of values would scarcely be possible if the substances that are expelled from the body were not doomed by their strong smells to share the fate which overtook olfactory stimuli after man adopted the erect posture. Anal erotism, therefore, succumbs in the first instance to the "organic repression" which paved the way to civilization. The existence of the social factor which is responsible for the further transformation of anal erotism is attested by the circumstance that, in spite of all man's developmental advances, he scarcely finds the smell of *his own* excreta repulsive, but only that of other people's. Thus a person who is not clean—who does not hide his excreta—is offending other people; he is showing no consideration for them. And this is confirmed by our strongest and commonest terms of abuse. It would be incomprehensible, too, that man should use the name of his most faithful friend in the animal world—the dog—as a term of abuse if that creature had not incurred his contempt through two characteristics: that it is an animal whose dominant sense is that of smell and one which has no horror of excrement, and that it is not ashamed of its sexual functions.

or death. For that reason the wise men of every age have warned us most emphatically against this way of life; but in spite of this it has not lost its attraction for a great number of people.

A small minority are enabled by their constitution to find happiness, in spite of everything, along the path of love. But far-reaching mental changes in the function of love are necessary before this can happen. These people make themselves independent of their object's acquiescence by displacing what they mainly value from being loved on to loving; they protect themselves against the loss of the object by directing their love, not to single objects but to all men alike; and they avoid the uncertainties and disappointments of genital love by turning away from its sexual aims and transforming the instinct into an impulse with an *inhibited aim*. What they bring about in themselves in this way is a state of evenly suspended, steadfast, affectionate feeling, which has little external resemblance any more to the stormy agitations of genital love, from which it is nevertheless derived. Perhaps St. Francis of Assisi went furthest in thus exploiting love for the benefit of an inner feeling of happiness. Moreover, what we have recognized as one of the techniques for fulfilling the pleasure principle has often been brought into connection with religion; this connection may lie in the remote regions where the distinction between the ego and objects or between objects themselves is neglected. According to one ethical view, whose deeper motivation will become clear to us presently, this readiness for a universal love of mankind and the world represents the highest standpoint which man can reach. Even at this early stage of the discussion I should like to bring forward my two main objections to this view. A love that does not discriminate seems to me to forfeit a part of its own value, by doing an injustice to its object; and secondly, not all men are worthy of love.

The love which founded the family continues to operate in civilization both in its original form, in which it does not renounce direct sexual satisfaction, and in its modified form as aim-inhibited affection. In each, it continues to carry on its function of binding together considerable numbers of people, and it does so in a more intensive fashion than can be effected through the interest of work in common. The careless way in which language uses the word "love" has its genetic justification. People give the name "love" to the relation between a man and a woman whose genital needs have led them to found a family; but they also give the name "love" to the positive feelings between parents and children, and between the brothers and sisters of a family, although *we* are obliged to describe this as "aim-inhibited love" or "affection". Love with an inhibited aim was in fact originally fully sensual love, and it is so still in man's unconscious. Both—fully sensual love and aim-inhibited love—extend outside the family and create new bonds with people who before were strangers. Genital love leads to the formation of new families, and aim-inhibited love to "friendships" which become valuable from a cultural standpoint because they escape some of the limitations of genital love, as, for instance, its exclusiveness. But in the course of development the relation of love to civilization loses its unambiguity. On the one hand love comes into opposition to the interests of civilization; on the other, civilization threatens love with substantial restrictions.

This rift between them seems unavoidable. The reason for it is not immediately recognizable. It expresses itself at first as a conflict between the family and the larger community to which the individual belongs. We have already perceived that one of the main endeavours of civilization is to bring people together into large unities. But the family will not give the individual up. The more closely the members of a family are attached to one another, the more often do they tend to cut themselves off from others, and the more difficult is it for them to enter into the wider circle of life. The mode of life in common which is phylogenetically the older, and which is the only one that exists in childhood, will not let itself be superseded by the cultural mode of life which has been acquired later. Detaching himself from his family becomes a task that faces every young person, and society often helps him in the solution of it by means of puberty and initiation rites. We get the impression that these are difficulties which are inherent in all psychical—and, indeed, at bottom, in all organic—development.

Furthermore, women soon come into opposition to civilization and display their retarding and restraining influence—those very women who, in the beginning, laid the foundations of civilization by the claims of their love. Women represent the interests of the family and of sexual life. The work of civilization has become increasingly the business of men, it confronts them with ever more difficult tasks and compels them to carry out instinctual sublimations of which women are little capable. Since a man does not have unlimited quantities of psychical energy at his disposal, he has to accomplish his tasks by making an expedient distribution of his libido. What he employs for cultural aims he to a great extent withdraws from women and sexual life. His constant association with men, and his dependence on his relations with them, even estrange him from his duties as a husband and father. Thus the woman finds herself forced into the background by the claims of civilization and she adopts a hostile attitude towards it.

The tendency on the part of civilization to restrict sexual life is no less clear than its other tendency to expand the cultural unit. Its first, totemic, phase already brings with it the prohibition against an incestuous choice of object, and this is perhaps the most drastic mutilation which man's erotic life has in all time experienced. Taboos, laws and customs impose further restrictions, which affect both men and women. Not all civilizations go equally far in this; and the economic structure of the society also influences the amount of sexual freedom that remains. Here, as we already know, civilization is obeying the laws of economic necessity, since a large amount of the psychical energy which it uses for its own purposes has to be withdrawn from sexuality. In this respect civilization behaves towards sexuality as a people or a stratum of its population does which has subjected another one to its exploitation. Fear of a revolt by the suppressed elements drives it to stricter precautionary measures. A high-water mark in such a development has been reached in our Western European civilization. A cultural community is perfectly justified, psychologically, in starting by proscribing manifestations of the sexual life of children, for there would be no prospect of curbing the sexual lusts of adults if the ground had not been prepared for it in childhood. But such a community cannot in any way be justified in going to the length of actually *disavowing* such easily demonstrable, and, indeed, striking phenomena. As regards the sexually mature individual, the choice of an object is restricted to the opposite sex, and most extra-genital satisfactions are forbidden as perversions. The requirement, demonstrated in these prohibitions, that there shall be a single kind of sexual life for everyone, disregards the dissimilarities, whether innate or acquired, in the sexual constitution of human beings; it cuts off a fair number of them from sexual enjoyment, and so becomes the source of serious injustice. The result of such restrictive measures might be that in people who are normal—who are not prevented by their constitution—the whole of their sexual interests would flow without loss into the channels that are left open. But heterosexual genital love, which has remained exempt from outlawry, is itself restricted by further limitations, in the shape of insistence upon legitimacy and monogamy. Present-day civilization makes it plain that it will only permit sexual relationships on the basis of a solitary, indissoluble bond between one man and one woman, and that it does not like sexuality as a source of pleasure in its own right and is only prepared to tolerate it because there is so far no substitute for it as a means of propagating the human race.

. . .

V

PSYCHO-ANALYTIC work has shown us that it is precisely these frustrations of sexual life which people known as neurotics cannot tolerate. The neurotic creates substitutive satisfactions for himself in his symptoms, and these either cause him suffering in themselves or become sources of suffering for him by raising difficulties in his relations with his environment and the society he belongs to. The latter fact is easy to understand; the former presents us with a new problem. But civilization demands other sacrifices besides that of sexual satisfaction.

We have treated the difficulty of cultural development as a general difficulty of development by tracing it to the inertia of the libido, to its disinclination to give up an old position for a new one. We are saying much the same thing when we derive the antithesis between civilization and sexuality from the circumstance that sexual love is a relationship between two individuals in which a third can only be superfluous or disturbing, whereas civilization depends on relationships between a considerable number of individuals. When a love-relationship is at its height there is no room left for any interest in the environment; a pair of lovers are sufficient to themselves, and do not even need the child they have in common to make them happy. In no other case does Eros so clearly betray the core of his being, his purpose of making one out of more than one; but when he has achieved this in the proverbial way through the love of two human beings, he refuses to go further.

So far, we can quite well imagine a cultural community consisting of double individuals like this, who, libidinally satisfied in themselves, are connected with one another through the bonds of common work and common interests. If this were so, civilization would not have to withdraw any energy from sexuality. But this desirable state of things does not, and never did, exist. Reality shows us that civilization is not content with the ties we have so far allowed it. It aims at binding the members of the community together in a libidinal way as well and employs every means to that end. It favours every path by which strong identifications can be established between the members of the community, and it summons up aim-inhibited libido on the largest scale so as to strengthen the communal bond by relations of friendship. In order for these aims to be fulfilled, a restriction upon sexual life is unavoidable. But we are unable to understand what the necessity is winch forces civilization along this path and which causes its antagonism to sexuality. There must be some disturbing factor which we have not yet discovered.

. . .

The element of truth behind all this, which people are so ready to disavow, is that men are not gentle creatures who want to be loved, and who at the most can defend themselves if they are attacked; they are, on the contrary, creatures among whose instinctual endowments is to be reckoned a powerful share of aggressiveness. As a result, their neighbour is for them not only a potential helper or sexual object, but also someone who tempts them to satisfy their aggressiveness on him, to exploit his capacity for work without compensation, to use him sexually without his consent, to seize his possessions, to humiliate him, to cause him pain, to torture and to kill him. *Homo homini lupus*. Who, in the face of all his experience of life and of history, will have the courage to dispute this assertion? As a rule this cruel aggressiveness waits for some provocation or puts itself at the service of some other purpose, whose goal might also have been reached by milder measures. In circumstances that are favourable to it, when the mental counter-forces which ordinarily inhibit it are out of action, it also manifests itself spontaneously and reveals man as a savage beast to whom consideration towards his own kind is something alien. Anyone who calls to mind the atrocities committed during the racial migrations or the invasions of the Huns, or by the people known as Mongols under Jenghiz Khan and Tamerlane, or at the capture of Jerusalem by the pious Crusaders, or even, indeed, the horrors of the recent World War—anyone who calls these things to mind will have to bow humbly before the truth of this view.

The existence of this inclination to aggression, which we can detect in ourselves and justly assume to be present in others, is the factor which disturbs our relations with our neighbour and which forces civilization into such a high expenditure [of energy]. In consequence of this primary mutual hostility of human beings, civilized society is perpetually threatened with disintegration. The interest of work in common would not hold it together; instinctual passions are stronger than reasonable interests. Civilization has to use its utmost efforts in order to set limits to man's aggressive instincts and to hold the manifestations of them in check by psychical reaction-formations. Hence, therefore, the use of methods intended to incite people into identifications and aim-inhibited relationships of love, hence the restriction upon sexual life, and hence too the ideal's commandment to love one's neighbour as oneself—a commandment which is really justified by the fact that nothing else runs so strongly counter to the original nature of man. In spite of every effort, these endeavours of civilization have not so far achieved very much. It hopes to prevent the crudest excesses of brutal violence by itself assuming the right to use violence against criminals, but the law is not able to lay hold of the more cautious and refined manifestations of human aggressiveness. The time comes when each one of us has to give up as illusions the expectations which, in his youth, he pinned upon his fellow-men, and when he may learn how much difficulty and pain has been added to his life by their ill-will. At the same time, it would be unfair to reproach civilization with trying to eliminate strife and competition from human activity. These things are undoubtedly indispensable. But opposition is not necessarily enmity; it is merely misused and made an *occasion* for enmity.

The communists believe that they have found the path to deliverance from our evils. According to them, man is wholly good and is well-disposed to his neighbour; but the institution of private property has corrupted his nature. The ownership of private wealth gives the individual power, and with it the temptation to ill-treat his neighbour; while the man who is excluded from possession is bound to rebel in hostility against his oppressor. If private property were abolished, all wealth held in common, and everyone allowed to share in the enjoyment of it, ill-will and hostility would disappear among men. Since everyone's needs would be satisfied, no one would have any reason to regard another as his enemy; all would willingly undertake the work that was necessary. I have no concern with any economic criticisms of the communist system; I cannot enquire into whether the abolition of private property is expedient or advantageous.[2] But I am able to recognize that the psychological premisses on which the system is based are an untenable illusion. In abolishing private property we deprive the human love of aggression of one of its instruments, certainly a strong one, though certainly not the strongest; but we have in no way altered the differences in power and influence which are misused by aggressiveness, nor have we altered anything in its nature. Aggressiveness was not created by property. It reigned almost without limit in primitive times, when property was still very scanty, and it already shows itself in the nursery almost before property has given up its primal, anal form; it forms the basis of every relation of affection and love among people (with the single exception, perhaps, of the mother's relation to her male child). If we do away with personal rights over material wealth, there still remains prerogative in the field of sexual relationships, which is bound to become the source of the strongest dislike and the most violent hostility among men who in other respects are on an equal footing. If we were to remove this factor, too, by allowing complete freedom of sexual life and thus abolishing the family, the germ-cell of civilization, we cannot, it is true, easily foresee what new paths the development of civilization could take; but one thing we can expect, and that is that this indestructible feature of human nature will follow it there.

It is clearly not easy for men to give up the satisfaction of this inclination to aggression. They do not feel comfortable without it. The advantage which a comparatively small cultural group offers of allowing this instinct an outlet in the form of hostility against intruders is not to be despised. It is always possible to bind together a considerable number of people in love, so long as there are other people left over to receive the manifestations of their aggressiveness. I once discussed the phenomenon that it is precisely communities with adjoining territories, and

[2] Anyone who has tasted the miseries of poverty in his own youth and has experienced the indifference and arrogance of the well-to-do, should be safe from the suspicion of having no understanding or good will towards endeavours to fight against the inequality of wealth among men and all that it leads to. To be sure, if an attempt is made to base this fight upon an abstract demand, in the name of justice, for equality for all men, there is a very obvious objection to be made—that nature, by endowing individuals with extremely unequal physical attributes and mental capacities, has introduced injustices against which there is no remedy.

related to each other in other ways as well, who are engaged in constant feuds and in ridiculing each other—like the Spaniards and Portuguese, for instance, the North Germans and South Germans, the English and Scotch, and so on. I gave this phenomenon the name of "the narcissism of minor differences", a name which does not do much to explain it. We can now see that it is a convenient and relatively harmless satisfaction of the inclination to aggression, by means of which cohesion between the members of the community is made easier. In this respect the Jewish people, scattered everywhere, have rendered most useful services to the civilizations of the countries that have been their hosts; but unfortunately all the massacres of the Jews in the Middle Ages did not suffice to make that period more peaceful and secure for their Christian fellows. When once the Apostle Paul had posited universal love between men as the foundation of his Christian community, extreme intolerance on the part of Christendom towards those who remained outside it became the inevitable consequence. To the Romans, who had not founded their communal life as a State upon love, religious intolerance was something foreign, although with them religion was a concern of the State and the State was permeated by religion. Neither was it an unaccountable chance that the dream of a Germanic world-dominion called for antisemitism as its complement; and it is intelligible that the attempt to establish a new, communist civilization in Russia should find its psychological support in the persecution of the bourgeois. One only wonders, with concern, what the Soviets will do after they have wiped out their bourgeois.

If civilization imposes such great sacrifices not only on man's sexuality but on his aggressivity, we can understand better why it is hard for him to be happy in that civilization. In fact, primitive man was better off in knowing no restrictions of instinct. To counterbalance this, his prospects of enjoying this happiness for any length of time were very slender. Civilized man has exchanged a portion of his possibilities of happiness for a portion of security. We must not forget, however, that in the primal family only the head of it enjoyed this instinctual freedom; the rest lived in slavish suppression. In that primal period of civilization, the contrast between a minority who enjoyed the advantages of civilization and a majority who were robbed of those advantages was, therefore, carried to extremes. As regards the primitive peoples who exist to-day, careful researches have shown that their instinctual life is by no means to be envied for its freedom. It is subject to restrictions of a different kind but perhaps of greater severity than those attaching to modern civilized man.

. . .

VI

. . .

Of all the slowly developed parts of analytic theory, the theory of the instincts is the one that has felt its way the most painfully forward. And yet that theory was so indispensable to the whole structure that something had to be put in its place. In what was at first my utter perplexity, I took as my starting-point a saying of the poet-philosopher, Schiller, that "hunger and love are what moves the world" Hunger could be taken to represent the instincts which aim at preserving the individual; while love strives after objects, and its chief function, favoured in every way by nature, is the preservation of the species. Thus, to begin with, ego-instincts and object-instincts confronted each other. It was to denote the energy of the latter and only the latter instincts that I introduced the term "libido". Thus the antithesis was between the ego-instincts and the "libidinal" instincts of love (in its widest sense) which were directed to an object. One of these object-instincts, the sadistic instinct, stood out from the rest, it is true, in that its aim was so very far from being loving. Moreover it was obviously in some respects attached to the ego-instincts: it could not hide its close affinity with instincts of mastery which have no libidinal purpose. But these discrepancies were got over; after all, sadism was clearly a part of sexual life, in the activities of which affection could be replaced by cruelty. Neurosis was regarded as the outcome of a struggle between the interest of self-preservation and the demands of the libido, a struggle in which the ego had been victorious but at the price of severe sufferings and renunciations.

Every analyst will admit that even to-day this view has not the sound of a long-discarded error. Nevertheless, alterations in it became essential, as our enquiries advanced from the repressed to the repressing forces, from the object-instincts to the ego. The decisive step forward was the introduction of the concept of narcissism—that is to say, the discovery that the ego itself is cathected with libido, that the ego, indeed, is the libido's original home, and remains to some extent its headquarters. This narcissistic libido turns towards objects, and thus becomes object-libido; and it can change back into narcissistic libido once more. The concept of narcissism made it possible to obtain an analytic understanding of the traumatic neuroses and of many of the affections bordering on the psychoses, as well as of the latter themselves. It was not necessary to give up our interpretation of the transference neuroses as attempts made by the ego to defend itself against sexuality; but the concept of libido was endangered. Since the ego-instincts, too, were libidinal, it seemed for a time inevitable that we should make libido coincide with instinctual energy in general, as G. G. Jung had already advocated earlier. Nevertheless, there still remained in me a kind of conviction, for which I was not as yet able to find reasons, that the instincts could not all be of the same kind. My next step was taken in *Beyond the Pleasure Principle* (1920*g*), when the compulsion to repeat and the conservative character of instinctual life first attracted my attention. Starting from speculations on the beginning of life and from biological parallels, I drew the conclusion that, besides the instinct to preserve living substance and to join it into ever larger units, there must exist another, contrary instinct seeking to dissolve those units and to bring them back to their primaeval, inorganic state. That is to say, as well as Eros there was an instinct of death. The phenomena of life could be explained from the concurrent or mutually opposing action of these two instincts. It was not easy, however, to demonstrate the activities of this supposed death instinct. The manifestations of Eros were conspicuous and noisy enough. It might be assumed that the death instinct operated silently within the organism towards its dissolution, but that, of course, was no proof. A more fruitful idea was that a portion of the instinct is diverted towards the external world and comes to light as an instinct of aggressiveness and destructiveness. In this way the instinct itself could be pressed into the service of Eros, in that the organism was destroying some other thing, whether animate or inanimate, instead of destroying its own self. Conversely, any restriction of this aggressiveness directed outwards would be bound to increase the self-destruction, which is in any case proceeding. At the same time one can suspect from this example that the two kinds of instinct seldom—perhaps never—appear in isolation from each other, but are alloyed with each other in varying and very different proportions and so become unrecognizable to our judgement. In sadism, long since known to us as a component instinct of sexuality, we should have before us a particularly strong alloy of this kind between trends of love and the destructive instinct; while its counterpart, masochism, would be a union between destructiveness directed inwards and sexuality—a union which makes what is otherwise an imperceptible trend into a conspicuous and tangible one.

. . .

The name "libido" can once more be used to denote the manifestations of the power of Eros in order to distinguish them from the energy of the death instinct. It must be confessed that we have much greater difficulty in grasping that instinct; we can only suspect it, as it were, as something in the background behind Eros, and it escapes detection unless its presence is betrayed by its being alloyed with Eros. It is in sadism, where the death instinct twists the erotic aim in its own sense and yet at the same time fully satisfies the erotic urge, that we succeed in obtaining the clearest insight into its nature and its relation to Eros. But even where it emerges without any sexual purpose, in the blindest fury of destructiveness, we cannot fail to recognize that the satisfaction of the instinct is accompanied by an extraordinarily high degree of narcissistic enjoyment, owing to its presenting the ego with a fulfilment of the latter's old wishes for omnipotence. The instinct of destruction, moderated and tamed, and, as it were, inhibited in its aim, must, when it is directed towards objects, provide the ego with the satisfaction of its vital needs and with control over nature. Since the assumption of the existence of the instinct is mainly based on theoretical grounds, we must also admit that it is not entirely proof against theoretical objections. But this is how things appear to us now, in the present state of our knowledge; future research and reflection will no doubt bring further light which will decide the matter.

In all that follows I adopt the standpoint, therefore, that the inclination to aggression is an original, self-subsisting instinctual disposition in man, and I return to my view that it constitutes the greatest impediment to civilization. At one point in the course of this enquiry I was led to the idea that civilization was a special process which mankind undergoes, and I am still under the influence of that idea. I may now add that civilization is a process in the service of Eros, whose purpose is to combine single human individuals, and after that families, then races, peoples and nations, into one great unity, the unity of mankind. Why this has to happen, we do not know; the work of Eros is precisely this. These collections of men are to be libidinally bound to one another. Necessity alone, the advantages of work in common, will not hold them together. But man's natural aggressive instinct, the hostility of each against all and of all against each, opposes this programme of civilization. This aggressive instinct is the derivative and the main representative of the death instinct which we have found alongside of Eros and which shares world-dominion with it. And now, I think, the meaning of the evolution of civilization is no longer obscure to us. It must present the struggle between Eros and Death, between the instinct of life and the instinct of destruction, as it works itself out in the human species. This struggle is what all life essentially consists of, and the evolution of civilization may therefore be simply described as the struggle for life of the human species. And it is this battle of the giants that our nurse-maids try to appease with their lullaby about Heaven.

. . .

Another question concerns us more nearly. What means does civilization employ in order to inhibit the aggressiveness which opposes it, to make it harmless, to get rid of it, perhaps? We have already become acquainted with a few of these methods, but not yet with the one that appears to be the most important. This we can study in the history of the development of the individual. What happens in him to render his desire for aggression innocuous? Something very remarkable, which we should never have guessed and which is nevertheless quite obvious. His aggressiveness is introjected, internalized; it is, in point of fact, sent back to where it came from—that is, it is directed towards his own ego. There it is taken over by a portion of the ego, which sets itself over against the rest of the ego as super-ego, and which now, in the form of "conscience", is ready to put into action against the ego the same harsh aggressiveness that the ego would have liked to satisfy upon other, extraneous individuals. The tension between the harsh super-ego and the ego that is subjected to it, is called by us the sense of guilt; it expresses itself as a need for punishment. Civilization, therefore, obtains mastery over the individual's dangerous desire for aggression by weakening and disarming it and by setting up an agency within him to watch over it, like a garrison in a conquered city.

As to the origin of the sense of guilt, the analyst has different views from other psychologists; but even he does not find it easy to give an account of it. To begin with, if we ask how a person comes to have a sense of guilt, we arrive at an answer which cannot be disputed: a person feels guilty (devout people would say "sinful") when he has done something which he knows to be "bad". But then we notice how little this answer tells us. Perhaps, after some hesitation, we shall add that even when a person has not actually *done* the bad thing but has only recognized in himself an *intention* to do it, he may regard himself as guilty; and the question then arises of why the intention is regarded as equal to the deed. Both cases, however, presuppose that one had already recognized that what is bad is reprehensible, is something that must not be carried out. How is this judgement arrived at? We may reject the existence of an original, as it were natural, capacity to distinguish good from bad. What is bad is often not at all what is injurious or dangerous to the ego; on the contrary, it may be something which is desirable and enjoyable to the ego. Here, therefore, there is an extraneous influence at work, and it is this that decides what is to be called good or bad. Since a person's own feelings would not have led him along this path, he must have had a motive for submitting to this extraneous influence. Such a motive is easily discovered in his helplessness and his dependence on other people, and it can best be designated as fear of loss of love. If he loses the love of another person upon whom he is dependent, he also ceases to be protected from a variety of dangers. Above all, he is exposed to the danger that this stronger person will show his superiority in the form of punishment. At the beginning, therefore, what is bad is whatever causes one to be threatened with loss of love. For fear of that loss, one must avoid it. This, too, is the reason why it makes little difference whether one has already done the bad thing or only intends to do it. In either case the danger only sets in if and when the authority discovers it, and in either case the authority would behave in the same way.

This state of mind is called a "bad conscience"; but actually it does not deserve this name, for at this stage the sense of guilt is dearly only a fear of loss of love, "social" anxiety. In small children it can never be anything else, but in many adults, too, it has only changed to the extent that the place of the father or the two parents is taken by the larger human community. Consequently, such people habitually allow themselves to do any bad thing which promises them enjoyment, so long as they are sure that the authority will not know anything about it or cannot blame them for it; they are afraid only of being found out. Present-day society has to reckon in general with this state of mind.

A great change takes place only when the authority is internalized through the establishment of a super-ego. The phenomena of conscience then reach a higher stage. Actually, it is not until now that we should speak of conscience or a sense of guilt. At this point, too, the fear of being found out comes to an end; the distinction, moreover, between doing something bad and wishing to do it disappears entirely, since nothing can be hidden from the super-ego, not even thoughts. It is true that the seriousness of the situation from a real point of view has passed away, for the new authority, the super-ego, has no motive that we know of for ill-treating the ego, with which it is intimately bound up; but genetic influence, which leads to the survival of what is past and has been surmounted, makes itself felt in the fact that fundamentally things remain as they were at the beginning. The super-ego torments the sinful ego with the same feeling of anxiety and is on the watch for opportunities of getting it punished by the external world.

At this second stage of development, the conscience exhibits a peculiarity which was absent from the first stage and which is no longer easy to account for. For the more virtuous a man is, the more severe and distrustful is its behaviour, so that ultimately it is precisely those people who have carried saintliness furthest who reproach themselves with the worst sinfulness. This means that virtue forfeits some part of its promised reward; the docile and continent ego does not enjoy the trust of its mentor, and strives in vain, it would seem, to acquire it. The objection will at once be made that these difficulties are artificial ones, and it will be said that a stricter and more vigilant conscience is precisely the hallmark of a moral man. Moreover, when saints call themselves sinners, they are not so wrong, considering the temptations to instinctual satisfaction to which they are exposed in a specially high degree —since, as is well known, temptations are merely increased by constant frustration, whereas an occasional satisfaction of them causes them to diminish, at least for the time being. The field of ethics, which is so full of problems, presents us with another fact: namely that ill-luck—that is, external frustration—so greatly enhances the power of the conscience in the super-ego. As long as things go well with a man, his conscience is lenient and lets the ego do all sorts of things; but when misfortune befalls him, he searches his soul, acknowledges his sinfulness, heightens the demands of his conscience, imposes abstinences on himself and punishes himself with penances.[3] Whole peoples have behaved in this way, and still do. This, however, is easily explained by the original infantile stage of conscience, which, as we see, is not given up after the introjection into the superego, but persists alongside of it and behind it. Fate is regarded as a substitute for the parental agency. If a man is unfortunate it means that he is no longer loved by this highest power; and, threatened by such a loss of love, he once more bows to the parental representative in his super-ego—a representative whom, in his days of good fortune, he was ready to neglect. This becomes especially clear where Fate is looked upon in the strictly religious sense of being nothing else than an expression of the Divine Will. The people of Israel had believed themselves to be the favourite child of God, and when the great Father caused misfortune after misfortune to rain down upon this people of his, they were never shaken in their belief in his relationship to them or questioned his power or righteousness. Instead, they produced the prophets, who held up their sinfulness before them; and out of their sense of guilt they created the overstrict commandments of their priestly religion. It is remarkable how differently a primitive man behaves. If he has met with a misfortune, he does not throw the blame on himself but on his fetish, which has obviously not done its duty, and he gives it a thrashing instead of punishing himself.

Thus we know of two origins of the sense of guilt: one arising from fear of an authority, and the other, later on, arising from fear of the super-ego. The first insists upon a renunciation of instinctual satisfactions; the second, as well as doing this, presses for punishment, since the continuance of the forbidden wishes cannot be concealed from the super-ego. We have also learned how the severity of the super-ego—the demands of conscience—is to be understood. It is simply a continuation of the severity of the external authority, to which it has succeeded and which it has in part replaced. We now see in what relationship the renunciation of instinct stands to the sense of guilt. Originally, renunciation of instinct was the result of fear of an external authority: one renounced one's satisfactions in order not to lose its love. If one has carried out this renunciation, one is, as it were, quits with the authority and no sense of guilt should remain. But with fear of the super-ego the case is different. Here, instinctual renunciation is not enough, for the wish persists and cannot be concealed from the super-ego. Thus, in spite of the renunciation that has been made, a sense of guilt comes about. This constitutes a great economic disadvantage in the erection of a super-ego, or, as we may put it, in the formation of a conscience. Instinctual renunciation now no longer has a completely liberating effect; virtuous continence is no longer rewarded with the assurance of love. A threatened external unhappiness—loss of love and punishment on the part of the external authority—has been exchanged for a permanent internal unhappiness, for the tension of the sense of guilt.

. . .

Some readers of this work may further have an impression that they have heard the formula of the struggle between Eros and the death instinct too often. It was alleged to characterize the process of civilization which mankind undergoes but it was also brought into connection with the development of the individual, and, in addition, it was said to have revealed the secret of organic life in general. We cannot, I think, avoid going into the relations of these three processes to one another. The repetition of the same formula is justified by the consideration that both the process of human civilization and of the development of the individual are also vital processes—which is to say that they must share in the most general characteristic

[3] This enhancing of morality as a consequence of ill-luck has been illustrated by Mark Twain in a delightful little story, *The First Melon I ever Stole*. This first melon happened to be unripe. I heard Mark Twain tell the story himself in one of his public readings. After he had given out the title, he stopped and asked himself as though he was in doubt: "*Was* it the first?" With this, everything had been said. The first melon was evidently not the only one.

of life. On the other hand, evidence of the presence of this general characteristic fails, for the very reason of its general nature, to help us to arrive at any differentiation [between the processes], so long as it is not narrowed down by special qualifications. We can only be satisfied, therefore, if we assert that the process of civilization is a modification which the vital process experiences under the influence of a task that is set it by Eros and instigated by Ananke—by the exigencies of reality; and that this task is one of uniting separate individuals into a community bound together by libidinal ties. When, however, we look at the relation between the process of human civilization and the developmental or educative process of individual human beings, we shall conclude without much hesitation that the two are very similar in nature, if not the very same process applied to different kinds of object. The process of the civilization of the human species is, of course, an abstraction of a higher order than is the development of the individual and it is therefore harder to apprehend in concrete terms, nor should we pursue analogies to an obsessional extreme; but in view of the similarity between the aims of the two processes—in the one case the integration of a separate individual into a human group, and in the other case the creation of a unified group out of many individuals—we cannot be surprised at the similarity between the means employed and the resultant phenomena.

In view of its exceptional importance, we must not long postpone the mention of one feature which distinguishes between the two processes. In the developmental process of the individual, the programme of the pleasure principle, which consists in finding the satisfaction of happiness, is retained as the main aim. Integration in, or adaptation to, a human community appears as a scarcely avoidable condition which must be fulfilled before this aim of happiness can be achieved. If it could be done without that condition, it would perhaps be preferable. To put it in other words, the development of the individual seems to us to be a product of the interaction between two urges, the urge towards happiness, which we usually call "egoistic", and the urge towards union with others in the community, which we call "altruistic". Neither of these descriptions goes much below the surface. In the process of individual development, as we have said, the main accent falls mostly on the egoistic urge (or the urge towards happiness); while the other urge, which may be described as a "cultural" one, is usually content with the role of imposing restrictions. But in the process of civilization things are different. Here by far the most important thing is the aim of creating a unity out of the individual human beings. It is true that the aim of happiness is still there, but it is pushed into the background. It almost seems as if the creation of a great human community would be most successful if no attention had to be paid to the happiness of the individual. The developmental process of the individual can thus be expected to have special features of its own which are not reproduced in the process of human civilization. It is only in so far as the first of these processes has union with the community as its aim that it need coincide with the second process.

Just as a planet revolves around a central body as well as rotating on its own axis, so the human individual takes part in the course of development of mankind at the same time as he pursues his own path in life. But to our dull eyes the play of forces in the heavens seems fixed in a never-changing order; in the field of organic life we can still see how the forces contend with one another, and how the effects of the conflict are continually changing. So, also, the two urges, the one towards personal happiness and the other towards union with other human beings must struggle with each other in every individual; and so, also, the two processes of individual and of cultural development must stand in hostile opposition to each other and mutually dispute the ground. But this struggle between the individual and society is not a derivative of the contradiction—probably an irreconcilable one—between the primal instincts of Eros and death. It is a dispute within the economics of the libido, comparable to the contest concerning the distribution of libido between ego and objects; and it does admit of an eventual accommodation in the individual, as, it may be hoped, it will also do in the future of civilization, however much that civilization may oppress the life of the individual to-day.

The analogy between the process of civilization and the path of individual development may be extended in an important respect. It can be asserted that the community, too, evolves a super-ego under whose influence cultural development proceeds. It would be a tempting task for anyone who has a knowledge of human civilizations to follow out this analogy in detail. I will confine myself to bringing forward a few striking points. The super-ego of an epoch of civilization has an origin similar to that of an individual. It is based on the impression left behind by the personalities of great leaders—men of overwhelming force of mind or men in whom one of the human impulsions has found its strongest and purest, and therefore often its most one-sided, expression. In many instances the analogy goes still further, in that during their lifetime these figures were—often enough, even if not always—mocked and maltreated by others and even despatched in a cruel fashion. In the same way, indeed, the primal father did not attain divinity until long after he had met his death by violence. The most arresting example of this fateful conjunction is to be seen in the figure of Jesus Christ—if, indeed, that figure is not a part of mythology, which called it into being from an obscure memory of that primal event. Another point of agreement between the cultural and the individual super-ego is that the former, just like the latter, sets up strict ideal demands, disobedience to which is visited with "fear of conscience". Here, indeed, we come across the remarkable circumstance that the mental processes concerned are actually more familiar to us and more accessible to consciousness as they are seen in the group than they can be in the individual man. In him, when tension arises, it is only the aggressiveness of the super-ego which, in the form of reproaches, makes itself noisily heard; its actual demands often remain unconscious in the background. If we bring them to conscious knowledge, we find that they coincide with the precepts of the prevailing cultural super-ego. At this point the two processes, that of the cultural development of the group and that of the cultural development of the individual, are, as it were, always interlocked. For that reason some of the manifestations and properties of the super-ego can be more easily detected in its behaviour in the cultural community than in the separate individual.

The cultural super-ego has developed its ideals and set up its demands. Among the latter, those which deal with the relations of human beings to one another are comprised under the heading of ethics. People have at all times set the greatest value on ethics, as though they expected that it in particular would produce especially important results. And it does in fact deal with a subject which can easily be recognized as the sorest spot in every civilization. Ethics is thus to be regarded as a therapeutic attempt—as an endeavour to achieve, by means of a command of the super-ego, something which has so far not been achieved by means of any other cultural activities. As we already know, the problem before us is how to get rid of the greatest hindrance to civilization—namely, the constitutional inclination of human beings to be aggressive towards one another; and for that very reason we are especially interested in what is probably the most recent of the cultural commands of the super-ego, the commandment to love one's neighbour as oneself. In our research into, and therapy of, a neurosis, we are led to make two reproaches against the super-ego of the individual. In the severity of its commands and prohibitions it troubles itself too little about the happiness of the ego, in that it takes insufficient account of the resistances against obeying them—of the instinctual strength of the id [in the first place], and of the difficulties presented by the real external environment [in the second]. Consequently we are very often obliged, for therapeutic purposes, to oppose the super-ego, and we endeavour to lower its demands. Exactly the same objections can be made against the ethical demands of the cultural super-ego. It, too, does not trouble itself enough about the facts of the mental constitution of human beings. It issues a command and does not ask whether it is possible for people to obey it. On the contrary, it assumes that a man's ego is psychologically capable of anything that is required of it, that his ego has unlimited mastery over his id. This is a mistake; and even in what are known as normal people the id cannot be controlled beyond certain limits. If more is demanded of a man, a revolt will be produced in him or a neurosis, or he will be made unhappy. The commandment, "Love thy neighbour as thyself", is the strongest defence against human aggressiveness and an excellent example of the unpsychological proceedings of the cultural super-ego. The commandment is impossible to fulfil; such an enormous inflation of love can only lower its value, not get rid of the difficulty. Civilization pays no attention to all this; it merely admonishes us that the harder it is to obey the precept the more meritorious it is to do so. But anyone who follows such a precept in present-day civilization only puts himself at a disadvantage vis-à-vis the person who disregards it. What a potent obstacle to civilization aggressiveness must be, if the defence against it can cause as much unhappiness as aggressiveness itself! "Natural" ethics, as it is called, has nothing to offer here except the narcissistic satisfaction of being able to think oneself better than others. At this point the ethics based on religion introduces its promises of a better after-life. But so long as virtue is not rewarded here on earth, ethics will, I fancy, preach in vain. I too think it quite certain that a real change in the relations of human beings to possessions would be of more help in this direction than any ethical commands; but the recognition of this fact among socialists has been obscured and made useless for practical purposes by a fresh idealistic misconception of human nature.

I believe the line of thought which seeks to trace in the phenomena of cultural development the part played by a super-ego promises still further discoveries. I hasten to come to a close. But there is one question which I can hardly evade. If the development of civilization has such a far-reaching similarity to the development of the individual and if it employs the same methods, may we not be justified in reaching the diagnosis that, under the influence of cultural urges, some civilizations, or some epochs of civilization—possibly the whole of mankind—have become "neurotic"? An analytic dissection of such neuroses might lead to therapeutic recommendations which could lay claim to great practical interest. I would not say that an attempt of this kind to carry psycho-analysis over to the cultural community was absurd or doomed to be fruitless. But we should have to be very cautious and not forget that, after all, we are only dealing with analogies and that it is dangerous, not only with men but also with concepts, to tear them from the sphere in which they have originated and been evolved. Moreover, the diagnosis of communal neuroses is faced with a special difficulty. In an individual neurosis we take as our starting-point the contrast that distinguishes the patient from his environment, which is assumed to be "normal". For a group all of whose members are affected by one and the same disorder no such background could exist; it would have to be found elsewhere. And as regards the therapeutic application of our knowledge, what would be the use of the most correct analysis of social neuroses, since no one possesses authority to impose such a therapy upon the group? But in spite of all these difficulties, we may expect that one day someone will venture to embark upon a pathology of cultural communities.

. . .

The fateful question for the human species seems to me to be whether and to what extent their cultural development will succeed in mastering the disturbance of their communal life by the human instinct of aggression and self-destruction. It may be that in this respect precisely the present time deserves a special interest. Men have gained control over the forces of nature to such an extent that with their help they would have no difficulty in exterminating one another to the last man. They know this, and hence comes a large part of their current unrest, their unhappiness and their mood of anxiety. And now it is to be expected that the other of the two "Heavenly Powers", eternal Eros, will make an effort to assert himself in the struggle with his equally immortal adversary. But who can foresee with what success and with what result?

Georg Simmel

Georg Simmel (1858–1918) is arguably the most original and far-ranging member of the founding generation of modern sociology. Never happy within the academic division of labor, he contributed to all of the social sciences but remained primarily a philosopher. His influence has been profound but subtle and diffuse.

Simmel was born in 1858 in Berlin, the youngest child in a family of prosperous and cultured Jews. He studied philosophy at the University of Berlin and soon acquired his lifelong taste for intellectual eclecticism, studying history, art, anthropology, and religion. His disdain for academic conventions was to serve him well as one of the most brilliant lecturers of his day, but it made him many enemies in his university career. He was also the target of overt anti-Semitism and suffered from pedants who derided his belletristic style as well as from prejudices against sociology that ran deep within the German academic establishment. For most of his life Simmel lectured and wrote without the security of a faculty appointment.

Simmel was greatly admired by Max Weber and Ernst Troeltsch, was a founder (with Weber and Ferdinand Tœnnies) of the German Sociological Society, and exerted great influence on Robert Park, who attended his lectures at the University of Berlin and subsequently founded the "Chicago School" of sociology. In spite of all this, Simmel regarded himself as a philosopher and made lasting contributions to aesthetics, ethics, and the theory of knowledge. His public lectures and cultural essays for the newspapers won a diverse following among European intellectuals, including Stefan George, Rainer Rilke, Edmund Husserl, George Lukacs, and Martin Buber. But his unorthodox work acknowledged no scholarly predecessors or contemporaries, nor did he recruit students to carry on his brand of inquiry. As many have argued, Simmel's marginality reinforced his nonconformist style and provided central themes for his thought. In his famous essay "The Stranger" and in "The Web of Group-Affiliations," he shows, for example, that the absence of strong social ties may provoke skepticism and even anxiety but also fosters objectivity and intellectual freedom.

Simmel was in quest of a subject matter for sociology that would distinguish it from the other social sciences and the humanistic disciplines. Following Immanuel Kant, he found this not in a new set of topics, but in a method, or, rather, in a special point of view on phenomena that might be the subjects of other sciences as well. The special task of sociology is to study the forms of social interaction apart from their content. Simmel assumes that the same social forms—competition, exchange, secrecy, domination—could encompass quite different content, and the same social content could be embodied in different forms. Forms arise as people interact with one another for the sake of certain purposes or to satisfy certain emotional needs. They are the processes by which individuals combine into supraindividual unities, stable or transient, solidary or antagonistic. Forms may gain autonomy from the demands of the moment, becoming larger, more solid structures that stand detached from, even opposed to, the continuity of life. Some of these forms involve structural changes over time and may be called forms of development; others are essentially cultural, such as the universalism that marks the principles of logic or justice. Unlike Marx, Durkheim, or Weber, however, Simmel never integrates his work into an overarching scheme. Instead he gathers a rich variety of contents under each abstract form, allowing for new and startling comparisons among social phenomena.

As might be expected, Simmel is more interested in how individual needs and goals create the forms of sociality than in how institutions mold and constrain their members. Individuality was his abiding concern, and his most insightful pages explore the social conditions that make it easier for persons to discover and express their individuality. In modern society, with its plurality of cultural and social groups, individuals are caught in the intersection of cross-cutting interests and expectations, where they sometimes thrive but also may perish. Expanding on Marx's idea of alienation, Simmel speaks of the "tragedy of culture." Our complex division of labor and highly developed money economy greatly magnify the distance between an immense realm of cultural products and the individual who cannot assimilate them. We risk becoming estranged from the products of our own creative spirit. Simmel treats the conflict between individual and society in his most famous essay, "The Stranger," and explores the development of individualism in "The Web of Group-Affiliations," one chapter of his *Sociology* (1922). But his greatest work on this theme is the authoritative *Philosophy of Money* (1900). Here he works out the implications of the money economy for social forms and for individual freedom. He draws attention to the phenomena of impersonality, the trivialization of human relationships, the calculating outlook, and the egocentrism, but also to the very real advantages of the money economy for individuals.

SOCIOLOGY

1922

"The Web of Group-Affiliations"

ANALOGIES BETWEEN PERCEPTION AND GROUP-FORMATION

. . .

. . . At first the individual sees himself in an environment which is relatively indifferent to his individuality, but which has implicated him in a web of circumstances. These circumstances impose on him a close coexistence with those whom the accident of birth has placed next to him. This close coexistence represents the first condition of the phylogenetic and ontogenetic development, whose continuation aims toward the association of homogeneous members from heterogeneous groups. Thus, the family comprises a number of different individuals, who are at first entirely dependent on this familial association. However, as the development of society progresses, each individual establishes for himself contacts with persons who stand outside this original group-affiliation, but who are "related" to him by virtue of an actual similarity of talents, inclinations, activities, and so on. The association of persons because of external coexistence is more and more superseded by association in accordance with internal relationships. Just as a higher concept binds together the elements which a great number of very different perceptual complexes have in common, so do practical considerations bind together like individuals, who are otherwise affiliated with quite alien and unrelated groups. New contacts are established between individuals which penetrate every nook and cranny of the contacts that are earlier, relatively more natural and that are held together by relationships of a more sensual kind.

PROPINQUITY AND INTEREST AS A BASIS OF GROUP-FORMATION

The independent groups, whose alliances used to constitute universities at an earlier time, were divided according to the nationality of the students. Later on, so-called faculties were developed in the place of such alliances. These faculties were academic departments according to common areas of study. Thus, a group whose cohesion depended upon geographic and physiological factors, *terminus a quo*, was entirely replaced by a group whose cohesion was based on purpose, on factual considerations, or, if one will, on individual interests.

The development of the English trade unions shows the same pattern, though its characteristics were somewhat more complex. Originally, the individual trade unions tended towards local exclusiveness: they were closed to workers who came from elsewhere. Frictions and petty jealousies between such separate groups were unavoidable. However, the tendency toward a uniform organization of trades throughout the country gradually eliminated this situation. The following example shows that this change had become inevitable. When the cotton weavers decided upon uniform piece rates, it was apparent that this would lead to a concentration of the industry in favorably located places and to losses for the more remote villages. Yet, even the representatives of these remote villages voted for uniform piece rates because this was deemed best for the industry as a whole.

Although from the beginning workers came together on the basis of their similar activities, their association depended largely on the fact that they were neighbors. Unquestionably this contributed to a close contact between a specific trade and the associations of the other trades, as long as the latter existed in the same locality. In the course of its development the association of workers in one trade was removed from this dependence on local relationships. Henceforth, the similarity in the occupation of the members became the only determinant of the relationship between the association and those in other trades. An historian of the trade unions has expressed this change by saying that the *trade* had become the governing principle of the workers' organizations in place of the *city*. There is an element of freedom operating here: for however much confinement there may be in the position of the worker, membership in a trade union implies more freedom of choice for the individual than belonging to the citizenry of a town.

In general, this type of development tends to enlarge the sphere of freedom: not because the affiliation with, and the dependence on groups, has been abandoned, but because it has become a matter of choice with whom one affiliates and upon whom one is dependent. Any association, which is based on local relationships or is otherwise brought about without the individual's participation, differs from affiliations which are freely chosen, because as a rule the latter will make it possible for the individual to make his beliefs and desires felt. Hence, such groupings may be based upon relationships which grow out of the nature of the individuals concerned.

. . .

ORGANIC AND RATIONAL CRITERIA OF GROUP-FORMATION

In relatively uncomplicated situations age groups may function as a sociological criterion and may become a basis of division for the entire group. Like the division between the sexes, age groups stand midway between the organic and the rational. For example, in Sparta around 200 B.C. political parties were designated as the elders, the young men, and the youngsters. Similarly, among different primitive peoples one finds men organized in age-groups, each of which has a special social significance and a special way of life. The basis of this solidarity is entirely personal and impersonal at the same time.

Obviously, age-groups provide such a basis of solidarity only when the culture is still without an extensive intellectual life. For this would immediately foster the unfolding of individual intellectual differences, of differences in the development of ideas, of political parties depending on ideologies. And as a result individuals of quite different age-groups would feel that they belong together. It is, indeed, this lack of an acquired education which is one of the reasons why youth as such shows a certain solidarity, why young people are attracted to one another much more so than are older people. Youths are often surprisingly indifferent towards each other's individuality.

The division by age-groups is a cause, though an extremely awkward cause, of group-formation, which combines personal and objective criteria. The organic and rational causes of group-formation, whose contrast is usually emphasized, are here brought together. A purely physiological aspect of individuals, their age, becomes a basis for joint action. Individuals are consciously brought together on this basis. Age is an entirely natural and personal fact which here works as a completely objective principle. It is understandable that this fact gains great importance for the social structure of primitive peoples, since age is relieved of all elements of caprice, since the fact of age is immediately apparent and as such readily determines one's outlook on life.

Group-affiliations which are formed according to objective criteria constitute a superstructure which develops over and above those group-affiliations which are formed according to natural, immediately given criteria. One of the simplest examples is the original cohesion of the family-group which is modified in such a way that the individual member introduces his family into other groups. One of the most complex examples is the "republic of scholars" which is in part an intellectual and in part a real association of all persons, who join in the pursuit of such a highly general goal as knowledge. In all other respects these scholars belong to the most varied groups —with regard to their nationality, their personal and special interests, their social position, and so on.

The period of the Renaissance demonstrated most clearly the power of intellectual and educational interests to bring together in a new community like-minded people from a large variety of different groups. Humanistic interests broke down the medieval isolation of social groups and of estates. They gave to people who represented the most diverse points of view and who often remained faithful to the most diverse occupations, a common interest in ideas and in knowledge. This common interest, whether one of active pursuit or of passive appreciation, cut across all previously established forms and institutions of medieval life. Humanism at that time entered the experience of all peoples and groups from the outside as something that was equally strange to all. And this very fact made it possible for Humanism to become a common area of interest for them all, or at any rate for certain people among them.

For example, the idea prevailed that all things famous belonged together. This is shown by the collections of biographies which began to appear in the 14th century. These biographies described in a single work people of excellence from many fields, whether they were theologians, or artists, statesmen or philologists. In their way, the secular rulers gave recognition to this new rank-order, which involved a new analysis and synthesis of social groups. Robert of Naples befriends Petrarch and makes him a gift of his own purple cape.

Two hundred years later this social action has shed its lyric guise and has assumed a more objective and strictly limited form. Francis I of France wanted to make that social group, which was concerned exclusively with the higher learning, completely independent and autonomous even in relation to the universities. These universities were charged with the education of theologians and jurists. But Francis I proposed a separate academy, whose members would devote themselves to investigation and teaching without having any practical purpose in mind. It was a consequence of this separation of what is intellectually significant from every other value that the Venetian Senate accompanied the extradition of Giordano Bruno with this letter to the Papal Court. Bruno was one of the worst heretics, it said, he had done the most reprehensible things, he had led a dissolute, even a devilish life. In other respects, however, he was one of the most distinguished intellects that could be imagined, a man of rare learning and spiritual greatness.

The restlessness and the adventurous spirit of the Humanists, their often unstable and unreliable character, were in keeping with the independence of the intellect, which was the central focus of their lives. This independence made them indifferent to all other obligations usually incumbent upon men. The individual humanist spent his life in a colorful variety of life-situations. This way of life was symbolic of the movement of Humanism, which embraced the poor scholar and the monk, the powerful General and the brilliant Duchess, in a single framework of intellectual interests. Thereby the way was opened for a most important, further differentiation of the social structure, though there are precedents for such a development in antiquity.

Criteria derived from knowledge came to serve as the basis of social differentiation and group-formation. Up to the Renaissance, social differentiation and group-formation had been based either on criteria of self-interest (economic, military, and political in a broad or narrow sense), or of emotion (religious), or of a mixture of both (familial). Now, intellectual and rational interests came to form groups, whose members were gathered from many other social groups. This is a striking example of the general trend, that the formation of groups, which has occurred more recently, often bears a rational character, and that the substantive purpose of these groups is the result of conscious reflection and intelligent planning. Thus, secondary groups, because of their rational formation, give the appearance of being determined by a purpose, since their affairs revolve around intellectually articulated interests.

. . .

GROUP-AFFILIATIONS AND THE INDIVIDUAL PERSONALITY

The groups with which the individual is affiliated constitute a system of coordinates, as it were, such that each new group with which he becomes affiliated circumscribes him more exactly and more unambiguously. To belong to any one of these groups leaves the individual considerable leeway. But the larger the number of groups to which an individual belongs, the more improbable is it that other persons will exhibit the same combination of group-affiliations, that these particular groups will "intersect" once again [in a second individual]. Concrete objects lose their individual characteristics as we subsume them under a general concept in accordance with one of their attributes. And concrete objects regain their individual characteristics as other concepts are emphasized under which their several attributes may be subsumed. To speak Platonically, each thing has a part in as many ideas as it has manifold attributes, and it achieves thereby its individual determination. There is an analogous relationship between the individual and the groups with which he is affiliated.

A concrete object with which we are confronted has been called the synthesis of perceptions. And each object has a more enduring configuration, so to speak, the more various the perceptions are, which have entered into it. Similarly as individuals, we form the personality out of particular elements of life, each of which has arisen from, or is interwoven with, society. This personality is subjectivity par excellence in the sense that it combines the elements of culture in an individual manner. There is here a reciprocal relation between the subjective and the objective. As the person becomes affiliated with a social group, he surrenders himself to it. A synthesis of such subjective affiliations creates a group in an objective sense. But the person also regains his individuality, because his pattern of participation is unique; hence the fact of multiple group-participation creates in turn a new subjective element. Causal determination of, and purposive actions by, the individual appear as two sides of the same coin. The genesis of the personality has been interpreted as the point of intersection for innumerable social influences, as the end-product of heritages derived from the most diverse groups and periods of adjustment. Hence, individuality interpreted as that particular set of constituent elements which in their quality and combination make up the individual. But as the individual becomes affiliated with social groups in accordance with the diversity of his drives and interests, he thereby expresses and returns what he has "received," though he does so consciously and on a higher level.

As the individual leaves his established position within *one* primary group, he comes to stand at a point at which many groups "intersect." The individual as a moral personality comes to be circumscribed in an entirely new way, but he also faces new problems. The security and lack of ambiguity in his former position gives way to uncertainty in the conditions of his life. This is the sense of an old English proverb which says: he who speaks two languages is a knave. It is true that external and internal conflicts arise through the multiplicity of group-affiliations, which threaten the individual with psychological tensions or even a schizophrenic break. But it is also true that multiple group-affiliations can strengthen the individual and reenforce the integration of his personality. Conflicting and integrating tendencies are mutually reinforcing. Conflicting tendencies can arise just because the individual has a core of inner unity. The ego can become more clearly conscious of this unity, the more he is confronted with the task of reconciling within himself a diversity of group-interests. The effect of marriage on both spouses is that they belong to several families; this has always been a source of enrichment, a way of expanding one's interests and relationships but also of intensifying one's conflicts. These conflicts may induce the individual to make internal and external adjustments, but also to assert himself energetically.

In primitive clan-organizations the individual would participate in several groups in such a way that he belonged to the kinship or totemic group of his mother, but also to the narrower, familial or local association of his father. Now these simple people are not equal to conflicts such as those just mentioned, which is basically due to the fact that they lack a firm awareness of themselves as personalities. With peculiar purposefulness these two kinds of association are therefore so differently arranged that they do not encroach upon each other. Relationships on the maternal side have a more ideal, spiritual nature, whereas on the paternal side they are real, material and directly effective. In the case of the Australian aborigines, i.e., the Hereros, and among many other hunting tribes, maternal kinship, and similarly the totemic association, do not constitute a basis for community-living. They have no effect on daily life, but only on festive occasions of deep significance, such as marriage ceremonies and ceremonies occasioned by death and blood revenge. The last of these has an ideal, abstract character in the lives of the primitive peoples. The totemic association is transmitted through maternal descent and, therefore, it is often scattered through many tribes and hordes. It is held together only by common taboos on food and common ceremonials, and particularly by means of special names and special symbols on weapons. On the other hand, the paternal kinship-relations encompass all of daily life, waging war, alliances, inheritance, hunting, and so on. They do not have these taboos and symbols and do not need them, because the bond of a community in one locality and the convergence of their direct interests provide the basis for a sense of group-cohesion. At this stage, each connection which is not local usually assumes a more ideal character. It is the sign of a higher social development that group-cohesion can transcend local ties and yet be thoroughly realistic and concrete. But if the individual in a primitive tribe belongs to both the paternal-local group and to the maternal clan, these groups must be separated from each other in terms of the distinctly concrete or distinctly abstract values which they embody. Given the undifferentiated character of the primitive mind, this separation is a precondition for the possibility that the same individual belongs to both groups.

GROUP-AFFILIATIONS AND THE FAMILY

The Catholic priesthood represents examples of multiple group-affiliations which are unique in kind and also in the degree to which they were successful. No estate was excluded from the recruitment of priests and monks. The power of the ecclesiastical estate greatly attracted both the highest and the lowest social elements. In medieval England strong aversions between social classes prevailed generally. However, the priesthood, although it formed a strong and compact class, did not engender real class-hatred because it originated from all classes and every family had some relative who belonged to it. A similar situation was created by the fact that church-property existed everywhere. Because there was some church-property in every province and almost every community, alongside the infinite number of property titles characteristic of the Middle Ages, there arose an inter-regional uniformity of the clerical estate, which was both cause and consequence of its purposive unity. To date, this is the greatest example in history of the formation of a social group which cuts across all other existing groups. But at the same time it is characterized by the fact that it actually produced no overlapping of group-affiliations in the individuals. The priesthood could establish a relationship to, and could communicate with, all existing social strata in a manner which was entirely unbiased, because the individual priest was completely released from the ties with his social stratum; he was not even permitted to retain his name. Otherwise, these ties would have determined the personality of the priest together with those which he had newly gained in the priesthood.

But the personality of the priest was determined instead by his affiliation with the priesthood and the consequences of this situation confirm our analysis, albeit by means of a contradiction. The priest may possess no individuality in the normal sense, he cannot possess any traits which would differentiate him from other priests. Since he is entirely a priest, he must be a priest to the exclusion of all other concerns. Thus, the overlapping of group-affiliations has no effect upon the individual in this case, but only upon the estate as a whole, which is made up of *former* members of *all* estates and groups. That the priesthood as a higher social form was determined sociologically on the basis of overlapping group-affiliations, was possible only because the priesthood stood in the same relationship to all of the groups. Among the means utilized by Catholicism, celibacy is the most radical method by which the individual priest was put outside the network of group-affiliations.

Marriage constitutes a sociological determination of such finality that the individual is no longer quite free to attain a position in a group other than his family which would correspond to his interest in this second group. It is significant that the lower Russian clergyman, whose task demanded that he live among the people, is generally married, while the higher, ruling clergy are celibate. On the other hand, even the lowest ranking, Roman Catholic priest occupies in his village a somewhat abstract position which isolates him from the community-life of his environment. To be sure, the priesthood of the Russian Church is only an approximation of the Protestant clergy, which as a matter of principle is entirely enmeshed in civil life. The Russian priesthood is almost completely endogenous: priests of the Greek Orthodox Church seldom marry anyone other than the daughters of priests. Marriage is often so significant for the other sociological ties of the husband, that associations are actually differentiated on the basis of whether or not the marriage of their members are of consequence for these associations.

In the Middle Ages and even later the marriage of a journeyman was regarded with displeasure by his fellows. Indeed, in several associations of journeymen difficulties were placed in the way of a married journeyman who desired membership. For marriage restricted the migration of journeymen, which was essential not only for the unity and inner solidarity of the journeymen's estate, but also for the ready mobility of the group in accordance with shifting opportunities for work. The marriage of a journeyman ran counter also to the homogeneity of interest, the independence of the group in relation to their masters, and the social cohesion of the estate. Because of the peculiar structure of marriage and the family, the overlapping of group-affiliations inevitably resulted in this case in the rather extensive withdrawal of the individual from all social ties.

It is apparent that, for similar reasons, celibacy was considered appropriate for the soldier wherever a clearly differentiated military estate [officer corps] existed. However, in the Macedonian regiments of the Ptolemies and afterwards in the era of the Roman Emperors, soldiers were permitted to marry or to have concubines. [This distinction between officers and men is similar to the distinction between the higher and the lower Russian clergy.] The regiments were often replenished from among the offspring of these unions. Only the thoroughgoing fusion of the modern army with the structure of national life has completely abolished the rule of celibacy for the officers.

It is also plain that the same formal pattern of social relations may occur with reference to other conditions, even though this is not so striking and basic a case as that of marriage. The old scholastic universities refused to accept students [who were native residents of the town]. In the city of Bologna the rights of membership in the university were withdrawn from those students who acquired citizenship after a residence of more than ten years. In like manner, the Hanseatic League of German merchants in Flanders excluded every compatriot who had acquired Flemish citizenship.

As a rule an overlapping of group-affiliations cannot occur if the social groups involved are too far apart with regard to their purpose and in terms of the demands they make upon the individual. And a group which wants its members to become absorbed unconditionally in its activities must regard it as incompatible with this principle if an individual is differentiated from other members by virtue of his simultaneous affiliation with another group. Of course, the element of jealousy between groups enters in as well.

. . .

MULTIPLE GROUP-AFFILIATIONS WITHIN A SINGLE GROUP

A typical example of multiple group-affiliations within a single group is the competition among persons who show their solidarity in other respects. On the one hand the merchant joins other merchants in a group which has a great number of common interests: legislation on issues of economic policy, the social prestige of business, representation of business-interests, joint action as over against the general public in order to maintain certain prices, and many others. All of these concern the world of commerce as such and make it appear to others as a unified group. On the other hand, each merchant is in competition with many others. To enter this occupation creates for him at one and the same time association and isolation, equalization and particularization. He pursues his interests by means of the most bitter competition with those with whom he must often unite closely for the sake of common interests. This inner contrast is probably most pronounced in the area of commerce, but it is present in some way in all other areas as well, down to the ephemeral socializing of an evening party.

An infinite range of individualizing combinations is made possible by the fact that the individual belongs to a multiplicity of groups, in which the relationship between competition and socialization varies greatly. It is a trivial observation that the instinctive needs of man prompt him to act in these mutually conflicting ways: he feels and acts *with* others but also *against* others. A certain measure of the one and the other, and a certain proportion between them, is a purely formal necessity for man, which he meets in the most manifold ways. Often this occurs in a manner, which makes an individual's action understandable not on the basis of its objective meanings, but on the basis of the satisfaction which it affords to the formal drives mentioned above. Individuality is characterized, both in regard to its natural striving and its historical development, by that proportion between socialization and competition which is decisive for it.

And the reverse tendency arises on the same basis: the individual's need for a clearer articulation and for a more unambiguous development of his personality, forces him to select certain groups. And from their combination he gains his maximum of individuality—the one group offering him opportunities for socialization, the other opportunities for competition. Thus, the members of a group in which keen competition prevails will gladly seek out such other groups as are lacking in competition as much as possible. As a result businessmen have a decided preference for social clubs. The estate-consciousness of the aristocrat, on the other hand, rather excludes competition within his own circle; hence, it makes supplementations of that sort [i.e., social clubs] largely superfluous. This suggests forms of socialization to the aristocrat which contain stronger competitive elements—for example, those clubs which are held together by a common interest in sports.

Finally, I shall mention here the frequent discrepancies which arise because an individual or a group are controlled by interests that are opposed to each other. This may permit individuals and groups to belong at the same time to parties which are opposed to each other. Individuals are likely to become affiliated with conflicting groups, if in a many-sided culture the political parties are intensely active. Under such conditions it usually happens that the political parties also represent the different viewpoints on those questions which have nothing at all to do with politics. Thus, a certain tendency in literature, art, religion, etc., is associated with one party, an opposite tendency with another. The dividing line which separates the parties is, thereby, extended throughout the entire range of human interests. Obviously, an individual who will not surrender completely to the dictates of the party, will join a group, say on the basis of his esthetic or religious convictions, which is amalgamated with his political enemies. He will be affiliated with two groups which regard each other as opponents.

RELIGION AS A FACTOR IN MULTIPLE GROUP-AFFILIATIONS

Religious affiliation is the most important and at the same time the most characteristic example [of individualization] ever since religion has been emancipated from racial, national, or local ties, a world-historical fact of immeasurable significance. Either the religious community embraces the civic community in terms of its other essential or comprehensive interests, or the religious community is entirely free of all solidarity with whatever is *not* religion. The nature of religion is completely expressed in both of these sociological types, though in a different language or at another level of development in each case.

It is understandable that the co-existence and the sharing of human interests is not possible with people who do not share one's faith. The deeply justified need for unity was satisfied, a priori so to speak, in all of ancient civilization, in the Semitic as well as the Graeco-Roman world. Religion was made an affair of the tribe or the state. With a few exceptions, the deity was identified with the interests of the political group, and the duties toward Him were identical with the all-embracing duties toward the latter.

Yet the power of religious motivation is equally apparent, where it is independent of all social ties originating from other motives, and where it is strong enough to bring together believers adhering to the same creed, in spite of all the differences between them which arise out of their other affiliations. This form of religious organization is obviously a highly individualistic one. The religious temper has lost the support which it had obtained from its integration with the entire complex of social ties. Now religious experience is based upon the soul of the individual and it is his responsibility; on that basis the individual seeks to establish a bond with others who are similarly qualified in terms of their religious experience, but perhaps in no other respect. Christianity in its pure sense is an entirely individualistic religion, and this has made possible its diffusion throughout the manifold of national and local groups. The Christian was conscious of the fact that he took with him his church-affiliation into every community of his choosing, regardless of the psychological influences and the duties which such a community exerted and made incumbent upon him. This consciousness must have created a feeling of individual determination and self-confidence.

This sociological significance of religion reflects its dual relationship to life. On the one hand, religion stands in contrast to the whole substance of human life; it is the counterpart and the equivalent of life itself, aloof from its secular movements and interests. On the other hand, religion takes sides among the parties in the secular life, though it had elevated itself above the world of affairs as a matter of principle. As such religion is an element of secular life alongside all its other elements; it becomes involved in the multitude of changing relationships though at the same time it rejects this involvement. As a result a remarkable involution occurs. The disavowal of all social ties, which is evidence of a deep religiosity, allows the individual and his religious group to come in contact with any number of other groups with whose members they do not share any common interests. And the relationships again serve to distinguish and to determine the individuals concerned as well as the religious groups.

This pattern is repeated in many specific religious situations and in the peculiar intertwining between the religious and the other interests of individuals. In the quarrels between France and Spain, the Huguenots placed themselves at one time at the service of the king, when the struggles turned against Catholic Spain and its friends in France. On another occasion, when they were oppressed by the king, they joined Spain directly. The cruel suppression of the Irish Catholics by England revealed a dual position of another type. One day the Protestants of England and Ireland would feel united against a common religious enemy without regard for their fellow countrymen; the next day the Protestants and Catholics of Ireland would be united against the suppressor of their common fatherland without consideration of religious differences. By way of contrast the European states intervened in Asia to defend Chinese or Turkish Christians; but this action seemed quite outrageous and incomprehensible to people like the Chinese, among whom the primitive identity of religious and political group-affiliation is still unbroken.

But where this unity has been broken as much as in Switzerland, the abstract nature of religion—which because of this abstract quality occupies a definite position in relation to all other interests—brings about immediately very characteristic patterns of group-affiliation. Because of the enormous differences between its cantons, Switzerland does not have a system of political parties such that politically like-minded people in the various cantons would divide themselves into major parties with regard to the national government. Only the *ultramontane people of all cantons*, [i.e., Catholics who follow the Papal authority in all questions of secular and ecclesiastical policy] form a joint group in political affairs.

One can assume without question that this emancipation of religious from political ties has also consequences in the opposite direction, in that it will make possible political mergers which would have been frustrated by the continuing unity of both. The most striking example is perhaps the union between Scotland and England in 1707. For both countries the advantages of becoming a *single* state were bound up with the continued existence of the two churches. Up to that time political and religious concepts had been closely interrelated in both countries. Only the separation of Church and State made the amalgamation of political interests between the two countries possible; otherwise the ecclesiastical interests would not have tolerated it. It was said of the two countries that they could preserve harmony only by agreeing to differ. Once this solution, together with its consequences for group-affiliation, had taken place, then it was no longer possible to abolish the freedom which had been gained. Hence the principle: *cuius regio eius religio*, is valid only if it does not need to be stated explicitly, but instead reflects the existence of a naive and undifferentiated condition in which Church and State are at one.

It is quite remarkable when the religious point of view overcomes all other bases of separation and amalgamates persons and interests despite their natural differentiation. Yet, this religious unity is thought of as quite parallel to those [other cases of organized solidarity] which arise merely on the basis of an objective differentiation. Thus in 1896 the Jewish workers of Manchester came together in an organization which was to include *all* categories of workers (mainly these were tailors, shoemakers, and bakers) and which intended to make common cause with the other trade unions in regard to the interests of labor. But the other trade unions were organized in accordance with the *objective* differences between types of work. This principle of organization was so important that the Trade Unions could not be induced to amalgamate with the International, because the latter was constituted without regard for the type of work in which its members were engaged. Although the case of the Jewish workers seems to go back to the undifferentiated community of interests in the religious as well as the social and economic sense, it reveals nevertheless the separation of these interests, at least on principle. The voluntary coordination of the Jewish workers with trade-unions organized on a purely objective basis [namely the division of labor] reveals that their organization was based on a practical purpose [rather than in accordance with religious belief].

The situation is manifestly different in the case of the Catholic trade unions of Germany, because of their great scope, because of the political significance of Catholicism in Germany, and because their religion does not place the Catholic workers in as conspicuous a position as the Jewish workers, (For example, in Germany the religious differentiation has produced special workers' associations within the general Catholic organizations. In Aachen a number of years ago, weavers, spinners, finishers, needlemakers, metal workers and construction workers were organized in this way.) Catholic organizations are large enough to allow for this division without involving an overlapping of group-affiliations such that each of these special associations would join with non-Catholic workers in the same trade. Still, this latter development has already occurred on occasion and that inner division is apparently the first step in this direction.

PRIESTHOOD AS A SPECIAL TYPE OF GROUP-FORMATION

Finally there arise overlapping group-affiliations on a higher level, in that religious forces become sublimated in the priesthood. The relationship between believers and priests involves representation and leadership, control and cooperation, veneration and the provision of material sustenance. To be sure, the sociological form of this relationship varies in some respects with each religion. But the relations between believers and priests have so much in common that one can, with reservations, speak of a formally similar position of the priest within groups, however much these differ in all other respects. Out of this there arises above all a solidarity of interests, a mutual understanding, a cohesiveness among the priests, which under certain conditions can even drown out the substantive antagonism between Evangelical ministers and Catholic priests.

A single priest or a kindred group of priests belong both to a national, a denominational, and in some sense a party-like association, and to that association of all clergies which arises partly from a sociological and partly from an ethical-metaphysical kinship. This overlapping of group-affiliations gives to the individual priest a peculiarly determined character which sets him apart from other members of the one group as well as of the other. [Simmel refers here to the contrast between the priest and the believers as a group within one church, and to the contrast between the priests of all churches and all believers.]

INDIVIDUALISM AND COLLECTIVISM IN MODERN SOCIETY

The development of the public mind shows itself by the fact that a sufficient number of groups is present which have form and organization. Their number is sufficient in the sense that they give an individual of many gifts the opportunity to pursue each of his interests in association with others. Such multiplicity of groups implies that the ideals of collectivism and of individualism are approximated to the same extent. On the one hand the individual finds a community for each of his inclinations and strivings which makes it easier to satisfy them. This community provides an organizational form for his activities, and it offers in this way all the advantages of group-membership as well as of organizational experience. On the other hand, the specific qualities of the individual are preserved through the combination of groups which can be a different combination in each case.

Thus one can say that society arises from the individual and that the individual arises out of association. An advanced culture broadens more and more the social groups to which we belong with our whole personality; but at the same time the individual is made to rely on his own resources to a greater extent and he is deprived of many supports and advantages associated with the tightly-knit, primary group. Thus, the creation of groups and associations in which any number of people can come together on the basis of their interest in a common purpose, compensates for that isolation of the personality which develops out of breaking away from the narrow confines of earlier circumstances.

. . .

CONCLUDING REMARKS

This is the principal pattern of the development of culture, which also comprises the sociological factors. Meaningful and profoundly significant institutions and behavior patterns are replaced by those which in themselves appear to be completely mechanical, external, and inanimate. But the latter have a higher purpose, which reaches beyond that of the earlier level of organization. And this higher purpose gives to the collective impact and to the consequences of institutions and behavior-patterns, an intellectual significance which is inevitably lacking in each single element. This is the characteristic of the modern soldier as over against the medieval knight, of factory work as over against handicraft work, of the modern levelling and uniformity of so many aspects of life, which were formerly left to the free and creative response of the individual.

On the one hand, organizations are too extensive and complex today to allow each of their members to express one idea completely, so to speak. Each of the members can have only mechanical significance without any meaning in themselves. Only as a member of the whole can he contribute his part toward the realization of an idea. On the other hand, the intellectual element in every activity is often differentiated so that the mechanical and the intellectual come to exist separately. For instance, the woman handling an embroidering machine engages in a much less imaginative activity than the woman embroidering by hand. The imaginative impulses of this activity have been transferred to the machine, they have become objectified. Thus, it is possible for social institutions, gradations, associations to become more mechanical and external, and yet, to serve cultural progress and the internal coherence of a whole group.

This is the case if a higher social purpose is at stake to which the individual must submit. This higher purpose will no longer permit them to retain the spirit and the rationale which under earlier social conditions gave to institutions and associations a terminus to their purposive activities. In this way we may explain the transition from the principle of kinship to the principle of social divisions by numbers, e.g., associations of ten, even though the latter principle involves an association of heterogeneous elements as opposed to the natural homogeneity of the family.

LESTER WARD

Lester Ward (1841–1913) was one of the founders of American sociology and the first to free it from the biological fetters of Darwinism. While his colleagues paid tribute to a free-enterprise economy that was already about to disappear, Ward stressed the need for social planning and reform, for a "sociocratic" society that later generations were to call a welfare state.

Like many American reformers in the Progressive age, Ward was a Midwesterner of modest origins. In time left over from factory jobs, he taught himself various languages as well as biology and physiology, and finally became a high school teacher. After two years in the Civil War, he moved to Washington, D.C.; worked in the civil service; and in his spare time succeeded in acquiring three more degrees in the arts, medicine, and the law. Still later he became a geologist, then chief paleontologist in the United States Geographical Survey. Only in 1906, near the end of his career, was Ward called to the Ivory Tower—as professor of sociology at Brown University.

The original subject of Ward's major book, the two-volume *Dynamic Sociology* (1883), was education. But his greatest achievement, called the theory of *social telesis*, was to refute social Darwinism by arguing that while natural evolution proceeded in an aimless manner, human evolution was informed by purposeful action. Therefore, such phenomena as survival of the fittest, laissez-faire economics, and Malthus's theory of overpopulation—the stock in trade of the evolutionists—did not apply to human development, which proceeds according to planned action by an enlightened government. Ward welcomed the many popular reform movements of his day. Education would enable the common man and woman to participate consciously in the self-government of democratic citizens. The bottom layers of society—the proletariat, women, even the underclass of the slums—are by nature the equals of the "aristocracy of brains" if only they could receive proper instruction. Ward was a strong supporter of feminism. His "gynecocentric theory"—that women were the originators of social life—was widely cited by feminists at the turn of the century. This theory was first explored in an essay "Our Better Halves" (1888), in *Forum.*

Ward's other major works include *The Psychic Factors of Civilization* (1893), *Outlines of Sociology* (1898), *Pure Sociology* (1903), *Applied Sociology* (1904), and the six-volume *Glimpses of the Cosmos*, his intellectual autobiography. Ward died in Washington, D.C., in 1913.

PURE SOCIOLOGY

1903

PART II, XIV

. . .

All these facts from both kingdoms, and the number that might be added is unlimited, combine to show that the female constitutes the main trunk, descending unchanged from the asexual, or presexual, condition; that the male element was added at a certain stage for the sole purpose of securing a crossing of ancestral strains, and the consequent variation and higher development; that it began as a simple fertilizer, assuming a variety of forms; that for reasons. hereafter to be considered, the male in most organisms gradually assumed more importance, and ultimately came to approach the size and general nature of the female; but that throughout nearly or quite the whole of the invertebrates, and to a considerable extent among the vertebrates, the male has remained an inferior creature, and has continued to devote its existence chiefly to the one function for which it was created. The change, or progress, as it may be called, has been wholly in the male, the female remaining unchanged. This is why it is so often said that the female represents heredity and the male variation. "The ovum is the material medium through which the law of heredity manifests itself, while the male element is the vehicle by which new variations are added. . . . The greater variability of the male is also shown by a comparison of the adult male and female with the immature birds of both sexes."

The last fact is the one usually adduced in support of the theory that in birds and mammals where the male is superior the female is an example of "arrested development." Such is, however, probably not the case, and the female simply represents the normal condition, while the condition of the male is abnormal due to his great powers of variability. That the female should resemble the young is quite natural, but the statement is an inverted one, due to the androcentric bias. The least unbiased consideration would make it clear that the colors of such male birds as Professor Brooks had in mind are not the normal colors of the species, but are due to some abnormal or supranormal causes. The normal color is that of the young and the female, and the color of the male is the result of his excessive variability. Females cannot thus vary. They represent the center of gravity of the biological system. They are that "stubborn power of permanency" of which Goethe speaks. The female not only typifies the race but, metaphor aside, she *is* the race.

Sexual Selection.—The fact that requires to be explained is that, as we have seen, the male, primarily and normally an inconspicuous and insignificant afterthought of nature, has in most existing organisms attained a higher stage of development and somewhat approached the form and stature of the primary trunk form which is now called the female. That which might naturally surprise the philosophical observer is not that the female is usually superior to the male, but that the male should have advanced at all beyond its primitive estate as either a fertilizing organ attached to the female, or at most a minute organism detached from her but devoted exclusively to the same purpose. In other words, while female

From *Pure Sociology: A Treatise on the Origin and Spontaneous Development of Society* by Lester Ward, 2nd ed. (New York: The Macmillan Company, 1911).

superiority is a perfectly natural condition, male development requires explanation. We have explained the origin of the male as a provision of nature for keeping up the difference of potential among biotic forces. This we found in Chapter XI to be one of the leading dynamic principles. But this principle does not explain the first step nor any subsequent step made by the male toward equality with the female. For this an entirely different principle must be found.

We saw at the outset that in order to fulfill his mission the male must be endowed with an innate interest in performing his work. This was supplied on the principle laid down in Chapter V, viz., appetition. This attribute was absolutely necessary to the success of the scheme, and throughout all nature we find the male always active and eager seeking the female and exerting his utmost powers to infuse into her the new hereditary *Anlagen* that often make up the greater part of his material substance. This intense interest in his work is the *natura naturans*, the voice of nature speaking through him and commanding him, in season and out of season, always and under all circumstances, to do his duty, and never on any pretext to allow an opportunity to escape to infuse into the old hereditary trunk of his species the new life that is in him. This duty he always performed, not only making extraordinary efforts but incurring enormous risks, often actually sacrificing his life and perishing at his post.

The sociological application of this is that the sexual irregularities of human society are chiefly due to this same principle. All attempts on the part of society to regulate the relations of the sexes, necessary though they may be to the maintenance of the social order, interfere with the biologic principle of crossing strains and securing the maximum variation, development, and vigor of the stock. The violation of human laws relating to this class of conduct is usually in obedience to that higher law of nature commanding such conduct. As Havelock Ellis says:

> A cosmic conservatism does not necessarily involve a social conservatism. The wisdom of Man, working through a few centuries or in one corner of the earth, by no means necessarily corresponds to the wisdom of Nature, and may be in flat opposition to it. This is especially the case when the wisdom of Man merely means, as sometimes happens, the experience of our ancestors gained under other conditions, or merely the opinions of one class or one sex. Taking a broad view of the matter, it seems difficult to avoid the conclusion that it is safer to trust to the conservatism of Nature than to the conservatism of Man. We are not at liberty to introduce any artificial sexual barrier into social concerns.

Such violations of the social code are called crimes and are thereby made such, but they are artificial crimes. Those who commit them may even think they are doing "wrong," because they have been taught so; nevertheless they continue to commit them and take the risks of punishment. They obey the biological imperative in the face of all danger in perfect analogy with the action of the male spider or mantis.

This part of the scheme was thus effectively carried out, and so far it was a complete success, and ample variation and consequent diversity and progress were secured in the organic world. The sacrifice of males was a matter of complete indifference, as much so as is the sacrifice of germs, because the supply was inexhaustible, and in fact, throughout the lower orders an excess of males over females is the normal condition, and often the number of males greatly exceeds that of the females. That a hundred males should live and die without once exercising their normal faculty is of less consequence than that one female should go unfecundated. Biologic economy consists in unlimited resources coupled with the multiplication of chances. Success in accomplishing the main purpose is the paramount consideration. The cost in effort, sacrifice, and life is a comparatively unimportant element.

But it is obvious that the interest of the male is wholly unlike the interest of the female. That the female has an interest there is no doubt. She also has to a limited extent the appetent interest of the male, but this is not usually strong enough to cause her even to move from her place, much less to seek the male. From this point of view she is comparatively indifferent, and is, as is so commonly said, the passive sex. But the female has another and wholly different interest and one which is wanting in the male. Through her nature secures another end which is second only to the two great ends thus far considered, viz., reproduction and fertilization. The male element is in a high degree centrifugal. Unlimited variation would be dangerous if not destructive. Mere difference is not all that is required by evolution. Quality is an element as important as degree. The female is the guardian of hereditary qualities. Variation may be retrogressive as well as progressive. It may be excessive and lead to abnormalities. It requires regulation. The female is the balance wheel of the whole machinery. As the primary, ancestral trunk she stands unmoved amid the heated strife of rivals and holds the scales that decide their relative worth to the race. While the voice of nature speaking to the male in the form of an intense appetitive interest, says to him: fecundate! it gives to the female a different command, and says: discriminate! The order to the male is: cross the strains! that to the female is: choose the best! Here the value of a plurality of males is apparent. In such a plurality there are always differences. The female recognizes these differences, and instinctively selects the one that has the highest value for the race. This quality must of course coincide with a subjective feeling of preference, a coincidence which is brought about by the action of the well-known laws of organic adaptation.

This subjective feeling it is which constitutes the distinctive interest of the female. It is clearly quite other than the interest of the male. It is wanting in the plant and in the lowest animals, but nevertheless makes its appearance at a very early stage in the history of sentient beings. In considering it we have to do with a psychic attribute a grade higher than that of pure appetency. In fact it represents the dawn of the esthetic faculty. We have already seen in Chapter VII how the advent of mind gave the world a new dispensation and seemed to reverse the whole policy of nature. We are now about to witness another profound transformation wrought by a special psychic faculty viz., the faculty of taste. This transformation is nothing less than the work of raising that miniature speck of existence, the primordial fertilizing agent, to the rank of a fully developed animal organism, approaching in varying degrees, and actually reaching in a few instances, the status of the original specific trunk, then called the female.

The foundation of the whole process is the fundamental law of heredity, that offspring inherit the qualities of both their parents. The qualities of the mother, being those of the species in general, are of course inherited and do not concern the transformation. This comes through the qualities of the male. The incipient esthetic tastes of the female cause her to select the qualities from among her suitors that she prefers, and to reject all males that do not come up to her standard. The qualities selected are transmitted to the offspring and the new generation again selects and again transmits. As all females may be supposed to have substantially the same preferences the effect is cumulative, and however slowly the transformation may go on, it is only necessary to multiply the repetitions a sufficient number of times to secure any required result. The particular characters thus selected are called secondary sexual characters; they are chiefly seen in the male because the female already has the normal development. There can be no doubt that in cases, like spiders, where the males are so exceedingly, small, one of the preferred qualities is a respectable stature and bulk, and that throughout the lower orders the chief selecting has been that of larger and larger males, until the observed present state of partial sex equality was attained. This is exactly the kind of facts that would be overlooked by the average investigator, attention being concentrated on certain more striking and apparently abnormal facts, such as brilliant coloration, peculiar markings, special ornamental organs, weapons of destruction, etc. These latter, under the joint action of the principle of selection and the law of parsimony, are often not only confined to the male, but do not appear until the age of maturity, at which time they can alone serve the purpose for which they were selected and created, viz., to attract the female and lead to the continued selection of those males in which they are best developed. It is upon these that biological writers chiefly dwell. They point to a certain degree of development in the tastes of the females which lies beyond the simply useful.

. . .

While the animal origin of man is now almost universally admitted by anthropologists and by well-informed persons generally, there is manifest a very tardy recognition of its full meaning. No blame ever attaches to the sexual relations of animals. They are usually or always such as best subserve the needs of different species; at least they are such as the conditions actually produced. It was the same with man when he emerged from the animal state, and, properly viewed, they have always been such since that date. The multitudinous forms of marriage have all been the products of the conditions of existence. A common error tacitly entertained is that animals carry on the process of reproduction and rearing of the young by a conscious attention to this important business. They are supposed to woo and mate for this purpose, and to care for their offspring with an eye to the interests of the species. The fact is that these functional results are the consequences of the law of adaptation, and the agents are wholly unconscious of them as anything to be attained by their actions. They only seek their interests in the form of feelings, which are so regulated by instinct as to secure the results. For example, as has already been said, animals can have no knowledge of the connection between mating and propagating. All they know is that they like to mate. The female brings forth her young with no conception of the part the male has had in it. She cares for her young because she is impelled to do so by an innate interest, in short, because she likes to do so. All this is true of all animal species, and it is not at all probable that the degree of reasoning power that enabled primitive man to perceive that the fertilization of the male was a necessary condition to reproduction was attained until long after the full human estate had been reached and man had advanced far into the protosocial stage. The fact that races still exist incapable of performing such an act of ratiocination proves that the inability to perform it must have once been general.

In such a state it was natural and necessary that everything should be traced to the mother. The father was unknown and unthought of. The idea of paternity did not exist. Maternity was everything. Fertilization and reproduction were as completely separated in thought as they have been shown to be in essence. That under such circumstances mother-rule and mother-right should prevail is among the necessities of existence. Amazonism, matriarchy, and all the forms of gynæcocracy that are found among primitive peoples, instead of being anomalies or curiosities, are simply survivals of this early and probably very long stage in the history of man and society of which no other evidence now exists, but which is the logical and inevitable conclusion that must follow the admission of the animal origin of man.

. . .

Androcracy.—At some point quite early in the protosocial stage it began slowly to dawn upon the growing intellect of man that a causal connection existed between these couplings of men and women and the birth of children. It was this simple act of ratiocination that literally reversed the whole social system. For the first time the man began to perceive that he, too, had a part in the continuance of the race, that the children were in part his, and not wholly the woman's. . . .

. . .

But the idea once firmly established that the family was a joint product of the woman and the man, it is easy to see the important results that would naturally follow. The same strengthening of the reasoning powers that made the discovery of paternity possible worked in all other directions. Paternity implied power over the child, which was now exercised by the father as well as by the mother. . . .

The passage from the gynæcocratic to the androcratic state was characterized, on the part of man by the loss of his normal chivalry and respect for the preferences of woman, and on the part of woman by the loss of her virtue. Both the time-honored assertion of authority by woman and submission to it by man were abrogated. In discovering his paternity and accompanying authority man also discovered his power, which at that stage meant simply physical strength. He began to learn the economic value of woman and to exert his superior power in the direction of exacting not only favors but service from her. The gynæcocratic régime once broken over the steps were short and rapid to complete androcracy. The patriarchate or patriarchal system, in which the man assumed complete supremacy, was the natural sequel to the process that had begun. It was all the product of the strengthening intellect which refused longer to be bound by the bonds of animal instinct and broke away from the functional restraints that adaptation had imposed upon the sexes. The man saw that he was the master creature, that woman was smaller, weaker, less shrewd and cunning than he, and at the same time could be made to contribute to his pleasure and his wants, and he proceeded to appropriate her accordingly.

"OUR BETTER HALVES"

1888

The practice of calling women better than men is purely chivalric—an empty compliment to the sex. The less enlightened regard them as inferior. The more enlightened consider them equal when all elements are taken into the account. The general opinion is that they are superior morally and inferior mentally and physically. But there are so many kinds of moral, mental, and physical qualities that each of these classes, when carefully analyzed, is found to contain some elements in which the one and some in which the other sex stands higher. It is therefore a difficult problem, increasing in intricacy with more thorough and candid investigation. Attempts have been made, often with much success, to point out the leading characteristics in which the sexes differ, especially in mental traits, and some have gone deeper and sought to explain these differences as arising from physical and social conditions.

It is not my purpose to treat the subject from this standpoint, nor to attempt in any way to show wherein superiority consists. I propose simply to predicate of the female sex a particular kind of superiority and to offer some proofs on this single point. Whatever may be woman's present condition in civilized, barbaric, or savage society, and whatever may be the condition of the female sex in the different departments of animal life, I shall undertake to contend that in the economy of organic nature the female sex is the primary, and the male a secondary element. If this be a law, its application to the human race is readily made and its importance to social life cannot be ignored.

That such a view should be looked upon as unsound, and even absurd, by those who have only studied men is quite natural, but one would suppose that close students of nature, particularly such as have chosen the world of life as their special field of research, would pause at this question and seek to give it such a final solution as to prevent its return into the arena of discussion. I am sorry to say that they have not done so. In fact, so far as I have observed, they have treated it from the most superficial standpoint. Writers of this class have frequently drawn important practical conclusions

"Our Better Halves" by Lester Ward (*Forum* 6, November 1888; reprint, *Against the Tide*, eds. Michael S. Kimmel and Thomas E. Mosmiller, Boston: Beacon Press, 1992).

from what I hope to show to be mere half-truths—conclusions bearing upon the future education, treatment, and position of woman in society. A quotation or two from authors of repute will make this point clear. Thus, in an article entitled "The Woman's Rights Question Considered from a Biological Point of View," in the "Quarterly Journal of Science" for October, 1878, the writer says:

> We propose, therefore, to examine this question in the light of the principles of natural selection, of differentiation and specialization, and to inquire whether the relations of the sexes in the human species and the distribution of their respective functions are or are not in general harmony with what is observed in that portion of the animal kingdom which lies nearest to man; to wit, in Mammalia. . . . Even a very superficial and popular survey of the class Mammalia will satisfy us that the structural differences between the males and the females of each species are by no means confined to the reproductive organs. The male ruminant, whale, bat, elephant, rodent, carnivore, or ape, is on the average a larger and heavier animal than his mate. The tiger, for instance, exceeds the tigress in size by a proportion of from ten to twenty per cent. In few, if any, species is the superior stature of the male more striking than in the one which approaches man most nearly in its physical development—the gorilla. But the mere difference in size is not all; the female is scarcely in any normal case a mere miniature copy of the male. Her proportions differ; the head and the thorax are relatively smaller, the pelvis broader, the bones slighter, the muscles less powerful. The male in many cases possesses offensive weapons which in the female are wanting. In illustration we need only to refer to the tusks of the elephant and the boar, and the horns of many species of deer. On the contrary, there is no instance of a female possessing any weapon which is not also found, to at least an equal degree, in the male. Further, the superior size of the head in the male is not merely due to the more massive osseous growth needful for the support of tusks, horns, etc., but to a proportionately larger development of brain.

And after much more in the same strain, this writer concludes:

> We have, therefore, in fine, full ground for maintaining that the "woman's rights movement" is an attempt to rear, by a process of "unnatural selection," a race of monstrosities—hostile alike to men, to normal women, to human society, and to the future development of our race.

Prof. W. K. Brooks, in a very able article in the "Popular Science Monthly" for June and July, 1879, succeeded, as I think, in proving that the well-known passivity of the female sex has the important significance that it represents the principle of heredity, or permanence of type, the male representing that of variability; thus completely reversing the *varium et mutabile semper femina*. But notwithstanding his lucid conceptions on this point, Prof. Brooks felt called upon in this article to write:

> Our conclusions have a strong leaning to the conservative or old-fashioned view of the subject—to what many will call "male" view of women. The positions which women already occupy in society and the duties which they perform are, in the main, what they should be if our view is correct; and any attempt to improve the condition of women by ignoring or obliterating the intellectual differences between them and men must result in disaster to the race, and the obstruction of that progress and improvement which the history of the past shows to be in store for both men and women in the future. So far as human life in this world is concerned, there can be no improvement which is not accomplished in accordance with the laws of nature; and, if it is a natural law that the parts which the sexes perform in the natural evolution of the race are complemental to each other, we cannot hope to accomplish anything by working in opposition to the natural method.

Utterances similar to those above quoted have constantly found place for the last twenty years in our best scientific literature, and it may be fairly said to be the fashion among scientific men to treat the woman question from this point of view. A great array of evidence is brought to show that woman is physically inferior to man, that she is smaller in stature, and that her brain is not only absolutely smaller, but is smaller in proportion to her body; that she has less strength in proportion to her size, less power of endurance, and a greater number of ailments. This, it is said, is the natural result of her sex.

Reproduction is so great a drain upon the female system that we should expect it to be attended with diminished strength and vitality. It is further argued that the smaller and weaker females of animals, as well as the young, are protected by the larger and stronger males, and the inference is freely drawn that the dependence of the females among animals is similar to that of women in society, which latter is therefore the natural condition.

I shall not deny the fact of woman's physical and mental inferiority, nor shall I deny that the differences are, in the main, due to causes analogous to those which have differentiated the sexes of the higher animals. I must, however, deny in toto that these causes are what they are assumed by these writers to be. It has always surprised me that those who start out avowedly from a Darwinian standpoint should so quickly abandon it and proceed to argue from pre-Darwinian premises. It was Darwin who taught us why the boar has tusks, the stag antlers, and the peacock gaudy tail-feathers. It is because the females chose mates that possessed these characters. The characters selected by the females have been, in the main, those that tended to insure success in rivalry for mates. The greater size and strength of the males, together with their powerful weapons, have not been acquired, as is implied in the argument above stated, for the purpose of protecting the dependent females; they have been acquired entirely for the purpose of combating rivals and winning mates. In very few such animals do the males ever attempt to protect the females, even where the latter have their young to take care of. When the hen with her brood of chickens is attacked, it is not the cock that ruffs his feathers and defends them with his spurs; it is the mother herself that defends them. The cock is always found with hens that have no chickens, and only uses his spurs in fighting with other cocks that have no notion of injuring the females. In the entire animal kingdom the cases where the male uses his great powers to protect the female or the young, or to bring them food, are so rare that where they are observed they are recorded as curious approximations to the social state of man. These "secondary sexual characters," as Darwin has named them, are generally adapted to aggressive warfare, not with the enemies of the species, but with the males of the same species for the possession of the females. All this has positively no analogy with the human condition, and those who cite these facts as a justification for retaining woman in a lower sphere of either mental or physical activity than that occupied by man, abandon the modern and correct interpretation of them and fall back upon the old interpretation which has been proved to be false.

That secondary sexual characters exist in man is, indeed, true. His beard is clearly one of the purely ornamental ones. His larger size and greater strength were doubtless acquired before his moral faculties had awakened, and are the result of his battles for his wives. The predominance of the male brain in the human species doubtless partakes of this nature, and is in a large degree attributable to this cause. The time came in the development of the race when brute force began to give way to sagacity, and the first use to which this growing power was put was that of circumventing rivals for female favor. Brain grew with effort, and like the other organs that are so strangely developed through this cause, it began to be more especially characteristic of the sex. The weaker sex admired success then as now, and the bright-witted became the successful ones, while the dull failed to transmit their dullness. There was a survival of the cunning.

The first use of mental power, as of physical power, was to defeat rivals and secure mates; it was not to protect female frailty or supply food to offspring. The females protected themselves and their progeny by maternal instinct. The females of all wild animals are more dangerous to encounter than the males, especially when they have young; and it has been observed that the male carnivores rarely attack man.

Nor do I deny that these agencies of selection are still at work, slowly, it is true, but perhaps as rapidly as at any previous period, producing physical modifications in man. But it is no longer simple female selection of male qualities, as in the lower animals; there is now going on an opposite class of influences by which a true male selection is bringing about modifications in woman, and this had progressed so far at the beginning of the historic period that the ornamental characters had been, as it were, transferred from the male to the female, and beauty, which in birds and many animals is the exclusive attribute of the males, had become the leading attribute of the women of the higher races. And while setting down this fact, let me call attention to its great significance as pointing to future possibilities in woman when men shall learn to select other qualities in their companions than mere beauty; for under the power of this comparatively modern male selection woman may become whatever man shall desire her to be, and the ideal woman, however high the standard, will become more and more the real woman.

The entire argument of those who would restrict woman's sphere because she is mentally and physically inferior to man would therefore fall to the ground, even if we were to admit that there was something in her sex that rendered that inferiority natural and essential. To be fully consistent, it would be necessary to insist that woman should defend both herself and her offspring from hostile influences of all kinds, and also assume the whole duty of supplying her children with food, while the sole function of man should be, as it is in most mammals and birds, to take care of himself and fight off rivals. This would be the "natural" state of society in the sense in which these philosophers employ that term. It is only distantly approached in a few of the very lowest tribes of savages.

But let us now inquire what grounds there are for accepting this mental and physical inferiority of women as something inherent in the nature of things. Is it really true that the larger part taken by the female in the work of reproduction necessarily impairs her strength, dwarfs her proportions, and renders her a physically inferior and dependent being? In most human races it may be admitted that women are less stalwart than men, although all the stories of Amazonian tribes are not mere fictions. It is also true, as has been insisted upon, that the males of most mammals and birds exceed the females in size and strength, and often differ from them greatly in appearance. But this is by no means always the case. The fable of the hedgehog that won the race with the hare by cunningly stationing Mrs. Hedgehog at the other end of the course, instructed to claim the stakes, is founded upon an exception which has many parallels. Among birds there are cases in which the rule is reversed. There are some entire families, as for example the hawks, in which the females exceed the males. If we go further down the scale, however, we find this attribute of male superiority to disappear almost entirely throughout the reptiles and amphibians, with a decided leaning toward female supremacy; and in the fishes, where male rivalry does not exist, the female, as every fisherman knows, is almost invariably the heavier game.

But it is not until we go below the vertebrate series and contemplate the invertebrate and vegetable worlds that we really begin to find the data for a philosophical study of the meaning of sex. It has been frequently remarked that the laws governing the higher forms of life can be rightly comprehended only by an acquaintance with the lower and more formative types of being. In no problem is this more true than in that of sex.

In studying this problem it is found that there is a great world of life that wholly antedates the appearance of sex—the world of asexual life—nor is the passage from the sexless to the distinctly male and female definite and abrupt. Between them occur parthenogenesis or virgin reproduction, hermaphroditism, in which the male being consists simply of an organ, and parasitic males, of which we shall presently speak, while the other devices of nature for perpetuating life are innumerable and infinitely varied. But so far as sex can be predicated of these beings, they must all be regarded as female. The asexual parent must be contemplated as, to all intents and purposes, maternal. The parthenogenetic aphis or shrimp is in all essential respects a mother. The hermaphrodite creature, whatever else it may be, is also necessarily a female. Following these states come the numberless cases in which the female form continues to constitute the type of life, the insignificant male appearing to be a mere afterthought.

The vegetable kingdom, except in its very lowest stages, affords comparatively few pointed illustrations of this truth. The strange behavior of the hemp plant, in which, as has long been known, the female plants crowd out the male plants by overshadowing them as soon as they have been fertilized by the latter, used to be frequently commented upon as a perverse anomaly in nature. Now it is correctly interpreted as an expression of the general law that the primary purpose of the male sex is to enable the female, or type form, to reproduce, after performing which function the male form is useless and a mere cumberer of the ground. But the hemp plant is by no means alone in possessing this peculiarity. I could enumerate several pretty well known species that have a somewhat similar habit. I will mention only one, the common cud-weed, or everlasting (*Antennaria plantaginifolia*), which, unlike the hemp, has colonies of males separate from the females, and these male plants are small and short-lived. Long after their flowering stalks have disappeared the female plants continue to grow, and they become large and thrifty herbs lasting until frost.

In the animal kingdom below the vertebrates female superiority is well-nigh universal. In the few cases where it does not occur it is generally found that the males combat each other, after the manner of the higher animals, for the possession of the females. The cases that I shall name are such as all are familiar with. The only new thing in their presentation is their application to the point at issue.

The superiority of the queen bee over the drone is only a well-known illustration of a condition which, with the usual variations and exceptions, is common to a great natural order of insects. The only mosquito that the unscientific world knows is the female mosquito. The male mosquito is a frail and harmless little creature that swarms with the females in the early season and passes away when his work is done. There are many insects of which the males possess no organs of nutrition in the imago state, their duties during their ephemeral existence being confined to what the Germans call the *Minnedienst*. Such is the life of many male moths and butterflies. But much greater inequalities are often found. I should, perhaps, apologize for citing the familiar case of spiders, in some species of which the miniature lover is often seized and devoured during his courtship by the gigantic object of his affections. Something similar, I learn, sometimes occurs with the mantis or "praying insect."

Merely mentioning the extreme case of Sphærularia, in which the female is several thousand times as large as the male, I may surely be permitted to introduce the barnacle, since it is one of the creatures upon which Prof. Brooks lays considerable stress in the article to which I have referred. Not being myself a zoologist, I am only too happy to quote him. He says:

> Among the barnacles there are a few species the males and females of which differ remarkably. The female is an ordinary barnacle, with all the peculiarities of the group fully developed, while the male is a small parasite upon the body of the female, and is so different from the female of its own species, and from all ordinary barnacles, that no one would ever recognize in the adult male any affinity whatever to its closest allies.

The barnacle, or cirripede, is the creature which Mr. Darwin so long studied, and from which he learned so many lessons leading up to his grand generalizations. In a letter to Sir Charles Lyell, dated September 14, 1849, he recounts some of his discoveries while engaged in this study. Having learned that most cirripedes, but not all, were hermaphrodite, he remarks:

> The other day I got a curious case of a unisexual instead of hermaphrodite cirripedge, in which the female had the common cirripedial character, and in two valves of her shell had two little pockets in each of which she kept a little husband. I do not know of any other case where a female invariably has two husbands. I have one still odder fact, common to several species, namely, that though they are hermaphrodite, they have small additional, or, as I call them, complemental males. One specimen, itself, hermaphrodite, had no less than seven of these complemental males attached to it.

Prof. Brooks brings forward facts of this class to demonstrate that the male is the variable sex, while the female is comparatively stable. However much we may doubt his further conclusion that variability rather than supplementary procreative power was the primary purpose of the separate male principle, we must, it would seem, concede that variability and adaptability are the distinguishing characteristics of the male sex everywhere, as the transmitting power and permanence of type are those of the female. But this is a very different thing from saying that the female sex is incapable of progress, or that man is destined to develop indefinitely, leaving woman constantly farther and farther in the rear. Does the class of philosophers to which reference has been made look forward to a time when woman shall become as insignificant an object compared to man as the male spider is compared to the female? This would be the logical outcome of their argument if based upon the relative variability of the male sex.

We have now seen that, whether we contemplate the higher animals, among which male superiority prevails, or the lower forms, among which female superiority prevails, the argument from biology that the existing relations between the sexes in the human race are precisely what nature intended them to be, that they ought not to be disturbed and cannot be improved, leads, when carried to its logical conclusion, to a palpable absurdity. But have we, then, profited nothing by the thoughtful contemplation of the subject from these two points of view? Those who rightly interpret the facts cannot avoid learning a most important lesson from each of these lines of inquiry. From the first the truth comes clearly forth that the relations of the sexes among the higher animals are widely abnormal, warped, and strained by a long line of curious influences, chiefly psychic, which are incident to the development of animal organisms under the competitive principle that prevails throughout nature. From the second comes now into full view the still more important truth with which we first set out, that the female sex is primary in point both of origin and of importance in the history and economy of organic life. And as life is the highest product of nature and human life the highest type of life, it follows that the grandest fact in nature is woman.

But we have learned even more than this, that which is certainly of more practical value. We have learned how to carry forward the progress of development so far advanced by the unconscious agencies of nature. Accepting evolution as we must, recognizing heredity as the distinctive attribute of the female sex, it becomes clear that it must be from the steady advance of woman rather than from the uncertain fluctuations of man that the sure and solid progress of the future is to come. The attempt to move the whole race forward by elevating only the sex that represents the principle of instability, has long enough been tried. The many cases of superior men the sons of superior mothers, coupled with the many more cases of degenerate sons of superior sires, have taught us over and over again that the way to civilize the race is to civilize woman. And now, thanks to science, we see why this is so. Woman is the unchanging trunk of the great genealogic tree; while man, with all his vaunted superiority, is but a branch, a grafted scion, as it were, whose acquired qualities die with the individual, while those of woman are handed on to futurity. Woman *is* the race, and the race can be raised up only as she is raised up. There is no fixed rule by which Nature has intended that one sex should excel the other, any more than there is any fixed point beyond which either cannot further develop. Nature has no intentions, and evolution has no limits. True science teaches that the elevation of woman is the only sure road to evolution of man.

Thorstein Veblen

Thorstein Veblen (1857–1929) was an American economist who argued that economics must consider aspects of human culture—people's customs and habits—that are relevant to economic life. Veblen spent most of his life trying to undermine the assumptions of the neoclassical economics that dominated the academic world and helped legitimate "free enterprise" in the Gilded Age. With biting wit and an almost gleeful disregard of convention, he criticized the leading institutions of American society in a way that was both playful and shrewd, winning himself an audience far beyond the social sciences. Veblen's theory of a "leisure class" that lives "off the industrial community rather than in it" led one commentator to brand him "a kind of Benjamin Franklin trapped in the age of the Great Gatsby."

Veblen was born in 1857 to Norwegian immigrants on the Wisconsin frontier and was moved to Minnesota by his father, an artisan-farmer, when he was eight years old. Like Lester Ward before him or the social critics V. L. Parrington and Charles Beard after him, Veblen was alienated from the genteel culture of the East. Unlike these men, however, who came from old Protestant American stock, Veblen was the son of foreigners who lived on a remote farmstead cut off from the surrounding world of the Yankees. After nine more years on the farm, he was sent off to Carleton, a small Congregational college in Minnesota. For the next ten years, he bounced from one teaching job to another, returned to the farm, lived a rather idle life, and was all but incomprehensible to the academic denizens of the Midwest.

In 1892 he landed an academic job at the University of Chicago, the first of many marginal jobs he would hold at Stanford, the University of Missouri, the New School for Social Research in New York City, in the civil service, and as an editor of a small magazine. Recalcitrant, amused, and detached, he failed at all of these jobs yet maintained the sturdiness of mind and outlook to laugh off his detractors and write six major books—four of them while living in the cellar of a colleague's house. Throughout these years, his wife kept leaving him and returning again, and Veblen took up with various women on campus, getting himself fired from Stanford after an affair with a colleague's wife. Veblen spent his final years in a shack within the woods near Stanford, where he died on August 3, 1929.

Veblen was effective as a critic because, as C. Wright Mills has said, he used the American value of efficiency to criticize American reality. Historical progress is rooted in an instinct of workmanship that fosters continuous improvement of the industrial arts. But in the course of history, predatory classes arise that seize the property of their enemies (especially the women), and booty rather than productive work becomes the symbol of prowess. The struggle for existence becomes a competition for "pecuniary emulation," a ceaseless striving for prestige, and conspicuous display of wealth becomes more important than production. This is the value of leisure for aristocratic societies. But when the higher classes must move in wider circles of urban strangers, they advertise their wealth through conspicuous and wasteful consumption. Thus, it is not the propensity to truck and barter that inspires people in the modern world, but the propensity to stand out.

In his writings on modern America, such as his first book, *The Theory of the Leisure Class* (1899), Veblen linked this theory with a theory of business enterprise that is half John Dewey, half Karl Marx. America, he believed, was split in two between the productive and the pecuniary, the benevolent forces of technology and the profit system that distorts them. He contrasted the rationality of work, of the machine process and its personnel, to the irrational caprices of speculators, financiers, and the wealthy who squander valuable goods so as to win prestige. The conflict between technicians and financiers was a class struggle as well as a combat for status, driving the economy through severe business cycles.

Veblen is best known for his mordant analysis of the workings of prestige, as in his essay on the economic function of women's dress. He saw that conspicuous consumption was not confined to the upper classes but rather spreads throughout society as the economic pie expands. Following the path he blazed, critics of a later era, such as David Riesman and C. Wright Mills, showed how status striving may serve to distract people from the abiding realities of social class. But Veblen has been widely criticized on several grounds. By focusing derisively on the upper class at play, he discounts their military, political, and economic activity and thus fails to see the consequences of all this monkey business: how prestige truly buttresses power. This is probably due to Veblen's overly rigid distinction between the idle rich and the industrious bourgeoisie. His leisure class owns much but controls nothing; in contrast to the managers and technicians who direct production and thereby make history, they are parasites and destined to decline. But in reality this is true of only one element of the upper classes, at one period in history; it is a theory of high society in the Gilded Age, not of a nationwide elite that has arisen with the development of the mass media, higher education, and large-scale bureaucratic organizations. Since Veblen's day, some critics assert, there has emerged a national system of prestige, with signs of a merger among the economic, political, and "status" elites: a system more stable than the one Veblen reviled.

THE THEORY OF THE LEISURE CLASS

1899

I INTRODUCTORY

The institution of a leisure class is found in its best development at the higher stages of the barbarian culture; as, for instance, in feudal Europe or feudal Japan. In such communities the distinction between classes is very rigorously observed; and the feature of most striking economic significance in these class differences is the distinction maintained between the employments proper to the several classes. The upper classes are by custom exempt or excluded from industrial occupations, and are reserved for certain employments to which a degree of honor attaches. Chief among the honorable employments in any feudal community is warfare; and priestly service is commonly second to warfare. If the barbarian community is not notably warlike, the priestly office may take precedence, with that of the warrior second. But the rule holds with but slight exceptions that, whether warriors or priests, the upper classes are exempt from industrial employments, and this exemption is the economic expression of their superior rank. Brahmin India affords a fair illustration of the industrial exemption of both these classes. In

From *The Theory of the Leisure Class: An Economic Study of Institutions* by Thorstein Veblen (1899; reprint, New York: New American Library, 1953).

the communities belonging to the higher barbarian culture there is a considerable differentiation of sub-classes within what may be comprehensively called the leisure class; and there is a corresponding differentiation of employments between these sub-classes. The leisure class as a whole comprises the noble and the priestly classes, together with much of their retinue. The occupations of the class are correspondingly diversified; but they have the common economic characteristic of being non-industrial. These non-industrial upper-class occupations may be roughly comprised under government, warfare, religious observances, and sports.

. . .

The evidence afforded by the usages and cultural traits of communities at a low stage of development indicates that the institution of a leisure class has emerged gradually during the transition from primitive savagery to barbarism; or more precisely, during the transition from a peaceable to a consistently warlike habit of life. The conditions apparently necessary to its emergence in a consistent form are: (1) the community must be of a predatory habit of life (war or the hunting of large game or both); that is to say, the men, who constitute the inchoate leisure class in these cases, must be habituated to the infliction of injury by force and stratagem; (2) subsistence must be obtainable on sufficiently easy terms to admit of the exemption of a considerable portion of the community from steady application to a routine of labor. The institution of a leisure class is the outgrowth of an early discrimination between employments, according to which some employments are worthy and others unworthy. Under this ancient distinction the worthy employments are those which may be classed as exploit; unworthy are those necessary everyday employments into which no appreciable element of exploit enters.

This distinction has but little obvious significance in a modern industrial community, and it has, therefore, received but slight attention at the hands of economic writers. When viewed in the light of that modern common sense which has guided economic discussion, it seems formal and insubstantial. But it persists with great tenacity as a commonplace preconception even in modern life, as is shown, for instance, by our habitual aversion to menial employments. It is a distinction of a personal kind—of superiority and inferiority. In the earlier stages of culture, when the personal force of the individual counted more immediately and obviously in shaping the course of events, the element of exploit counted for more in the everyday scheme of life. Interest centered about this fact to a greater degree. Consequently a distinction proceeding on this ground seemed more imperative and more definitive then than is the case today. As a fact in the sequence of development, therefore, the distinction is a substantial one and rests on sufficiently valid and cogent grounds.

. . .

. . . A distinction is still habitually made between industrial and non-industrial occupations; and this modern distinction is a transmuted form of the barbarian distinction between exploit and drudgery. Such employments as warfare, politics, public worship, and public merrymaking, are felt, in the popular apprehension, to differ intrinsically from the labor that has to do with elaborating the material means of life. The precise line of demarcation is not the same as it was in the early barbarian scheme, but the broad distinction has not fallen into disuse.

The tacit, common-sense distinction today is, in effect, that any effort is to be accounted industrial only so far as its ultimate purpose is the utilization of non-human things. The coercive utilization of man by man is not felt to be an industrial function; but all effort directed to enhance human life by taking advantage of the non-human environment is classed together as industrial activity. By the economists who have best retained and adapted the classical tradition, man's "power over nature" is currently postulated as the characteristic fact of industrial productivity. This industrial power over nature is taken to include man's power over the life of the beasts and over all the elemental forces. A line is in this way drawn between mankind and brute creation.

. . .

. . . Those employments which are to be classed as exploit are worthy, honorable, noble; other employments, which do not contain this element of exploit, and especially those which imply subservience or submission, are unworthy, debasing, ignoble. The concept of dignity, worth, or honor, as applied either to persons or conduct, is of first-rate consequence in the development of classes and of class distinctions, and it is therefore necessary to say something of its derivation and meaning. Its psychological ground may be indicated in outline as follows.

As a matter of selective necessity, man is an agent. He is, in his own apprehension, a center of unfolding impulsive activity—"teleological" activity. He is an agent seeking in every act the accomplishment of some concrete, objective, impersonal end. By force of his being such an agent he is possessed of a taste for effective work, and a distaste for futile effort. He has a sense of the merit of serviceability or efficiency and of the demerit of futility, waste, or incapacity. This aptitude or propensity may be called the instinct of workmanship. Wherever the circumstances or traditions of life lead to an habitual comparison of one person with another in point of efficiency, the instinct of workmanship works out in an emulative or invidious comparison of persons. The extent to which this result follows depends in some considerable degree on the temperament of the population. In any community where such an invidious comparison of persons is habitually made, visible success becomes an end sought for its own utility as a basis of esteem. Esteem is gained and dispraise is avoided by putting one's efficiency in evidence. The result is that the instinct of workmanship works out in an emulative demonstration of force.

During that primitive phase of social development, when the community is still habitually peaceable, perhaps sedentary, and without a developed system of individual ownership, the efficiency of the individual can be shown chiefly and most consistently in some employment that goes to further the life of the group. What emulation of an economic kind there is between the members of such a group will be chiefly emulation in industrial serviceability. At the same time the incentive to emulation is not strong, nor is the scope for emulation large.

When the community passes from peaceable savagery to a predatory phase of life, the conditions of emulation change. The opportunity and the incentive to emulation increase greatly in scope and urgency. The activity of the men more and more takes on the character of exploit; and an invidious comparison of one hunter or warrior with another grows continually easier and more habitual. Tangible evidences of prowess—trophies—find a place in men's habits of thought as an essential feature of the paraphernalia of life. Booty, trophies of the chase or of the raid, come to be prized as evidence of preeminent force. Aggression becomes the accredited form of action, and booty serves as prima facie evidence of successful aggression. As accepted at this cultural stage, the accredited, worthy form of self-assertion is contest; and useful articles or services obtained by seizure or compulsion, serve as a conventional evidence of successful contest. Therefore, by contrast, the obtaining of goods by other methods than seizure comes to be accounted unworthy of man in his best estate. The performance of productive work, or employment in personal service, falls under the same odium for the same reason. An invidious distinction in this way arises between exploit and acquisition by seizure on the one hand and industrial employment on the other hand. Labor acquires a character of irksomeness by virtue of the indignity imputed to it.

. . .

II PECUNIARY EMULATION

In the sequence of cultural evolution the emergence of a leisure class coincides with the beginning of ownership. This is necessarily the case, for these two institutions result from the same set of economic forces. In the inchoate phase of their development they are but different aspects of the same general facts of social structure.

It is as elements of social structure—conventional facts—that leisure and ownership are matters of interest for the purpose in hand. An habitual neglect of work does not constitute a leisure class; neither does the mechanical fact of use and consumption constitute ownership. The present inquiry, therefore, is not concerned with the beginning of indolence, nor with the beginning of the appropriation of useful articles to individual consumption. The point in question is the origin and nature of a conventional leisure class on the one hand and the beginnings of individual ownership as a conventional right or equitable claim on the other hand.

The early differentiation out of which the distinction between a leisure and a working class arises is a division maintained between men's and women's work in the lower stages of barbarism. Likewise the earliest form of ownership is an ownership of the women by the able-bodied men of the community. The facts may be expressed in more general terms, and truer to the import of the barbarian theory of life, by saying that it is an ownership of the woman by the man.

There was undoubtedly some appropriation of useful articles before the custom of appropriating women arose. The usages of existing archaic communities in which there is no ownership of women is warrant for such a view. In all communities the members, both male and female, habitually appropriate to their individual use a variety of useful things; but these useful things are not thought of as owned by the person who appropriates and consumes them. The habitual appropriation and consumption of certain slight personal effects goes on without raising the question of ownership; that is to say, the question of a conventional, equitable claim to extraneous things.

The ownership of women begins in the lower barbarian stages of culture, apparently with the seizure of female captives. The original reason for the seizure and appropriation of women seems to have been their usefulness as trophies. The practice of seizing women from the enemy as trophies, gave rise to a form of ownership-marriage, resulting in a household with a male head. This was followed by an extension of slavery to other captives and inferiors, besides women, and by an extension of ownership-marriage to other women than those seized from the enemy. The outcome of emulation under the circumstances of a predatory life, therefore, has been on the one hand a form of marriage resting on coercion, and on the other hand the custom of ownership. The two institutions are not distinguishable in the initial phase of their development; both arise from the desire of the successful men to put their prowess in evidence by exhibiting some durable result of their exploits. Both also minister to that propensity for mastery which pervades all predatory communities. From the ownership of women the concept of ownership extends itself to include the products of their industry, and so there arises the ownership of things as well as of persons.

In this way a consistent system of property in goods is gradually installed. And although in the latest stages of the development, the serviceability of goods for consumption has come to be the most obtrusive element of their value, still, wealth has by no means yet lost its utility as a honorific evidence of the owner's prepotence.

. . .

The end of acquisition and accumulation is conventionally held to be the consumption of the goods accumulated—whether it is consumption directly by the owner of the goods or by the household attached to him and for this purpose identified with him in theory. This is at least felt to be the economically legitimate end of acquisition, which alone it is incumbent on the theory to take account of. Such consumption may of course he conceived to serve the consumer's physical wants—his physical comfort—or his so-called higher wants—spiritual, æsthetic, intellectual, or what not; the latter class of wants being served indirectly by an expenditure of goods, after the fashion familiar to all economic readers.

But it is only when taken in a sense far removed from its naïve meaning that consumption of goods can be said to afford the incentive from which accumulation invariably proceeds. The motive that lies at the root of ownership is emulation; and the same motive of emulation continues active in the further development of the institution to which it has given rise and in the development of all those features of the social structure which this institution of ownership touches. The possession of wealth confers honor; it is an invidious distinction. Nothing equally cogent can be said for the consumption of goods, nor for any other conceivable incentive to acquisition, and especially not for any incentive to the accumulation of wealth.

It is of course not to be overlooked that in a community where nearly all goods are private property the necessity of earning a livelihood is a powerful and ever-present incentive for the poorer members of the community. The need of subsistence and of an increase of physical comfort may for a time be the dominant motive of acquisition for those classes who are habitually employed at manual labor, whose subsistence is on a precarious footing, who possess little and ordinarily accumulate little; but it will appear in the course of the discussion that even in the case of these impecunious classes the predominance of the motive of physical want is not so decided as has sometimes been assumed. On the other hand, so far as regards those members and classes of the community who are chiefly concerned in the accumulation of wealth, the incentive of subsistence or of physical comfort never plays a considerable part. Ownership began and grew into a human institution on grounds unrelated to the subsistence minimum. The dominant incentive was from the outset the invidious distinction attaching to wealth, and, save temporarily and by exception, no other motive has usurped the primacy at any later stage of the development.

Property set out with being booty held as trophies of the successful raid. So long as the group had departed but little from the primitive communal organization, and so long as it still stood in close contact with other hostile groups, the utility of things or persons owned lay chiefly in an invidious comparison between their possessor and the enemy from whom they were taken. The habit of distinguishing between the interests of the individual and those of the group to which he belongs is apparently a later growth. Invidious comparison between the possessor of the honorific booty and his less successful neighbors within the group was no doubt present early as an element of the utility of the things possessed, though this was not at the outset the chief element of their value. The man's prowess was still primarily the group's prowess, and the possessor of the booty felt himself to be primarily the keeper of the honor of his group. This appreciation of exploit from the communal point of view is met with also at later stages of social growth, especially as regards the laurels of war.

But so soon as the custom of individual ownership begins to gain consistency, the point of view taken in making the invidious comparison on which private property rests will begin to change. Indeed, the one change is but the reflex of the other. The initial phase of ownership, the phase of acquisition by naïve seizure and conversion, begins to pass into the subsequent stage of an incipient organization of industry on the basis of private property (in slaves); the horde develops into a more or less self-sufficing industrial community; possessions then come to be valued not so much as evidence of successful foray, but rather as evidence of the prepotence of the possessor of these goods over other individuals within the community. The invidious comparison now becomes primarily a comparison of the owner with the other members of the group. Property is still of the nature of trophy, but, with the cultural advance, it becomes more and more a trophy of successes scored in the game of ownership carried on between the members of the group under the quasi-peaceable methods of nomadic life.

Gradually, as industrial activity further displaces predatory activity in the community's everyday life and in men's habits of thought, accumulated property more and more replaces trophies of predatory exploit as the conventional exponent of prepotence and success. With the growth of settled industry, therefore, the possession of wealth gains in relative importance and effectiveness as a customary basis of repute and esteem. Not that esteem ceases to be awarded on the basis of other, more direct evidence of prowess; not that successful predatory aggression or warlike exploit ceases to call out the approval and admiration of the crowd, or to stir the envy of the less successful competitors; but the opportunities for gaining distinction by means of this direct manifestation of superior force grow less available both in scope and frequency. . . .

. . .

Those members of the community who fall short of this, somewhat indefinite, normal degree of prowess or of property suffer in the esteem of their fellowmen; and consequently they suffer also in their own esteem, since the usual basis of self-respect is the respect accorded by one's neighbors. Only individuals with an aberrant temperament can in the long run retain their self-esteem in the face of the disesteem of their fellows. Apparent exceptions to the rule are met with, especially among people with strong religious convictions. But these apparent exceptions are scarcely real exceptions, since such persons commonly fall back on the putative approbation of some supernatural witness of their deeds.

So soon as the possession of property becomes the basis of popular esteem, therefore, it becomes also a requisite to that complacency which we call self-respect. In any community where goods are held in severalty it is necessary, in order to ensure his own peace of mind, that an individual should possess as large a portion of goods as others with whom he is accustomed to class himself; and it is extremely gratifying to possess something more than others. But as fast as a person makes new acquisitions, and becomes accustomed to the resulting new standard of wealth, the new standard forthwith ceases to afford appreciably greater satisfaction than the earlier standard did. . . .

. . .

What has just been said must not be taken to mean that there are no other incentives to acquisition and accumulation than this desire to excel in pecuniary standing and so gain the esteem and envy of one's fellowmen. The desire for added comfort and security from want is present as a motive at every stage of the process of accumulation in a modern industrial community; although the standard of sufficiency in these respects is in turn greatly affected by the habit of pecuniary emulation. To a great extent this emulation shapes the methods and selects the objects of expenditure for personal comfort and decent livelihood.

Besides this, the power conferred by wealth also affords a motive to accumulation. That propensity for purposeful activity and that repugnance to all futility of effort which belong to man by virtue of his character as an agent do not desert him when he emerges from the naïve communal culture where the dominant note of life is the unanalyzed and undifferentiated solidarity of the individual with the group with which his life is bound up. When he enters upon the predatory stage, where self-seeking in the narrower sense becomes the dominant note, this propensity goes with him still, as the pervasive trait that shapes his scheme of life. The propensity for achievement and the repugnance to futility remain the underlying economic motive. The propensity changes only in the form of its expression and in the proximate objects to which it directs the man's activity. Under the regime of individual ownership the most available means of visibly achieving a purpose is that afforded by the acquisition and accumulation of goods; and as the self-regarding antithesis between man and man reaches fuller consciousness, the propensity for achievement—the instinct of workmanship—tends more and more to shape itself into a straining to excel others in pecuniary achievement. . . .

III CONSPICUOUS CONSUMPTION

. . .

In the earlier phases of the predatory culture the only economic differentiation is a broad distinction between an honorable superior class made up of the able-bodied men on the one side, and a base inferior class of laboring women on the other. According to the ideal scheme of life in force at that time it is the office of the men to consume what the women produce. Such consumption as falls to the women is merely incidental to their work; it is a means to their continued labor, and not a consumption directed to their own comfort and fullness of life. Unproductive consumption of goods is honorable, primarily as a mark of prowess and a perquisite of human dignity; secondarily it becomes substantially honorable in itself, especially the consumption of the more desirable things. The consumption of choice articles of food, and frequently also of rare articles of adornment, becomes tabu to the women and children; and if there is a base (servile) class of men, the tabu holds also for them. With a further advance in culture this tabu may change into simple custom of a more or less rigorous character; but whatever be the theoretical basis of the distinction which is maintained, whether it be a tabu or a larger conventionality, the features of the conventional scheme of consumption do not change easily. When the quasi-peaceable stage of industry is reached, with its fundamental institution of chattel slavery, the general principle, more or less rigorously applied, is that the base, industrious class should consume only what may be necessary to their subsistence. In the nature of things, luxuries and the comforts of life belong to the leisure class. Under the tabu, certain victuals, and more particularly certain beverages, are strictly reserved for the use of the superior class.

The ceremonial differentiation of the dietary is best seen in the use of intoxicating beverages and narcotics. If these articles of consumption are costly, they are felt to be noble and honorific. Therefore the base classes, primarily the women, practice an enforced continence with respect to these stimulants, except in countries where they are obtainable at a very low cost. From archaic times down through all the length of the patriarchal regime it has been the office of the women to prepare and administer these luxuries, and it has been the perquisite of the men of gentle birth and breeding to consume them. Drunkenness and the other pathological consequences of the free use of stimulants therefore tend in their turn to become honorific, as being a mark, at the second remove, of the superior status of those who are able to afford the indulgence. . . .

. . .

The quasi-peaceable gentleman of leisure, then, not only consumes of the staff of life beyond the minimum required for subsistence and physical efficiency, but his consumption also undergoes a specialization as regards the quality of the goods consumed. He consumes freely and of the best, in food, drink, narcotics, shelter, services, ornaments, apparel, weapons and accoutrements, amusements, amulets, and idols or divinities. In the process of gradual amelioration which takes place in the articles of his consumption, the motive principle and the proximate aim of innovation is no doubt the higher efficiency of the improved and more elaborate products for personal comfort and wellbeing. But that does not remain the sole purpose of their consumption. The canon of reputability is at hand and seizes upon such innovations as are, according to its standard, fit to survive. Since the consumption of these more excellent goods is an evidence of wealth, it becomes honorific; and conversely, the failure to consume in due quantity and quality becomes a mark of inferiority and demerit.

This growth of punctilious discrimination as to qualitative excellence in eating, drinking, etc., presently affects not only the manner of life, but also the training and intellectual activity of the gentleman of leisure. He is no longer simply the successful, aggressive male—the man of strength, resource, and intrepidity. In order to avoid stultification he must also cultivate his tastes, for it now becomes incumbent on him to discriminate with some nicety between the noble and the ignoble in consumable goods. He becomes a connoisseur in creditable viands of various degrees of merit, in manly beverages and trinkets, in seemly apparel and architecture, in weapons, games, dances, and the narcotics. This cultivation of the æsthetic faculty requires time and application, and the demands made upon the gentleman in this direction therefore tend to change his life of leisure into a more or less arduous application to the business of learning how to live a life of ostensible leisure in a becoming way. Closely related to the requirement that the gentleman must consume freely and of the right kind of goods, there is the requirement that he must know how to consume them in a seemly manner. His life of leisure must be conducted in due form. Hence arise good manners in the way pointed out in an earlier chapter. High-bred manners and ways of living are items of conformity to the norm of conspicuous leisure and conspicuous consumption.

. . .

In the later development of peaceable industry, the usage of employing an idle corps of uniformed men-at-arms gradually lapses. Vicarious consumption by dependents bearing the insignia of their patron or master narrows down to a corps of liveried menials. In a heightened degree, therefore, the livery comes to be a badge of servitude, or rather of servility. Something of a honorific character always attached to the livery of the armed retainer, but this honorific character disappears when the livery becomes the exclusive badge of the menial. The livery becomes obnoxious to nearly all who are required to wear it. We are yet so little removed from a state of effective slavery as still to be fully sensitive to the sting of any imputation of servility. This antipathy asserts itself even in the case of the liveries or uniforms which some corporations prescribe as the distinctive dress of their employees. In this country the aversion even goes the length of discrediting—in a mild and uncertain way—those government employments, military and civil, which require the wearing of a livery or uniform.

With the disappearance of servitude, the number of vicarious consumers attached to any one gentleman tends, on the whole, to decrease. The like is of course true, and perhaps in a still higher degree, of the number of dependents who perform vicarious leisure for him. In a general way, though not wholly nor consistently, these two groups coincide. The dependent who was first delegated for these duties was the wife, or the chief wife; and, as would be expected, in the later development of the institution, when the number of persons by whom these duties are customarily performed gradually narrows, the wife remains the last. In the higher grades of society a large volume of both these kinds of service is required; and here the wife is of course still assisted in the work by a more or less numerous corps of menials. But as we descend the social scale, the point is presently reached where the duties of vicarious leisure and consumption devolve upon the wife alone. In the communities of the Western culture, this point is at present found among the lower middle class.

And here occurs a curious inversion. It is a fact of common observance that in this lower middle class there is no pretense of leisure on the part of the head of the household. Through force of circumstances it has fallen into disuse. But the middle-class wife still carries on the business of vicarious leisure, for the good name of the household and its master. In descending the social scale in any modern industrial community, the primary fact—the conspicuous leisure of the master of the household—disappears at a relatively high point. The head of the middle-class household has been reduced by economic circumstances to turn his hand to gaining a livelihood by occupations which often partake largely of the character of industry, as in the case of the ordinary business man of today. But the derivative fact—the vicarious leisure and consumption rendered by the wife, and the auxiliary vicarious performance of leisure by menials—remains in vogue as a conventionality which the demands of reputability will not suffer to be slighted. It is by no means an uncommon spectacle to find a man applying himself to work with the utmost assiduity, in order that his wife may in due form render for him that degree of vicarious leisure which the common sense of the time demands.

The leisure rendered by the wife in such cases is, of course, not a simple manifestation of idleness or indolence. It almost invariably occurs disguised under some form of work or household duties or social amenities, which prove on analysis to serve little or no ulterior end beyond showing that she does not occupy herself with anything that is gainful or that is of substantial use. As has already been noticed under the head of manners, the greater part of the customary round of domestic cares to which the middle-class housewife gives her time and effort is of this character. Not that the results of her attention to household matters, of a decorative and mundificatory character, are not pleasing to the sense of men trained in middle-class proprieties; but the taste to which these effects of household adornment and tidiness appeal is a taste which has been formed under the selective guidance of a canon of propriety that demands just these evidences of wasted effort. The effects are pleasing to us chiefly because we have been taught to find them pleasing. There goes into these domestic duties much solicitude for a proper combination of form and color, and for other ends that are to be classed as æsthetic in the proper sense of the term; and it is not denied that effects having some substantial æsthetic value are sometimes attained. Pretty much all that is here insisted on is that, as regards these amenities of life, the housewife's efforts are under the guidance of traditions that have been shaped by the law of conspicuously wasteful expenditure of time and substance. If beauty or comfort is achieved—and it is a more or less fortuitous circumstance if they are—they must be achieved by means and methods that commend themselves to the great economic law of wasted effort. The more reputable, "presentable" portion of middle-class household paraphernalia are, on the one hand, items of conspicuous consumption, and on the other hand, apparatus for putting in evidence the vicarious leisure rendered by the housewife.

The requirement of vicarious consumption at the hands of the wife continues in force even at a lower point in the pecuniary scale than the requirement of vicarious leisure. At a point below which little if any pretence of wasted effort, in ceremonial cleanness and the like, is observable, and where there is assuredly no conscious attempt at ostensible leisure, decency still requires the wife to consume some goods conspicuously for the reputability of the household and its head. So that, as the latter-day outcome of this evolution of an archaic institution, the wife, who was at the outset the drudge and chattel of the man, both in fact and in theory—the producer of goods for him to consume—has become the ceremonial consumer of goods which he produces. But she still quite unmistakably remains his chattel in theory; for the habitual rendering of vicarious leisure and consumption is the abiding mark of the unfree servant.

This vicarious consumption practiced by the household of the middle and lower classes can not be counted as a direct expression of the leisure-class scheme of life, since the household of this pecuniary grade does not belong within the leisure class. It is rather that the leisure-class scheme of life here comes to an expression at the second remove. The leisure class stands at the head of the social structure in point of reputability; and its manner of life and its standards of worth therefore afford the norm of reputability for the community. The observance of these standards, in some degree of approximation, becomes incumbent upon all classes lower in the scale. In modern civilized communities the lines of demarcation between social classes have grown vague and transient, and wherever this happens the norm of reputability imposed by the upper class extends its coercive influence with but slight hindrance down through the social structure to the lowest strata. The result is that the members of each stratum accept as their ideal of decency the scheme of life in vogue in the next higher stratum, and bend their energies to live up to that ideal. On pain of forfeiting their good name and their self-respect in case of failure, they must conform to the accepted code, at least in appearance.

The basis on which good repute in any highly organized industrial community ultimately rests is pecuniary strength; and the means of showing pecuniary strength, and so of gaining or retaining a good name, are leisure and a conspicuous consumption of goods. Accordingly, both of these methods are in vogue as far down the scale as it remains possible; and in the lower strata in which the two methods are employed, both offices are in great part delegated to the wife and children of the household. Lower still, where any degree of leisure, even ostensible, has become impracticable for the wife, the conspicuous consumption of goods remains and is carried on by the wife and children. The man of the household also can do something in this direction, and indeed, he commonly does; but with a still lower descent into the levels of indigence—along the margin of the slums—the man, and presently also the children, virtually cease to consume valuable goods for appearances, and the woman remains virtually the sole exponent of the household's pecuniary decency. No class of society, not even the most abjectly poor, foregoes all customary conspicuous consumption. The last items of this category of consumption are not given up except under stress of the direst necessity. Very much of squalor and discomfort will be endured before the last trinket or the last pretense of pecuniary decency is put away. There is no class and no country that has yielded so abjectly before the pressure of physical want as to deny themselves all gratification of this higher or spiritual need.

From the foregoing survey of the growth of conspicuous leisure and consumption, it appears that the utility of both alike for the purposes of reputability lies in the element of waste that is common to both. In the one case it is a waste of time and effort, in the other it is a waste of goods. Both are methods of demonstrating the possession of wealth, and the two are conventionally accepted as equivalents. The choice between them is a question of advertising expediency simply, except so far as it may be affected by other standards of propriety, springing from a different source. On grounds of expediency the preference may be given to the one or the other at different stages of the economic development. The question is, which of the two methods will most effectively reach the persons whose convictions it is desired to affect. Usage has answered this question in different ways under different circumstances.

So long as the community or social group is small enough and compact enough to be effectually reached by common notoriety alone—that is to say, so long as the human environment to which the individual is required to adapt himself in respect of reputability is comprised within his sphere of personal acquaintance and neighborhood gossip—so long the one method is about as effective as the other. Each will therefore serve about equally well during the earlier stages of social growth. But when the differentiation has gone farther and it becomes necessary to reach a wider human environment, consumption begins to hold over leisure as an ordinary means of decency. This is especially true during the later, peaceable economic stage. The means of communication and the mobility of the population now expose the individual to the observation of many persons who have no other means of judging of his reputability than the display of goods (and perhaps of breeding) which he is able to make while he is under their direct observation.

The modern organization of industry works in the same direction also by another line. The exigencies of the modern industrial system frequently place individuals and households in juxtaposition between whom there is little contact in any other sense than that of juxtaposition. One's neighbors, mechanically speaking, often are socially not one's neighbors, or even acquaintances; and still their transient good opinion has a high degree of utility. The only practicable means of impressing one's pecuniary ability on these unsympathetic observers of one's everyday life is an unremitting demonstration of ability to pay. In the modern community there is also a more frequent attendance at large gatherings of people to whom one's everyday life is unknown; in such places as churches, theaters, ballrooms, hotels, parks, shops, and the like. In order to impress these transient observers, and to retain one's self-complacency under their observation, the signature of one's pecuniary strength should be written in characters which he who runs may read. It is evident, therefore, that the present trend of the development is in the direction of heightening the utility of conspicuous consumption as compared with leisure.

It is also noticeable that the serviceability of consumption as a means of repute, as well as the insistence on it as an element of decency, is at its best in those portions of the community where the human contact of the individual is widest and the mobility of the population is greatest. Conspicuous consumption claims a relatively larger portion of the income of the urban than of the rural population, and the claim is also more imperative. The result is that, in order to keep up a decent appearance, the former habitually live hand-to-mouth to a greater extent than the latter. So it comes, for instance, that the American farmer and his wife and daughters are notoriously less modish in their dress, as well as less urbane in their manners, than the city artisan's family with an equal income. It is not that the city population is by nature much more eager for the peculiar complacency that comes of a conspicuous consumption, nor has the rural population less regard for pecuniary decency. But the provocation to this line of evidence, as well as its transient effectiveness, is more decided in the city. This method is therefore more readily resorted to, and in the struggle to outdo one another the city population push their normal standard of conspicuous consumption to a higher point, with the result that a relatively greater expenditure in this direction is required to indicate a given degree of pecuniary decency in the city. The requirement of conformity to this higher conventional standard becomes mandatory. The standard of decency is higher, class for class, and this requirement of decent appearance must be lived up to on pain of losing caste.

Consumption becomes a larger element in the standard of living in the city than in the country. Among the country population its place is to some extent taken by savings and home comforts known through the medium of neighborhood gossip sufficiently to serve the like general purpose of pecuniary repute. These home comforts and the leisure indulged in—where the indulgence is found—are of course also in great part to be classed as items of conspicuous consumption; and much the same is to be said of the savings. The smaller amount of the savings laid by by the artisan class is no doubt due, in some measure, to the fact that in the case of the artisan the savings are a less effective means of advertisement, relative to the environment in which he is placed, than are the savings of the people living on farms and in the small villages. Among the latter, everybody's affairs, especially everybody's pecuniary status, are known to everybody else. Considered by itself simply—taken in the first degree—this added provocation to which the artisan and the urban laboring classes are exposed may not very seriously decrease the amount of savings; but in its cumulative action, through raising the standard of decent expenditure, its deterrent effect on the tendency to save cannot but be very great.

. . .

VI PECUNIARY CANONS OF TASTE

It is not only with respect to consumable goods —including domestic animals—that the canons of taste have been colored by the canons of pecuniary reputability. Something to the like effect is to be said for beauty in persons. . . .

. . .

In modern communities which have reached the higher levels of industrial development, the upper leisure class has accumulated so great a mass of wealth as to place its women above all imputation of vulgarly productive labor. Here the status of women as vicarious consumers is beginning to lose its place in the affections of the body of the people; and as a consequence the ideal of feminine beauty is beginning to change back again from the infirmly delicate, translucent, and hazardously slender, to a woman of the archaic type that does not disown her hands and feet, nor, indeed, the other gross material facts of her person. In the course of economic development the ideal of beauty among the peoples of the Western culture has shifted from the woman of physical presence to the lady, and it is beginning to shift back again to the woman; and all in obedience to the changing conditions of pecuniary emulation. The exigencies of emulation at one time required lusty slaves; at another time they required a conspicuous performance of vicarious leisure and consequently an obvious disability; but the situation is now beginning to outgrow this last requirement, since, under the higher efficiency of modern industry, leisure in women is possible so far down the scale of reputability that it will no longer serve as a definitive mark of the highest pecuniary grade.

. . .

VII DRESS AS AN EXPRESSION OF THE PECUNIARY CULTURE

It will be in place, by way of illustration, to show in some detail how the economic principles so far set forth apply to everyday facts in some one direction of the life process. For this purpose no line of consumption affords a more apt illustration than expenditure on dress. It is especially the rule of the conspicuous waste of goods that finds expression in dress, although the other, related principles of pecuniary repute are also exemplified in the same contrivances. Other methods of putting one's pecuniary standing in evidence serve their end effectually, and other methods are in vogue always and everywhere; but expenditure on dress has this advantage over most other methods, that our apparel is always in evidence and affords an indication of our pecuniary standing to all observers at the first glance. It is also true that admitted expenditure for display is more obviously present, and is, perhaps, more universally practiced in the matter of dress than in any other line of consumption. No one finds difficulty in assenting to the commonplace that the greater part of the expenditure incurred by all classes for apparel is incurred for the sake of a respectable appearance rather than for the protection of the person. And probably at no other point is the sense of shabbiness so keenly felt as it is if we fall short of the standard set by social usage in this matter of dress. It is true of dress in even a higher degree than of most other items of consumption, that people will undergo a very considerable degree of privation in the comforts or the necessaries of life in order to afford what is considered a decent amount of wasteful consumption; so that it is by no means an uncommon occurrence, in an inclement climate, for people to go ill clad in order to appear well dressed. And the commercial value of the goods used for clothing in any modern community is made up to a much larger extent of the fashionableness, the reputability of the goods than of the mechanical service which they render in clothing the person of the wearer. The need of dress is eminently a "higher" or spiritual need.

This spiritual need of dress is not wholly, nor even chiefly, a naïve propensity for display of expenditure. The law of conspicuous waste guides consumption in apparel, as in other things, chiefly at the second remove, by shaping the canons of taste and decency. In the common run of cases the conscious motive of the wearer or purchaser of conspicuously wasteful apparel is the need of conforming to established usage, and of living up to the accredited standard of taste and reputability. It is not only that one must be guided by the code of proprieties in dress in order to avoid the mortification that comes of unfavorable notice and comment, though that motive in itself counts for a great deal; but besides that, the requirement of expensiveness is so ingrained into our habits of thought in matters of dress that any other than expensive apparel is instinctively odious to us. Without reflection or analysis, we feel that what is inexpensive is unworthy. "A cheap coat makes a cheap man." "Cheap and nasty" is recognized to hold true in dress with even less mitigation than in other lines of consumption. On the ground both of taste and of serviceability, an inexpensive article of apparel is held to be inferior, under the maxim "cheap and nasty." We find things beautiful, as well as serviceable, somewhat in proportion as they are costly. With few and inconsequential exceptions, we all find a costly hand-wrought article of apparel much preferable, in point of beauty and of serviceability, to a less expensive imitation of it, however cleverly the spurious article may imitate the costly original; and what offends our sensibilities in the spurious article is not that it falls short in form or color, or, indeed, in visual effect in any way. The offensive object may be so close an imitation as to defy any but the closest scrutiny; and yet so soon as the counterfeit is detected, its æsthetic value, and its commercial value as well, declines precipitately. Not only that, but it may be asserted with but small risk of contradiction that the æsthetic value of a detected counterfeit in dress declines somewhat in the same proportion as the counterfeit is cheaper than its original. It loses caste æsthetically because it falls to a lower pecuniary grade.

But the function of dress as an evidence of ability to pay does not end with simply showing that the wearer consumes valuable goods in excess of what is required for physical comfort. Simple conspicuous waste of goods is effective and gratifying as far as it goes; it is good prima facie evidence of pecuniary success, and consequently *prima facie* evidence of social worth. But dress has subtler and more far-reaching possibilities than this crude, first-hand evidence of wasteful consumption only. If, in addition to showing that the wearer can afford to consume freely and uneconomically, it can also be shown in the same stroke that he or she is not under the necessity of earning a livelihood, the evidence of social worth is enhanced in a very considerable degree. Our dress, therefore, in order to serve its purpose effectually, should not only be expensive, but it should also make plain to all observers that the wearer is not engaged in any kind of productive labor. In the evolutionary process by which our system of dress has been elaborated into its present admirably perfect adaptation to its purpose, this subsidiary line of evidence has received due attention. A detailed examination of what passes in popular apprehension for elegant apparel will show that it is contrived at every point to convey the impression that the wearer does not habitually put forth any useful effort. It goes without saying that no apparel can be considered elegant, or even decent, if it shows the effect of manual labor on the part of the wearer, in the way of soil or wear. The pleasing effect of neat and spotless garments is chiefly, if not altogether, due to their carrying the suggestion of leisure—exemption from personal contact with industrial processes of any kind. Much of the charm that invests the patent-leather shoe, the stainless linen, the lustrous cylindrical hat, and the walking-stick, which so greatly enhance the native dignity of a gentleman, comes of their pointedly suggesting that the wearer cannot when so attired bear a hand in any employment that is directly and immediately of any human use. Elegant dress serves its purpose of elegance not only in that it is expensive, but also because it is the insignia of leisure. It not only shows that the wearer is able to consume a relatively large value, but it argues at the same time that he consumes without producing.

The dress of women goes even farther than that of men in the way of demonstrating the wearer's abstinence from productive employment. It needs no argument to enforce the generalization that the more elegant styles of feminine bonnets go even farther towards making work impossible than does the man's high hat. The woman's shoe adds the so-called French heel to the evidence of enforced leisure afforded by its polish; because this high heel obviously makes any, even the simplest and most necessary manual work extremely difficult. The like is true even in a higher degree of the skirt and the rest of the drapery which characterizes woman's dress. The substantial reason for our tenacious attachment to the skirt is just this: it is expensive and it hampers the wearer at every turn and incapacitates her for all useful exertion. The like is true of the feminine custom of wearing the hair excessively long.

But the woman's apparel not only goes beyond that of the modern man in the degree in which it argues exemption from labor; it also adds a peculiar and highly characteristic feature which differs in kind from anything habitually practiced by the men. This feature is the class of contrivances of which the corset is the typical example. The corset is, in economic theory, substantially a mutilation, undergone for the purpose of lowering the subject's vitality and rendering her permanently and obviously unfit for work. It is true, the corset impairs the personal attractions of the wearer, but the loss suffered on that score is offset by the gain in reputability which comes of her visibly increased expensiveness and infirmity. It may broadly be set down that the womanliness of woman's apparel resolves itself, in point of substantial fact, into the more effective hindrance to useful exertion offered by the garments peculiar to women. This difference between masculine and feminine apparel is here simply pointed out as a characteristic feature. The ground of its occurrence will be discussed presently.

So far, then, we have, as the great and dominant norm of dress, the broad principle of conspicuous waste. Subsidiary to this principle, and as a corollary under it, we get as a second norm the principle of conspicuous leisure. In dress construction this norm works out in the shape of divers contrivances going to show that the wearer does not and, as far as it may conveniently be shown, can not engage in productive labor. Beyond these two principles there is a third of scarcely less constraining force, which will occur to any one who reflects at all on the subject. Dress must not only be conspicuously expensive and inconvenient; it must at the same time be up to date. No explanation at all satisfactory has hitherto been offered of the phenomenon of changing fashions. The imperative requirement of dressing in the latest accredited manner, as well as the fact that this accredited fashion constantly changes from season to season, is sufficiently familiar to every one, but the theory of this flux and change has not been worked out. We may of course say, with perfect consistency and truthfulness, that this principle of novelty is another corollary under the law of conspicuous waste. Obviously, if each garment is permitted to serve for but a brief term, and if none of last season's apparel is carried over and made further use of during the present season, the wasteful expenditure on dress is greatly increased. This is good as far as it goes, but it is negative only. Pretty much all that this consideration warrants us in saying is that the norm of conspicuous waste exercises a controlling surveillance in all matters of dress, so that any change in the fashions must conform to the requirement of wastefulness; it leaves unanswered the question as to the motive for making and accepting a change in the prevailing styles, and it also fails to explain why conformity to a given style at a given time is so imperatively necessary as we know it to be.

For a creative principle, capable of serving as motive to invention and innovation in fashions, we shall have to go back to the primitive, non-economic motive with which apparel originated—the motive of adornment. Without going into an extended discussion of how and why this motive asserts itself under the guidance of the law of expensiveness, it may be stated broadly that each successive innovation in the fashions is an effort to reach some form of display which shall be more acceptable to our sense of form and color or of effectiveness, than that which it displaces. The changing styles are the expression of a restless search for something which shall commend itself to our æsthetic sense; but as each innovation is subject to the selective action of the norm of conspicuous waste, the range within which innovation can take place is somewhat restricted. The innovation must not only be more beautiful, or perhaps oftener less offensive, than that which it displaces, but it must also come up to the accepted standard of expensiveness.

It would seem at first sight that the result of such an unremitting struggle to attain the beautiful in dress should be a gradual approach to artistic perfection. We might naturally expect that the fashions should show a well-marked trend in the direction of some one or more types of apparel eminently becoming to the human form; and we might even feel that we have substantial ground for the hope that today, after all the ingenuity and effort which have been spent on dress these many years, the fashions should have achieved a relative perfection and a relative stability, closely approximating to a permanently tenable artistic ideal. But such is not the case. It would be very hazardous indeed to assert that the styles of today are intrinsically more becoming than those of ten years ago, or than those of twenty, or fifty, or one hundred years ago. On the other hand, the assertion freely goes uncontradicted that styles in vogue two thousand years ago are more becoming than the most elaborate and painstaking constructions of today.

The explanation of the fashions just offered, then, does not fully explain, and we shall have to look farther. It is well known that certain relatively stable styles and types of costume have been worked out in various parts of the world; as, for instance, among the Japanese, Chinese, and other Oriental nations; likewise among the Greeks, Romans, and other Eastern peoples of antiquity; so also, in later times, among the peasants of nearly every country of Europe. These national or popular costumes are in most cases adjudged by competent critics to be more becoming, more artistic, than the fluctuating styles of modern civilized apparel. At the same time they are also, at least usually, less obviously wasteful; that is to say, other elements than that of a display of expense are more readily detected in their structure.

These relatively stable costumes are, commonly, pretty strictly and narrowly localized, and they vary by slight and systematic gradations from place to place. They have in every case been worked out by peoples or classes which are poorer than we, and especially they belong in countries and localities and times where the population, or at least the class to which the costume in question belongs, is relatively homogeneous, stable, and immobile. That is to say, stable costumes which will bear the test of time and perspective are worked out under circumstances where the norm of conspicuous waste asserts itself less imperatively than it does in the large modern civilized cities, whose relatively mobile wealthy population today sets the pace in matters of fashion.

The countries and classes which have in this way worked out stable and artistic costumes have been so placed that the pecuniary emulation among them has taken the direction of a competition in conspicuous leisure rather than in conspicuous consumption of goods. So that it will hold true in a general way that fashions are least stable and least becoming in those communities where the principle of a conspicuous waste of goods asserts itself most imperatively, as among ourselves. All this points to an antagonism between expensiveness and artistic apparel. In point of practical fact, the norm of conspicuous waste is incompatible with the requirement that dress should be beautiful or becoming. And this antagonism offers an explanation of that restless change in fashion which neither the canon of expensiveness nor that of beauty alone can account for.

The standard of reputability requires that dress should show wasteful expenditure; but all wastefulness is offensive to native taste. The psychological law has already been pointed out that all men—and women perhaps even in a higher degree—abhor futility, whether of effort or of expenditure—much as Nature was once said to abhor a vacuum. But the principle of conspicuous waste requires an obviously futile expenditure; and the resulting conspicuous expensiveness of dress is therefore intrinsically ugly. Hence we find that in all innovations in dress, each added or altered detail strives to avoid condemnation by showing some ostensible purpose, at the same time that the requirement of conspicuous waste prevents the purposefulness of these innovations from becoming anything more than a somewhat transparent pretense. Even in its freest flights, fashion rarely if ever gets away from a simulation of some ostensible use. The ostensible usefulness of the fashionable details of dress, however, is always so transparent a make-believe, and their substantial futility presently forces itself so baldly upon our attention as to become unbearable, and then we take refuge in a new style. But the new style must conform to the requirement of reputable wastefulness and futility. Its futility presently becomes as odious as that of its predecessor; and the only remedy which the law of waste allows us is to seek relief in some new construction, equally futile and equally untenable. Hence the essential ugliness and the unceasing change of fashionable attire.

Having so explained the phenomenon of shifting fashions, the next thing is to make the explanation tally with everyday facts. Among these everyday facts is the well-known liking which all men have for the styles that are in vogue at any given time. A new style comes into vogue and remains in favor for a season, and, at least so long as it is a novelty, people very generally find the new style attractive. The prevailing fashion is felt to be beautiful. This is due partly to the relief it affords in being different from what went before it, partly to its being reputable. As indicated in the last chapter, the canon of reputability to some extent shapes our tastes, so that under its guidance anything will be accepted as becoming until its novelty wears off, or until the warrant of reputability is transferred to a new and novel structure serving the same general purpose. That the alleged beauty, or "loveliness," of the styles in vogue at any given time is transient and spurious only is attested by the fact that none of the many shifting fashions will bear the test of time. When seen in the perspective of half-a-dozen years or more, the best of our fashions strike us as grotesque, if not unsightly. Our transient attachment to whatever happens to be the latest rests on other than æsthetic grounds, and lasts only until our abiding æsthetic sense has had time to assert itself and reject this latest indigestible contrivance.

The process of developing an æsthetic nausea takes more or less time; the length of time required in any given case being inversely as the degree of intrinsic odiousness of the style in question. This time relation between odiousness and instability in fashions affords ground for the inference that the more rapidly the styles succeed and displace one another, the more offensive they are to sound taste. The presumption, therefore, is that the farther the community, especially the wealthy classes of the community, develop in wealth and mobility and in the range of their human contact, the more imperatively will the law of conspicuous waste assert itself in matters of dress, the more will the sense of beauty tend to fall into abeyance or be overborne by the canon of pecuniary reputability, the more rapidly will fashions shift and change, and the more grotesque and intolerable will be the varying styles that successively come into vogue.

There remains at least one point in this theory of dress yet to be discussed. Most of what has been said applies to men's attire as well as to that of women; although in modern times it applies at nearly all points with greater force to that of women. But at one point the dress of women differs substantially from that of men. In woman's dress there is obviously greater insistence on such features as testify to the wearer's exemption from or incapacity for all vulgarly productive employment. This characteristic of woman's apparel is of interest, not only as completing the theory of dress, but also as confirming what has already been said of the economic status of women, both in the past and in the present.

As has been seen in the discussion of woman's status under the heads of Vicarious Leisure and Vicarious Consumption, it has in the course of economic development become the office of the woman to consume vicariously for the head of the household; and her apparel is contrived with this object in view. It has come about that obviously productive labor is in a peculiar degree derogatory to respectable women, and therefore special pains should be taken in the construction of women's dress, to impress upon the beholder the fact (often indeed a fiction) that the wearer does not and can not habitually engage in useful work. Propriety requires respectable women to abstain more consistently from useful effort and to make more of a show of leisure than the men of the same social classes. It grates painfully on our nerves to contemplate the necessity of any well-bred woman's earning a livelihood by useful work. It is not "woman's sphere." Her sphere is within the household, which she should "beautify," and of which she should be the "chief ornament." The male head of the household is not currently spoken of as its ornament. This feature taken in conjunction with the other fact that propriety requires more unremitting attention to expensive display in the dress and other paraphernalia of women, goes to enforce the view already implied in what has gone before. By virtue of its descent from a patriarchal past, our social system makes it the woman's function in an especial degree to put in evidence her household's ability to pay. According to the modern civilized scheme of life, the good name of the household to which she belongs should be the special care of the woman; and the system of honorific expenditure and conspicuous leisure by which this good name is chiefly sustained is therefore the woman's sphere. In the ideal scheme, as it tends to realize itself in the life of the higher pecuniary classes, this attention to conspicuous waste of substance and effort should normally be the sole economic function of the woman.

At the stage of economic development at which the women were still in the full sense the property of the men, the performance of conspicuous leisure and consumption came to be part of the services required of them. The women being not their own masters, obvious expenditure and leisure on their part would redound to the credit of their master rather than to their own credit; and therefore the more expensive and the more obviously unproductive the women of the household are, the more creditable and more effective for the purpose of reputability of the household or its head will their life be. So much so that the women have been required not only to afford evidence of a life of leisure, but even to disable themselves for useful activity.

It is at this point that the dress of men falls short of that of women, and for sufficient reason. Conspicuous waste and conspicuous leisure are reputable because they are evidence of pecuniary strength; pecuniary strength is reputable or honorific because, in the last analysis, it argues success and superior force; therefore the evidence of waste and leisure put forth by any individual in his own behalf cannot consistently take such a form or be carried to such a pitch as to argue incapacity or marked discomfort on his part; as the exhibition would in that case show not superior force, but inferiority, and so defeat its own purpose. So, then, wherever wasteful expenditure and the show of abstention from effort is normally, or on an average, carried to the extent of showing obvious discomfort or voluntarily induced physical disability, there the immediate inference is that the individual in question does not perform this wasteful expenditure and undergo this disability for her own personal gain in pecuniary repute, but in behalf of some one else to whom she stands in a relation of economic dependence; a relation which in the last analysis must, in economic theory, reduce itself to a relation of servitude.

To apply this generalization to women's dress, and put the matter in concrete terms: the high heel, the skirt, the impracticable bonnet, the corset, and the general disregard of the wearer's comfort which is an obvious feature of all civilized women's apparel, are so many items of evidence to the effect that in the modern civilized scheme of life the woman is still, in theory, the economic dependent of the man—that, perhaps in a highly idealized sense, she still is the man's chattel. The homely reason for all this conspicuous leisure and attire on the part of women lies in the fact that they are servants to whom, in the differentiation of economic functions, has been delegated the office of putting in evidence their master's ability to pay.

. . .

"THE ECONOMIC THEORY OF WOMAN'S DRESS"

1894

Under the patriarchal organisation of society, where the social unit was the man (with his dependents), the dress of the women was an exponent of the wealth of the man whose chattels they were. In modern society, where the unit is the household, the woman's dress sets forth the wealth of the household to which she belongs. Still, even today, in spite of the nominal and somewhat celebrated demise of the patriarchal idea, there is that about the dress of women which suggests that the wearer is something in the nature of a chattel; indeed, the theory of woman's dress quite plainly involves the implication that the woman is a chattel. In this respect the dress of women differs from that of men. . . .

Woman, primarily, originally because she was herself a pecuniary possession, has become in a peculiar way the exponent of the pecuniary strength of her social group; and with the progress of specialisation of functions in the social organism this duty tends to devolve more and more entirely upon the woman. The best, most advanced, most highly developed societies of our time have reached the point in their evolution where it has (ideally) become the great, peculiar, and almost the sole function of woman in the social system to put in evidence her economic unit's ability to pay. That is to say, woman's place (according to the ideal scheme of our social system) has come to be that of a means of conspicuously unproductive expenditure. . . . "Dress," therefore, from the economic point of view, comes pretty near being synonymous with "display of wasteful expenditure." . . .

It is not that the wearers or the buyers of these wasteful goods desire the waste. They desire to make manifest their ability to pay. What is sought is not the de facto waste, but the appearance of waste. Hence there is a constant effort on the part of the consumers of these goods to obtain them at as good

From "The Economic Theory of Woman's Dress" by Thorstein Veblen (*Popular Science Monthly* 46, November 1894; reprint, *Against the Tide*, eds. Michael S. Kimmel and Thomas E. Mosmiller, Boston: Beacon Press, 1992).

a bargain as may be; and hence also a constant effort on the part of the producers of these goods to lower the cost of their production, and consequently to lower the price. But as fast as the price of the goods declines to such a figure that their consumption is no longer prima facie evidence of a considerable ability to pay, the particular goods in question fall out of favor, and consumption is diverted to something which more adequately manifests the wearer's ability to afford wasteful consumption. . . . [T]here is the evidence of expenditure afforded by a constant supersession of one wasteful garment or trinket by a new one. This principle inculcates the desirability, amounting to a necessity wherever circumstances allow, of wearing nothing that is out of date. . . .

This requirement of novelty is the underlying principle of the whole of the difficult and interesting domain of fashion. Fashion does not demand continual flux and change simply because that way of doing is foolish; flux and change and novelty are demanded by the central principle of all dress—conspicuous waste. . . .

But apart from the exhibition of pecuniary strength afforded by an aggressive wasteful expenditure, the same purpose may also be served by conspicuous abstention from useful effort. The woman is, by virtue of the specialisation of social functions, the exponent of the economic unit's pecuniary strength, and it consequently also devotes on her to exhibit the unit's capacity to endure this passive form of pecuniary damage. She can do this by putting in evidence the fact (often a fiction) that she leads a useless life. Dress is her chief means of doing so. The ideal of dress . . . is to demonstrate to all observers, and to compel observation of the fact, that the wearer is manifestly incapable of doing anything that is of any use. The modern civilised woman's dress attempts this demonstration of habitual idleness, and succeeds measurably.

Herein lies the secret of the persistence, in modern dress, of the skirt and of all the cumbrous and otherwise meaningless drapery which the skirt typifies. The skirt persists because it is cumbrous. It hampers the movements of the wearer and disables her, in great measure, for any useful occupation. So it serves as an advertisement (often disingenuous) that the wearer is backed by sufficient means to be able to afford the idleness, or impaired efficiency, which the skirt implies. The like is true of the high heel, and in less degree of several other features of modern dress.

Herein is also to be sought the ground of the persistence (probably not the origin) of the one great mutilation practiced by civilised occidental womankind—the constricted waist, as well as of the analogous practice of the abortive foot among their Chinese sisters. This modern mutilation of woman is perhaps not to be classed strictly under the category of dress; but it is scarcely possible to draw the line so as to exclude it from the theory, and it is so closely coincident with that category in point of principle that an outline of the theory would be incomplete without reference to it.

. . . The fact that voluntarily accepted physical incapacity argues the possession of wealth practically establishes the futility of any attempted reform of woman's dress in the direction of convenience, comfort, or health. It is of the essence of dress that it should (appear to) hamper, incommode, and injure the wearer, for in so doing it proclaims the wearer's pecuniary ability to endure idleness and physical incapacity.

. . . [T]his requirement, that women must appear to be idle in order to be respectable, is an unfortunate circumstance for women who are compelled to provide their own livelihood. They have to supply not only the means of living, but also the means of advertising the fiction that they live without any gainful occupation; and they have to do all this while encumbered with garments specially designed to hamper their movements and decrease their industrial efficiency. . . .

. . .

W. E. B. Du Bois

For over thirty years, W. E. B. Du Bois (1868–1963) was the most articulate, original, and widely read spokesperson for the civil rights of black people. A social scientist, political militant, essayist, and poet, he wrote nineteen books and hundreds of articles, edited four periodicals, and was a founder of the NAACP (National Association for the Advancement of Colored People) and the Pan-African movement. In a lifetime of nearly a century, Du Bois moved steadily leftward, from the prudent assimilationism of Booker T. Washington to a version of socialism that stressed the economic advancement of people of color around the world. His life and writings form a bridge between the nineteenth century and the civil rights movement of the 1960s.

Du Bois was well prepared for his multifaceted career. Born into a rural New England community with no experience of segregation, he entered Fisk University in 1885 to study liberal arts and "suddenly came to a region where the world was split into white and black halves, and where the darker half was held back by race prejudice and legal bonds, as well as by deep ignorance and dark poverty." Faced by an all-white faculty yet immersed in the world of Jim Crow laws, Du Bois was kept constantly aware of worlds both black and white. In a famous passage in *The Souls of Black Folk*, he described the conflict: "One feels ever his two-ness—an American, a Negro, two souls, two thoughts, two unreconciled strivings; two warring ideals in one dark body, whose dogged strength alone keeps it from being torn asunder."

From Fisk, Du Bois proceeded to Harvard, where once again he lived two lives. He pursued a second baccalaureate degree with teachers, such as William James, George Santayana, and Josiah Royce, but after hours preferred to mingle in the company of long-established black families of Boston. His professors treated him seriously, with no condescension, and Du Bois began to nurture that keen sense of his own individuality and mission that became something of a legend. After graduating cum laude in 1890, Du Bois went on to receive his Ph.D. from Harvard in 1895, traveling for two years in Germany and submitting a thesis on the African slave trade. His degree was the first to be conferred by Harvard on an American black and only the fifth to be awarded to any black person by an American university.

By this time Du Bois had reached the conclusion that race was the defining feature of American society, that, as he put it, "the problem of the twentieth century was the problem of the color line," and therefore that the most significant contribution he could make toward achieving racial justice would be a series of scientific studies of the Negro. In 1899 he published *The Philadelphia Negro*, the first study of its kind and often praised as his best book. At Atlanta University, where he was professor of history and economics from 1897 to 1910, he established a program of studies of the American Negro and published works on the Negro church and common school and on the Negro artisan. Rigorous and carefully informed, these works nevertheless failed to satisfy him because they appeared to prove nothing to the white population of the United States.

Around this time, Du Bois became disturbed over the immense influence wielded by the doctrines of Booker T. Washington, whose aim it was to gain the sympathy and cooperation of whites, especially in the South. *The Souls of Black Folk* (1903) represents Du Bois's turn from scientific scholarship, which would never claim his undivided attention again, toward political exhortation and personal essays, as well as from Washington's meliorism toward the building of autonomous black peoples' movements. He organized the Niagara Movement (1905–1910) in opposition to Washington. From it emerged the NAACP, with which Du Bois was affiliated during much of the rest of his life. In his new position as director of research and editor of *The Crisis*, he pressed hard for recognition of Negro rights, urging the white liberals on the NAACP board to stand up against social, not only legal, discrimination. He was also a passionate champion of women's equality, as the editorial "Votes for Women" and essay from *Darkwater* make clear.

Du Bois came to question the premises of the NAACP, its legalism and almost exclusive focus on the courts. Race relations in the 1920s, marked by riots, lynchings, and the battle to widen voting privileges of blacks, seemed to demand a more radical approach. Du Bois called for an increase in the power and economic organization of blacks themselves and began to link their struggle with the anticolonial movements that arose overseas in the wake of World War I. In 1919 he organized the Pan-African Congress in Paris, cajoling funds from the NAACP, and during the 1920s battled with Marcus Garvey over leadership of the Pan-African movement.

By 1930 Du Bois began openly to criticize the NAACP. His study of *Black Reconstruction* (1933), one of the best works on the period, argued that Reconstruction failed not because of its own weakness but because of the economic pressure and relentless violence used by Southern whites. From its failure Du Bois drew a lesson for the present day. Legal remedies were insufficient when "the essential need was to guard and better the chances of Negroes, educated and ignorant, to earn a living, safeguard their income, and raise the level of their employment." When in 1934 the board opposed his use of *The Crisis* to advance these ends, Du Bois cut his ties with the organization, and at the age of sixty-six set off on his own.

After 1935 Du Bois's influence waned, yet for more than thirty years he was a leader in the world Pan-African movement, continued to study in new areas, and moved steadily toward socialism, finally becoming a member of the Communist Party of the United States. He founded and edited *Phylon: The Atlanta University Review of Race and Culture* (1940), returned to the NAACP as director of special research (1944–1948), organized conferences on world peace, and traveled extensively in the U.S.S.R. and China. In 1961 he accepted the invitation of President Nkrumah to come to Ghana as director of the *Encyclopedia Africana* project, planned by Du Bois in 1909 but never financed in the United States. He became a citizen of Ghana and died there in 1963.

Of all Du Bois's works, *The Souls of Black Folk* is the most widely read and most successful. Organized as fourteen brief essays and stories, it is many things at once: as one writer put it, the book is a moving, even lyrical meditation on the consciousness of color, a biting critique of Booker T. Washington, a scholarly examination of certain phases of black history, and an evaluation of some central strands of African American culture. In form as well as in subject, it expresses Du Bois's own restless and divided consciousness, as elite intellectual and oppressed minority, as liberal reformer and radical militant, as social scientist and poet. *The Souls of Black Folk*, Saunders Redding wrote, "may be seen as fixing that moment in history when the American Negro began to reject the idea of the world belonging to white people."*

---

*J. Saunders Redding, "Portrait of W. E. Burghardt Du Bois," *American Scholar*, 18, Winter, 1948–1949, p. 94.

THE SOULS OF BLACK FOLK: ESSAYS AND SKETCHES

1903

OF MR. BOOKER T. WASHINGTON AND OTHERS

From birth till death enslaved; in word, in deed, unmanned!
Hereditary bondsmen! Know ye not
Who would be free themselves must strike the blow!

—Byron

Easily the most striking thing in the history of the American Negro since 1876 is the ascendancy of Mr. Booker T. Washington. It began at the time when war memories and ideals were rapidly passing; a day of astonishing commercial development was dawning; a sense of doubt and hesitation overtook the freedmen's sons—then it was that his leading began. Mr. Washington came, with a single definite programme, at the psychological moment when the nation was a little ashamed of having bestowed so much sentiment on Negroes, and was concentrating its energies on Dollars. His programme of industrial education, conciliation of the South, and submission and silence as to civil and political rights, was not wholly original; the Free Negroes from 1830 up to war-time had striven to build industrial schools, and the American Missionary Association had from the first taught various trades; and Price and others had sought a way of honorable alliance with the best of the Southerners. But Mr. Washington first indissolubly linked these things; he put enthusiasm, unlimited energy, and perfect faith into this programme, and changed it from a by-path into a veritable Way of Life. And the tale of the methods by which he did this is a fascinating study of human life.

It startled the nation to hear a Negro advocating such a programme after many decades of bitter complaint; it startled and won the applause of the South, it interested and won the admiration of the North; and after a confused murmur of protest, it silenced if it did not convert the Negroes themselves.

To gain the sympathy and coöperation of the various elements comprising the white South was Mr. Washington's first task; and this, at the time Tuskegee was founded, seemed, for a black man, well-nigh impossible. And yet ten years later it was done in the words spoken at Atlanta: "In all things purely social we can be as separate as the five fingers, and yet one as the hand in all things essential to mutual progress." This "Atlanta Compromise" is by all odds the most notable thing in Mr. Washington's career. The South interpreted it in different ways: the radicals received it as a complete surrender of the demand for civil and political equality; the conservatives, as a generously conceived working basis for mutual understanding. So both approved it, and to-day its author is

From *The Souls of Black Folk: Essays and Sketches* by W. E. B. Du Bois (Chicago: A. C. McClurg, 1903).

certainly the most distinguished Southerner since Jefferson Davis, and the one with the largest personal following.

Next to this achievement comes Mr. Washington's work in gaining place and consideration in the North. Others less shrewd and tactful had formerly essayed to sit on these two stools and had fallen between them; but as Mr. Washington knew the heart of the South from birth and training, so by singular insight he intuitively grasped the spirit of the age which was dominating the North. And so thoroughly did he learn the speech and thought of triumphant commercialism, and the ideals of material prosperity, that the picture of a lone black boy poring over a French grammar amid the weeds and dirt of a neglected home soon seemed to him the acme of absurdities. One wonders what Socrates and St. Francis of Assisi would say to this.

And yet this very singleness of vision and thorough oneness with his age is a mark of the successful man. It is as though Nature must needs make men narrow in order to give them force. So Mr. Washington's cult has gained unquestioning followers, his work has wonderfully prospered, his friends are legion, and his enemies are confounded. To-day he stands as the one recognized spokesman of his ten million fellows, and one of the most notable figures in a nation of seventy millions. One hesitates, therefore, to criticise a life which, beginning with so little, has done so much. And yet the time is come when one may speak in all sincerity and utter courtesy of the mistakes and shortcomings of Mr. Washington's career, as well as of his triumphs, without being thought captious or envious, and without forgetting that it is easier to do ill than well in the world.

The criticism that has hitherto met Mr. Washington has not always been of this broad character. In the South especially has he had to walk warily to avoid the harshest judgments—and naturally so, for he is dealing with the one subject of deepest sensitiveness to that section. Twice—once when at the Chicago celebration of the Spanish-American War he alluded to the color-prejudice that is "eating away the vitals of the South," and once when he dined with President Roosevelt—has the resulting Southern criticism been violent enough to threaten seriously his popularity. In the North the feeling has several times forced itself into words, that Mr. Washington's counsels of submission overlooked certain elements of true manhood, and that his educational programme was unnecessarily narrow. Usually, however, such criticism has not found open expression, although, too, the spiritual sons of the Abolitionists have not been prepared to acknowledge that the schools founded before Tuskegee, by men of broad ideals and self-sacrificing spirit, were wholly failures or worthy of ridicule. While, then, criticism has not failed to follow Mr. Washington, yet the prevailing public opinion of the land has been but too willing to deliver the solution of a wearisome problem into his hands, and say, "If that is all you and your race ask, take it."

Among his own people, however, Mr. Washington has encountered the strongest and most lasting opposition, amounting at times to bitterness, and even to-day continuing strong and insistent even though largely silenced in outward expression by the public opinion of the nation. Some of this opposition is, of course, mere envy; the disappointment of displaced demagogues and the spite of narrow minds. But aside from this, there is among educated and thoughtful colored men in all parts of the land a feeling of deep regret, sorrow, and apprehension at the wide currency and ascendancy which some of Mr. Washington's theories have gained. These same men admire his sincerity of purpose, and are willing to forgive much to honest endeavor which is doing something worth the doing. They coöperate with Mr. Washington as far as they conscientiously can; and, indeed, it is no ordinary tribute to this man's tact and power that, steering as he must between so many diverse interests and opinions, he so largely retains the respect of all.

But the hushing of the criticism of honest opponents is a dangerous thing. It leads some of the best of the critics to unfortunate silence and paralysis of effort, and others to burst into speech so passionately and intemperately as to lose listeners. Honest and earnest criticism from those whose interests are most nearly touched—criticism of writers by readers, of government by those governed, of leaders by those led—this is the soul of democracy and the safeguard of modern society. If the best of the American Negroes receive by outer pressure a leader whom they had not recognized before, manifestly there is here a certain palpable gain. Yet there is also irreparable loss—a loss of that peculiarly valuable education which a group receives when by search and criticism it finds and commissions its own leaders. The way in which this is done is at once the most elementary and the nicest problem of social growth. History is but the record of such group-leadership; and yet how infinitely changeful is its type and character! And of all types and kinds, what can be more instructive than the leadership of a group within a group?—that curious double movement where real progress may be negative and actual advance be relative retrogression. All this is the social student's inspiration and despair.

Now in the past the American Negro has had instructive experience in the choosing of group leaders, founding thus a peculiar dynasty which in the light of present conditions is worth while studying. When sticks and stones and beasts form the sole environment of a people, their attitude is largely one of determined opposition to and conquest of natural forces. But when to earth and brute is added an environment of men and ideas, then the attitude of the imprisoned group may take three main forms—a feeling of revolt and revenge; an attempt to adjust all thought and action to the will of the greater group; or, finally, a determined effort at self-realization and self-development despite environing opinion. The influence of all of these attitudes at various times can be traced in the history of the American Negro, and in the evolution of his successive leaders.

Before 1750, while the fire of African freedom still burned in the veins of the slaves, there was in all leadership or attempted leadership but the one motive of revolt and revenge—typified in the terrible Maroons, the Danish blacks, and Cato of Stono, and veiling all the Americas in fear of insurrection. The liberalizing tendencies of the latter half of the eighteenth century brought, along with kindlier relations between black and white, thoughts of ultimate adjustment and assimilation. Such aspiration was especially voiced in the earnest songs of Phyllis, in the martyrdom of Attucks, the fighting of Salem and Poor, the intellectual accomplishments of Banneker and Derham, and the political demands of the Cuffes.

Stern financial and social stress after the war cooled much of the previous humanitarian ardor. The disappointment and impatience of the Negroes at the persistence of slavery and serfdom voiced itself in two movements. The slaves in the South, aroused undoubtedly by vague rumors of the Haytian revolt, made three fierce attempts at insurrection—in 1800 under Gabriel in Virginia, in 1822 under Vesey in Carolina, and in 1831 again in Virginia under the terrible Nat Turner. In the Free States, on the other hand, a new and curious attempt at self-development was made. In Philadelphia and New York color-prescription led to a withdrawal of Negro communicants from white churches and the formation of a peculiar socio-religious institution among the Negroes known as the African Church—an organization still living and controlling in its various branches over a million of men.

Walker's wild appeal against the trend of the times showed how the world was changing after the coming of the cotton-gin. By 1830 slavery seemed hopelessly fastened on the South, and the slaves thoroughly cowed into submission. The free Negroes of the North, inspired by the mulatto immigrants from the West Indies, began to change the basis of their demands, they recognized the slavery of slaves, but insisted that they themselves were freemen, and sought assimilation and amalgamation with the nation on the same terms with other men. Thus, Forten and Purvis of Philadelphia, Shad of Wilmington, Du Bois of New Haven, Barbadoes of Boston, and others, strove singly and together as men, they said, not as slaves; as "people of color," not as "Negroes." The trend of the times, however, refused them recognition save in individual and exceptional cases, considered them as one with all the despised blacks, and they soon found themselves striving to keep even the rights they formerly had of voting and working and moving as freemen. Schemers of migration and colonization arose among them; but these they refused to entertain, and they eventually turned to the Abolition movement as a final refuge.

Here, led by Remond, Nell, Wells-Brown, and Douglass, a new period of self-assertion and self-development dawned. To be sure, ultimate freedom and assimilation was the ideal before the leaders, but the assertion of the manhood rights of the Negro by himself was the main reliance, and John Brown's raid was the extreme of its logic. After the war and emancipation, the great form of Frederick Douglass, the greatest of American Negro leaders, still led the host. Self-assertion, especially in political lines, was the main programme, and behind Douglass came Elliot, Bruce, and Langston, and the Reconstruction politicians, and, less conspicuous but of greater social significance Alexander Crummell and Bishop Daniel Payne.

Then came the Revolution of 1876, the suppression of the Negro votes, the changing and shifting of ideals, and the seeking of new lights in the great night. Douglass, in his old age, still bravely stood for the ideals of his early manhood—ultimate assimilation *through* self-assertion, and on no other terms. For a time Price arose as a new leader, destined, it seemed, not to give up, but to re-state the old ideals in a form less repugnant to the white South. But he passes away in his prime. Then came the new leader. Nearly all the former ones had become leaders by the silent suffrage of their fellows, had sought to lead their own people alone, and were usually, save Douglass, little known outside their race. But Booker T. Washington arose as essentially the leader not of one race but of two—a compromiser between the South, the North, and the Negro. Naturally the Negroes resented, at first bitterly, signs of compromise which surrendered their civil and political rights, even though this was to be exchanged for larger chances of economic development. The rich and dominating North, however, was not only weary of the race problem, but was investing largely in Southern enterprises, and welcomed any method of peaceful coöperation. Thus, by national opinion, the Negroes began to recognize Mr. Washington's leadership; and the voice of criticism was hushed.

Mr. Washington represents in Negro thought the old attitude of adjustment and submission; but adjustment at such a peculiar time as to make his programme unique. This is an age of unusual economic development, and Mr. Washington's programme naturally takes an economic cast, becoming a gospel of Work and Money to such an extent as apparently almost completely to overshadow the higher aims of life. Moreover, this is an age when the more advanced races are coming in closer contact with the less developed races, and the race-feeling is therefore intensified; and Mr. Washington's programme practically accepts the alleged inferiority of the Negro races. Again, in our own land, the reaction from the sentiment of war time has given impetus to race-prejudice against Negroes, and Mr. Washington withdraws many of the high demands of Negroes as men and American citizens. In other periods of intensified prejudice all the Negro's tendency to self-assertion has been called forth; at this period a policy of submission is advocated. In the history of nearly all other races and peoples the doctrine preached at such crises has been that manly self-respect is worth more than lands and houses, and that a people who voluntarily surrender such respect, or cease striving for it, are not worth civilizing.

In answer to this, it has been claimed that the Negro can survive only through submission. Mr. Washington distinctly asks that black people give up, at least for the present, three things—first, political power, second, insistence on civil rights, third, higher education of Negro youth—and concentrate all their energies on industrial education, the accumulation of wealth, and the conciliation of the South. This policy has been courageously and insistently advocated for over fifteen years, and has been triumphant for perhaps ten years. As a result of this tender of the palm-branch, what has been the return? In these years there have occurred:

1. The disfranchisement of the Negro.
2. The legal creation of a distinct status of civil inferiority for the Negro.
3. The steady withdrawal of aid from institutions for the higher training of the Negro.

These movements are not, to be sure, direct results of Mr. Washington's teachings; but his propaganda has, without a shadow of doubt, helped their speedier accomplishment. The question then comes: Is it possible, and probable, that nine millions of men can make effective progress in economic lines if they are deprived of political rights, made a servile caste, and allowed only the most meagre chance for developing their exceptional men? If history and reason give any distinct answer to these questions, it is an emphatic *No*. And Mr. Washington thus faces the triple paradox of his career:

1. He is striving nobly to make Negro artisans business men and property-owners; but it is utterly impossible, under modern competitive methods, for workingmen and property-owners to defend their rights and exist without the right of suffrage.
2. He insists on thrift and self-respect, but at the same time counsels a silent submission to civic inferiority such as is bound to sap the man hood of any race in the long run.
3. He advocates common-school and industrial training, and depreciates institutions of higher learning; but neither the Negro common-schools, nor Tuskegee itself, could remain open a day were it not for teachers trained in Negro colleges, or trained by their graduates.

This triple paradox in Mr. Washington's position is the object of criticism by two classes of colored Americans. One class is spiritually descended from Toussaint the Savior, through Gabriel, Vesey, and Turner, and they represent the attitude of revolt and revenge; they hate the white South blindly and distrust the white race generally, and so far as they agree on definite action, think that the Negro's only hope lies in emigration beyond the borders of the United States. And yet, by the irony of fate, nothing has more effectually made this programme seem hopeless than the recent course of the United States toward weaker and darker peoples in the West Indies, Hawaii, and the Philippines—for where in the world may we go and be safe from lying and brute force?

The other class of Negroes who cannot agree with Mr. Washington has hitherto said little aloud. They deprecate the sight of scattered counsels, of internal disagreement; and especially they dislike making their just criticism of a useful and earnest man an excuse for a general discharge of venom from small-minded opponents. Nevertheless, the questions involved are so fundamental and serious that it is difficult to see how men like the Grimkes, Kelly Miller, J. W. E. Bowen, and other representatives of this group, can much longer be silent. Such men feel in conscience bound to ask of this nation three things:

1. The right to vote.
2. Civic equality.
3. The education of youth according to ability.

They acknowledge Mr. Washington's invaluable service in counselling patience and courtesy in such demands; they do not ask that ignorant black men vote when ignorant whites are debarred, or that any reasonable restrictions in the suffrage should not be applied; they know that the low social level of the mass of the race is responsible for much discrimination against it, but they also know, and the nation knows, that relentless color-prejudice is more often a cause than a result of the Negro's degradation; they seek the abatement of this relic of barbarism, and not its systematic encouragement and pampering by all agencies of social power from the Associated Press to the Church of Christ. They advocate, with Mr. Washington, a broad system of Negro common schools supplemented by thorough industrial training; but they are surprised that a man of Mr. Washington's insight cannot see that no such educational system ever has rested or can rest on any other basis than that of the well-equipped college and university, and they insist that there is a demand for a few such institutions throughout the South to train the best of the Negro youth as teachers, professional men, and leaders.

This group of men honor Mr. Washington for his attitude of conciliation toward the white South; they accept the "Atlanta Compromise" in its broadest interpretation, they recognize, with him, many signs of promise, many men of high purpose and fair judgment, in this section; they know that no easy task has been laid upon a region already tottering under heavy burdens. But, nevertheless, they insist that the way to truth and right lies in straightforward honesty, not in indiscriminate flattery; in praising those of the South who do well and criticising uncompromisingly those who do ill; in taking advantage of the opportunities at hand and urging their fellows to do the same, but at the same time in remembering that only a firm adherence to their higher ideals and aspirations will ever keep those ideals within the realm of possibility. They do not expect that the free right to vote, to enjoy civic rights, and to be educated, will come in a moment; they do not expect to see the bias and prejudices of years disappear at the blast of a trumpet; but they are absolutely certain that the way for a people to gain their reasonable rights is not by voluntarily throwing them away and insisting that they do not want them; that the way for a people to gain respect is not by continually belittling and ridiculing themselves; that, on the contrary, Negroes must insist continually, in season and out of season, that voting is necessary to modern manhood, that color discrimination is barbarism, and that black boys need education as well as white boys.

In failing thus to state plainly and unequivocally the legitimate demands of their people, even at the cost of opposing an honored leader, the thinking classes of American Negroes would shirk a heavy responsibility—a responsibility to themselves, a responsibility to the struggling masses, a responsibility to the darker races of men whose future depends so largely on this American experiment, but especially a responsibility to this nation—this common Fatherland. It is wrong to encourage a man or a people in evil-doing; it is wrong to aid and abet a national crime simply because it is unpopular not to do so. The growing spirit of kindliness and reconciliation between the North and South after the frightful difference of a generation ago ought to be a source of deep congratulation to all, and especially to those whose mistreatment caused the war; but if that reconciliation is to be marked by the industrial slavery and civic death of those same black men, with permanent legislation into a position of inferiority, then those black men, if they are really men, are called upon by every consideration of patriotism and loyalty to oppose such a course by all civilized methods, even though such opposition involves disagreement with Mr. Booker T. Washington. We have no right to sit silently by while the inevitable seeds are sown for a harvest of disaster to our children, black and white.

First, it is the duty of black men to judge the South discriminatingly. The present generation of Southerners are not responsible for the past, and they should not be blindly hated or blamed for it. Furthermore, to no class is the indiscriminate endorsement of the recent course of the South toward Negroes more nauseating than to the best thought of the South. The South is not "solid"; it is a land in the ferment of social change, wherein forces of all kinds are fighting for supremacy; and to praise the ill the South is to-day perpetrating is just as wrong as to condemn the good. Discriminating and broad-minded criticism is what the South needs—needs it for the sake of her own white sons and daughters, and for the insurance of robust, healthy mental and moral development.

To-day even the attitude of the Southern whites toward the blacks is not, as so many assume, in all cases the same; the ignorant Southerner hates the Negro, the workingmen fear his competition, the money-makers wish to use him as a laborer, some of the educated see a menace in his upward development, while others—usually the sons of the masters—wish to help him to rise. National opinion has enabled this last class to maintain the Negro common schools, and to protect the Negro partially in property, life, and limb. Through the pressure of the money-makers, the Negro is in danger of being reduced to semi-slavery, especially in the country districts; workingmen, and those of the educated who fear the Negro, have united to disfranchise him, and some have urged his deportation; while the passions of the ignorant are easily aroused to lynch and abuse any black man. To praise this intricate whirl of thought and prejudice is nonsense; to inveigh indiscriminately against "the South" is unjust; but to use the same breath in praising Governor Aycock, exposing Senator Morgan, arguing with Mr. Thomas Nelson Page, and denouncing Senator Ben Tillman, is not only sane, but the imperative duty of thinking black men.

It would be unjust to Mr. Washington not to acknowledge that in several instances he has opposed movements in the South which were unjust to the Negro; he sent memorials to the Louisiana and Alabama constitutional conventions, he has spoken against lynching, and in other ways has openly or silently set his influence against sinister schemes and unfortunate happenings. Notwithstanding this, it is equally true to assert that on the whole the distinct impression left by Mr. Washington's propaganda is, first, that the South is justified in its present attitude toward the Negro because of the Negro's degradation; secondly, that the prime cause of the Negro's failure to rise more quickly is his wrong education in the past; and, thirdly, that his future rise depends primarily on his own efforts. Each of these propositions is a dangerous half-truth. The supplementary truths must never be lost sight of: first, slavery and race-prejudice are potent if not sufficient causes of the Negro's position; second, industrial and common-school training were necessarily slow in planting because they had to await the black teachers trained by higher institutions—it being extremely doubtful if any essentially different development was possible, and certainly a Tuskegee was unthinkable before 1880; and, third, while it is a great truth to say that the Negro must strive and strive mightily to help himself, it is equally true that unless his striving be not simply seconded, but rather aroused and encouraged, by the initiative of the richer and wiser environing group, he cannot hope for great success.

In his failure to realize and impress this last point, Mr. Washington is especially to be criticised. His doctrine has tended to make the whites, North and South, shift the burden of the Negro problem to the Negro's shoulders and stand aside as critical and rather pessimistic spectators; when in fact the burden belongs to the nation, and the hands of none of us are clean if we bend not our energies to righting these great wrongs.

The South ought to be led, by candid and honest criticism, to assert her better self and do her full duty to the race she has cruelly wronged and is still wronging. The North—her co-partner in guilt—cannot salve her conscience by plastering it with gold. We cannot settle this problem by diplomacy and suaveness, by "policy" alone. If worse comes to worst, can the moral fibre of this country survive the slow throttling and murder of nine millions of men?

The black men of America have a duty to perform, a duty stern and delicate—a forward movement to oppose a part of the work of their greatest leader. So far as Mr. Washington preaches Thrift, Patience, and Industrial Training for the masses, we must hold up his hands and strive with him, rejoicing in his honors and glorying in the strength of this Joshua called of God and of man to lead the headless host. But so far as Mr. Washington apologizes for injustice, North or South, does not rightly value the privilege and duty of voting, belittles the emasculating effects of caste distinctions, and opposes the higher training and ambition of our brighter minds—so far as he, the South, or the Nation, does this—we must unceasingly and firmly oppose them. By every civilized and peaceful method we must strive for the rights which the world accords to men, clinging unwaveringly to those great words which the sons of the Fathers would fain forget: "We hold these truths to be self-evident: That all men are created equal; that they are endowed by their Creator with certain unalienable rights; that among these are life, liberty, and the pursuit of happiness."

. . .

OF OUR SPIRITUAL STRIVINGS

. . . Between me and the other world there is ever an unasked question: unasked by some through feelings of delicacy; by others through the difficulty of rightly framing it. All, nevertheless, flutter round it. They approach me in a half-hesitant sort of way, eye me curiously or compassionately, and then, instead of saying directly, How does it feel to be a problem? they say, I know an excellent colored man in my town; or, I fought at Mechanicsville; or, Do not these Southern outrages make your blood boil? At these I smile, or am interested, or reduce the boiling to a simmer, as the occasion may require. To the real question, How does it feel to be a problem? I answer seldom a word.

And yet, being a problem is a strange experience—peculiar even for one who has never been anything else, save perhaps in babyhood and in Europe. . . .

Why did God make me an outcast and a stranger in mine own house? The shades of the prison-house closed round about us all: walls strait and stubborn to the whitest, but relentlessly narrow, tall, and unscalable to sons of night who must plod darkly on in resignation, or beat unavailing palms against the stone, or steadily, half hopelessly, watch the streak of blue above.

After the Egyptian and Indian, the Greek and Roman, the Teuton and Mongolian, the Negro is a sort of seventh son, born with a veil, and gifted with second-sight in this American world—a world which yields him no true self-consciousness, but only lets him see himself through the revelation of the other world. It is a peculiar sensation, this double-consciousness, this sense of always looking at one's self through the eyes of others, of measuring one's soul by the tape of a world that looks on in amused contempt and pity. One ever feels his twoness—an American, a Negro; two souls, two thoughts, two unreconciled strivings; two warring ideals in one dark body, whose dogged strength alone keeps it from being torn asunder.

The history of the American Negro is the history of this strife—this longing to attain self-conscious manhood, to merge his double self into a better and truer self. In this merging he wishes neither of the older selves to be lost. He would not Africanize America, for America has too much to teach the world and Africa. He would not bleach his Negro soul in a flood of white Americanism, for he knows that Negro blood has a message for the world. He simply wishes to make it possible for a man to be both a Negro and an American, without being cursed and spit upon by his fellows, without having the doors of Opportunity closed roughly in his face.

This, then, is the end of his striving; to be a co-worker in the kingdom of culture, to escape both death and isolation, to husband and use his best powers and his latent genius. These powers of body and mind have in the past been strangely wasted, dispersed, or forgotten. The shadow of a mighty Negro past flits through the tale of Ethiopia the Shadowy and of Egypt the Sphinx. Throughout history, the powers of single black men flash here and there like falling stars, and die sometimes before the world has rightly gauged their brightness. Here in America, in the few days since Emancipation, the black man's turning hither and thither in hesitant and doubtful striving has often made his very strength to lose effectiveness, to seem like absence of power, like weakness. And yet it is not weakness—it is the contradiction of double aims. The double-aimed struggle of the black artisan—on the one hand to escape white contempt for a nation of mere hewers of wood and drawers of water, and on the other hand to plough and nail and dig for a poverty-stricken horde—could only result in making him a poor craftsman, for he had but half a heart in either cause. By the poverty and, ignorance of his people, the Negro minister or doctor was tempted toward quackery and demagogy; and by the criticism of the other world, toward ideals that made him ashamed of his lowly tasks. The would-be black *savant* was confronted by the paradox that the knowledge his people needed was a twice-told tale to his white neighbors, while the knowledge which would teach the white world was Greek to his own flesh and blood. The innate love of harmony and beauty that set the ruder souls of his people a-dancing and a-singing raised but confusion and doubt in the soul of the black artist; for the beauty revealed to him was the soul-beauty of a race which his larger audience despised, and he could not articulate the message of another people. This waste of double aims, this seeking to satisfy two unreconciled ideals, has wrought sad havoc with the courage and faith and deeds of ten thousand thousand people—has sent them often wooing false gods and invoking false means of salvation, and at times has even seemed about to make them ashamed of themselves. . . .

The Nation has not yet found peace from its sins; the freedman has not yet found in freedom his promised land. Whatever of good may have come in these years of change, the shadow of a deep disappointment rests upon the Negro people—a disappointment all the more bitter because the unattained ideal was unbounded save by the simple ignorance of a lowly people.

The first decade was merely a prolongation of the vain search for freedom, the boon that seemed ever barely to elude their grasp—like a tantalizing will-o'-the-wisp, maddening and misleading the headless host. The holocaust of war, the terrors of the Ku Klux Klan, the lies of carpetbaggers, the disorganization of industry, and the contradictory advice of friends and foes, left the bewildered serf with no new watchword beyond the old cry for freedom. As the time flew, however, he began to grasp a new idea. The ideal of liberty demanded for its attainment powerful means, and these the Fifteenth Amendment gave him. The ballot, which before he had looked upon as a visible sign of freedom, he now regarded as the chief means of gaining and perfecting the liberty with which war had partially endowed him. And why not? Had not votes made war and emancipated millions? Had not votes enfranchised the freedmen? Was anything impossible to a power that had done all this? A million black men started with renewed zeal to vote themselves into the kingdom. So the decade flew away, the revolution of 1876 came, and left the half-free serf weary, wondering but still inspired. Slowly but steadily, in the following years, a new vision began gradually to replace the dream of political power—a powerful movement, the rise of another ideal to guide the unguided, another pillar of fire by night after a clouded day. It was the ideal of "book-learning"; the curiosity, born of compulsory ignorance, to know and test the power of the cabalistic letters of the white man, the longing to know. Here at last seemed to have been discovered the mountain path to Canaan; longer than the highway of Emancipation and law, steep and rugged, but straight, leading to heights high enough to overlook life.

Up the new path the advance guard toiled, slowly, heavily, doggedly; only those who have watched and guided the faltering feet, the misty minds, the dull understandings, of the dark pupils of these schools know how faithfully, how piteously, this people strove to learn. It was weary work. The cold statistician wrote down the inches of progress here and there, noted also where here and there a foot had slipped or some one had fallen. To the tired climbers, the horizon was ever dark, the mists were often cold, the Canaan was always dim and far away. If, however, the vistas disclosed as yet no goal, no resting-place, little but flattery and criticism, the journey at least gave leisure for reflection and self-examination; it changed the child of Emancipation to the youth with dawning self-consciousness, self-realization, self-respect. In those sombre forests of his striving his own soul rose before him, and he saw himself—darkly as through a veil; and yet he saw in himself some faint revelation of his power, of his mission. He began to have a dim feeling that, to attain his place in the world, he must be himself, and not another. For the first time he sought to analyze the burden he bore upon his back, that dead-weight of social degradation partially masked behind a half-named Negro problem. He felt his poverty; without a cent, without a home, without land, tools, or savings, he had entered into competition with rich, landed, skilled neighbors. To be a poor man is hard, but to be a poor race in a land of dollars is the very bottom of hardships. He felt the weight of his ignorance—not simply of letters, but of life, of business, of the humanities; the accumulated sloth and shirking and awkwardness of decades and centuries shackled his hands and feet. Nor was his burden all poverty and ignorance. The red stain of bastardy, which two centuries of systematic legal defilement of Negro women had stamped upon his race, meant not only the loss of ancient African chastity, but also the hereditary weight of a mass of corruption from white adulterers, threatening almost the obliteration of the Negro home.

A people thus handicapped ought not to be asked to race with the world, but rather allowed to give all its time and thought to its own social problems. But alas! while sociologists gleefully count his bastards and his prostitutes, the very soul of the toiling, sweating black man is darkened by the shadow of a vast despair. Men call the shadow prejudice, and learnedly explain it as the natural defence of culture against barbarism, learning against ignorance, purity against crime, the "higher" against the "lower" races. To which the Negro cries Amen! and swears that to so much of this strange prejudice as is founded on just homage to civilization, culture, righteousness, and progress, he humbly bows and meekly does obeisance. But before that nameless prejudice that leaps beyond all this he stands helpless, dismayed, and well-nigh speechless; before that personal disrespect and mockery, the ridicule and systematic humiliation, the distortion of fact and wanton license of fancy, the cynical ignoring of the better and the boisterous welcoming of the worse, the all-pervading desire to inculcate disdain for everything black, from Toussaint to the devil—before this there rises a sickening despair that would disarm and discourage any nation save that black host to whom "discouragement" is an unwritten word.

But the facing of so vast a prejudice could not but bring the inevitable self-questioning, self-disparagement, and lowering of ideals which ever accompany repression and breed in an atmosphere of contempt and hate. Whispering and portents came borne upon the four winds: Lo! we are diseased and dying, cried the dark hosts; we cannot write, our voting is vain; what need of education, since we must always cook and serve? And the Nation echoed and enforced this self-criticism, saying: Be content to be servants, and nothing more; what need of higher culture for half-men? Away with the black man's ballot, by force or fraud—and behold the suicide of a race! Nevertheless, out of the evil came something of good—the more careful adjustment of education to real life, the clearer perception of the Negroes' social responsibilities, and the sobering realization of the meaning of progress.

So dawned the time of *Sturm und Drang*: storm and stress to-day rocks our little boat on the mad waters of the world-sea; there is within and without the sound of conflict, the burning of body and rending of soul; inspiration strives with doubt, and faith with vain questionings. The bright ideals of the past—physical freedom, political power, the training of brains and the training of hands—all these in turn have waxed and waned, until even the last grows dim and overcast. Are they all wrong—all false? No, not that, but each alone was over-simple and incomplete—the dreams of a credulous race-childhood, or the fond imaginings of the other world which does not know and does not want to know our power. To be really true, all these ideals must be melted and welded into one. The training of the schools we need to-day more than ever—the training of deft hands, quick eyes and ears, and above all the broader, deeper, higher culture of gifted minds and pure hearts. The power of the ballot we need in sheer self-defence—else what shall save us from a second slavery? Freedom, too, the long-sought, we still seek—the freedom of life and limb, the freedom to work and think, the freedom to love and aspire. Work, culture, liberty—all these we need, not singly but together, not successively but together, each growing and aiding each, and all striving toward that vaster ideal that swims before the Negro people, the ideal of human brotherhood, gained through the unifying ideal of Race; the ideal of fostering and developing the traits and talents of the Negro, not in opposition to or contempt for other races, but rather in large conformity to the greater ideals of the American Republic, in order that some day on American soil two world-races may give each to each those characteristics both so sadly lack. We the darker ones come even now not altogether empty-handed: there are to-day no truer exponents of the pure human spirit of the Declaration of Independence than the American Negroes; there is no truer American music but the wild sweet melodies of the Negro slave; the American fairy tales and folk-lore are Indian and African; and, all in all, we black men seem the sole oasis of simple faith and reverence in a dusty desert of dollars and smartness. Will America be poorer if she replace her brutal dyspeptic blundering with light-hearted but determined Negro humility? or her coarse and cruel wit with loving jovial good-humor? or her vulgar music with the soul of the Sorrow Songs?

Merely a concrete test of the underlying principles of the great republic is the Negro Problem, and the spiritual striving of the freedmen's sons is the travail of souls whose burden is almost beyond the measure of their strength, but who bear it in the name of an historic race, in the name of this the land of their fathers' fathers, and in the name of human opportunity.

And now what I have briefly sketched in large outline let me on coming pages tell again in many ways, with loving emphasis and deeper detail, that men may listen to the striving in the souls of black folk.

DARKWATER: VOICES FROM WITHIN THE VEIL

1920

THE DAMNATION OF WOMEN

. . . As I remember through memories of others, backward among my own family, it is the mother I ever recall—the little, far-off mother of my grandmother who sobbed her life away in song, longing for her lost palm-trees and scented waters; the tall and bronzen grandmother, with beaked nose and shrewish eyes, who loved and scolded her black and laughing husband as he smoked lazily in his high oak chair; above all, my own mother, with all her soft brownness—the brown velvet of her skin, the sorrowful black-brown of her eyes, and the tiny brown-capped waves of her midnight hair as it lay new parted on her forehead. All the way back in these dim distances it is mothers and mothers of mothers who seem to count, while fathers are shadowy memories.

Upon this African mother-idea, the westward slave trade and American slavery struck like doom. In the cruel exigencies of the traffic in men and in the sudden, unprepared emancipation the great pendulum of social equilibrium swung from a time, in 1800—when America had but eight or less black women to every ten black men—all too swiftly to a day, in 1870—when there were nearly eleven women to ten men in our Negro population. This was but the outward numerical fact of social dislocation; within lay polygamy, polyandry, concubinage, and moral degradation. They fought against all this desperately, did these black slaves in the West Indies, especially among the half-free artisans; they set up their ancient household gods, and when Toussaint and Christophe founded their kingdom in Haiti, it was based on old African tribal ties and beneath it was the mother-idea.

The crushing weight of slavery fell on black women. Under it there was no legal marriage, no legal family, no legal control over children. To be sure, custom and religion replaced here and there what the law denied, yet one has but to read advertisements like the following to see the hell beneath the system:

> One hundred dollars reward will be given for my two fellows, Abram and Frank. Abram has a wife at Colonel Stewart's, in liberty County, and a mother at Thunderbolt, and a sister in Savannah.
>
> William Roberts

> Fifty dollars reward—Ran away from the subscriber a Negro girl named Maria. She is of a copper color, between thirteen and fourteen years of age—bareheaded and barefooted. She is small for her age—very sprightly and very likely. She stated she was going to see her mother at Maysville.
>
> Sanford Thompson

> Fifty dollars reward—Ran away from the subscriber his Negro man Pauladore, commonly called Paul. I understand General R. Y. Hayne has purchased his wife and children from H. L. Pinckney, Esq., and has them now on his plantation at Goose Creek, where, no doubt, the fellow is frequently lurking.
>
> T. Davis

The Presbyterian synod of Kentucky said to the churches under its care in 1835: "Brothers and sisters, parents and children, husbands and wives, are torn asunder and permitted to see each other no more. These acts are daily occurring in the midst of

From *Darkwater: Voices from within the Veil* by W. E. B. Du Bois (New York: Schocken, 1920).

us. The shrieks and agony often witnessed on such occasions proclaim, with a trumpet tongue, the iniquity of our system. There is not a neighborhood where these heartrending scenes are not displayed. There is not a village or road that does not behold the sad procession of manacled outcasts whose mournful countenances tell that they are exiled by force from all that their hearts hold dear."

A sister of a president of the United States declared: "We Southern ladies are complimented with the names of wives, but we are only the mistresses of seraglios."

Out of this, what sort of black women could be born into the world of to-day? There are those who hasten to answer this query in scathing terms and who say lightly and repeatedly that out of black slavery came nothing decent in womanhood; that adultery and uncleanness were their heritage and are their continued portion.

Fortunately so exaggerated a charge is humanly impossible of truth. The half-million women of Negro descent who lived at the beginning of the 19th century had become the mothers of two and one-fourth million daughters at the time of the Civil War and five million granddaughters in 1910. Can all these women be vile and the hunted race continue to grow in wealth and character? Impossible. Yet to save from the past the shreds and vestiges of self-respect has been a terrible task. I most sincerely doubt if any other race of women could have brought its fineness up through so devilish a fire.

Alexander Crummell once said of his sister in the blood: "In her girlhood all the delicate tenderness of her sex has been rudely outraged. In the field, in the rude cabin, in the press-room, in the factory she was thrown into the companionship of coarse and ignorant men. No chance was given her for delicate reserve or tender modesty. From her childhood she was the doomed victim of the grossest passion. All the virtues of her sex were utterly ignored. If the instinct of chastity asserted itself, then she had to fight like a tiger for the ownership and possession of her own person and ofttimes had to suffer pain and lacerations for her virtuous self-assertion. When she reached maturity, all the tender instincts of her womanhood were ruthlessly violated. At the age of marriage—always prematurely anticipated under slavery—she was mated as the stock of the plantation were mated, not to be the companion of a loved and chosen husband, but to be the breeder of human cattle for the field or the auction block."

Down in such mire has the black motherhood of this race struggled—starving its own wailing offspring to nurse to the world their swaggering masters; welding for its children chains which affronted even the moral sense of an unmoral world. Many a man and woman in the South have lived in wedlock as holy as Adam and Eve and brought forth their brown and golden children, but because the darker woman was helpless, her chivalrous and whiter mate could cast her off at his pleasure and publicly sneer at the body he had privately blasphemed.

I shall forgive the white South much in its final judgment day: I shall forgive its slavery, for slavery is a world-old habit; I shall forgive its fighting for a well-lost cause, and for remembering that struggle with tender tears; I shall forgive its so-called "pride of race," the passion of its hot blood, and even its dear, old, laughable strutting and posing; but one thing I shall never forgive, neither in this world nor the world to come: its wanton and continued and persistent insulting of the black womanhood which it sought and seeks to prostitute to its lust. I cannot forget that it is such Southern gentlemen into whose hands smug Northern hypocrites of today are seeking to place our women's eternal destiny—men who insist upon withholding from my mother and wife and daughter those signs and appellations of courtesy and respect, which elsewhere he withholds only from bawds and courtesans.

The result of this history of insult and degradation has been both fearful and glorious. It has birthed the haunting prostitute, the brawler, and the beast of burden; but it has also given the world an efficient womanhood, whose strength lies in its freedom and whose chastity was won in the teeth of temptation and not in prison and swaddling clothes.

. . .

As I look about me today in this veiled world of mine, despite the noisier and more spectacular advance of my brothers, I instinctively feel and know that it is the five million women of my race who really count. Black women (and women whose grandmothers were black) are today furnishing our teachers; they are the main pillars of those social settlements which we call churches; and they have with small doubt raised three-fourths of our church property. If we have today, as seems likely, over a billion dollars of accumulated goods, who shall say how much of it has been rung from the hearts of servant girls and washer-women and women toilers in the fields? As makers of two million homes these women are today seeking in marvelous ways to show forth our strength and beauty and our conception of the truth . . .

What is today the message of these black women to America and to the world? The uplift of women is, next to the problem of the color line and the peace movement, our greatest modern cause. When, now, two of these movements—woman and color—combine in one, the combination has deep meaning.

In other years women's way was clear: to be beautiful, to be petted, to bear children. Such has been their theoretic destiny and if perchance they have been ugly, hurt, and barren, that has been forgotten with studied silence. In partial compensation for this narrowed destiny the white world has lavished its politeness on its womankind—its chivalry and bows, its uncoverings and courtesies—all the accumulated homage disused for courts and kings and craving exercise. The revolt of white women against this preordained destiny has in these latter days reached splendid proportions, but it is the revolt of an aristocracy of brains and ability—the middle class and rank and file still plod on in the appointed path, paid by the homage, the almost mocking homage, of men.

From black women of America, however (and from some others, too, but chiefly from black women and their daughters' daughters), this gauze has been withheld and without semblance of such apology they have been frankly trodden under the feet of men. They are and have been objected to, apparently for reasons peculiarly exasperating to reasoning human beings. When in this world a man comes forward with a thought, a deed, a vision, we ask not, how does he look—but what is his message? It is of but passing interest whether or not the messenger is beautiful or ugly—the *message* is the thing. This, which is axiomatic among men, has been in past ages but partially true if the messenger was a woman. The world still wants to ask that a woman primarily be pretty and if she is not, the mob pouts and asks querulously, "What else are women for?" Beauty "is its own excuse for being," but there are other excuses, as most men know, and when the white world objects to black women because it does not consider them beautiful, the black world of right asks two questions: "What is beauty?" and, "Suppose you think them ugly, what then? If ugliness and unconventionality and eccentricity of face and deed do not hinder men from doing the world's work and reaping the world's reward, why should it hinder women?"

Other things being equal, all of us, black and white, would prefer to be beautiful in face and form and suitably clothed; but most of us are not so, and one of the mightiest revolts of the century is against the devilish decree that no woman is a woman who is not by present standards a beautiful woman. This decree the black women of America have in large measure escaped from the first. Not being expected to be merely ornamental, they have girded themselves for work, instead of adorning their bodies only for play. Their sturdier minds have concluded that if a woman be clean, healthy, and educated, she is as pleasing as God wills and far more useful than most of her sisters. If in addition to this she is pink and white and straight-haired, and some of her fellow-men prefer this, well and good; but if she is black or brown and crowned in curled mists (and this to us is the most beautiful thing on earth), this is surely the flimsiest excuse for spiritual incarceration or banishment.

The very attempt to do this in the case of Negro Americans has strangely over-reached itself. By so much as the defective eyesight of the white world rejects black women as beauties, by so much the more it needs them as human beings—an enviable alternative, as many a white woman knows. Consequently, for black women alone, as a group, "handsome is that handsome does" and they are asked to be no more beautiful than God made them, but they are asked to be efficient, to be strong, fertile, muscled, and able to work. If they marry, they must as independent workers be able to help support their children, for their men are paid on a scale which makes sole support of the family often impossible. . . .

What does this mean? It forecasts a mighty dilemma which the whole world of civilization, despite its will, must one time frankly face: the unhusbanded mother or the childless wife. God send us a world with woman's freedom and married motherhood inextricably wed, but until He sends it. I see more of future promise in the betrayed girl-mothers of the black belt than in the childless wives of the white North, and I have more respect for the colored servant who yields to her frank longing for motherhood than for her white sister who offers up children for clothes. Out of a sex freedom that today makes us shudder will come in time a day when we will no longer pay men for work they do not do, for the sake of their harem; we will pay women what they earn and insist on their working and earning it; we will allow those persons to vote who know enough to vote, whether they be black or female, white or male; and we will ward race suicide, not by further burdening the over-burdened, but by honoring motherhood, even when the sneaking father shirks his duty.

"Wait till the lady passes," said a Nashville white boy.

"She's no lady; she's a nigger," answered another.

So some few women are born free, and some amid insult and scarlet letters achieve freedom; but our women in black had freedom thrust contemptuously upon them. With that freedom they are buying an untrammeled independence and dear as is the price pay for it, it will in the end be worth every taunt and groan. Today the dreams of the mothers are coming true. We have still our poverty and degradation, our lewdness and our cruel toil; but we have, too, a vast group of women of Negro blood who for strength of character, cleanness of soul, and unselfish devotion of purpose, is today easily the peer of any group of women in the civilized world. And more than that, in the great rank and file of our five million women we, have the up-working of new revolutionary ideals, which must in time have vast influence on the thought and action of the land.

For this, their promise, and for their hard past, I honor the women of my race. Their beauty—their dark and mysterious beauty of midnight eyes, crumpled hair, and soft, full-featured faces—is perhaps more to me than to you, because I was born to its warm and subtle spell; but their worth is yours as well as mine. No other women on earth could have emerged from the hell of force and temptation which once engulfed and still surrounds black women in America with half the modesty and womanliness that they retain. I have always felt like bowing myself before them in all abasement, searching to bring some tribute to these long-suffering victims, these burdened sisters of mine, whom the world, the wise, white world, loves to affront and ridicule and wantonly to insult. I have known the women of many lands and nations—I have known and seen and lived beside them, but none have I known more sweetly feminine, more unswervingly loyal, more desperately earnest, and more instinctively pure in body and in soul than the daughters of my black mothers. This, then—a little thing—to their memory and inspiration.

"VOTES FOR WOMEN"

1917

Let us answer frankly, there is not the slightest reason for supposing that white American women under ordinary circumstances are going to be any more intelligent, liberal or humane toward the black, the poor and unfortunate than white men are. On the contrary, considering what the subjection of a race, a class or a sex must mean, there will undoubtedly manifest itself among women voters at first more prejudice and petty meanness toward Negroes than we have now. It is the awful penalty of injustice and oppression to breed in the oppressed the desire to oppress others. The southern white women who form one of the most repressed and enslaved groups of modern civilized women will undoubtedly, at first, help willingly and zealously to disfranchize Negroes, cripple their schools and publicly insult them.

Nevertheless, votes for women must and ought to come and the Negroes should help bring this to pass for these reasons:

1. Any extension of democracy involves a discussion of the fundamentals of democracy.
2. If it is acknowledged to be unjust to disfranchise a sex it cannot be denied that it is absurd to disfranchise a color.
3. If the North enfranchises women, the proportion of unselfish intelligent voters among Negroes will be increased, and the proportion of Negro voters whom white politicians have trained to venality will be decreased.
4. If when the North enfranchises women the South refuses, or enfranchises only the whites, then the discrepancy between North and South in the votes cast will be even greater than now; at present the southern white voter has from five to seven times the power of the northern voter. How long would the nation endure an increase or even a doubling of this power? It would not take long before southern representatives in Congress would be cut down or colored women enfranchised.
5. Granting that first tendencies would make the woman voter as unfair in race rights as the man, there would be in the long run a better chance to appeal to a group that knows the disadvantage and injustice of disfranchisement by experience, than to one arrogant and careless with power. And in all cases the broader the basis of democracy the surer is the universal appeal for justice to win ultimate hearing and sympathy.

Therefore: Votes for Women.

"Votes for Women" by W. E. B. Du Bois (*Crisis* 15, no. 1, November 1917; reprint, *Against the Tide*, eds. Michael S. Kimmel and Thomas E. Mosmiller, Boston: Beacon Press, 1992).

CHARLOTTE PERKINS GILMAN

Charlotte Perkins Gilman (1860–1935) is best known for "The Yellow Wallpaper," a fictionalized account of her nervous breakdown, which culminated in 1888. At that time, her husband and her doctor developed a treatment plan that forced her to abandon all intellectual labor. Eventually she defied their regimen and worked her way out of her depression, publishing a series of satiric poems, lecturing on behalf of the progressivist Nationalist Movement, and divorcing Charles Stetson in 1894. After the divorce she moved to California and with her daughter rebuilt a life.

In 1893 Gilman collected about seventy-five poems into a volume entitled *In This Our World*, which failed commercially but came to be regarded as a classic statement on the women's movement. Its author was, as the novelist William Dean Howells put it, "the only optimist reformer" he ever met. Gilman began lecturing widely on feminism, and as a public intellectual bridged the worlds of public affairs and academic scholarship.

Women and Economics (1898), originally entitled *Economic Relation of the Sexes as a Factor in Social Development*, is Gilman's most original book. Building on some of Lester Ward's ideas, she explores the origin of women's subordination and its function in evolution. Woman makes a living by marriage, not by the work she does, and so man becomes her economic environment. As a consequence, her female qualities dominate her human ones because it is the female traits through which she earns her living. Women, Gilman puts it, are oversexed: They are raised to market their feebleness, their docility, and so on, and these qualities are called feminine.

Gilman was one of the first to see the need for innovations in child rearing and home maintenance that would ease the burdens of working women. She envisaged housework as being like any other kind of work—as a public, social activity no different from shoemaking or shipbuilding. In her fiction she imagines a range of institutions that overcome the isolation of women and children, such as communal kitchens, day care centers, and city plans that foster camaraderie rather than withdrawal.

In the first decade of the century, Gilman developed her social theory in the pages of the *American Journal of Sociology* and in three influential books: *Concerning Children* (1900), *The Home* (1904), and *Human Work* (1904). In the latter, she explored the elements of work—the work of both sexes—that give it purpose and dignity, as well as the alienating effects of the modern labor process.

In 1909 Gilman began the arduous seven-year editorship of her monthly periodical, *The Forerunner*. Every word of it, including advertising copy, she wrote herself: a total that in her own estimation amounted to four books a year. The periodical contained articles on social and economic issues as they pertained to women, poetry and stories, and two full-length novels, *What Diantha Did* (1910) and *The Crux* (1911).

After *The Forerunner* folded, Gilman's influence declined, but Gilman remained characteristically productive and personally content. In 1923 she published *His Religion and Hers*, an idiosyncratic work that contrasts the male conception of life (as postponement and preparation for the afterlife) with the female perspective (as paradise in the present time and place). Echoing earlier works, she distinguishes women's practicality from the mundane narrowing of horizons imposed by their current state and argues for the value of this practicality in public and political life.

Gilman's last work was her autobiography, *The Living of Charlotte Perkins Gilman*, published in 1935—an excellent source for understanding her life, temperament, and multifaceted career.

Suffering from cancer and surviving her second husband's unexpected death in 1934, she lived for a time near her daughter in Pasadena, California, then committed suicide by chloroform. In her autobiography she concludes, "The one predominant duty is to find one's work and do it, and I have striven mightily at that. The religion, the philosophy, set up so early, have seen me through."

WOMEN AND ECONOMICS

1898

I

. . .

The economic status of the human race in any nation, at any time, is governed mainly by the activities of the male: the female obtains her share in the racial advance only through him.

Studied individually, the facts are even more plainly visible, more open and familiar. From the day laborer to the millionnaire, the wife's worn dress or flashing jewels, her low roof or her lordly one, her weary feet or her rich equipage,—these speak of the economic ability of the husband. The comfort, the luxury, the necessities of life itself, which the woman receives, are obtained by the husband, and given her by him. And, when the woman, left alone with no man to "support" her, tries to meet her own economic necessities, the difficulties which confront her prove conclusively what the general economic status of the woman is. None can deny these patent facts,—that the economic status of women generally depends upon that of men generally, and that the economic status of women individually depends upon that of men individually, those men to whom they are related. But we are instantly confronted by the commonly received opinion that, although it must be admitted that men make and distribute the wealth of the world, yet women earn their share of it as wives. This assumes either that the husband is in the position of employer and the wife as employee, or that marriage is a "partnership," and the wife an equal factor with the husband in producing wealth.

Economic independence is a relative condition at best. In the broadest sense, all living things are economically dependent upon others,—the animals upon the vegetables, and man upon both. In a narrower sense, all social life is economically interdependent, man producing collectively what he could by no possibility produce separately. But, in the closest interpretation, individual economic independence among human beings means that the individual pays for what he gets, works for what he gets, gives to the other an equivalent for what the other gives him. I depend on the shoemaker for shoes, and the tailor for coats; but, if I give the shoemaker and the tailor enough of my own labor as a house-builder to pay for the shoes and coats they give me, I retain my personal independence. I have not taken of their product, and given nothing of mine. As long as what I get is obtained by what I give, I am economically independent.

From *Women and Economics* by Charlotte Perkins Gilman (Boston: Small, Maynard, 1898).

Women consume economic goods. What economic product do they give in exchange for what they consume? The claim that marriage is a partnership, in which the two persons married produce wealth which neither of them, separately, could produce, will not bear examination. A man happy and comfortable can produce more than one unhappy and uncomfortable, but this is as true of a father or son as of a husband. To take from a man any of the conditions which make him happy and strong is to cripple his industry, generally speaking. But those relatives who make him happy are not therefore his business partners, and entitled to share his income.

Grateful return for happiness conferred is not the method of exchange in a partnership. The comfort a man takes with his wife is not in the nature of a business partnership, nor are her frugality and industry. A housekeeper, in her place, might be as frugal, as industrious, but would not therefore be a partner. Man and wife are partners truly in their mutual obligation to their children,—their common love, duty, and service.. But a manufacturer who marries, or a doctor, or a lawyer, does not take a partner in his business, when he takes a partner in parenthood, unless his wife is also a manufacturer, a doctor, or a lawyer. In his business, she cannot even advise wisely without training and experience. To love her husband, the composer, does not enable her to compose; and the loss of a man's wife, though it may break his heart, does not cripple his business, unless his mind is affected by grief. She is in no sense a business partner, unless she contributes capital or experience or labor, as a man would in like relation. Most men would hesitate very seriously before entering a business partnership with any woman, wife or not.

If the wife is not, then, truly a business partner, in what way does she earn from her husband the food, clothing, and shelter she receives at his hands? By house service, it will be instantly replied. This is the general misty idea upon the subject,—that women earn all they get, and more, by house service. Here we come to a very practical and definite economic ground. Although not producers of wealth, women serve in the final processes of preparation and distribution. Their labor in the household has a genuine economic value.

For a certain percentage of persons to serve other persons, in order that the ones so served may produce more, is a contribution not to be overlooked. The labor of women in the house, certainly, enables men to produce more wealth than they otherwise could; and in this way women are economic factors in society. But so are horses. The labor of horses enables men to produce more wealth than they otherwise could. The horse is an economic factor in society. But the horse is not economically independent, nor is the woman. If a man plus a valet can perform more useful service than he could minus a valet, then the valet is performing useful service. But, if the valet is the property of the man, is obliged to perform this service, and is not paid for it, he is not economically independent.

The labor which the wife performs in the household is given as part of her functional duty, not as employment. The wife of the poor man, who works hard in a small house, doing all the work for the family, or the wife of the rich man, who wisely and gracefully manages a large house and administers its functions, each is entitled to fair pay for services rendered.

To take this ground and hold it honestly, wives, as earners through domestic service, are entitled to the wages of cooks, housemaids, nursemaids, seamstresses, or housekeepers, and to no more. This would of course reduce the spending money of the wives of the rich, and put it out of the power of the poor man to "support" a wife at all, unless, indeed, the poor man faced the situation fully, paid his wife her wages as house servant, and then she and he combined their funds in the support of their children. He would be keeping a servant: she would be helping keep the family. But nowhere on earth would there be "a rich woman" by these means. Even the highest class of private housekeeper, useful as her services are, does not accumulate a fortune. She does not buy diamonds and sables and keep a carriage. Things like these are not earned by house service.

But the salient fact in this discussion is that, whatever the economic value of the domestic industry of women is, they do not get it. The women who do the most work get the least money, and the women who have the most money do the least work. Their labor is neither given nor taken as a factor in economic exchange. It is held to be their duty as women to do this work; and their economic status bears no relation to their domestic labors, unless an inverse one. Moreover, if they were thus fairly paid,—given what they earned, and no more,—all women working in this way would be reduced to the economic status of the house servant. Few women—or men either—care to face this condition. The ground that women earn their living by domestic labor is instantly forsaken, and we are told that they obtain their livelihood as mothers. This is a peculiar position. We speak of it commonly enough, and often with deep feeling, but without due analysis.

In treating of an economic exchange, asking what return in goods or labor women make for the goods and labor given them,—either to the race collectively or to their husbands individually,—what payment women make for their clothes and shoes and furniture and food and shelter, we are told that the duties and services of the mother entitle her to support.

If this is so, if motherhood is an exchangeable commodity given by women in payment for clothes and food, then we must of course find some relation between the quantity or quality of the motherhood and the quantity and quality of the pay. This being true, then the women who are not mothers have no economic status at all; and the economic status of those who are must be shown to be relative to their motherhood. This is obviously absurd. The childless wife has as much money as the mother of many,—more; for the children of the latter consume what would otherwise be hers; and the inefficient mother is no less provided for than the efficient one. Visibly, and upon the face of it, women are not maintained in economic prosperity proportioned to their motherhood. Motherhood bears no relation to their economic status. Among primitive races, it is true,—in the patriarchal period, for instance,—there was some truth in this position. Women being of no value whatever save as bearers of children, their favor and indulgence did bear direct relation to maternity; and they had reason to exult on more grounds than one when they could boast a son. To-day, however, the maintenance of the woman is not conditioned upon this. A man is not allowed to discard his wife because she is barren. The claim of motherhood as a factor in economic exchange is false to-day. But suppose it were true. Are we willing to hold this ground, even in theory? Are we willing to consider motherhood as a business, a form of commercial exchange? Are the cares and duties of the mother, her travail and her love, commodities to be exchanged for bread?

It is revolting so to consider them; and, if we dare face our own thoughts, and force them to their logical conclusion, we shall see that nothing could be more repugnant to human feeling, or more socially and individually injurious, than to make motherhood a trade. Driven off these alleged grounds of women's economic independence; shown that women, as a class, neither produce nor distribute wealth; that women, as individuals, labor mainly as house servants, are not paid as such, and would not be satisfied with such an economic status if they were so paid; that wives are not business partners or co-producers of wealth with their husbands, unless they actually practise the same profession; that they are not salaried as mothers, and that it would be unspeakably degrading if they were,—what remains to those who deny that women are supported by men? This (and a most amusing position it is),—that the function of maternity unfits a woman for economic production, and, therefore, it is right that she should be supported by her husband.

The ground is taken that the human female is not economically independent, that she is fed by the male of her species. In denial of this, it is first alleged that she is economically independent,—that she does support herself by her own industry in the house. It being shown that there is no relation between the economic status of woman and the labor she performs in the home, it is then alleged that not as house servant, but as mother, does woman earn her living. It being shown that the economic status of woman bears no relation to her motherhood, either in quantity or quality, it is then alleged that motherhood renders a woman unfit for economic production, and that, therefore, it is right that she be supported by her husband. Before going farther, let us seize upon this admission,—that she *is* supported by her husband.

Without going into either the ethics or the necessities of the case, we have reached so much common ground: the female of genus homo is supported by the male. Whereas, in other species of animals, male and female alike graze and browse, hunt and kill, climb, swim, dig, run, and fly for their livings, in our species the female does not seek her own living in the specific activities of our race, but is fed by the male.

Now as to the alleged necessity. Because of her maternal duties, the human female is said to be unable to get her own living. As the maternal duties of other females do not unfit them for getting their own living and also the livings of their young, it would seem that the human maternal duties require the segregation of the entire energies of the mother to the service of the child during her entire adult life, or so large a proportion of them that not enough remains to devote to the individual interests of the mother.

Such a condition, did it exist, would of course excuse and justify the pitiful dependence of the human female, and her support by the male. As the queen bee, modified entirely to maternity, is supported, not by the male, to be sure, but by her co-workers, the "old maids," the barren working bees, who labor so patiently and lovingly in their branch of the maternal duties of the hive, so would the human female, modified entirely to maternity, become unfit for any other exertion, and a helpless dependent.

Is this the condition of human motherhood? Does the human mother, by her motherhood, thereby lose control of brain and body, lose power and skill and desire for any other work? Do we see before us the human race, with all its females segregated entirely to the uses of motherhood, consecrated, set apart, specially developed, spending every power of their nature on the service of their children?

We do not. We see the human mother worked far harder than a mare, laboring her life long in the service, not of her children only, but of men; husbands, brothers, fathers, whatever male relatives she has; for mother and sister also; for the church a little, if she is allowed; for society, if she is able; for charity and education and reform,—working in many ways that are not the ways of motherhood.

It is not motherhood that keeps the housewife on her feet from dawn till dark; it is house service, not child service. Women work longer and harder than most men, and not solely in maternal duties. The savage mother carries the burdens, and does all menial service for the tribe. The peasant mother toils in the fields, and the workingman's wife in the home. Many mothers, even now, are wage-earners for the family, as well as bearers and rearers of it. And the women who are not so occupied, the women who belong to rich men,—here perhaps is the exhaustive devotion to maternity which is supposed to justify an admitted economic dependence. But we do not find it even among these. Women of ease and wealth provide for their children better care than the poor woman can; but they do not spend more time upon it themselves, nor more care and effort. They have other occupation.

In spite of her supposed segregation to maternal duties, the human female, the world over, works at extra-maternal duties for hours enough to provide her with an independent living, and then is denied independence on the ground that motherhood prevents her working!

If this ground were tenable, we should find a world full of women who never lifted a finger save in the service of their children, and of men who did *all* the work besides, and waited on the women whom motherhood prevented from waiting on themselves. The ground is not tenable. A human female, healthy, sound, has twenty-five years of life before she is a mother, and should have twenty-five years more after the period of such maternal service as is expected of her has been given. The duties of grandmotherhood are surely not alleged as preventing economic independence.

The working power of the mother has always been a prominent factor in human life. She is the worker par excellence, but her work is not such as to affect her economic status. Her living, all that she gets,—food, clothing, ornaments, amusements, luxuries,—these bear no relation to her power to produce wealth, to her services in the house, or to her motherhood. These things bear relation only to the man she marries, the man she depends on,—to how much he has and how much he is willing to give her. The women whose splendid extravagance dazzles the world, whose economic goods are the greatest, are often neither houseworkers nor mothers, but simply the women who hold most power over the men who have the most money. The female of genus homo is economically dependent on the male. He is her food supply.

. . .

XI

. . .

. . . Each mother slowly acquires some knowledge of her business by practising it upon the lives and health of her family and by observing its effect on the survivors; and each daughter begins again as ignorant as her mother was before her. This "rule of thumb" is not transmissible. It is not a genuine education such as all important work demands, but a slow animal process of soaking up experience,—hopelessly ineffectual in protecting the health of society. As the ultimate selecting agent in feeding humanity, the private housewife fails, and this not by reason of any lack of effort on her part, but by the essential defect of her position as individual purchaser. Only organization can oppose such evils as the wholesale adulteration of food; and woman, the house-servant, belongs to the lowest grade of unorganized labor.

Leaving the selection of food, and examining its preparation, one would naturally suppose that the segregation of an entire sex to the fulfilment of this function would insure most remarkable results. It has, but they are not so favorable as might be expected. The art and science of cooking involve a large and thorough knowledge of nutritive value and of the laws of physiology and hygiene. As a science, it verges on preventive medicine. As an art, it is capable of noble expression within its natural bounds. As it stands among us to-day, it is so far from being a science and akin to preventive medicine, that it is the lowest of amateur handicrafts and a prolific source of disease; and, as an art, it has developed under the peculiar stimulus of its position as a sex-function into a voluptuous profusion as false as it is evil. Our innocent proverb, "The way to a man's heart is through his stomach," is a painfully plain comment on the way in which we have come to deprave our bodies and degrade our souls at the table.

On the side of knowledge it is permanently impossible that half the world, acting as amateur cooks for the other half, can attain any high degree of scientific accuracy or technical skill. The development of any human labor requires specialization, and specialization is forbidden to our cook-by-nature system. What progress we have made in the science of cooking has been made through the study and experience of professional men cooks and chemists, not through the Sisyphean labors of our endless generations of isolated women, each beginning again where her mother began before her.

. . .

There was a time when kings and lords retained their private poets to praise and entertain them; but the poet is not truly great until he sings for the world. So the art of cooking can never be lifted to its true place as a human need and a social function by private service. Such an arrangement of our lives and of our houses as will allow cooking to become a profession is the only way in which to free this great art from its present limitations. It should be a reputable, well-paid profession, wherein those women or those men who were adapted to this form of labor could become cooks, as they would become composers or carpenters. Natural distinctions would be developed between the mere craftsman and the artist; and we should have large, new avenues of lucrative and honorable industry, and a new basis for human health and happiness.

This does not involve what is known as "co-operation." Co-operation, in the usual sense, is the union of families for the better performance of their supposed functions. The process fails because the principle is wrong. Cooking and cleaning are not family functions. We do not have a family mouth, a family stomach, a family face to be washed. Individuals require to be fed and cleaned from birth to death, quite irrespective of their family relations. The orphan, the bachelor, the childless widower, have as much need of these nutritive and excretive processes as any patriarchal parent. Eating is an individual function. Cooking is a social function. Neither is in the faintest degree a family function. That we have found it convenient in early stages of civilization to do our cooking at home proves no more than the allied fact that we have also found it convenient in such stages to do our weaving and spinning at home, our soap and candle making, our butchering and pickling, our baking and washing.

As society developes, its functions specialize; and the reason why this great race-function of cooking has been so retarded in its natural growth is that the economic dependence of women has kept them back from their share in human progress. When women stand free as economic agents, they will lift and free their arrested functions, to the much better fulfilment of their duties as wives and mothers and to the vast improvement in health and happiness of the human race.

Co-operation is not what is required for this, but trained professional service and such arrangement of our methods of living as shall allow us to benefit by such service. When numbers of people patronize the same tailor or baker or confectioner, they do not co-operate. Neither would they co-operate in patronizing the same cook. The change must come from the side of the cook, not from the side of the family. It must come through natural functional development in society, and it is so coming. Woman, recognizing that her duty as feeder and cleaner is a social duty, not a sexual one, must face the requirements of the situation, and prepare herself to meet them. A hundred years ago this could not have been done. Now it is being done, because the time is ripe for it.

If there should be built and opened in any of our large cities to-day a commodious and well-served apartment house for professional women with families, it would be filled at once. The apartments would be without kitchens; but there would be a kitchen belonging to the house from which meals could be served to the families in their rooms or in a common diningroom, as preferred. It would be a home where the cleaning was done by efficient workers, not hired separately by the families, but engaged by the manager of the establishment; and a roof-garden, day nursery, and kindergarten, under well-trained professional nurses and teachers, would insure proper care of the children. The demand for such provision is increasing daily, and must soon be met, not by a boarding-house or a lodging-house, a hotel, a restaurant, or any makeshift patching together of these; but by a permanent provision for the needs of women and children, of family privacy with collective advantage. This must be offered on a business basis to prove a substantial business success; and it will so prove, for it is a growing social need.

. . .

XIV

. . .

What the human race requires is permanent provision for the needs of individuals, disconnected from the sex-relation. Our assumption that only married people and their immediate relatives have any right to live in comfort and health is erroneous. Every human being needs a home,—bachelor, husband, or widower, girl, wife, or widow, young or old. They need it from the cradle to the grave, and without regard to sex-connections. We should so build and arrange for the shelter and comfort of humanity as not to interfere with marriage, and yet not to make that comfort dependent upon marriage. With the industries of home life managed professionally, with rooms and suites of rooms and houses obtainable by any person or persons desiring them, we could live singly without losing home comfort and general companionship, we could meet bereavement without being robbed of the common conveniences of living as well as of the heart's love, and we could marry in ease and freedom without involving any change in the economic base of either party concerned.

Married people will always prefer a home together, and can have it; but groups of women or groups of men can also have a home together if they like, or contiguous rooms. And individuals even could have a house to themselves, without having, also, the business of a home upon their shoulders.

Take the kitchens out of the houses, and you leave rooms which are open to any form of arrangement and extension; and the occupancy of them does not mean "housekeeping." In such living, personal character and taste would flower as never before; the home of each individual would be at last a true personal expression; and the union of individuals in marriage would not compel the jumbling together of all the external machinery of their lives,—a process in which much of the delicacy and freshness of love, to say nothing of the power of mutual rest and refreshment, is constantly lost. The sense of lifelong freedom and self-respect and of the peace and permanence of one's own home will do much to purify and uplift the personal relations of life, and more to strengthen and extend the social relations. The individual will learn to feel himself an integral part of the social structure, in close, direct, permanent connection with the needs and uses of society.

This is especially needed for women, who are generally considered, and who consider themselves, mere fractions of families, and incapable of any wholesome life of their own. The knowledge that peace and comfort may be theirs for life, even if they do not marry,—and may be still theirs for life, even if they do,—will develope a serenity and strength in women most beneficial to them and to the world. It is a glaring proof of the insufficient and irritating character of our existing form of marriage that women must be forced to it by the need of food and clothes, and men by the need of cooks and housekeepers. We are absurdly afraid that, if men or women can meet these needs of life by other means, they will cheerfully renounce the marriage relation. And yet we sing adoringly of the power of love!

In reality, we may hope that the most valuable effect of this change in the basis of living will be the cleansing of love and marriage from this base admixture of pecuniary interest and creature comfort, and that men and women, eternally drawn together by the deepest force in nature, will be able at last to meet on a plane of pure and perfect love. We shame our own ideals, our deepest instincts, our highest knowledge, by this gross assumption that the noblest race on earth will not mate, or, at least, not mate monogamously, unless bought and bribed through the common animal necessities of food and shelter, and chained by law and custom.

The depth and purity and permanence of the marriage relation rest on the necessity for the prolonged care of children by both parents,—a law of racial development which we can never escape. When parents are less occupied in getting food and cooking it, in getting furniture and dusting it, they may find time to give new thought and new effort to the care of their children. The necessities of the child are far deeper than for bread and bed: those are his mere racial needs, held in common with all his kind. What he needs far more and receives far less is the companionship, the association, the personal touch, of his father and mother. When the common labors of life are removed from the home, we shall have the time, and perhaps the inclination, to make the personal acquaintance of our children. They will seem to us not so much creatures to be waited on as people to be understood. As the civil and military protection of society has long since superseded the tooth-and-claw defence of the fierce parent, without in the least endangering the truth and intensity of the family relation, so the economic provision of society will in time supersede the bringing home of prey by the parent, without evil effects to the love or prosperity of the family. These primitive needs and primitive methods of meeting them are unquestionably at the base of the family relation; but we have long passed them by, and the ties between parent and child are not weakened, but strengthened, by the change.

. . .

The present economic basis of family life holds our friendly and familiar intercourse in narrow grooves. Such visiting and mingling as is possible to us is between families rather than between individuals; and the growing specialization of individuals renders it increasingly unlikely that all the members of a given family shall please a given visitor or he please them. This, on our present basis, either checks the intercourse or painfully strains the family relation. The change of economic relation in families from a sex-basis to a social basis will make possible wide individual intercourse without this accompanying strain on the family ties.

. . .

JOHN DEWEY

John Dewey is one of the most significant philosophers in modern American history. During his distinguished career, his enormous influence extended throughout both academic circles and the world of progressive politics. His educational ideas, which many consider to be the foundation for the progressive education movement, have had a lasting effect on educational systems around the world, including those of the United States, China, Japan, and the former Soviet Union.

Dewey was born in Burlington, Vermont on October 20, 1859. His father was a Civil War veteran and the owner of a local grocery store, who was known less for his moneymaking zeal than for his wit and endearing personality. Dewey's mother was an ardent evangelical Congregationalist, known for her tireless work with Burlington's poor. In 1875, John and his older brother, Davis, enrolled at the University of Vermont. During his first two years at the university, Dewey took a rather lackadaisical approach to his studies, but by the end of his undergraduate career, he had done well enough to graduate Phi Beta Kappa.

Upon graduation, Dewey, with the help of a cousin who told him about the opening, obtained a high school teaching position in Oil City, Pennsylvania, where he joined a three-member faculty. After two years in Pennsylvania Dewey returned to Vermont, where he continued to teach high school and took a year's tutorial with one of his former philosophy professors at the University of Vermont, H. A. P. Torrey. Shortly thereafter, Dewey submitted two manuscripts to William Torrey Harris, who was the editor of the *Journal of Speculative Philosophy*. He asked Harris to evaluate the manuscripts and to inform him as to whether his work showed any promise. Harris not only told Dewey to keep up with his philosophical endeavors, but agreed to publish both articles. On the basis of Harris's encouragement and Dewey's ongoing frustration with the discipline in his high school classes, Dewey decided to apply to the graduate program in philosophy at Johns Hopkins University.

Dewey was accepted to the program, but he was not offered any financial assistance. Undeterred, he borrowed five hundred dollars from an aunt and enrolled at Johns Hopkins in the fall of 1882. By 1884, Dewey had completed his Ph.D., and, after several months of unemployment, he took a position at the University of Michigan, where his adviser from Johns Hopkins, George S. Morris, had also taken a position. Dewey was to remain in Ann Arbor for the next ten years, with the exception of a brief stint in Minneapolis at the University of Minnesota. During those ten years, Dewey cemented a reputation for himself as an up-and-coming star in American philosophy—a reputation that he would live up to and even eclipse during the remainder of his academic career, which he spent first at the University of Chicago and later at Columbia University.

Serving as the foundation for Dewey's prodigious writings was his philosophical conceptualization of human action and knowledge. Arguing against an idealist philosophy that accorded thought an elevated metaphysical importance in human behavior, Dewey insisted that thought is not an innate attribute preprogrammed into all humans. Instead, he posited that thought is part and parcel of our experiences of and interactions with the world. When faced with a puzzling situation in which no readily apparent course of action is to be taken, Dewey believed that thought arises out of functional necessity, as a means of resolving the contradictions of that experience. Thus, knowledge is as much something that one does as something that one has; it is accumulated in the process of engaging with one's world and in applying inquiry and problem solving to overcome the difficulties that one may encounter. Regardless of the subject matter to which inquiry is directed, what is required of knowledgeable individuals, in Dewey's eyes, is the application of methodical thought and the self-correction of hypotheses through empirical testing. While empirically testing hypotheses is often presumed to be wholly the province of scientists, Dewey believed that it is a part of all human inquiry, so that, for example, experimenting how best to interact with a troublesome neighbor is done in much the same way as scientists conduct experiments in their laboratories. Dewey's vision of inquiry even extended to a subject matter long thought to be beyond the scope of rational application of thought—morality. For Dewey, morals are not abstract concepts that one is said to "believe in" or "possess"; they emerge through the course of our everyday lives as we evaluate our experiences, determine them to be either good or bad, and then conduct a line of action that is likely to ensure the presence of the good and the absence of the bad.

What follows from all this is that the ideal societal configurations, according to Dewey, are ones that continually place individuals in positions in which they are challenged to grow through the use of inquiry, because such challenges grant individuals the greatest degree of freedom possible. Consequently, the ideal forms of government are ones that consciously embrace the interests of all members of society and facilitate interaction between individuals with different cultural beliefs, which ensures that all individuals will encounter a diversity of viewpoints from which to learn. Although it was Dewey's view that participatory democracies were best suited for carrying out these functions, his support of democracies should not be interpreted as simply a belief in a given set of governmental institutions or election laws. His support for democracies was premised on the notion that democracy is not only or most closely a form of government; for Dewey, democracy is also an end, something to be striven for, a way of life, "a form of moral and spiritual association" in which individuals actively exchange ideas and air grievances as a means of learning from one another and arriving at a more inclusive understanding of what goods should be pursued. Since democracy, as a collective enterprise, extends beyond the institutions of government, if it is to persist, new generations must acquire the basic dispositions that are needed for democratic engagement and inquiry. It was Dewey's belief that the most effective way for this process to happen is for the educational institutions of a society to inculcate children with a desire for learning and growth that will continue later in life and lead them to seek out and participate in democratic forms of association. Thus, for Dewey, education is much more than simply imparting basic knowledge upon an individual, as many traditional theories of education would have it. For him, it is the process through which the basic dispositions of individuals toward their fellow citizens and toward life as a whole are created. As he put it, "Democracy has to be born anew every generation, and education is its midwife."

While Dewey's intellectual influence continues in philosophical and sociological circles today, this is hardly the only legacy he left behind. During much of his career, Dewey was just as likely to tackle the pressing political problems of his day as he was important philosophical questions. For example, his writings debated such issues as what role should a government play in responding to economic depression, the threat that communism posed to the world, whether or not the United States should enter the World Wars I and II, and the relative merits of everything from the Treaty of Versailles to displaying art in post offices. Dewey also traveled extensively, including trips to China, Mexico, Russia, South Africa, and Turkey, to give lectures and to carry out studies of educational systems. He was a frequent contributor to progressive news sources, such as the *New Republic* and the *Nation*. He was involved in numerous political causes, including the fight for women's suffrage and the unionization of schoolteachers. He participated in the Commission of Inquiry into the Charges Against Leon Trotsky at the Moscow Trial, which exposed the political machinations behind the Moscow trials of the mid-1930s. Dewey remained active to the end of his ninety-two years, continuing to write and to clarify ideas. He even remarried at the age of eighty-seven (his first wife died when he was sixty-eight), and shortly thereafter he and his new wife adopted two war orphans.

Perhaps there is no better testament to Dewey's contribution to political and social thought than that offered by one of his most vehement critics, Morris Cohen, who suggested that "If there could be such an office as that of national philosopher, no one else [besides Dewey] could be properly mentioned for it." Indeed, there are few who could measure up to the contributions made by a man whose prodigious writings span thirty-seven volumes and whose thinking has so profoundly affected our attitudes toward democracy and education.

DEMOCRACY AND EDUCATION

1916

When it is said that education is development everything depends upon *how* development is conceived. Our net conclusion is that life is development, and that developing, growing, is life. Translated into its educational equivalents, that means (*i*) that the educational process has no end beyond itself; it is its own end; and that (*ii*) the educational process is one of continual reorganizing, reconstructing, transforming.

1. Development when it is interpreted in *comparative* terms, that is, with respect to the special traits of child and adult life, means the direction of power into special channels: the formation of habits involving executive skill, definiteness of interest, and specific objects of observation and thought. But the comparative view is not final. The child has specific powers; to ignore that fact is to stunt or distort the organs upon which his growth depends. The adult uses his powers to transform his environment, thereby occasioning new stimuli which redirect his powers and keep them developing. Ignoring this fact means arrested development, a passive accommodation. Normal child and normal adult alike, in other words, are engaged in growing. The difference between them is not the difference between growth and no growth, but between the modes of growth appropriate to different conditions. With respect to the development of powers devoted to coping with specific scientific and economic problems we may say the child should be growing in manhood. With respect to sympathetic curiosity, unbiased responsiveness, and openness of mind, we may say that the adult should be growing in childlikeness. One statement is as true as the other.

Three ideas which have been criticized, namely, the merely privative nature of immaturity, static adjustment to a fixed environment, and rigidity of habit, are all connected with a false idea of growth or development,—that it is a movement toward a fixed goal. Growth is regarded as *having* an end, instead of *being* an end. The educational counterparts of the three fallacious ideas are first, failure to take account of the instinctive or native powers of the young; secondly, failure to develop initiative in coping with

From *Democracy and Education* by John Dewey (New York: Macmillan Company, 1916).

novel situations; thirdly, an undue emphasis upon drill and other devices which secure automatic skill at the expense of personal perception. In all cases, the adult environment is accepted as a standard for the child. He is to be brought up *to* it.

Natural instincts are either disregarded or treated as nuisances—as obnoxious traits to be suppressed, or at all events to be brought into conformity with external standards. Since conformity is the aim, what is distinctively individual in a young person is brushed aside, or regarded as a source of mischief or anarchy. Conformity is made equivalent to uniformity. Consequently, there are induced lack of interest in the novel, aversion to progress, and dread of the uncertain and the unknown. Since the end of growth is outside of and beyond the process of growing, external agents have to be resorted to to induce movement toward it. Whenever a method of education is stigmatized as mechanical, we may be sure that external pressure is brought to bear to reach an external end.

2. Since in reality there is nothing to which growth is relative save more growth, there is nothing to which education is subordinate save more education. It is a commonplace to say that education should not cease when one leaves school. The point of this commonplace is that the purpose of school education is to insure the continuance of education by organizing the powers that insure growth. The inclination to learn from life itself and to make the conditions of life such that all will learn in the process of living is the finest product of schooling.

When we abandon the attempt to define immaturity by means of fixed comparison with adult accomplishments, we are compelled to give up thinking of it as denoting lack of desired traits. Abandoning this notion, we are also forced to surrender our habit of thinking of instruction as a method of supplying this lack by pouring knowledge into a mental and moral hole which awaits filling. Since life means growth, a living creature lives as truly and positively at one stage as at another, with the same intrinsic fullness and the same absolute claims. Hence education means the enterprise of supplying the conditions which insure growth, or adequacy of life, irrespective of age. We first look with impatience upon immaturity, regarding it as something to be got over as rapidly as possible. Then the adult formed by such educative methods looks back with impatient regret upon childhood and youth as a scene of lost opportunities and wasted powers. This ironical situation will endure till it is recognized that living has its own intrinsic quality and that the business of education is with that quality.

Realization that life is growth protects us from that so-called idealizing of childhood which in effect is nothing but lazy indulgence. Life is not to be identified with every superficial act and interest. Even though it is not always easy to tell whether what appears to be mere surface fooling is a sign of some nascent as yet untrained power, we must remember that manifestations are not to be accepted as ends in themselves. They are signs of possible growth. They are to be turned into means of development, of carrying power forward, not indulged or cultivated for their own sake. Excessive attention to surface phenomena (even in the way of rebuke as well as of encouragement) may lead to their fixation and thus to arrested development. What impulses are moving toward not what they have been is the important thing for parent and teacher.

. . .

Summary

Power to grow depends upon need for others and plasticity. Both of these conditions are at their height in childhood and youth. Plasticity or the power to learn from experience means the formation of habits. Habits give control over the environment, power to utilize it for human purposes. Habits take the form both of habituation, or a general and persistent balance of organic activities with the surroundings, and of active capacities to readjust activity to meet new conditions. The former furnishes the background of growth; the latter constitute growing. Active habits involve thought, invention, and initiative in applying capacities to new aims. They are opposed to routine which marks an arrest of growth. Since growth is the characteristic of life, education is all one with growing; it has no end beyond itself. The criterion of the value of school education is the extent in which it creates a desire for continued growth and supplies means for making the desire effective in fact.

. . .

3. Education as Reconstruction

In its contrast with the ideas both of unfolding of latent powers from within, and of the formation from without, whether by physical nature or by the cultural products of the past, the ideal of growth results in the conception that education is a constant reorganizing or reconstructing of experience. It has all the time an immediate end, and so far as activity is educative, it reaches that end—the direct transformation of the quality of experience. Infancy, youth, adult life,—all stand on the same educative level in the sense that what is really *learned* at any and every stage of experience constitutes the value of that experience and in the sense that it is the chief business of life at every point to make living thus contribute to an enrichment of its own perceptible meaning.

We thus reach a technical definition of education: It is that reconstruction or reorganization of experience which adds to the meaning of experience, and which increases ability to direct the course of subsequent experience. (1) The increment of meaning corresponds to the increased perception of the connections and continuities of the activities in which we are engaged. The activity begins in an impulsive form; that is, it is blind. It does not know what it is about; that is to say, what are its interactions with other activities. An activity which brings education or instruction with it makes one aware of some of the connections which had been imperceptible. To recur to our simple example, a child who reaches for a bright light gets burned. Henceforth he *knows* that a certain act of touching in connection with a certain act of vision (and vice-versa) means heat and pain; or, a certain light means a source of heat. The acts by which a scientific man in his laboratory learns more about flame differ no whit in principle. By doing certain things, he makes perceptible certain connections of heat with other things, which had been previously ignored. Thus his acts in relation to these things get more meaning; he knows better what he is doing or "is about" when he has to do with them; he can *intend* consequences instead of just letting them happen—all synonymous ways of saying the same thing. At the same stroke, the flame has gained in meaning; all that is known about combustion, oxidation, about light and temperature, may become an intrinsic part of its intellectual content.

(2) The other side of an educative experience is an added power of subsequent direction or control. To say that one knows what he is about, or can intend certain consequences, is to say, of course, that he can better anticipate what is going to happen; that he can, therefore, get ready or prepare in advance so as to secure beneficial consequences and avert undesirable ones. A genuinely educative experience, then, one in which instruction is conveyed and ability increased, is contradistinguished from a routine activity on one hand, and a capricious activity on the other. (*a*) In the latter one "does not care what happens"; one just lets himself go and avoids connecting the consequences of one's act (the evidences of its connections with other things) with the act. It is customary to frown upon such aimless random activity, treating it as willful mischief or carelessness or lawlessness. But there is a tendency to seek the cause of such aimless activities in the youth's own disposition, isolated from everything else. But in fact such activity is explosive, and due to maladjustment with surroundings. Individuals act capriciously whenever they act under external dictation, or from being told, without having a purpose of their own or perceiving the bearing of the deed upon other acts. One may learn by doing something which he does not understand; even in the most intelligent action, we do much which we do not mean, because the largest portion of the connections of the act we consciously intend are not perceived or anticipated. But we learn only because after the act is performed we note results which we had not noted before. But much work in school consists in setting up rules by which pupils are to act of such a sort that even after pupils have acted, they are not led to see the connection between the result—say the answer—and the method pursued. So far as they are concerned, the

whole thing is a trick and a kind of miracle. Such action is essentially capricious, and leads to capricious habits. (*b*) Routine action, action which is automatic, may increase skill to do a *particular* thing. In so far, it might be said to have an educative effect. But it does not lead to new perceptions of bearings and connections; it limits rather than widens the meaning-horizon. And since the environment changes and our way of acting has to be modified in order successfully to keep a balanced connection with things, an isolated uniform way of acting becomes disastrous at some critical moment. The vaunted "skill" turns out gross ineptitude.

The essential contrast of the idea of education as continuous reconstruction with the other one-sided conceptions which have been criticized in this and the previous chapter is that it identifies the end (the result) and the process. This is verbally self-contradictory, but only verbally. It means that experience as an active process occupies time and that its later period completes its earlier portion; it brings to light connections involved, but hitherto unperceived. The later outcome thus reveals the meaning of the earlier, while the experience as a whole establishes a bent or disposition toward the things possessing this meaning. Every such continuous experience or activity is educative, and all education resides in having such experiences.

It remains only to point out (what will receive more ample attention later) that the reconstruction of experience may be social as well as personal. For purposes of simplification we have spoken in the earlier chapters somewhat as if the education of the immature which fills them with the spirit of the social group to which they belong, were a sort of catching up of the child with the aptitudes and resources of the adult group. In static societies, societies which make the maintenance of established custom their measure of value, this conception applies in the main. But not in progressive communities. They endeavor to shape the experiences of the young so that instead of reproducing current habits, better habits shall be formed, and thus the future adult society be an improvement on their own. Men have long had some intimation of the extent to which education may be consciously used to eliminate obvious social evils through starting the young on paths which shall not produce these ills, and some idea of the extent in which education may be made an instrument of realizing the better hopes of men. But we are doubtless far from realizing the potential efficacy of education as a constructive agency of improving society, from realizing that it represents not only a development of children and youth but also of the future society of which they will be the constituents.

Summary

Education may be conceived either retrospectively or prospectively. That is to say, it may be treated as process of accommodating the future to the past, or as an utilization of the past for a resource in a developing future. The former finds its standards and patterns in what has gone before. The mind may be regarded as a group of contents resulting from having certain things presented. In this case, the earlier presentations constitute the material to which the later are to be assimilated. Emphasis upon the value of the early experiences of immature beings is most important, especially because of the tendency to regard them as of little account. But these experiences do not consist of externally presented material, but of interaction of native activities with the environment which progressively modifies both the activities and the environment. The defect of the Herbartian theory of formation through presentations consists in slighting this constant interaction and change.

The same principle of criticism applies to theories which find the primary subject matter of study in the cultural products—especially the literary products—of man's history. Isolated from their connection with the present environment in which individuals have to act, they become a kind of rival and distracting environment. Their value lies in their use to increase the meaning of the things with which we have actively to do at the present time. The idea of education advanced in these chapters is formally summed up in the idea of continuous reconstruction of experience, an idea which is marked off from education as preparation for a remote future as unfolding, as external formation, and as recapitulation of the past.

THE DEMOCRATIC CONCEPTION IN EDUCATION

To say that education is a social function, securing direction and development in the immature through their participation in the life of the group to which they belong, is to say in effect that education will vary with the quality of life which prevails in a group. Particularly is it true that a society which not only changes but which has the ideal of such change as will improve it, will have different standards and methods of education from one which aims simply at the perpetuation of its own customs. To make the general ideas set forth applicable to our own educational practice, it is, therefore, necessary to come to closer quarters with the nature of present social life.

1. The Implications of Human Association

Society is one word, but many things. Men associate together in all kinds of ways and for all kinds of purposes. One man is concerned in a multitude of diverse groups, in which his associates may be quite different. It often seems as if they had nothing in common except that they are modes of associated life. Within every larger social organization there are numerous minor groups: not only political subdivisions, but industrial, scientific, religious, associations. There are political parties with differing aims, social sets, cliques, gangs, corporations, partnerships, groups bound closely together by ties of blood, and so on in endless variety. In many modern states and in some ancient, there is great diversity of populations, of varying languages, religions, moral codes, and traditions. From this standpoint, many a minor political unit, one of our large cities, for example, is a congeries of loosely associated societies, rather than an inclusive and permeating community of action and thought. (See *ante*, p. 20.)

The terms society, community, are thus ambiguous. They have both a eulogistic or normative sense, and a descriptive sense; a meaning de jure and a meaning de facto. In social philosophy, the former connotation is almost always uppermost. Society is conceived as one by its very nature. The qualities which accompany this unity, praiseworthy community of purpose and welfare, loyalty to public ends, mutuality of sympathy, are emphasized. But when we look at the facts which the term *denotes* instead of confining our attention to its intrinsic *connotation*, we find not unity, but a plurality of societies, good and bad. Men banded together in a criminal conspiracy, business aggregations that prey upon the public while serving it, political machines held together by the interest of plunder, are included. If it is said that such organizations are not societies because they do not meet the ideal requirements of the notion of society, the answer, in part, is that the conception of society is then made so "ideal" as to be of no use, having no reference to facts; and in part, that each of these organizations, no matter how opposed to the interests of other groups, has something of the praiseworthy qualities of "Society" which hold it together. There is honor among thieves, and a band of robbers has a common interest as respects its members. Gangs are marked by fraternal feeling, and narrow cliques by intense loyalty to their own codes. Family life may be marked by exclusiveness, suspicion, and jealousy as to those without, and yet be a model of amity and mutual aid within. Any education given by a group tends to socialize its members, but the quality and value of the socialization depends upon the habits and aims of the group.

Hence, once more, the need of a measure for the worth of any given mode of social life. In seeking this measure, we have to avoid two extremes. We cannot set up, out of our heads, something we regard as an ideal society. We must base our conception upon societies which actually exist, in order to have any assurance that our ideal is a practicable one. But, as we have just seen, the ideal cannot simply repeat the traits which are actually found. The problem is to extract the desirable traits of forms of community life which actually exist, and employ them to criticize undesirable features and suggest improvement. Now in any social group whatever, even in a gang of thieves, we find some interest held in common, and we find a certain amount of interaction and coöperative intercourse with other groups. From these two traits we derive our standard. How numerous and varied are the interests which are consciously shared? How full and free is the interplay with other forms of association? If we apply these considerations to, say, a criminal band, we find that the ties which consciously hold the members together are few in number, reducible almost to a common interest in plunder; and that they are of such a nature as to isolate the group from other groups with respect to give and take of the values of life. Hence, the education such a society gives is partial and distorted. If we take, on the other hand, the kind of family life which illustrates the standard, we find that there are material, intellectual, æsthetic interests in which all participate and that the progress of one member has worth for the experience of other members—it is readily communicable—and that the family is not an isolated whole, but enters intimately into relationships with business groups, with schools, with all the agencies of culture, as well as with other similar groups, and that it plays a due part in the political organization and in return receives support from it. In short, there are many interests consciously communicated and shared; and there are varied and free points of contact with other modes of association.

I. Let us apply the first element in this criterion to a despotically governed state. It is not true there is no common interest in such an organization between governed and governors. The authorities in command must make some appeal to the native activities of the subjects, must call some of their powers into play. Talleyrand said that a government could do everything with bayonets except sit on them. This cynical declaration is at least a recognition that the bond of union is not merely one of coercive force. It may be said, however, that the activities appealed to are themselves unworthy and degrading—that such a government calls into functioning activity simply capacity for fear. In a way, this statement is true. But it overlooks the fact that fear need not be an undesirable factor in experience. Caution, circumspection, prudence, desire to foresee future events so as to avert what is harmful, these desirable traits are as much a product of calling the impulse of fear into play as is cowardice and abject submission. The real difficulty is that the appeal to fear is *isolated*. In evoking dread and hope of specific tangible reward—say comfort and ease—many other capacities are left untouched. Or rather, they are affected, but in such a way as to pervert them. Instead of operating on their own account they are reduced to mere servants of attaining pleasure and avoiding pain.

This is equivalent to saying that there is no extensive number of common interests; there is no free play back and forth among the members of the social group. Stimulation and response are exceedingly one-sided. In order to have a large number of values in common, all the members of the group must have an equable opportunity to receive and to take from others. There must be a large variety of shared undertakings and experiences. Otherwise, the influences which educate some into masters, educate others into slaves. And the experience of each party loses in meaning, when the free interchange of varying modes of life-experience is arrested. A separation into a privileged and a subject-class prevents social endosmosis. The evils thereby affecting the superior class are less material and less perceptible, but equally real. Their culture tends to be sterile, to be turned back to feed on itself; their art becomes a showy display and artificial; their wealth luxurious; their knowledge overspecialized; their manners fastidious rather than humane.

Lack of the free and equitable intercourse which springs from a variety of shared interests makes intellectual stimulation unbalanced. Diversity of stimulation means novelty, and novelty means challenge to thought. The more activity is restricted to a few definite lines—as it is when there are rigid class lines preventing adequate interplay of experiences—the more action tends to become routine on the part of the class at a disadvantage, and capricious, aimless, and explosive on the part of the class having the materially fortunate position. Plato defined a slave as one who accepts from another the purposes which control his conduct. This condition obtains even where there is no slavery in the legal sense. It is found wherever men are engaged in activity which is socially serviceable, but whose service they do not understand and have no personal interest in. Much is said about scientific management of work. It is a narrow view which restricts the science which secures efficiency of operation to movements of the muscles. The chief opportunity for science is the discovery of the relations of a man to his work—including his relations to others who take part—which will enlist his intelligent interest in what he is doing. Efficiency in production often demands division of labor. But it is reduced to a mechanical routine unless workers see the technical, intellectual, and social relationships involved in what they do, and engage in their work because of the motivation furnished by such perceptions. The tendency to reduce such things as efficiency of activity and scientific management to purely technical externals is evidence of the one-sided stimulation of thought given to those in control of industry—those who supply its aims. Because of their lack of all-round and well-balanced social interest, there is not sufficient stimulus for attention to the human factors and relationships in industry. Intelligence is narrowed to the factors concerned with technical production and marketing of goods. No doubt, a very acute and intense intelligence in these narrow lines can be developed, but the failure to take into account the significant social factors means none the less an absence of mind, and a corresponding distortion of emotional life.

II. This illustration (whose point is to be extended to all associations lacking reciprocity of interest) brings us to our second point. The isolation and exclusiveness of a gang or clique brings its antisocial spirit into relief. But this same spirit is found wherever one group has interests "of its own" which shut it out from full interaction with other groups, so that its prevailing purpose is the protection of what it has got, instead of reorganization and progress through wider relationships. It marks nations in their isolation from one another; families which seclude their domestic concerns as if they had no connection with a larger life; schools when separated from the interest of home and community; the divisions of rich and poor; learned and unlearned. The essential point is that isolation makes for rigidity and formal institutionalizing of life, for static and selfish ideals within the group. That savage tribes regard aliens and enemies as synonymous is not accidental. It springs from the fact that they have identified their experience with rigid adherence to their past customs. On such a basis it is wholly logical to fear intercourse with others, for such contact might dissolve custom. It would certainly occasion reconstruction. It is a commonplace that an alert and expanding mental life depends upon an enlarging range of contact with the physical environment. But the principle applies even more significantly to the field where we are apt to ignore it—the sphere of social contacts.

Every expansive era in the history of mankind has coincided with the operation of factors which have tended to eliminate distance between peoples and classes previously hemmed off from one another. Even the alleged benefits of war, so far as more than alleged, spring from the fact that conflict of peoples at least enforces intercourse between them and thus accidentally enables them to learn from one another, and thereby to expand their horizons. Travel, economic and commercial tendencies, have at present gone far to break down external barriers; to bring peoples and classes into closer and more perceptible connection with one another. It remains for the most part to secure the intellectual and emotional significance of this physical annihilation of space.

2. The Democratic Ideal

The two elements in our criterion both point to democracy. The first signifies not only more numerous and more varied points of shared common interest, but greater reliance upon the recognition of mutual interests as a factor in social control. The second means not only freer interaction between social groups (once isolated so far as intention could keep up a separation) but change in social habit—its continuous readjustment through meeting the new situations produced by varied intercourse. And these two traits are precisely what characterize the democratically constituted society.

Upon the educational side, we note first that the realization of a form of social life in which interests are mutually interpenetrating, and where progress, or readjustment, is an important consideration, makes a democratic community more interested than other communities have cause to be in deliberate and systematic education. The devotion of democracy to education is a familiar fact. The superficial explanation is that a government resting upon popular suffrage cannot be successful unless those who elect and who obey their governors are educated. Since a democratic society repudiates the principle of external authority, it must find a substitute in voluntary disposition and interest; these can be created only by education. But there is a deeper explanation. A democracy is more than a form of government; it is primarily a mode of associated living, of conjoint communicated experience. The extension in space of the number of individuals who participate in an interest so that each has to refer his own action to that of others, and to consider the action of others to give point and direction to his own, is equivalent to the breaking down of those barriers of class, race, and national territory which kept men from perceiving the full import of their activity. These more numerous and more varied points of contact denote a greater diversity of stimuli to which an individual has to respond; they consequently put a premium on variation in his action. They secure a liberation of powers which remain suppressed as long as the incitations to action are partial, as they must be in a group which in its exclusiveness shuts out many interests.

The widening of the area of shared concerns, and the liberation of a greater diversity of personal capacities which characterize a democracy, are not of course the product of deliberation and conscious effort. On the contrary, they were caused by the development of modes of manufacture and commerce, travel, migration, and intercommunication which flowed from the command of science over natural energy. But after greater individualization on one hand, and a broader community of interest on the other have come into existence, it is a matter of deliberate effort to sustain and extend them. Obviously a society to which stratification into separate classes would be fatal, must see to it that intellectual opportunities are accessible to all on equable and easy terms. A society marked off into classes need be specially attentive only to the education of its ruling elements. A society which is mobile, which is full of channels for the distribution of a change occurring anywhere, must see to it that its members are educated to personal initiative and adaptability. Otherwise, they will be overwhelmed by the changes in which they are caught and whose significance or connections they do not perceive. The result will be a confusion in which a few will appropriate to themselves the results of the blind and externally directed activities of others.

. . .

One of the fundamental problems of education in and for a democratic society is set by the conflict of a nationalistic and a wider social aim. The earlier cosmopolitan and "humanitarian" conception suffered both from vagueness and from lack of definite organs of execution and agencies of administration. In Europe, in the Continental states particularly, the new idea of the importance of education for human welfare and progress was captured by national interests and harnessed to do a work whose social aim was definitely narrow and exclusive. The social aim of education and its national aim were identified, and the result was a marked obscuring of the meaning of a social aim.

This confusion corresponds to the existing situation of human intercourse. On the one hand, science, commerce, and art transcend national boundaries. They are largely international in quality and method. They involve interdependencies and coöperation among the peoples inhabiting different countries. At the same time, the idea of national sovereignty has never been as accentuated in politics as it is at the present time. Each nation lives in a state of suppressed hostility and incipient war with its neighbors. Each is supposed to be the supreme judge of its own interests, and it is assumed as matter of course that each has interests which are exclusively its own. To question this is to question the very idea of national sovereignty which is assumed to be basic to political practice and political science. This contradiction (for it is nothing less) between the wider sphere of associated and mutually helpful social life and the narrower sphere of exclusive and hence potentially hostile pursuits and purposes, exacts of educational theory a clearer conception of the meaning of "social" as a function and test of education than has yet been attained.

Is it possible for an educational system to be conducted by a national state and yet the full social ends of the educative process not be restricted, constrained, and corrupted? Internally, the question has to face the tendencies, due to present economic conditions, which split society into classes some of which are made merely tools for the higher culture of others. Externally, the question is concerned with the reconciliation of national loyalty, of patriotism, with superior devotion to the things which unite men in common ends, irrespective of national political boundaries. Neither phase of the problem can be worked out by merely negative means. It is not enough to see to it that education is not actively used as an instrument to make easier the exploitation of one class by another. School facilities must be secured of such amplitude and efficiency as will in fact and not simply in name discount the effects of economic inequalities, and secure to all the wards of the nation equality of equipment for their future careers. Accomplishment of this end demands not only adequate administrative provision of school facilities, and such supplementation of family resources as will enable youth to take advantage of them, but also such modification of traditional ideals of culture, traditional subjects of study and traditional methods of teaching and discipline as will retain all the youth under educational influences until they are equipped to be masters of their own economic and social careers. The ideal may seem remote of execution, but the democratic ideal of education is a farcical yet tragic delusion except as the ideal more and more dominates our public system of education.

The same principle has application on the side of the considerations which concern the relations of one nation to another. It is not enough to teach the horrors of war and to avoid everything which would stimulate international jealousy and animosity. The emphasis must be put upon whatever binds people together in coöperative human pursuits and results, apart from geographical limitations. The secondary and provisional character of national sovereignty in respect to the fuller, freer, and more fruitful association and intercourse of all human beings with one another must be instilled as a working disposition of mind. If these applications seem to be remote from a consideration of the philosophy of education, the impression shows that the meaning of the idea of education previously developed has not been adequately grasped. This conclusion is bound up with the very idea of education as a freeing of individual capacity in a progressive growth directed to social aims. Otherwise a democratic criterion of education can only be inconsistently applied.

Summary

Since education is a social process, and there are many kinds of societies, a criterion for educational criticism and construction implies a *particular* social ideal. The two points selected by which to measure the worth of a form of social life are the extent in which the interests of a group are shared by all its members, and the fullness and freedom with which it interacts with other groups. An undesirable society, in other words, is one which internally and externally sets up barriers to free intercourse and communication of experience. A society which makes provision for participation in its good of all its members on equal terms and which secures flexible readjustment of its institutions through interaction of the different forms of associated life is in so far democratic. Such a society must have a type of education which gives individuals a personal interest in social relationships and control, and the habits of mind which secure social changes without introducing disorder.

Elsie Clews Parsons

Elsie Clews Parsons was born into a prominent New York family in 1874. Her father was the founder of a New York bank, and her mother, Lucy Madison Worthington, was a descendent of President James Madison. Parsons's formative years bore the marks of wealth and privilege that she experienced as a child of New York "society." She was home schooled by the family's governesses until the age of ten; spent many of her summers exploring the outdoors at her family's cottage in Newport, Rhode Island; and spent still other summers with her mother in Europe. By the age of thirteen, she was fluent in both French and German.

Ever serious, Parsons exhibited a strong devotion to intellectual pursuits from an early age. When she graduated high school, her family pushed her to become a debutante, which they felt would only be fitting for a woman of her upbringing. Parsons, however, insisted on charting her own course, and she decided to enroll in the newly founded Barnard College in 1892. Following the completion of her junior year at Barnard, her mother asked Parsons to accompany her to Paris for the summer. Parsons refused to go, stating that she simply had too much studying to do. The next summer, she was all but forced to spend the summer with her mother in France. Again, though, Parsons's studious side showed through, as she eschewed other more youthful activities in favor of spending her days studying in the Biblioteque Nationale. By the end of the summer, Parsons had managed to translate, in its entirety, Gabriel Tarde's *Laws of Imitation*. In the fall of 1897, against the wishes of her family, Parsons entered the Ph.D. program in education at Columbia University, where she would later finish her degree in 1899 with minors in philosophy, sociology, and statistics.

After completing her Ph.D., Parsons taught at Barnard from 1899 to 1902 and lectured there from 1902 to 1905, but with the exception of a brief stint at the newly formed new School for Social Research in 1919, she did not teach again because her financial independence allowed her to concentrate almost exclusively on research and writing. She became active in settlement work, chairing the finance committee at Greenwich House and participating in the College Settlements Association. In 1900 she married Herbert Parsons, a young lawyer, who was himself active in political and social reform movements. Mirroring her life's interest in examining how individuals might challenge societal conventions, her marriage to Herbert was far from conventional. Initially, Parsons had been hesitant to marry because of her concern that marriage might hamper her career. Eventually, however, she came to see it as a worthwhile "experiment" for her to carry out. Together, she and Herbert had four children and tragically lost three others, who died during childhood. While they remained married until his death, their marriage, in many ways, continued to be an experiment, in that it became quite "open" in its later years.

In 1906, Parsons published her first major work, *The Family*, which grew out of her lectures on the family at Barnard. In it, she explored the subjects of sexual education and sexual morality while attempting to combat the mistruths and inaccuracies that she felt pervaded the debates about sexuality at that time. The book drew particularly heated criticisms from many sources, including the opinion pages of newspapers and church pulpits, for its suggestion that "trial marriage" was a sensible option for women to consider, and one that could help ensure their "full development." According to Parsons, while marriage should generally be viewed as a permanent commitment, if it proved unsatisfactory and no children involved were, then divorce should be a legitimate option that should be open to all women.

In addition to challenging familial conventions and sexual mores, Parsons also challenged traditional understandings of gender. Presaging the postmodern arguments of many contemporary gender scholars, *Old-Fashioned Woman* (1912) questions the validity of the category "woman." For Parsons, the idea of an essential "femininity" that all women are said to possess was a myth perpetuated via social and cultural rituals that contributed to the further subjugation of woman. As she put it: "the more thoroughly a woman is classified, the more easily is she controlled." Consequently, Parsons considered the main purpose of feminism to be contesting the usefulness of "woman" as a coherent category so that women were seen first and foremost as human beings and/or personalities—not simply women as such. Not willing to allow her feminist ideals to fall on deaf ears, Parsons was closely associated with the new "feminist" movement, which began to coalesce between 1909 and 1913. Among other things, she was a frequent participant in Heterodoxy, a weekly discussion group for feminists, which met in New York City.

As her career progressed, Parsons gradually moved away from sociology and began to focus more on anthropology. Concurrent with her shift in disciplinary focus was her shift in interest away from social reform and toward scientific research. Parsons grew increasingly convinced that the best way to promote her egalitarian ideals was through the use of scientific research that interrogated the concrete realities of social life, rather than relying on philosophical or sociological generalizations. Sparked by a trip to the southwest United States in 1915, during which she met the anthropologists Franz Boas and Pliny Goodard, Parsons embarked on some twenty-five years of ethnographic research and writing on Native Americans that led to such works as *Mitla, Town of the Souls* (1936); *Pueblo Indian Religion* (1939); and *Peguche, Canton of Otavalo* (1945). By the end of those twenty-five years, she had established herself as one of the leading authorities on Native American cultures. Testifying to the respect that she had earned from her colleagues, she became the first woman to be elected president of the American Anthropological Association in 1941.

While the name Parsons is now almost exclusively, at least within sociology, associated with the contributions made by Talcott Parsons, there remains much to be learned from the legacy bequeathed to us by *Elsie Clews* Parsons. Parsons's intellectual approach—characterized by a heavy dose of skepticism for socially accepted truths and an incisiveness, which was used to sift carefully through the particulars of cultural artifacts and the rituals of everyday life—stands as a striking exemplar for all social scientists to emulate. Perhaps more than anything, though, her life and career serve as direct evidence that cold, rigorous, scientific observation need not be seen as antithetical to passionate political and moral engagement. For Parsons, the two were hardly at odds with one another—they were intimately intertwined. As Alfred Kroeber, a colleague of Parsons and a distinguished anthropologist in his own right, commented, Parsons "studied the science of society the better to fight back against society." Her life, research, and the degree to which she continually combined the two to challenge existing societal conventions suggest that there are few who were more adept at the pugilistic arts of social science than Else Clews Parsons.

WOMEN IN PUBLIC LIFE

1914

A few years ago there was discussion in academic circles over differentiating the college curriculum of women from that of men. Surely the curriculum for men is not so satisfactory, it was urged, that it cannot be improved. Besides, the educational needs of women may be different, if only a little, from the needs of men. "True, perhaps," was the answer of the advocates of an identical curriculum, "but even so, we can't *afford* to differentiate, as yet at least. To give women as 'good' an education as men, we must give them the *same* education. That is the only way we can keep up the standard." And hitherto in the colleges this plea, right or wrong, has governed. It is the same argument that underlies feminist effort in other fields. That women may have as *ample* opportunities throughout society as men, they must have, it is felt, more or less consciously, the *same* opportunities. Society is after all very simple minded, one new idea at a time is its measure. Let not feminism confuse its issues. Before women can improve on men's ways, those ways, one and all, must be open to women.

Whether or not this is sound feminist doctrine, it is the clue to an understanding of much of the feminist agitation of today. It suggests, too, some of the directions still to be taken by the feminist movement. It may be profitable therefore to consider some of the differentiations[1] in habits and customs that have arisen in society for the lives of men and women, the differentiations of daily life and of life at crises, not overlooking, where we can discern them, the psychological reasons for these differentiations.

"So long as a lady shall deem herself in need of some gentleman's arm to conduct her properly out of a dining or ballroom," wrote an American publicist over half a century ago, "so long as she shall consider it dangerous or unbecoming to walk half a mile alone by night—I cannot see how the Woman's Rights' theory is ever to be anything more than a logically defensible abstraction." If this opinion of Horace Greeley is to be taken as a prediction that the Woman's Rights' platform of his time would not be enacted until another measure of freedom was secure to women, it has not been justified by the course of events. Property disqualifications have been entirely removed from women, the right of guardianship has become theirs (to the extent it was originally desired), and the days are counted to their possession, throughout the country, of the right of suffrage. These rights are theirs and yet it still embarrasses a woman to stand alone in a ballroom or sit with other women after the men have come out from the smoking-room; and it may be that the woman allured by the mystery of solitude under the stars is still rare.

[1] Not all; feministic discussion must confine itself, for example, to the exclusiveness of men, trusting that the exclusiveness of women will some day be a matter for hominist agitation. The farseeing feminist trusts, too, that the legal inequalities of men will cease to be neglected—inequalities before the law in responsibility for crime, for example, and in matters of property (damages for breach of promise, alimony, or any legal obligation to support women).

From *Women in Public Life*, ed. James P. Lichtenberger, *Annals of the American Academy of Political and Social Science*, 56 (November 1914).

But perhaps what Greeley meant to say was that economic or political reform would not greatly affect women as long as the conventionalities of their daily life remained unchanged. If so, was he not, in the main, right and for his period extraordinarily discerning? Even today, many a suffragist, however ardent, is unpossessed of this insight. Anxious beyond measure for the vote, she is wholly unperturbed by the constraints of her daily life. Loath to be wholly dependent upon men in the limited number of matters which make up government, she is willing enough to be dependent upon them and upon women too in those endless details of daily life any woman might be expected to determine for herself. I recently attended a political convention at Saratoga where several women were lobbying for suffrage. One evening one of them wanted to go with a man to a dance, but she would not go, I overheard her declare, unless another woman went with them. The following afternoon another suffragist who had started to motor to New York took the train at Albany because, thanks to an unforeseen emergency, one of the two men motoring with her had to remain in Albany. "I couldn't think of getting into New York after midnight with only one man. . . ." Is not chaperonage a more important question for women, I wonder, than suffrage?

Comparative inability to choose either solitariness or their company is not characteristic merely of modern women. In no culture have women shown desire to do anything which requires running the risks of being alone. Women hermits are extremely scarce, there are few women explorers, there are no women vagabonds, even the licensed adventuress, too restricted in her activity for any real adventure, is outcasted in a group. Rarely indeed do women go off by themselves—into the corner of a ballroom, into the wilderness, to the play, to the sacred high places of the earth or to the Islands of the Blessed. Penelope stays at home. Her reasons for staying at home vary, of course. She has to help her mother; she will be raped by a licentious male, a man or perhaps a god; she owes obedience to her parents; she will lose her reputation; she will give birth to a monster or her baby will die; she has to get the dinner ready; she has to look after the baby; she will bring disgrace to her family, dishonor to her husband, shame upon her children, disaster to her clan.

Whatever the sanctions, whatever the necessities or the excuses, woman's place having been in the home, her acquaintances have been restricted to the family circle and to the segments of the other family circles it overlaps. And with these friends and relatives her intercourse is unbroken and more or less incessant. The womanly woman has ever been an available woman, "always there when you wanted her." From such "home life" there have been for all women two prime outcomes. The unfamiliar person, the stranger, has been feared and shunned, more feared and shunned by women even than by men. Women in other words are peculiarly apprehensive of people of other localities, of other tribes or nations, of other castes, of other sets; and with such outlanders or outsiders they have as little to do as possible. Women are "inhospitable." They are "snobs." They are "full of prejudices." They are not "good mixers."

But to this characteristic tendency of women to keep to themselves, there are two exceptions. Within the home itself women associate with strangers, i.e., with those unlike themselves, unlike in age and in sex, and seldom, too, are the times when women do not have to put up with this association. Being "home bodies," they cannot get away, like men, from their children or their parents, they have to make the best of their brothers or their husbands. Face to face with these heterogeneities of sex or age, women have raised up barriers against them, carefully regulating their relations with their juniors and seniors and with the other sex. Their attitude is very conventional with members of different age classes and with men, more conventional, I mean, than that of men with women or with those unlike in age—and this is the second important outcome for women of their home life. Upon women age and sex taboos are heavier than upon men. And it is they who are the foremost teachers of the proprieties, of politeness, of good manners, of the amenities—all rules of conduct for life with others more or less unlike yourself and yet not to be avoided.

With beings unlike yourself the alternative to conventionality is avoidance. And that alternative is taken on the whole by men in relation both to their juniors and seniors[2] and to women. More or less unconsciously they avoid women and more or less deliberately they exclude them from their interests and their places of assembly—from their economic pursuits, from their learned professions, from their games and pastimes, from their club-houses, churches,[3] forums, council halls, universities, and play-houses. Even the initiative in the avoidance practiced within the family group is taken, I surmise, by men.[4] At home and away from it such seclusiveness and exclusiveness in men result, of course, in increasing the differences between them and women. Increased differences stimulate to greater seclusiveness or exclusiveness; we get a closed circle.

For the moment let us turn away from this closed circle to consider certain sex differentiations in customs at times of crisis. We noted that the heterogeneities of sex and of age are more constantly under the noses of women, so to speak, than of men. Women are closer to life, we sometimes say, meaning that they are face to face with birth and growth, decay and death. And so it is to be expected that they, rather than men, will play the leading parts in the policy human beings have chosen to meet the changes of life—the policy of ignoring the change until it is inevitable and then mitigating the shock of it through the diversion of ceremonial.[5] And women do play in the ceremonial of crisis the more prominent or lasting rôles. Mourning observances are far more elaborate for women than for men and far more prolonged. So are wedding and honeymoon observances, although in them of course the character of duality must preclude any great differentiation.[6] As for puberty or initiation ceremonial, that curious means of breaking the shock of realizing that the young have grown up, if women appear to take a less important part in it than men, reasons consistent with our general interpretation are not hard to find. The initiation of boys means they are leaving home. No amount of ceremonial can disguise that break. Were they to stay on at home in a different relation to it, then the women might enter more strikingly into their man-making rites.[7] As it is, all women can do is to express ceremonially their distress at "losing" their boys. Andamanese women "weep over" an initiate the morning after he breaks his turtle fast. Throughout the first night of an initiation Mita-Koodi women are expected to wail. The kinswomen of an Euahlayi initiate are supposed to be so much in need of comforting that the old men bring them presents of food. In other Australian tribes we find rites to symbolize the separation imminent between the initiate and his kinswomen. Among the Kurnai he sprinkles his mother with water, among the Arunta he throws his boomerang towards her spirit camp to show her, the ethnographers suggest, that all

[2] Although classification by age is characteristic of every society, our specific data on age classes are scant and very scattered; but from what I have from others and have observed at first hand I am inclined to believe that seniority is more of a bar in daily intercourse between adult men than between women. The fact that men see comparatively little of children hardly needs mention. Seeing them seldom, they can afford, they feel, to treat them as contemporaries. This is a reason why children "take to men" and not, as a fond mother sometimes alleges, because men are novelties. Children, like women, dread the Stranger.

[3] From religious exclusiveness almost all other forms of exclusiveness can be traced just as all the professions were differentiated from the priesthood and as games and the arts had religious origins. But the exclusion of women from the derivatives of ecclesiasticism in no mere historical sequence or survival. History gives it the sanction of the past in given cases, but it has an ever fresh psychological spring.

[4] Among us it is the son-in-law who avoids his mother-in-law and there appears to be no evidence that it is the other way round among savages where this practice is more formal. At any rate it is the father-in-law in every society who avoids his daughter-in-law and not vice versa. Everywhere, too, it is "up to" the boy to stop "hanging round" his mother and playing with his sisters.

[5] Under the rubric of *Ceremonial Reluctance* I am preparing a fuller statement of this shock absorber theory of ceremonial.

[6] The veiling of the bride and her seclusiveness before and after the wedding are the most notable. But the bridal couple apart, the women of the family are more concerned with the marriage ceremonial than the men.

[7] As they do at the nubility of girls; for the "coming out" rites of girls do not mean a break with family life.

is at an end between them.[8] But the initiates are turning their backs on their mother only to turn their faces towards their father and their father's friends. For these seniors, upon taking into their life youthful participants, an adjustment is necessary, and it is for them to get it over with as quickly and easily as possible. Naturally they resort to the usual social method, the method of ceremonial. It is plain enough why men figure rather than women in the puberty or initiation rites to celebrate a boy's growing up.

But there are other conditions in the life of men besides an adjustment to their juniors to be met with ceremonial or with conventionality. Their contacts with all their non-familial groups, the groups they resort to when they leave home, when they go out "to meet a man," all these associations have to be entered upon with ceremonial and, their membership never entirely homogeneous, safeguarded with conventionalities. Hence presentations and introductions of all kinds, the conferring of orders or degrees, the induction into office, "treating" and the "sacred laws of hospitality." Hence tribal or patriotic standards, professional etiquette, chivalry, the code of a gentleman, and many other caste taboos or rules. In all these matters women figure far less than men, of course, for the simple enough reason that they are out of touch with the different groups concerned. They have avoided them or they have been excluded from them. Then when they do begin to seek admission into these non-familial groups we may note that very often they ride roughshod over their conventionalities,[9] breaking their rules, either because they are ignorant of them or because they see in them little or no value. This procedure, whatever its explanation, is very disturbing to men, distasteful to them and even abhorrent. And often enough it is the more or less unconscious anticipation of such violations by women, of such misbehaviour, that sets men so bitterly against opening the doors to them. Merely to lessen masculine apprehensiveness and to overcome masculine antagonism women might do well to adopt quickly and unquestioningly masculine conventionalities.

But even if women develop a sense of honor and a respect for masculine routine, even if they shear their hair and dress like men, even if they keep men's hours, and work and play like men, even if they smoke and swear and get drunk like men, even if they succeed in getting from the outside the loyalty and esprit du corps that usually come only with participation in the life of the group, learning to swim, in other words, without going near the water, even if they conform in all these ways, differences will still exist between them and men, natural differences, urges the anti-feminist, and should not these natural differences receive appreciation and be given social expression? However we may answer this question, it does not quite meet the point of masculine exclusiveness. It is *apprehension of difference* rather than actual difference which bulks so large now and always in the social regulation of sex. It is fear of the unlike rather than the fact of it. The anti-feminist wishes to keep women apart from men not because he values sex differences, but because he fears them. He or she is not so anxious to preserve them as to get away from them, to be protected from the danger of being disturbed by them. Differences in age, in caste, in family, and in race, have filled mankind with analogous apprehensions and prompted analogous methods and plans of self-protection.

Age-class, caste group, family, and race, each has its own closed circle—from unlikeness to exclusion or seclusion, from exclusion or seclusion to unlikeness—but each of these vicious circles the modern spirit has begun to invade and break down. In the spirit of our time fear of the unlike is waning, and *pari passu* intolerance. Fear of the unlike and intolerance are due to fear of change, and that fear, whether of change wrought by life or of change threatened by the stranger, that great fear, is passing. With it are bound to go the devices of self-protection it prompted—ceremonial, conventionality, and segregation. In this general movement of the human spirit feminism was born; upon its march the hopes of feminism ultimately must depend.

[8] The rigid separation of initiates from females is also more of a symbol of sex segregation, I think, than a practical measure against sexual intercourse. It is a concentration rite, a synopsis, so to speak, of the life ahead of them, life apart from women.

[9] An infraction we recognize when we say, for example, that women have no sense of honor, or that women dislike "red tape."

VIRGINIA WOOLF

Virginia Woolf (1882–1941) was one of the originators of the modern novel and a distinguished critic of her time. Like most upper middle-class women, she was educated at home; hers was a highly intellectual household ruled by her publicly eminent but personally demanding father. The stresses of her home life may have contributed to the episodes of madness that plagued her life and work. After her father's death in 1904, Woolf and her three siblings moved to Gordon Square, London, which became the center of the "Bloomsbury Group."

Virginia married Leonard Woolf in 1912 and soon afterward completed her first novel, *The Voyage Out* (1915). Two years later they founded the Hogarth Press, which published her books. In the years that followed, periods of peace and astonishing creativity in which she produced novels and critical essays alternated with periods of mental illness.

After the appearance in 1919 of her second novel, *Night and Day*, Woolf began to explore the "stream of consciousness" style. Rather than character or event, she wanted to stress the texture of experience itself, the impression of time present and time passing in individual lives. In *Mrs. Dalloway* (1925) and *To the Lighthouse* (1927), she used time shifts, flashbacks, and multiple points of view in an attempt to convey the world of intuitive consciousness and spontaneous feelings. In *The Waves* (1931) the emphasis again is on the inner life, as the reader experiences the mind of one or another of six characters from their childhood to old age. And the action in *Between the Acts* (1941), as in *Mrs. Dalloway*, takes place on a single day, but history is suggested by the staging of a village pageant that records English life, while the reader is also reminded of impending war.

Feminism pervades Woolf's novels, which often center upon a female character struggling to grasp or to defend her individuality. Her most famous essay, *A Room of One's Own* (1929), describes the troubles encountered by women writers in a man's world and calls for economic independence and privacy for women, as well as for control of marriage and reproduction and the opportunity for advanced education.

It is in *Three Guineas*, however, that Woolf's feminism is most political and transformative. Published in 1938, it is her most urgent and least charming work, a book that critics decried as propaganda and that discomfited even her friends. With an angry eloquence, Woolf makes the case that men's heaviest burden is the values they inevitably acquire from the institutions that are the route to public success. Men grow accustomed to competition, hierarchy, and the profit motive until even the potentially valuable qualities of ambition and patriotism are corrupted. Public life becomes heartless and exploitative, and, moreover, men bring these attitudes and practices back into the home.

The emphasis in *Three Guineas* is not on woman's role as nurturer and therefore peacemaker so much as on fears of co-optation and assimilation, not on legal equality so much as on how power and institutions have disadvantaged women, and not on specific reforms called for by the women's movement so much as on the importance of this movement as a source of support even after these reforms have been achieved.

THREE GUINEAS

1938

. . .

The word "influence" then has changed. The educated man's daughter has now at her disposal an influence which is different from any influence that she has possessed before. It is not the influence which the great lady, the Siren, possesses; nor is it the influence which the educated man's daughter possessed when she had no vote; nor is it the influence which she possessed when she had a vote but was debarred from the right to earn her living. It differs, because it is an influence from which the charm element has been removed; it is an influence from which the money element has been removed. She need no longer use her charm to procure money from her father or brother. Since it is beyond the power of her family to punish her financially she can express her own opinions. In place of the admirations and antipathies which were often unconsciously dictated by the need of money she can declare her genuine likes and dislikes. In short, she need not acquiesce; she can criticize. At last she is in possession of an influence that is disinterested.

Such in rough and rapid outlines is the nature of our new weapon, the influence which the educated man's daughter can exert now that she is able to earn her own living. The question that has next to be discussed, therefore, is how can she use this new weapon to help you to prevent war? And it is immediately plain that if there is no difference between men who earn their livings in the professions and women who earn their livings, then this letter can end; for if our point of view is the same as yours then we must add our sixpence to your guinea; follow your methods and repeat your words. But, whether fortunately or unfortunately, that is not true. The two classes still differ enormously. And to prove this, we need not have recourse to the dangerous and uncertain theories of psychologists and biologists; we can appeal to facts. Take the fact of education. Your class has been educated at public schools and universities for five or six hundred years, ours for sixty. Take the fact of property. Your class possesses in its own right and not through marriage practically all the capital, all the land, all the valuables, and all the patronage in England. Our class possesses in its own right and not through marriage practically none of the capital, none of the land, none of the valuables, and none of the patronage in England. That such differences make for very considerable differences in mind and body, no psychologist or biologist would deny. It would seem to follow then as an indisputable fact that "we"—meaning by "we" a whole made up of body, brain and spirit, influenced by memory and tradition—must still differ in some essential respects from "you," whose body, brain and spirit have been so differently trained and are so differently influenced by memory and tradition. Though we see the same world, we see it through different eyes. Any help we can give you must be different from that you can give yourselves, and perhaps the value of that help may lie in the fact of that difference. Therefore before we agree to sign your manifesto or join your society, it might be well to discover where the difference lies, because then we may discover where the help lies also. Let us then by way of a very elementary beginning lay before you a photograph—a crudely coloured photograph—of your world as it appears to us who see it from the threshold of the private house; through the shadow of the veil that St. Paul still lays upon our eyes; from the bridge which connects the private house with the world of public life.

Your world, then, the world of professional, of public life, seen from this angle undoubtedly looks queer. At first sight it is enormously impressive. Within quite a small space are crowded together St. Paul's, the Bank of England, the Mansion House, the massive if funereal battlements of the Law Courts; and on the other side, Westminster Abbey and the Houses of Parliament. There, we say to ourselves, pausing, in this moment of transition on the bridge, our fathers and brothers have spent their lives. All these hundreds of years they have been mounting those steps, passing in and out of those doors, ascending those pulpits, preaching, money-making, administering justice. It is from this world that the private house (somewhere, roughly speaking, in the West End) has derived its creeds, its laws, its clothes and carpets, its beef and mutton. And then, as is now permissible, cautiously pushing aside the swing doors of one of these temples, we enter on tiptoe and survey the scene in greater detail. The first sensation of colossal size, of majestic masonry is broken up into a myriad points of amazement mixed with interrogation. Your clothes in the first place make us gape with astonishment. How many, how splendid, how extremely ornate they are—the clothes worn by the educated man in his public capacity! Now you dress in violet; a jewelled crucifix swings on your breast; now your shoulders are covered with lace; now furred with ermine; now slung with many linked chains set with precious stones. Now you wear wigs on your heads; rows of graduated curls descend to your necks. Now your hats are boatshaped, or cocked; now they mount in cones of black fur; now they are made of brass and scuttleshaped; now plumes of red, now of blue hair surmount them. Sometimes gowns cover your legs; sometimes gaiters. Tabards embroidered with lions and unicorns swing from your shoulders; metal objects cut in star shapes or in circles glitter and twinkle upon your breasts. Ribbons of all colours—blue, purple, crimson—cross from shoulder to shoulder. After the comparative simplicity of your dress at home, the splendour of your public attire is dazzling.

But far stranger are two other facts that gradually reveal themselves when our eyes have recovered from their first amazement. Not only are whole bodies of men dressed alike summer and winter—a strange characteristic to a sex which changes its clothes according to the season, and for reasons of private taste and comfort—but every button, rosette and stripe seems to have some symbolical meaning. Some have the right to wear plain buttons only; others rosettes; some may wear a single stripe; others three, four or five. And each curl or stripe is sewn on at precisely the right distance apart—it may be one inch for one man, one inch and a quarter for another. Rules again regulate the gold wire on the shoulders, the braid on the trousers, the cockades on the hats—but no single pair of eyes can observe all these distinctions, let alone account for them accurately.

Even stranger, however, than the symbolic splendour of your clothes are the ceremonies that take place when you wear them. Here you kneel; there you bow; here you advance in procession behind a man carrying a silver poker; here you mount a carved chair; here you appear to do homage to a piece of painted wood; here you abase yourselves before tables covered with richly worked tapestry. And whatever these ceremonies may mean you perform them always together, always in step, always in the uniform proper to the man and the occasion.

Apart from the ceremonies, such decorative apparel appears to us at first sight strange in the extreme. For dress, as we use it, is comparatively simple. Besides the prime function of covering the body, it has two other offices—that it creates beauty for the eye, and that it attracts the admiration of your sex. Since marriage until the year 1919—less than twenty years ago—was the only profession open to us, the enormous importance of dress to a woman can hardly be exaggerated. It was to her what clients are to you—dress was her chief, perhaps her only, method of becoming Lord Chancellor. But your dress in its immense elaboration has obviously another function. It not only covers nakedness, gratifies vanity, and creates pleasure for the eye, but it serves to advertise the social, professional, or intellectual standing of the wearer. If you will excuse the humble illustration, your dress fulfils the same function as the tickets in a grocer's shop. But, here, instead of saying, "This is margarine; this pure butter; this is the finest butter in the market," it says, "This man is a clever man—he is Master of Arts; this man is a very clever man—he is Doctor of Letters; this man is a most clever man—he is a Member of the Order of Merit." It is this function—the advertisement function—of your dress that seems to us most singular. In the opinion of St. Paul, such advertisement, at any rate for our sex, was unbecoming and immodest; until a very few years ago we were denied the use of it. And still the tradition, or belief, lingers among us that to express worth of any kind, whether intellectual or moral, by wearing pieces of metal, or ribbon, coloured hoods or gowns, is a barbarity which deserves the ridicule which we bestow upon the rites of savages. A woman who advertised her motherhood by a tuft of horsehair on the left shoulder would scarcely, you will agree, be a venerable object.

But what light does our difference here throw upon the problem before us? What connection is there between the sartorial splendours of the educated man and the photograph of ruined houses and dead bodies? Obviously the connection between dress and war is not far to seek; your finest clothes are those that you wear as soldiers. Since the red and the gold, the brass and the feathers are discarded upon active service, it is plain that their expensive and not, one might suppose, hygienic splendour is invented partly in order to impress the beholder with the majesty of the military office, partly in order through their vanity to induce young men to become soldiers. Here, then, our influence and our difference might have some effect; we, who are forbidden to wear such clothes ourselves, can express the opinion that the wearer is not to us a pleasing or an impressive spectacle. He is on the contrary a ridiculous, a barbarous, a displeasing spectacle. But as the daughters of educated men we can use our influence more effectively in another direction, upon our own class—the class of educated men. For there, in courts and universities, we find the same love of dress. There, too, are velvet and silk, fur and ermine. We can say that for educated men to emphasize their superiority over other people, either in birth or intellect, by dressing differently, or by adding titles before, or letters after their names are acts that rouse competition and jealousy—emotions which, as we need scarcely draw upon biography to prove, nor ask psychology to show, have their share in encouraging a disposition towards war. If then we express the opinion that such distinctions make those who possess them ridiculous and learning contemptible, we should do something, indirectly, to discourage the feelings that lead to war. Happily we can now do more than express an opinion; we can refuse all such distinctions and all such uniforms for ourselves. This would be a slight but definite contribution to the problem before us—how to prevent war; and one that a different training and a different tradition puts more easily within our reach than within yours.

. . .

. . . Let us turn to the public press and see if we can discover from the opinions aired there any hint that will guide us in our attempt to decide the delicate and difficult question as to the aroma, the atmosphere that surrounds the word "Miss" in Whitehall. We will consult the newspapers.

First:

> I think your correspondent . . . correctly sums up this discussion in the observation that woman has too much liberty. It is probable that this so-called liberty came with war, when women assumed responsibilities so far unknown to them. They did splendid service during those days. Unfortunately, they were praised and petted out of all proportion to the value of their performances.

That does very well for a beginning. But let us proceed:

> I am of the opinion that a considerable amount of the distress which is prevalent in this section of the community [the clerical] could be relieved by the policy of employing men instead of women, wherever possible. There are today in Government

> offices, post offices, insurance companies, banks and other offices, thousands of women doing work which men could do. At the same time there are thousands of qualified men, young and middle-aged, who cannot get a job of any sort. There is a large demand for women labour in the domestic arts, and in the process of re-grading a large number of women who have drifted into clerical service would become available for domestic service.

The odour thickens, you will agree.

Then once more:

> I am certain I voice the opinion of thousands of young men when I say that if men were doing the work that thousands of young women are now doing the men would be able to keep those same women in decent homes. Homes are the real places of the women who are now compelling men to be idle. It is time the Government insisted upon employers giving work to more men, thus enabling them to marry the women they cannot now approach.

There! There can be no doubt of the odour now. The cat is out of the bag; and it is a Tom.

After considering the evidence contained in those three quotations, you will agree that there is good reason to think that the word "Miss," however delicious its scent in the private house, has a certain odour attached to it in Whitehall which is disagreeable to the noses on the other side of the partition; and that it is likely that a name to which "Miss" is attached will, because of this odour, circle in the lower spheres where the salaries are small rather than mount to the higher spheres where the salaries are substantial. As for "Mrs.," it is a contaminated word; an obscene word. The less said about that word the better. Such is the smell of it, so rank does it stink in the nostrils of Whitehall, that Whitehall excludes it entirely. In Whitehall, as in heaven, there is neither marrying nor giving in marriage.

Odour then—or shall we call it "atmosphere"?—is a very important element in professional life; in spite of the fact that like other important elements it is impalpable. It can escape the noses of examiners in examination rooms, yet penetrate boards and divisions and affect the senses of those within. Its bearing upon the case before us is undeniable. For it allows us to decide in the case of *Baldwin* v. *Whitaker* that both the Prime Minister and the *Almanack* are telling the truth. It is true that women civil servants deserve to be paid as much as men; but it is also true that they are not paid as much as men. The discrepancy is due to atmosphere.

Atmosphere plainly is a very mighty power. Atmosphere not only changes the sizes and shapes of things; it affects solid bodies, like salaries, which might have been thought impervious to atmosphere. An epic poem might be written about atmosphere, or a novel in ten or fifteen volumes. But since this is only a letter, and you are pressed for time, let us confine ourselves to the plain statement that atmosphere is one of the most powerful, partly because it is one of the most impalpable, of the enemies with which the daughters of educated men have to fight. If you think that statement exaggerated, look once more at the samples of atmosphere contained in those three quotations. We shall find there not only the reason why the pay of the professional woman is still so small, but something more dangerous, something which, if it spreads, may poison both sexes equally. There, in those quotations, is the egg of the very same worm that we know under other names in other countries. There we have in embryo the creature, Dictator as we call him when he is Italian or German, who believes that he has the right, whether given by God, Nature, sex or race is immaterial, to dictate to other human beings how they shall live; what they shall do. Let us quote again: "Homes are the real places of the women who are now compelling men to be idle. It is time the Government insisted upon employers giving work to more men, thus enabling them to marry the women they cannot now approach." Place beside it another quotation: "There are two worlds in the life of the nation, the world of men and the world of women. Nature has done well to entrust the man with the care of his family and the nation. The woman's world is her family, her husband, her children, and her home." One is written in English, the other in German. But where is the difference? Are they not both saying the same thing? Are they not both the voices of Dictators, whether they speak English or German, and are we not all agreed that the dictator when we meet him abroad is a very dangerous as well as a very ugly animal? And he is here among us, raising his ugly head, spitting his poison, small still, curled up like a caterpillar on a leaf, but in the heart of England. Is it not from this egg, to quote Mr. Wells again, that "the practical obliteration of [our] freedom by Fascists or Nazis" will spring? And is not the woman who has to breathe that poison and to fight that insect, secretly and without arms, in her office, fighting the Fascist or the Nazi as surely as those who fight him with arms in the limelight of publicity? And must not that fight wear down her strength and exhaust her spirit? Should we not help her to crush him in our own country before we ask her to help us to crush him abroad? And what right have we, Sir, to trumpet our ideals of freedom and justice to other countries when we can shake out from our most respectable newspapers any day of the week eggs like these?

Here, rightly, you will check what has all the symptoms of becoming a peroration by pointing out that though the opinions expressed in these letters are not altogether agreeable to our national self-esteem they are the natural expression of a fear and a jealousy which we must understand before we condemn them. It is true, you will say, that these gentlemen seem a little unduly concerned with their own salaries and their own security, but that is comprehensible, given the traditions of their sex, and even compatible with a genuine love of freedom and a genuine hatred of dictatorship. For these gentlemen are, or wish to become, husbands and fathers, and in that case the support of the family will depend upon them. In other words, Sir, I take you to mean that the world as it is at present is divided into two services; one the public and the other the private. In one world the sons of educated men work as civil servants, judges, soldiers and are paid for that work; in the other world, the daughters of educated men work as wives, mothers, daughters—but are they not paid for that work? Is the work of a mother, of a wife, of a daughter, worth nothing to the nation in solid cash? That fact, if it be a fact, is so astonishing that we must confirm it by appealing once more to the impeccable Whitaker. Let us turn to his pages again. We may turn them, and turn them again. It seems incredible, yet it seems undeniable. Among all those offices there is no such office as a mother's; among all those salaries there is no such salary as a mother's. The work of an archbishop is worth £15,000 a year to the State; the work of a judge is worth £5,000 a year; the work of a permanent secretary is worth £3,000 a year; the work of an army captain, of a sea captain, of a sergeant of dragoons, of a policeman, of a postman—all these works are worth paying out of the taxes, but wives and mothers and daughters who work all day and every day, without whose work the State would collapse and fall to pieces, without whose work your sons, Sir, would cease to exist, are paid nothing whatever. Can it be possible? Or have we convicted Whitaker, the impeccable, of errata?

Ah, you will interpose, here is another misunderstanding. Husband and wife are not only one flesh; they are also one purse. The wife's salary is half the husband's income. The man is paid more than the woman for that very reason—because he has a wife to support. The bachelor then is paid at the same rate as the unmarried woman? It appears not—another queer effect of atmosphere, no doubt; but let it pass. Your statement that the wife's salary is half the husband's income seems to be an equitable arrangement, and no doubt, since it is equitable, it is confirmed by law. Your reply that the law leaves these private matters to be decided privately is less satisfactory, for it means that the wife's half-share of the common income is not paid legally into her hands, but into her husband's. But still a spiritual right may be as binding as a legal right; and if the wife of an educated man has a spiritual right to half her husband's income, then we may assume that the wife of an educated man has as much money to spend, once the common household bills are met, upon any cause that appeals to her as her husband. Now her husband, witness Whitaker, witness the wills in the daily paper, is often not merely well paid by his profession, but is master of a very considerable capital sum. Therefore this lady who asserts that £250 a year is all that a woman can earn today in the professions is evading the question; for the profession of marriage in the educated class is a highly paid one, since she has a right, a spiritual right, to half her husband's salary. The puzzle deepens; the mystery thickens. For if the wives of rich men are themselves rich women, how does it come about that the income of the W.S.P.U. was only £42,000 a year; how does it come about that the honorary treasurer of the college rebuilding fund is still asking for £100,000; how does it come about that the treasurer of a society for helping professional women to obtain employment is asking not merely for money to pay her rent but will be grateful for books, fruit or cast-off clothing? It stands to reason that if the wife has a spiritual right to half her husband's income because her own work as his wife is unpaid, then she must have as much money to spend upon such causes as appeal to her as he has. And since those causes are standing hat in hand a-begging we are forced to conclude that they are causes that do not take the fancy of the educated man's wife. The charge against her is a very serious one. For consider—there is the money—that surplus fund that can be devoted to education, to pleasure, to philanthropy when the household dues are met; she can spend her share as freely as her husband can spend his. She can spend it upon whatever causes she likes; and yet she will not spend it upon the causes that are dear to her own sex. There they are, hat in hand a-begging. That is a terrible charge to bring against her.

But let us pause for a moment before we decide that charge against her. Let us ask what are the causes, the pleasures, the philanthropies upon which the educated man's wife does in fact spend her share of the common surplus fund. And here we are confronted with facts which, whether we like them or not, we must face. The fact is that the tastes of the married woman in our class are markedly virile. She spends vast sums annually upon party funds; upon sport; upon grouse moors; upon cricket and football. She lavishes money upon clubs—Brooks', White's, the Travellers', the Reform, the Athenaeum—to mention only the most prominent. Her expenditure upon these causes, pleasures and philanthropies must run into many millions every year. And yet by far the greater part of this sum is spent upon pleasures which she does not share. She lays out thousands and thousands of pounds upon clubs to which her own sex is not admitted; upon racecourses where she may not ride; upon colleges from which her own sex is excluded. She pays a huge bill annually for wine which she does not drink and for cigars which she does not smoke. In short, there are only two conclusions to which we can come about the educated man's wife—the first is that she is the most altruistic of beings who prefers to spend her share of the common fund upon his pleasures and causes; the second, and more probable, if less creditable, is not that she is the most altruistic of beings, but that her spiritual right to a share of half her husband's income peters out in practice to an actual right to board, lodging and a small annual allowance for pocket money and dress. Either of these conclusions is possible; the evidence of public institutions and subscription lists puts any other out of the question. For consider how nobly the educated man supports his old school, his old college; how splendidly he subscribes to party funds; how munificently he contributes to all those institutions and sports by which he and his sons educate their minds and develop their bodies—the daily papers bear daily witness to those indisputable facts. But the absence of her name from subscription lists, and the poverty of the institutions which educate her mind and her body seem to prove that there is something in the atmosphere of the private house which deflects the wife's spiritual share of the common income impalpably but irresistibly towards those causes which her husband approves and those pleasures which he enjoys. Whether creditable or discreditable, that is the fact. And that is the reason why those other causes stand a-begging.

. . .

It is a thought not without its glamour. Consider what it would mean if among us there were now a woman motor-car manufacturer who, with a stroke of her pen, could endow the women's colleges with two or three hundred thousand pounds apiece. The honorary treasurer of the rebuilding fund, your sister at Cambridge, would have her labours considerably lightened then. There would be no need of appeals and committees, of bazaars and strawberries and cream. And suppose that there were not merely one rich woman, but that rich women were as common as rich men. What could you not do? You could shut up your office at once. You could finance a woman's party in the House of Commons. You could run a daily newspaper committed to a conspiracy, not of silence, but of speech. You could get pensions for spinsters; those victims of the patriarchal system, whose allowance is insufficient and whose board and lodging are no longer thrown in. You could get equal pay for equal work. You could provide every mother with chloroform when her child is born; you could bring down the maternal death-rate from four in every thousand to none at all, perhaps. In one session you could pass Bills that will now take you perhaps a hundred years of hard and continuous labour to get through the House of Commons. There seems at first sight nothing that you could not do, if you had the same capital at your disposal that your brothers have at theirs. Why not, then, you exclaim, help us to take the first step towards possessing it? The professions are the only way in which we can earn money. Money is the only means by which we can achieve objects that are immensely desirable. Yet here you are, you seem to protest, haggling and bargaining over conditions. But consider this letter from a professional man asking us to help him to prevent war. Look also at the photographs of dead bodies and ruined houses that the Spanish Government sends almost weekly. That is why it is necessary to haggle and to bargain over conditions.

For the evidence of the letter and of the photographs when combined with the facts with which history and biography provide us about the professions seem together to throw a certain light, a red light, shall we say, upon those same professions. You make money in them; that is true; but how far is money in view of those facts in itself a desirable possession? A great authority upon human life, you will remember, held over two thousand years ago that great possessions were undesirable. To which you reply, and with some heat as if you suspected another excuse for keeping the pursestring tied, that Christ's words about the rich and the Kingdom of Heaven are no longer helpful to those who have to face different facts in a different world. You argue that as things are now in England extreme poverty is less desirable than extreme wealth. The poverty of the Christian who should give away all his possessions produces, as we have daily and abundant proof, the crippled in body, the feeble in mind. The unemployed, to take the obvious example, are not a source of spiritual or intellectual wealth to their country. These are weighty arguments; but consider for a moment the life of Pierpont Morgan. Do you not agree with that evidence before us that extreme wealth is equally undesirable, and for the same reasons? If extreme wealth is undesirable and extreme poverty is undesirable, it is arguable that there is some mean between the two which is desirable. What then is that mean—how much money is needed to live upon in England today? And how should that money be spent? What is the kind of life, the kind of human being, you propose to aim at if you succeed in extracting this guinea? Those, Madam, are the questions that I am asking you to consider and you cannot deny that those are questions of the utmost importance. But alas, they are questions that would lead us far beyond the solid world of actual fact to which we are here confined. So let us shut the New Testament, Shakespeare, Shelley, Tolstoy and the rest, and face the fact that stares us in the face at this moment of transition—the fact of the procession; the fact that we are trapesing along somewhere in the rear and must consider that fact before we can fix our eyes upon the vision on the horizon.

There it is then, before our eyes, the procession of the sons of educated men, ascending those pulpits, mounting those steps, passing in and out of those doors, preaching, teaching, administering justice, practising medicine, making money. And it is obvious that if you are going to make the same incomes from the same professions that those men make you will have to accept the same conditions that they accept. Even from an upper window and from books we know or can guess what those conditions are. You will have to leave the house at nine and come back to it at six. That leaves very little time for fathers to know their children. You will have to do this daily from the age of twenty-one or so to the age of about sixty-five. That leaves very little time for friendship, travel or art. You will have to perform some duties that are very arduous, others that are very barbarous. You will have to wear certain uniforms and profess certain loyalties. If you succeed in those professions the words "For God and the Empire" will very likely be written, like the address on a dog-collar, round your neck. And if words have meaning, as words perhaps should have meaning, you will have to accept that meaning and do what you can to enforce it. In short, you will have to lead the same lives and profess the same loyalties that professional men have professed for many centuries. There can be no doubt of that.

If you retaliate, what harm is there in that? Why should we hesitate to do what our fathers and grandfathers have done before us? let us go into greater detail and consult the facts which are nowadays open to the inspection of all who can read their mother tongue in biography. There they are, those innumerable and invaluable works upon the shelves of your own library. Let us glance again rapidly at the lives of professional men who have succeeded in their professions. Here is an extract from the life of a great lawyer. "He went to his chambers about half-past nine. . . . He took briefs home with him . . . so that he was lucky if he got to bed about one or two o'clock in the morning." That explains why most successful barristers are hardly worth sitting next at dinner—they yawn so. Next, here is a quotation from a famous politician's speech. ". . . since 1914 I have never seen the pageant of the blossom from the first damson to the last apple—never once have I seen that in Worcestershire since 1914, and if that is not a sacrifice I do not know what is." A sacrifice indeed, and one that explains the perennial indifference of the Government to art—why, these unfortunate gentlemen must be as blind as bats. Take the religious profession next. Here is a quotation from the life of a great bishop. "This is an awful mind- and soul-destroying life. I really do not know how to live it. The arrears of important work accumulate and crush." That bears out what so many people are saying now about the Church and the nation. Our bishops and deans seem to have no soul with which to preach and no mind with which to write. Listen to any sermon in any church; read the journalism of Dean Alington or Dean Inge in any newspaper. Take the doctor's profession next. "I have taken a good deal over £13,000 during the year, but this cannot possibly be maintained, and while it lasts it is slavery. What I feel most is being away from Eliza and the children so frequently on Sundays, and again at Christmas." That is the complaint of a great doctor; and his patient might well echo it, for what Harley Street specialist has time to understand the body, let alone the mind or both in combination, when he is a slave to thirteen thousand a year? But is the life of a professional writer any better? Here is a sample taken from the life of a highly successful journalist. "On another day at this time he wrote a 1,600 words article on Nietzsche, a leader of equal length on the railway strike for the *Standard*, 600 words for the *Tribune* and in the evening was at Shoe Lane." That explains among other things why the public reads its politics with cynicism, and authors read their reviews with foot-rules—it is the advertisement that counts; praise or blame have ceased to have any meaning. And with one more glance at the politician's life, for his profession after all is the most important practically, let us have done. "Lord Hugh *loitered in the lobby*. . . . The Bill [the Deceased Wife's Sister Bill] was in consequence dead, and the further chances of the cause were relegated to the chances and mischances of another year." That not only serves to explain a certain prevalent distrust of politicians, but also reminds us that since you have the Pensions Bill to steer through the lobbies of so just and humane an institution as the House of Commons, we must not loiter too long ourselves among these delightful biographies, but must try to sum up the information which we have gained from them.

. . .

. . . What can it be? Simply, you reply, that we, daughters of educated men, are between the devil and the deep sea. Behind us lies the patriarchal system; the private house, with its nullity, its immorality, its hypocrisy, its servility. Before us lies the public world, the professional system, with its possessiveness, its jealousy, its pugnacity, its greed. The one shuts us up like slaves in a harem; the other forces us to circle, like caterpillars head to tail, round and round the mulberry tree, the sacred tree, of property. It is a choice of evils. Each is bad. Had we not better plunge off the bridge into the river; give up the game; declare that the whole of human life is a mistake and so end it?

But before you take that step, Madam, a decisive one, unless you share the opinion of the professors of the Church of England that death is the gate of life—*Mors Janua Vitae* is written upon an arch in St. Paul's—in which case there is, of course, much to recommend it, let us see if another answer is not possible.

Another answer may be staring us in the face on the shelves of your own library, once more in the biographies. Is it not possible that by considering the experiments that the dead have made with their lives in the past we may find some help in answering the very difficult question that is now forced upon us? At any rate, let us try. The question that we will now put to biography is this: For reasons given above we are agreed that we must earn money in the professions. For reasons given above those professions seem to us highly undesirable. The question we put to you, lives of the dead, is how can we enter the professions and yet remain civilized human beings; human beings, that is, who wish to prevent war?

This time let us turn to the lives not of men but of women in the nineteenth century—to the lives of professional women. But there would seem to be a gap in your library, Madam. There are no lives of professional women in the nineteenth century. A Mrs. Tomlinson, the wife of a Mr. Tomlinson, F.R.S., F.C.S., explains the reason. This lady, who wrote a book "advocating the employment of young ladies as nurses for children," says: ". . . it seemed as if there were no way in which an unmarried lady could earn a living but by taking a situation as governess, for which post she was often unfit by nature and education, or want of education." That was written in 1859—less than 100 years ago. That explains the gap on your shelves. There were no professional women, except governesses, to have lives written of them. And the lives of governesses, that is the written lives, can be counted on the fingers of one hand. What then can we learn about the lives of professional women from studying the lives of governesses? Happily old boxes are beginning to give up their old secrets. Out the other day crept one such document written about the year 1811. There was, it appears, an obscure Miss Weeton, who used to scribble down her thoughts upon professional life among other things when her pupils were in bed. Here is one such thought. "Oh! how I have burned to learn Latin, French, the Arts, the Sciences, anything rather than the dog trot way of sewing, teaching, writing copies, and washing dishes every day. . . . Why are not females permitted to study physics, divinity, astronomy, etc., etc., with their attendants, chemistry, botany, logic, mathematics, &c.?" That comment upon the lives of governesses, that question from the lips of governesses, reaches us from the darkness. It is illuminating, too. But let us go on groping; let us pick up a hint here and a hint there as to the professions as they were practised by women in the nineteenth century. Next we find Anne Clough, the sister of Arthur Clough, pupil of Dr. Arnold, Fellow of Oriel, who, though she served without a salary, was the first principal of Newnham, and thus may be called a professional woman in embryo—we find her training for her profession by "doing much of the housework . . . earning money to pay off what had been lent by their friends, pressing for leave to keep a small school, reading books her brother lent her, and exclaiming, 'If I were a man, I would not work for riches, to make myself a name or to leave a wealthy family behind me. No, I think I would work for my country, and make its people my heirs.'" The nineteenth-century women were not without ambition it seems. Next we find Josephine Butler, who, though not strictly speaking a professional woman, led the campaign against the Contagious Diseases Act to victory, and then the campaign against the sale and purchase of children "for infamous purposes"—we find Josephine Butler refusing to have a life of herself written, and saying of the women who helped her in those campaigns: "The utter absence in them of any desire for recognition, of any vestige of egotism in any form, is worthy of remark. In the purity of their motives they shine out 'clear as crystal.'" That, then, was one of the qualities that the Victorian woman praised and practised—a negative one, it is true; not to be recognized; not to be egotistical; to do the work for the sake of doing the work. An interesting contribution to psychology in its way. And then we come closer to our own time; we find Gertrude Bell, who, though the diplomatic service was and is shut to women, occupied a post in the East which almost entitled her to be called a pseudo-diplomat—we find rather to our surprise that "Gertrude could never go out in London without a female friend or, failing that, a maid. . . . When it seemed unavoidable for Gertrude to drive in a hansom with a young man from one tea party to another, she feels obliged to write and confess it to my mother." So they were chaste, the women pseudo-diplomats of the Victorian Age? And not merely in body; in mind also. Gertrude "was not allowed to read Bourget's *The Disciple* for fear of contracting whatever disease that book may disseminate. Dissatisfied but ambitious, ambitious but austere, chaste yet adventurous—such are some of the qualities that we have discovered. But let us go on looking—if not at the lines, then between the lines of biography. And we find, between the lines of their husbands' biographies, so many women practising—but what are we to call the profession that consists in bringing nine or ten children into the world, the profession which consists in running a house, nursing an invalid, visiting the poor and the sick, tending here an old father, there an old mother?—there is no name and there is no pay for that profession; but we find so many mothers, sisters and daughters of educated men practising it in the nineteenth century that we must lump them and their lives together behind their husbands' and brothers', and leave them to deliver their message to those who have the time to extract it and the imagination with which to decipher it. Let us ourselves, who as you hint are pressed for time, sum up these random hints and reflections upon the professional life of women in the nineteenth century by quoting once more the highly significant words of a woman who was not a professional woman in the strict sense of the word, but had some nondescript reputation as a traveller nevertheless—Mary Kingsley:

> "I don't know if I ever revealed the fact to you that being allowed to learn German was *all* the paid-for education I ever had. £2,000 was spent on my brother's. I still hope not in vain."

That statement is so suggestive that it may save us the bother of groping and searching between the lines of professional men's lives for the lives of their sisters. If we develop the suggestions we find in that statement, and connect it with the other hints and fragments that we have uncovered, we may arrive at some theory or point of view that may help us to answer the very difficult question, which now confronts us. For when Mary Kingsley says, ". . . being allowed to learn German was *all* the paid-for education I ever had," she suggests that she had an unpaid-for education. The other lives that we have been examining corroborate that suggestion. What then was the nature of that "unpaid-for education" which, whether for good or for evil, has been ours for so many centuries? If we mass the lives of the obscure behind four lives that were not obscure, but were so successful and distinguished that they were actually written, the lives of Florence Nightingale, Miss Clough, Mary Kingsley and Gertrude Bell, it seems undeniable that they were all educated by the same teachers. And those teachers, biography indicates, obliquely, and indirectly, but emphatically and indisputably none the less, were poverty, chastity, derision, and—what word however covers "lack of rights and privileges"? Shall we press the old word "freedom" once more into service? "Freedom from unreal loyalties," then, was the fourth of their teachers; that freedom from loyalty to old schools, old colleges, old churches, old ceremonies, old countries which all those women enjoyed, and which, to a great extent, we still enjoy by the law and custom of England. We have no time to coin new words, greatly though the language is in need of them. Let "freedom from unreal loyalties" then stand as the fourth great teacher of the daughters of educated men.

Biography thus provides us with the fact that the daughters of educated men received an unpaid-for education at the hands of poverty, chastity, derision and freedom from unreal loyalties. It was this unpaid-for education, biography informs us, that fitted them, aptly enough, for the unpaid-for professions. And biography also informs us that those unpaid-for professions had their laws, traditions, and labours no less certainly than the paid-for professions. Further, the student of biography cannot possibly doubt from the evidence of biography that this education and these professions were in many ways bad in the extreme, both for the unpaid themselves and for their descendants. The intensive childbirth of the unpaid wife, the intensive money-making of the paid husband in the Victorian age had terrible results, we cannot doubt, upon the mind and body of the present age. To prove it we need not quote once more the famous passage in which Florence Nightingale denounced that education and its results; nor stress the natural delight with which she greeted the Crimean war; nor illustrate from other sources—they are, alas, innumerable—the inanity, the pettiness, the spite, the tyranny, the hypocrisy, the immorality which it engendered as the lives of both sexes so abundantly testify. Final proof of its harshness upon one sex at any rate can be found in the annals of our "great war," when hospitals, harvest fields and munition works were largely staffed by refugees flying from its horrors to their comparative amenity.

But biography is many-sided; biography never returns a single and simple answer to any question that is asked of it. Thus the biographies of those who had biographies—say Florence Nightingale, Anne Clough, Emily Brontë, Christina Rossetti, Mary Kingsley—prove beyond a doubt that this same education, the unpaid for, must have had great virtues as well as great defects, for we cannot deny that these, if not educated, still were civilized women. We cannot, when we consider the lives of our uneducated mothers and grandmothers, judge education simply by its power to "obtain appointments," to win honour, to make money. We must, if we are honest, admit that some who had no paid-for education, no salaries and no appointments were civilized human beings—whether or not they can rightly be called "English" women is matter for dispute; and thus admit that we should be extremely foolish if we threw away the results of that education or gave up the knowledge that we have obtained from it for any bribe or decoration whatsoever. Thus biography, when asked the question we have put to it—how can we enter the professions and yet remain civilized human beings, human beings who discourage war, would seem to reply: If you refuse to be separated from the four great teachers of the daughters of educated men—poverty, chastity, derision and freedom from unreal loyalties—but combine them with some wealth, some knowledge, and some service to real loyalties then you can enter the professions and escape the risks that make them undesirable.

Such being the answer of the oracle, such are the conditions attached to this guinea. You shall have it, to recapitulate, on condition that you help all properly qualified people, of whatever sex, class or colour, to enter your profession; and further on condition that in the practise of your profession you refuse to be separated from poverty, chastity, derision and freedom from unreal loyalties. Is the statement now more positive, have the conditions been made more clear and do you agree to the terms? You hesitate. Some of the conditions, you seem to suggest, need further discussion. Let us take them, then, in order. By poverty is meant enough money to live upon. That is, you must earn enough to be independent of any other human being and to buy that modicum of health, leisure, knowledge and so on that is needed for the full development of body and mind. But no more. Not a penny more.

By chastity is meant that when you have made enough to live on by your profession you must refuse to sell your brain for the sake of money. That is you must cease to practise your profession, or practise it for the sake of research and experiment; or, if you are an artist, for the sake of the art; or give the knowledge acquired professionally to those who need it for nothing. But directly the mulberry tree begins to make you circle, break off. Pelt the tree with laughter.

By derision—a bad word, but once again the English language is much in need of new words—is meant that you must refuse all methods of advertising merit, and hold that ridicule, obscurity and censure are preferable, for psychological reasons, to fame and praise. Directly badges, orders, or degrees are offered you, fling them back in the giver's face.

By freedom from unreal loyalties is meant that you must rid yourself of pride of nationality in the first place; also of religious pride, college pride, school pride, family pride, sex pride and those unreal loyalties that spring from them. Directly the seducers come with their seductions to bribe you into captivity, tear up the parchments; refuse to fill up the forms.

. . .

Such then are some of the methods by which the society, the anonymous and secret Society of Outsiders would help you, Sir, to prevent war and to ensure freedom. Whatever value you may attach to them you will agree that they are duties which your own sex would find it more difficult to carry out than ours; and duties moreover which are specially appropriate to the daughters of educated men. For they would need some acquaintance with the psychology of educated men, and the minds of educated men are more highly trained and their words subtler than those of working men. There are other duties, of course—many have already been outlined in the letters to the other honorary treasurers. But at the risk of some repetition let us roughly and rapidly repeat them, so that they may form a basis for a society of outsiders to take its stand upon. First, they would bind themselves to earn their own livings. The importance of this as a method of ending war is obvious; sufficient stress has already been laid upon the superior cogency of an opinion based upon economic independence over an opinion based upon no income at all or upon a spiritual right to an income to make further proof unnecessary. It follows that an outsider must make it her business to press for a living wage in all the professions now open to her sex; further that she must create new professions in which she can earn the right to an independent opinion. Therefore she must bind herself to press for a money wage for the unpaid worker in her own class—the daughters and sisters of educated men who, as biographies have shown us, are now paid on the truck system, with food, lodging and a pittance of £40 a year. But above all she must press for a wage to be paid by the State legally to the mothers of educated men. The importance of this to our common fight is immeasurable; for it is the most effective way in which we can ensure that the large and very honourable class of married women shall have a mind and a will of their own, with which, if his mind and will are good in her eyes, to support her husband, if bad to resist him, in any case to cease to be "his woman" and to be her self. You will agree, Sir, without any aspersion upon the lady who bears your name, that to depend upon her for your income would effect a most subtle and undesirable change in your psychology. Apart from that, this measure is of such importance directly to yourselves, in your own fight for liberty and equality and peace, that if any condition were to be attached to the guinea it would be this: that you should provide a wage to be paid by the State to those whose profession is marriage and motherhood. Consider, even at the risk of a digression, what effect this would have upon the birth-rate, in the very class where the birth-rate is falling, in the very class where births are desirable—the educated class. Just as the increase in the pay of soldiers has resulted, the papers say, in additional recruits to the force of arms-bearers, so the same inducement would serve to recruit the child-bearing force, which we can hardly deny to be as necessary and as honourable, but which, because of its poverty, and its hardships, is now failing to attract recruits. That method might succeed where the one in use at present—abuse and ridicule—has failed. But the point which, at the risk of further digression, the outsiders would press upon you is one that vitally concerns your own lives as educated men and the honour and vigour of your professions. For if your wife were paid for her work, the work of bearing and bringing up children, a real wage, a money wage, so that it became an attractive profession instead of being as it is now an unpaid profession, an unpensioned profession, and therefore a precarious and dishonoured profession, your own slavery would be lightened. No longer need you go to the office at nine-thirty and stay there till six. Work could be equally distributed. Patients could be sent to the patientless. Briefs to the briefless. Articles could be left unwritten. Culture would thus be stimulated. You could see the fruit trees flower in spring. You could share the prime of life with your children. And after that prime was over no longer need you be thrown from the machine on to the scrap heap without any life left or interests surviving to parade the environs of Bath or Cheltenham in the care of some unfortunate slave.

No longer would you be the Saturday caller, the albatross on the neck of society, the sympathy addict, the deflated work slave calling for replenishment; or, as Herr Hitler puts it, the hero requiring recreation, or, as Signor Mussolini puts it, the wounded warrior requiring female dependants to bandage his wounds. If the State paid your wife a living wage for her work which, sacred though it is, can scarcely be called more sacred than that of the clergyman, yet as his work is paid without derogation so may hers be—if this step which is even more essential to your freedom than to hers were taken the old mill in which the professional man now grinds out his round, often so wearily, with so little pleasure to himself or profit to his profession, would be broken; the opportunity of freedom would be yours; the most degrading of all servitudes, the intellectual servitude, would be ended; the half-man might become whole. But since three hundred millions or so have to be spent upon the arms-bearers, such expenditure is obviously, to use a convenient word supplied by the politicians, "impracticable" and it is time to return to more feasible projects.

The outsiders then would bind themselves not only to earn their own livings, but to earn them so expertly that their refusal to earn them would be a matter of concern to the work master. They would bind themselves to obtain full knowledge of professional practices, and to reveal any instance of tyranny or abuse in their professions. And they would bind themselves not to continue to make money in any profession, but to cease all competition and to practise their profession experimentally, in the interests of research and for love of the work itself, when they had earned enough to live upon. Also they would bind themselves to remain outside any profession hostile to freedom, such as the making or the improvement of the weapons of war. And they would bind themselves to refuse to take office or honour from any society which, while professing to respect liberty, restricts it, like the universities of Oxford and Cambridge. And they would consider it their duty to investigate the claims of all public societies to which, like the Church and the universities, they are forced to contribute as taxpayers as carefully and fearlessly as they would investigate the claims of private societies to which they contribute voluntarily. They would make it their business to scrutinize the endowments of the schools and universities and the objects upon which that money is spent. As with the educational, so with the religious profession. By reading the New Testament in the first place and next those divines and historians whose works are all easily accessible to the daughters of educated men, they would make it their business to have some knowledge of the Christian religion and its history. Further they would inform themselves of the practice of that religion by attending Church services, by analysing the spiritual and intellectual value of sermons; by criticizing the opinions of men whose profession is religion as freely as they would criticize the opinions of any other body of men. Thus they would be creative in their activities, not merely critical. By criticizing education they would help to create a civilized society which protects culture and intellectual liberty. By criticizing religion they would attempt to free the religious spirit from its present servitude and would help, if need be, to create a new religion based, it might well be, upon the New Testament, but, it might well be, very different from the religion now erected upon that basis. And in all this, and in much more than we have time to particularize, they would be helped, you will agree, by their position as outsiders, that freedom from unreal loyalties, that freedom from interested motives which are at present assured them by the State.

It would be easy to define in greater number and more exactly the duties of those who belong to the Society of Outsiders, but not profitable. Elasticity is essential; and some degree of secrecy, as will be shown later, is at present even more essential. But the description thus loosely and imperfectly given is enough to show you, Sir, that the Society of Outsiders has the same ends as your society—freedom, equality, peace; but that it seeks to achieve them by the means that a different sex, a different tradition, a different education, and the different values which result from those differences have placed within our reach. Broadly speaking, the main distinction between us who are outside society and you who are inside society must be that whereas you will make use of the means provided by your position—leagues, conferences, campaigns, great names, and all such public measures as your wealth and political influence place within your reach—we, remaining outside, will experiment not with public means in public but with private means in private. Those experiments will not be merely critical but creative. To take two obvious instances:—the outsiders will dispense with pageantry not from any puritanical dislike of beauty. On the contrary, it will be one of their aims to increase private beauty; the beauty of spring, summer, autumn; the beauty of flowers, silks, clothes; the beauty which brims not only every field and wood but every barrow in Oxford Street; the scattered beauty which needs only to be combined by artists in order to become visible to all. But they will dispense with the dictated, regimented, official pageantry, in which only one sex takes an active part—those ceremonies, for example, which depend upon the deaths of kings, or their coronations to inspire them. Again, they will dispense with personal distinctions—medals, ribbons, badges, hoods, gowns—not from any dislike of personal adornment, but because of the obvious effect of such distinctions to constrict, to stereotype and to destroy. Here, as so often, the example of the Fascist States is at hand to instruct us—for if we have no example of what we wish to be, we have, what is perhaps equally valuable, a daily and illuminating example of what we do not wish to be. With the example then, that they give us of the power of medals, symbols, orders and even, it would seem, of decorated ink-pots to hypnotize the human mind it must be our aim not to submit ourselves to such hypnotism. We must extinguish the coarse glare of advertisement and publicity, not merely because the limelight is apt to be held in incompetent hands, but because of the psychological effect of such illumination upon those who receive it. Consider next time you drive along a country road the attitude of a rabbit caught in the glare of a head-lamp—its glazed eyes, its rigid paws. Is there not good reason to think without going outside our own country, that the "attitudes," the false and unreal positions taken by the human form in England as well as in Germany, are due to the limelight which paralyses the free action of the human faculties and inhibits the human power to change and create new wholes much as a strong head-lamp paralyses the little creatures who run out of the darkness into its beams? It is a guess; guessing is dangerous; yet we have some reason to guide us in the guess that ease and freedom, the power to change and the power to grow, can only be preserved by obscurity; and that if we wish to help the human mind to create, and to prevent it from scoring the same rut repeatedly, we must do what we can to shroud it in darkness.

. . .